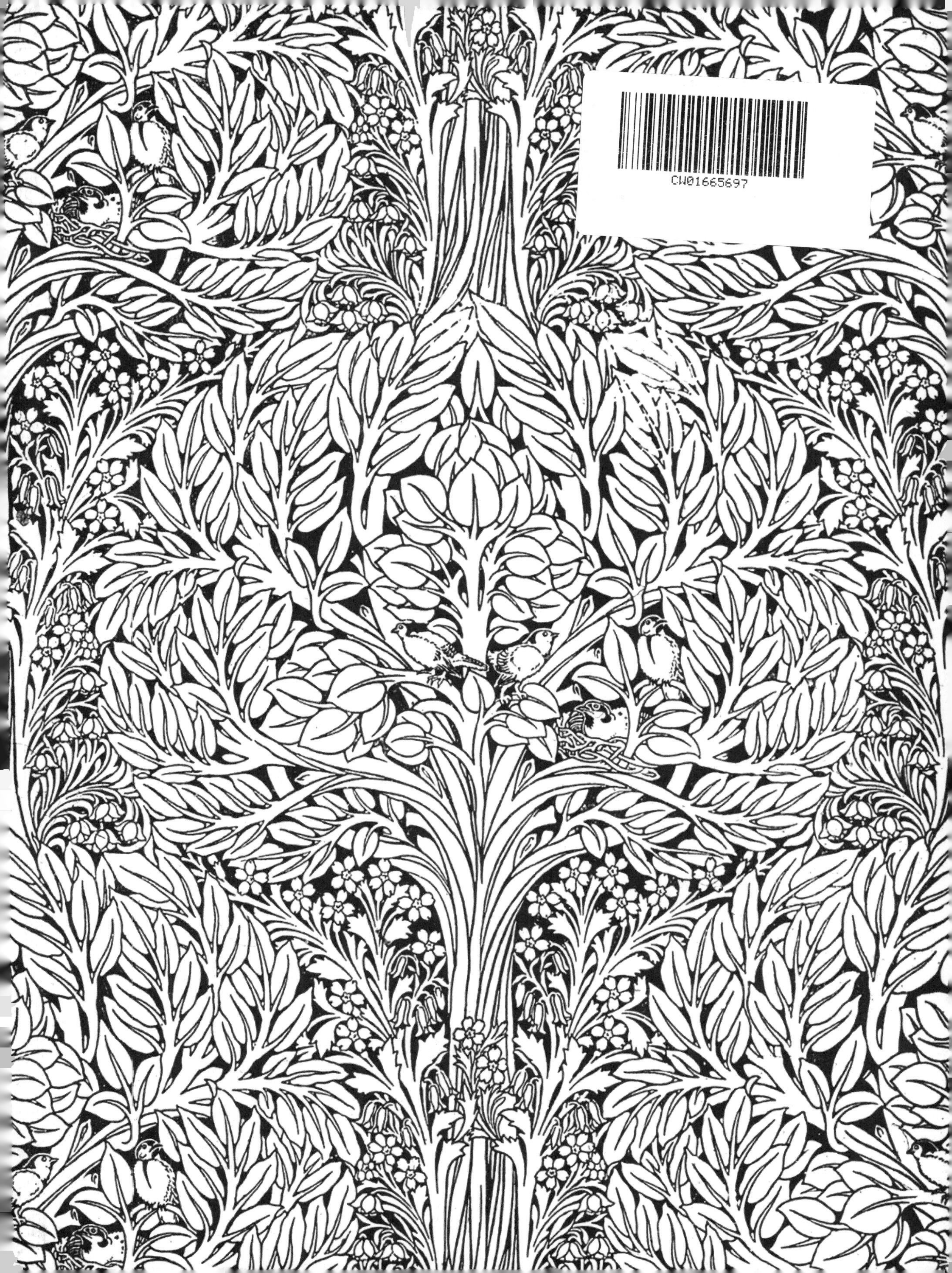

Cyndy Manton – 12/10/51 – 31/08/21
Keith Gillies – 1/09/50 – 22/11/21

15th December '21

Steve,

Something by two of my favourite people.

Thank you
Catriona

HENRY WILSON

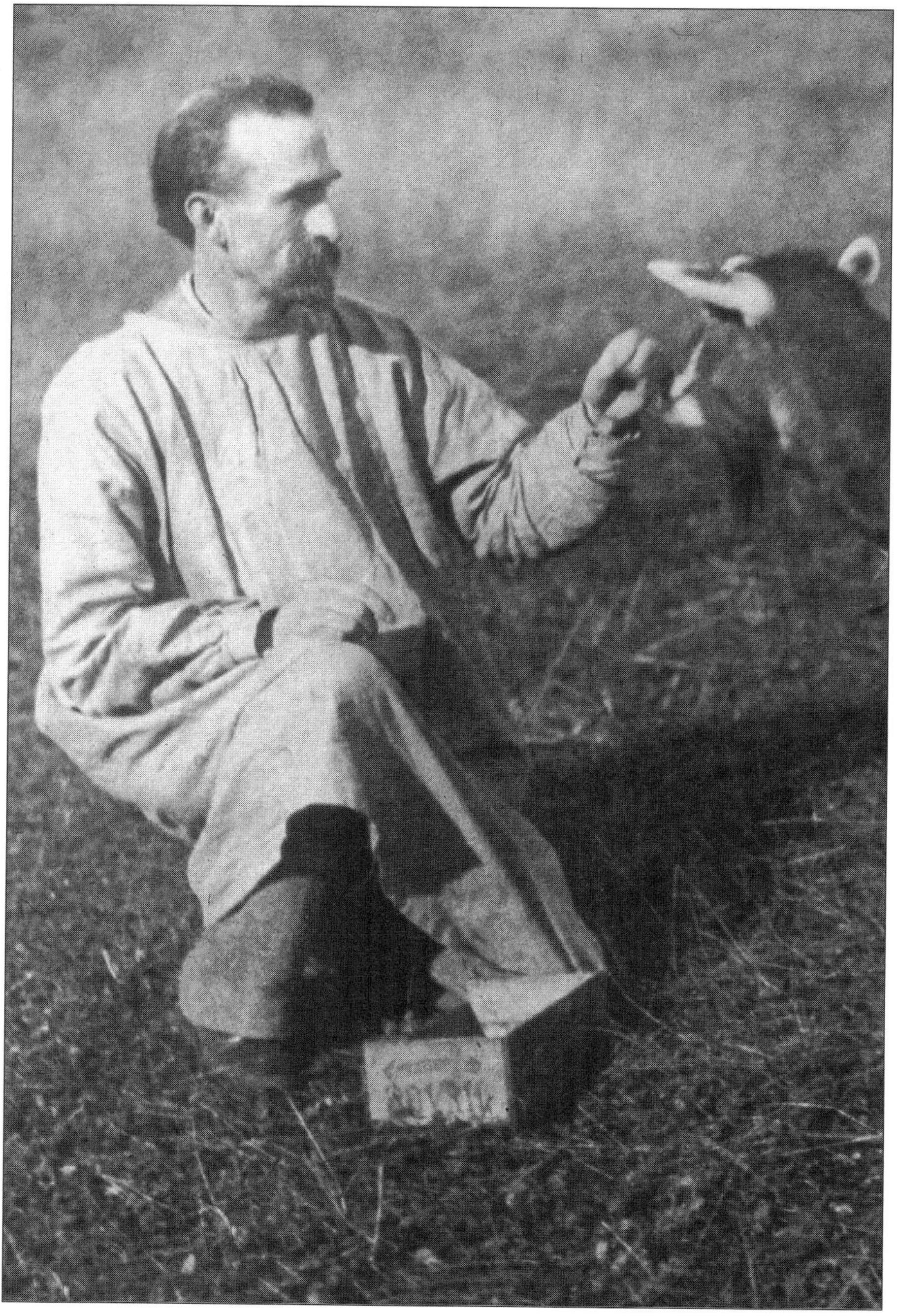

Henry Wilson 1864 -1934, at the family home in Kent, c. 1910.

HENRY WILSON
PRACTICAL IDEALIST

Cyndy Manton

The Lutterworth Press

First published in in 2009 by
The Lutterworth Press,
PO Box 60,
Cambridge,
CB1 2NT,
England

www.lutterworth.com
publishing@lutterworth.com

British Library Cataloguing in Publication Data
A record is available from the British Library

ISBN 978 0 7188 3097 7 (hardback)
ISBN 978 0 7188 3098 4 (paperback)

Design and origination
by Keith Gillies

Printed in UK by the MPG Books Group

For additional material about Henry Wilson
visit www.henrywilson.eu

HENRY WILSON
PRACTICAL IDEALIST

CONTENTS

LIST OF PLATES

COLOUR PLATES BETWEEN PAGES 96-97 & 168-169

ACKNOWLEDGEMENTS

My thanks are due to many people: the late Orrea Pernel, the violinist - Pernel, or 'Pernie' Wilson - shared with me her memories of her father, giving precious insights into the man and his art; the late Isobel Howden, Edgar Wilson's daughter, provided similarly key recollections of her uncle Harry; the late Yvor Wilson – Edgar's son – and Patten's grandson Edwin Patten Wilson, also contributed unique family reminiscences.

For sharing their enthusiasm and knowledge, and for their invaluable advice, I thank fellow enthusiasts Alan Crawford and Peter Cormack, who constructively criticised the manuscript in its earliest form, and made many helpful suggestions along the way.

I am privileged to have had the ever-resourceful comments of Jon Harris, the book's final incarnation owing much to his expert observations and to his patient and creative encouragement.

Collectors and connoisseurs who have marvelled with me at Wilson's craftsmanship and vision include Elizabeth Bonython, David Beasley, Geoffrey Munn, David Ottewill and Lionel Lambourne.

I am pleased to acknowledge the curators of the museums and galleries who make Wilson's work accessible to public view: the Victoria and Albert Museum; Goldsmiths' Hall; Cheltenham Art Gallery and Museum; the Fitzwilliam Museum, Cambridge; Birmingham Museums and Art Gallery; Glasgow Museum; the William Morris Gallery.

The staff of those libraries that preserve the documents of Wilson's career gave indispensable assistance, including those at the Wilson Archive held by the Royal College of Art; at the British Art Library in the Victoria and Albert Museum, with its drawings and biographical material; at the Royal Institute of British Architects; and at countless metropolitan and local history centres who have helped me trace information on individual commissions.

For making their records available I am grateful to the incumbents, wardens, historians and archivists of the churches and cathedrals in the UK, USA, Canada, and India that Wilson built, restored or enriched, and to the owners and guardians of his privately commissioned architectural projects for the access they offered me.

Photographs were taken in USA by Penny Sparke and Linda Greyser; in UK by Geoff Harris, Colin Manton, Jonathan H. Robbins, David J. Ovens, Peter Grosvenor, Kate Cooper, Rob Orland, John Taylor, Freda Raphael, Doug Houghton and Keith Gillies.

The sponsors whose generosity made this publication possible include: The Paul Mellon Centre for Studies in British Art; Albert Dawson Educational Trust; The Duke of Portland's Charitable Trust; The Harley Foundation; The Great Britain Sasakawa Foundation; Birmingham Assay Office; Lord Londonderry; the HWB Fund.

This book is dedicated to the memory of my parents,
Maud and Alfred Manton, whose faith in it never wavered.

INTRODUCTION
'PERHAPS THE GREATEST ARTIST OF THE LOT'

By all accounts Henry Wilson was a quiet man, modest to a fault. At first sight, apart from his distinctive aquiline profile, his appearance was unremarkable. He was not widely known to the general public, and even amongst friends it was hard to get him to talk much about his own works, which were mostly unsigned. When he died in Menton, France in 1934, he was buried in a leased plot, long since obliterated.

Such unassuming worldly credentials belie the powerful originality of his work and his prodigious skills as a craftsman. In dramatic architectural schemes, and in the expressiveness of his executed buildings and sculptures; in his richly evocative jewellery and fine metalwork, in inspirational lectures and writings; in all these, he displays an exceptional intensity of invention and insight. The works summon up deep-seated meanings which often surpass their material reality. They, and the thinking that underlies them, most thoroughly represent Henry Wilson. And it is through the diverse, yet linked, aspects of his creativity that his character and impact is most properly revealed. As he himself wrote in 1902 'design is the expression of your personality in terms of the material in which you work'.[1]

Janet, the astute and observant wife of Wilson's fellow designer and ideologist C.R. Ashbee, testified to the admiration felt for Wilson in arts and crafts circles when she described a group of Art Workers' Guild members gathering for a rehearsal of their masque *Beauty's Awakening* in May 1899. Gradually they assemble:

> *Selwyn Image, Walter Crane, Louis Davis ... and Wilson, who looks like a seedy bank clerk and is perhaps the greatest artist of the lot.*[2]

Ashbee bemoaned the fact that frankly, England 'wasted'[3] Henry Wilson, and it is true that several of his most impressive schemes, including two cathedrals, remained unexecuted. Hermann Muthesius, architect, critic and international apostle of the English Arts and Crafts movement, sounded similarly aggrieved in his 1904-5 book, *Das Englische Haus*:

> *It is a matter of profound regret for English art that an artist of Wilson's brilliance has not found greater opportunity to express his splendid artistic powers.*[4]

The time is long overdue to fully recognise these powers, to set Wilson firmly in his context, and at last to properly celebrate this gifted architect, designer, craftsman, writer, teacher and Arts and Crafts publicist.

The Arts and Crafts movement was well-established by the time Wilson started work in the 1880s, and it was against this backdrop that his attitudes to design developed. It was a movement that delighted in a fresh, non-copyist approach led by individuality and inspiration. Its buildings were typically endowed with a sense of purpose and their own *genius loci*, and like its designs in other media, showed dedicated originality and craftsmanship. Tradition was respected, but never allowed to fossilise. Wilson's adherence to craft ideals was flexible enough to evolve with the changing times – times which were scarred by the Great War and shaped by mass production. Such developments were met with an inexhaustible blend of vision and pragmatism by Wilson, one of the most talented architects and designer-craftsmen of the period.

An examination of Wilson's career could be approached from several angles. Investigating his work according to profession or style, for example, would be convenient, in that a broad pattern is discernable. At times he was most readily identifiable as, say, an architect, or sculptor, or silversmith, working in the Arts and Crafts style or in an Art Nouveau mood. But the relative ease of compartmentalising him, most famously as a jeweller, along with his own humility and a tendency to regard him as the 'closest' and 'best'[5] pupil of the architect J.D. Sedding who drifted off into the crafts, has undoubtedly contributed to the absence so far of an all-embracing analysis of his achievements. But only an interlinked overview can present an accurate picture of his importance within late-nineteenth and early-twentieth century architecture and design.

In his consideration of Sedding's career published in *The Architectural Review* of 1897-98, Wilson declared that the 'best critic [is] he who can divine most of the artist's thoughts'.[6] As with William Morris, to look in isolation at what Wilson *made* is not enough. To understand how, why and in what context he was working is crucial. Highlighting the links between the different elements of Wilson's cross-disciplinary vision is fundamental. Each aspect of his work forms part of a cohesive whole which, as well as conforming to many of the stylistic preoccupations of the day, also illuminates Wilson's intense individuality.

At the core of this individuality lies the desire he himself identified: to 'reach down to the lower levels of mental life'[7] and tap into a store of 'unconscious memories'.[8] In so doing he developed a highly articulate visual language that mingles conventional symbolism and personal insight. The resulting blend is both eclectic and original. So whilst the process of unpicking particular threads can provide helpful focal points, it remains a misleading one if these threads are not rewoven and seen relative to each other and to his life as a whole. Dissecting him and leaving it at that militates against the concept of 'the all-round man'[9] which he proposed as the ideal, and which he himself surely fulfilled.

This all-round approach was expressed from the very outset of Wilson's career in the architectural profession, and persisted through every area into which architecture naturally, and logically, led him. His early architectural training, especially during his last formal appointment between 1888 and 1891 as John Sedding's chief assistant, would influence the whole of his subsequent career. There, in the office of this free Gothic architect, he worked alongside other pupils including Ernest Gimson and John Paul Cooper, each of whom absorbed Sedding's special instinct for the crafts. It was an environment in which the connections between the crafts, and between them and architecture as a whole, were actively and enthusiastically explored. An ethos had been created of using tradition without being bound by it, and of getting the craftsmen involved in a building to work, as Ruskin advocated, as a team.

Sedding's sudden death in 1891 effectively propelled Wilson into the role of fully-fledged Arts and Crafts architect. Out of loyalty Wilson dedicated unconscionable hours to completing, in some cases improving, his late master's projects-in-hand. At the same time he produced some strikingly original works of his own in which familiar historical elements were boldly transformed into novel, dramatic forms. Just such a transformation is evident in one of his 'wasted' schemes, for St. Andrew's, Boscombe (1895). This proposal, for a Dorset parish church with the resonance of a cathedral, sadly never progressed beyond Wilson's drawing board.

In his *Memoirs*, reviewing the year 1902, Ashbee listed some of the 'real architects' then at work in Britain as 'Bodley, Webb, Lethaby, Harry Wilson and Charles Holden'.[10] George Frederick Bodley (1827-1907) and Philip Webb (1831-1915) were both of an older generation and had established their styles and principles already – Bodley as one of the great Victorian Gothic revivalists, Webb as the figurehead of Arts and Crafts vernacular architecture. But the three younger architects, fully alive to their predecessors' pioneering work and impatient of designs that framed form without feeling, were poised to exploit new creative possibilities.

As much as any of his early buildings, it was Lethaby's 1891 book *Architecture, Mysticism and Myth* that set ripples rolling through his generation of designers and craftsmen. Its range of cosmic allusions and its exploration of ancient shapes, symbols and meanings were embodied in his own arcane little Herefordshire church at Brockhampton; but this was not built until 1901-2. Meanwhile, no one manifested his book's theories more coherently and consistently than Wilson. In him, its ideas fused with the liberating impulses bequeathed him by Sedding, and were channelled into intriguing new directions. It was in following these paths in the 1890 Ladbroke Grove library design, or in his bold church schemes for Lynton (1892) or Highgate (1896), that he most clearly entered into creative interchange with other innovators including Charles Nicholson, Charles Harrison Townsend and Charles Rennie Mackintosh.

Given his distinctive contribution to architecture, it is not difficult to see why Wilson was offered honorary membership of the Royal Institute of British Architects – nor, however, is it hard to understand why he declined it. From both experience and instinct he shrank from a body which seemed more concerned with academicism, or worse, business-led professionalism, than with the flesh and breath of real building. Any message which could be conveyed through architecture's formal qualities alone struck Wilson as a distinctly partial message. His, by contrast, was a multifaceted one into which craft experience had been thoroughly absorbed. Consequently it was inevitable that in time he 'ceased to practice architecture as generally understood',[11] and sought instead to approach it through what he called the 'building arts'.[12] His telling phrase effectively summed up those crafts which made a vital contribution to architecture and in turn derived their strength from it. As the various elements of Wilson's career unfold he can be seen to step back from architectural practice and into the building crafts – and at times, away from both, towards the ornamental crafts, notably jewellery. Significantly, though his essays in this art were intensely architectural in the broadest, architectonic sense of the word. Making precious metalwork seems very different from putting up buildings, but throughout it all there remains a latent sense of the miniature, intrinsically architectural world it inhabits. In this sense, though he disengaged from architectural practice, Wilson never gave up his architectural vocation.

The claim made by D.S. MacColl, artist, National Gallery curator and writer sympathetic to the Arts and Crafts, that Wilson had been 'a gifted architect who went off into the minor crafts'[13] would have left Wilson bemused. For him no craft was 'minor', rather '... all are worthy of the best energies of the artist'.[14] By 1891 his interests were already diversifying. At Holy Trinity Church, Sloane Street, he fulfilled roles as both architect and craftsman-decorator, playing an integral part, as Sedding's right-hand man and successor, in its building and furnishing. These roles reappeared at Welbeck Abbey, Nottinghamshire, where between 1893 and 1897 he completed the creation and decoration of the new library and chapel; and at St. Mark's, Brithdir, which Wilson built and decorated between 1895 and 1898. Because of its seclusion this Welsh mountain church has received relatively slight attention, though it is certainly amongst the best work he ever carried out. But alongside his talents as architect and decorator must be ranged his skills in sculpture and stained glass, plaster and woodwork, lettering and stage design. Each has an important bearing on the others, the last casting an interesting light on the deliberate theatricality of his architectural and interior design work.

Taking pride of place amongst all these attainments, however, are Wilson's unsurpassed talents in goldwork, silverwork and jewellery – the crafts for which he is most widely known. A review of his seminal book *Silverwork and Jewellery* when, in 1912, it went into its second edition was unequivocal in its praise, calling him 'unquestionably the most brilliant of the craftsmen engaged in the design and making of silverwork and jewellery'.[15] As for Wilson himself, he insisted in 1908 that he would 'rather be known as a goldsmith than as anything else in the world'.[16] The crafts of fine metalwork and jewellery would receive renewed interest from the Arts and Crafts in the period following 1900. It was during this time that Wilson moved from London to rural Kent, where he built a family home and set up his own metalwork and jewellery studio.

By this time he had produced some of his most symbolically-charged silverwork, including his chalices for St. Bartholomew's Church, Brighton (1898) and for Gloucester Cathedral (1900). He had also started to make his naturalistic, evocative jewellery, from brooches and rings to necklaces and tiaras. The influence of Sedding and the researches of Lethaby mingle with his own idiosyncratic vision and sensational expertise. Intricate gold and silverwork tendrils and stems enmesh semi-precious stones or border pools of glowing enamel. The techniques at which Wilson excelled – including, most difficult amongst the whole repertoire, transparent network enamel or *plique-à-jour* – were so sophisticated that they amazed critics and clients alike. Fellow craftsmen, too, were thrilled by the work, like the Scottish silversmith James Cromar Watt. His response is all the more potent in springing from informed admiration: 'apart altogether from their beauty,' he enthused in a letter to Wilson, 'the making of the things beats everything....'[17] The finished pieces trap and translate themes of nature, Christianity, myth and astrology, and for all their meticulous order and craftsmanship, still manage to seem spontaneous.

The workers in fine metals with whom Wilson shared common interests were all innovators, individualists. The jewels of Arthur and Georgie Gaskin, for example, were refreshingly naturalistic, often comprising tight clusters of small leaves set with semi-precious stones and enriched with touches of enamel. Alexander Fisher's experiments with painted enamel were being made in the 1890s, when he and Wilson entered a brief working partnership, the technique finding expression in both men's work. And Paul Cooper, whose work would evolve its own modern idioms, had started out in architecture, like Wilson himself, before moving successfully into the metalworking arts. Wilson's impact on him in the 1900s was so pronounced that during this period it is occasionally difficult to differentiate their work. As in architecture, a web of influences and cross-borrowings surrounded Wilson's fine metalwork and jewellery, though none of his fellow smiths and jewellers displays such enthralling fluency in so wide a range of symbolic allusions and technical coups.

Amongst the assortment of architect-decorators for whom Wilson's example was naturally a source of interest were three significant exponents of the new domestic architecture and design – Baillie Scott, Gimson and Ashbee. In creating his carefully-harmonised early interiors, Mackay Hugh Baillie Scott drew on the styles of both Townsend and Edgar Wood, but also on the forms and nuances of Wilson's, his style finding colourful expression in his designs of 1897 for the drawing-room of the Grand Ducal Palace, Darmstadt. Ernest Gimson was an exponent with whom Wilson would collaborate on several projects; like Wilson, he had learned to love traditional skills in Sedding's office, but after some memorable essays in vernacular architecture, he would concentrate on furniture design, plasterwork and metalwork. Each thread endured throughout his working life, though without his encompassing, or aspiring to, such a broadly-based stance as Wilson's. By contrast, C.R. Ashbee, one of the most impressive Arts and Crafts figures of all, in common with Wilson embraced both practice and theory: he collaborated on the Darmstadt commission, built his celebrated asymmetrical houses of 1899 in Chelsea, and, with equal facility, designed flowing, Art Nouveau silverwork and jewellery for his Guild of Handicraft. That enterprise, established in 1888, forms an interesting parallel with Wilson's ideas about self-supporting craft villages. Wilson admired Ashbee's energy and devotion to craft ideals, but Ashbee never attained Wilson's expertise as a craftsman. Indeed, with his generous praise for Wilson's brilliance, Ashbee would have been the first to admit the disparity between them in this respect. As Christopher Whall, artist in stained glass and plasterwork, remarked 'he [Ashbee] has great ideas, but one contrasts them with his personal work and one trembles....'[18]

Contemplating Wilson's achievements as a sculptor – the art which, in his latter years, embodied Wilson's highest ambitions – Ashbee judiciously put him on a par with the renowned nineteenth century sculptors Alfred Gilbert and Alfred Stevens. To his own admiration for these figures, Wilson added an affinity with the medieval masters, with Rodin, and with the emotional and spiritual universes of Burne-Jones and William Blake. He was elected to the Council of the International Society of Painters, Sculptors and Gravers in 1899, remaining a staunch member until its dissolution in 1925. Soon after, his energies unabated, he was writing to his brother Edgar

> *I want all the Wilson family to be on top in everything. I haven't got to the top in sculpture yet but I hope to before I go over to the other side.*[19]

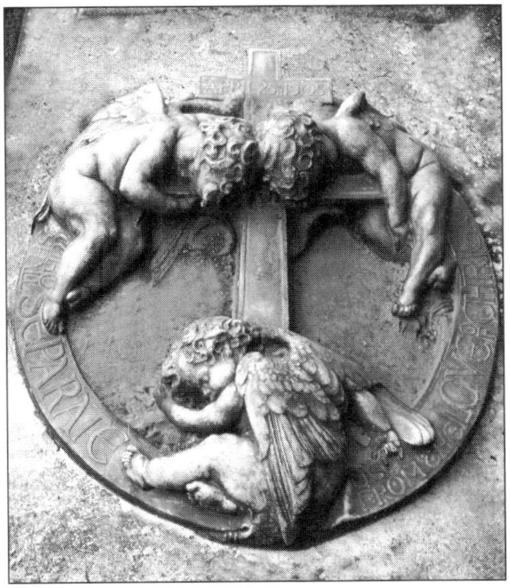

Figure 1. Church of St. Mary the Virgin, Kemsing, Kent: Henry Wilson, bronze cherubs on top of Collet family tomb in churchyard, 1905-6.

Within a few months, he had won the Silver Medal at the 1927 Paris Salon. His exhibit, a pair of bronze doors for an American tea company's headquarters, told in their relief panels the story of tea culture from planting to export. Some of Wilson's associates, including a former workshop assistant, H. Brown-Morrison, felt sure he would be remembered 'chiefly as a sculptor', and indeed there can be no doubt that Wilson's sculptural achievements deserve to be ranked alongside the great masters like those mentioned by Ashbee. Brown-Morrison adds with conviction, 'Some of the most lovely modern figures I know are by him on a tombstone in Kemsing....'[20] He meant the pillared tomb of 1905-06, which is infused with symbols of life, the soul and the elements. Upon it three bronze cherubs – emblems of the Trinity – sleep, as Wilson's own notes explain, 'within the circle of eternity around the cross'.[21] (Fig. 1). His old friend and colleague, the architect Francis William Troup, believed that Wilson's fame would rest on the Elphinstone Tomb with its eloquent bronze personifications of the Virtues and Vices, which he created for King's College, Aberdeen between 1909 and 1926. However, at the summit of Wilson's achievements in sculpture, the culmination of the four commissions for bronze doors that he would undertake, must be placed his final work, the most conspicuously-sited and ambitiously-sized of all his creations, the huge bronze doors which he designed between 1927 and 1931 for the Cathedral of St. John the Divine, New York: they present, in their sequence of 48 relief panels, gripping scenes from the Old and New Testaments and the Apocalypse.

So expressive and emotionally charged are Wilson's designs in whatever medium he chose to work that often they 'speak' visually, while his ability to communicate with an audience manifested itself more literally in his work as writer, teacher and lecturer. These talents appeared in numerous articles, which continued well into the 1920s in periodicals such as *The Architectural Review,* of which he himself was editor from 1896 to 1901. In them he would debate topics ranging from architecture, advertising and education to post-war reconstruction, creativity, and the meaning of art itself.

But it is in his book *Silverwork and Jewellery*, completed in 1902 and published by John Hogg in January 1903, that his writing blends most fully with personal, practical insight. While his designs unite consummate skill and vitality, his book links the authoritative voice of experience with an empathetic, I'm-here-at-your-shoulder tone. Familiar with the joys of creativity, he knew its pitfalls all too well: '... the joint looks perfectly soldered, but on filing ... immediately falls to pieces....'[22] It is easy to share the response of one contemporary reporting back to him – 'we read your book and felt able to sit down and do it all'.[23]

The captivating character of *Silverwork and Jewellery* found a voice in real life in Wilson's own workshop, where he was renowned for his patience, clarity and enthusiasm. This is not to say that every worker would feel at ease with him. His manner could be disconcerting: as Brown-Morrison vividly recounted

> *I admired rather than liked Wilson. He was often sarcastic and cynical which worried me as a boy. His highest praise of any work was 'Quite amusing'.*[24]

Nevertheless, his students (Wilson teaching variously between 1896 and 1917 at the Central School of Arts and Crafts, the Royal College of Art, and Birmingham's Vittoria Street School for Jewellers and Silversmiths) were unanimous in their respect and affection for their tutor. Sedding's niece, who studied under Wilson at the Central School, recalled

> *how able and inspiring was his teaching, and how devoted to him were all who owed their training to him. By his charm this ideal companion of the adolescent could in a moment turn a lesson into an amusing game.*[25]

It was typical of Wilson to break into French or Italian. Favourite phrases were 'jamais, jamais de la vie' and 'je m'en doute'[26], but such fragments disclosed little of his outstanding gifts as a linguist. It was he who could happily translate Marinetti's original Futurist Manifesto into English, and when the Arts and Crafts Exhibition Society showed their members' work in Paris in 1914 it was Wilson who contributed, in French, the catalogue's introductory essay on the current renaissance of English jewellery. In fact, in French he was fluent, and even acquired a competency in the principles of an Oriental language when a Japanese helper joined the household at their home in Kent from 1902.

Wilson's magnetism as a public speaker radiates from his lecture notes. The galvanising effect of his 'Gates of Wonder' talk is almost palpable. It urges, pleads with every one of his listeners to recognise, and express, their creativity: 'you can all be great, you can all be individuals'.[27] His active part in promoting the public face of the crafts formed a natural corollary to his teaching, and he became an influential commentator on pivotal twentieth century design initiatives such as the Deutscher Werkbund and the Design and Industries Association. In 1920 he became one of the nine founding governors of the British Institute of Industrial Art (a direct forerunner of the Design Council), which was established primarily to improve design standards in manufactured goods. His communication skills found yet another incarnation as a tenacious and resourceful exhibition organiser for the Arts and Crafts – a talent informed, in part at least, by the same theatrical instincts that moulded his several stage designs. Despite inevitably problematic circumstances, he steered to fruition the 1916 exhibition of the Arts and Crafts Exhibition Society. And in 1925 he was the chief organiser of the British Pavilion at the legendary International Exposition of Decorative and Industrial Arts in Paris.

In 1917, Wilson became Master of the Art Workers' Guild, Ashbee rating him as one of the greatest the group had ever had. His year of office ran concurrently with his seven-year presidency of the Arts and Crafts Exhibition Society, a role that Lethaby urged him to accept in 1915, confident that he would be a much-needed 'guiding force' who 'would certainly confer great benefit on it and the country'.[28]

This encouragement, from so longstanding and valued a friend, underlines the parallels between the two men. Gimson highlighted their complementary qualities when he wrote to Wilson 'you and he are the brains and wisdom of the movement'.[29] Of all the comparisons to be made between

Wilson and his peers, that with the architect and theorist Lethaby is perhaps the closest. Lethaby neither sought nor acquired Wilson's supreme skill in so wide a range of crafts; but both were architecturally trained designer-teachers driven by a desire to promote design as 'part of the cosmic process'.[30]

Looking back in 1952 Brown-Morrison confronted the daunting task of summing up his former master's complex and inspirational career. 'He seemed to have taken the lead in any sphere in which he operated' he mused. Indeed, he concluded, 'he seemed intellectually a giant'.[31] It is timely, more than a lifetime after Wilson's death, to hold up to the light the traces this giant left behind.

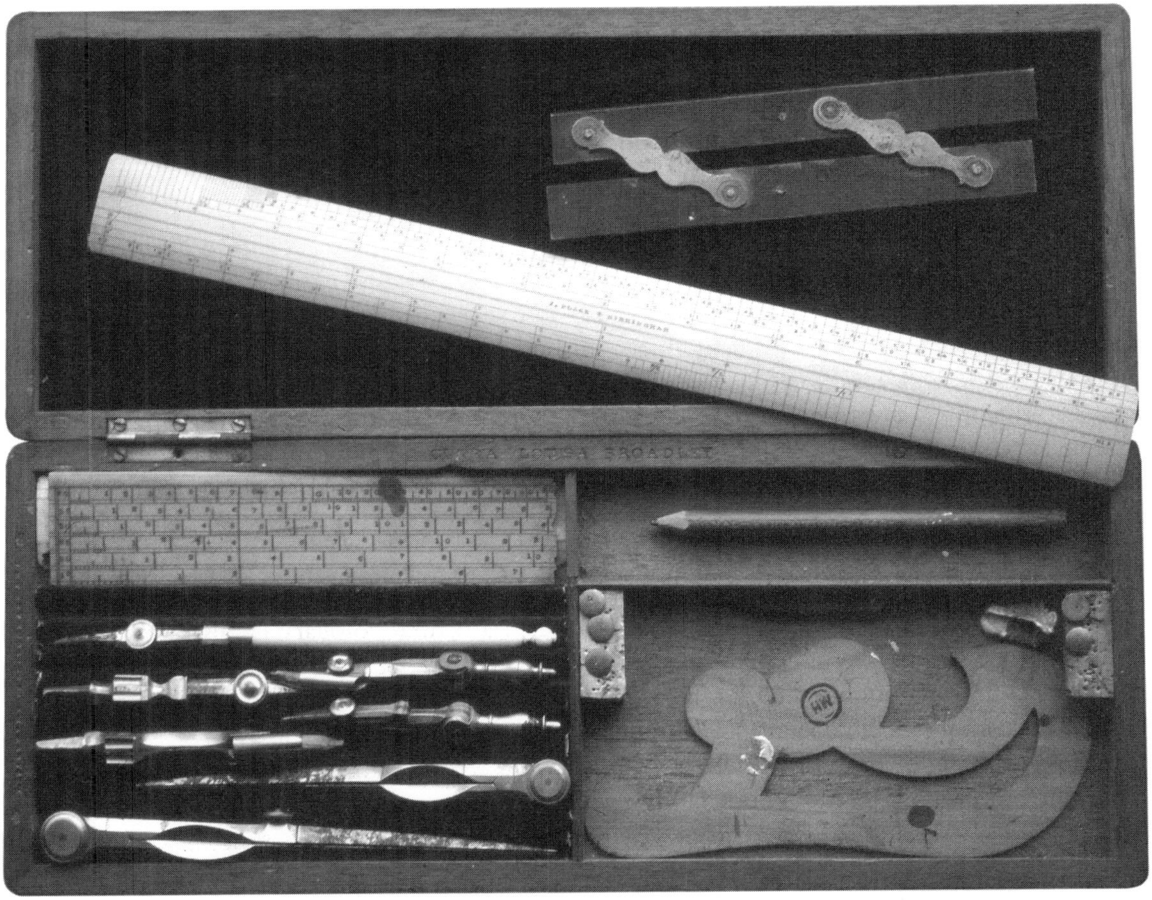

Private Collection

Figure 2. Drawing box, inherited by Wilson from his mother, whose maiden name, Clara Louisa Broadley, is stamped into the hinge-edge of the bottom portion; his own initials appear on the French curve.

CHAPTER ONE
FIRST INFLUENCES

In everyday life Wilson used his real name, Harry, and this was how family, friends and even some reviewers knew him. The more formal-sounding Henry appeared in official contexts – for public correspondence, for articles and longer publications, for exhibition catalogues and in his role as a teacher. His choice of this style of address may have stemmed from respect for the Henry in his father's name, and from its having a more serious ring to it, lending gravitas when needed; but its use was never explained. The notorious reticence that he displayed in talking about his work applied as much to this topic as to his own early life and training. And so while Henry was the name by which he would become most widely known, and under which he registered his official assay mark, at heart he was Harry. It was by this name that both his birth and marriage were recorded, and in so momentous a document as his last will and testament, he firmly declared himself: 'I, Harry Wilson'.[1]

He was born on 12 March 1864 at 91 Red Rock Street, West Derby, Liverpool, but soon he would move with his family to Shropshire. His father, William Henry Wilson, was Assistant Master at Liverpool Collegiate School, where he met and become engaged to Clara Broadley, who taught in the school's elementary department; they married in 1863 at Kirkheaton, near her native Huddersfield. William resigned his post in the spring of 1866, prior to taking up the headship of the Endowed School in the small market town of Cleobury Mortimer, some ten miles east of Ludlow. By April, the couple were settling into the Old School House in Viols Walk (Fig. 3), with two-year old Harry and baby Marion. Their new home was a commanding five-bay ashlar building of around 1740, with pedimented doorway, hipped roof and tall lantern, forming part of the free school founded through the endowment of Sir William Lacon Childe. Two newer parts, dating from 1863, stand in nearby Childe Road: built by G.E. Street with – prophetically for Harry – his assistant J.D. Sedding, they were the junior school, a gabled structure with turreted porch, and the elementary school, the plain pitched-roof building beside it, where Clara took charge until 1881.[2] After completing his early education at the Old School House (Fig. 4), Harry returned to Liverpool, to the Collegiate School in Shaw Street. In term-time, he lodged in Everton; but for the holidays he would make his way home to 'Clibbery'.

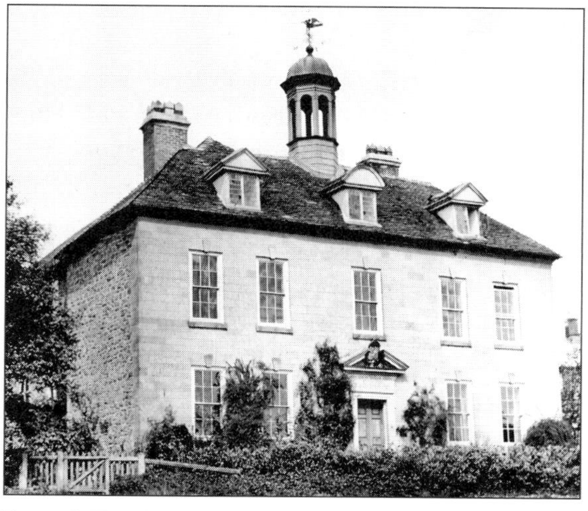

Private Collection

Figure 3. The Old School House, Cleobury Mortimer, Shropshire: c. 1740.

The son of a farmer from Snodland, Kent, William Wilson had entered teaching only after being dissuaded from taking up engineering. A practical man, and a talented amateur artist-craftsman, he encouraged his son to make art his career. 'After a childhood whose chiefest delights were pencil and paper', recalled Harry in a cursory autobiographical note of 1910, 'I was set at the age of ten to make studies of the Dyce and Forster Drawing Copies, issued by the Department of Science and Art ... '.[3] Clara, famously green-fingered, was a close observer of nature with a great understanding of planting and propagation. Both parents were intensely religious, and the family lived frugally in an

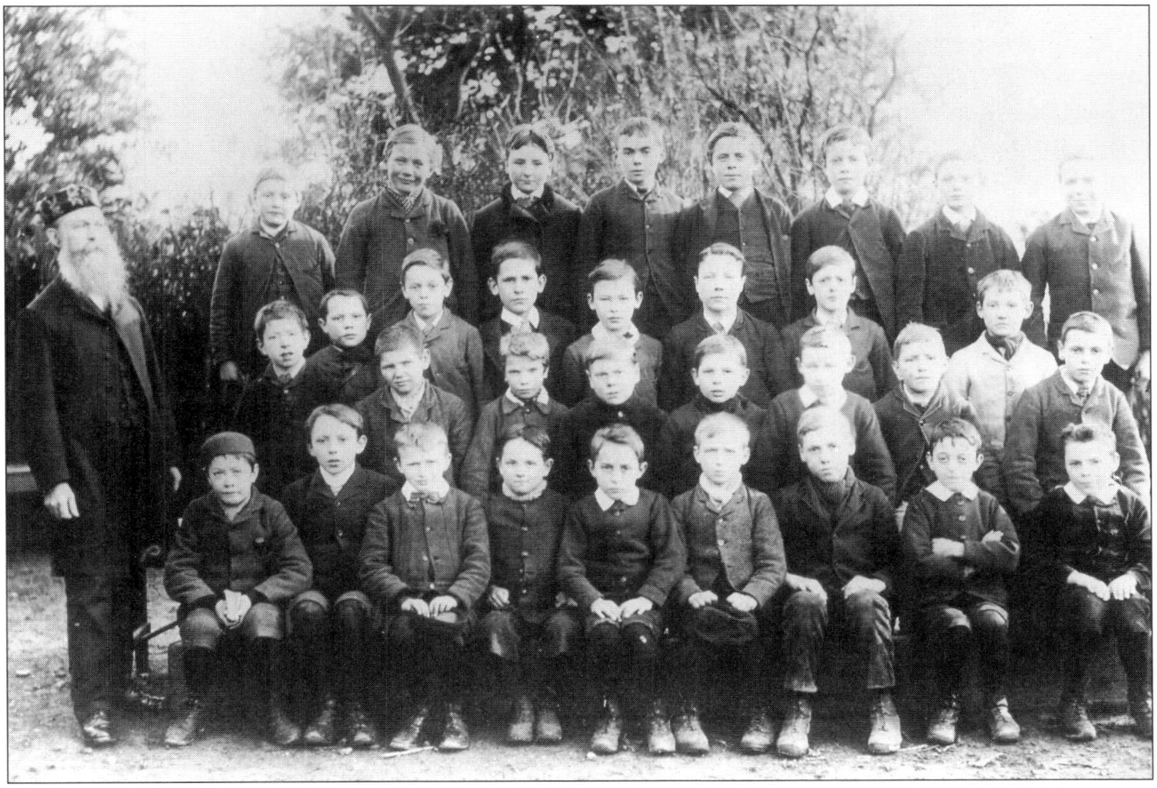

Private Collection

Figure 4. School photograph: headmaster William Henry Wilson stands to the left, Harry Wilson is the 5th boy from the left, 3rd row from the front, c. 1876.

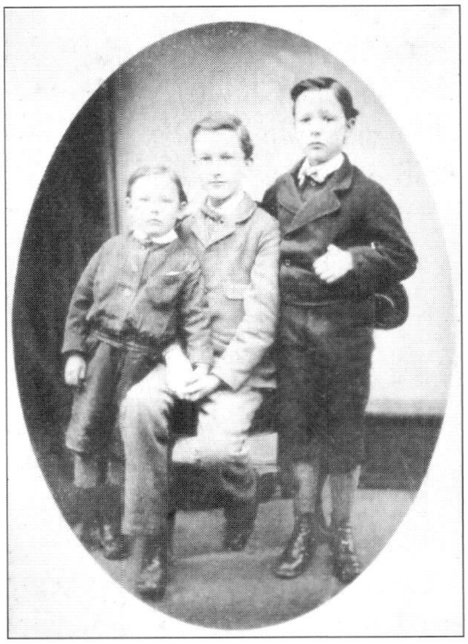

Private Collection

Figure 5. Edgar, Harry and Patten Wilson, c. 1880.

atmosphere of keen debate and enquiry. Harry was the eldest of three surviving boys. Marion would die of scarlet fever aged four-and-a-half, while a younger brother, Theodore, died at two months as a result of a fall from his nurse's lap. The middle son, Patten, born in 1869, followed Harry to school in Liverpool; he would become an illustrator and commercial artist. The youngest, Edgar, nine years Harry's junior, was destined to pursue an adventurous career in the shipping business in the Middle East, running trade routes for the Euphrates & Tigris Corporation, in time becoming its Joint Managing Director (Fig. 5). Both Patten and their father would help Harry on assorted commissions, Patten, for instance, collaborating with him in 1893 on the font for the chapel at Welbeck Abbey; two years later his father worked on the altar cross for St. Martin's, Marple, and in 1896, on the beaten brass doors for St. Peter's, Ealing. In subject matter and style, Patten's Pre-Raphaelitesque illustrations, like those published in *The Builder* of 1896,[4] could not help but share elements of his brother's designs, since the work of both was steeped in the romance of tradition.[5]

On leaving the Collegiate School at 16, Harry enrolled at the Kidderminster School of Art, to follow (as his 1910 note records) 'the usual course set for designers, including nature study, light and shade drawings in various media, and courses of applied design, historical ornament and architecture'.[6] His word 'usual' aptly evokes his feelings about the dullness of the instruction he encountered, a pitfall he vowed to avoid in the teaching he himself undertook later, in which he would foster personal creativity above all.

In 1882, his studies successfully completed, Wilson chose to become articled to the Maidenhead architect Edward Shrewsbury (1848-1924), an associate member of the Royal Institute of British Architects and a founder member of the Berkshire Archaeological Society. The practice was firmly rooted in the Maidenhead area, building several churches, the Technical Institute, and the Jubilee clocktower; it was in the office at Queen Street Chambers, designed in 1877 by Shrewsbury himself, that Wilson worked out his articles.[7]

Shrewsbury's approach to architecture was an essentially local one. He met Maidenhead's requirements in a direct, unpretentious manner with unassuming buildings of stone or Thames Valley stock-brick, leavened on occasions with decorative pargetting. His responsiveness to the needs of the district was an early factor in the development of Wilson's own sensitivity to locale. Shrewsbury was renowned for his dislike of office-based architecture, preferring on-site supervision of his designs. This involvement with the building process would find reaffirmation in Wilson's philosophy of architecture, in which the exchange of ideas between workman and architect was vital.

By 1884 Wilson had moved to the London practice of Sir George Gilbert Scott's younger architect son, the gifted if rather staid John Oldrid Scott (1841-1913). Here he was employed for eighteen months as an 'improver' – a supervised apprentice, working part-time on a nominal wage, for the privilege of honing his professional skills and gaining experience. On two days a week, office work was exchanged for study at the Westminster School of Art, where the Professor, Fred Brown, would frequently despatch his students to the National Gallery to make studies in oil or watercolour after selected Old Masters.

One of the leading Gothic Revival architects of the day, Oldrid Scott, had worked for his father – the most prolific of all the Revivalists – from 1860 to 1878, when he had succeeded to the practice. His own predilection was for fourteenth century Gothic, which he used for two major projects during Wilson's time with him: St. Mary's, Slough, built between 1875 and 1913, and an unsuccessful entry in 1886 for the first Liverpool Cathedral competition.[8] Scott's preference for a specific phase of Gothic, albeit an advanced one, alerted Wilson to the huge creative potential of the Gothic style, but also prompted him, by the very limits it imposed, to find ways of freeing the Gothic spirit from strict academic restraints.

Scott influenced Wilson in another direction too, in advocating a thorough professional grasp of all the trades and skills that contributed to a building's overall effect. Although the scholarly and reserved Scott shunned the role of self-publicist, his designs for the crafts embodied the importance he attached to these elements of a building. For example, his set of forty-four oak chancel stalls for St. Alban's Cathedral, made in 1882 to his specifications by the ecclesiastical furnishers Farmer and Brindley, are vigorous in form but respectful of their context, a sensitivity seen again in his numerous designs for church plate.[9]

In 1886 Wilson moved to the more congenial and creative office of Scott's exact contemporary, John Belcher, while pursuing his studies at the Westminster School of Art with Mouat Loudon as his Professor, Fred Brown having left to become Principal of the Slade School. John Belcher had inherited his father's prosperous City practice, where he had served his own apprenticeship. His student years in Paris had inclined him to French classicism, but his strong affinity with Gothic survived. Features of Belcher's practice form striking parallels with that of J.D. Sedding, his 'old and sincere friend,' in whose office Wilson would complete his apprentice years. Both were affected by the light, spacious Gothicism of G.E. Street, and by the richly patterned effects of William Burges, whose style was reflected in the diapered brickwork of Belcher's 1873 Church of St. Mary, Camberwell New Road.

Belcher attached considerable importance to the unity of architecture and its 'sister' arts,[10] and he would chair the first meeting of the Art Workers' Guild in 1884. His views on the crafts, corresponding closely with those of both Sedding and Wilson, were summed up in his declaration:

> *I have always contended for their collaboration ... even when such an idea was regarded as quite utopian. In all cases the artists should work together ab initio.*[11]

Even in the latter part of his career, when he was concentrating on commercial and civic buildings in an urban Baroque style, Belcher continued to marry art with architecture. His best-known design, the Institute of Chartered Accountants of 1888-93, was the winning entry in the competition to create that organisation's Moorgate Place headquarters. With sculptures by Hamo Thornycroft and Harry Bates, both prominent Art Workers' Guildsmen, it fully adopts his unifying principles. Its exterior, a sure integration of structural and plastic arts, combines the Baroque style and Arts and Crafts tenets in a synthesis that would profoundly influence individuals from the next generation, such as Charles Holden in his commissioning in 1908 of both Jacob Epstein for the sculptures on Rhodesia House in the Strand, and Wilson himself, both as architect and as sculptural embellisher of other architects' buildings.

Belcher's views on the good sense of architects employing the same building team on successive projects matched a fundamental maxim of Sedding's; as Belcher put it,

> *The more frequently the same men work together the more thoroughly will they ... acquire an intelligent insight into [the architect's] thoughts .... He on his part will be able to allow a certain amount of freedom of expression to the men under him.*[12]

Although his restorations of old churches would be fewer than Sedding's, his approach was no less painstaking. In his Architect's Report preliminary to his 1886 refurbishment of the Wiltshire Church of St. Mary Magdalene, South Marston, whose earliest parts were known to date from the twelfth century, Belcher outlined his strategy:

> *In restoring and adding to this church I propose to preserve as far as possible every feature of interest .... The timbers of the nave roof at present covered up, I expect to find of oak. Some may be sound enough for re-use; if not short lengths at least could be worked into the lychgate ... .*[13]

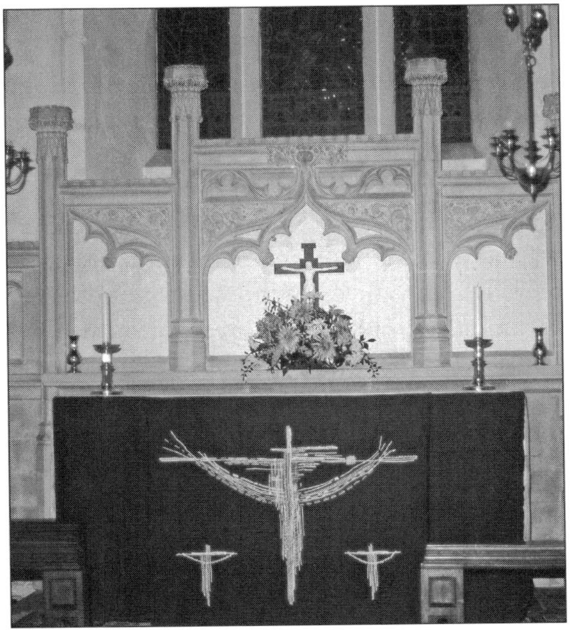

Figure 6. Church of St. Mary Magdalene, South Marston, Wiltshire: Wilson's first recorded work, reredos, 1886.

It was here, for John Belcher, that Wilson's earliest recorded design was executed – the carved and painted stone reredos (Fig. 6). Its richly crocketed and crowned pinnacles show his sensitivity to the Gothic idiom, and emphasise the architectural feeling of the work, while his emerging individual vision might be glimpsed in the heads at the ends of the cusping. Originally it was painted with angels on each side panel, and 'symbolical decorated crosses'[14] in the centre; now much of the intended effect is lost under a coat of distemper.

However, the paths of Belcher and Sedding diverged dramatically with Belcher's gravitation towards the Baroque style, this reaching its fullest expression in the Town Hall for Colchester of 1897-1902. Variations on the style had been gaining popularity since the late 1880s with works by John Brydon, Norman Shaw and Belcher himself, but neither Sedding nor Wilson showed any inclination to engage with such secular grandeur, nor with the range of large-scale civic and commercial architecture on which Belcher's reputation would come to rest. Coincidentally, the parting of their ways is personified in Wilson, who, in 1888, the year work began on the Chartered Accountants' building, left Belcher to become Chief Assistant in Sedding's office.

Two former colleagues from Belcher's practice, Beresford Pite (1861-1934) and Thomas Phillips Figgis (1858-1948), would nevertheless exert a lasting effect on Wilson. Pite had become Belcher's partner in 1885; in quite a different context, and many years later, Wilson and Pite would became colleagues again, when both found themselves teaching at the Royal College of Art under W.R. Lethaby, Pite holding the Professorship of Architecture from 1900 until 1923. Wilson had greatly admired Pite's architectural drawings ever since he had first seen them in Belcher's office. His own impressive draughtsmanship had evolved in Shrewsbury's and Oldrid Scott's offices, but its dynamic impressionism seems the perfect embodiment of Pite's assertion that 'though actual building is [the Architect's] goal ... these documentary Designs have beauties of their own'.[15] Pite's maverick inventiveness was to have a strong impact on Wilson, the boldness of the schemes it produced often seeming to place him one step ahead of his contemporaries. When Pite left Belcher to set up his own practice, his first commission was Christ Church, Brixton, for which he chose a neo-Byzantine style 'when every one else was Gothic'. His own house at 82 Mortimer Street (1896) was decorated with giant Michaelangelesque caryatids 'while his brother architects were playing with little terracotta dolls'.[16] Like him, Wilson would develop a personal architectural style drawing on a range of unexpected sources but owing complete allegiance to none. In combination with threads leading from J.F. Bentley's Westminster Cathedral of 1895-1903, and from research into Byzantine art by Lethaby and Robert Weir Schultz,[17] Pite's Brixton church, under construction from 1897 to 1903, would give Wilson the confidence to pursue his own extravagant Byzantine scheme of decoration at St. Bartholomew's, Brighton from 1898.

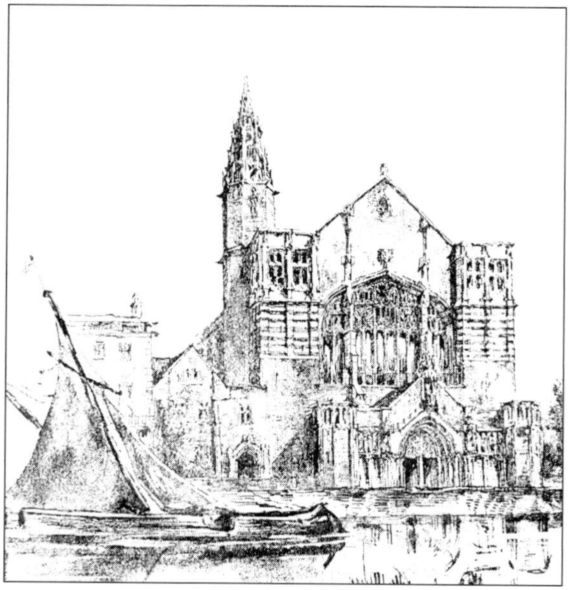

Figure 7. John Belcher: church on the Regent's Canal, 1889, illustrated in *The Architect*, 27 February 1891.

A further intriguing link between Wilson and Pite exists in the design for a church on the Regent's Canal, in Paddington, submitted to the Royal Academy in 1889 and illustrated in *The Architect* of 27 February 1891 (Fig. 7). Although displayed in Belcher's name, something of its design must be attributed on stylistic grounds to either Wilson, or Pite, or both. The proposal daringly blends Gothic and Romanesque elements with wholly underived original features. Assuming it to be the work of

Belcher himself, the architect Mervyn Macartney, a pupil of Norman Shaw and founder-member of the Art Workers' Guild, hailed it as the prototype of Sedding's Holy Trinity, Sloane Street of 1888-91.[18] Yet Sedding's church was three-quarters finished by the time Belcher's Paddington design was published. The Sedding-trained architect Charles Nicholson concluded that Belcher and Sedding should properly be regarded as joint originators of fresh, freer ideas in Gothic.[19] If, however, Wilson is acknowledged as a constant factor in both designs, perhaps sharing early ideas with Pite in the Paddington scheme, certainly collaborating with Sedding on Holy Trinity, then the link between the two buildings becomes less a question of precedent and more one of common authorship.

Although T.P. Figgis left Belcher's office soon after Wilson arrived, their duties overlapped long enough for a friendship to form, and in 1890, by which time Wilson had moved on to join Sedding, and Figgis had his own practice, the pair became successful joint entrants in a limited competition for the Free Public Library, Ladbroke Grove. So important was this, the first purpose-built library in the area, that it was arranged that William Gladstone, the Liberal leader, should open it.

The winning design was published in *The Architect* of 20 June 1890 (Fig. 8). The façade of the proposed building is neo-Elizabethan, and, as befitting its West London setting, essentially of stock-brick. In this original scheme, a Tree of Knowledge, in carved stone bas-relief, symbolises the building's overall purpose as it grows from ground level, upwards between the large windows, themselves divided into graduated panes; linking arches and lunettes above them unify the main gable and entrance bay. At its summit, the tree's branches spread into the undulating line of a pierced parapet which forms a backdrop for figures of Milton, Shakespeare and Spenser. Presiding over them

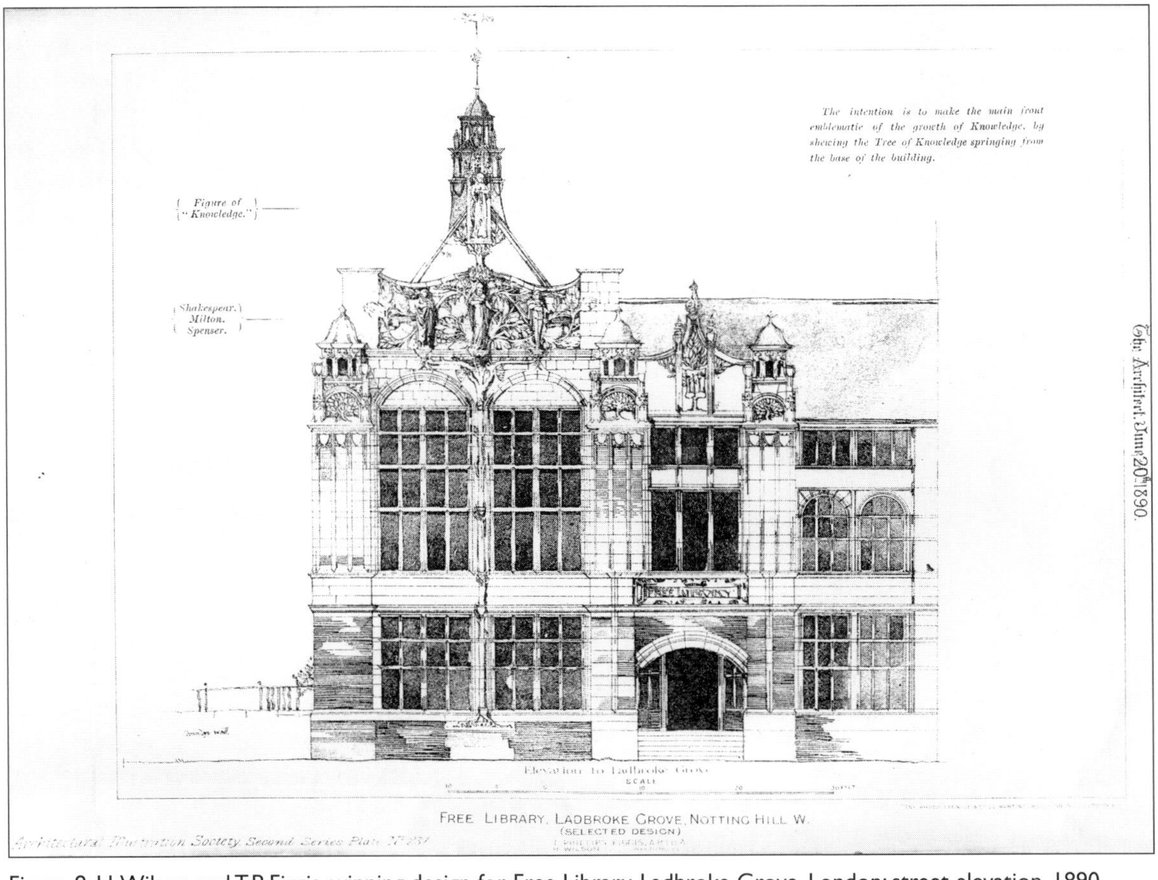

Figure 8. H. Wilson and T.P. Figgis, winning design for Free Library, Ladbroke Grove, London: street elevation, 1890.

all, in a pillared niche, is the figure of Knowledge. The steeply-pitched slate roof is crowned with an intricate lantern – a symbolic temple of Knowledge at the summit of learning.

The foliage adorning this proposed design immediately brings to mind the decorative friezes of C.H. Townsend's Bishopsgate Institute of 1892-94 and Horniman Museum of 1896-1901. The three domed turrets on the Ladbroke Grove façade, and especially the large spire-topped roof-lantern, may draw on Wilson's memories of his childhood home, the Old School House in Cleobury, with its dormered tiled roof and central lantern, a source of his enduring passion for the satisfying silhouette. At the same time, the library's cupolas, the striking geometry of its windows and the naturalistic decoration foreshadow aspects of C.R. Mackintosh's design for a railway terminus shown in the 1893 Soane Medallion Competition.[20]

While most of the symbolic impact of the library's proposed exterior would be lost in execution, the interior plan survived intact. The busy ground floor, with News Room and book-lending counter, was organised around a spacious entrance hall. On the first floor, three Reading Rooms led off a central landing. Every opportunity was taken to economise on the interior fixtures and fittings while preserving the general effect; as part of that ambience the large General Reading Room was to have a fireplace designed by Wilson, and modelled by him and F.W. Pomeroy. Its frieze, depicting the water nymph Undine amidst swirling streams, fishes and waterweed, was exhibited, before installation, at the third Arts and Crafts Exhibition in 1890.[21]

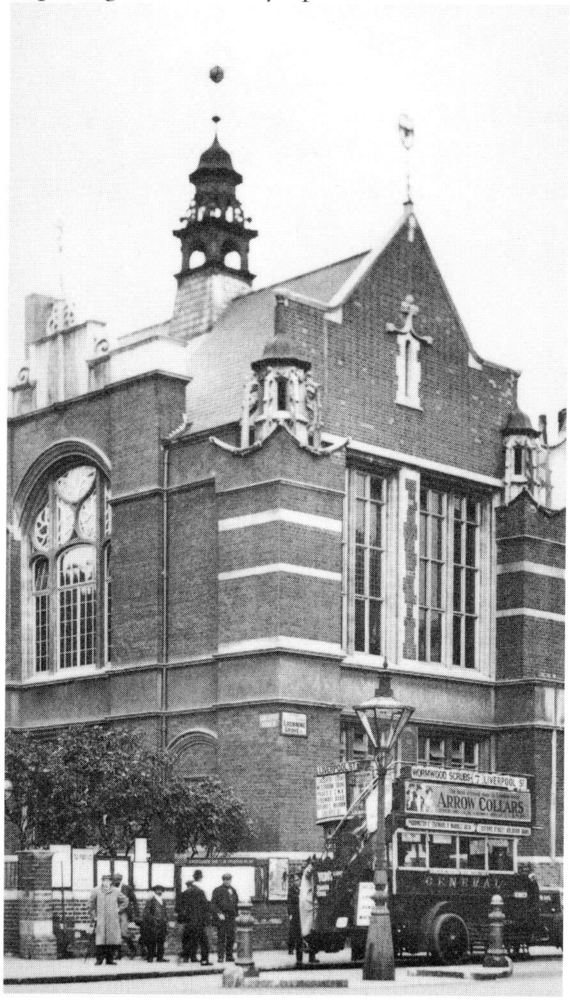

Royal Borough of Kensington & Chelsea

Figure 9. Ladbroke Grove Library as built, c. 1910.

The Commissioners for Public Libraries saw to it that, as erected by the firm of John Greenwood, the exterior of the library would be much plainer than Wilson and Figgis had envisaged it (Fig. 9). Some of the special features that had given the scheme its distinctive character were retained, but many more were abandoned so as to cut costs. The trio of domed turrets facing Ladbroke Grove, and the lantern crowning the roof were saved, so too the arched, asymmetrically-placed main entrance and the round-headed side window with its flamboyant tracery (Plate 1). But the tree, the sculpted figures, the elaborate iconographical scheme of the kind intrinsic to Wilson's later work and to his ambition to evolve a symbolism relevant to everyday life, all this was scrapped.

Further casualties of the cuts that swept away the building's proto-Art Nouveau overlay were its rhythms and coherence: the dished tops of the brick piers, hastily conceived to pick up the wave-form of the plain stone gable, serve as reminders of the intended interplay of squared and fluid elements, but their curtailment is abrupt and looks incomplete. The narrow lancet topped by three forlorn clusters of foliage in an otherwise featureless main gable is a poor substitute for a flourishing Tree of Knowledge. The broad stone band dividing the ground floor from the upper levels, together with three narrow stone courses and an intrusive cornice over the main window, adds some variety to a starved-looking frontage. Ironically, though, these features succeed in creating a 'streaky bacon' façade of the very kind its architects had set out to eschew; all in all, the 'Reductions' that the Commissioners had exacted rendered the finished building almost unrecognisable as the winning design.

Figgis sounded pragmatic when, on 15 January 1890, he read out to the assembled Committee members details of the first swathe of economies that he and Wilson had been pressed into making: 'The front of the Building has been re-modelled and made much less ornate, the carving being omitted in the principal gable, with the exception of the topmost niche ... '.

As yet, however, the specifications remained exemplary. The walls, for instance, were to be

> *built of best hard burnt stocks, faced with red brick and stone. The dressings, sills and mullions to the windows also of stone. The roofs to be covered with green slates, and ventillating fléche and angle turrets to have copper domes. All timber will be best quality Baltic fir. The floors to be fireproof on Lindsay's patent system of steel and concrete. The ground floor will be finished with wood block flooring. All walls to be plastered and the News Room to have a tiled dado ... .*[22]

But the deeper cuts the architects found themselves inflicting on their design just two and a half months later were more painful. This second round of savings, in which almost all their preferred options were exchanged for cheaper substitutes, enabled Wilson and Figgis to reduce the 'Amount of Tender' from £4,299-0-0 to £3,591-12-2; even then it marginally exceeded the limit of £3,590 set by the Commissioners, and the high specifications the architects had tried to preserve had been compromised. The greatest economy came with the use of Bath stone 'in lieu of Doulting', and, inevitably, 'less ... carving', which reduced the total by £144-0-0. Their January 'Report' was superseded item by item in the final account of 1 April, with each saving costed to the last penny:

stock facing instead of red (except piers to porch); omit ¼-brick projection for plinth	*£20-6-3*
Saving on gable in Lancaster Road, substitution of plain coping and red facing, and of plain finials for canopies	*£85-0-0*
Ashton and Green's permanent green slates instead of Eureka	*£5-0-0*
Ordinary plastering in lieu of trowelled stucco throughout	*£12-10-0*
Wood instead of iron casements	*£40-0-0*
Omission of grilles to circular headed windows and to staircase window	*£33-6-0*
Reduce fireproofing	*£67-15-0*
Ordinary floors & fillets instead of woodblocks to basement and ground floor	*£65-0-0*
Keen's cement dado and skirting painted instead of tiles for News Room	*£37-0-0*
Distempering instead of plastering to Book Stores in basement	*£6-10-0*
Reduce the price of sanitary fittings	*£10-0-0*

The architects even resorted to second-hand items in their bid to meet their budget: the use of 'old ranges and stoves and chimney pieces throughout basement and second floor' saved £15.[23]

As luck would have it, the opening ceremony was also subject to alteration. Due to pressing political duties, Mr. Gladstone had no time to spare, but Sir John Lubbock – whose achievements as Liberal MP for Maidstone included the Public Libraries Act and establishing, in 1871, the annual August Bank Holiday[24] – was a popular stand-in on the day, 29 October 1891. The library's social impact was clear, as was the effect of the building itself, or rather, of its original published design, which came as a revelation to other rising architects, especially Charles Harrison Townsend and Charles Rennie Mackintosh. However, so ruthless a transformation of his (albeit collaborate) first independent building must have provided Wilson with an early lesson in the difficult compromises – and sacrifices – sometimes demanded of an architect.

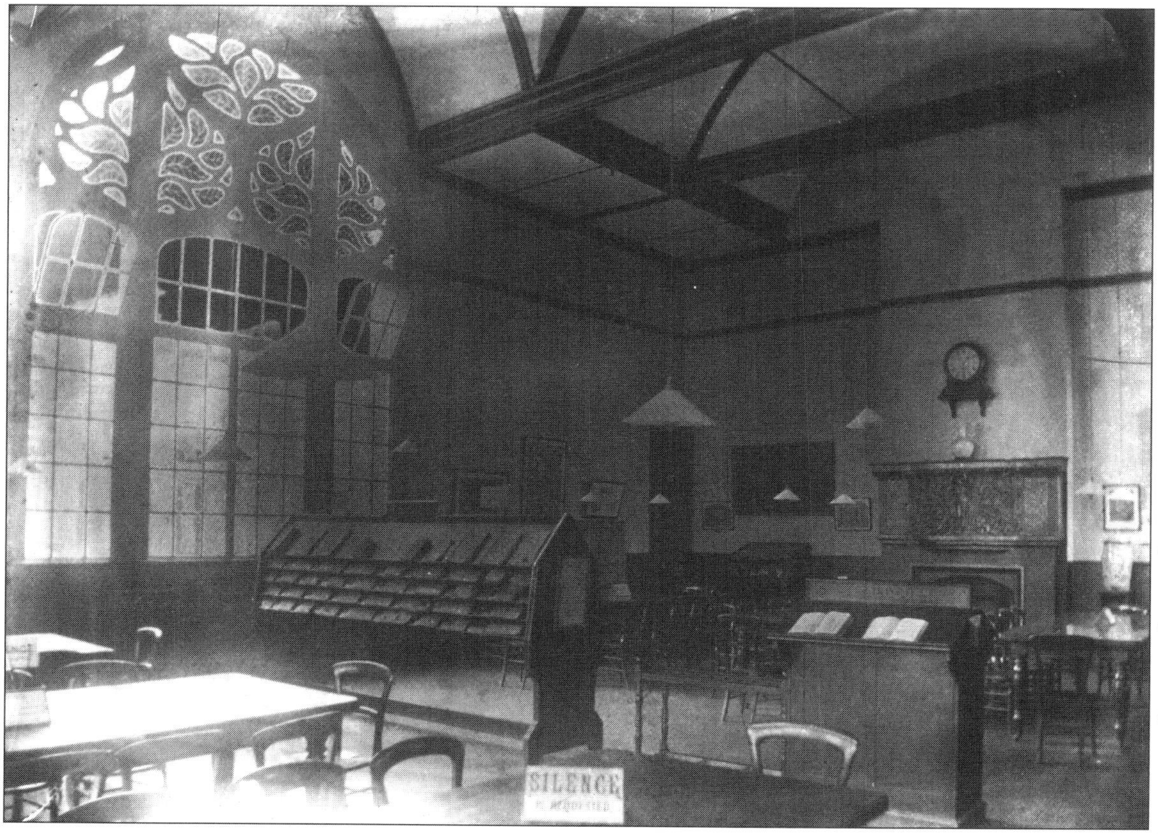

Royal Borough of Kensington & Chelsea

Figure 10. (top) Ladbroke Grove Library, General Reading Room, with Wilson's Undine fireplace frieze *in situ*, c. 1910; (below) Frieze from library fireplace: designed by H. Wilson, modelled by F.W. Pomeroy and H. Wilson, displayed at Arts and Crafts Exhibition 1890, illustrated in *The Architect,* 16 January 1891.

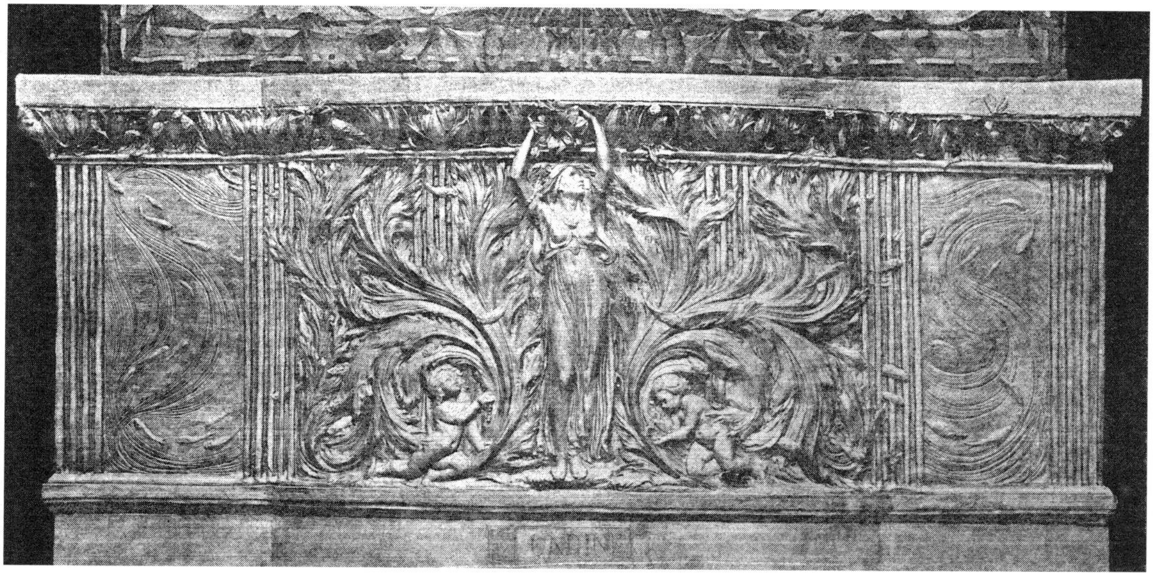

CHAPTER TWO

SEDDING AND HIS IMPACT

Henry Wilson left Belcher's practice in 1888 to become chief architectural assistant to J.D. Sedding, in his office at 447 Oxford Street, next door to the showrooms of Morris & Co. at 449. Throughout his relatively short career, John Dando Sedding (1838-91) combined an unflagging talent with an evident formal sensitivity, restoring many West Country churches and designing new buildings in styles ranging from free Gothic to Renaissance revisited. He had completed his articles with the Gothic Revival architect G.E. Street (1824-81), through whose office had passed as assistants William Morris, Philip Webb and Norman Shaw. From 1863 Sedding worked for some five years in Penzance with his ill-fated elder brother Edmund; then in Bristol, until 1874, before setting up his own London practice in 1875. He was deeply committed to the Arts and Crafts movement, believing earnestly in the need for modern architects to work closely with craftsmen, sculptors and painters. Sedding's first encounter with Wilson was at the Art Workers' Guild, of which Sedding had been an enthusiastic member since its inception in 1884. He sat on its first committee, becoming its Master in 1886, two years after John Belcher. Wilson had been attending its meetings during his time with Belcher, but did not officially join until 1892.

The three years Wilson spent in Sedding's office shaped many of his most deeply-held beliefs. The period of their collaboration combined incessant activity with a creative freedom that stood in sharp contrast to some of Wilson's previous experiences. His sadness at the rapid passage of his time with Sedding and its abrupt close with the 53-year-old Sedding's sudden death in 1891, pervades his affectionate tributes to his master. Sedding had died at the peak of his career, just as his progressive attitudes towards architecture were reaching their fullest expression. Some of his most important buildings, including the Church of the Holy Redeemer, Clerkenwell and Holy Trinity, Sloane Street, lay unfinished at the time of his death. Wilson's immense sorrow at the thought of Sedding's unfulfilled potential was only mitigated by the conviction that it was the *ideas* he was seeking to embody that would have the most enduring significance.

By the time of Sedding's death, Wilson had lived in London for seven years, lodging for the greater part of that time at 32 Bedford Gardens. In 1889 Wilson's father retired, and the family moved from Cleobury Mortimer into the rented house Harry found for them in Harrow, where he himself would join them. His determination to carry on the Oxford Street office and complete his master's unfinished works was one of total commitment. It sprang partly from feelings of loyalty, and partly from a sense of duty to clients to whom work had been promised. Wilson seemed practically to *become* Sedding in order to finish the jobs left undone. Bearing in mind his unreserved devotion to Sedding's ideas, it would not have been difficult for him to complete these commissions in the spirit of their initial conception.[1] As Sedding's right-hand man, he had in any case been fully involved from the outset with any commissions accepted between 1888 and 1891.

Nevertheless, during and immediately following his time with Sedding, Wilson was establishing his own architectural identity. This had already been expressed in the 1890 Ladbroke Grove Library design quite separately from Sedding. It reappeared in some of his independent additions to Sedding commissions, for instance in the clergy house and campanile at Holy Redeemer, Clerkenwell. Even more striking demonstrations of Wilson's autonomy are to be seen in those cases where he diverged from Sedding's drawings and substituted ideas of his own. This occurred, for instance, in his re-design of the tower for St. Clement's, Bournemouth, added in 1893 to Sedding's church of 1873; and in his 1896 proposal for the west end of St. Augustine's, Highgate, another dramatic departure from

Sedding's design. Besides, entirely fresh commissions were beginning to reach Wilson, notably, in 1895, that for St. Mark's, Brithdir.

Wilson's portrayals of Sedding consistently suggest a man who was exceptional on both a personal and a professional level. The many small incidents of Sedding's life which Wilson recounts in illustration of his architectural achievements show these two facets inseparably intermingled. Wilson recalls, for example, an occasion when he and Sedding had quarrelled:

> *I remember once when there had been a slight disagreement between us I wrote to explain. Next morning when he entered the office he came straight to the desk where I was working, quietly put his arm round me, took my free hand in his and pressed it to him without a word. It was more than enough.*[2]

Nor was Wilson alone in feeling the power of Sedding's 'electric' personality:

> *All who knew him – clients, workmen, friends and acquaintances – long to have known him more. Those in his office were his friends whose criticism he invited, and on whose collaboration he relied with a loving trustfulness as rare as it was delightful.*[3]

United in their grief and admiration for their master, Wilson and J.P. Cooper (a pupil in the office at the time of Sedding's death) together wrote an illuminating series of articles on Sedding's career for *The Architectural Review* in 1897-98 which form a moving tribute. They distinguished three broad phases, the first two being vital forerunners to the innovative third – when Wilson was working for him – and which did most to secure Sedding's justifiable reputation as one of the most original and expressive architects of his time.

Looking back on the first phase of his career, articled to and then working with G.E. Street between 1858 and 1863, Sedding himself would speak impatiently of the Gothic Revival's obsession with 'classification'. This he regarded as a soulless and destructive process in that it reduced the essentially 'informal elements of old art to formulae'.[4] Worse still in his view was the Revival's tendency to create specialists not just in Gothic architecture, but in particular *kinds* of Gothic. As the arch-Goth himself, Sir Gilbert Scott, admitted in his autobiography, some Revivalists were as hostile to certain varieties of Gothic as they were to classical architecture.

Such attitudes were characterised by Sedding as both 'defective' and 'abnormal'[5] – indictments which must have struck a chord with Wilson when he remembered his former boss Oldrid Scott's almost exclusive pursuit of fourteenth century Gothic. Sedding had been trained at a time when the foremost second generation Goths, Street himself, White, Butterfield, Burges, Brooks, Pearson, and Bodley, were producing some of their major works. While the Gothic Revival exerted a lifelong influence on Sedding, it never transformed him into one of those blinkered specialists that it made of some of his contemporaries. Street, after all, had taught that an architect should be capable of decorating his own buildings, an ideal which Sedding in turn passed on to Wilson. It was probably Street's influence, as much as some early advice given him by Ruskin, that stimulated Sedding's interest in the crafts. Sedding's own particular skills lay in stone carving and wrought ironwork:

> *He would tell how he spent his evenings in his rooms, where he must have had a most amenable landlady, at work with mallet and chisel on a block of stone ... .*[6]

Street and Sedding shared many fundamental architectural ideas. Like Viollet-le-Duc, Street had a strong streak of practicality, regarding the pointed architecture of Gothicism as essentially rational. The most knowledgeable and well-travelled of the Revivalists, he encompassed a broad range of inspiration. Most significantly, he was aware of the possibility of the 'development'[7] of the Gothic language that might be achieved by drawing on the medieval styles of England and Europe, and even on classicism.

Some of his principal urban churches were built during Sedding's employment with him, for example the red brick St. James-the-Less, Westminster, of 1859-61, with its polychromatic decoration and its freestanding tower, reminiscent of the campaniles of Northern Italy. The furnishings were designed by Street himself, who was renowned for the care that he gave to every detail of his buildings.

> *Yet a fundamental opposition of temperaments between the two men finally made a parting of the ways inevitable; as Wilson and Cooper wrote, 'their natures were entirely unsympathetic, and Sedding, when the opportunity offered, left ...'.*[8]

The second phase of John Sedding's career thus began in 1863, soon, he had moved to Cornwall, and entered into partnership with his elder brother Edmund, an architect with a successful practice in Penzance, but whose precarious health was causing concern. At the time, Edmund was considered the more gifted of the two, having completed his articles with Street, then running an office in Bristol, and later, in London. Certainly their partnership helped John develop his personal style. The first commission completed entirely by John Sedding, St. Martin's Church, Marple (1869-70), had actually been entrusted to Edmund, but in 1868 his health finally broke down and he died, leaving only fragmentary sketches before work could begin. The commission thereby passed to John as a windfall, and he was able to proceed on his own, free from the constraints of his London training.

St. Martin's is built of local Cheshire sandstone with a bellcote and half-timbered porch at the West end. Inside, its barrel roof, widely-spaced piers, broad chancel arch and lavishly decorated chancel create a spacious mood. Not surprisingly, some remnants of Sedding's debt to the Gothic Revival, and to Edmund's more historicist style, remain. Wilson himself remarked on its 'comparative hardness of detail' and the 'general rectilinearity of the design'.[9] But clear signs of John Sedding's individuality also emerge, for example, in the richness of the chancel and the sensitive control of massing. It was significant, also, that he went to Ford Madox Brown for the design of the chancel window, and to Morris & Co. to execute it. The finished window, representing in its figures the combined skills of Burne-Jones, Rossetti, Morris and Brown, forms a clear demonstration of Sedding's belief in the need for architect and craftsman to collaborate. Later Wilson himself would contribute to St. Martin's, producing some of his best work in adding the Lady Chapel, font cover, Christopher Chapel and memorial plaque.

Living and working in Cornwall had a profound effect on Sedding: Wilson and Cooper declared that it was there that he 'first studied building',[10] implying that in contrast with the formal training in drawing and measuring provided by Street, he was really beginning to understand and learn from old wrought stones *in situ*. The word 'building' is consciously chosen by them instead of the more academic 'architecture' to suggest the actual making of buildings by craftsmen working within a 'living' tradition. It was in his Cornish period that Sedding began to concentrate on the restoration of old churches, making appropriate modern additions where necessary. The growth of a deep affinity with the landscape and character of Cornwall enabled him to effect creative alterations to buildings in the spirit of their original conception.

The implications that the study of old Cornish work had on Sedding's own commissions parallel the approach adopted by the Society for the Protection of Ancient Buildings (SPAB) which William Morris was to found in 1877, and which, by the time of Wilson's maturity in the late 1880s onwards, would include many up-and-coming young architects and designers; Ernest Gimson, Sidney Barnsley, Emery Walker, Sydney Cockerell and Detmar Blow, and Lethaby and Sedding regularly attended its meetings. Though he never became a member, Wilson himself attended some committee meetings as a visitor.[11] Lethaby explained how this 'Antiscrape' society, ostensibly focused on the past, in fact supplied a key to the present and the future:

dealing with the common facts of traditional building in ... hundreds of examples, it became, under the technical guidance of Philip Webb the architect, a real school of practical building. It is a curious fact that, ... engaged in an intense study of antiquity, [it] became a school of rational builders and modern building.[12]

The SPAB's stance evolved in the 1890s with Philip Webb's appeal for 'essential, modern' work on old buildings to be 'simple, unpretentious' and 'frankly the production of the present day'. The idea won the approval of some of Sedding's closest associates – including Ernest Gimson[13] - and Sedding's intelligent, sympathetic restorations, like those which he carried out in 1888 at Burford, Gloucestershire, were the apogee of SPAB thought.

In attempting to define the special character of Cornish church building, Sedding had distinguished three main features – a feeling for nature, a distinct local identity, and a marked 'emotional'[14] dimension. It is no surprise that these elements formed the major concerns of his own subsequent buildings.

For Sedding, a Cornishman 'by adoption'[15] (his having been born in Eton, Berkshire), the first of these had indeed become a major source of inspiration, and it remained a vital consideration in buildings he erected later, far away from Cornwall. He shared Ruskin's contention that 'You cannot love art well till you love what she mirrors better' (Lethaby cited these words in Sedding's obituary in *The Builder*), and maintained that a young architect would gain more from strolling in a garden than sketching in a museum. Even the way he worked, here vividly evoked by Wilson, seemed to resemble the workings of nature:

In his half shy yet eager way ... he would go straight to his drawing board and, settling on his stool like a bird alighting on a bough, would fall to vigorously. The design would sprout in new and unexpected places, only to be ruthlessly pruned down. Phase succeeded phase until the vision in his mind's eye was more-or-less nearly presented; when after covering half the paper with notes, he would ... proceed to something else. These little birdy ways ... kept us constantly ... alert, for we never quite knew what he would do next ... .[16]

In his book *Garden-Craft Old and New*, published in the last year of his life, Sedding explained how, as well as its simple aesthetic value, a garden can have have a symbolic one too, as a 'memorial of Paradise Lost'.[17] The same may be said of the portrayals of nature in his work, notably at Holbeton, Devon, where in 1884 he began one of his most influential schemes of restoration. He added a new South porch to the church, but elsewhere left the building's structure unaltered. Any repairs were made sparingly and invisibly. Additional features like the new chancel screen, seats, altar, reredos and marble floor were carefully gauged to blend with the old. This sympathetic approach, along with that of other restorations Sedding carried out in the 1880s, won the SPAB's approval and were a fertile source of inspiration for other architects. Wilson's and Cooper's articles likened Holbeton's restored nave to a 'garden full of flowers on either side', leading to a chancel yet 'more finely carved, with lizards, squirrels, frogs and every sort of creeping thing, with birds and flowers innumerable';[18] the work would form an example for Wilson's own choir stalls at Brithdir in 1895-98.

Sedding himself was especially pleased with his new doors of ironwork enriched with enamel, declaring that it was by these above all that he would choose to be remembered, and that his gravestone should read 'He made the doors at Holbeton and was an artist in his way'.[19] For Wilson, they did not epitomise the entirety of Sedding's spirit as craftsman, 'excellent in execution'[20] though they were, and he made no mention of them on the headstone he made for his master. Several other features of Sedding's Holbeton work would leave a deep impression on other architects. Colour flowed into the Holbeton church from panels of stained glass designed by Heywood Sumner, while the green-tinged 'bottle glazing'[21] of the aisle windows and tower screen suited Sedding's eclectic approach, it being made like late-medieval church windows, whose ringed texture derived from each disc of molten glass having been spun on a rod. The technique was popularised in the 'Domestic Revival' by William Morris, Norman Shaw and others in the 1860s, and reappeared in St. Osmund's, Poole, by Edward Prior, who had trained in Shaw's office and was a co-founder of the Art Workers' Guild. Wilson, involved in the furnishing of this astonishing church in 1904, may well have suggested bottle glazing; certainly he encouraged Christopher Whall to use it in his own comission of the Chapel and Library at Welbeck.

This local aspect, the singularity of 'type' Sedding had observed in Cornwall's architecture, manifests itself in the architecture of *every* district: as Sedding explained in his book *Art and Handicraft*, published posthumously in 1893:

> *Our national architecture, like our national language is pretty much a matter of dialects ... your knowledge of the English of Yorkshire will not frank you in a tramp across Sussex or Devon.*[22]

In other words, it was no use building in a Barnsley 'dialect' in Chichester, or vice versa. This perception of ways of building that reflected the personality of an area provided a way into 'free' design. Aspects of Sedding's sensitivity to the localness of architecture translated easily into the self-expression of the best new work of his latter years. Regional identity in his buildings had become *personal* identity, giving rein in turn to the romantic, 'emotional quality'[23] which he invariably sought to reveal, a sense of vital self-expression which distanced Sedding decisively from his Revivalist forerunners and contemporaries.

Therefore, in the third and unfinished phase of his career, the influences Sedding had absorbed from his Gothic training and Cornish experience fused with an increasingly open-minded and innovative approach, which drew added impetus from Wilson's arrival in the office in 1888. Now his stance became most thoroughly the 'despair of the classifying bookmaker',[24] so that the eclectic Edwardian Baroque architect E.W. Mountford, in trying to pinpoint the indefinable quality of Sedding's style, could only conclude that

> *It would puzzle most people, and probably was intended to. He took the best from everything and made it part of himself.*[25]

Sedding's reluctance to be locked into one single style showed in his deliberate mingling of different periods of Gothic, and his using other styles with equal fluency alongside Gothic forms. So, too, did it manifest itself in the variety of his commissions, from his neo-Jacobean castle at Netley near Southampton, to the modest vernacular West Country vernacular of Flete Lodge, Holbeton (both 1889); and in the range of expression between the decorative detailing of some of his restoration schemes, to the externally austere Cardiff church of St. Dyfrig. The initial submission for this church had demonstrated Sedding's early predilection, dating back to a revelatory visit to Italy, for Renaissance forms. But by the time St. Dyfrig's was finally built in 1888-89 the design had been drastically simplified, its exuberance confined to the interior with its brightly painted ceiling and the reredos – Wilson's – depicting the Adoration. Nevertheless, it stands as the precursor to one of the great buildings of Sedding's final years, the Church of the Holy Redeemer, Clerkenwell (1887-88).

The impact of Holy Redeemer, with its powerful evocation of the Renaissance at a time when received opinion more-or-less assumed that churches would be Gothic, was enormous. After all, it was, with individual works by Charles Dance, Philip Hardwick, and Herbert Gribble's 1878 Brompton Oratory, one of the few specimens of Renaissance church architecture to be erected in London since the time of Wren. By building in this style Sedding was resisting the Ruskinian taboo on Renaissance architecture; but then he did not share Ruskin's belief in the innate expressive superiority of Gothic forms, preferring, like Lethaby, to acknowledge the possibility that expressiveness might flow simply and directly from the geometry of a building.[26]

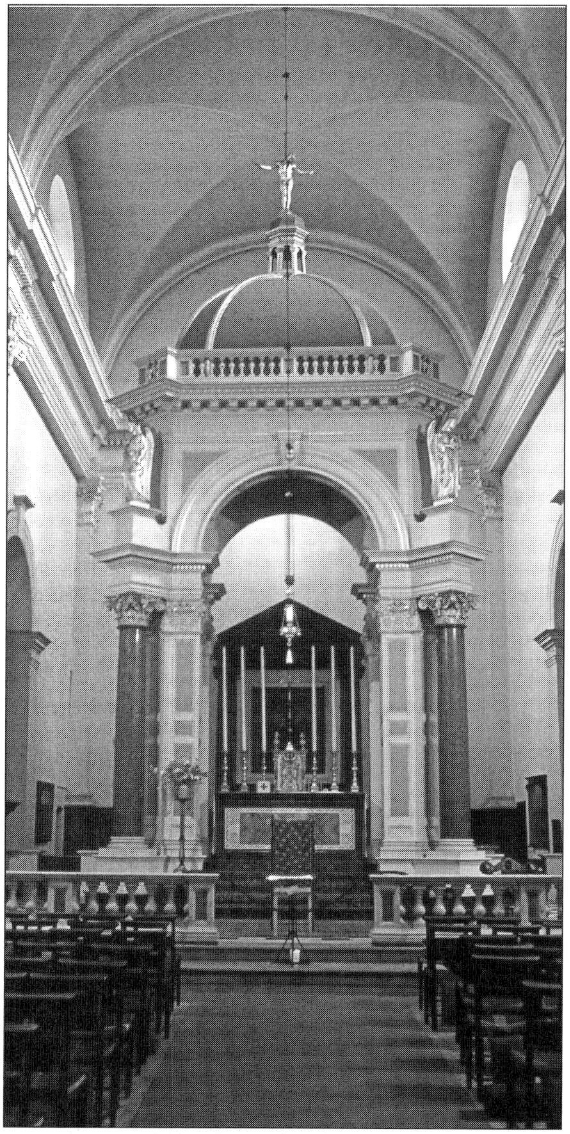

Figure 11. J.D. Sedding, Church of the Holy Redeemer, Clerkenwell, 1887-88: interior looking East, baldacchino with decoration by H. Wilson and F.W. Pomeroy, 1891-4

Outside, above the round-headed West door, is an inscribed Roman frieze dedicating the church CHRISTO LIBERATORI – to Christ the Redeemer. A circular window pierces the upper wall. This West wall, banded in broad stripes of stone and brick, is surmounted by a plain pediment of Portland stone. Cruciform in plan, the interior is wide, tall and light (Fig. 11). The nave is divided from narrow aisles by widely-spaced Corinthian columns. Springing from a deep entablature, groined vaults arch over large, oeil-de-boeuf clerestory windows, while a series of round-headed aisle windows maximise the general sense of spaciousness.

The church depends for its effect chiefly on its proportions, but also on the grandeur of form and space that Sedding sensed could be gained through structural innovation. Holy Redeemer was one of the first churches in London to be built around a framework of steel stanchions and girders encased in moulded concrete columns and entablatures. He proudly referred to it as 'constructionally an engineer's church'.[27] With proposals to fresco the interior's East wall unexecuted, the little applied decoration is restricted to F.W. Pomeroy's acanthus leaf mouldings on the capitals of the columns, and the carved golden angels (Plate 5), Wilson's contribution, on the structurally independent marble-pillared baldacchino.

As soon as it was open to inspection, the writer Walter Pater observed with admiration that it seems to draw the viewer's imagination almost irresistibly to the Renaissance churches of Venice.[28] Yet Sedding, a self-confessed opponent of the blind introduction of undigested foreign features, would have seen nothing un-English about it. Wilson himself played down any direct foreign or historical precedent, regarding Holy Redeemer as essentially modern, the 'legitimate offspring of necessity and convenience' and as a unique expression of Sedding's personality. His explanation that the 'Italian element' observable in the decoration of its Cardiff forbear had been 'left out' here in Clerkenwell, and his identification of Holy Redeemer's apparently Italianate flavour as merely unconscious or coincidental, perhaps strikes an unnecessarily defensive note:

> *Holy Redeemer's singular grace [and spaciousness] insensibly recall the best works of fifteenth century Italy, simply because works of genius, whether of nations or individuals, have much in common; ... all buildings of beams and arches, the method employed because of its cheapness, must have a family resemblance ... .*[29]

But his claim for the 'singular grace' of the church is well-founded. While its Cardiff prototype is unquestionably derivative and Italianate, Holy Redeemer has evolved for itself a genuinely English Renaissance style which handles light, space and mass with a resounding sense of freshness and originality.

The plainness of St. Dyfrig's exterior had resulted, partly at least, from financial trimming, but may also suggest a certain unease on Sedding's part at building in the heart of the city rather than in a natural landscape. Wilson readily admitted that so sensitive was Sedding to his environment that his town churches characteristically give the impression that he was 'glad to get inside and shut out the view'.[30] Yet despite Holy Redeemer's unrelievedly urban site in Exmouth Market – at the time a poor area, many of whose inhabitants were incidentally of Italian descent – the district did at least have its own bustling identity, which seemed to inspire Sedding and would absorb Wilson in his turn.

Another inspirational factor for both men was the building's dual role. On one hand, as a local parish church, it had to fit into the Clerkenwell streetscape. This was assured by its predominantly brick envelope and its proximity to its neighbours – a succession of commercial concerns starting with Hales Stores, then Woolworth's, and others including a betting shop, have occupied the premises abutting the clergy house. On the other hand, it was also a mission church, and had to declare itself to the neighbourhood. This it does, with confident, uncluttered calmness.

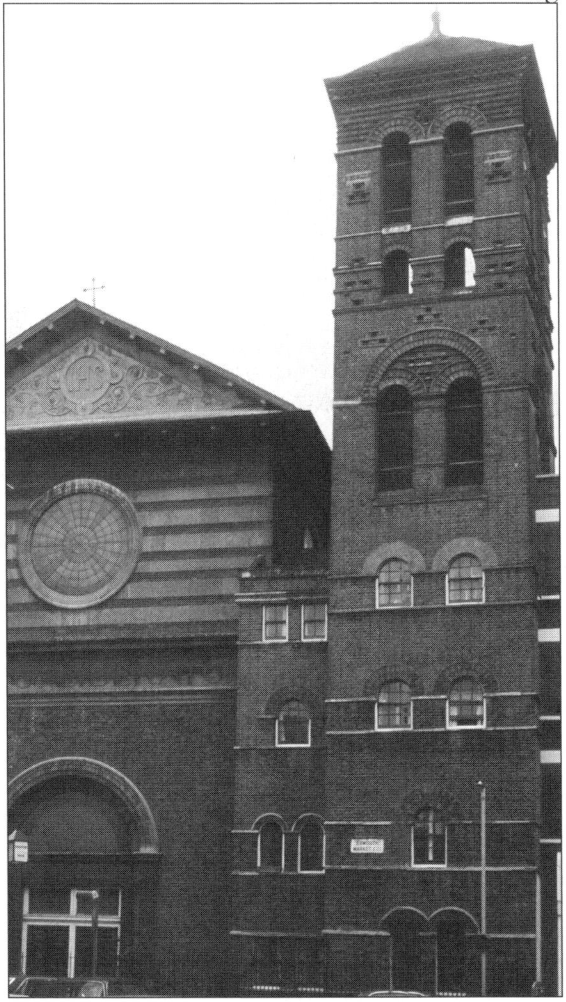

Figure 12. J.D. Sedding, Church of the Holy Redeemer 1887-88, with Wilson's clergy house and campanile, 1904.

Amongst Wilson's priorities after Sedding's death was to complete the unfinished East end of the church. When funds faltered and building came to a temporary halt in 1888, Sedding had avoided supplying anything more permanent than a corrugated iron partition, surmising that a brick wall, even a makeshift one, would not provide sufficient impetus to finish the building as it was meant to be. In 1894, when building resumed, it was Wilson who supervised the Southwark firm of Messrs T. Rider in extending the church for a further thirty-five feet to form the Lady Chapel.

The most substantial and original project Wilson undertook at Holy Redeemer was the integrated clergy house and campanile, built adjoining the church in 1904 (Fig. 12). This new building, in stock-brick and stone with tile and terracotta detailing, while still evoking a late-fifteenth century mood, gives a less formal impression than the church. The first four floors of the tower form the ingeniously-planned clergy house. The entrance hall and two visitors' waiting rooms occupy the ground floor, with a study and bedrooms for resident priests on each of the three floors above. Built onto the back of the clergy house, like a buttress with little gabled dormers, are further rooms: on the ground floor is the kitchen; the first floor houses the dining room, the second a guest room, the third and fourth were intended as servants' bedrooms and a bathroom. A spiral staircase conveniently connected the servants' quarters and the kitchen, which was linked to the dining room by a dumb waiter to facilitate the serving of meals.

Above the house the campanile, or bell tower, is structurally a hollow shell (Plate 4). Here, the stone coursing which marks each floor of the clergy house changes to horizontal bands of tile. On each face of the tower is a large, semicircular-headed relieving arch headed with radiating terracotta bricks, and with two smaller open arches set as widely as possible in the bay. This motif is reminiscent of the interplay of arched forms in Pite's neo-Byzantine Christ Church, Brixton (1897-1903), while the voussoirs above them recall those of Townsend's Church of St. Martin, Blackheath, Surrey (1892-95). As is often the case with Wilson and his contemporaries, such recurring features underline a subtle sense of peer group synchronicity.

The top tier of the tower forms an open belfry with four narrow arched openings in rising linked pairs, small below, taller above, on each face. Above are square dove-holes framed in terracotta projections that create, below cornice and roof, not only unusual textural variation, but also perches for the birds traditionally associated with message-carrying, as if to stress Holy Redeemer's missionary role.

Wilson's association with the church was a long and productive one, and despite lengthy periods of residence abroad, he would remain its official architect until 1930. In 1908 he designed the massive Portland stone font whose bowl alone weighs one and a half tons. In 1916 he completed the adjacent parish room, a practical and economical building in red brick with, for its sole decoration, the semi-circular, herringbone-patterned spandrel to the entrance arch (Plate 6). Inside the church, the walnut-doored mortuary chamber of 1918, which opens off the North aisle, and All Souls' Chapel nearby, were both designed by Wilson as war memorials, the latter in 1921 in memory of parishioner Arthur Gladstone Shaw. The Chapel's sombre bronze reredos reworks the design Wilson had modelled in 1903 for the pietà in the Welbeck Abbey chapel. The dead Christ is supported by two of the three Marys, his left arm hanging heavily beyond the walnut frame as if to stress the grim, three-dimensional reality of the scene.

Wilson sent his final contribution to the church, the Eyre memorial, from his Paris studio in 1927: a sculpture in gilded bronze of the resurrected Christ, commemorating Holy Redeemer's first vicar. The statue takes its inspiration from the youthful figure of Michaelangelo's Risen Christ in S. Spirito, Florence. It had been Sedding's memories of that very church and its baldacchino, visited by him some thirty years earlier, that had inspired him to create his own interpretation in London. A previous embodiment of the Eyre memorial's Christ-figure had appeared in 1919 as part of the Great War memorial gate that Wilson had created for the chapel of Tonbridge School, where its boyish appearance had a particularly poignant resonance. He had not anticipated the heated and, in his opinion, absurd controversy that it would generate when it was used at Clerkenwell. Congregation and clerics alike criticised its resemblance to a naked classical god, and for not being 'religious'[31] enough. Initially, it had been installed alongside the baldacchino, on a pedestal made by the sculptor F.T. Foulger; but so vehement and unremitting were the complaints about it that after thirteen years it was moved to its present, less provocative, position on top of the baldacchino.

Holy Redeemer had been remarkable for its distinctively modern reformulation of the English Renaissance style. Sedding's last and greatest church, Holy Trinity, Sloane Street (1888-91), proved equally controversial, in this case for the freedom with which it treated the more familiar forms of Gothic. In their tributes, Wilson and Cooper claimed that at Holy Trinity, Sedding had transcended convention to find 'his own solution to Gothic'.[32] It was a 'solution' that had been evolving throughout all his earlier work, most markedly in St. Clement's, Bournemouth, which already, in the early 1870s, gave clear pointers towards the Sloane Street church.

At St. Clement's, Sedding had mingled late fourteenth and early fifteenth century Gothic forms with no pretensions to scholastic correctness. To pull off this blend so successfully, he had used the extensive studies that he had made over the years of old architecture as a basis for design – as reminders of the effects of light, shade and proportion. His studies were never a taxonomy of pre-ordained forms. When preparing drawings for his new buildings, he would make sketches which conveyed the effect and atmosphere he was hoping to achieve, rather than flawless, stringently accurate architectural perspectives. This was a working practice he tried to communicate to everyone he trained.

> *If a pupil wished to enter his office, he would never ask for measured drawings – pencil notes and sketches told him all he wanted to know.*[33]

Wilson, on whom this approach was to leave such a strong impression, likened Sedding's methods to Baldassari's freehand elevations for the great fifteenth century church of St. Petronius in Bologna. Lethaby, appreciative of Sedding's freehand skills, applauded him as 'one of the first architects to really learn how to *draw*'.[34]

Holy Trinity, Sloane Street, has been called the cathedral of the Arts and Crafts movement. It is an expansive yet inclusive building, grand in scale, refined in detail, and in its creative expression, a triumph of collaboration. Whereas Edward Prior's Church of St. Andrew, Roker (1904-07), the other claimant to the title, has a self-denying, solid monumentality, Holy Trinity's claim is based on its richness and on the glamour of its inventiveness.

In design and detail, Holy Trinity's West front brings to mind St. George's Chapel, Windsor, or even Gloucester Cathedral. With its twin turrets, its crenellated parapet, and its impressive window rising to a Tudor point, it clearly draws on Gothic forms. But these are combined with strikingly original features, such as the elaborate freestone coursing, the window's vigorous tracery, and the delicate cupolas surmounting the turrets, all of which suggest Wilson's exuberance above Sedding's gentle restraint. Significantly, too, each feature finds a counterpart in other designs by Wilson in which Sedding had no hand: the Ladbroke Grove Library, the tower of St. Clement's, Bournemouth. The Sloane Street façade apart, the remaining elevations are of plain brickwork, expertly handled by the Lambeth contractors Higgs and Hill, but Wilson's presence is strongly felt in the exterior railings. Installed in front of the building in 1902, their springy vine motifs skilfully complement the energetic mood of the West window's tracery (Plate 13).

Inside, the wide vaulted nave and chancel, the large East and West windows, the slender pillars between aisles and nave, and the airy openness of the whole unite to produce a feeling of pure, unobstructed spaciousness – a sensation Sedding had pioneered in his 1887-90 Church of All Saints', Falmouth. The stylistic freedom by which he achieved this unfettered atmosphere at Holy Trinity caused some consternation, even amongst his closest allies. Heywood Sumner admitted that he found Sedding's unconventional approach 'rather bewildering',[35] different styles of Gothic being interspersed with free Renaissance elements, as in the chancel gates, and with forms drawn from Sedding's own invention. Christopher Whall expressed similar disquiet during the tour Sedding had given him, but Sedding's response suggests he was rather pleased at such puzzlement:

> *I looked at it in silence, trying to take it in. He cocked his head on one side and said 'Well? is it too naughty? I hope it's not too naughty?'*[36]

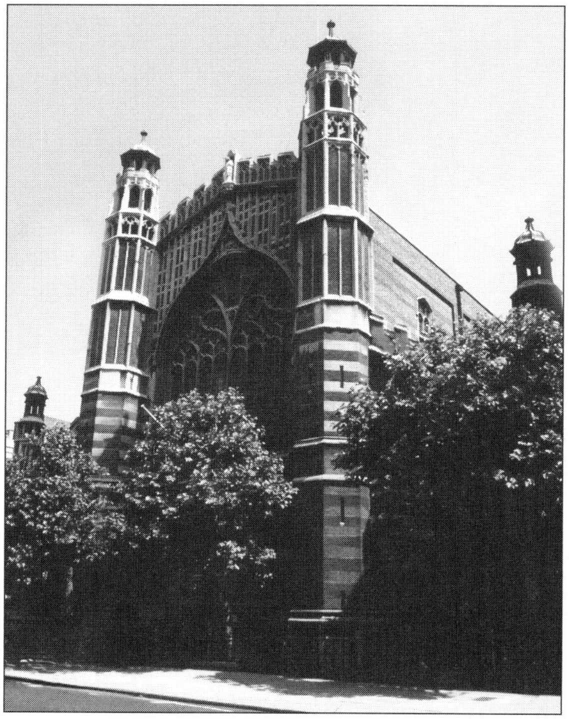

Figure 13. (above) Holy Trinity Church, Sloane Street, London, 1888-91: West front, J.D. Sedding with H. Wilson.

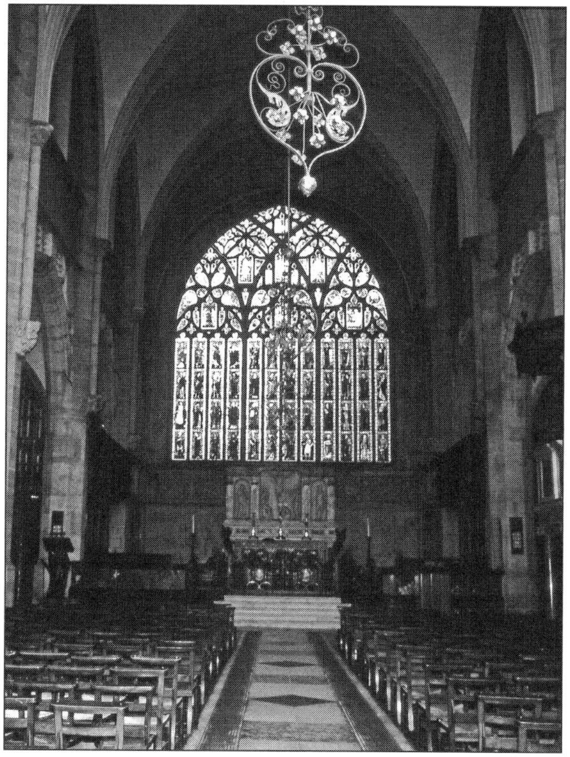

Figure 14. (above) Holy Trinity: interior of sanctuary.

Collaborating closely with Wilson, Sedding had produced in Holy Trinity a virtually unclassifiable synthesis of imagination and the styles that had most deeply affected him; the remarkable totality of effect represents an exciting, seamless fusion. (Figs. 13, 14) Wilson himself hailed the building as 'an attempt to raise the architecture of the future'.[37] But as he said, it was still 'an attempt,' and a comment Whall had made during his visit remains a valid one: 'I don't see your point in mixing styles. It's using Style all the same.'[38] Sedding's reply is not recorded, but the unique, essentially personal mixture of elements within the church provides a vivid indication of how his unlikely blend of individual and traditional impulses might have developed had he lived beyond 1891.

Just as important, though, as what was built at Sloane Street, was the way in which the project was organised. Holy Trinity is the working out, in this respect, of ideas explored earlier at St. Clement's. In the Bournemouth church Sedding had ensured an exceptionally high standard of craftsmanship by searching out the best workmen and promoting in them the sense of belonging to a community, or guild, of craftsmen.

He treated his workmen as pupils, pointing out what effects he wanted them to aim at, often handling the mallet and chisel himself. Most of his designs for stone and woodcarving he drew on the material, either in the workshop or on the site, and it was difficult for those who saw him thus at work not to catch some of his spirit.[39]

That Sedding was forced to plan his building in such detail, even to the extent of scoring designs on blocks of stone for the masons to carve, was a measure of the difficulty of reproducing a guild-like environment under modern conditions. In reality, the industrialised world was reshaping attitudes and economies, and the sense of tradition intrinsic to Sedding's approach was dying.

When Wilson characterised Sedding as a 'medieval builder born two hundred years too late',[40] he was highlighting not only Sedding's frustrations in the 1880s, but also the dilemma which he himself would experience in the following decade – a dilemma which would lead him increasingly into fields outside the architectural mainstream. It could not be denied that some workmen were efficient, co-operative, enthusiatic even, and receptive; but none of these qualities quite added up to the Ruskinian vision of spontaneous creativity which Sedding, and later Wilson, yearned to elicit from each employee. And yet, both were convinced that if only craftsmen could rediscover how to invent rather than to imitate, a truly original, modern style would spontaneously emerge.

In the absence of such intuitive creativity Sedding turned to other means of achieving sincere, relevant, vital architecture. In the first place, although his commissions did not justify retaining a standing army of craftsmen, whenever work arose he could call on particular, sympathetic talents. Thus most of his woodwork was executed in the Somerset workshop of Charles Trask and Son, of Norton-sub-Hamdon – a long-established family concern where traditional methods were still in use. Wilson continued to use them after Sedding's death, for instance between 1894 and 1896, for the oak woodwork in the chapel of Douglas Castle, Lanarkshire, and the walnut furnishings of 1907 for the Lady Chapel at Holy Redeemer, Clerkenwell. Similarly, most of Sedding's ironwork was made by Longden & Co., whose proprietor, Henry Longden, was an old friend and fellow member of the Art Workers' Guild. Longden's Phoenix Foundry was on Furnace Hill, Sheffield, but his London showrooms were at 447 Oxford Street, directly below Sedding's office. He carried out many important commissions for Sedding, such as the metal fittings for Holy Trinity, Sloane Street, and continued to work for Wilson, casting the bowl of the Welbeck font, for example. By working regularly with the same firms Sedding established a rapport with their craftsmen based upon mutual confidence and continuity. Indeed, by employing such tried-and-tested workmen he had, in Wilson's estimation, 'well-nigh formed a new school'.[41]

The second recourse Sedding adopted in his pursuit of 'living'[42] architecture was simplification. Rather than erode still further the modern workman's already diminished expressiveness by *prescribing* idiosyncracies of form or detail, in itself a futile contradiction in terms, Sedding preferred to assume a lack of old-fashioned virtuosity in his workmen and to rely instead on the building's plan, proportions and sense of unity for effect. The success initiated at St. Clement's in this respect was turned into the major achievements of Holy Redeemer and Holy Trinity.

The third measure Sedding used to counteract the shortfall in creative vision – the use of leading artists – found fullest, though still incomplete, articulation in the Sloane Street church. His resolve to encourage creativity in every craftsman remained undiminished, and found redoubled optimism in Wilson's career. Collaboration with established artists represented an interim expedient, and provides an insight into the two men's enthusiasm both for the activities of the Art Workers' Guild and to their aspirations for what it might achieve in the future.

> *Sedding's hope for Architecture lay in the co-operation amongst Artists ... Guilds for artists first; those for workmen would follow in due course.*[43]

Insofar as Holy Trinity marked a compromise of approach, its success as an expression of Sedding's ideals was qualified, and partial. Wilson's verdict on the church as 'a magnificent failure',[44] might to some degree be justified. The absence of an underlying, truly integrated tradition could not be substituted by simply mixing together what were ultimately separate works of art and craft by selected stars. Nevertheless, the range of artists engaged on the project was impressive, and their several contributions to the scheme individually striking. First and foremost was Sedding himself, who as architect devised the overall plan and concept, as well as setting out preliminary ideas for font and pulpit. It was he who was responsible for the silver and brass altar-cross, an elegant design embellished with topaz, amethyst, carbuncle and crystal with, on its stem, his enamel medallion of Man's expulsion from Paradise. Sedding's understanding of metalworking radiates from his working drawings, diagrams and cross-sections of its parts, as well as from the finished work.[45] Longden executed Sedding's designs for the chancel rail with its Renaissance-inspired metal scrollwork, and for the gilded heart-shaped wrought iron electroliers illuminating the nave; the organ case, made to Sedding's design, was installed in 1891 by J.W. Walker & Sons.[46]

Among the artist-craftsmen recruited by Sedding to adorn the church was the sculptor F.W. Pomeroy: his bronze angels, seated and bearing scrolls, surmount the green marble pillars flanking the chancel gates; his, too, are the carved figures on the chancel stalls. The marble altar frontal showing the Entombment was carved by Harry Bates. Onslow Ford made the font with its broad, shallow bowl of onyx marble, in collaboration with the French carver F. Boucher, who created the bronze cherubim encircling the stem. Hamo Thornycroft's proposal to carve the twelve apostles on the nave piers had Sedding's full approval, as did Burne-Jones's fresco for the upper nave walls, for which the artist prepared studies. Both elements are depicted in Sedding's drawing of a nave bay, published in *The Builder* of 12 October 1889, but in the event neither was pursued.[47] Burne-Jones is represented, however, in the East window, with its forty-eight prophets, apostles and saints, the design using cartoons drawn up for previous commissions. It was made by Morris and Co., William Morris himself designing the red-robed St. Bartholomew and collaborating with his glass-painting workshop's foreman on the foliage around Burne-Jones's figures. Christopher Whall designed and made the clerestory windows depicting various angelic orders, and those in the South aisle – the Adoration and the Holy Spirit – while the work of the leading Arts and Crafts metalworker and sculptor Henry Armstead appears in the lectern: a bronze angel of peace.

With the exception of Sedding, Wilson was the most prolific participant in the planning and decoration of the interior space of Holy Trinity. The tragedy of Sedding's death could not weaken the team's dedication, and though mourning his loss, their work continued. As common sense decreed, they were anxious to avoid costly delays; they also knew that this project was bigger than any one individual. Wilson made important additions of his own while co-ordinating the work, and succeeded Sedding as the official Church Architect, as which he served until 1916 when F.C. Eden took over. In 1891 his hammered gilt panels enhanced Sedding's wrought iron chancel gates, but the first major task Wilson undertook was done in Sedding's stead: finishing and installing the pulpit in 1891-92 (Plate 12). Sedding's ideas for it were well advanced, and its pillared alabaster and marble design accords fully with his chancel gates, whose curving lines and Renaissance mood is echoed in the pulpit's lobed plan and richly-coloured surfaces. Wilson's privileged insights into his late master's approach gave clues whenever alterations were needed during the job, like those required as the pulpit was set in place, when its contours had to be aligned with the adjacent column, and the arc of its wrought iron handrail adjusted to Wilson's specifications by Longden's.[48]

Models by Wilson were used as guides by Armstead to carve the prophets on the stone medallions (or 'cheeses') in the spandrels of the nave arches, but only two, above the South choir stalls, would be installed: finished between October 1904 and February 1905, depicting Jonah and Isaiah.[49] Wilson's relief panel of white plaster in the baptistry, its inclusive mood well-matched to its setting beside the font, was made in 1907. At its centre is Christ blessing a group of infants against the backdrop of a distant city. The whole scene, within its gold-chequered frame, gains extra vitality from Christ's halo interrupting the frame as he leans forward – a typical Wilson device to give life to a moment in time.

Two bronze figures by Wilson flank the entrance to the Memorial Chapel, which Eden created in the South aisle in 1920. These praying child angels, originally intended for the altar rail, were moved so as to stand, heads bowed, either side of its beaten copper archway. This entrance by Wilson corresponds with the one he had already created for the Lady Chapel in the opposite aisle. Its capitals depict gods of the ancient world, such as Mercury and Saturn, while the young male figure in its central roundel tends a garden: the concerns of war have become those of fruitful peace. The same scene recurs on Wilson's reredos of 1903-05 at Sydenham (Plate 8), the angels by the entrance echo his 1898 Tinling memorial in Gloucester Cathedral, and the stylised waves on the capitals resemble those on the 1900 Gloucester chalice. The Memorial Chapel itself embodied a concept Wilson would have been swift to endorse – he would become a frequent memorial-maker in the wake of the Great War.

However, his most significant personal contribution to Holy Trinity's interior is the Lady Chapel in the North aisle, begun in 1892. As it stands, it represents only the central portion of a far more elaborate scheme – Wilson was planning to add a rood screen and stained glass, designs that would involve Christopher Whall and Louis Davis, the glass-painter and illustrator, who became a colleague of Wilson's in 1899 on the life-drawing course at the Central School of Arts and Crafts. According to the critic for *The Architectural Review*, Wilson's original Lady Chapel scheme (Plate 9) seemed 'translumined with the fire of passion', its effect captivating: '... such invention in the details of decoration, such an appeal to heart and brain ...'.[50] In fact, Wilson intended to screen his chapel from the rest of the church by a colonnade and romanesque archways. The main columns would be organic compositions of twining stems and foliage interspersed with robed figures, alternating with a series of light, silver-sheathed archways. Metal cladding on this ambitious scale foreshadows what would prove to be one of his favourite techniques. The original brown and gold patterning that once decorated the walls was later painted over by Eden, who, as it happened, disapproved of the chapel in almost every particular.[51]

The deliberate separateness of Wilson's Lady Chapel suggests the idea of a church-within-a-church, and like the tower he added to Sedding's Bournemouth church, hints at his growing independence from his late master's syle. Only a fraction of his scheme may have been carried out, yet even in its abbreviated form the chapel conveys a sense of quiet, focused seclusion. As planned, Wilson's green and white marble baldacchino, resting on four red marble pillars, forms its centre. Beneath this canopy is the Lady Altar, with its green marble retable and a frontal painted by W. Reynolds-Stephens; on it stands Wilson's silver-gilt and enamel cross. The symbols of the four Evangelists – repoussé medallions set against squares of foliage – adorn its crosspieces: the winged man for St. Matthew, the lion of St. Mark, St. John's eagle, and St. Luke's bull. At the centre the rose, the emblem of faith and life, is surrounded by a circlet, complementing the smooth sheen of the knopped shaft and foot. The whole sanctuary is set on marble steps and enclosed within a low green marble rail supported on brass balusters (Figs. 15, 16).

The wrought iron and gilt organ screen filling the arches behind the baldacchino was carried out to Wilson's design by Nelson Dawson in 1899.[52] The verticals of its grid-like framework (Fig. 17) support golden vine leaves, while simple interlinked rings hang from the horizontals to evoke the fullness and translucency of grapes. Such bold abstraction was a measure of Wilson's sensitivity to the two-dimensional function of his design, when such innovation was likely to provoke the kind of critical disdain which *The Builder* poured on it:

> *It is deficient in ... style; such a detail as the hanging clusters of interlocking rings ... is not beautiful and has (as far as we can see) no meaning; they seem to be put there for the sake of putting something....*[53]

Access to the organ chamber is through an archway at the back of the Lady Chapel, the one fragment executed of Wilson's proposal to enclose the chapel (Plate 10). Scattered over its beaten copper surface are simple raised flowers. Centrally placed are two doves in a tree of life,

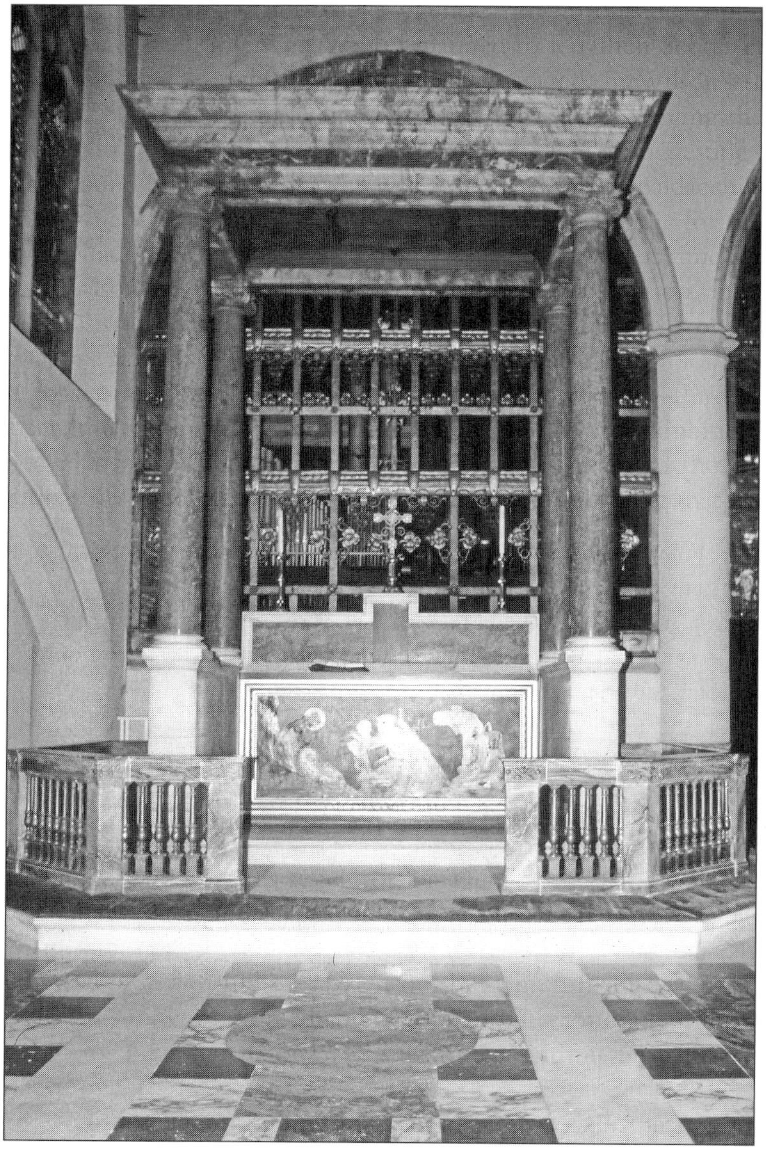

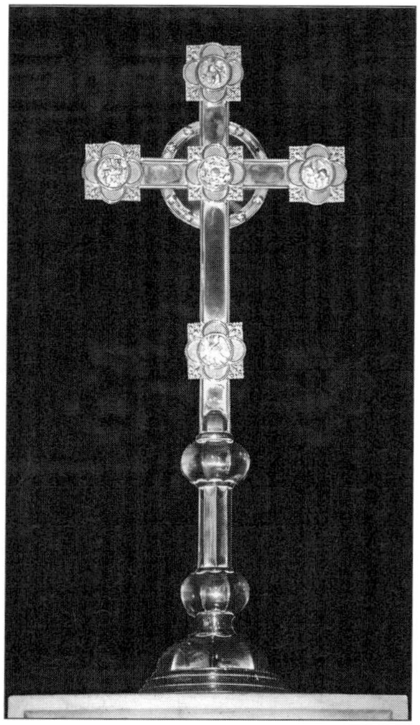

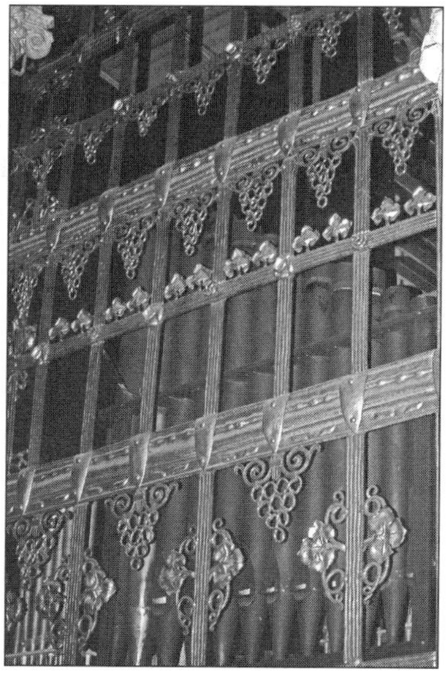

Figure 15. (above) Holy Trinity: the Lady Chapel sanctuary, H.Wilson, 1892-99.
Figure 16. (top right) Lady Chapel altar cross.
Figure 17. (bottom right) Organ screen with vine motifs.

beneath a text of compact yet lucid lettering (Plate 11), which takes on a visually satisfying dimension of its own, just as that on his chancel gates at Salcombe made around 1890. His interest in lettering as a decorative device was affirmed during the five years he taught at the Central School. W.R. Lethaby, the School's director, was himself an advocate of well-arranged lettering directly carved on buildings, and in 1900 he gave the inscription equal status with the architecture of the façade of his Eagle Insurance Building in Birmingham. Keen to instigate a modern revival of printing and type design, Lethaby set up a pioneer lettering course at the Central in 1900. Running the classes was the expert calligrapher and innovative typographic designer Edward Johnston. And at Holy Trinity, in 1902, a rising star in the lettering arts was given his first carving commission: Wilson's collaborator on the text over the organ-chamber arch was Johnston's pupil, Eric Gill.

Thus far, Wilson's authority as Sedding's successor as architect to Holy Trinity had gone unchallenged. Not so when it came to the finishing of the East end of the chancel. In 1894 he submitted drawings for a tall, elaborate reredos, incorporating two large panels showing the Adoration and the Crucifixion flanked and framed by niches holding figures of the saints and prophets, the whole rising to an openwork pinnacle comprising the angelic host. The end wall was principally occupied by Sedding's window, already glazed by Burne-Jones assisted by Morris himself. The effect of the reredos would have been to mask the window for three quarters its height and most of its width; Wilson already had his answer ready for the objectors:

> *The attention of the spectator should be compelled to some object of interest before passing to the real end of the building. By these means only can mystery be obtained. To say that because a certain window has been designed nothing else should be placed there is to assume that the building was made for the window, and not the window for the building.*[54]

The editor of *The Builder* appreciated Wilson's argument, but remained unconvinced:

> *We still have the impression that ... a large and elaborate east window is meant to be seen from the church. But we are quite sure that our readers will enjoy Mr. Wilson's characteristic defence of his position as much as we do*[55]

... and Wilson's climactic reredos was rejected in favour of a modest marble depiction of the crucifixion, commissioned from the sculptor John Tweed.

Wilson was all too aware of the huge challenge Sedding had undertaken at Holy Trinity, and understood the frustrations inherent in the project – frustrations which had coloured Sedding's career as a whole. Consequently, when he came to evaluate Sedding's impact on architecture, Wilson set as much store by his ideas as by the material achievements that they had produced:

> *His claim on our regard does not rest on the invention of a new style nor on the modification of an old one; nor does it rest on the mass of work he left behind, beautiful as much of it is. It rests upon his personal influence; on the intellectual stimulus he provided.*[56]

Sedding's influence manifested itself in the work of many younger architects, especially those who trained in his office, like J.P. Cooper, Ernest Gimson and Arthur Grove, as well as those of independent mind beyond it, such as Edward Prior, Walter J. Tapper and Leonard Stokes, who shared his impatience with formulaic historicism and sterile professionalism. All were determined to embrace a 'simpler, more natural'[57] approach. Foremost amongst them was his heir apparent, Henry Wilson.

It was natural, therefore, that Sedding's grave in the churchyard at St. John's, West Wickham, should be marked by a headstone designed by Wilson. In 1889, a year after moving to the village from London's Charlotte Street, Sedding – himself an accomplished organist – had accepted a commission to design the organ-chamber for the church. The finely clipped hedges of the Seddings' garden, within sight of the churchyard that would be his final resting place, testified to his new-found delight in topiary. His unexpected death on 7 April 1891 was followed within the week by that of his wife, Rose. Thus Wilson found himself designing their shared headstone (Fig. 18), and chose to set the carved figure of the crucified Christ between panels of birds and lilies, as if to endorse Sedding's own dictum that church buildings should be 'wrought ... with everything which has life and beauty, in frank and fearless naturalism'.[58] In the work and person of Wilson, Sedding's commitment to breaking 'the coercion of the "styles"'[59] and achieving a truly 'living'[60] union of the arts would indeed continue unabated.

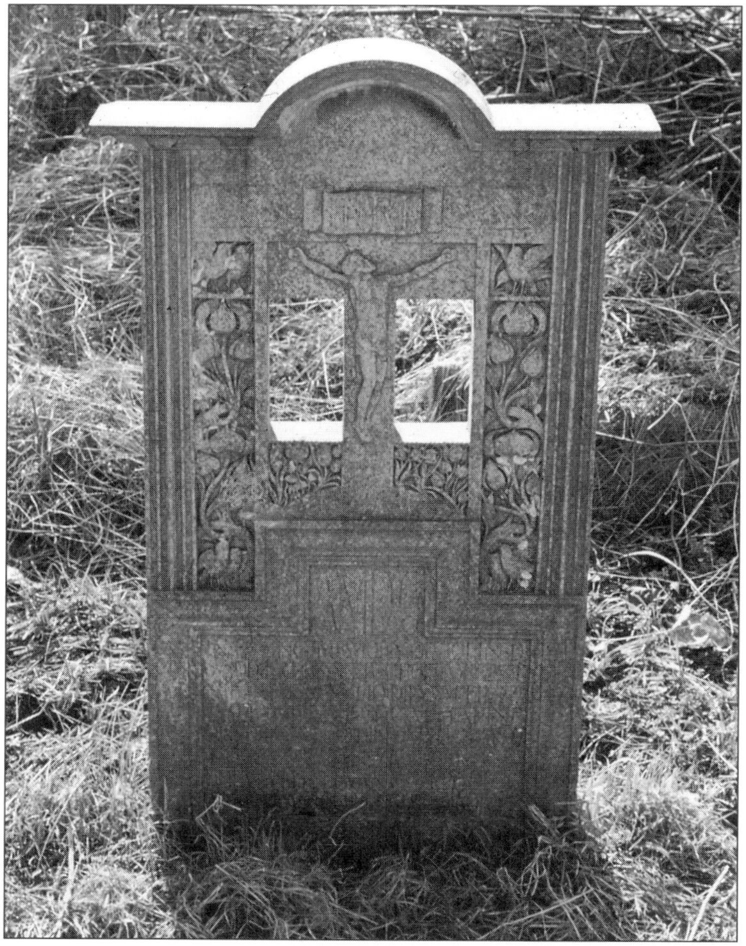

Figure 18. St. John's Church, West Wickham, Kent, Henry Wilson: gravestone of J.D. Sedding and his wife, Rose, 1891.

CHAPTER THREE

LIFE AFTER SEDDING

At work in Sedding's office were several individuals with whom Wilson was to form lasting attachments, and who were themselves, destined to make outstanding contributions to contemporary Arts and Crafts. By the time Wilson joined it in 1888, Ernest Gimson had worked with Sedding for about two years, and Alfred Powell and Charles Nicholson for one. Arthur Grove took up articles with Sedding in 1890. Ernest Barnsley had left only recently, in October 1887, to practice in his native Birmingham, but he stayed in close contact with the office; in 1894, he joined forces with his brother Sidney and Gimson, in their craft workshop at Pinbury, in the Cotswolds.[1]

The Barnsleys and Gimson would distinguish themselves as makers of craft furniture, and Powell as a pottery decorator.[2] Grove was to follow a more orthodox architectural career. The son of a vicar in the Welsh borders, he continued to work with Wilson after 1891 in Sedding's old office, then established his own practice in 1897 within Wilson's new premises in Kensington. In 1906, he moved his practice to 1, Hare Court, off Fleet Street, where for some years the Arts and Crafts Exhibition Society also had its office. Of the several Welsh commissions Grove would carry out, two were associated with Sedding or Wilson: his font of 1895 for Wilson's church at Brithdir, and the completion in 1906-08 of Sedding's Cardiff church, where he was responsible for the West end, as well as later adding the clergy house and parish hall, and designing the lectern.[3]

Charles Nicholson, who would remain a lifelong friend of Wilson, stayed on until 1893, when he left to set up on his own, forming a partnership with H.C. Corlette two years later. In 1898 he was commissioned to enlarge St. Matthew's Church, Yiewsley, Middlesex, for which, during the works, Wilson made a bronze altar cross and candlesticks. Nicholson's spacious new nave and chancel, with painted barrel ceiling and large clear glass windows, relegated Sir Gilbert Scott's 1859 nave to serve as the North aisle;[4] the new portion stands in distinct contrast to that dimly lit, intricately patterned earlier work, Nicholson's fresh element demonstrating how far Sedding's pupils had moved on from doctrinaire Revivalism.

Although never a trainee architect, Christopher Whall, craftsman in stained glass, plasterwork and mural painting, was as good as inseparable from Sedding's enterprises during the late 1880s, subsequently remaining one of Wilson's closest friends and collaborators. He had begun his career working for commercial glass manufacturers such as W.G. Saunders and Hardman's, but was instinctively drawn to Arts and Crafts ideals. One of his earliest designs, 'The Elements', which would form the five stained glass windows of Gloucester Cathedral's Lady Chapel, was exhibited in 1888 at the first Arts and Crafts Exhibition at the New Gallery, and afterwards at the Liverpool Art Congress. Sedding saw the work and was impressed enough to invite Whall firstly to join the team working on Holy Trinity, Sloane Street, and then to design new glass for St. Mary's, Stamford, Lincolnshire, where Sedding had restored the medieval chancel in the last year of his life. Whall signed up with the Art Workers' Guild in 1889, becoming its Master in 1912, and was co-author with Wilson of its 1889 masque, *Beauty's Awakening*, for which Wilson designed sets and costumes. Like Wilson, he taught at the Central School (in his case, from 1896-1904) and at the Royal College (1898); he would contribute to the Liverpool Cathedral scheme submitted by Lethaby and Wilson in 1902, and in 1905 published a monograph on his art, *Stained Glass Work*, in the Technical Handbooks series.[5]

Another of the close collaborative friendships Wilson struck up at Sedding's was with John Paul Cooper, who would distinguish himself as a silversmith and jeweller. Son of a partner in the

Leicester hosiery works Cooper, Corah & Sons, Cooper was following Lethaby's advice when in 1889 he joined Sedding's practice; but by 1892 his interests were turning decisively to the decorative arts, and he soon embarked on a naturally evolving creative journey of the kind Wilson himself had already begun. Wilson was Cooper's architectural mentor in the office, supervising his articles after Sedding's death. He seems to have cast Wilson in the same role as that in which Wilson had initially cast Sedding – the stage designer and director Gordon Craig recalls, in a letter of about 1910, the unique authority that Wilson held for the younger man:

> *How's Paul? I suppose he was quite a boy when you first helped him: 'Wilson says' and 'Wilson that –'. Lovely!*[6]

Francis Cooper called to mind his father's and Wilson's love of reading and travel as 'a bond of mutual understanding' between them, and remembered the constant exchange of ideas between the young assistants in Sedding's office:

> *... long hours spent in discussion, ... holidays abroad, and letters sent home to the 'office' revealed a tremendous vigour and keen interest in detail. Architecture was studied in its widest sense.*[7]

Such were the future colleagues and allies Wilson encountered at Sedding's. Meanwhile, in a comparable creative powerhouse, the office of Sedding's exact contemporary Richard Norman Shaw, were several young men destined to have an equally formative effect on architecture and the crafts. Edward Prior, a founder member of the Art Workers' Guild, had joined Shaw in 1872, remaining until the late 1880s, when the outstanding originality of his own architectural work revealed itself.[8] W.R. Lethaby, the most creatively influential of all Wilson's friends, was with Shaw between 1879 and 1890; the independently-thinking Arts and Crafts architect Robert Weir Schultz (Schultz Weir after the outbreak of the Great War), from 1884 to 1891. Sidney Barnsley came to Shaw's in 1886, soon after his brother Ernest started at Sedding's. It was the Barnsleys who formed the crucial link between the offices: through them the aspiring designers in both practices met and mingled, and for a few months in 1888 and 1889, all these young architects were, in effect, working alongside one another.

Many themes in Wilson's work can be traced back to these early exchanges within and between the offices of Sedding and Shaw. A warm regard would always exist between Ernest Gimson and Wilson, even though they did not maintain particularly close contact in later years and their careers took very different paths. Following his involvement with the short-lived furniture venture Kenton & Co., Gimson moved permanently, in April 1893, to Gloucestershire, where he relished being 'as far as possible from the railway'.[9] He undertook architectural renovations and built a few new houses in and around his native Leicester; but by 1902, he was concentrating on furniture design, mostly plain, solid oak pieces; he would later establish a workshop in Sapperton with Ernest Barnsley and the Dutch cabinet maker Peter Waals, settling unobtrusively in the cottage he built further up the valley. Wilson, by contrast, would pursue a public role as designer-craftsman as well as teacher and apologist for the Arts and Crafts, remaining no less eloquent in his pronouncements after his move to France in 1922. Gimson's quiet achievements in fine plasterwork and increasingly rich furniture in walnut and inlay may have diverged from Wilson's proselytising visions of 'federated workshops, craft villages, agriculture, and the intensive culture of every human being',[10] yet important similarities existed between them: both were characterised by an individuality and idealism exceptional even within the Arts and Crafts movement. Both, Gimson albeit in a less consistently 'hands-on' sense, were architecturally-trained craftsmen; both would ultimately abandon mainstream architecture, prompted by disillusionment and frustration with the situation the profession found itself in during the 1890s.[11]

A particular enthusiasm that overflowed between Shaw's assistants and Sedding's was their fascination with Byzantine architecture and iconography. William Morris had lectured on the art of Byzantium in 1879, but it was the return to Shaw's office of three of his young assistants from study-tours of Greece in 1888 and 1889-90 that drew renewed attention to the style. A mere fraction of their research was brought together in a monograph issued under the joint names of Sidney Barnsley and Weir Schultz, though in the preface they acknowledge Lethaby as the instigator of their expeditions.[12] Back home, no time was lost in proving the pudding: Barnsley's Byzantium-inspired St. Sophia's, or Church of the Wisdom of God, was built at Lower Kingswood, Surrey in 1891. Weir Schultz in 1896 supplied the editor of *The Architectural Review* – Henry Wilson – with an extended article on Byzantine architecture,[13] and in 1912 created the Chapel of St. Andrew in that apotheosis of the free Byzantine style, G.F. Bentley's Westminster Cathedral.

In 1894 Lethaby himself published with Harold Swainson a meticulously researched book on the cathedral of S. Sophia, Constantinople.[14] Wilson observed how, in Byzantine work, inspiration drawn from a variety of sources could combine with the spirit of the age to create a new and unique identity, arguing that Byzantine art had developed its own special character by uniting 'passion, common-sense, exquisite skill [and] Greek precision, [with] Gothic and Eastern mystery, simplicity and richness'.[15] Such a fertile combination would have huge relevance to his search for a style which, whilst making use of past experience, would still belong in the present. Material expression of his interest in Byzantine art occurs in several of his works, such as his liturgical fittings of 1898-1908 for Edmund Scott's tremendous, unfinished St. Bartholomew's Church in Brighton, and the *mise en scène* he devised for the 1916 Arts and Crafts Exhibition. Affinities with such elemental blending of passion, practicality and precision, would indeed underpin Wilson's entire career.

The symbolic language of architecture was another common interest of the young Sedding/Shaw group. Wilson felt sure that it was their pervasive, quasi-magical sense of 'other-worldliness'[16] that gave extra force to Sedding's designs. Truly expressive symbolism, Wilson contended, was not a matter of mere surface detailing, but must extend throughout the building as a whole. He himself had already shown a sensitivity to such overtones in his Tree of Knowledge design for the Ladbroke Grove Library, and it would reappear in the conception of the 'beyond' he sought at Holy Trinity, Sloane Street. Gradually his work encripted an increasingly diverse range of mythical, biblical and astrological references which united to form his personal visual language.

One man, if any, had a crucial influence on Wilson's work and thought – W.R. Lethaby, with his lifelong enquiry into a universal symbolism, into 'the ultimate facts behind all architecture'.[17] Many examples in his book *Architecture, Mysticism and Myth* concerning the 'influence of known and imagined facts of the universe on architecture',[17] were to find manifest form in Wilson's work soon after the book's publication late in 1891, though undoubtedly the two men would have discussed the ideas it contains well before that date. Thus, in 1893, Wilson's oviform lamps for the chapel at Welbeck Abbey deliberately embodied the shape that lies at the heart of Lethaby's chapter on 'The Symbol of Creation'. Wilson's eagle lectern for the same chapel clearly relates to Lethaby's account of this emblematic creature in his account of 'The Golden Gates of the Sun'. Eagles had been lecterns in England since the 1300s, traditionally denoting the spirit of the gospels – but Wilson's version, incorporating an unfamiliar range of images and planetary allusions, lifts the idea onto a stranger plane of eclectism and myth.

A close, productive friendship had grown up between Lethaby and Wilson, whose careers complemented and reinforced one another's. After running his own architectural practice between 1891 and 1902, Lethaby ceased to be an active member of the profession, feeling that the language of the coming century was steel and concrete, and that he himself was out of step with its idioms.

Thereafter he devoted himself to teaching and writing; having been a founder-member of the Art Workers' Guild, Lethaby became the Arts and Crafts movement's most consistently challenging ideologist, just as Wilson was arguably its most talented designer-craftsman. The two men collaborated on projects that show the breadth of design they were each able to tackle. On one hand they could work together to create the processional cross shown at the 1899 Arts and Crafts Exhibition;[19] on the other, they could mobilise an entire architectural team comprising F.W. Troup, Stirling Lee, Whall, Halsey Ricardo and Weir Schultz to produce a startling concrete design for the second Liverpool Cathedral Competition in 1902.

Again, in striving to improve teaching standards in the applied arts, Wilson and Lethaby worked easily alongside one another. From 1896 to 1910 Lethaby was Principal of the Central School of Arts and Crafts; under his aegis Wilson taught life drawing. Wilson was also instructor in goldsmithing at the Royal College of Art for the first twelve years of Lethaby's Professorship of Design there, from 1901 to 1918.

The presence of Lethaby in Shaw's office, and Wilson in Sedding's, led to a lively cross-fertilisation of ideas between the two establishments, and beyond, the young men's imaginations embracing the crucial concerns of Sedding's and Shaw's contemporaries in architecture and the applied arts, such as William Morris and Philip Webb. Wilson and his peers were gaining experience in an intellectual world whose roots could be traced directly to Ruskin – a world characterised by a faith in original, honest design, by a sympathetic yet innovatory attitude to tradition, and by a commitment to the reintegration of architecture and the crafts. This intense and absorbing period in the 1890s left a vivid imprint on them all. 'Do you recall,' wrote Gimson to Wilson some twenty-five years later,

> *... those meetings in Ossington Street, and the walk across the Park, and Butler, and the interminable discussions on perspective, and Ruskin, and how you scorned me because I could admire the primitives and yet see something wonderful in Doré, whom I was nurtured on from infancy. And the incomparable, giggling Meredith, and Finch ... And that trick of locking the back room without a key. And your lovely, perfect, pale drawings – my despair and admiration. And Cook's Monday lectures, which made you sick. Oh, an army walks past when I think of you! And Longden: then JD ... .*

Gimson's memories, even at a distance of a quarter-century, could transport him in a moment to his former lodgings in Notting Hill, to debates about themes carried over from previous generations, to contemporary topics hotly contested with his fellow architectural trainees – his close friend W.R. Butler, who emigrated to Australia in 1890; Edward Meredith, who took Gimson's place at Sedding's before setting up his own practice in 1898; Henry Finch, with whom Wilson and Cooper shared an office in Manchester Square while the Oxford Street practice was being transferred to Kensington; and Henry Longden, to whose family ironworks most of the metalwork commissions of that Oxford Street era had been entrusted, and who would rise to the rank of major in the Great War. But always, without fail, their enduring affection and admiration for one supremely inspirational figure would lead Wilson and Gimson into reminiscences of their master, J.D. Sedding.[20]

For Wilson, one of the most influential aspects of that master's career was his restorations and his way of going about them. The necessary additions he made to numerous churches always sought to catch the spirit of the building, and the equally necessary repairs were tempered with restraint. A case in point was Sedding's last job, the restoration between 1889 and 1891 of the church of St. Mary Magdalene, Winsford, Somerset. The immediate reaction amongst the carpenters mending its eighteenth century roof was that the medieval nave walls were sloping dangerously outwards. On closer examination, Sedding discovered that the effect came from a conscious strategy on the part of the old builders. Rather than being out of true, the walls were externally perpendicular – the 'slope' was due simply to their being cut away on their upper inside surfaces to create a deliberate outward 'batter', guaranteeing the building's stability. There was no emergency, and the old walls still stand. But Winsford would always be linked in Wilson's memory not just with that eureka moment, but with sadder associations: the final stages of the job in March 1891 proved to be Sedding's last days too. As he drove in his trap the few miles from the station to the church he took a sudden chill in the wind slicing through the Dulverton valley, and died a few days later in Winsford vicarage.[21]

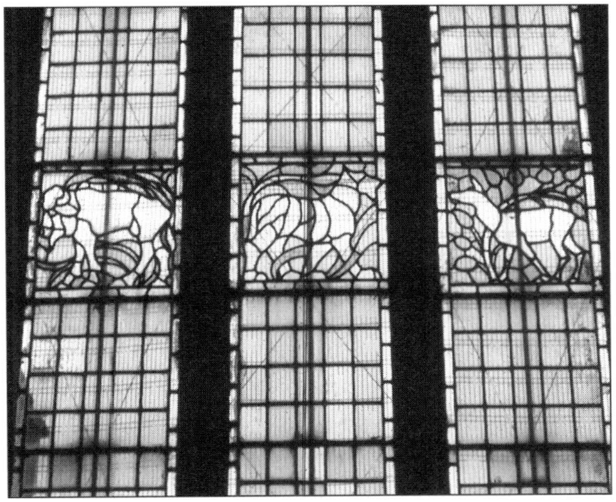

Figure 19. St. Mary's Church, Pitstone, Buckinghamshire: Henry Wilson, nave window detail, South wall, 1893.

The death of the man who had been infinitely more than a boss to him, more even than a friend, was a stunning blow to Wilson. Sedding had been his guiding force, and his influence was to live on through all Wilson's subsequent work. The deep respect he had inherited for nature, craftsmanship and locale passed into his own restorations after Sedding's death, like that of the thirteenth century church of St. Mary, Pitstone, in the Buckinghamshire Chilterns. Between 1891 and 1893 he restored the building, added a new South door, and devised new windows for the East end and in the nave, to be made by Cakebread Robey & Co. His three-light East window, dedicated to the first vicar of the consolidated parish of Pitstone and Ivinghoe, shows Mary as the Virgin, robed in blue; in the centre is Christ clad in regal red, an orb with cross in one hand, the other raised in blessing; in the third lancet is green-robed Mary Magdalene, with her emblem, the phial of ointment. For the nave's South wall Wilson designed five lancets, single and grouped, in water-green glass; Art Nouveau tracery at their tips evokes growing foliage, while a deep band across their midriff (Fig.19) depicts stylised flowers, a bull, a lion and a deer.[22]

With the Pitstone work underway, Wilson began a two-year restoration of the fifteenth century church of St. Mary Magdalene, Launceston, where he redecorated the chancel, reseated the nave and installed parclose screens and oak choir stalls; then in 1894, as that job neared completion, he was already turning his attention to the fifteenth century church of Holy Trinity, Ilfracombe, for which he had been commissioned to add new vestries and a timber-pillared lychgate.

This lychgate, with its tiled pavilion roof, was built in memory of the Rev. John Chanter, brother-in-law of the author-clergyman Charles Kingsley.[23] Formally, it reprises one he had created a year earlier in 1893, during his restoration of St. Mary's, Lynton, just to the East along the North Devon coast, there with the addition of a knopped spirelet. Wilson's introduction to the church at Lynton had been via a commission to supplement the existing Norman tower, situated at the South-West corner of the building, with a new bell tower. At the Academy show of 1892 he had exhibited a sprightly variant of the traditional West Country campanile, topped with an upswept, broad-eaved roof.[24] It was much admired, and never built (Figs. 20, 21).

His proposal for the church itself, though, to return it, in the spirit of Sedding, to its authentic roots, was approved without hesitation. *The Builder*'s characterisation of the style of the nave and North aisle as they had come down to Wilson after successive eighteenth and nineteenth century rebuilds and additions, was that they were of 'bastard Egyptian design'.[25] Employing Bryants of Barnstaple, he had their five bays rebuilt in keeping with what survived of the late Romanesque

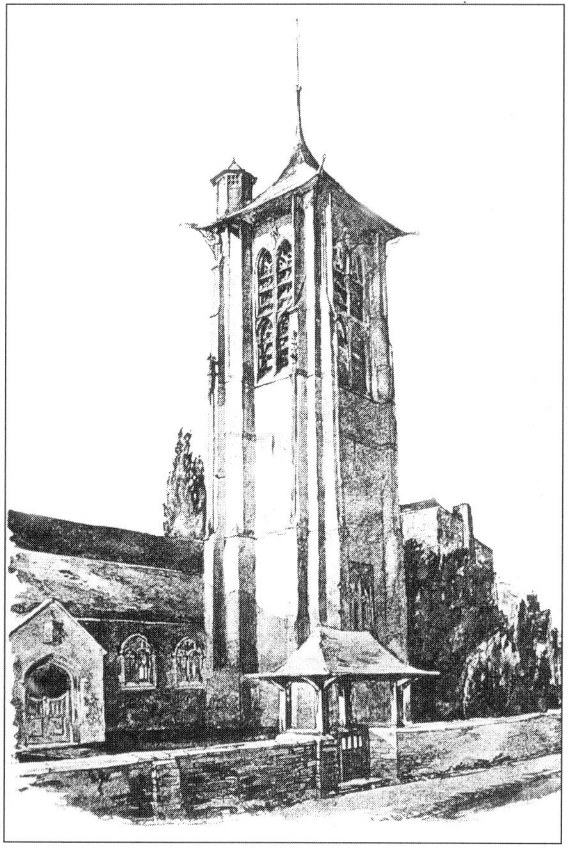

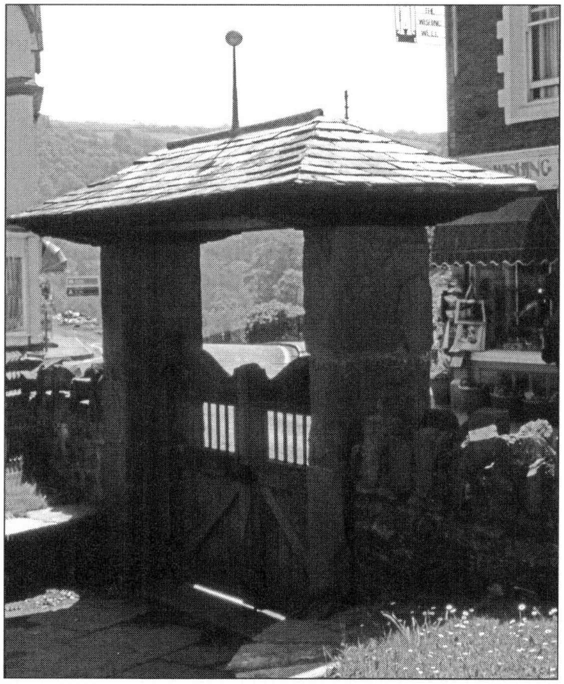

Figure 20. (left) St. Mary's Church, Lynton, Devon: Wilson's proposal for new bell-tower and lychgate, *Academy Architecture,* 1892.

Figure 21. (above) St. Mary's, Lynton: lychgate as built, with stone piers, 1893.

origins of the building, with octagonal piers and pointed arches. A fourteenth century wagon roof was revealed and restored, and for the central niche of the old porch, he asked Pomeroy to carve a sculpture of the Virgin and Child. With the exception of the tower and the eighteenth century wall of the South aisle – the nave of the original church – Wilson produced, between 1893 and 1894, an almost entirely new building. Yet it was a reconstruction guided by respect for original forms, and within which, especially throughout the North aisle, a remarkable assemblage of Arts and Crafts design would be brought together.

The success of the recreation of the body of the church led to further distinctive contributions from Wilson, with the completion of the neo-Romanesque chancel, and the fitting out of the Lady Chapel in the North aisle, both in 1904-06. Remodelling the chancel entailed creating low segmental arches, and an East window depicting the Nativity, its lights separated simply by the smooth intervening wall-surfaces; the Lady Chapel, the Reverend Cox explained in March 1905, must be 'ready for use as soon as may be'.[26] Instantly recalling his recent Brithdir designs (see below), the sheen of Wilson's repoussé copper Lady Altar lends the space an inviting glow, intensified by the subtle textures of the Tree of Life and twin reeded crosses of its frontal (Plate 52). In response to the vicar's enquiry as to whether he 'might happen to have a simple cross that would do', Wilson supplied one that was ideal for the purpose, its transoms terminating in openwork leaf-like shapes composed of vines and bunches of grapes, reminiscent of motifs he had used in miniature in a gold pendant-cross of the 1890s.[27] To accompany it he sent a pair of plain copper altar candlesticks; all were in place by the following spring, and he turned his mind to the chapel's three-light East window, over his Lady

Altar and arcaded retable. He proposed it be glazed by Whall, who, in 1896, had designed the two-light tower window on the theme of Life's Pilgrimage. Cox reluctantly but firmly put paid to the idea:

> *I don't know what we shall do about the E. window; at present we have only allowed about £100, & I fear that not a great deal more will come in ... I spoke to Whall and he said his charge would be £5 per foot, but this did not include the design, carriage fixing and making, so I am afraid three lights are quite out of the question as each contains about 12 square feet ... .*[28]

A speedy compromise was required, and so the old chancel window, created in all its Victorian brightness for an earlier restoration back in 1866, became the Lady Chapel's East window. While appreciating the expediency of the decision, Wilson was still determined to have glass by Whall in the chapel; this was achieved in the North lancet of 1907 which, made to Wilson's design, portrays in its single light St. Ann and the Virgin, illuminated by the calm greens, blues and purples of Whall's glass. For the adjacent four-light window, enlivened by the seagulls that typify his work, Wilson collaborated with Heywood Sumner, the designer of the main sequence of windows in the church. Proceeding eastwards, the North aisle's windows resume the theme of the Benedicite – a psalm in which the world in all its diversity is invited to praise its creator – culminating in the Creation design, again by Sumner, for the finely-traced West window. The sequence is interrupted in the aisle's fourth window, designed by Wilson and made by Shrigley & Hunt, depicting four virtues.[29] Wilson's impressive octagonal oak pulpit is adorned with carved foliage swags and animals, and ingeniously-mingled images of the zodiac in low relief on each side (Plate 51); like his lectern of oak and ebony, carved with woodland creatures and enriched with fruitwood chequerwork, floral inlays and an openwork frieze, it was made in the workshops of Charles Trask.[30]

Arresting examples of Wilson putting his responses to nature into his work appear in the little Somerset church of St. Mary, Norton-sub-Hamdon, which he restored between 1894 and 1895 after its tower had been struck by lightning. Trask, whose woodworking business was located in the village, had recommended Wilson for the task, and it was workmen from this traditional family firm who, under Wilson's supervision, undertook vital structural repairs. Wilson himself designed a new West window using Prior's 'Early English Glass', and an oak tower-screen to replace the original fifteenth century one which had been reduced to ashes. The biblical text extending across it and around the panelled ringing chamber testifies to Wilson's skill in using decorative letter-forms, while the marble fluting swirling around his font simultaneously evokes the waters of baptism and the natural element of the four sinuous fishes sculpted at its base (Fig. 22), their forms fiercer than those carved by him for Welbeck Abbey's font the previous year. But it is the carved and painted upper portion of the new exterior tower door that most fully acknowledges the natural world, with a profusion of wild creatures – fox, hedgehog, rabbit, crow (Plate 14). Their unmannered interpretation by Trask's country craftsmen reflects the spontaneity of the living world of which the church, its golden hamstone

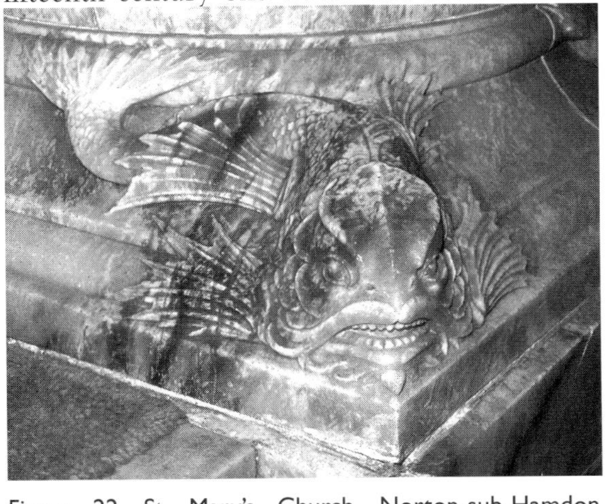

Figure 22. St. Mary's Church, Norton-sub-Hamdon, Somerset: base of Wilson's font showing carved alabaster fish detail, 1894-95.

hewn from the slopes of Ham Hill above the village, forms a part. Trask understood Wilson's affinity with the place and – unlike the Diocesan Court, which ordered changes to its design – wholeheartedly endorsed the window, with its images of Life, Work and Pity, created by Wilson to mark the Trasks' fiftieth wedding anniversary in 1904.[31]

In 1896 Wilson became uncommonly exercised by the controversial remedial work proposed at Peterborough Cathedral. The Dean and Chapter had been warned in two reports by John Pearson, who had recently completed his restoration of the central tower and crossing, that the early thirteenth century West front with its three tall arches was in a dangerous state. Its North gable was indeed on the point of collapse: the great towers flanking the façade rested on the vaults of the two outer arches which, poorly constructed and weakened with age, could hardly bear the load – there were cracks in the arches and bulges in the gables. The spring storms of 1895 had already blown down four pinnacles. Pearson, assisted by Arthur Blomfield, was immediately engaged to underpin the whole West front, but so bad was the state of the gable that he could see no alternative to its being taken down and rebuilt. *The Builder* and the RIBA agreed with him; not so the Society of Antiquaries and the SPAB, both of whom strongly opposed the idea, even offering to repair it free of charge: the problem, they insisted after their limited survey, was internal, and could be cured by recoring – replacing the core of loose and degraded rubble with concrete. The bitter row that ensued spread far beyond professional circles: public opinion also demanded a say. *The Times* was showered with letters that took one or other polarised view concerning this nationally important building, and even *Punch* pitched in with witty sketches on the debate. Wilson took the Anti-Scrape line in resisting the dismantling of the gable, and joined Lethaby, Detmar Blow, J.T. Micklethwaite, Weir Schultz, Troup, Prior, Mervyn Macartney, Ernest Newton, Ashbee and, from the Sedding generation, Philip Webb and the engineer John Carruthers, in signing a letter to *The Builder.* In an article of his own in *The Architectural Review,*[32] he condemned the destructive drift of the scheme as an architectural scandal, and aired his fears that the 'accidental beauty' of the gable's ancient awkwardnesses and eccentricities was about to be sacrificed.

His opinion was widely respected, though in reality the dire violation he had feared had never been on the cards; after the radical option had been successfully executed, he gladly conceded that the gable's demolition and reassembly had been sensible and well-considered. With his unassuming approach to restoration, he must have shared the relief expressed in follow-up letters from Prior and Micklethwaite clarifying their antipathy not to Pearson, but rather, to the perceived risk of the Cathedral being given a neat replica gable instead of the genuine article intelligently repaired. In the event some 2,000 stones had been removed and numbered, with 1,800 of them being accurately returned to their places. Only those past preservation had been renewed. This was the same anti-interpretive approach which, on a tiny scale, had distinguished Wilson's frank yet inconspicuous repairs of 1892 to the choir stalls and pulpit of the church of St. Peter and St. Paul at Charlton Adam, nine miles north-east of Norton-sub-Hamdon, and it was rooted in fundamental principles: if these applied at one extreme of the scale, then they applied equally at the other.

> *The world slips away as we enter the doors; the tall pillars have something eternal about them; the gloom and mystery seem infinite; like a great sea-shell the roof is full of whispers … .*[33]

His words, describing Westminster Abbey, convey something of Wilson's reverence for Gothic architecture; the Gothic Revival was warmly saluted by him as a reawakening of the English spirit 'after centuries of eclipse',[34] but he was careful to endorse only its rare, truly sensitive, manifestations. It was his contention that 'inspiration' in art and design was actually the 'rush of unconscious memory'[35] stretching back, unbroken, through countless generations of craftsmanship. The belief forms a crucial component of Wilson's attitude to the Gothic style – since we are so strongly linked to our spiritual ancestors, certain types of architecture appeal spontaneously, tapping a pool of shared unconscious memory. Particular buildings may trigger 'an instinctive organic recognition, dim ... remembrances reaching down to the lower levels of mental life'.[36] The idea finds parallels in Lethaby's thought, and was to be developed most fully later, in Jung's concept of the collective unconscious.

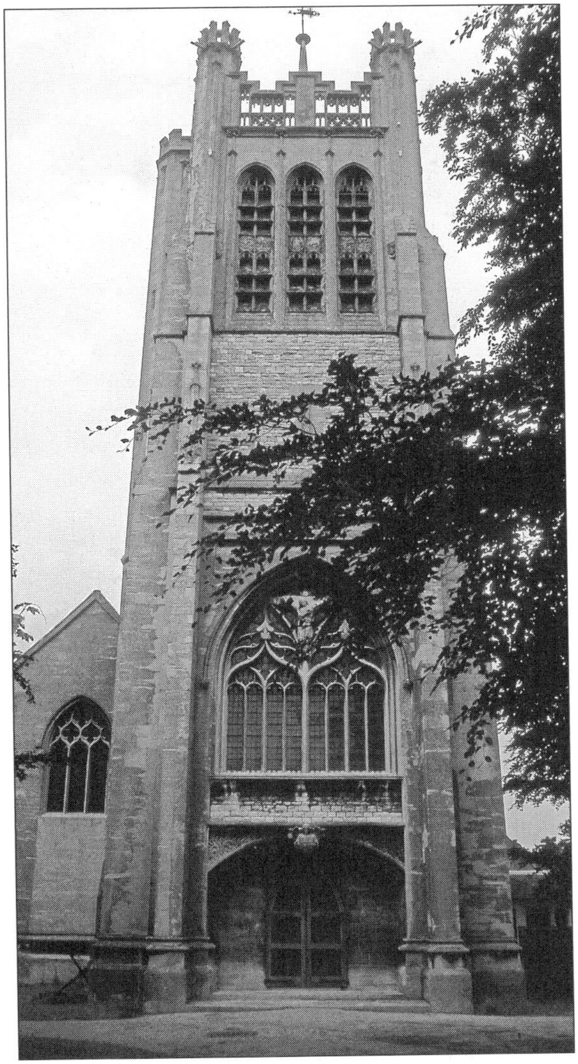

Figure 23. St. Clement's, Bournemouth: Wilson's West tower, added 1889-93 to Sedding's church of 1871.

Wilson gave expression to his belief in Gothic as a living, deeply-felt architectural language in his new tower for St. Clement's, Bournemouth (Fig. 23), completing the church Sedding had built in 1871. In 1889, when the go-ahead for the tower reached Sedding's office, Wilson was his chief assistant, and – presumably with Sedding's approval – he replaced Sedding's draft of a low, square tower and compact spire with his own slender design. This, with its turrets and traceried parapet, carries unmistakeable echoes of fifteenth century West Country towers, like St. Mary's, Taunton, and St. Peter's, Evercreech, as if affirming Wilson's faith in the continuity of building types – those enduring local styles that he and Cooper identified when writing about Sedding. Within such a 'type', however, Wilson adds exuberant details and an explicit iconography which are all his own.

The slightly uneasy marriage between Sedding's church and Wilson's tower emphasises his growing readiness to produce a building untrammelled by pre-ordained stylistic norms, even those of his beloved Sedding His loyalty here belongs to age-old Gothic forms blended with a distinct personal element. Gothic was providing Wilson with a powerful design impetus, one that was being felt as the century neared its end by numerous Gothic-inspired architects: by the unclassifiable Leonard Stokes, by Temple Moore in his airy interpretations of church spaces, by Ninian Comper with his doctrine of 'unity by inclusion'. It is implicit, too, in the monumental Gothicism of Giles Gilbert Scott with which he won the 1902 Liverpool Cathedral competition, and in the Arts and Crafts Gothic of the Birmingham architect W.H. Bidlake, best evidenced in his church of St. Agatha, Sparkbrook (1899-1901), the parapet and cupolas of which involuntarily recall Wilson's tower at Bournemouth.

St. Clement's tall and elegant tower has a stair turret at its north-east angle and minor turrets to the other three. The tracery of the eight-light West window shows the martyrdom of St. Clement, tied to an anchor and thrown into the Black Sea. The stone figure of the saint is depicted bound to the window's central mullion, which branches above his head to form the shape of an anchor.

The tracery on either side cascades outwards in flamboyant, surging wave-forms.[37] On completion of the window and the ringing chamber, work came to a halt while the contract with the builders, Merrick & Son of Tewkesbury, was renewed. When work resumed in 1892, Sedding was dead and Wilson officially in charge of finishing the job. The next stage, the belfry, was embellished with a band of carving by F.W. Pomeroy. The lacy fretwork of the parapet, though singularly inappropriate to the corrosive sea air, lends a fine delicacy to the tower's top stage. For all the vicar's initial anxiety about its Art Nouveau overtones, he had no need to worry: Wilson's tower successfully and seriously melds originality with tradition, its effect overtaking the vagaries of any temporary fashion to form one of his finest architectural works – indeed, in Charles Nicholson's view, probably his best.[38]

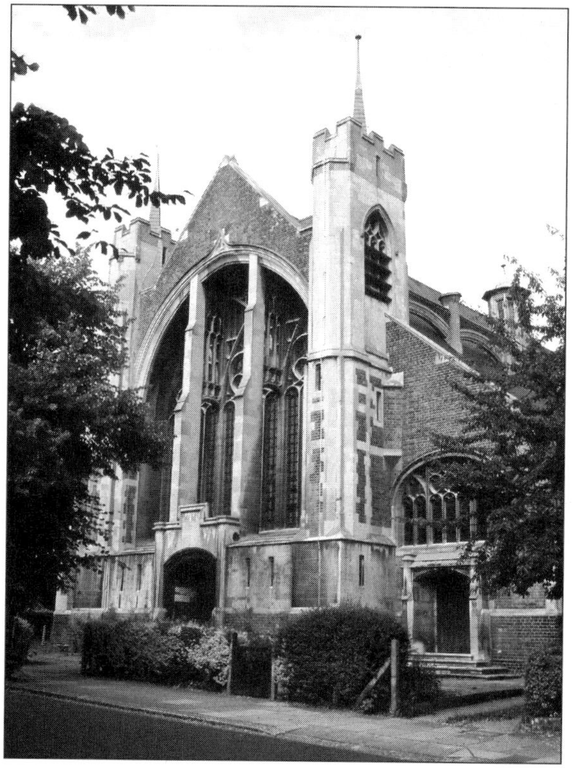

Figure 24. St. Peter's Church, Ealing: J.D. Sedding and H.Wilson, West front, 1889-93.

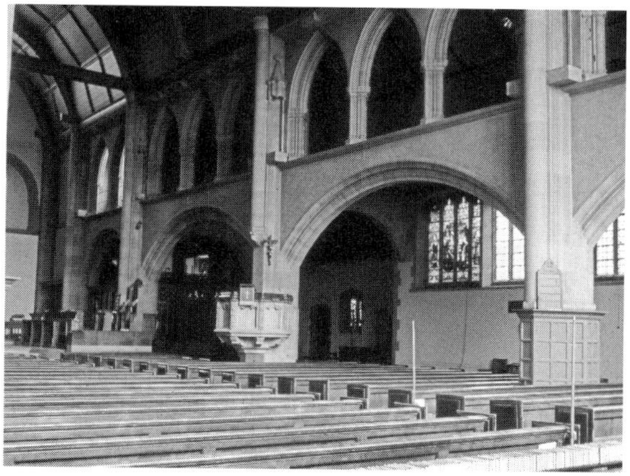

Figure 25. St Peter's, Ealing: nave and sanctuary.

An altogether larger task came for Wilson with St. Peter's Church, Ealing (Figs. 24, 25). Like Sedding, he consistently maintained that it was not the precise forms embodied in the shells of old buildings that were of really lasting value. More significant were the feelings which their makers had been striving to express. Consequently, he was dismissive of architects who adopted too material a standpoint, and who undervalued the inner vision, the spiritual message, and the psychological import of architecture. Despite his faith in the tenacity of the Gothic spirit, Wilson realised how brutally it could be misinterpreted by architectural copyists mimicking, with 'sheeplike'[39] conformity, the outward forms of old buildings as they jumped onto the Revivalist bandwagon. To him the spectacle of some of his uninspired contemporaries 'eagerly gathering capitals, cornices, pinnacles and profiles with the pathetic confidence of boys in their grotto' was risible. In his graphic imagination these so-called architects became 'human hermit-crabs ... huddling their inglorious quarters into the cast shell of some dead creature'.[40]

Wilson was convinced that it was the modern architect's role to draw on eternal, emotional qualities, just as it had been the old master-builder's. Even in the most humdrum life, the human mind may experience moments, perhaps while gazing at a landscape as dusk falls, when

the business of life shows small and inconsequent; then the secret of existence seems to be disengaging itself, waiting to be seized.[41]

Present-day practitioners must continue the paths which their predecessors had begun, and find methods and sources which would be as expressive in their own time as those their forbears had found in theirs. After all, 'what is most precious in our work is what we unconsciously reveal of ourselves, our race, our society'.[42] It was with this in mind that in 1892 Wilson began directing the construction of St. Peter's Church, in whose design he must surely have been involved from the outset and which headed the list F.W. Troup compiled from Wilson's own notes of his more important works in architecture.

The commission had been awarded to Sedding in 1889, perspectives and plan of the proposed building appearing first in *The Builder*,[43] then in *The Architect*. While having features in common, especially in their handling of space, the design differs from Holy Trinity, Sloane Street in being plainer in detail, more daring in structure, less literal in its Gothic allusions. When the project began, Sedding himself was busier than ever, not only with the Sloane Street church, All Saints', Falmouth, and the Industrial Schools, Bristol, but also with restoring or adding to old churches: St. Mary's, Stamford, St. John's, West Wickham and St. Mary's, Winsford. It was both opportune and just to give Wilson, increasingly playing the role of partner, more of the independence for which his talents and ambition pleaded. Charles Nicholson, working successively under Sedding and Wilson as St. Peter's took shape, was unequivocal in attributing the work done 'entirely to Wilson', Sedding having left only brief notes at his death; his conclusion is endorsed in an account by the Reverend William Petty, St. Peter's first vicar.[44] To be sure, the interior perspective published in *The Builder* of 16 November 1889, is headed 'John D. Sedding archt'. Exactly how much his assistant contributed to the concept remains a matter for conjecture, but it is fair to assume that while Sedding controlled the office and its output, Wilson's insights were by now decidedly influential throughout the design process.

The title of the Architect's Report, 'New and Old',[45] submitted to the Commissioners with perpective and transverse and longitudinal sections, testifies to the way the new church, though acknowledging the past, vigorously embraces the present. The flowing lines of its pared down Gothic accord easily with the Art Nouveau idiom pervading the West window, while the building's bold spatial qualities readily accommodate the distinctly modern role it had been assigned. Significantly, its Gothic references, like those of St. Clement's and of Holy Trinity, Sloane Street, are to the fourteenth century forms of the style – a style which in its own medieval context had represented a search for fresh inspiration, and which at Ealing found expression in bold structural and spatial innovation.

In replacing a temporary corrugated iron church, the new St. Peter's had to be suitable for 'congregational' purposes in a town district. But it was also seeking 'breadth of effect' and 'picturesqueness'[46] in its simple masses and arched forms. Practical considerations, such as unimpeded sound and sight lines, and a separate south door for schoolchildren, combine with an originality of design to make this the most striking of the churches commissioned in the Sedding era and realised by Wilson. The free openness of planning that characterised Sedding's church designs seems reaffirmed, emboldened even, by the touch of his chief assistant, a dynamic force in the office since 1888; on a par, in its Sedding heritage, with Sloane Street and Clerkenwell, the Ealing church looks forward to Wilson's proposed completion of St. Augustine's, Highgate and to the fearless interior spaces of his entry for the British Columbia cathedral competition of 1893.

Erected by Joseph Dorey and Co. of Brentford, St. Peter's is an expansive structure with a broad nave and wide aisles, its internal length some 130', able to accommodate over a thousand worshippers. The nave and chancel, each with aisles, occupy four bays, while shallow transepts create a Latin cross plan. In the chancel, the stone cornice is carved with wild animals, including a bear and an elephant (Plate 15), the latter giving an early glimpse in sculptural form of a creature that would achieve symbolic import in Wilson's metalwork, and contemporary cultural resonance in his twentieth century bronzework in America. In a sketch of 1898, eight elephants bear the arched base of a chalice on their backs,[47] the motif emphasising his cross-disciplinary, archetypal vision.

Sweeping arches link the moulded brick nave piers. Above are galleries, screened from the nave by a series of pointed arches. These galleries were available if required for extra space, but were primarily included 'for their effect, and light and shade'.[48] Here, distinctively architectural intuition produces both practical effect and visual impact: the way a building becomes architecture – or, as Lethaby put it, 'architecture interpenetrates building not for the satisfaction of the simple needs of the body, but the complex ones of the intellect'.[49]

Wilson continued the commission following Sedding's death under the established 'Sedding and Wilson' banner – drawings, for example, of the screen between vestry and tower, and for the organ chamber were prepared in May 1893. Empty niches in the nave piers at gallery level, intended to hold full-size statues of the apostles, testify that the embellishment of the church was never finished. The wooden roof, of simple trussed construction in the nave, is panelled in the chancel to throw out sound to the congregation, and in anticipation of ceiling paintings which again were never executed. A plan to sheath the interior face of the west doors in flower-embossed brass incorporated the craft skills of Wilson's father, William. A single door was displayed at the Arts and Crafts Exhibition of 1896,[50] but for reasons of time and cost, only sections finally appeared, in beaten brass strips across the doors' width. Installed by Farmer & Brindley in 1910, the plain Gothic freestone pulpit, a memorial to William Petty, was designed, as if to keep his spirit alive, by Sedding's nephew, Edmund.

One of the most remarkable features of the building's structure is the way the nave piers pierce the roof, rising eighteen feet above it, to form a series of octagonal turrets with lead cupolas. Between them are set smaller pinnacles, linked by light, loping arches. As well as relieving the unbroken visual effect of the roof and creating a fine interplay of verticals and horizontals, the arrangement has a functional role, contributing to the structural integrity of the church.

True visual energy is achieved in the play of bulk and delicacy in the façade of the church, fulfilling the aim embodied in 'New and Old' that the church present 'as great an effect as possible to the road'. The massive West wall of box ground stone is fifteen feet thick at its base, allowing for the window to be dramatically recessed to a depth of eight feet within a great buttressed arch. The arrangement is reminiscent of the fifteenth century West front of Gloucester Cathedral with its buttressed mullions and large recessed window, well known to both Wilson and Sedding. Twelve slim lancets compose the lower part of Wilson's window, swirling tracery the upper part. Plain, pale glazing, purposely uncluttered, intensifies its effect, while two castellated turrets flank it, each surmounted by an elegant spirelet. One, the South, was to act as a temporary bell-tower until the intended square belfry could be built above the North transept. Frustrated by cost, this was never executed, nor were the statues intended for the buttress arches – a fortunate omission, it might be judged, for the satisfying unimpeded curves their absence permits.

St. Peter's represented the successful culmination of a commission which had been given to Sedding and Wilson on the strength not just of their design proposal but also of the practice's style and reputation. About the alternative way of gaining work – through the open architectural competition system – Wilson had enormous reservations. As a challenger in four of them, he was doubtful about their producing architecture of real worth, for while competitions gave a few the chance to advance their career, they also had severe drawbacks. It was quite usual to compete for as long as ten years before winning one – a fact which highlights Wilson's unusually early success as co-author of the successful Ladbroke Grove Library design. Persistent lack of success could have a demoralising effect on an architect, and lead him to compromise his personal style in order to improve his chances of winning. On the whole, the system tended to nurture safe mediocrity and to gradually stifle schemes of true originality.

'New and Old' reappeared as Wilson's motto for the proposal he submitted, with high hopes, to the 1893 competition for a new cathedral in Victoria, British Columbia (Fig. 26). Its wide vaulted nave and chancel, its large East and West windows, the elegant piers, and above all, an exhilarating sense of space, all featured in *The Builder*'s review of Wilson's design, which noted that 'the mantle of his former principal had fallen on him in more senses than one'.[51] But however many similarities exist between this design and projects that he had worked on with his late master, it is the links, both backwards and forwards, to Wilson's independent designs of the late 1880s and the 1890s that are most in evidence. The square, buttressed West towers, for example, their tiers clearly delineated by setbacks, clearly relate to that he added to the Bournemouth church. The sculpted crucifix on the West front prefigures the emotionally charged one in his 1896 submission for St. Augustine's, Highgate. Wilson's propensity for blending bulk and dainty elegance finds expression in the cupolas, finials and spires surmounting his huge cathedral, and his feeling for mass is explored with a theatrical gusto unknown in Sedding's designs.

So epic a composition, of local stone with a slate roof, was to be built in stages, with morning chapel, cloisters and chapter house to be added later, beyond the North chancel. At a cost of £20,000, Wilson's cathedral would have held some 1,200 people. Soaring piers and vaulted roof emphasise the vastness of its interior. (Fig. 27). While Sedding's design tenets had been assimilated by his loyal assistant, the furnishings – chequered marble chancel rail, pillared pulpit, stylised fig trees painted on aisle vaults, Lethaby-inspired lamps – show the subtle allusiveness of Wilson's maturing style. However, while *The Builder* admired this 'fine and picturesque'[52] design, it lacks the confidence of the Ealing church. What presents itself, rather, is a somewhat unwieldy profusion of form and

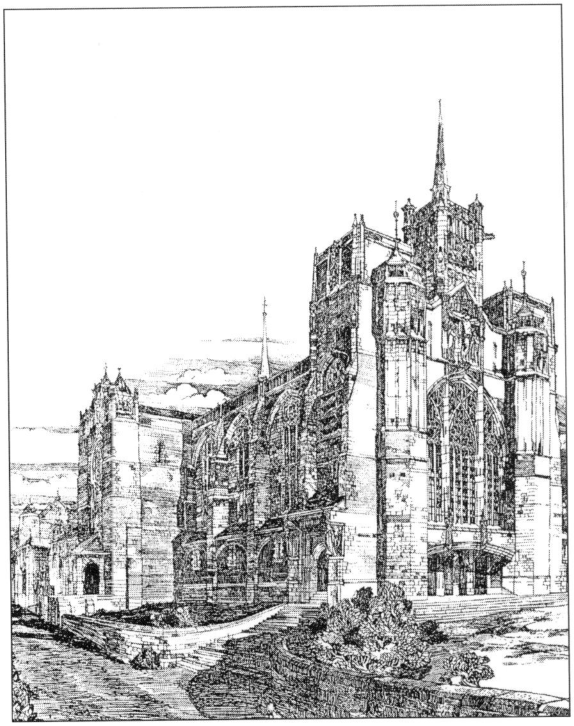

Figure 26. (above) Victoria B.C., competition for new Cathedral: 'New and Old' design by Henry Wilson, 1893.

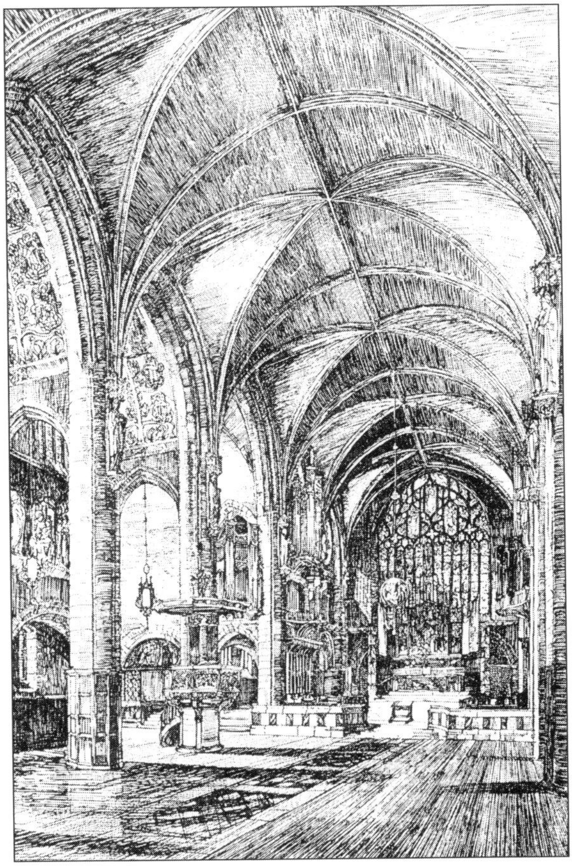

Figure 27. (right) Victoria Cathedral competition: 'New and Old' interior showing sanctuary and crossing.

mood. The separate ingredients are Wilson at his best, but the impression is of a superlative mixture of every conceivable idea. A comment once made by Whall about Sedding might be applied here to Wilson: 'what one chiefly wished for in him was repose'.[53] The competition judge, the Revivalist Sir Arthur Blomfield, placed him in the ten finalists, but a Wilson victory was denied by the more predictable 'Fides', by the home firm of Keith and Evers, of Victoria, B.C.[54] Nevertheless, Wilson's entry, exhibited at Church House, had real impact and, if allowed to evolve in construction, must surely have resulted in a sensational building.

The Ladbroke Grove Library would, in the end, prove to be Henry Wilson's one competition success: his subsequent designs were invariably too outspoken to gain the unanimous approval of any team of judges. In 1895, increasingly assured in his ideas, he decided to try his luck in the contest for a brand new church of St. Andrew's, Boscombe. This held a special piquancy, in bringing him into direct rivalry with his former master Oldrid Scott, whose office he had left nine years previously. Their entries underlined the divergence of their paths. In collaboration with C.T. Miles of Bournemouth, Scott produced a straight Gothic scheme in line with the tenets of Revivalism that he had followed for some thirty years,[55] while Wilson, aspiring towards fresh, original architecture, designed a church operatic in its aura,[56] and which, four years after Sedding's death, was to all intents and purposes free of all Sedding features.

In Wilson's proposal (Fig. 28), two round-headed doorways lead into a prow-like porch. Above is a dramatically recessed West window, flanked by massive square buttresses with side wings forming a barbican the width and height of the entire church. At roof level is arcading in an almost Townsendian spirit, flanking a belfry whose fancifulness contrasts sharply with the plainness of the West front.

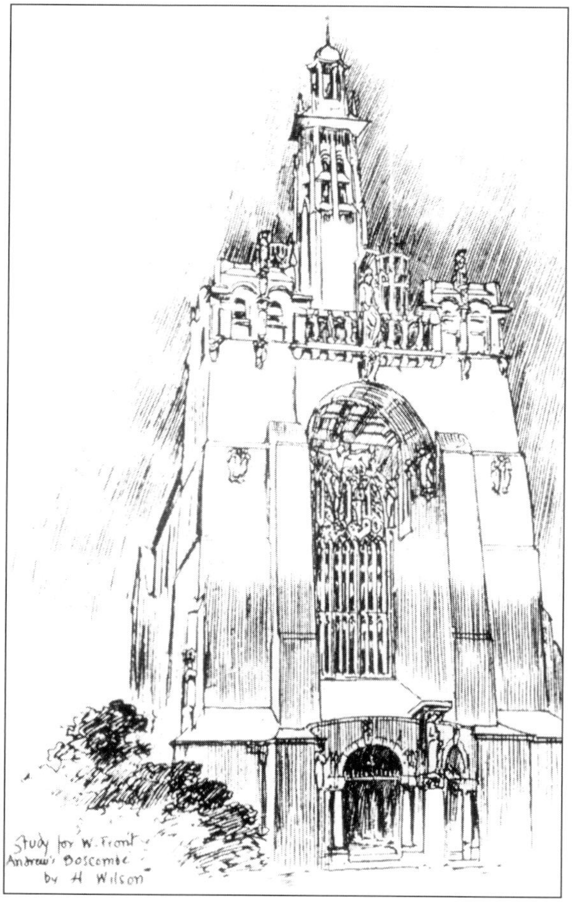

Figure 28. Proposed church of St. Andrew, Boscombe, Dorset: Wilson's competition sketch for West front, 1895.

Executed in watercolour to portray a warm golden stone church rearing up against a blue sky, Wilson's design won considerable attention at the Royal Academy summer exhibition of 1895. He had drawn it as if from ground level, and its lofty perspective and the handling of mass and detail seemed to suggest that even a country or suburban church could invoke a cathedral's grandeur. It was never intended literally as a towering structure of vast proportions. But it was meant to function as an impressive, inspirational building within its own context.

Naturally, it was Scott's 'proper' but more pedestrian design that was adopted: but Wilson who, having taken his explorations significantly further, gained the kudos. His Boscombe proposal had an important future, feeding decisively into the work of other architects as far away as Glasgow, where James Miller's 1904 church of St. Andrew-in-the-East suggests close attentiveness to Wilson's drawings for the Boscombe competion.

At this stage in his career, though, a single first prize and the income accruing from a solid contract, fulfilled with no loss of his original vision, would have been timely: by 1895 he and Margaret Morse had been engaged to be married for four years, but he still felt insufficiently established or secure to make her his wife.

Still, his personal devotion to creative truth endured. Despite the distance Wilson interposed with such energy between himself and academic Revivalism, he knew that his attempts at free design were in constant danger of being swamped by the stream of formulaic work being turned out by countless professors of the style. He parodied their typical office advertisements with one of his own, seeking assistants 'versed in Gothic and Classic detail, with some knowledge of Spanish Renaissance ... '.[57] or some other more-or-less irrelevant historical specialism. The antidote he proposed to such chimeras was to go back to fundamentals – to practical expertise and a true understanding of nature. Both were vital if architects were to find a genuinely creative approach to the structural and decorative challenges of a new age.

The key lay – for anyone who had read Ruskin or watched Sedding at work – in the material process of making the building. As Wilson pointed out, 'if Architecture be the Art of Building, Building is based on the crafts [thus] the first thing an Architect should learn is not how to design, nor draw, but how to Build',[58] to *make* things through the practice of a craft or building trade.

Wilson himself was a craftsman of extraordinary capacity, knowledgeable of many materials, personally adept at modelling in plaster, carpentry, sculpting and metalwork from jewellery to foundry work.[59] For him, the raw materials of building held a mysterious potency, forming a bond with the impulses of architecture closer than mere stylistic fluency ever could. He spoke optimistically around 1900 of the handful of young architects who, like the Barnsleys, were abandoning office work to learn a craft, or to gain experience of actually working on buildings, like Detmar Blow with his great house at Happisburgh, Norfolk. Then there were those who had chosen to familiarise themselves with a building trade, like F.W. Troup and Arthur Grove, both of whom learnt leadwork and later taught the skill at the Central School of Arts and Crafts. Wilson admired those who had become 'plasterers, builders, cabinet-makers ...' welcoming these 'signs of a wiser attitude to building and ... to our lives, mental and physical'.[60] Such immediate experience was the ideal: but the architect must at least show sensitivity to the process of building. Writing to the architect and town planner Patrick Geddes, Wilson characterised several fellow architects according to this theme:

> *... E.S. Prior is a really gifted person and a builder – Baillie Scott is no builder, neither is Voysey, I do not think that Mackintosh is, but both he and Voysey have grit and tenacity, a belief in themselves and a certain strange originality of which Scott is innocent. The works of each I avoid ... Lorimer I know and admire. He is a real worker.*[61]

As for developing a true understanding of nature, this could only render an architect's art and ideals 'freer and saner'[62] by bringing him into harmony with the environment within which he was working. 'We see the result of the craftsman's knowledge and nature study', Wilson insisted, in the work of 'all the men who have really achieved anything. The work of Philip Webb, Burges and Sedding comes upon the mind with the fragrance of new creation ... '.[63] The way these architects worked was direct, simple and natural, like that of the medieval builders – largely site-based, and absolutely focused on the peculiarities of the job in hand.

Their road led to architectural riches; the 'poverty'[64] of much modern architecture was due to the remoteness of the office, of the process of design from the building site. Prestigious architectural perspectives were produced to give clients an idea of how their building would look, and to show it off to maximum advantage at the Royal Academy. Minutely detailed working drawings would then be generated, and enacted by run-of-the-mill building firms. Worse still, there were times when an architect might be involved in so many concurrent commissions that he would have no chance to make his own perspectives and drawings, delegating them instead to his draughtsmen. In consequence, all meaningful exchanges between architect, builder and craftsman were lost. 'One might as well play blindman's buff by telegraph as hope to produce works of art by our present methods',[65] was Wilson's comment. A painter could not paint 'by proxy' – why then expect an architect to solve problems of height, thickness, colour, material, light, shade and atmosphere on paper, in an office miles away from the work?[66]

Not for Wilson the role of a 'paper architect' who made 'specifications [rather than] buildings'.[67] His own methods were closer to those of a master-builder, for whom craftsmanship infinitely outweighed graphic exactitude.[68]

> *[The] function of a master-builder engaged on one building at a time ... is that of the preparation of the scheme of the building, and the translation of that scheme into comprehensible diagrams for the use of the workmen under him; these diagrams should ... contain only the essential facts. They are the skeletons on which the craftsman builds up a body of beauty.*[69]

That concept of the *scheme* of a building was central to his approach, and the word acquired a special meaning in his personal vocabulary. He used it to describe an impressionistic, emotional portrayal, or study, of the proposed building. Such schemes – more subjective, freer versions of the architectural perspective – should convey not just how the finished building would look, but also, how it would affect the viewer. In combination with clear, informative *diagrams* it would act as a valuable guide for the builders, highlighting the overall effect for which they should aim, but not in such a way as to prevent its being embellished or adjusted through dialogue with the architect as site and materials prompted.

However, though a valiant core of individuals, mostly Art Workers' Guild members, adopted this flexible attitude as to how drawing related to building, there were no mass conversions. Wilson's fluent, summary graphic style had been shaped by Sedding's creative interpretation of drawings and designs. The drawings of Lethaby, Newton, Prior and Gimson showed an equally sensitive understanding of texture, massing and mood. But such flexibility belonged to a minority, while the rest of the profession became increasingly deskbound. It was an irony, noted Wilson, that

> *at our ... institutes and societies [architects] read papers on ... the freedom and naturalness of ancient work, [then] go home and draw out plans for a building from concrete to cornice, all figured before a brick has been laid.*[70]

It was above all through his powerful, individualistic *schemes* that Wilson gained a reputation as one of the truly creative draughtsmen of his day. His old friend Pite described how his 'genius' for draughtsmanship that had been 'quietly developing' under Belcher 'had flowered in a quite extraordinary way' under Sedding, and for many years, as with his 1895 Boscombe design, 'his dramatically picturesque drawings gave life to the Architecture Room of the Royal Academy'.[71]

Another striking Wilson 'scheme', for the West front of St. Augustine's Church, Highgate, London, was shown at the Academy in 1896 (Fig. 29). The chancel and one bay of the nave had been built by Sedding nine years earlier; in 1893 Wilson had built the Lady Chapel, incorporating Sedding's design for a reredos. The painted altarpiece showing the Annunciation is by Whall, and flanking the altar are wrought-iron screens by Wilson, each depicting a golden World Tree, springing, as explained in Lethaby's book, from a perfect sphere, its branches terminating in seven stars.[72] By 1895 Wilson had completed the five further nave bays in accordance with Sedding's drawings, but with some modification of detail, as in the vaulting at the North-West corner, and the intriguing arched passageway that forms the North aisle.

At this point the church authorities decided to part company with Sedding's drawings and, rather than give Wilson *carte blanche*, to open the completion of the West front to competition. Wilson, naturally, was one of the entrants, and his 'scheme' shows a façade with the elemental drama of a cliff face, owing nothing to Sedding's 1885 proposal.[73] These are no longer the sunny stone planes of Boscombe, but shadowy, sombre tones that fix the building in its urban context, Archway Road. The composition is boldly asymmetrical, a massive octagonal turret with flattened ogee cap marking its North corner, a slighter version with less emphatic dome to the South. This roof-form had already featured in Wilson's Victoria cathedral proposal, and would recur on the proposed tower (1892) and the executed lychgate (1893) at St. Mary's Church, Lynton. Cued by this Wilsonian shape, Harrison Townsend borrowed from it in 1898 for the porch of a house – Cliff Towers – he was designing in Salcombe.[74]

In Wilson's design for St. Augustine's, the gabled front was to be crowned with an arched, two-tier temple-like structure, seemingly scaled up from the silver wafer-box he designed, also in 1895, for St. Martin's, Marple. The jambs of the central arches continue downwards as buttresses, framing the three slender lights of the West window. Beneath it, the condemned Christ and two thieves are depicted in a lifesize crucifixion sculpted (on the evidence of the drawing) with harrowing intensity. Reviewing Wilson's scheme, the *The Builder* wisely read it as 'a study, in a picturesque rather than an architectural sense', and praised it as 'a very original architectural conception, with plenty of room for ingenious working out in detail'. This was precisely what Wilson, with his belief in drawings being suggestive rather than prescriptive, had intended. But when evaluating Wilson's attempt to summon up feeling at the expense of exact specifications, the writer was less convinced: in the materials available, and in this site, 'the actual building could hardly have the effect conveyed in the drawing ...'.[75]

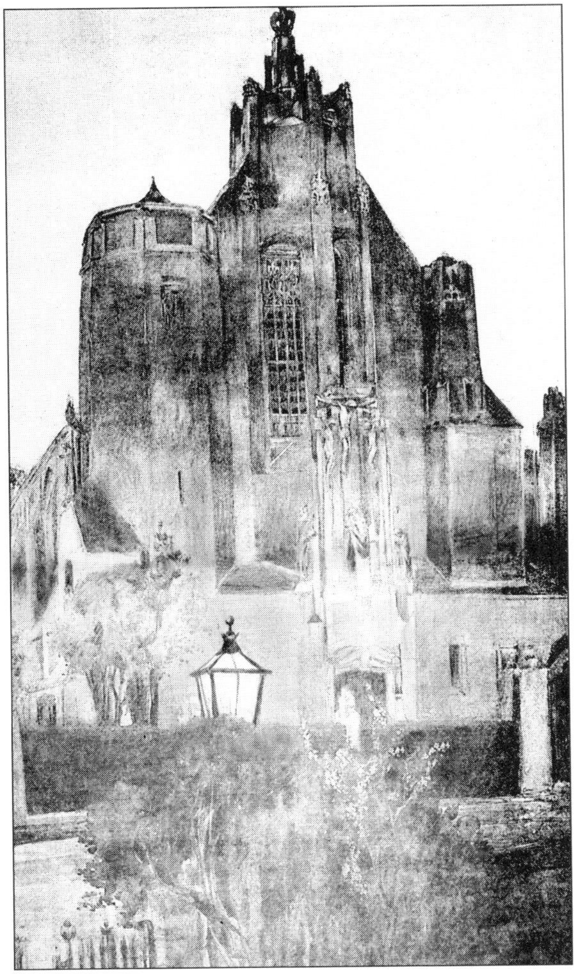

Figure 29. St. Augustine's Church, Highgate: scheme by Wilson for the new West end, *Academy Architecture*, 1896.

In the event, Wilson's scheme was held back for sixteen years, before being rejected in favour of a cheaper solution submitted by J. Harold Gibbons (1878-1958). With its buttresses, its strongly-traced window and its crucifix (albeit much reduced in size and emotional effect), the new design borrowed much from Wilson's proposal, but the momentous impact promised in the original concept was now diluted and irretrievably tamed.[76]

Wilson fully recognised the dilemma facing progressive architects of the day: their artistic hunches might pull them in one direction, but professional custom even more strongly in the other. His idealism constantly sought to redress the balance, and to reinstate individualism over the formulaic trend of modern architectural practice. To these ends he consistently proposed the renaissance of the guild system; although industrial society had produced trades unions and building corporations, such bodies, he noted, ignored the essential unity which the old guilds had implied. Regulating hours and wages had overtaken the urge to produce the finest work: the 'methods of the counting house'[77] had ousted inspiration. The remedy surely lay in the architects relinquishing their hermetically-sealed, office-bound practices and, by being craftsmen themselves, increasing the investment of their fellow-workers in the project-in-hand.

For a while, in the late 1890s, it seemed that this could happen, and that architecture might be restored to its role as a 'music' art, with the architect acting as a 'composer'[78] for an orchestra of craftsmen. This dream of a root-and-branch craft revival would have had only limited impact on the all-important field of commercial architecture, but at that hopeful, fervent stage, all seemed possible. As might be expected, the form into which Wilson's ambitions crystallised for such truly collaborative architecture, the exponent of his 'ideal', craft-inspired building, was that of a church:

> *imagine a building erected by the Art Workers' Guild – a mere barn boldly buttressed, showing high above the roofs of some town … and rising from them sheer and rugged as a cliff, entered … by a pillared porch arched over with a mosaic vault. Through a door covered with stories in beaten metal you step into a solemn and simple hall with walls recessed to give shadow and surface change, the windows few and lofty … The Guild should fill these with opaline glazing. Others might decorate the upper walls with frescoes … Beneath them should be marble sheeting of rich, plain colour. The floor should be a chequer of sombre-tinted stone, the roof timbers quaintly coloured and enlivened by gold; some of the architects might design pavements like the sea and ceilings like the sky. Imagine a sudden rise of steps at choir level, like a wave in a sea of stone, then a further lift to … the baldachin, glowing with colour like an altar fire. The altar itself, a piece of solemn sculpture, or a master work wrought with all the resources of the modern Goldsmith's Art set with enamels and reliefs in beaten silver. The lamps, the chandeliers, the chalices would all be enriched with reverent fancies. Here might be endless opportunities for the Artist and the Craftsman; I am convinced it only needs organisation … to be realised. Naturally, I shall be told that all this is impractical and visionary, but so much the better … .*[79]

The description bears an uncanny resemblance to the remarkable church that Wilson himself had just been commissioned to furnish, St. Bartholomew's in Brighton. He was not its architect, that role had been filled some fifteen years earlier by the short-lived Sussex architect Edmund Scott, but he had been appointed to fit and finish this daringly-scaled masterpiece. Although not conforming fully to the *ab initio* spirit he had described, Wilson was able to achieve at Brighton a similarly magisterial outcome in his thrilling neo-Byzantine transformation of the interior of Scott's incomplete building: echoes of his fantasy church resound throughout.

A few months before visualising his ideal church, Wilson had gathered together a group of leading artist-craftsmen to decorate the family chapel at Douglas Castle, Lanarkshire, the eighteenth century seat of the Earls of Home. On the death of his father, Charles, the twelfth Earl and second Baron Douglas, had decided to proceed with improvements to the estate, and in 1888, had the chapel built by the Edinburgh partnership Wardrop and Reid, with additions by George Henderson.[80] The architects had left a bare interior relieved only by its plain glazed brickwork, oak wainscotting and perfunctory acanthus ceiling corbels. Wilson captivated the new Earl's imagination with a decorative scheme that embraced nature, colour and craftsmanship (Fig. 30). He began the transformation of the insipid single-cell interior by plastering the upper walls in preparation for frescoes, by replacing

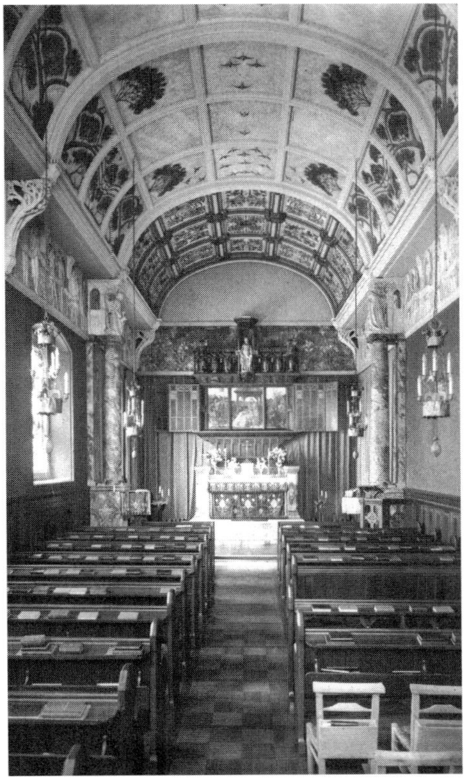
Courtesy of the Royal Commision on the Ancient and Historical Monuments of Scotland

Figure 30. Douglas Castle: the private chapel with Wilson's scheme of redecoration, 1896.

the corbels with figures of saints leaning from clustered forest branches, and by changing its proportions with the creation of a separate chancel with steps leading up to it, divided from the nave by a pair of giant freestanding red marble columns. The patterned marble floor, steps and altar, and the alabaster retable were entrusted to Raffles Davison working closely with Wilson, who himself designed the marble altar rail. The reredos – a vibrant painted triptych by Christopher Whall – was an Adoration with shepherds and Magi; the frame to each panel, of oak inlaid with ebony chevrons, was designed by Wilson together with the oak and ebony organ-case, and made by Trask's craftsmen in Somerset.

In carved oak niches along the top of the reredos stood a row of saints, with the crowned mother Mary at its centre, executed by F.W. Pomeroy, who 'did much of the modelling on the spot in plaster and gesso'.[81] His, too, were the figures surmounting the chancel columns, and the frieze of woodland scenes in low-relief, painted by Whall. The skills of Whall as a colourist reappeared on the nave ceiling in boughs of Scots pine enclosing a circling flock of swallows, and on the chancel ceiling with its wreathed willow fronds; the intended cycle of wall-paintings, however, remained unexecuted. The natural lighting was transmuted with coloured and leaded glass: using Prior's 'Early English' slab glass, Whall's two-light chancel window illustrated the Annunciation and Visitation, while those in the nave, using 'ornamental leading',[82] showed heraldic elements from the Douglas arms, and details that mirrored the ceiling's pine boughs. Bronze hanging lamps, each a mysterious, arched structure with five candleholders rising above it and a pendant egg-form beneath, made resplendent replacements for dull wall-mounted lights.

The chapel's collaborative approach, unified under Wilson's leadership, attracted critical comment that fully vindicated his artistic aims – *The Builder,* for example, thought it 'an interesting example of what we want to see more of, a building carried out and decorated by architect, sculptor and painter working in conjunction with each other'.[83] Castle and chapel have long gone, but in contemporary illustrations, and in photographs of the chapel taken before its demolition in 1956, features of that ideal 'visionary' building described by Wilson at the end of the 1890s are plain to see.

On a wholly greater scale of ambition than the Douglas Castle chapel in Sedding's and Wilson's collaboration, was the major commission at Welbeck Abbey, near Worksop, Nottinghamshire. Taken on by Sedding in 1889, it was carried through in stages, between his death in 1891 and 1913, by Wilson. The young 6th Duke of Portland had succeeded, in 1879, the reclusive 5th (or 'Underground') Duke, notorious for the subterranean rooms he had had built beneath the Abbey. The 22 year-old heir was dismayed, at first sight, at the unworkable layout and delapidated state of the property. The opportunity to convert the neglected, old-fashioned house into an agreeable modern residence would be supplied in 1900 by a major roof fire: the commission fell to a past-master in comfort and convenience, Sir Ernest George.

Sedding's 1889 assignment was to create a chapel and library within an existing freestanding building, the Old Riding School. This stone structure, some distance to the south-west of the L-shaped main house, had been built for Sir William Cavendish in 1622-23 by John Smythson. As Earl of Mansfield, Cavendish had spent his years of Commonwealth exile in the 1650s compiling his celebrated treatise on the equestrian arts, 'La Nouvelle Méthode'. Created 1st Duke of Newcastle at the Restoration, he was able to return to his estates in the English Midlands and pursue his passion for haute-école horsemanship. This enthusiasm would be shared by the 5th Duke of Portland, who, taking possession of the house in 1854, radically altered the Oxford wing and embarked on his extraordinary 'New Works' well to the West, with their plethora of farm and domestic innovations: poultry yard, hay barn, gasworks, traction engines, workers' cottages, cow houses, stables around a yard 180' square, a 1270' gallop for his racehorses. He had Smythson's Old Riding School enlarged and re-roofed; then abandoned it for an even bigger glass-roofed one adjacent to the stables.

While boasting impressive rooms dating from the 1770s by John Carr, external trimmings from the 1790s by Humphrey Repton, and a remarkable early Gothick hall, the Abbey had no chapel – Carr's had disappeared and the room built for the purpose by the 5th Duke had never been consecrated. The suggestion that Sedding should design one came from Frank Mildmay – he had been charmed by the 1887 gate-lodge Sedding had built at Flete, Devon, for the house of Mildmay's father (itself revamped by Shaw and Lethaby). The Old Riding School would ideally serve the twin purposes of chapel and library, the latter nearer the main house, the chapel approached through it and oriented East-West. The 5th Duke's roof-trusses would remain, as would his copper-tiled roof – indeed, its pale, dragon-scaled effect, a distinctive feature of the Abbey's buildings, would be repeated both on Wilson's curved Print Corridor and Ernest George's main block.

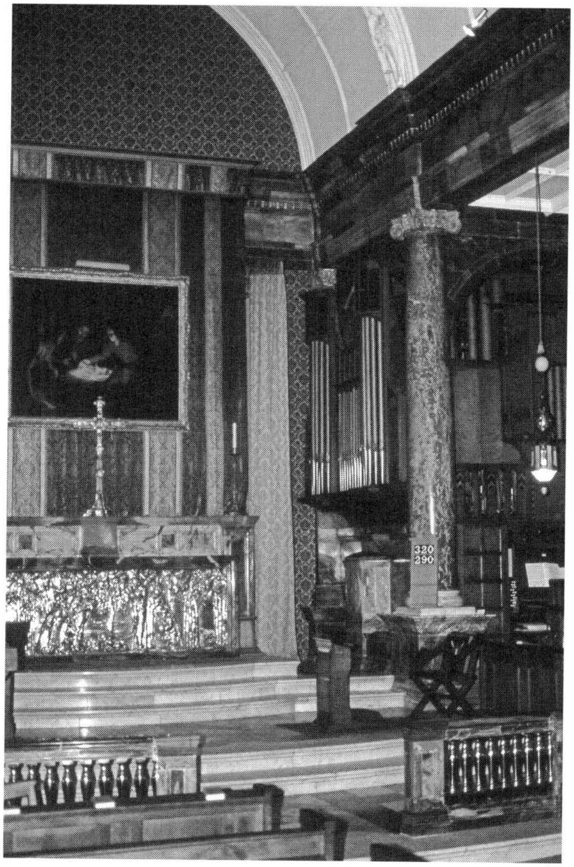

Figure 31. Welbeck Abbey, Nottinghamshire: the Chapel, with altar frontal completed by Wilson to Sedding's design, 1889-93.

Sedding began his task with the structural division of the inside space of the Old Riding School in the ratio of three to two. The Library, occupying the larger portion, would have a low, wagon ceiling, with gently canted side-slopes running down to the window-heads. The Chapel, by contrast, would exploit the full height offered by the 5th Duke's hammerbeam trusses: the logical form was a central barrel-vault flanked by flat ceilings – the Church of the Holy Redeemer, Clerkenwell, scaled down and simplified.

In addition to the cross-wall three structural additions were needed – a blower-room on the West elevation for the organ, a fireplace-bay with chimney in the Library's North wall, and a stair-hall to bring family and friends down from the Print Corridor which, straddling Carr's office-quadrant, linked the old and new elements of the Abbey. Sedding had discussed his ideas for setting out and furnishing the Chapel with Wilson, and his drawing for the altar frontal was ready for the 1890 show of the Arts and Crafts Exhibition Society.[84] Its display was at the invitation of the 6th Duke, who was President of the Society that year. The design, an Adoration scene set amid trees and flowers evoking the Abbey's setting in Sherwood Forest, was faithfully translated (Fig. 31) into repousée silver by Wilson, and exhibited, with his own altar cross and lectern (Plate 16), at the Society's 1893 show. It was installed in the Chapel in time for its consecration that autumn.

In preparation for the complex architectural interventions, though scarcely in anticipation of his master's death, Wilson acquainted himself with every aspect of the Abbey and its history. By this point in his career, he would have been well-qualified to carry out such major remodelling on his own, but work had already started on the wall dividing Library from Chapel when Sedding died. The main task of resolving the new rooms fell to Wilson, working now as the conscientious executor of his late master's artistic ideals. Several parts of the chapel hint at Sedding's Renaissance inspiration, such as its tunnel-vault, resting on columns of russet Fauld alabaster, crowned with cream alabaster capitals, a translation into noble stone of those at Clerkenwell. But the Byzantine references and the naturalism of the carved detail betray Wilson's mind at work, with plasterwork arching across the ceiling in bands of openwork foliage peopled with saints and apostles, while the choir stalls, with their exuberantly carved saints and Wise Virgins, show him in his most confident stride. The windows are simple squares, each filled by Whall with circular bottle-glass panes set around a single pale blue flower.

In the sanctuary – demarcated by a green marble altar rail with silver balusters – patterned marble steps approach the altar, on which stands the silver altar cross, designed by Wilson and made by Longden's. Its enamel roundels, showing the Expulsion and Crucifixion, recall Sedding's cross for Holy Trinity Church, Sloane Street, but with its subtle Byzantine allusions mingling with a distinctively 1890s mood, it achieves its own stylistic autonomy.

The silver lectern, set on the front edge of the plain marble pulpit, is an eagle, perching on a cross (Plate 16): in the enamel plaque at its centre, the yellow rays of the sun of heaven stretch towards the green globe of earth, establishing the eagle's identity as the 'solar bird' of Lethaby's book, crouching with outstretched wings at the mouth of the Sun Temple at Baalbek – a bird able to fly to the sun and gaze at it unblinking, in this evoking the spiritual principle of release from earthly bondage.[85] Here, at Welbeck, it represents both Christ steadily looking on the glory of God, and his Ascension. The scroll of God's laws unfurls at its feet, and its crown (denoting sovereignty), and breastplate (protection and preservation) are studded with opals; on its outspread wings rests a metal circlet embossed with the signs of the zodiac, as if enclosing the Bible within the movement of the spheres: diverse belief systems have been effortlessly linked, and their universality confirmed.

Just as in Wilson's 'visionary' building, the elaborate hanging lamps at Welbeck are enriched with 'reverent fancies' (Plate 19). A large alabaster egg incorporated into each lamp's suspension-chain recalls Lethaby's 'symbol of Creation': his description of such hanging eggs in churches, mosques and tombs across the world illustrates their role as symbols of 'the origin of life', 'the world floating in the void', 'the hope of the resurrection'. Lethaby's claim for 'something inherently mysterious in the perfect form of a very large egg'[86] fascinated Wilson, and found expression amidst the chapel's menu of interwoven symbolic references. Suspended below each egg, a brass globe represents the world; beneath it, an openwork sphere of swirling forms embodies the element of water, or the firmament, and below that, the lamp burns within a pillared temple, standing 'foursquare'[87] on a bowl containing the lamp oil.

The chapel's baptistry, set in the first bay of the South aisle, contains a small but sumptuous font (Fig. 33), designed by Wilson and executed by a distinguished group of artist-craftsmen in time for the christening of the Duke's eldest son in 1893. Pomeroy carved the elongated trees and angels on

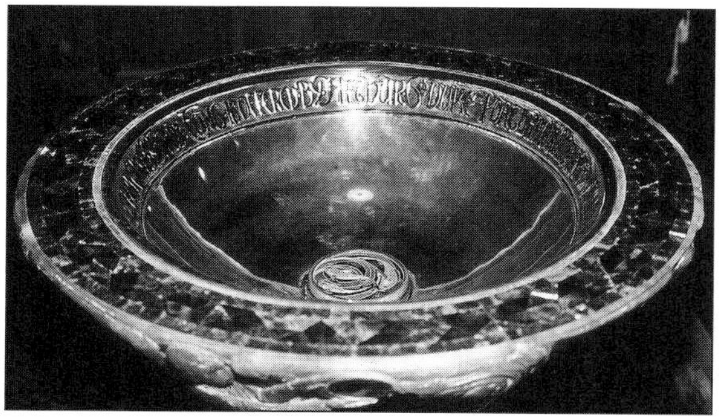

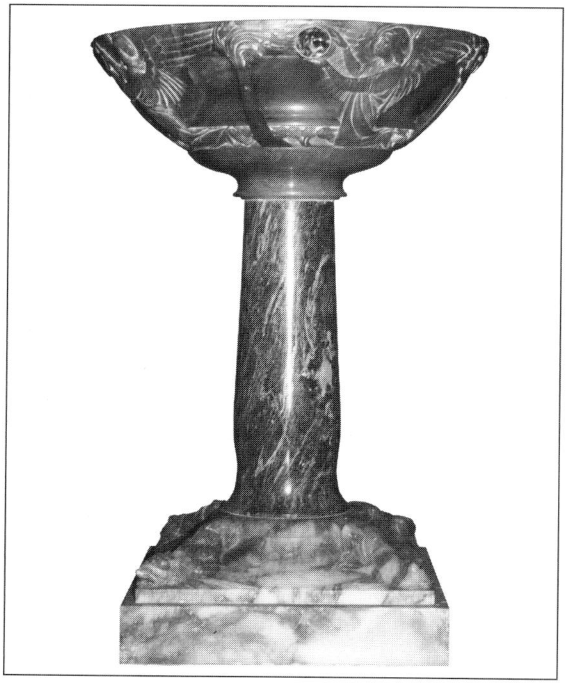

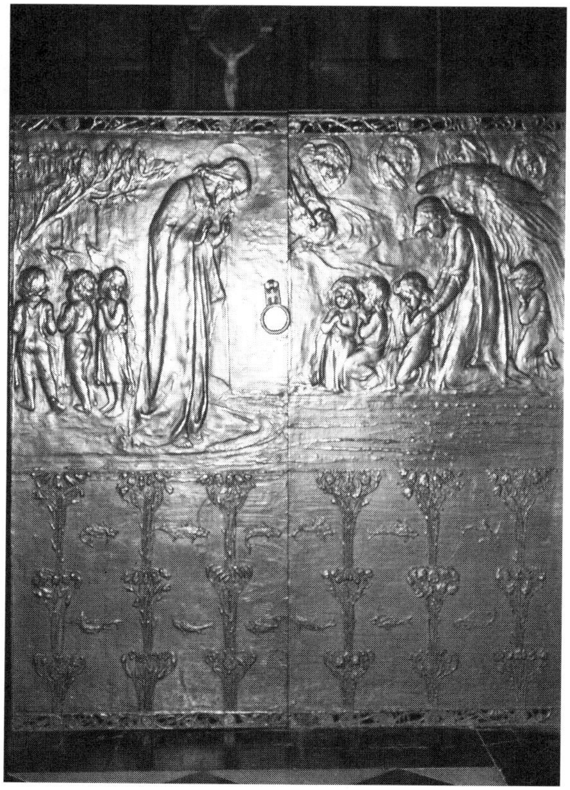

Figure 32. (left) Welbeck Abbey Chapel: font, design by Henry Wilson, marble carving by F.W. Pomeroy, 1893.

Figure 33. (top left) Welbeck Abbey Chapel: font bowl, mosaic rim by Raffles Davison, inlaid symbols by Patten Wilson, enamel plug by Henry Wilson.

Figure 34. (above) Welbeck Abbey Chapel: baptistry gates design by Henry Wilson, made by F.W. Pomeroy, 1896.

the underside of its marble bowl; Longden's lined it with brass and embellished the plug (Plate 18) with a blue-green enamel disc made by Wilson: its eye-catching motif, three fishes swimming tip to tail in the compact manner of a netsuke icon, is illustrated in Wilson's *Silverwork and Jewellery*. The font's rim is inlaid with glistening pearl mosaics by Raffles Davison, and enriched at intervals with semi-precious stones forming astrological symbols, designed by Patten Wilson, who embraced this opportunity to collaborate with his older brother. Inside the rim (Fig. 32), a brass circlet with its unbroken ring of words denoting the promise of eternal life through baptism,[88] records the font's first use, its inscription foreshadowing Wilson's 1906 design for the edge and surface of the gravestone of the Reverend Walter Stables, vicar of Far Headingley, where lettering without beginning or end suggests the continuity of life after death.[89]

Three years after the completion of the Welbeck font, Wilson's designs for bronze baptistry gates (Fig. 34) were interpreted by Pomeroy.[90] On the upper panels, in bas-relief, are angels and children kneeling in prayer on the banks of a river; beneath are panels of stylised waterweed. The *Studio* admired them for showing 'freshness without any undue straining after novelty', comparing their perception of natural growth to 'the way the Japanese masters of lacquer loved to depict it'.[91] The comparison is an apt reminder of Wilson's interest in 'the miraculous skill' of Japanese methods, some of which would be described in the second edition of *Silverwork and Jewellery* with its chapters on Japanese casting, 'woodgrain' metal, and patinas; one reproduced a lecture on Japanese metalworking by Professor Unno Bisei of Tokyo's Fine Art College, delivered at Wilson's invitation at the Central School.[92]

The impressive bronze double doors (Plate 17) Wilson designed for the chapel break away from any Sedding precedent, prefiguring those at St. Mary's Church, Nottingham, of 1904-05, and at Boston and New York in the 1920s. On the chapel face, six bas-relief panels show the Nativity, the Adoration, the sacrifice of Isaac, and scenes in Eden. Such well-rehearsed stories always released Wilson's talent for finding the unexpected in the familiar. Thus, the twin queues of people waiting to pay tribute to the infant Christ gain fresh meaning in their composition: in the first line, facing left, women and children, evidently of humble origin, have joined the stream of visitors reported in the Gospels, the Magi at their head, the shepherds bringing up the rear. In the second, facing right, the Wise Virgins, whose lyrical linearity recalls figures in a Burne-Jones painting, have been co-opted into the procession, one of them leading a fetterless, docile bull whose form, extending across adjacent panels, accentuates the scene's continuity of movement.

The creation of the doors from commission to completion can be traced through the detailed correspondence relating to the project. Wilson sent his drawings for the proposed doors to Welbeck in the spring of 1909; in his accompanying letter to the Duke's secretary, Mr. Stevens, he agreed that the Welbeck clerk-of-works and his maintenance team should fit his cast bronze panels to the oak that would form their core. In his reply, Stevens enclosed the doors' dimensions, requesting in return estimates of the cost and the time needed to complete the work, and full-size sketches of the designs which could be pinned to the existing doors to give an impression of their final effect. In his letter of 6 May 1909, Wilson wrote that he was 'going on carefully' with the doors; their cost,

> *approximately £225 each side, that is to say £450 the pair of doors. This includes the pairs of modelled handles for each half of the door. The work would take about three months to model, and six weeks or so to reproduce, but I should like to have six clear months if that were possible.*[93]

The Duke's acceptance of the price was communicated by return, along with his desire to to see the cartoons of the panels as mentioned. Yet a year and a half passed with no news from Wilson. On 26 September 1910 Stevens reminded him that 'the Duke still wishes to adhere to the original arrangement' of 'seeing and approving sketches of everything you propose to do'. Wilson sent them in November, assuring him that there had been 'no delay' in the modelling process.

> *The work is being pushed forward as rapidly as I can. I have made special effort to get it hastened forward and will report progress a little later. All the panels are in hand and all well advanced.*[94]

But by the following spring, two years since the initial agreement, patience at Welbeck was growing thin: 'I wish I could induce you to see things from his Grace's point of view' wrote Mr. Stevens in May 1911, returning, as requested, Wilson's full-size elevation drawings; in June, Wilson announced:

> *Two panels are already moulded in plaster. The third is about to be moulded and the fourth is nearly ready. The two remaining are well in hand. The fittings and mouldings will not take long to do. The work is being carried on continuously.*[95]

Studio work continued through the autumn, and on 12 December 1911, Wilson informed Stevens that the panels were all but complete:

I have just finished the last panel for the doors and as soon as the cast is ready I shall take all the panels over to Paris [to] have them reproduced in metal. I have had all the moulds fixed upon a model of the doors so that I can get the whole to work together without any awkward joins …[96]

This trip to the foundry of LeBlanc Barbedienne, the first of two that Wilson made to deliver the casts personally, underlines the professional rapport that he and the Paris founder enjoyed; having used the firm for a variety of jobs, Wilson fully trusted its workmanship. The models for the Welbeck doors were complete, and on 5 January 1912, Wilson confirmed that the plaster casts of the last two panels were safe in the Paris foundry. This was news that he was especially glad to impart, after a slight disagreement that had arisen over a bronze tablet he was designing for the Library.[97]

Stevens had one last request of him: to have sight of the original sketch '… in order that we may know what arrangement of panelling you have in mind'. Wilson sent it straightaway, its arriving at Welbeck comfortably in advance of the bronze casts. The completed doors, assembled in accordance Wilson's directions, won the Duke's immediate approval. Indeed, so deeply affected was he by the gentle depiction of the Wise Virgins that he added an inscription in honour of his mother-in-law, who had died earlier that year: 'Frances Dallas Yorke 1912: loving she lived, loved she lives.'

Above the doors is Wilson's semi-circular bronze pietà – expansive compared with the later version at Holy Redeemer, Clerkenwell, it forms a memorial to the Duke's brother, Lord William Bentinck, a major in the Tenth Royal Hussars: its dedication records that he served 'without a day's intermission' throughout the whole Boer War, but 'died suddenly on board the S.S. Arabia in the Suez Canal on his way to India November 5 1903'.[98] The dramatic power of this life-size pietà is intense. Christ's drooping hand hangs heavily from its frame, to point directly at each individual passing beneath it (Plate 20).

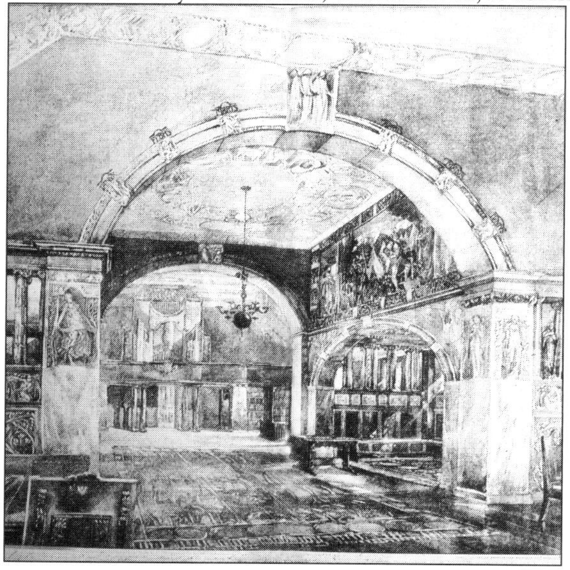

Figure 35. Welbeck Abbey: Wilson's original proposal for the library interior, *The Builder* 23 September 1893.

The spacious library, Eastwards beyond the vestibule, was considerably simplified by Wilson in execution so as to reduce the time the commission was taking. Thus, while his sketch of 1893 (Fig. 35) shows an inglenook midway along the library's length, with two enclosing arches springing from it to span the whole room to create a virtual room-within-a-room; but practical constraints dicated its scaling down. Even so, as executed, an alcove, punctuating the North wall and lit by its own side-windows gives this large, wagon-roofed room focus, and provides a foil to both the gallery at the chapel end and the giant-piered portal at the entrance end. In the main library-space, the ceiling rose with its zodiac figures survived, but the arched screens by Alfred Powell, to be painted with murals by Whall, were omitted,[99] and only the inglenook with its alabaster fireplace was fully realised. Jointly conceived by Wilson and Pomeroy, this is carved with portraits of the great teachers of the ancient world and enriched with nacre medallions.[100] The *Studio* was effusive, admiring how the 'luxurious opulence' of the fireplace's 'well-ordered riot of carving' is emphasised by the 'plain surfaces of the jambs' – a comment epitomising exactly the effect Wilson had been seeking.[101]

Screening the library's entrance doors is Wilson's pair of tall wrought-iron gates, set within a red marble archway, which perpetuates the form of the seventeenth-century outer portal that had been obliterated by the new stair-lobby, but whose twin is preserved on the parallel 'kitchen' range. During 1897 Wilson prepared decorations for the hallway and the double oak staircase leading up to the first floor quadrant – the 'Virgins' Wing' – housing the maidservants' quarters[102] and linking with the south-east wing. Murals by Whall decorate the walls of this corridor, while the long curve of its ceiling is enlivened by vigorously sculpted birds and animals in low relief, in which Wilson was joined by Louis Davis to create a fine vista of plasterwork; its splendour lies its detail, its variety and in the lightness of touch with which aspects of the natural world are modelled.

The stairhead room above the new porch, where quadrant meets main house, is a collaboration between Pomeroy and Wilson in which the two men put all their inventive skills into the carving of the stone frieze, especially the winged dragon. Circling the space in its scaly coils, the creature seems to embody both the breath of life and life-giving waters as it guards the treasure-house of the library beyond. As for the quadrant's exterior, the upper storey to the courtyard is Wilson's alone. The concave curve, smoothly rendered in contrast to the surrounding ashlar, defers neither to Carr nor Smythson,[103] nor in the sharp profile of its pale metal roof, to Ernest George's skyline.

The collaborative efforts overseen by Wilson at Douglas and Welbeck[104] form visible embodiments of his contention that his was an era of extraordinary, if undervalued, artistic possibilities:

> *Architects ... have it in their power to create a school of associated craftsmen who might do for the buildings of today what the Associated Craftsmen of North Italy – led by such men as Orcagna, Pisano, Maetani, Mino da Fiesole – did for the buildings of their day. When we have sculptors like Alfred Gilbert, Thornycroft, Pomeroy, Stirling Lee; painters galore; metalworkers like Alexander Fisher, Nelson Dawson, Reynolds – what more could we desire?*[105]

The potential was there, but it was not being intelligently exploited. The problem was not the lack of talent, but how to harness its richness and diversity. This, essentially, had been the task he had set himself and his band of colleagues at both Ducal houses. Reverting to his favourite metaphor, of architecture as music, Wilson warned his contemporaries that in architecture, 'that Art of all Arts', the spectator was witnessing 'a leaderless orchestra playing on untuned instruments without a score'.[106]

After so many emotive pleas for integrated, inclusive architecture, and his own demonstrations of it in actual terms, Wilson understood that his argument would cut more ice if it were based on more coherent and widespread evidence. If valid reform was to be achieved, it was not going to come through isolated triumphs such as those at Welbeck or Holy Trinity, Sloane Street, or the individual campaigns of his like-minded contemporaries. Such works, though well-received, would not be enough to halt the growing trend towards architectural bureaucracy, or to significantly disturb the public's acceptance of it. By 1900, he was shifting his position, acknowledging that it was necessary for the crafts themselves – the very ingredients of great architecture – first of all to be reborn, and then to be sympathetically reorganised. It was to this end, therefore, that he now began to direct all the power of his eloquence and practical energy.

CHAPTER FOUR
CREATIVE TRANSITION

Certain British architects, as the turn of the century approached, were 'devoting themselves to being arty', while engineers were creating beauty of 'a more ferocious and monumental kind'.[1] So wrote D.S. MacColl some thirty years later, having observed it all from his curator's desk at the National Gallery. Henry Wilson, no doubt, was among those architects. Yet Wilson was not averse to engineering honestly done, and he readily acknowledged its role in the expansion of commerce. What distressed him was that the times seemed so much more in tune with the engineer and commercial contractor than with the master builder and creative craftsman. He warned against the blurring of the distinctions between engineering and 'true Architecture'[2] which, he maintained, resulted in nothing more than 'veneered engineering'.[3] His strongest words, though, were reserved for the rampant stylistic borrowing which permeated turn of the century architecture. Flemish and French Renaissance, Baroque and English Classical were all at call, and were adopted often with no particular rationale behind the choice. And it was his locking horns with the advocates of one of these, the baroque, which led to his forfeiting the editorship of *The Architectural Review*, a post he had held since the magazine's inception.

Throughout the 1880s and 1890s Baroque had been steadily gathering popularity for commercial and civic buildings: impressive essays in the style were commissioned in 1897 for the town halls in Cardiff and Colchester – the latter from Wilson's former master, John Belcher, who became one of the style's most enthusiastic exponents. The following year, the imposing ashlar War Office by the Scottish architect William Young, rose with baroque force in Whitehall, and in 1899 further baroque designs were accepted for the Central Library at Hull and the Cartwright Library at Bradford, for Woolwich Town Hall, and for Imperial College, Kensington.[4]

Wilson's departure from Belcher's office in 1888 coincided with the start of work on the Chartered Accountants' Building. In fully integrating embellishments with structure, this baroque design stood for much that any designer, keen to ratify the arts and crafts in modern life, might applaud. With a magnificent sculptural frieze by Hamo Thornycroft, sympathetic details by Harry Bates, and a conscious harmonising of architecture and the associated arts, the building champions a central tenet of the Arts and Crafts – the Unity of the Arts. This unity struck Wilson all the more strongly given his regard for Thornycroft and Bates, both protagonists in Sedding's Sloane Street church, and for Belcher himself, a founder member of the Art Workers' Guild and renowned for his commitment to bringing the arts under the wing of architecture. But the realm the building inhabits, that of corporate, commercial grandeur, was one that Wilson never entered. In leaving Belcher for Sedding, Wilson had moved to an office where the ideal of unity prevailed, but would be expressed in different contexts, whether vernacular or spiritual, and on an essentially human scale.

Wilson articulated his antipathy to grandiose public-building baroque in the pages of *The Architectural Review* in 1900, in his critique of the entries submitted for the Old Bailey competition. Most, including Edward Mountford's winning design, were in the baroque style. All, from Brydon's to Hare's, were roundly condemned by Wilson, both for their anodyne character: 'Do any of these designs *look* like a Sessions House?' and for their lack of cohesion between plan and elevation: 'it is impossible to admire both, for they contradict one another, with the result we admire neither'.[5]

On the evidence of his Ladbroke Grove Library design, Wilson would have preferred a free style building evocative of the theme of justice. Nevertheless, Mountford's building, with its instantly recognisable silhouette, its Portland stone façade and its painted and marble interiors, slots skilfully into its cramped location on the site of the old Newgate Prison. It recognisably reprises the quoins and voussoirs of George Dance's demolished building – and despite Wilson's qualms, represents one of the best examples of official Edwardian baroque.

Wilson's uncompromising attacks on the whole sheaf of Old Bailey designs set him at odds with much contemporary architectural opinion, not least that of the *Review's* incoming editorial committee of 1901, which numbered some of the very architects whose work he had denigrated. When the Professional and Trade Papers Company had launched *The Architectural Review* in 1896, three architects were billed as its editors, C.E. Mallows, F. Hamilton Maugham and H. Wilson – though Wilson was regarded as the 'real'[6] editor. His policies took a *Gazette des Beaux Arts* stance, embracing more cultural and scholarly interests than the other architectural periodicals of the time. The 'finely imaginative cover'[7] Wilson designed for the magazine graced the first nine volumes, before being superseded by a baroque, Inigo Jones-style replacement. Discussions of contemporary building and contributions from practicing architects were included, but space was also devoted to the appraisal of earlier masters and to arts other than building. Wilson's own articles, from those on Burne-Jones, Sedding and Persian art to practical considerations of the restoration of St. Mary's Church, Oxford, effectively characterised its tone.[8]

When Professional and Trade Papers went bankrupt in 1900, the *Review* passed into the hands of the Technical Journals company, and Belcher, Arthur Blomfield, Horsley, Macartney, Ernest Newton, Prior, Halsey Ricardo and Stokes were co-opted onto a new editorial committee. Wilson found himself passed over; but he had already presided over the *Review*'s first four years and so, given the tenor of the times, did not feel it entirely a matter of regret to leave.

As he himself stressed in his retiring article, it had been his consistent policy to dedicate the *Review* to 'the artistic as distinguished from the business side of architecture'.[9] His idealism frequently left him out of step with the price ethos. Brown-Morrison, his metalwork student at The Thatched House from 1906-08, later admitted that

> *As a businessman I believe he was hopeless – often out of pocket over commissions. But that was the Artist who finishes his work to his satisfaction despite the cost ... .*[10]

The architectural commissions Wilson carried out in the late 1890s and early 1900s show how careful he was in selecting work, only accepting commissions from sympathetic clients who would allow him freedom of expression. Not surprisingly, such jobs tended to be confined to particular churches and houses. These could hardly justify his concentrating full-time on architecture. Of the five private houses he designed, only two were built as initially envisaged. The earliest of his designs, an entrance lodge for Welbeck Abbey, featured in *Academy Architecture*'s Annual Architectural Review of 1892. His imposing gatehouse was designed to give access access to the estate from the Ollerton road, its turret and pillared cupola echoing the lines of the square-piered quadrant walls flanking it. The gates themselves were set in a gothic arch, with a mullioned window above, and on either side, buttresses with setbacks emphasising the building's strength, as if anticipating the 1896 proposal for St. Augustine's, Highgate.[11] In the event, a conventional solution was favoured: tall iron gates between piers supporting lions – the Lion Gates – while the lodge, rendered with Dutch gable and formally grouped chimneys, stands to one side.

Also published in 1892 was a design in watercolour for a hunting lodge near Malmesbury (Fig. 36). Typically in Wilson's work, its style follows local tradition, yet is spiced with some individual touches, buttressed chimneys and a front door set obliquely in the semi-octagonal bay. This double-storey feature rising past the main eaves, has hints of Sedding's Flete Lodge, and the unbuilt design provides a tantalising glimpse of what Wilson might have achieved on a more monumental scale.

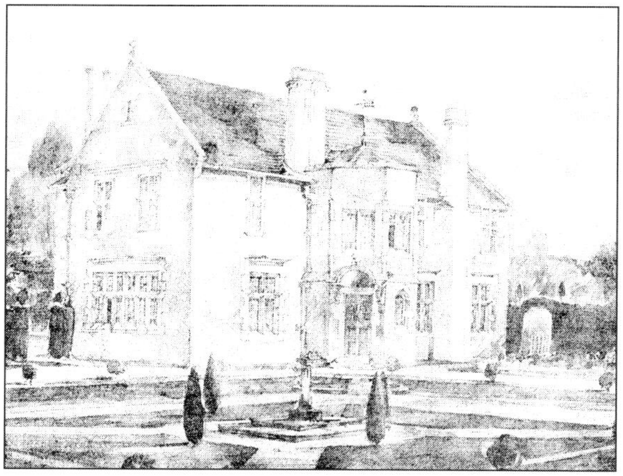

Figure 36. Henry Wilson: Proposal for Hunting Lodge near Malmesbury, Wiltshire, *The Architect* September 1892.

In its use of stone throughout, with mullioned windows and crowning entablatures, it points to Stokes, Prior and Blow in grand vernacular mode.[12]

Two years later, Wilson's links with Welbeck led to a commission, Maybury Cottage, on the southern edge of Woking, Surrey, for Miss Graham, the Duchess of Portland's aunt. Supervision of the whole job, comprising a main house with lodge (Plate 7), was entrusted to J.P. Cooper. Each structure was to have elaborate interior plasterwork with geometric and natural motifs. Casements set flush in pebbledash walls aligned the main house with Voysey's work, while the chief accents of its entrance front – the leaded gallery window over a broad segmental arch – were reminiscent both of Harrison Townsend and of Wilson's own Ladbroke Grove library drawings of 1890. They lent the façade an expansive air, and the chimneys, in arched and painted render, had a surprisingly modernist look. Groaning with extensions and hemmed in (the grounds having been sold off in the 1950s) by bungalows, the main structure was just identifiable as Wilson's original design until its demolition in 2002. The lodge, however, survives intact – roughcast, its roof tiled, a tall brick chimney dominating its uncluttered vernacular style.[13]

In 1900 Wilson drew up designs for a cottage near Welwyn, Hertfordshire, but like the Malmesbury Hunting Lodge, it was never built. However, the house that came closest to his heart came about soon after: between 1901 and 1902 he designed his own home in Kent. The Thatched House was ompleted shortly after his marriage to Margaret Morse, and here the Wilsons remained, between lengthy work forays abroad, until 1922.[14]

To this degree, then, of being selective and maintaining his creative integrity at all costs, Wilson was resigned to being a poor businessman. He was even prepared to eschew potentially lucrative contracts on offer in commerce and competitions rather than sacrifice his personal architectural vision. When, in 1889, his father retired on £50 p.a., and it was time for his parents and brother Patten to vacate the schoolhouse in Cleobury, it was Harry who volunteered to find a new home for the whole family, himself included. His youngest brother Edgar, who had been sharing Harry's digs in Bedford Gardens, joined him in the search; and it was Harry who finally chose a suitable home for them all, semi-detached and gabled, at 2 Sheepcote Road, Harrow.[15]

Edgar, however, did not stay long. He had become apprenticed in 1890 to the stationers Farmer & Sons in Kensington High Street. A year later Harry was to meet Margaret Morse, and would ask her to be his wife. Their marriage, though, would not take place for several years; his income at Sedding's was reasonable, but his earnings were, in effect, the financial mainstay of the household. Edgar's situation at Farmer's was not a happy one, and he left after three months. It was Harry who sensibly encouraged him to study for further qualifications, at St. Mark's College, Chelsea. The plan was an evident success – Edgar soon gained a clerkship at 11/6d a week with the Southwark broom makers Crowther and Garrod; in 1892, a position arose at the London and County Bank, and there he stayed, working steadily, for nine years. It was Harry, once again, who found him an opportunity with more stirring prospects. A friend, John Lynch, had mentioned that his company had an opening for a young man in Ahwaz, Persia, at £250 p.a. The new recruit would trade Karun wheat, linseed, sesame, gum arabic and wool by paddle-steamer along the Tigris, and by mule-train over the Bakhtiari road to Isfahan. Harry arranged an interview for Edgar, who, having made a favourable impression at Lynch Bros., set sail in April 1901 for the Middle East, to commence the new occupation that Harry had helped him find.

Meanwhile, Wilson's commitment to the family budget continued: Patten's earnings from his occasional commercial art commissions were at best sporadic, so until Edgar was able to contribute, Harry's income was stretched. But as he himself said, he did not build 'for the money there was in architecture',[16] and scorned the way it was instantly identifiable as a middle and upper class preserve. His indignation was well-founded: obscure but capable tradesmen were excluded, Jude-like, from a profession dominated by the class barrier, as Thomas Hardy, an ex-architect himself, showed in his novel of 1892-95; while boys with the right social connections were as likely to hit the jackpot with architecture as in the Stock Exchange.

Incongruous as it may seem, given his financial position, Wilson was gradually scaling down Sedding's practice during the 1890s. Some who knew him suspected that this retrenchment was born of expediency – an assumption lent credence by Wilson's self-confessed indifference to dedicated money-making. But his contraction of the office stemmed mainly from principle, not ineptitude, and was driven by an imperative more profound than his own domestic circumstances. He remained convinced that regenerating architecture hinged on reawakening the crafts, a belief he expounded in a lecture to the Architectural Association in 1889. In his paper he sarcastically dismissed the notion of architecture as the mother of the arts as 'one of those buttered aphorisms containing more-or-less microscopical portions of truth which only pass muster in those expansive, thumb-in-armhole, after dinner moments',[17] since actually, the reverse was true. Humans had painted and carved long before they had built. Historical precedent seemed to endorse the pioneering path his career was about to take: the pursuit of the crafts, with the revitalisation of architecture as its long-term objective.

In an exchange of letters in 1915 Wilson's former colleague at Birmingham Municipal School of Art, Arthur Griffith, recalled with disappointment how twenty years before – just at the moment when Wilson was preparing to leave the profession – he had hoped he would lead architecture out of the 'Renaissance desert'. Wilson quietly replied:

> *Don't be scornful of what you thought me capable of twenty years ago. Then I felt not able to create a new renaissance, or destroy an old one. But I did feel the need of preparing myself ... for the coming revolution by attacking the problem with my own hands. The fact is that no man, however great his intellect, can accomplish a revolution unless the soil has been prepared.*[18]

The craft revival, then, represented a new lease of life for architecture, not a clearcut alternative to it. It was never Wilson's intention to abdicate entirely from architecture and lose himself in the 'minor crafts',[19] as MacColl chose to interpret his decision. Rather, he planned to devote himself to re-energising the crafts (which, he maintained, were all equal and interdependent), and thereby to bring about a genuine marriage between them and architecture.

Apart from his ideological justification for approaching architecture via the crafts, Wilson was in any case more temperamentally in tune with the applied arts than with current architectural practice. As his contemporaries agreed, and as his most successful works demonstrate, the decoration of buildings simply interested him more than their structural problems. This propensity is clear in an assignment he undertook in 1904, when he added a wagon-roofed refectory to the Industrial Schools in Knowle, Bristol, in completion of Sedding's 1890 commission. As an entity, this 'shared' project is as significant for its interior features by Wilson as for its architectural conception by Sedding.[20] Throughout the part-timbered vernacular complex, Wilson's plasterwork ceilings are alive with patterns of twining rose stems, while his stone-hooded fireplace in the range South of the central quadrangle is dramatic in its austerity.

'The routine work of an architect's practice was always irksome to him,' wrote Charles Nicholson of Wilson in the years following Sedding's death,

> *though he stuck to the post manfully as long as he was able to serve the interests of Sedding's family. His architectural works do not fill up a long list, but they are all worth looking at and none of them is stupid. Nevertheless he was eventually to concentrate on work other than building … .*[21]

Wilson's interest in one of these other pursuits – metalwork – had been encouraged by Sedding, whose own feeling for the art had emerged early in his career. Taking Ruskin's advice he had applied himself to sketching nature and architecture, and to metalwork. As his architectural commitments increased in the 80s, so his designs for crosses and pastoral staves for the cathedrals at Wells and St. David's were entrusted to the church furnishers Barkentin and Krall for execution; further designs for chalices, altar crosses and the altar rail at Holy Trinity, Sloane Street went to Longden's. Both firms employed diligent craftsmen, but even so, the work, lacking the direct attention of its designer, was, according to Wilson, 'only an imperfect translation of Sedding's conceptions.'[22] Wilson's own affinity for the craft was reinforced by Ruskin's assertion that every artist should be apprenticed to a joiner, a stonecutter, or best of all, to a metalworker. Where Sedding had taken heed of the summons and attached himself to a blacksmith, Wilson, after completing the balance of his master's outstanding buildings, set himself to work for almost two years in a bronze foundry 'to acquire first hand knowledge of that difficult art'.[23]

Metalwork, particularly gold and silversmithing, suggested to him a fresh way into the more monumental arts. Besides, in metalwork, collaboration and delegation were optional, not inevitable. Accordingly, it became his desire to follow 'the methods of medieval Italy', where sculptor, painter and architect served an apprenticeship as a goldsmith or metalworker 'before taking up the work of their lives'.[24]

Wilson stayed on in Sedding's office for six years after his master's death, maintaining the practice on behalf of Sedding's son George alongside his own incoming work, but in 1897 he finally packed up at Oxford Street and took a house at 17 Vicarage Gate, Kensington. 'A great trial' was how he described the move, 'it disturbed business so much', but it was necessary, 'because the other place was far too small for any practical use, and much too noisy'.[25] The move held significance for his career, too: from the new premises he would indeed continue with Sedding's unfinished commissions, but also concentrate on the building crafts – plasterwork, metalwork, decorative schemes, sculpture. His north-facing studio was on the top floor. Two of Sedding's former assistants, Arthur Grove and George Briley (the latter having joined the practice shortly before Sedding's death) transferred to Kensington and occupied an architectural office on the ground floor. Here, Spencer Carey Curtis, articled to Wilson since 1896, worked out the remaining two years of his architectural training; he would assist with the silver wafer-box Wilson designed for St. Martin's, Marple, establishing his own interest in fine metalwork.

One floor was taken for a time by Alexander Fisher, with whom Wilson entered into a short-lived partnership. A fashionable goldsmith and enameller executing commissions for society clients, his Warwick Square studio had been of the 'drawing room type',[26] thickly carpeted and with comfortable armchairs focused on the pair of enamelling stoves. Here, smartly dressed in swallow-tail coat and pinstripe trousers, he would entertain patrons before showing them into the adjoining workshop to see how their commissions were progressing in the hands of his two assistants. It had been at the Central School of Arts and Crafts that he and Wilson first become acquainted – they taught there concurrently from 1896-9 – and soon Wilson, fully aware that it was Fisher more than anyone who was responsible for the development of enamelling, particularly in its painted form, within the Arts and Crafts style, had suggested he move his business to Vicarage Gate. Fisher's influence, disseminated through his classes at the Finsbury Technical College in the early 90s, would induce many craftsmen to cultivate enamelling skills: the Birmingham-based Gaskins, for example, and in London, Nelson Dawson, a founder of the Artificers' Guild, through which Wilson would sell items of his own silverwork and jewellery.

Fisher's influence flowed not only from his work, his teaching and his highly-prized personal tuition of a few wealthy lady clients, but also from articles in the *Studio*. Wilson himself, as editor of *The Architectural Review*, published Fisher's essay, 'The Renaissance of the Art of Enamelling', in clear acknowledgement of the renewed interest in art and of Fisher's role as its moving spirit. A working relationship between the two craftsmen promised much, not least the opportunity for Wilson to learn more about the technique; having Fisher close at hand was both instructive and inspiring.

As the partnership began, Fisher's workshop and assistants installed themselves at Vicarage Gate, and while continuing with their own work, he and Wilson joined forces on several metalwork commissions. These served to confirm the metalworking talents of each, highlighting Wilson's allusive vision and Fisher's enamelling finesse. One of their most representative pieces was a covered chalice, silver enriched with opal and lapis lazuli. Designed by Wilson and made by Fisher, its base incorporates seven turrets rising from the sea, while the finial embodies and depicts the Aether. A tabernacle of beaten bronze set with opal was another joint project, designed and made by Wilson, Fisher adding its cloisonné enamel embellishments.[27] Both men for a time recognised the mutual benefits of their arrangement.

Nevertheless, in however well-regulated a workplace, there was bound to be friction between two such disparate characters, one fundamentally worldly, the other idealistic: within the year the partnership was dissolved. While Fisher moved away, resurrecting his own workshop and becoming instructor of enamelling at Brighton's Art and Technical School, his two workmen stayed on at Vicarage Gate, in the metalworkshop Wilson had created in the basement. Lorenzo Colarossi remained as a general worker, and Luigi Movio, an experienced craftsman aged about sixty, became the workshop's first foreman.[28] By now, with his income from teaching and writing, from architectural and restoration commissions, and from his increased output in metalwork and jewellery, Wilson could afford to bring in five more assistants. John Innocent, a trade jeweller, succeeded Movio on his departure to teach metalwork at Birmingham Municipal School of Art. Felice Signorelli worked as chaser, George Romer as silversmith. S. Cowell, a hammerman, concentrated on raised work, and young Sidney Wiseman entered as second general worker. Harry Murphy was the shop boy, paid a penny a week by each of the men for running errands. Within a few years Wiseman and Murphy emerged as distinguished metalworkers under Wilson's influence, and were the key workers who accompanied him to Kent in 1902.

In addition, the workshop used occasional workers including Wilson's brother Patten, their father William, Herbert Maryon (author in 1912 of *Metalwork and Enamelling*), and not least, the architect J.P. Cooper, who stayed in close contact with Wilson after Oxford Street, taking charge of several of his decorative plasterwork commissions. By 1897 he had become interested enough in metalwork to take lessons in jewellery from Wilson's foreman, Innocent. He opened his own studio in Aubrey Walk in 1899, but as he had done at Sedding's, he took his direction from Wilson, often calling at Vicarage Gate to discuss projects where he might be of use.

Cooper found his true métier as silversmith and jeweller, his actual architecture being limited mostly to additions to his family's Leicester homes and factory. The Gothic style of his first mature pieces shows a complete absorption of Wilson's ideas; but soon he was experimenting independently with the neglected medium of shagreen – the decorative overlay of exotically-textured sharkskin

– and, as he grew in confidence and the Wilson echoes became less pronounced, his work took on a distinctively twentieth century look, prefiguring Art Deco. In 1904 he followed Wilson into teaching. When – on Movio's death – Birmingham Municipal School of Art sought a new headmaster for its silverwork and jewellery studio at Vittoria Street, Wilson, declining the post for himself, had recommended Cooper, but his protégé was deemed too inexperienced. It was a temporary doubt: soon Cooper was appointed head of metalwork, as which he served until 1907. Again like Wilson, he moved to Kent, building a family home and studio at Betsom's Hill, Westerham, in 1911.

Wilson's first serious engagement with architectural metalwork came in 1889-90, when Sedding was adding a chancel to James Ball's 1844 church of the Holy Trinity, Salcombe, Devon, and handed his chief assistant charge of the gates between the nave and his new East end. Wilson repaid Sedding's trust with a work of muted splendour (Plate 3) in solid oak, sheathed in copper, into which a spare tracery of raised foliage and text was beaten, and whose subtle texture was enhanced by cruciform, blue-crimson enamelled panels.[29]

The success of this early work encouraged Wilson to acquire yet more sophisticated skills to encompass the flow of his ever-growing symbolic language that had developed under Lethaby's influence. Between 1895 and 1900, Wilson added the North aisle, the Lady Chapel and a remarkable font cover to Sedding's picturesque little church of St. Martin, at Marple, in the Cheshire Pennines. The chapel's barrel vault, decorated in collaboration with Christopher Whall, is animated by a flock of plasterwork swallows, flittering in circles around a wreath of foliage and in free flight across the spandrel (Fig. 37). A sense of the living world is felt throughout the chapel's bas-relief frieze of trees, a watchful owl – just one of these branches' myriad inhabitants – perching loftily amongst them. The chapel's reredos was painted by Whall with the Annunciation, and like vault and plasterwork, it shows a clear affinity with the recent collaborative work at Douglas Castle. It was Charles Trask who undertook Wilson's design for the Lady Altar frontal, its broad chevrons of oak and ebony repeated in the ebony-chevroned oak altar rail.[30]

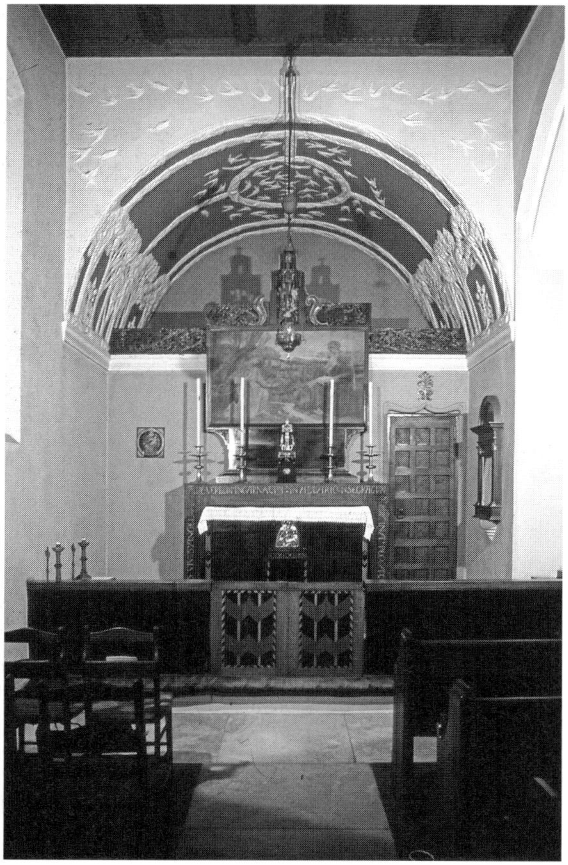

Figure 37. St. Martin's Church, Marple: Lady Chapel, H. Wilson, with plaster decoration by C. Whall, 1895-96.

The dual-transomed cross of Lorraine, for the St. Martin's Lady Altar, was made by Wilson himself, with the help of his father and of Longden & Co., in beaten copper (Plate 23). A monogram on each arm, the letter M for Martin, suggests a crown. Incorporating the patron saint's initial into his church designs not only marks Wilson's fidelity to tradition, but also his interest in lettering as a decorative device. Silver-gilt figures of Mary and John the Baptist stand in prayer alongside the crucified Christ. Issuing from the base of the cross, the four rivers of Paradise, as described by Lethaby in *Architecture, Mysticism and Myth*,[31] are translated into broad streams of bright blue-green enamel. Seeing it displayed in the 5th Arts and Crafts Exhibition of 1896, the *Studio's* reviewer seized on its visual impact, admiring its 'sumptuous colour ... employed with much mastery'.[32]

Along with the cross Wilson designed four copper candlesticks (whose distinctively Art Nouveau leaves and tendrils would reappear in his 1898 Yiewsley cross and candlesticks), and a silver wafer box whose sides, bearing the text 'Hoc est corpus meum ... ', rise from dome-like mounds embossed with flowers. Its cover, architectural in conception, is surmounted by a 'temple' of four arches, at their summit a dome enclosing a lapis lazuli sphere. Wilson's first sketch[33] shows a dove on top of the temple, but his final choice of motif brings a more satisfying coherence to the piece.

Four years later, in 1900, Wilson was to produce his crowning achievement at the Marple church, the oak font cover (Plate 24). Its octagonal edge is carved in a rhythmic pattern of waves and fishes, the rest veneered in ebony and inlaid with chevroned bands of fruit wood radiating from the centre. Acting as an elaborate knop is a large openwork globe of leafy branches in gilded cast iron. High above, and connected by a chain which incorporates three monograms of Saint Martin, a gilt dove hovers beneath a circle of golden stars. The chain epitomises the link between heaven and baptism, while the dove, the Holy Spirit, appears as a messenger between them.

Wilson's final coup at Marple was architectural: the Christopher Chapel (Plate 25). But this had to wait another nine years, during which other work and other clients were claiming his attention. From the late 1890s, sculpture was becoming one of his major preoccupations, leading him in 1899 to join the International Society of Sculptors, Painters and Gravers, of which he would remain a member until it disbanded in 1925. In recognition of his powers the Society displayed several of his sculptures, including the Welbeck pietà prior to installation, and adopted a design by him for their ceremonial medallion. Throughout his career Wilson regarded Orcagna, Leonardo and Pisano as his multi-talented mentors and models.[34] His own sculptural pieces, just as much as his decorative schemes and metalwork, harmonised with his architecture. Crucially, his work in each area overlapped the others in both fact and feeling, to form an unbroken network centred on architecture and giving true significance to his term 'the building arts'.[35]

Sedding always asserted that the architect's job resembled that of the sculptor, in that both employed 'the shaping faculty'[36] in their manipulation of outline, mass, space and texture. Wilson restated the idea by insisting on the collaboration of sculptor and architect, their roles being effectively inseparable. 'Architecture is really sculpture applied to the *n*th degree',[37] he argued, citing the great cathedrals of Amiens, Rheims and Notre Dame as his evidence; in his lectures he was apt to substitute the term 'sculptor-builder'[38] for architect. This habit of linking two concepts to form a fresh composite is typical of his speaking and writing style – descriptive, and full of the impact he needed to detonate contemporary assumptions. To him, it seemed dishonest to treat buildings merely as functional scaffolding for random works of applied art, since art in its most authentic sense should reside in the building as an entity.

His Boscombe and Highgate schemes, although unrealised, had shown Wilson experimenting with the fertile role he had assigned to the sculptor-builder. His finished church of St. Mark, Brithdir, provides a complete expression of the ideal. All the decorative and structural features are integrated into its overall arrangement, and every part fulfils a role within the essentially sculptural thrust of the whole.

St. Mark's was commissioned in 1895 by Mrs. Louisa Tooth. She and her husband, the Reverend Charles Tooth, had moved for the sake of his health from the English Midlands to Tuscany. In Florence, Tooth had founded and built St. Mark's English Church for the resident Anglican congregation and for the benefit of visitors. Returning to Britain on his death, his widow commissioned Wilson to design a small memorial church on land she owned in Merionethshire – now part of Gwynedd

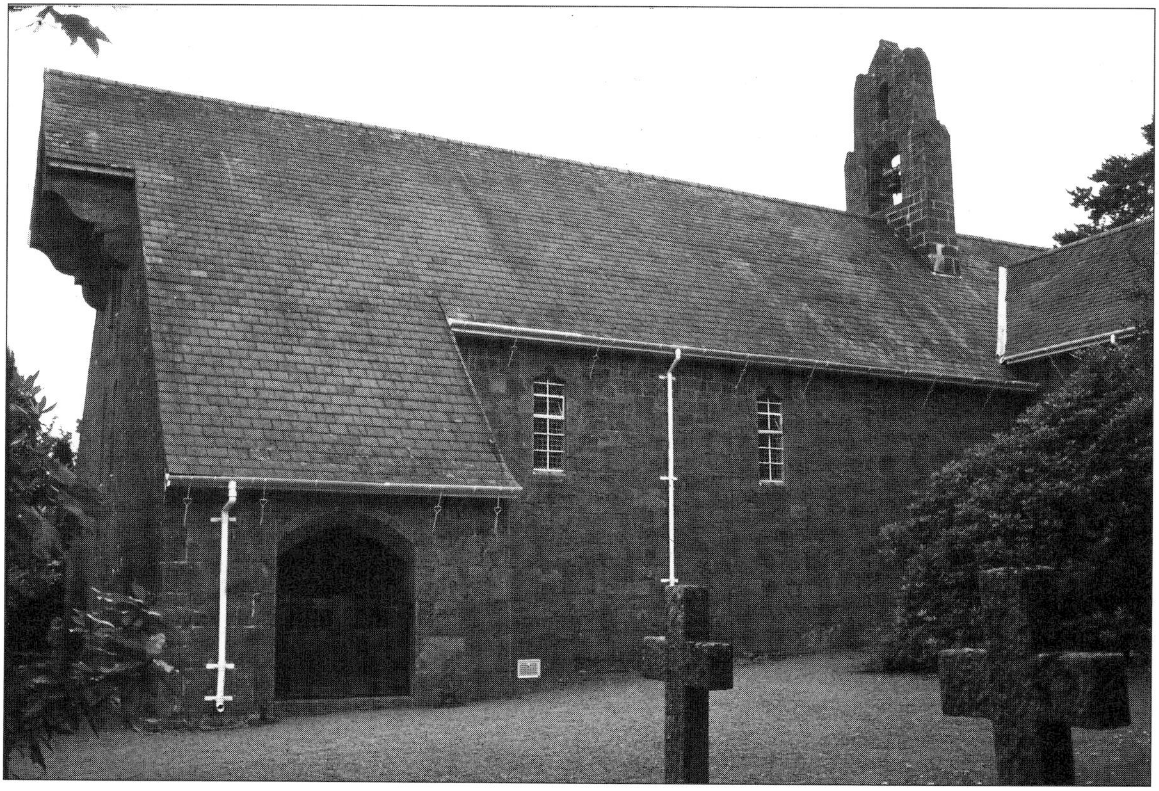

Figure 38. Brithdir, Gwynedd: St. Mark's Church, designed by Henry Wilson 1895-98.

– near Dolgellau. The modest building he created is of local granite with a steeply pitched roof of Aberllefenni slate, surmounted by a simple bellcote at the point where nave and chancel meet (Fig. 38). On the West wall, beneath a semi-circular stone hood – itself a strongly sculptural invention – is a massive granite cross. Partly because in a sense the church had originated in Italy where Tooth had seen out his final ministry, and partly because of the similarities of landscape, Wilson kept in his mind's eye some of the early churches 'just south of the Alps, where all the effect comes from their management of light and proportions'.[39] His small grey church seems to grow naturally from its Welsh hillside; nevertheless, at the same time, the sight of it unfailingly evokes the thrill of sudden discovery (Plate 46).

From the outset Wilson had stipulated that St. Mark's should be original and personal, while maintaining a quintessentially local identity. He staked out the site in person, and selected the roof-slates from the local quarry. He attended the building at each stage of its evolution; but he appointed two hand-picked assistants to remain on site for stretches of three or four weeks, supervising the local builder so as 'to get my ideas in the execution of details attended to, and avoid errors'. One, C.H.B. Quennell, was to 'see after the joinery and woodwork'.[40] In the future, he would win the RIBA Silver Medal and the National Gold Medal for his own architectural designs, though his real reputation later came to rest on his authorship of the *Everyday Life and Everyday Things* series.[41] He made it his task to buy timber from the local timber merchant and have it worked 'on the spot', the best and cheapest way, to Wilson's mind.[42] The other assistant, locally born and apprenticed, and with an exhaustive knowledge of traditional masonry practice, was given control of that part of the work. He was H.L. North, who would subsequently achieve fame for his vernacular slate houses around Llanlairfechan.[43] The labour was carried out by the occasionally wayward local contractor Mr. Williams, backed up by some of Mrs. Tooth's estate workers.

Wilson was assiduous in explaining every decision to client and workforce alike, these instructions forming a step-by-step account of the birth of the church and its growth. The letters exchanged with Mrs. Tooth deal with the project detail by detail, but also conceptually. She had envisaged a cruciform ground plan, Wilson pressed for a single cell, in-line format: 'Quite apart from the individuality of my arrangement, it is a peculiarly Welsh treatment. The cross-shaped plan descends at once to the ordinary level, and destroys what is most valuable in this design, the long-waisted look....'[44] Mrs. Tooth's suggestion that the roof be tiled received an equally swift rebuttal:

> *Tiles are quite a foreign element in a slate country. The rocks and stones, the grass and trees are all part of the landscape ... what is beautiful in Dolgelly seen from the station side is the sense of appropriateness in the slate roofs and grey and white walls. When the eye passes from the town to Cader Idris ... there is a kind of family likeness. The art must be part of the place, not imported into it ... I hope that you will refrain from compelling me to commit this artistic solecism.*[45]

In this matter Mrs. Tooth indeed acceded to her architect. Wilson's instructions to the builder were equally lucid, but even with such precautions, the drawbacks of working at one remove from the site embodied exactly the sort of frustration which, in hindsight, makes his withdrawal from architecture inevitable. His letter to Mrs. Tooth of August 1895 brims with the vexation that sometimes went with delegating tasks: '... as to Williams not knowing the length of the church it only needed the application of a two foot rule to any part of the plans as they are all drawn to scale. I am sending another set of working drawings ... to a large scale, but if he does not understand the small scale I fear about the larger ... '.[46] On another occasion, he flatly dismissed any expertise Williams might have claimed: 'he has no more knowledge of building than a cat, and has been persistently misrepresenting my methods and proposals'.[47] Wilson's intention, which left Williams aghast, was for the exposed wall-stones to be left untooled, to preserve their natural variations of colour and texture. 'Not squaring all the stones with mathematical accuracy ... will not only be an improvement in their looks, but an economy as well, a rare conjuncture!'[48] If he couldn't win Williams over on aesthetic grounds, he could at least appeal to him on those of economy.

Though they might be expected to have a natural affinity with the the local landscape and materials, Wilson – well-aware of the workforce's limitations – kept the building simple; 'in order that the work may be done locally I have omitted anything like carving or elaborate masonry.'[49] Even so, delays occurred as his careful explanations worked their way through. 'Mr. Williams does not quite understand that we want to make the roof at the same time as the walls so that the timbers may have time to season....'[50] As far as possible Wilson involved himself directly with all aspects of the building of St. Mark's. 'Most men I know delegate all the most important part of their work to others. I have not the conscience to do that, and whatever work I undertake I must do myself.'[51]

As the construction of the church neared completion, Wilson grew increasingly confident that an individual yet compatible effect was being achieved. 'Every time I see the church it gives me greater pleasure, it is so massively built and almost Egyptian in its solidity.'[52] The allusion to Egypt, an unlikely one to apply to a remote Welsh church, gains deeper resonance in the light of Wilson's friendship with Sir Lawrence Alma Tadema, painter of the life and buildings of the ancient world. Following their wedding, Harry and Margaret Wilson left London and stayed briefly at Alma Tadema's home at Fairseat, while, a few miles away at St. Mary's Platt, The Thatched House was being completed.

The contrast between the 'studious[ly] severe'[53] exterior of St. Mark's and its rich interior is breathtaking. The impression it creates reminded Wilson himself of the 'lonely hillside shrines' of Cornwall which had been such a profound influence on Sedding, and of Malory's overgrown 'wayside chapels ... enclosing fair silver altars'.[54] Inherent in the very form of the building were suggestions for its strongly coloured interior – Mrs. Tooth having insisted on extra windows which Wilson was reluctant to add for fear of making the space too light. As he explained, he had based the balance of natural light in St. Mark's on a small church at nearby Caerynwch, and with fastidious politeness insisted

> *it is really impossible for a stranger to the design, however gifted, to pronounce on the amount of light needed in any building in process. I had a case at a house in Lincolnshire. The client craved more light. I stuck to my guns and the result is a beautifully lighted staircase. I do not think you need fear in the present instance.*[53] *... To put a window on the south side to match the new one you already asked for on the north would besides spoil one of the few wall spaces we possess.*[55]

This last comment brings to mind his admiration for the power of the 'mere blank wall' in Burne-Jones's painting 'Danae's Tower'. 'Here we have a barbaric building,' he wrote, '... but how instructive for us! How well the rare windows are spaced! How simple and organic it all is!'[56]

Wilson's confidence in his specifications was based on a firm vision of the intended effect, thus the colours which he proposed and which largely survive today were integral to the essentially sculptural completeness of the church as a whole. The distempering, which, he told Mrs. Tooth, would take about ten days, would be carried out by Sidney Pullen, who had trained in the workshop of William Morris.

> *The nave walls would be distempered a rich red, those of the chancel and sanctuary a warm cream, almost yellow. The roof ... would be dark blue, the whole church looks so very pale now. Getting the right colour is very important because it must be the permanent and lasting one.*[57]

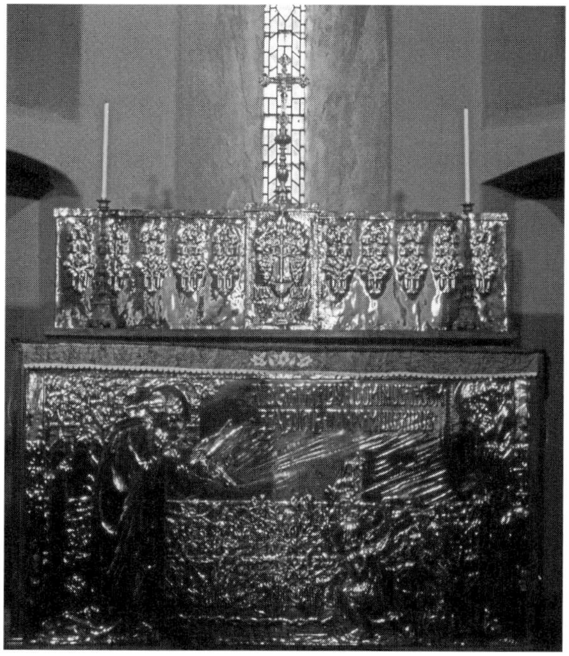

Figure 39. St. Mark's Church, Brithdir: altar frontal in copper, raised design of Mary, dove and child angel.

The initial visual impact of the interior of St. Mark's lies in its all-enveloping sense of colour; but, both liturgically and compositionally, all is made to focus on the altar. As a whole the church functions as a piece of architectural jewellery, with the altar as its gemstone and the building as its 'simple beautiful setting'.[58] Sheathed in copper, the altar bears repoussé figures of Mary and a child angel set against a bank of flowers (Fig. 39). Hovering before Mary is the dove of the Holy Spirit (Fig. 42). In the background stand the figures of Charles Tooth and his Guardian Angel. Unforeseen difficulties arose in the frontal's execution: no space had been reserved for the text, 'benedicta tu in mulieribus'. This had to be fitted into the design as work in Wilson's studio progressed – very satisfactorily in the event, since the lettering thereby becomes an integral part of the composition. The frontal also took longer to complete than Wilson had anticipated, and he wrote to Mrs. Tooth with a readily understandable excuse that emphasises the degree of his personal involvement. The reason,

> *though real enough and worrying enough, sounds a little ridiculous. The model who sat for the child angel was so restless that the sittings had to be indefinitely multiplied, a little being done each time. I could not change the model because he was just the type I wanted.*[59]

For all his calm explanations to Mrs. Tooth, Wilson's sharp retort to one of her queries about delays in the work betrays more than mild irritation at her impatience. At that moment, her attitude perhaps seemed to him to epitomise the contemporary indifference he had observed towards the creative process.

> *I want you to please believe ... that I have put my very best into the work, the more as I have taken as long as possible over it. The rapid rate of production in modern times is absolutely destructive of real quality ... [and] prevents any possibility of getting the artist's best. Rodin, the finest artist of today – Gilbert is a child compared to him – shewed me a model for his statue of Balzac. He has been at work on it for seven years, and is not yet half-way through. But those of us who know how important to ... art the modifying power of what Stephenson (R.L.) calls unconscious thought is ... realise what a fine work will result....*[60]

It was in this spirit that Wilson half-humorously confessed that he 'was quite resigned to making everyone's life miserable until it is done'.[61] Along with the altar, the pulpit (Fig. 40) was also taking shape in his London workshop. In the centre of each of its six sides is a repoussé wreath encircling a bunch of grapes, and the text 'Now gird up thy loins....' Wishing to make the pulpit subordinate to the altar, Mrs. Tooth suggested it might be framed in wood. Wilson had to marshal his best powers of persuasion to refute the idea:

> *Really, the Pulpit does not look like a pot at all. Logically to frame a metal panel in wood is wrong, and aesthetically also. The strength should be in the frame, and the eye, however strong the frame may really be, always gives more importance to metal. Moreover, there is no possibility, in a framed pulpit, of avoiding the idea of something seen before.*[62]

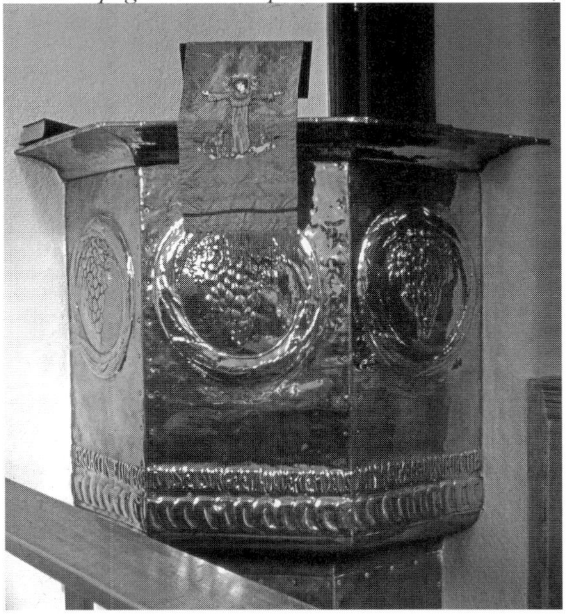

Figure 40. Brithdir, St. Mark's Church: copper pulpit, 1896-7.

It was about this time that Wilson moved his business to Kensington. He wrote to Mrs. Tooth with his new address, inviting her to visit to see 'the many interesting things' he was working on, including the Brithdir pieces.[63] Their friendly regard for one another would remain undented despite their creative skirmishes over the church. Yet another of these threatened to arise over the door giving access from the chancel to the pulpit. Wilson again defended his scheme in terms of the all-round effect of the church: 'From the beginning I designed it there.... I attach great importance to it. You see if I had done the ordinary thing, everyone would have accepted it and been pleased.'[64] Wilson's argument prevailed. Pulpit and door were completed exactly as he had designed them.

At Brithdir, Wilson had deliberately curbed any temptation to over-elaborate the interior. 'The desire to be severely plain was much weakened when I saw how the place could be richly decorated.... But I forbear....' He therefore gave up ideas for a rood, for carved angel heads at either end of the chancel beam, but also, most significantly, for a black marble and copper lectern: this he rejected in favour of a plain wooden one, which Mrs. Tooth purchased from him for £16.[65]

However, the Spanish chestnut choir stalls provided a perfect opportunity for Wilson to add embellishments in an entirely fitting and expressive way. Reassuring Mrs. Tooth that 'dull' as they may have looked when being unloaded from the packing cases in which they had been sent from Trask's workshop, they would 'just *make* the chancel,'[66] since they were meant to be seen from below, when the carved animals, half-hidden in their nooks and crannies, would come to life. In these stalls, decoration has not been artificially foisted onto structure: instead, fancy and function are genuinely united. A mouse at the end of one row of stalls (Fig. 41) pausing beneath a curvaceous Art Nouveau 'SM' for St. Mark, is reminiscent of the old misericord tradition, where idiosyncratic designs fit resourcefully into the available space. A multitude of creatures – an owl, a rabbit, a tortoise, a dolphin – bear witness to Wilson's belief in the vital interrelationship between the elements of the natural world. Far from being merely pretty, these living creatures, carved into the living wood, embody Wilson's vision of 'the mazes of existence'.[67]

The North and South doors at the West end provided the opportunity for craftsmanship of restrained but innovative richness (Plate 48). Paired bands of teak and ebony chevrons, each varying slightly from its neighbour, express Wilson's delight in unusual materials, interspersed with lustrous insets of abalone shell, a device quickly taken up by Townsend and Reynolds-Stephens (1902-4) in

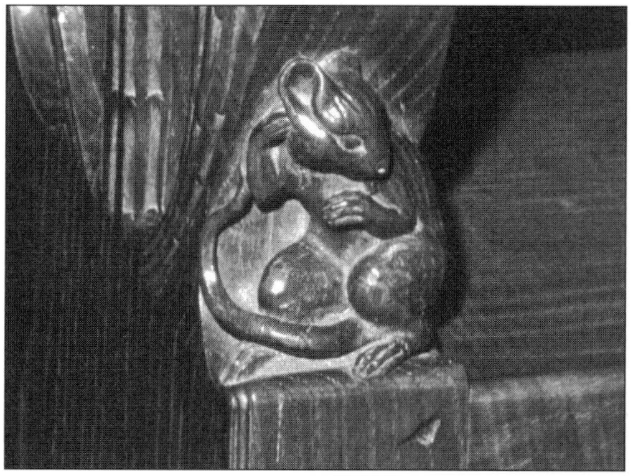

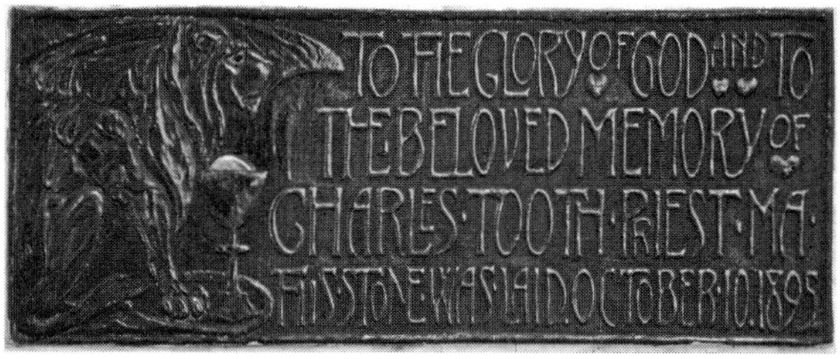

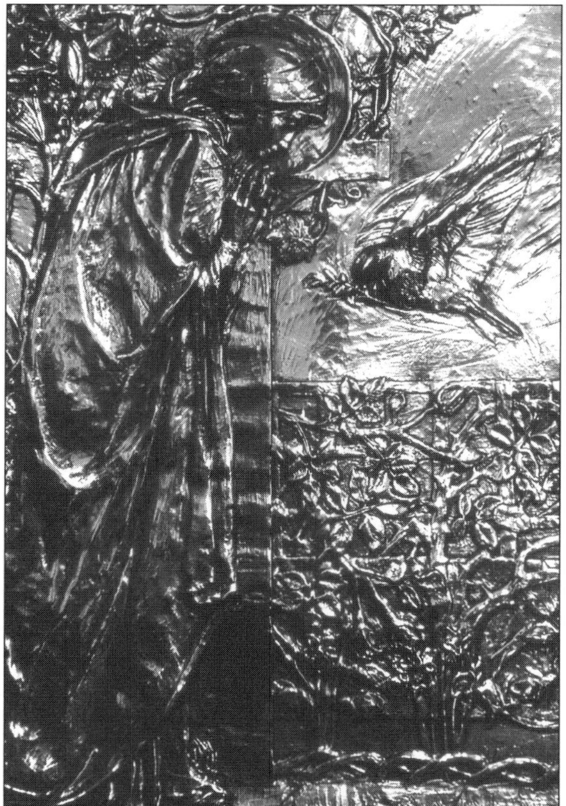

Figure 41. (top left) Brithdir, St. Mark's: choir-stall mouse.

Figure 42. (right) Brithdir, altar frontal: detail showing the Holy Spirit in the form of a dove approaching Mary.

Figure 43. (above) Brithdir, lettering of foundation plaque.

the Essex church of St. Mary the Virgin, Great Warley. Recalling jewellery techniques, their glint echoes the segments of cut pearl of the bronze foundation plaque behind the font, where they are set into the wings and eye of the lion of St. Mark. These, he explained, would lend the plaque a 'gleam ... which it might otherwise lack'. He insisted, in deference to the donor, that the expense would be 'inconsiderable ... about 1/- a piece' for cutting and setting the pearl. In the plaque Wilson's square and compact raised lettering (Fig. 43) accords perfectly with the rest of this memorial to the memory of one man.[68]

Unlike the pulpit and altar, which were integral to the arrangement of the church, the organ and font (Plate 47) were isolated objects capable, if badly managed, of fragmenting its coherence. Wilson therefore left these till last. The simple oak-panelled organ-case, raised on a shallow plinth to enhance the sound, was made by Trask, while the lead font basin, set on an octagonal tooled ashlar stem, was designed by Wilson, modelled by Arthur Grove and cast by William Dodds, a master plumber who taught at the Central School from 1896. The outer bowl is encircled by palm fronds – emblems of welcome and blessing – between wave-lines signifying the waters of baptism, which undulate around the surface in an uncluttered, quasi-Celtic manner, rejoicing in the solidity of lead.

In opting for a lead bowl, Wilson may have had local leadmining in mind, but was also fully aware – alert as ever to the possibilities of innovation within tradition – of the renaissance in the art of leadwork highlighted in Lethaby's volume of 1893. *The Builder* of 1900 would carry an article illustrating the Brithdir font among recent examples of the creative use of lead, and in 1909 Troup praised its flat-cast, 'bent round' technique,[69] which, though awkward to do, produced better quality lead than that made by conventional milling techniques.

By the time the final accounts were rendered, Wilson's estimated cost of £1,450, despite his meticulous attention to economy, had more than doubled. 'I do not know how the work has run up so,' he wrote; '... It is not as if it had been very elaborate in design....' He forestalled possible complaints from Mrs. Tooth with the assertion: 'The only thing I know is that I believe it is going to be one of the best bits of work this end of the century! If that be any comfort'.[70] Wilson was right on both counts. It isn't very elaborate in terms of size, or decoration, or expensive materials. But it *is* creative, carefully considered and crafted by hand – all costly ingredients. As for its being one of the best bits of work of the late 90s, its impact and integrity rank with the finest craft-inspired work of designers such as Lethaby or Gimson. 'Much of it may never be seen,' wrote Wilson to Mrs. Tooth, 'but there are only few other persons in England at the present time who could have given you as much'.[71]

Musing on this in the course of what proved to be his last letter to her, he wished it 'were nearer London: I should send many to see it'.[72] With the project complete, he admitted feeling 'a certain amount of pride in knowing that good work is there'.[73] For him, its true value lay in qualities more precious than purely financial ones. 'The chief merit' of the church, he concluded, 'is that it is *personal*.... I cannot tell you how I have thought about it nor ... what it has cost me. Now I have no hesitation in saying that what is done [there] must live, because it has come out of my own life.'[74]

The months that saw the completion of Mrs. Tooth's commission were a period of reflection for Wilson, to take stock of his professional and personal achievements so far. It was also at about this time, May 1898, that his mother succumbed to cancer, and it fell to Harry to take charge of the arrangements surrounding the funeral. She was to be laid to rest in Birling churchyard, Kent, among Wilsons of previous generations. That morning, Harry went ahead with Edgar to Ryarsh, to decorate the cart that he had specially hired with spring flowers and greenery, while his father and Patten made the journey by train, accompanying the coffin, from Harrow to Snodland station. There the horse and cart were waiting to bear the coffin on the last part of its journey. Loving plants and flowers as Clara Wilson did, this seemed a fitting farewell.

Besides displaying a rich originality of manner and detail, the Welsh church had demonstrated an essential concept underlying Wilson's creative vision: the crucial correlation of architecture and sculpture. As the building's architect, he had explored its inherent sculptural qualities, and he urged sculptors to observe broadly architectural qualities in their turn. In each of his sculptural commissions, the energies of architecture and sculpture fuse in a powerful unity, so that the strength of one art reinforces the structure and mood of the other.

Sculpture, as distinct from modelling, must, he said, be 'monumental'.[75] In other words, imagination must be dignified by the creative disciplines of form and proportion. At the same time, he was wary of diluting the gestural human forms of sculpture with intrusive architectural features such as pillars or plinths. Unless these added genuine emphasis, they should be omitted altogether. But he knew how to make effective use of such formal detail, as in his pietà for Welbeck, where Christ's hand, reaching lifeless beyond its frame, lends a peculiar intensity to the scene. Again, in the plaster sanctuary panel which he contributed in 1906 as part of the restoration of T.L. Donaldson's Holy Trinity Church of 1829 in Brompton Road, London, the interaction of the figurative and formal elements amplifies the message. Its trio of figures is capable of interpretation both as the Trinity, and as the Word of God with Truth and Wisdom in attendance; the viewer is drawn in by the almost three-dimensional flow of force from the majestic central figure, whose arms, outstretched in blessing, reach across the pillars flanking the throne, and whose halo clips the panel's upper frame.

Wilson's point about the monumental quality of good sculpture crystalises in his appreciation of Alfred Stevens's formidable Wellington catafalque in St. Paul's Cathedral: 'One feels the architect in the lines of his figures, and the sculptor in the fullness of his architectural forms'.[76] Similar interaction, though on a far more intimate scale, is seen in a memorial Wilson himself created for Gloucester Cathedral in 1898. Canon Edward Tinling had been one of Her Majesty's Inspectors of Schools, and a Canon of Gloucester for thirty years; Wilson had been responsible, some seven years previously, for the headstone of Tinling's daughter, none other than Rose Sedding. The subject of the memorial (Fig. 44) was therefore known to him, and he depicts the Canon with his back to us, in prayer on a marble rostrum, at the summit of the stair to heaven. His cope bears the image of Christ in a chasuble. A child-angel, an allusion to his work in education, replicates the pair of figures guarding the Remembrance Chapel at Holy Trinity, Sloane Street; it points him to the entrance of the walled citadel of Paradise, where the youthful Christ stands, crowned and with open arms, to greet him. The form of this welcoming figure suggests the stylised manner of a medieval effigy, while the architectural qualities of the memorial's mass and outline reinforce the disconcertingly physical immediacy of the group as a whole. The three polished bronze figures take on the static yet strangely lifelike drama of a tableau performed against a stage set of black marble.[77]

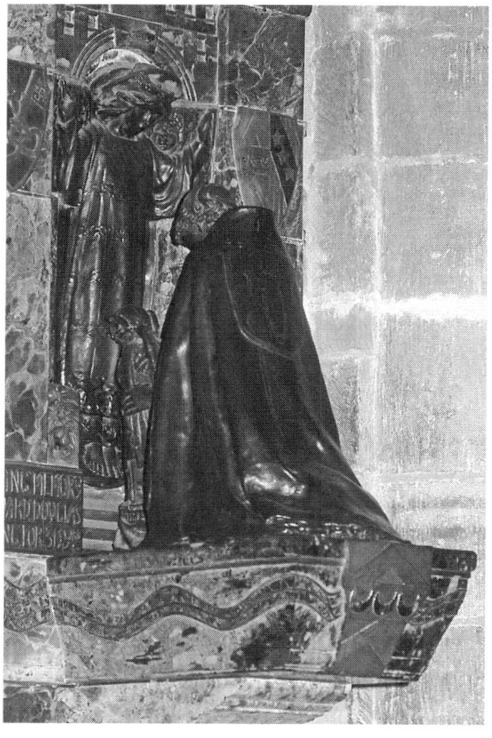

Figure 44. Gloucester Cathedral: Henry Wilson, Tinling Memorial, bronze and marble, 1898.

The kinship that unites architecture and sculpture in Wilson's work is echoed in the overlapping and intermeshing of symbolic systems. Astrology, astronomy, aspects of world religion, legend and Christian myth come together to form a unique visual grammar whose implications Wilson would exploit to their fullest potential, and to which the unlikely coherence of his vision lends an extraordinary intensity. His designs for the Welbeck chapel and the Marple cross had united cross-cultural systems of faith and Christianity. Subsequent commissions continued the search for correspondence, underlining his – and Lethaby's – contention that the boundaries dividing one set of belief-symbols from another are not as rigid or exclusive as they might at first seem.

In Wilson's case, this enabled him to construct a multi-layered visual language occupying the interstices and ambiguities between conventional symbolic frameworks. The process was a complicated one, his inspiration at once eclectic and original, personal and universal. At times it is as though passages of Lethaby's research on mysticism and myth – ideas to which Wilson himself was acutely sensitive – have been directly translated into the third dimension. As in architecture, where Wilson had expressed a 'desire to reach down to the lower levels of mental life', so, too, in his language of visual signs did he endeavour to activate an 'endless chain'[78] of potent human memories.

An interesting parallel might be drawn between Wilson's practice of reinvigorating half-forgotten symbols through unexpected syntheses, and the arcane art of alchemy. The alchemical link is not entirely far-fetched, the art reputedly spanning the space between matter and spirit, and transcending traditional dogma and religions. Wilson was fascinated by its theories, and it is no surprise to find him alluding to it with a matter-of-fact directness in a lecture about 'learning by doing'. As he explained, its origins, like those of the more orthodox branches of human endeavour, could be traced back to the crafts.

> *All art is linked with the handicrafts. Knowledge, or science, is rooted in handicraft. Chemistry has its roots in alchemy, alchemy in metallurgy, metallurgy in the founding of metals ...*[79].

Thus the eagle of the Welbeck chapel lectern (Plate 16) and the dragon encircling the Virgins' Wing stairhead both resemble, or allusively embody, alchemical symbols of the Great Work – the production of the Philosopher's Stone which could change base metal to gold. Such creatures inhabit the mysterious charts of the alchemists, signifying various stages of this process. Yet simultaneously, each carries other messages, the eagle denoting the gospels, the dragon the worlds of water and air. Similarly, the large egg-forms incorporated into the design of the chapel lamps evoke the Philosophic Egg – the sealed vessel in which the Great Work occurred. But in a Christian context they act as symbols of new life. In integrating these visual discourses Wilson consolidates his message about the universality of belief, and the complex convergence of faith systems. Within his transcendent iconography such symbols embrace birth and life, power and transformation, art and meaning.

Wilson's affection for the West Country, inherited from Sedding, and his excursions to France made with Gimson during their time as fellow assistants, stood him in good stead when he was commissioned to design the wall-clock (Fig. 45) for the North transept of Gloucester Cathedral – that is to say, the clockface and hands for the Cathedral clock, whose movement was located in the crossing tower. Though its bells had long kept the hours and quarters, successive Chapters had regarded an exterior dial as incompatible with the tower's architecture, and spurned the idea. But in 1899, the movement was overhauled by the makers of the Palace of Westminster's clock, Dent & Co. of Eastcheap, who devised an ingenious system (since replaced with an electric motor behind the dial) to link it, through gearboxes and layshafts reaching hundreds of feet over roofs and through walls, to a clockface *inside* the building. Given in memory of Canon Bartholomew Price, Master of Pembroke College, Oxford and Professor of Philosophy in the University, the clockface that Wilson

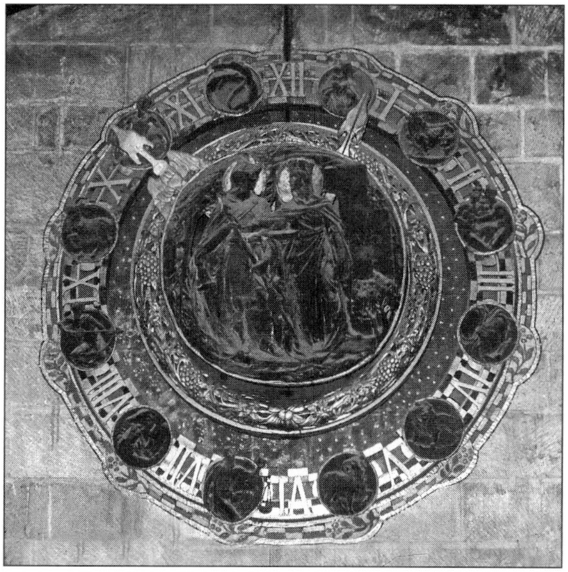

Figure 45. Gloucester Cathedral: Henry Wilson, clockface with bronze relief at its centre, 1899-1900.

designed in 1900 naturally drew on medieval examples he was familiar with, the astronomical clock in Wells Cathedral and the Grand Horloge at Rouen. To those he added his own propensity for manipulating symbol systems, giving that at Gloucester a particular allure.

Its central bronze relief plaque, 3*ft* in diameter and weighing almost a hundredweight, stands forward of the hands and brings the viewer metaphorically in sight of Heaven. To the left, is St. Michael holding a spear; beside him a crowned female saint reaches across as if to restrain him from using it. In the background is an arch inscribed PORTA MORTIS IANUA COELI – death's gate, heaven's doorway – through which the figures have just passed. With his helmet, tunic and sandals, Wilson's Michael is strikingly suggestive of Mercury – a typically Wilsonian merging of Christian and pagan taxonomy. The scene is surrounded by a gilded wreath of vines, the symbol of life, set like a giant bezel on a chequered band. A blue border, scattered with gold stars and suggesting the all-enveloping heavens, is painted straight onto the wall-ashlar. On the gilded quarter hand, with spread wings, rides a dove, the Christian God's words; from its beak springs a flame which, like that forming the hour hand, is a Christian emblem of divine revelation. A message is being sent symbolically from the centre to touch the earth, the rim of green and white chequerwork sprigged with red roses.

Alternating with Roman numerals, twelve bronze plaques depict the signs of the zodiac. Significantly, though, the usual planetary order has been changed by transposing Aries and Virgo, which seamlessly brings together astrology and Christianity. Aries, the ram of Jupiter, god of the ancient world, should in astrological terms appear between Pisces and Taurus at the top of the sequence. Instead, this elevated position is given to Virgo, who appears not as a solitary maiden but as the Madonna holding the infant Christ. Wilson had tried such a reordering already, though less confidently, in a sketch for another astrological clock, in which Virgo has become the Madonna, but has not made the crucial move from her place between Leo and Libra. The sense this move conveys, of the feminine principle of divinity at the centre of Christian myth, would reappear in Wilson's 1910 chapel at Wynyard Hall, Co. Durham, where the chancel beam bears an Annunciation rather than the usual rood figures of St. Mary and St. John on either side of the crucifix. In emphasising the feminine within the astrological cycle at Gloucester, he affirms the notion of synthesis. Christianity is not overturning pagan belief; rather, the tenets of both have been integrated.[80]

Wilson's astrological imagery exactly suits the time-measuring role of the Gloucester clock, and accords with local tradition. Carved zodiacs appear on many West Country churches, notably featuring on the twelfth century doorway of Kilpeck church, Herefordshire, which Wilson had known since boyhood, with Cleobury Mortimer twenty-five miles away. Coiling itself round each jamb is the dragon which would inspire him at Welbeck, while the carved zodiac framing the door is bordered with chevrons – a hallmark of Wilson's work, whether in wood, like the doors at Brithdir, or in plate, like his silver alms dish for St. John's, Cirencester, of 1902 (Plate 56), where it appears as black and green enamel margins to heraldic emblems and ship motifs.[81]

Wilson had never forgotten the imaginary building he had conjured up in 1896, richly fitted yet essentially a 'mere barn, rising high above the roofs of some town....' In the event, Brighton was that town, and the barn St. Bartholomew's Church, which with almost prophetic accuracy came under his hand the very next year. In 1897 he was commissioned to make six hammered brass candlesticks, each almost 5*ft* tall, for St. Bartholomew's high altar. The church had been built by Edmund Scott in 1872-74, but never completed, affording precisely the backdrop Wilson needed to enact the rest of his vision. St. Bartholomew's was one of the fifteen or so 'Wagner churches' commissioned in Brighton during the mid- and late nineteenth century by Henry Wagner (Vicar of Brighton 1824-70) and his son Arthur (perpetual curate of St. Paul's, until his death in 1902). In number, size and architectural importance – several being by leading architects such as Carpenter, Bodley, Burges, George Cheesman and Somers Clarke – they made a considerable impact on the town. Each was dictated by the ritualistic Anglo-Catholic views of the Wagners, whose fortune, deriving from their forbears' role as Hatters to the Hanoverian Kings and the Army, funded their building works and their welfare and educational schemes.[82]

The architect of St. Bartholomew's, Edmund Scott (unrelated to Sir Gilbert), had moved from London to Brighton in 1853, establishing his office at 26a Regency Square. His massive, sheer-sided, 'picked stock' brick church was by far his grandest work. The transverse stone dressings on its West façade, and its 30*ft* wheel window with four lancets beneath it and a four-light belfry window above, contributed to its staggering effect, and it acquired the nicknames 'Wagner's Folly' and, more accurately, 'Noah's Ark': the younger Wagner had favoured Scott's design because its elemental Gothic outline, steeply-pitched roof and lancet clerestory windows evoked a mighty Christian Ark – and because its huge scale would be sure to catch the attention of passengers arriving for work or pleasure by the adjacent railway. It would have been hard to miss: its height of 135*ft* from ground to roof-ridge made it the tallest parish church in Britain, just 2*ft* shy of the nave of Westminster Abbey – an apt benchmark for this, the cathedral of the so-called 'London, Brighton and South Coast Religion'. Its concentrated plan (just a nave without transepts or chancel, 170*ft* by 58*ft*) make its towering effect all the more impressive. There was a third and, in the circumstances, highly germane nickname favoured by the local residents: for the householders of Ann Street, complaining that the downdraughts it caused made their chimneys smoke, it became 'The Barn'.[83]

The following year, 1898, with the full approval of Arthur Wagner, the vicar, Father Cocks, commissioned Wilson to make a chalice (Plate 21). For both vicar and patron, unshakeable in their High Church sympathies, Wilson, with his reputation for the rich use of materials and thoughtful symbolism, was the obvious candidate for the commission. The silver bowl rests in a tracery of carved ivory, which forms an enclosing vine. Both silver and ivory are emblematic of purity, while the chryselephantine, or layered, construction is typical of Byzantine work. The stem of the chalice sustains the theme of the vine, this seeming to grow from the five-sided silver boss of the flanged base. The raised letters on the boss proclaim HIC EST CALIX MEUS NOVUM TESTM – here is my cup of the new covenant – while the stem's large enamelled silver knot embodies two dragons locked in mortal combat, to signify the self-destructive powers of evil. The idea is subtly reinforced by their enamel decoration in blue, symbolic of truth, and green, of hope and faith.

The base of the chalice is embellished with a garden of five trees, and five streams of blue-green enamel denoting the original river that watered Eden, and Pison, Gihon, Heddekel and Euphrates, the four rivers into which it divided. Wilson is using natural forms not only for their decorative value, but equally for their inherent symbolic and structural properties.[84]

His allusive approach to the major commission that ensued – the furnishing of the church itself – is accurately prefigured in this chalice. Now, at the request of Fr. Cocks, Wilson would apply his creativity on a grand scale. Into the unfinished interior he introduced a series of lavish fittings which transformed Scott's 'solemn, simple hall' into what he understood church-builders throughout the ages had sought to create: 'a visible presentiment of the invisible wonder city'.[85] Something of the impact of the interior that resulted from his contribution was conveyed by one writer who claimed that 'an involuntary gasp of surprise ...'[86] is generally the visitor's first response; the overwhelming impression is indeed one of space, radiant with moments of brilliant colour, all the more luminous against the mysterious shadows beyond.

As he had often pointed out, Wilson hated the idea of churches becoming galleries for mere 'exhibition excellence'.[87] This he had avoided at Brithdir by treating the whole building as a sculptural entity: at St. Bartholomew's he made the existing interior into a sacred theatre where each fitting should play its role in the spiritual enactment. It was with the sanctuary that his vision began to take shape: to dramatic effect, between 1898 and 1900, he recomposed Scott's space around a projecting baldacchino. Drawing heavily on Byzantine forms, the new structure reinterprets the unassuming altar-canopy of Sloane Street on a truly monumental scale (Plate 22). Clad in vivid green and red marble with alabaster capitals, it stands a full 45' high, glowing with colour 'like an altar fire': the embodiment of the baldacchino in Wilson's ideal church. The domed ceiling glistens with gold and mother-of-pearl mosaic, a dove hovering directly over the altar. Set high on twelve wide steps and a paved floor of black, grey and red marble this sumptuous canopy, erected at a cost of more than £2,000, stands like the perfect temple Lethaby described, 'four square at the centre of the earth',[88] symbolising both the authority of the Church and, at the same time, Paradise. Only the figure of Christ for the baldaccino's interior – contingent on the building of an extended East end – is missing.

In the centre of the marble retable with which he enriched the existing high altar, Wilson added a tabernacle door of beaten silver, depicting the crowned figure of perpetual youth, which here stands for the Church constantly renewed by the encircling True Vine.[89] Wilson completed the East end furnishings over the next eight years, during which the original patron, Fr. Arthur Wagner, died. Flanking the baldacchino stand the free-standing columns in Tuscan marble, dating from 1908, half the height of the baldacchino's piers and surmounted by bronze candlesticks

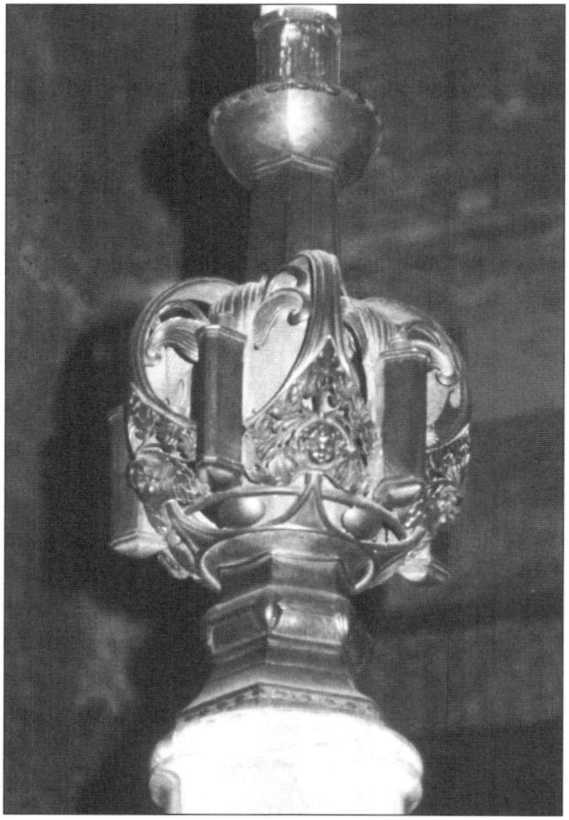

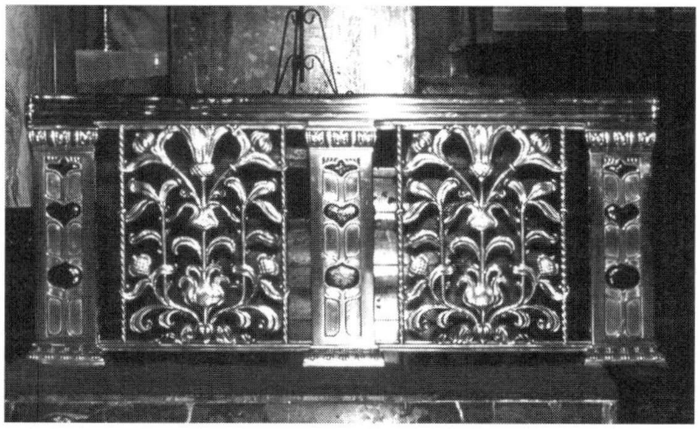

Figure 46. Furnishings by Wilson for St. Bartholomew's Church, Brighton: (top) bronze candlesocket, 1908; (bottom) brass and enamel altar rail, 1905.

or flambeaux (Fig. 46), and linked by Wilson's brass altar rails of 1905 (Fig. 46), low screens of thistles which take their cue from Genesis 3.17 in symbolising earthly sorrow. The blue enamel medallions enlivening their square piers recall the vivid medievalising architectural enamels of William Burges. Against the sanctuary walls are Wilson's oak choir stalls of 1907, their seats inlaid with ebony and inscribed with the Latin opening of Psalm 98, Cantate Domino, inviting songs of praise to the Lord. The oak had its own seasoned quality, the timber having been salvaged from an old house in Somerset.

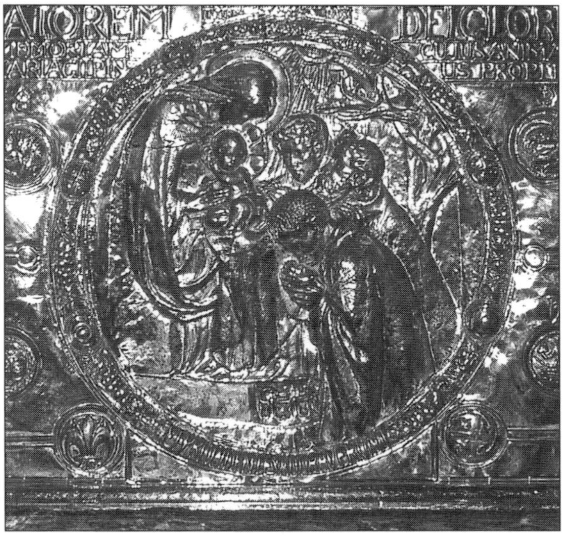

Figure 47. St. Bartholomew's, Brighton: Henry Wilson, Adoration scene from silver-plated Lady Altar, 1902.

Wilson's Sheffield plate Lady Altar of 1902 is the embodiment of the one in his imaginary church – 'a masterwork wrought with fine reliefs in beaten silver'. The central motif (Fig. 47) shows the Adoration of the Magi wreathed by vine. Around it are seven roundels, each using an Assyrian emblem to suggest the planetary system circling this central Christian image. To the left, a maned lion symbolises Apollo the sun god. Next is a wolf, sacred to Mars, then, representing Jupiter, is a hand grasping a thunderbolt. To the right is a chained serpent evoking the volatile nature of Mercury, a stag symbolising the hunter Diana, an owl signifying Venus, and a scorpion, guardian of the gateway of the sun and the emblem of Saturn. The four roundels beneath show versions of the swastika, ancient symbol of the sun or, in Christian thought, of the four evangelists with Christ at their centre. The last roundel encloses a fleur-de-lis, associated with the Trinity. This final emblem brings the total to twelve, reiterating Wilson's readiness to draw together Christian symbol and pagan myth into a rich new iconography.

The inscription along the top edge of the altar frontal forms a characteristically legible yet decorative frieze. At each end is a small repoussé square, the one showing the lamb of God lying on a book of scriptural law, the other, a dove bearing an olive twig as a symbol of the Annunciation, well-suited to a Lady Altar. But a dove carrying an olive twig also denotes the souls of the faithful departed in peace – an apt image for an altar made in memory of Louisa Gilpin, one of the longest-serving members of the congregation.[90]

On the retable, behind the altar's polished red alabaster top, are raised symbols of the four evangelists – the winged lion of St. Mark, the winged man depicting St. Matthew, the winged bull of St. Luke, and the eagle of St. John. All four would reappear on Wilson's last work, the New York cathedral doors. The Lady Altar's silver crucifix was originally designed by Wilson for the high altar, but that place was taken by a grandiose Oberammagau-style cross by McCulloch of Kennington, donated in 1912. Though larger than he might otherwise have made it, Wilson's crucifix accords well with its Lady Altar site. Praying angels kneel at either end of its crosspiece and at its foot, an arrangement which has much in common with a design made and exhibited in 1888 by his friend Whall.[91] The figure of Christ is represented in formalised low-relief, rather as he is shown in the Gloucester Cathedral Tinling Memorial, in which the drooping head, the only conspicuously three-dimensional part of the composition, brings a frisson of corporeality to the image.

The Lady Altar was destined to stand in the lofty Lady Chapel which, ever since 1898, Wilson had been planning to build at the East end of St. Bartholomew's. The abrupt curtailment of the building, particularly noticeable when seen from outside, confirms that an Eastward continuation had always been intended. Wilson planned to lengthen Scott's church by a further three bays – an enlargement the architect himself had envisaged. In Wilson's scheme, a screen would have been created between the nave and new Lady Chapel by piercing the existing back wall with three tall arches; in this, his sensitivity to 'vista', and his skill at suggesting 'the infinite by the finite',[92] would have found full expression. The wall at the back of the baldacchino was then to have been decorated in mosaic with a young Christ as King, while the mosaic for the new East wall would depict a 30' high Madonna in Glory – a controversial subject at that time for an Anglican church.

Wilson was justifiably proud of his proposed extension, and of the European interest it created. His design in chalk and watercolour was displayed at the Royal Academy in 1905, and illustrated in *Moderne Bauformen*.[93] The director of the Düsseldorf Exhibition of Christian Art (1909) offered Wilson a 20' square room all to himself, on the strength of a one-third size mock-up of the proposal having been 'the culminating point of the whole [church art] exhibition'[94] at Aix-la-Chapelle (Aachen) the previous year. Wilson wrote with evident satisfaction to the churchwarden of St. Bartholomew's, citing these accolades and explaining the careful planning that had gone into the plan:

> *In Oct. last when Fr Cocks asked me to put the work in hand … I told him that the first preliminary was the preparation of a model 1/3 lifesize … I told him also that the work would take over a year to do, & this was a minimum time. The reason is obvious. [It] is on a colossal scale: the figure of Christ standing upright (within the baldacchino) would be nearly 18 feet high – the figure on my 1/3 size model is fully lifesize. Not only so – as the work has to be enlarged the model has to be … minutely finished or every flaw gets magnified, necessitating the utmost care & frequent revisions. I began at the earliest moment to construct the wooden model of the baldacchino arch. This being very large … took the carpenters six weeks to finish and put up in the studio … .*[95]

In 1910, however, Fr. Cocks left St. Bartholomew's to join the Roman Catholic Church. Early the next year his successor, Fr. Henry Ross, shelved Wilson's plans in favour of a cheaper, doctrinally safer, and far less interesting design. It was by F. Hamilton Jackson, a member of the Birmingham Art Workers' Guild and a contributor to *The Architectural Review* during Wilson's editorship, and would be carried out by church furnishers Barkentin and Krall. The existing East wall was simply reinforced and decorated with a mosaic of four large archangels, while a cramped design of Christ in Glory was substituted within the baldacchino for the Christ-figure Wilson had proposed.

No subsequent commission would offer Wilson the opportunity for a decorative scheme on so vast a scale, and in so spectacular an idiom, and it was immediately clear that the rejection of his proposals had done an 'injustice' both to him and to the building as a whole:

> *… almost all my staff has been engaged in them for some months.… Throughout my work for Brighton I have spared no time, no thought, no energy, in order to produce a perfect result – a result worthy of the noblest church of modern times … .*[96]

But protestation was futile. Fr. Ross's dismissal of the carefully prepared drawings and models not only frustrated Wilson's vision for the church, but also means that no figurative work in mosaic by him survives: the only other example, his reredos for Holy Trinity, Fareham, commissioned in 1910-13, made by one of his Italian craftsmen and installed in 1922, was obliterated in the 1950s on the grounds that so eye-catching an image – a seated Christ holding a sceptre, with a crucifixion superimposed over his heart, cherubs on his lap, and angels and signs of the zodiac declaring him Lord of the Universe[97]- was distracting rather than aiding the congregation's devotions.

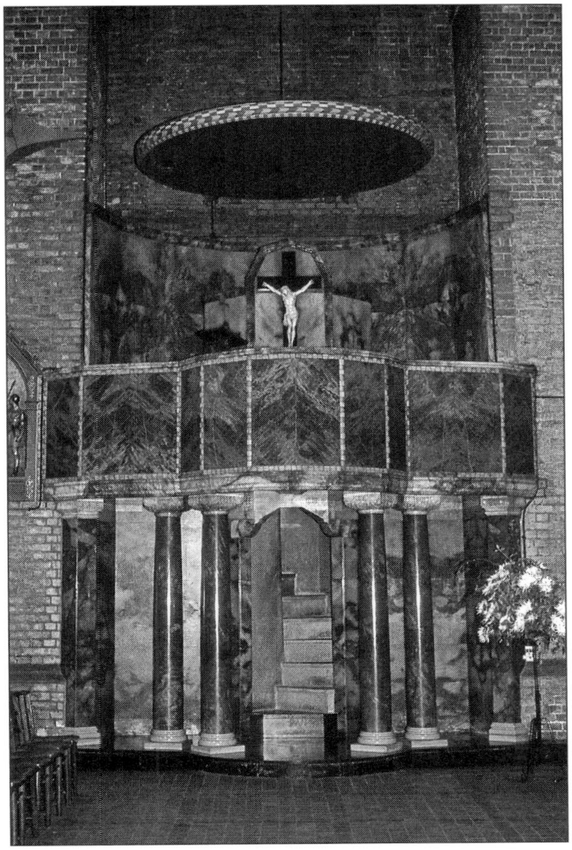

Figure 48. St. Bartholomew's, Brighton: pulpit; Wilson set its green marble gallery on six red marble columns, 1906.

However, during the enabling days of Fr. Cocks's incumbency, there was time at least to enact three further components of Wilson's vision for St. Bartholomew's. Facing the Lady Altar stands Wilson's imposing marble pulpit of 1906 (Fig. 48). Its polygonal gallery of green Irish marble, each panel framed in alabaster, is crowned with a circular tester edged with bright inlay, and rests on six columns of red African marble with alabaster capitals rising from a bow-fronted plinth of black Belgian marble. Six, the number of the days of creation, signified perfection, and was thereby appropriate to a pulpit's function. Access is by the stone spiral stairs which lead up between its pillars. This quirky but calculated manipulation of visual and structural elements perfectly embodies the 'quintessence of Wilsonism'.[98] The size of this half-concealed staircase is not in itself incongruous – but the curious disparity of narrow steps and robust pillars both stimulates the senses and excites the imagination.

Each alabaster capital is carved with a phrase of the exhortation: PRO NOBIS – Raphael it is God who heals us, Uriel who art the brightness of God, Gabriel who art the strength of God, Michael who is like unto God – ORATE. The four Archangels figure in the liturgy of the Byzantine Church, but just as significant for Wilson was their presence in some of William Blake's most important prints, like that from *Paradise Lost* where Raphael rebukes Adam and Eve beneath a canopy of curling fronds, themselves foreshadowing the curlicues of Wilson's Sloane Street railings and his Brighton chalice.[99] He valued Blake's engravings, especially those of Westminster Abbey, as a source of personal inspiration and, more broadly, as a stimulus for the Gothic Revival and Pre-Raphaelitism.

In the same year, Wilson's oak panelled organ gallery was completed at the West end of the church, while his copper-rimmed green marble font, set on a three-stepped base of black marble, took form in 1908. The gallery, as well as accommodating the organ, provides fifty extra seats, bringing the capacity of the church to 1,500.[100] The font, traditionally octagonal to evoke thoughts of rebirth and Paradise, is almost six feet in diameter. Yet, despite its size, it recalls the chunky gilded gesso boxes made by J.P. Cooper in the early 1900s, and anticipates his elegant silver-mounted shagreen caskets of the 1920s. Green marble panels line the baptistry, to which the statue of John the Baptist, made by W.D. Gough to the design of Sir Giles Gilbert Scott, was added long after Wilson's involvement with St. Bartholomew's, in 1925.

Wilson's consistent emphasis on artistic sincerity is clear in St. Bartholomew's. As he had done at Brithdir, so at Brighton he dedicated himself to infusing distinctively individual yet appropriate elements into his work. Again, like Blake, he had identified the timeless, universal 'invisible world' as the proper territory of the imaginative artist:

In all noble work it is the inner vision which signifies. Art is the cry of spirit to spirit; it is mind stretching out to mind across the body's prison's bars.[101]

It is precisely this spiritual bond that is affirmed by the interior of this vast, truncated church in Brighton.

Many of the devices Wilson used at St. Bartholomew's reappear in his final commission for Gloucester Cathedral: the chalice of 1900, made with Sidney Wiseman and Harry Murphy, which, like his work at the architectural scale, has the same Wilsonian capacity to manipulate scale, proportion and complicated symbolic languages (Plate 26). Its silver bowl is set in an openwork calyx of vines, akin to that on the Brighton chalice. The crystal-pillared knop represents the Temple of the Lamb: within a ring of columns a silver-gilt lamb lies on a golden Holy Mountain, that mountain whose summit, according to Lethaby, 'reached heaven' and from whence flowed the four rivers of Paradise, here rendered as four bosses of blue-green enamel.[102] Between the temple's four gabled arches stand enamel and jewel-studded pinnacles. The scaling down of these overtly architectural features attracts our attention as the pulpit stairs in St. Bartholomew's do, their use in a silverwork design intensifying their effect. Conventional boundaries between disciplines become blurred as the ordinary rules of form and material are creatively transgressed.

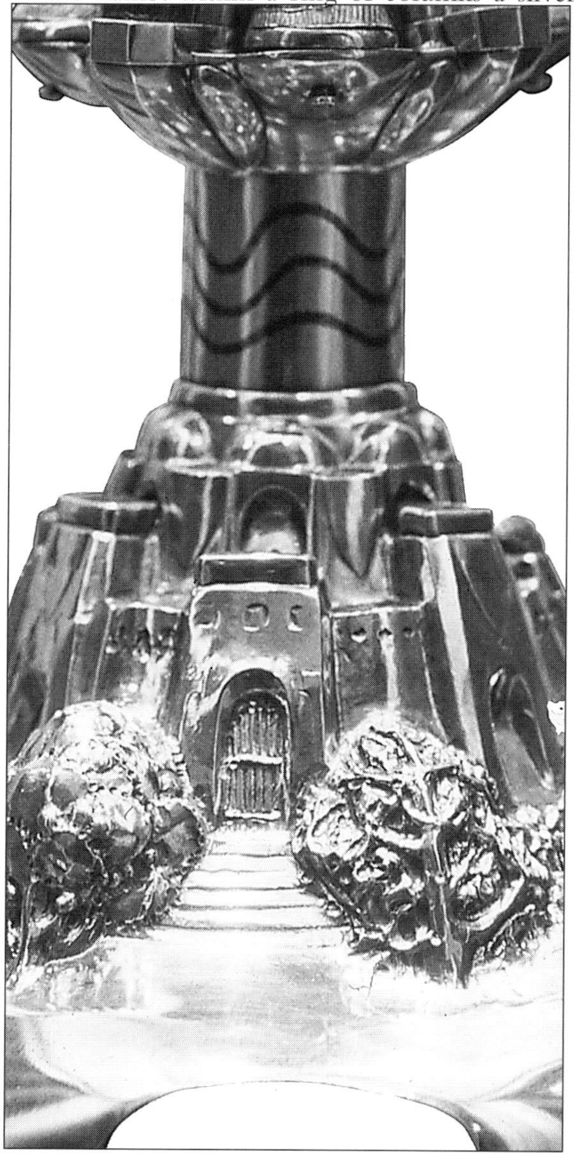

Figure 49. Gloucester Cathedral: Henry Wilson, chalice, silver 'earth-mountain' detail, with opal and niello, 1900.

The undulating niello lines on the stem of the Gloucester chalice suggest sea, or clouds. From its broadly splayed base rise seven domes like those on Marple's wafer box, surmounting seven archways, each the setting for a fire opal. Lethaby's symbology has the planets equated with self-lustrous metals or gems, allowing Wilson to allude, with his seven opals, to the seven planets – and to Lethaby's description of those planets circling 'the earth mountain,' with the Lamb of God on its summit, as well as to his contention that seven 'is written in the sky'.[103] The sevens pervading the chalice's structure reiterate Wilson's own sensitivity to number symbolism. Besides denoting the planets, sets of seven might signify the seven ages of man, or the seven precious substances. Here, though, Wilson has in mind 'the seven domed heavens'.[104] Planted amongst them are seven trees, evoking Paradise, between which rise seven flights of six steps, leading to heavenly gate-arches (Fig. 49), miniatures of the one in the Tinling memorial.

Just as each of Wilson's designs evolved

naturally and personally, so did his routes to fresh commissions. The Gloucester clock and the Brighton chalice both opened doors to further work, another example of one commission generating another being that for the private chapel for Walmsgate Hall, Langworth, north-east of Lincoln. The link was with his earlier work, at Welbeck. Winifred, Duchess of Portland, née Dallas-Yorke, had grown up at Walmsgate. On the death of her brother Haliburton in the Boer War, she persuaded her parents to commission Wilson for a family chapel next to the house. The work was completed between 1900 and 1901; the builder was Dunn of Horncastle. Wilson's chapel survived the demolition of Walmsgate Hall in 1960-62: in a new brick carcass on a new site, and stretched by a bay, the chapel's interior and its exterior stonework were faithfully reassembled to serve as St. Hugh's, the new parish church of Langworth.

The building's small bellcote, hipped roof and simple arched windows give it a slightly Italianate flavour; the overall effect is unostentatious, with the external decoration limited to carved shields on the stone window surrounds, while the clear glass of the windows makes the interior light and bright, appropriate both to the youth of the dead soldier whom the building commemorates, and to modern Anglican worship. As an entity, Wilson's design forms an exceptionally creative synthesis of the impulses of Art Nouveau and the Arts and Crafts.

Above a plain marble altar and against the light of the East window is suspended a square wooden canopy, richly carved and coloured. In the gilded vine tendrils of its border, vigorous growth is met with formal control. The blue underside of the canopy is sprinkled with gold circles and edged with spring flowers, while four bands of gilded chequerwork springing from its corners converge on a central diamond-shaped hatchment, whose plumes and Tudor rose are an acknowledgement of the dead soldier's regiment.

For its earlier incarnation as a domestic chapel, the Duchess's mother had been keen that Wilson make a pictorial altar frontal in beaten silver to the same pattern as the one at Welbeck, which she knew well. But by 1905, Wilson's typically persuasive argument had convinced her that a panelled treatment, like his recently-installed bronze doors at St. Mary's, Nottingham, was a more appropriate solution:

> *We now feel that we like your suggestion of the panels taken from your Nottingham doors much better than the Welbeck nativity picture. So we have quite come round to your way of thinking … .*[105]

There was talk, too, of creating a baldacchino, using the existing altar canopy as its roof. In the event neither altar frontal nor baldacchino materialised, though their omission – especially that of the baldacchino (due to lack of time and ready funds) – was probably a fortunate mischance, leaving the building's naturalness unspoilt.

Wilson's silver altar cross conforms, in its broadness and flatness, to this simplicity, while the crucified Christ is firmly three-dimensional and the crosspieces terminate in fleurs-de-lis. It is flanked on the altar-table by straight, oval-section silver candlesticks set on four-lobed bases. The sanctuary, paved with grey marble and wainscotted with exotically-veined green, recalls the steps of Wilson's ideal church, which form 'a wave in a sea of stone', and Lethaby's 'pavements like the sea'.[106]

In the chapel's reconstruction as a church, it proved impossible to rescue Wilson's plaster decoration for the chancel, but the carved chancel beam was saved and reinstated. It adopts motifs from the altar canopy, reiterating them in seductive colour. Twisting stems of a golden vine grow irrepressibly across it, between vivid queues of red, green and gold chevrons and chequerwork. The two original beams spanning the nave are painted with simple circles, squares and zigzags. A third beam, serving the added western bay, is shaped like the others but painted plain white like the tunnel-vaulted ceiling (Fig. 50).

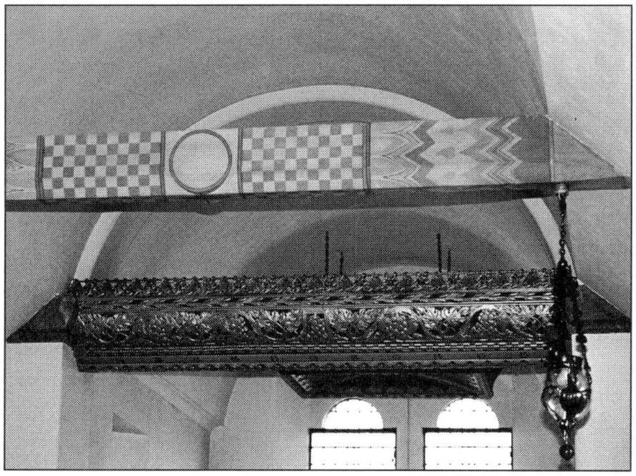

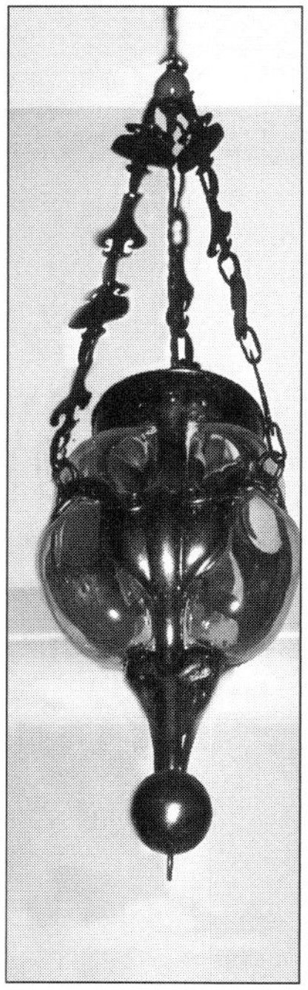

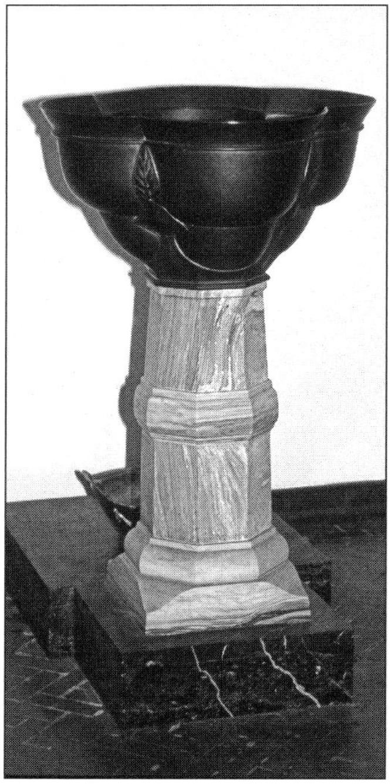

Figure 50. (above) St. Hugh's Church, Langworth, Lincs.: reconstruction of Wilson's commission for Walmsgate Hall chapel, altar canopy, nave and chancel beams, 1900-01.

Figure 51. (right) St. Hugh's, Langworth: hanging lamp, bronze and glass.

Figure 52. (far right) St. Hugh's, Langworth: font, copper and marble.

The symbolic language of the hanging lamps Wilson made for the Walmsgate Chapel may not be as detailed as that he had used seven years earlier, in the first flush of enthusiasm for Lethaby's researches, for the grander interior at Welbeck; nevertheless, their symbolism shares the same mythic impulses. Suspended from three ornate chains, each lamp (at Walmsgate they were oil, in St. Hugh's, electric bulbs are used) was designed to glow within a bulbous glass vessel enmeshed in fronds of beaten bronze, from which hung a globe representing the world (Fig. 51). The lamplight was meant to be diffused in mysterious, flickering rays; so subtle, however, was the illumination that, after several fraught services, Mrs. Dallas-Yorke was moved to chide their designer:

> *Your artistic lamps draw out and lose all the light and we must worship in semi-darkness with shadows cast over everything. A small acetylene plant might help … .*[107]

Her comment irresistibly recalls the lamps Wilson had produced for the Art Workers' Guild masque in 1892, which, 'so beautiful on paper ... turned out such dull, shapeless masses of silk, their subtle symbolism quite lost in the half light'.[108]

His font (Fig. 52), a simple lobed tulip-shape formed of copper and set on a faceted green marble column, stands in an alcove on the North side; closing the new West bay is the gallery that, at Walmsgate, received the Dallas-Yorkes' relations and visitors. Beneath it are sliding walnut entrance doors, with bronze angel-mask handles anticipating the ones Wilson would devise in 1904-05 for his doors at St. Mary's, Nottingham. Over them, is set his quiet portrayal in plaster of the young Haliburton. Uniformed and wearing a cloak whose folds define a broad arc, he kneels at an altar beneath a frond of palm, the symbol of honour. His sword is held point downwards in a gesture of peace and submission. Towards the end of 1905 Mrs. Dallas-Yorke had taken a mild dig at Wilson for his slowness in delivering this semi-circular panel:

> *I wonder what is happening to the memorial? As you said it was cast long ago. Will it be here for Xmas? I don't want to hurry you vexatiously, but that has happened which I feared – my husband despaired of its*

coming and spent the put-aside money on a horse. There is £25 gone on the transaction. If you don't bring the memorial soon he will buy another horse, and then all the money will be gone ... .[109]

That had done the trick. Soon, she was acknowledging the installation of the memorial with unreserved appreciation; her words make clear how the work of Wilson, a conscientious, inspired designer-architect, was still capable of attracting attention in a fast-changing world.

I want nothing in the chapel that has not the stamp of your approval. In these motor-car days it has gained such notoriety.... When I see the work of other architects I thank God that we owe our chapel to you![110]

In the late summer of 1901 Wilson finally felt in a position to marry his fiancée of ten years, and on the first day of August, in the Chapel of the Savoy, Margaret Ellinor Morse became Mrs. Harry Wilson. They had been introduced at the Arts and Crafts Exhibition Society, their relationship blossoming as they discussed craft and design, nature, and religion – her father, Francis Morse, was the incumbent of St. Mary's, Nottingham, and her brother Sidney was the vicar of Shelford, Radcliffe-on-Trent, who, with Paul Cooper, stood witness at the ceremony. One of five sisters, the beautiful and intelligent Miss Morse was an accomplished embroidress, and a chalice veil on which she and Wilson had collaborated was exhibited by her in 1899.[110] Despite his reputation as Sedding's heir, it was not until he was 37 that Wilson could consider either the income or security he earned from his commissions sufficient to marry on. Besides, as the oldest son, he felt a responsibility to see the other two married before himself: Patten first, the previous summer in the fashionable West End church, St. George's, Hanover Square, whilst Edgar's wedding, to the nurse who had tended their dying mother, followed in April 1901 at Christchurch, Streatham, hastened by his impending departure for the Middle East to start the job Harry had helped him find.

It had always been Margaret's and Harry's intention to live in the country, and so, towards the end of 1901, they closed up Vicarage Gate and left for Kent, to stay at Sir Lawrence Alma Tadema's house at Fairseat. From there, Wilson was ideally placed to supervise the construction of their new home two miles away.

Sidney's wedding gift to his sister had been a plot of slightly over 2½ acres in the parish of St. Mary's Platt, near Sevenoaks; here, their new home would come to represent a landmark of considerable symbolic weight for Wilson, his designing it at a crossroads in his life and its coinciding with his commitment in the early 1900s to metalwork and the arts *associated with* architecture, as against architecture itself. If William Morris's aspirations were reflected in his Red House, then Wilson's deliberate disconnection from the architectural 'profession' was mirrored in The Thatched House. It was built by local builders Curtis and Caine, over the years 1901 and 1902. Wilson was constantly on site as building progressed, his aim in its design being to trap as much sun as possible,[112] and to work in the spirit of the domestic vernacular of that corner of Kent – walls either roughcast or boarded, roofs thatched with eyebrows over upper windows and with half-hips to the gables (Plate 27).

Situated on the northern edge of the village, the house is set back from the road and cradled in the fold of wooded hill that rises steeply behind. The porch, projecting square to the wing that contained the reception room and Wilson's studio, masks a deliberate crank in the building's plan, the domestic quarters shying away to the left. The oak front door is accentuated by a segmental arch of tiles, and by its splayed reveal, with its plinth of hand-picked stones (Fig. 53). Kept small but emphasised by diagonal modelling, the paired chimneys are of local red brick, and the windows are simple flat-headed casements flush with the outer walls. Inside, exposed beams, iron window and door latches, wood-block floors, and window-reveals that show the thickness of the masonry, sustain the homely appearance of the exterior. Upstairs the bedrooms preserve the traditional theme, with sloping ceilings and latched doors. But Wilson made sure that part of the floor to the right of the house, the bathroom and a section of the landing, was of cast concrete, demontrating his readiness to combine modern techniques with craft-based ones. W.R. Lethaby, working at the same time in Herefordshire on his masterpiece, All Saints' Church, Brockhampton, was likewise uniting thatch and concrete; soon the two old allies would be submitting their joint proposal for the new Liverpool Cathedral, conceived entirely in concrete, the essential material of the twentieth century.

At the end of the landing, next to – but not connected to – his studio, was Wilson's oak-panelled study. His daughter Pernel recalled the long hours he spent in it:

> *My father often worked till late at night, so he generally had his breakfast by himself with a Loeb's Classic for company, or else a book in French, German or Italian. He was a very good linguist and really felt much more at home in Europe than in England. Depending on priorities he might then work in his study, coping with correspondence in connection with his architectural jobs, his work for the Art Workers' Guild and the Arts and Crafts Exhibition Society, or writing reports on the work of students at various goldsmiths' colleges, not to mention speeches on the importance of the Arts and Crafts in education.*[113]

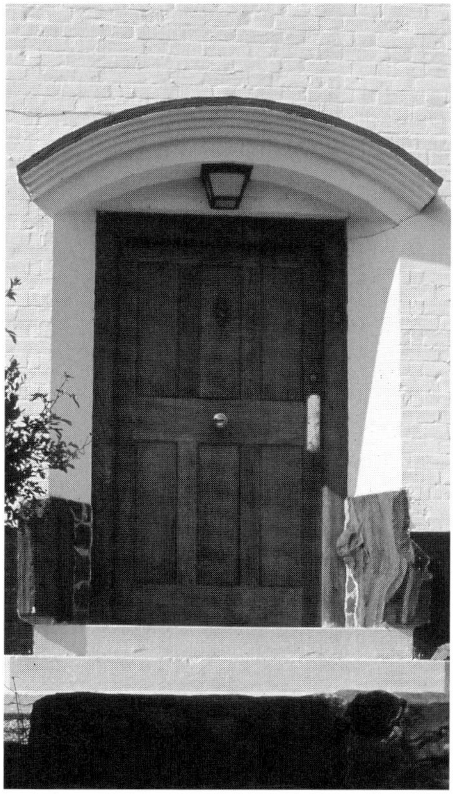

Figure 53. St. Mary's Platt, Kent: The Thatched House, front door with tile arch, 1901-02.

Running on from the right-hand wing of the house was the studio, a plain barn of one-and-a-half storeys, differentiated by its structure – frame and black boarding – but, except for a full-height studio light in its rear elevation, with windows matching those of the domestic part of the house (Plate 27).

A stone's throw to the East, Wilson built a carpentry shed and two workshops – one for metalwork and jewellery, the other for sculpture. Later, for Harry Murphy, his former apprentice at Vicarage Gate, and Sidney Wiseman, whom he appointed foreman, he built a pair of cottages. These two would become his closest associates on the metalwork commissions of the early 1900s, Wiseman concentrating on jewellery, Murphy on ecclesiastical pieces. After periods of teaching under Wilson at the Royal College and the Central School of Arts and Crafts, Murphy moved to Berlin, spending 1912 in the atelier of the silversmith Emil Lettré, whose work reflected some stylishly modern trends. By the time he returned to England, his designs had gravitated towards a formally plainer, less symbol-loaded idiom, but always retained the technical expertise and the resourcefulness that his training with Wilson had nurtured. The one-time penny-an-errand apprentice would in 1937 become Principal of the Central School.

The Thatched House swiftly became an unofficial craft academy. Wilson's own working time at Platt was divided between the studio, where he would plan his commissions, and the workshops, where he would supervise them when not executing them himself. J.D. Sedding's children, George – who, after briefly working alongside Wilson in the Oxford Street office, was officially apprenticed to him from 1901 to 1904 – and Rose, came to work for two years in the Platt metalwork and jewellery workshop. They took rooms in a local farmhouse, returning to London in 1907, where George, having studied modelling at the Royal College, set up his own studio at 11, Noel Street, to make silver and copper jewellery set with semi-precious gems. With the growth of his business came larger ecclesiastical pieces, in which something of the Wilsonian spirit persisted.

One of the closest allies and collaborators from the Sedding days, Paul Cooper, followed the Wilsons to Kent in 1902, settling in Westerham in 1911 in the house he had designed for himself and his family, Betsom's Green. Again, Curtis and Caine did the building work, incorporating studio and workshop into the design. The close creative association continued for ten years; indeed, Cooper's use – from as early as 1906 – of *mokumé*, a sophisticated technique combining silver with copper, sprang from their discussions as Wilson was preparing new chapters on Japanese metalwork for the second edition of *Silverwork and Jewellery*, which came out in 1912. This was the year when, needing to supervise at first hand the casting of the bronzework for his monumental Elphinstone Tomb, Wilson relocated to Venice, where he and his family would remain until the outbreak of war.

Wilson took delight in the prospect The Thatched House offered. Here he had the chance to write, work or simply think at will. Rural life brought 'peace and continual self recreation indispensible to creative work'.[114] His American friend, the architect Ralph Cram, believed the naturalness of the setting enabled Wilson to tap sources of inspiration inaccessible to the city dweller.

> *The gulf that yawns between The Thatched House and London or Birmingham is more than that of ... miles of English countryside. The chasm is one of time and spirit, and as one approaches the low thatched roofs and white walls of the house [and] the rough workshops where artists, artisans and apprentices are labouring, one slips back a century into the past.*[115]

Invited to address the Art Workers' Guild – on whose committee he had sat since 1898 – Wilson prefaced an authoritative disquisition on commemorative sculpture with a playful reference to this gulf:

> *When the Committee's request for a lecture floated down into my obscurity I felt like a sleeper newly awakened; and as I stepped outside on my way to work and glanced from white wall to purple thatch, thence to the golden dome of the beech and the infinite azure beyond, my daily thrill of ecstasy was checked... .*[116]

However, unlike the deliberately remote rural retreats sought by contemporaries like Gimson, Platt was within an hour of central London by direct train. Easy access to the capital was vital for Wilson. His former pupil at The Thatched House, Brown-Morrison, remembered his master departing for the station at Borough Green:

> *He always wore light homespun tweed (from H. Bill) and on several afternoons a week he cycled to the station at a great pace to catch the London train.*[117]

Among Wilson's commitments to educational and Arts and Crafts bodies, those to the Art Workers' Guild and the Arts and Crafts Exhibition Society were of chief importance. Until 1913, when it moved into its own premises at 6 Queen Square with a Guild Hall freshly embellished by Troup, the A.W.G. had been based at Clifford's Inn; the Society, however, continued from June 1907 right up to March 1918, to rent space within Edward Prior's office at 1, Hare Court, Temple, when it took a share in the Queen Square building. Prior was on close terms with many of the leading craftsmen, and several, Wilson included, would be drawn in to contribute to his crowning work, the brawny completion of the neo-Byzantine Church of St. Osmund, Parkstone, Dorset.

The style had been set by the chancel of 1904-05, by local architect G.A. Livesay of Bournemouth. In 1911, Prior was commissioned to continue the church from crossing to West end, taking on Arthur Grove as partner; Grove brought Wilson in to participate in making the chancel screen. The talents of Bainbridge Reynolds, MacDonald Gill and his brother Eric were discharged in metalwork, mural decoration and inscriptions, while Prior used his own Early English 'slab' glass to create the abstract configurations of the windows. Prior's virtuoso completion in 1916 in red, brown and yellow brick, with stone reserved on the exterior for wheel windows, has as many Anglo-Saxon overtones as Byzantine forms, and seems almost to anticipate Germany's immediate post-war Expressionist architecture.[118]

The Parkstone commission confirmed the creative ease that had coloured Wilson's and Grove's working relationship since the 1890s, when the core of their preferred team had been established; this rapport had been re-established in an intermediate commission of Grove's, at the Church of St. John the Divine, Richmond, Surrey. In 1905 Grove was asked to build a Gothic chancel onto Lewis Vulliamy's 1830s brick nave.[119] He approached Richard Garbe, a sculptor known to Wilson from the Central School, to design a Crucifixion for the exterior of the East gable. Wilson had used this archetypal format both at an architectural scale and in his silverwork; Garbe seems, in his relief of 1907-10, to be paying conscious homage, compressing the figure group tellingly sketched by Wilson in 1896 for the West front of St. Augustine's, Highgate, to focus attention on the two half-turning Marys at the foot of the cross. Wilson must surely have made his drawings available to Garbe.

Contenting himself at Richmond with interior works, Wilson created a notable bronze-effect plaster bas-relief, completed in 1910, for the Children's Corner. It shows the boy Jesus amid foliage and angel masks, his stance recalling that of the child-angel on the memorial of twelve years before, to Canon Tinling. There is a second Gloucester reminder in the silver repoussée tabernacle door Wilson made above the new altar of the Richmond church: the central figure on this miniature door recalls the bas-relief Christ on the Canon's cope.[120] Invited by Grove, Gimson, Bainbridge Reynolds and Whall collaborated on pulpit, wrought-iron work and stained glass; Eric Gill carved the lettering on the sacristy door and triptych, and his brother MacDonald Gill executed the chancel paintings.

A single, insubstantial shadow falls across Wilson's afternoons in London, cast by the reminiscences of Arthur Grove's son. In his later years, Peter Grove insinuated that the railway provided an opening for 'a loose life in London during the week'.[121] This hardly accords with the amount of work Wilson got through in the Platt years, nor with his standing as a 'clean man whom it is a privilege to have known'.[121] While correctly recalling Prior's subletting rooms to his father, MacDonald Gill and Wilson at Hare Court, Peter Grove had drawn fanciful conclusions as to the use of the 'big room', which Arthur Grove would take over from Wilson in 1918. To be sure, with Vicarage Gate gone, it was a useful occasional business address for Wilson, and callers could arrange to see him there to discuss jewellery, teaching or sculpture commissions.[123] But its primary use, until the Society's move to Queen Square, was for meetings of the Arts and Crafts Exhibition Society, one of Wilson's most enduring commitments and on whose behalf he was leasing the space. The allusion Peter Grove makes, to his father moving into *Wilson's* big room confirms how easily its comings and goings may have been misconstrued by an impressionable young observer.

Unlike some more introverted craftsmen of the time, Henry Wilson never sought to cut himself off from the mainstream of events; with The Thatched House he achieved his ideal – a measure of insulation, rather than isolation, from the issues confronting the craftsman in modern society. In a lecture he gave during the war years, he stressed the interdependence of city and country. His need for both is manifest in his own trenchant words:

> *The country is for food, for spirit, mind and body. The city is for stimulus, conference and market. Each is the complement of the other. The city is indispensable but in the country ... the craftsman may achieve ... the peace and self-recreation indispensable to creative work.*[124]

CHAPTER FIVE

FOCUS ON THE METALWORKING ARTS

If Wilson's tenancy of Vicarage Gate and his brief partnership with Alexander Fisher were early steps in his withdrawal from professional architecture, his move to Kent as the new century began set the seal on his commitment to the metalworking arts. From the time of Brithdir it was clear that his interests in architecture and metalwork were developing side by side, their impulses feeding into and strengthening one another. In 1896, while he was still working to complete Sedding's unfinished commissions, an article by Fred Miller about contemporary art metalworkers appeared in the *Art Journal*, placing Wilson firmly among the most notable.[1] Three years later, the art critic of the *New York Sun* seized on the apparent duality of his career, marvelling at the fact that this 'leading architect' yet finds time to produce 'these brooches, rings and necklaces'.[2]

Though we may now see the two sides of his career as inextricable, the focus on metalwork was envisaged by Wilson, at least initially, as a temporary excursion, designed to strengthen his creative powers as a whole before he made a homecoming to architecture. As he said, 'the fineness of touch, the habits of precision and decision and the coordination of mind and hand implicit in fine metalworking make the acquisition of the more spacious arts an easy matter'.[3]

In the end Wilson never did make that return journey, and 1908 found him insisting that he 'would rather be known as a goldsmith than as anything else in the world'.[4] Ralph Cram seemed to understand this change in his English colleague, noting in that year that despite having produced 'several unearthly and curiously emotional designs', architecture was for him 'largely a thing of the past'.[5]

That 'curiously emotional' quality, though, took on new life in Wilson's metalwork and jewellery. Like his architectural work, these designs are typefied by their free symbolism and intensely creative use of materials and techniques. Semi-precious gems, smoothly rounded or cabuchon-cut to enhance what he called their 'mysterious, magical quality, [their] inner lustre of liquid light',[6] are made to convey powerful, atavistic messages. Trees, vines, rose bushes and living creatures, set within borders of enamel chevrons or chequerwork, encapsulate a knowledge, a recognition, of the throbbing energy of the natural world. Through their technical virtuosity, there breathes an irrepressible spontaneity, recreating nature in silver and allied materials in a way both fresh and familiar. Elements may unite with an almost ecclesiastical preciousness: in the 1905 gold pendant and chain Wilson sold through the Artificers' Guild in Maddox Street,[7] a cross-shape is formed by an oval opal with cabochon emeralds and pearls on each side. Below it, a cast gold plaque, with green enamel columns and three opals set in its arched top, has an angel holding a dove; on the reverse gleams a Tudor rose (Plates 54-55).

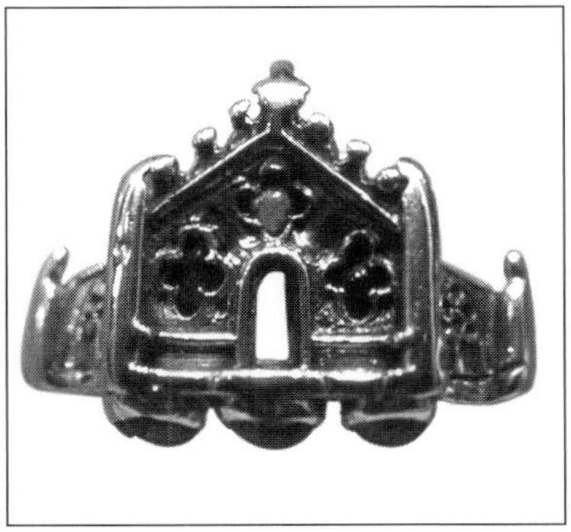

Victoria & Albert Museum

Figure 54. Wedding ring: made by Henry Wilson for W.R. Lethaby, gold with gemstones, 1901.

Furthermore, at a scale at which *natural* forms might be thought to have exclusive rights, influences from the world of architecture are omnipresent. These are seen explicitly in the gold wedding ring (Fig. 54) he made for William Lethaby, the design of which the two of them probably devised together, where instead of a simple stone-setting we find a miniature ecclesiastical façade enriched with amethyst, emerald, sapphire and rubies.[8] Elsewhere, the unembellished composition of a piece, its instinct for shape, space and effect, contains the inherent architectural feeling.

The careful logic Wilson applied to his transition into metalworking – as a preparation for, or renewal of, architecture – differed markedly from the less resolute, even accidental, paths taken by some fellow craftsmen. Alexander Fisher, for example, had followed in his father's footsteps as an enameller on pottery, only later turning his hand to enamelling on metal and in time to metalworking itself, while another contemporary, Nelson Dawson, had discovered by trial and error via architecture, then painting in watercolours, his skills in metalwork. His training in architecture meant that his metalwork often invoked architectural forms, leaving his enamels – the technique taught him by Fisher – to exploit imagery from nature. But his work lacked the symbolic and formal complexities of Wilson's, and he concentrated on making desireable objects for retail rather than to commission: jewellery, jewel boxes, candlesticks and doorplates, to be sold through the Artificers' Guild, which he set up with Edward Spenser in 1901.

Some similarities might be seen in the backgrounds of Wilson and Bainbridge Reynolds, both having their grounding in ecclesiastical architecture; Reynolds had been articled to J.P. Seddon, then worked for Street in his last years. But while Wilson explored the conceptual impulses shared by architecture and metalwork, the connection Reynolds made was more literal: alongside his architecture he focused on architectural metalwork – typically, geometrical and Gothic designs for gates and railings made in his own workshops and forges.

If there is a parallel for Wilson's progression from architecture to metalwork, it is the road taken by Charles Robert Ashbee. Each started off articled to a leading architect (in Ashbee's case, G.F. Bodley), yet both ended up playing a crucial role within the aesthetic and social reappraisal that accompanied the craft revival. Founded with four members in 1888, Ashbee's Guild of Handicraft had its first premises in Commercial Street, Whitechapel, before moving briefly in 1901 to the Mile End Road. Its membership concentrated mainly on cabinet making, fine metalwork and jewellery. Silverwork was where Ashbee's own designs were at their most distinctive, with their instantly recognisable signature features: multi-strand wire handles, dully polished surfaces, sparely used semi-precious stones. The patterns in his designs grew from natural forms, especially carnations or roses, or from abstract shapes suggested by the ductility of the metal itself. Ashbee agreed with Wilson on the conditions needed to produce good craft and design: only small workshops could guarantee silverwork and jewellery of 'feeling and character'.[9] Wilson admired the guild socialism the group was pursuing in making its dramatic move from the East End to the Cotswolds in 1902 – the very year he himself left London to establish his smaller, more personal enterprise in Kent.

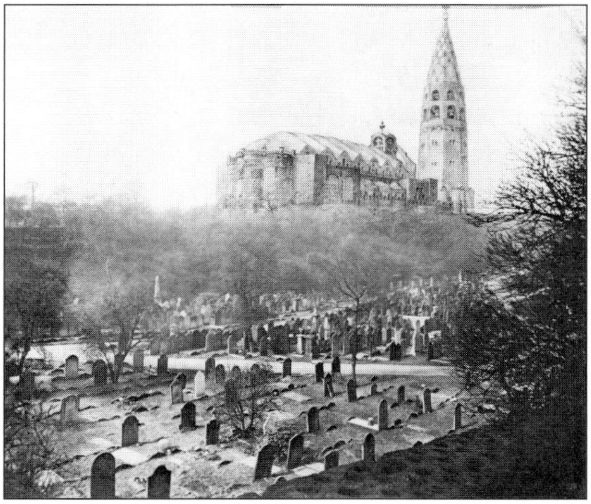

Victoria & Albert Museum

Figure 55. Anglican Cathedral, Liverpool: competition entry, photomontage with pencil rendering, 1902.

Wilson's architectural practice only just survived into the 1900s: the private chapel of 1901 at Walmsgate was his last actual commission to build. But what followed Walmsgate a year later proved to be one of the most radical proposals of early-twentieth century British architecture, even if it was unexecuted and largely unappreciated at the time. The design team he was leading jointly with Lethaby submitted, under Wilson's name, a daring entry for Liverpool's Anglican cathedral (Fig. 55). The team – Robert Weir Schultz, Troup, Halsey Ricardo, Christopher Whall and the sculptor

Stirling Lee – represented the leading edge of Arts and Crafts conviction, and their design fully answered a brief which required the creation of spacious, spiritual grandeur.

What was revolutionary about the team's thinking was the unprecedented material chosen for the carcass of the building and its expressive forms – concrete – in which by now both Wilson and Lethaby had practical experience. In reality, their unconventional proposal had little hope of success: as well as being the most innovative, it was also the most misunderstood of all the entries. Its adventurous free design was infused with subtle symbols and allusions to Byzantine forms, while its 'poured' qualities confidently proclaimed its concrete identity. Lethaby, who was responsible for the structural idea, was convinced, following Brockhampton, that concrete was the material for the new century. Nine years after the Liverpool competition he was still publicly advocating concrete, urging that 'we ... sweep away our fear that it is an inartistic material and boldly build ... a museum or a cathedral, wide and simple and amply lighted.'[10] In 1913, as if in response, a museum, or more accurately, a great exhibition hall, appeared in Max Berg's Century Hall at Breslau, its broad curves and spaces and continuous clerestory bands relishing concrete as a building material.

According to Weir Schultz, the other Byzantinist in the group, they had 'many jolly meetings and arguments'[11] while working on their startling design. Seen now, its dynamism generates a sense of contained strength, a quality that Wilson had discerned in relation to Sedding's church at Truro, which to him evoked a poised, crouching animal. In the Liverpool design, an undulating roof enclosing deep nave vaults seems to ripple with waves captured in solid form, to create an extraordinary 'ridge and furrow surface'.[11] Intricate, surging tracery fills the rounded window bays of nave and apse. The squat, square West gable bellcote contrasts with the tall, conical tower marking the climax of the building, and this most suggests the hand of Henry Wilson with his predilection for the manipulation of scale.

The 'chimney-like'[12] octagon belfry-tower with its two high tiers of arches, its bells visible within, recalls the Byzantine studies Lethaby and Weir Schultz made in the 1890s. But these arches, both here and inside the nave, also echo features of Wilson's Highgate and Ealing designs, while with typical cross-disciplinary ease, the double row of arcading on the base of his Gloucester chalice has been reborn in architectural form. The soaring spire with its ascending series of overlapping arches resounds with indefinable mythic suggestions, yet remains decisively modern in impact. Just how modern it would have seemed is implicit in the lines of the grand pinnacle of William van Alen's Chrysler Building of 1930, though this *tour de force* of Jazz Age architecture is clad in silvery Nirosta metal and designed to be enhanced, in a way that Wilson would surely have approved, with built-in floodlighting.

The model and plans for their cathedral were exhibited alongside the other competitors' designs at the Walker Art Gallery, Liverpool, in July 1902. Given the unusual and challenging forms chosen by the Wilson/Lethaby team, the proposal was condemned as austere and eccentric by reviewers and judges alike.

> *Some attempt should be made to treat the exterior in a more decorative manner. The sketch of the tower looks almost like a joke,*[13]

pronounced *The Builder*'s correspondent, insensitive to the heroic endeavour to find, *de novo*, a structural aesthetic appropriate to the new material. While the reviewer for the *Building News* was by turns facetious and disparaging.

> *The design ... by six well-known men who belong to an advanced school is remarkable ... the exterior [shows] a pointed, tapering tower, ludicrously suggesting ... a huge cigar, or torpedo set on end.*[14]

The overall effect he judged to be 'lumpy'; maybe, but there was enough skill within the team to have ironed out any such anomalies in execution. Some of the other entries, like Pite's massive

Byzantine design or Mackintosh's sweeping free Gothic proposal, were indeed inventive, but only that of Wilson and his colleagues was positively experimental. The judge appointed to evaluate the entries was the eminent senior Goth G.F. Bodley; his assistant Richard Norman Shaw (Lethaby's and Schultz's old master) at least had a progressive interest in steel frames and fireproof structures. It is understandable that Bodley should have been overwhelmed by Giles Gilbert Scott's ambitious and fluent essay in fourteenth-century Gothic to be built in red Woolston sandstone – with its lofty twin towers (reduced to one after Bodley's death) and 2,500-person capacity. More remarkable was the post-verdict discovery that the twenty-two year old Scott had yet to complete his training under Temple Moore. Consequently, Bodley himself was appointed to work alongside the inexperienced winner, supervising the setting-out and construction of the first part, the Lady Chapel.[15]

The indifference, even hostility, that met the concrete cathedral proposed by the Wilson/Lethaby team effectively clinched the two men's new career directions, Wilson gravitating towards the crafts, especially silverwork and jewellery, and Lethaby towards teaching and design theory. Wilson was exasperated, but not surprised, at the rejection of so brave and original an architectural proposal – though in any case his course was set. In fact, in the year of the Liverpool competition, Wilson completed two of his most important metalwork commissions – the Lady Altar at St. Bartholomew's, Brighton and an alms dish for St. John's, Cirencester (Plate 56) – as well as taking a prestigious new one from the Birmingham Constitutional Club for a ceremonial casket to be presented to the town's famous son, the Liberal statesman Joseph Chamberlain. Most significantly, The Thatched House, with its ample workshop facilities, was completed, and Wilson's book, *Silverwork and Jewellery*, was with the publisher.

The volume was one of a series of Handbooks on the Artistic Crafts produced under the general editorship of W.R. Lethaby, who outlined in a common preface their three aims – to provide a guide to good workmanship, to emphasise that design and craftsmanship are inseparable, and to present artistic craft as an occupation in which every diligent workman could earn a reasonable livelihood. The titles and authors aimed to embrace the whole gamut of craft skills: *Writing and Illuminating* by Edward Johnston, *Bookbinding* by Douglas Cockerell, *Woodblock Printing* by Frank Morley Fletcher, *Woodcarving* by George Jack, *Embroidery and Tapestry Weaving* by Mrs. Grace Christie, *Stained Glass Work* by Christopher Whall, *Dress Design* by Talbot Hughes, *Heraldry for Craftsmen and Designers* by William St. John Hope. Wilson's own volume, its individual Preface both personal and pragmatic, would prove to be one of the most influential. It bore out Lethaby's claims for the series as a whole, and provided the best possible guide, plain and direct, to the twin crafts of its title.

> *The worst fault of such a text-book ... would be vagueness. I have attempted to avoid this by describing ... each process from beginning to end ... round diagrams inserted in the text.*[16]

Over and above the technical aspects, Wilson tackles the enigmatic theme of creativity. This he does in a confidence-building and, paradoxically, *practical* way. Without presuming to prescribe formulae, he successfully describes how elusive springs of inspiration might be stimulated, activated and materially interpreted.

While acknowledging the difficulties implicit in trying to encapsulate such 'limitless'[17] arts as silverwork and jewellery between two covers, he confesses himself quite satisfied, despite inevitable restrictions of space, with the book as a straightforward guide to techniques and starting points. It was not his aim to dictate actual designs, only to describe the methods 'which had given the best results'[18] in his own workshop; for 'if the worker has any imagination – few are really without it – then he will find the way for himself'.[19]

He was adamant that self-expression must be distinguished from self-indulgence. Workers would only stunt their 'native powers'[20] if they succumbed to arrogance or pretentiousness. Careful workmanship and humility of approach were the only legitimate routes to the priceless quality of individuality:

> *If a student will study methods, materials and natural forms, feed his imagination on old work, and attend faithfully to his instincts, his personality can safely be left to attend to itself.*[21]

The statement forms the basis of Wilson's message to his readers, and serves to highlight the five focal points around which the book, and Wilson's lifelong design philosophy, was organised: methods, materials, nature, tradition and instinct.

In a handbook intended, and still used, as a manual for working craftsmen, the description of methods predominates: in Chapter IX, for example, Wilson describes in lucid terms and conversational tone how to set about making a spoon:

> *First take a piece of silver say 10 gauge, mark on it the shape of the bowl (fig. 30) – avoid the ugly modern shapes – and beat it with a boxwood mallet into a suitable hollow in the beating block.... You may find that as the metal extends it will crack at the edge, if so file away the crack with a triangular file; this prevents the crack from spreading.*[22]

With the same calm attention to detail, and unfailingly preempting the most common queries, Wilson explains the making of rings, brooches, cups, pendants, hair ornaments, bracelets and candlesticks. All the basic hand-metalworking techniques, polishing, soldering, chasing and repoussé, are methodically laid out; the mechanical processes of die-stamping and electro-plating are omitted altogether on the grounds that they have 'too little connection with art to be considered'.[23] Towards the end of the book a section is devoted to Practical Recipes: 'cement for engravers', 'good solder for gold'; and to avoid any possible confusion, Wilson provides a glossary of terms from 'alloy' and 'annealing' to 'riffle' and 'tang'.

Such clear instructions must have furnished timely assistance to the growing number of technically illiterate artist-jewellers in Britain at the turn of the twentieth century. The period might well be characterised as that of the gifted amateur, condemned, without the specialised training Continental workmen were required to undergo, to fall short of the standards of workmanship achieved by commercial firms such as Hennell's, Hancock's, Mappin & Webb, Garrard's or Elkington's. An *Art Journal* critic reviewing the 1901 International Exhibition in Glasgow pointed an acerbic finger at the failings of such amateurs: 'it is a pity that so many of these modern craftsmen have so much to learn from the trade jewellers they look down on ... .'[24]

Shining through his descriptions of metalworkers' methods is Wilson's faith in the special 'educational value of process'.[25] The crucial role he ascribed it is lent weight by the childhood memories of his daughter, Pernel:

> *He was a great believer in ... training the mind by means of training the hands from an early age, and we were all expected to do a daily stint in the jeweller's workshop. He insisted on our making our own designs and carrying them out. Naturally he would always help if we got into difficulties, but however arduous the work we had to carry it out ourselves.*[26]

Her sister Dione was a competent silversmith as a girl; Lady Collet of Kemsing was pleased to own two silver spoons she made for her.[27]

Along with its emphasis on craft dexterity, the inspirational value of materials themselves is emphasised in Wilson's handbook. He devotes a whole chapter to discussing the best suppliers from which to obtain silver, gold, tin, brass, borax, pitch, acid – all the materials the fine metalworker needs – and with disarming directness, shares privileged tricks of the trade, recommending a tea strainer for applying powdered enamel, stale beer for polishing repoussé work, horseradish for colouring bronze, and suet, well-kneaded with fine wood ash, for holding gems steady during polishing. Always his tone is unaffected and to the point:

> *A pound or two of best boxwood sawdust will be wanted and kept in an ordinary biscuit box. It is used for drying the work after washing ... .*[28]

In the value it set on careful technique and thoughtful use of materials, *Silverwork and Jewellery* reinforced the artistic mood of the times, one which Wilson himself had a strong hand in creating, and which was correctly summed up by the artist and critic Aymer Vallance in 1901 when he noted that the jewellery of the last 'ten or fifteen years' had represented a concerted movement, many pieces sharing a distinct 'family likeness'.[29] Emphasising meaning before status, and individuality before convention, Wilson consistently advocated the use of semi-precious gems, simply shaped and polished, instead of more flashy and expensive types, cut with 'infinite ingenuity and intolerable hideousness',[30] into regular, geometrical facets. Freed from the inhibitions imposed by precious stones, inventive jewellers of the Arts and Crafts and Art Nouveau styles were using moonstones, opals, peridots, garnets, chrysophrase and turquoise, gems which in conventional commercial terms were unremarkable.

A gold necklace Wilson made around 1905, and chosen by him to illustrate the second edition of *Silverwork and Jewellery*, is alive with such gems (Plate 40). Suspended from a square gold-wire boss studded with blister pearls and cabuchon emeralds, the central medallion is a gold angel with wings enamelled red (Fig. 56), loosely framed in a double wreath of gold vines set with emeralds, opal, blister pearls and sapphire, from which hangs a large island-like drop opal. In the decorated part of the chain, curved oblong opals, each framed in gold, alternate with pearl and emerald bosses, from two of which, balancing the red-winged angel, hang small vine wreaths encircling a wild baroque pearl. These accents, along with the small gold spurs on the settings of the oblong chain-opals, emphasise the natural 'radial lines'[31] he recommends for necklaces. Leading up to the clasp, the chain

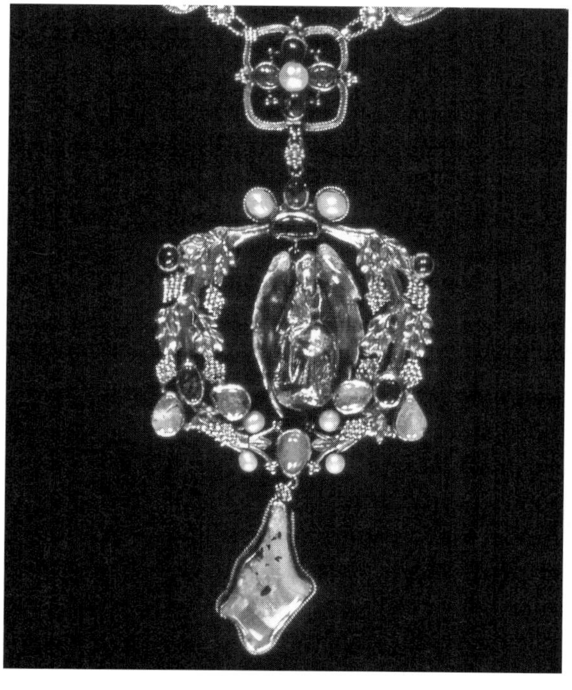

Private Collection

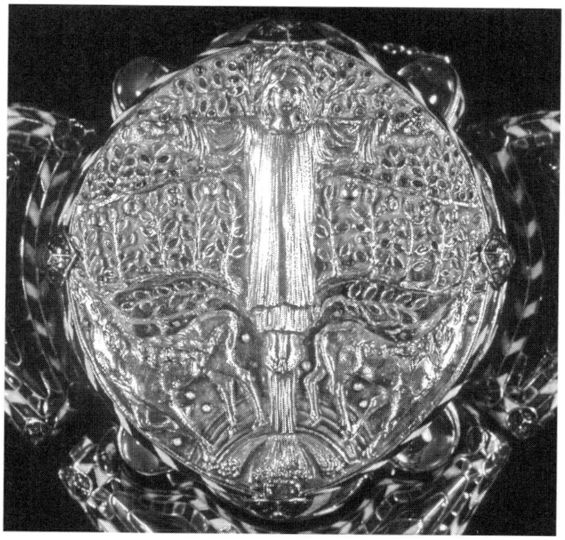

Private Collection

Figure 56. (left) Gold enamel necklace, chosen as an illustration in *Silverwork and Jewellery (2nd ed.)*, c.1905.

Figure 57. (above) Gold enamel morse, central repoussé medallion with Christ against the Tree of Life, 1910.

is of gold and plain, though made specifically for the piece; in Wilson's opinion, shop-made chains were best avoided, since 'they spoil the effect of the most carefully devised necklace. The way to secure a good chain is to coil the links yourself....'[32]

These jewels were for *wearing* – the whole point, as far as Wilson was concerned. The look was one thing; but the jewel's flexibility, its being comfortable in use, was paramount. Nowhere is Wilson's care for such articulation better demonstrated than in a morse – the heavy clasp of an ecclesiastical cope – made by him in 1910 (Plate 41). Its four display elements, three triangles around a central medallion, are carefully linked together so as to allow the wearer ease of movement. Each triangular portion bears a gold openwork relief of a rose tree, against a field of pale green enamel edged with rows of green and blue zigzags, mauve and green chequerwork, and white and green chevrons. A large oval moonstone bordered in green and white enamel enriches the three outermost points. At the centre of the morse – secured by two fine gold pins and chains to its own backing frame, which itself is set with moonstones and enamelled with holly berries and leaves – is a detachable oval repoussé medallion (Fig. 57), the climax of Wilson's art in this piece. Christ, open-armed before a pleached and budding Tree of Life, is flanked by springing harts, emblems of spiritual fervour, on an enamelled lawn fringed by the waters of Paradise. The invention and interplay here of miniature geometrical forms – favoured motifs in his decorative vocabulary – comprised a satisfying part of his skill to be passed on to readers of his book:

> *Lozenges, zigzags, chevrons – any one of these elementary forms, repeated rhythmically, will produce the pleasantest effect.*[33]

Wilson's disdain for the trade jewellers' use of expensive gems had its basis in aesthetic and creative considerations. It was all too easy to use valuable stones as a 'substitute for design' rather than as a 'medium of expression',[34] which accounts for why the sole reference to diamonds in *Silverwork and Jewellery* is to their dust, a cutting medium in engraving. His lavish use of diamonds in the 5' tall, silver-plated Lumley Memorial cross for Exeter Cathedral, commissioned in 1923 (together with a 12" replica, locked away except for special days), in memory of Mary Lumley by her husband Frederick and her brother Lord Mamhead, might seem out of character. Here, though, it was the clients' express wish that Wilson incorporate specific gemstones which belonged to Mrs. Lumley's estate. While the figure of Christ standing beneath a silver canopy at the centre of the cross replicates Clerkenwell's Eyre Memorial, the arms of the cross terminate in enamelled bosses, their centres originally set with large cut diamonds on the front, and cabuchon amethysts on the reverse.

Wilson had always suspected the pecuniary appeal of spectacular autonomous gems. The completed cross stood on the High Altar of the Cathedral until its theft one July night in 1950; when it was discovered the next day dumped in a field beside the Homerton road, it was precisely those fine diamonds that were missing. The rescued cross, minus diamonds, was given a new home on the rood beam of nearby Kenton church, opposite Powderham Castle.

Wilson's use of the rich, though not costly, medium of enamel is thoroughly discussed in *Silverwork and Jewellery*. He describes five types, including champlevé (for which the precious metal ground is indented to receive the enamel), limoges (enamel pictures 'painted' onto a copper plaque using powdered colours on a gum base), and intaglio (where a design is carved in a shallow 'pit' in the metal, then coated with enamel).

The cloisonné technique (Wilson's own favourite) is introduced to his readers in simple terms: a cloisonné enamel brooch might typically be made by attaching a gold wire rim around a 22 carat domed base, a linear design of flattened gold wire soldered within this rim, and the 'cloisons' between filled with enamel colours. At the other extreme of expertise stands a gold buckle made by Wilson at Platt just after the workshops opened (Plate 38); this is a masterwork of the technique, elevating it to the height of accomplishment.

The buckle is in two matching halves, each centred on a triple-tiered mount presenting a cabuchon sapphire. Each generous blue stone is secured in a black and white chequered cloisonné annule set on a circlet of gold vines, which in turn sits on a green cloisonné wreath of holly. Surrounding each sapphire, five large pearls thrust forward in cylindrical blue enamel pods held in place by red cloisonné fronds, which curl close around the pearls, dynamically heightening the three-dimensional, sculptural energy of the piece. From beneath each sapphire, growing into the spaces between the pearls, unfold five speckled pale green cloisonné leaves, gold-veined with cloison wires and tipped with cabuchon emeralds. No detail has been neglected, and the effect, intensified by the multiplicity of invention, is of a glimmering depth and sculptural force seemingly beyond the range of jewellery. But, as if to cap his own exercise in virtuosity, Wilson has a further trick in reserve: by providing one half of the buckle with a concealed gem-studded loop, he allows it an independent existence as a pendant (Plate 39).

In his resumé of enamelling, Wilson left plique-à-jour, the most elusive method of all, until last. Like miniature stained glass windows, this transparent variant derives its strength from an invisible 'network' of metal within the thickness of the enamel. Such an intricate technique was suitable only for a very limited range of pieces, like tiaras, which would allow the 'peep of day' to shine through them. It was more popular among the French Art Nouveau designers like Lalique and Eugène Feuillâtre than with English jewellers, but the number who had acquired the enormous technical proficiency or confidence to carry it off was strictly limited. Wilson was one of the élite, but even he found few opportunities to justify its use. Nevertheless, a gold cloak clasp he made in the early Thatched House years is a breathtaking example of the technique (Plate 42).

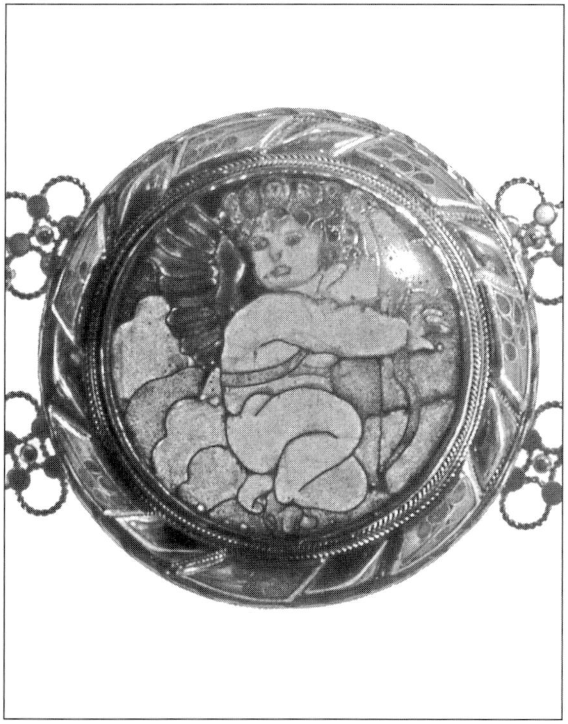

Private Collection

Figure 58. Plique-à-jour medallion at centre of gold cloak clasp, Cupid with bow and clouds, early 1900s.

Suspended in space, between the two edges of a cloak, the clasp's central plique-à-jour medallion was calculated to occupy an open position, its background constantly changing with the wearer's movement. Cupid kneels amongst billowing clouds, turning as he prepares to release his arrow (Fig. 58). A pair of fine gold chains link this scene, whose importance is emphasised by the depth of its frame, to two smaller satellite roundels, one depicting a red rose, one a white, perhaps conjuring up the Wars of the Roses but certainly making Cupid the conduit between opposites. Each rose roundel is linked in turn to a short vertical crystal rod, itself encircled with green cloisonné bands and tipped with semi-precious gems, to be attached to the cloak-edges. These green bands alone were enough to astonish Wilson's friend and colleague, James Cromar Watt, who had organised the Edinburgh exhibition to which Wilson submitted this piece in 1906: his letter of receipt marvelled at how Wilson had made the bands 'fit so closely round the crystal' that they looked 'as if they were flexible!'[35] As a fellow silversmith and leading member of the Scottish Arts and Crafts, Watt's admiration was born of a full understanding of the materials Wilson typically used, and a shared skill in fashioning them. In the same letter he jumps on a slightly unworldly streak in his friend:

But aren't you dreadful? You haven't sent the prices, so I can't insure them: consequently I daresay I shall get no sleep for fear of burglars or fire or earthquake. I wonder whether I should save first your box of enamels or my cloisonné vase?[36]

Wilson's recognition of Sedding's ability to make the tracery of windows and screens spring 'as the branch from a tree trunk' is often reflected in *Silverwork and Jewellery*. Here, freely mixing terms from nature and from craft usage, Wilson is describing how to make a hair ornament:

make twigs of thick wire … soldered together in a simple interlacing pattern. Then make a calix setting for each rose and solder it on the tip of each principle twig….[37]

In his 1896 article in the *Art Journal*, Fred Miller applauded the way 'Mr. Wilson works in the spirit of natural forms instead of adopting conventions as though they were precedents in law'. Going straight to nature as his source, Wilson advises his readers to do likewise: 'Remember always to have a bit of natural foliage near you as a guide …'.[38] Nature's translation into art must be direct, spontaneous, epitomising the organic feeling of life itself. In suggesting a nightingale as a motif for a pendant, he is recording his own observation, maybe in the garden at Platt, and his response to it.

Watch one…. Take an opera glass and find the spot most frequented by the birds…. You will never forget your first sight of the little brown-backed bird against the sky and leaves, his head thrown back in an ecstasy of song. Make as many sketches as you can, and when you get home take a piece of silver, size 8….[39]

However, the craftsman must take care to adapt nature sensitively to his requirements. Wilson's advice recalls William Morris's warning not to 'imitate' nature but to work 'the way she does',[40] naturally, within the constraints of the chosen medium.

Your studies cannot be too painstaking. But when you translate these studies into work, learn to leave out. The artist seeks forms typical of his subject and yet suitable to his material.[41]

Such judicious 'leaving out' can be seen in an enamelled silver locket Wilson made in the early 1900s (Plate 37). A 'typical' rambling rose strays with a fluency 'suitable' to its painted technique, across a square blue enamel panel, bordered with uprights of green enamel, crowned by a gable of green and white chequerwork, giving the frame the look of simple architecture. At each angle is a cabuchon emerald, while three gems – an amethyst above two emeralds – are grouped at its tip. Corresponding elements – gemstones and a rambling rose – enrich the reverse. Hinged along one of its uprights, the locket opens to reveal a bright green compartment, though the shades of the two halves are not an exact match. Rather than regarding such lack of uniformity as a flaw, chance variations like this appealed to Wilson as something natural, as 'a trace of the human touch which makes the meanest material precious'.[42] The chain of the necklace is sprinkled with individually-crafted silver lozenge beads, some with cloisonné patterns, the rest with beaded silver wire wound tightly around them.

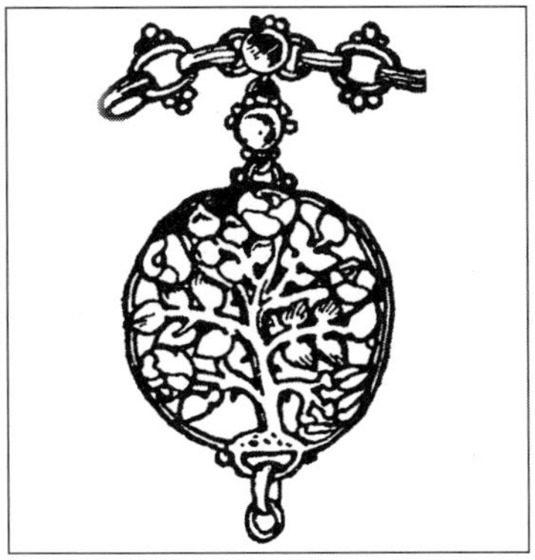

Figure 59. *Silverwork and Jewellery, Ch. XIV, Necklaces*: a design idea.

The rose reappeared in 1912, this time as a prize bloom; using all his mastery as modeller and and enameller Wilson gave it positively sculptural embodiment in a gold enamel brooch, within which he achieved one of his most vivacious combinations of colour (Plate 43). The commission came from Harry's youngest brother Edgar, who in 1904 had lost his wife to typhoid in Basra. Now, after eight years, he was embarking on a second marriage; this jewel would be his gift to his new mother-in-law (Plates 44). Its centrepiece is a full-bodied red rose, at its heart a lustrous blue moonstone, encircled by a ring of pearls for dewdrops.[43] The outer petals rest on a circlet of cream enamel, laced with white cross-bands dotted with tiny green leaves. Suspended from it are three pendants, each comprising a small crystal sphere and a larger moonstone drop set in gold, separated by gold links and tapering crystal rods, whose ends are tipped by green and white enamel bands, and capped with tiny green domes. The effect is opulent, but it is the opulence of simplicity.

The brooch was designed to invoke thoughts of home: the wedding was taking place as far from English hedgerow and rosebed as could be imagined, in Teheran, where by now Edgar's work in the shipping business had led him and where Winifred, his wife-to-be, had grown up, the daughter of the manager of the Indo-European Telegraph Company. For Edgar's wedding present to his bride, Harry made an enamelled gold pendant on a simple gold chain (Plate 45). Suspended from a round moonstone, it descends in three stages, articulated by a chain of three tiny gold roses. First an inverted crescent, a symbol of shielding and embracing, embellished with green and white patterned cloisonné enamel, and set with small cabuchon rubies; at each tip, ringed with gold, an oval chalcedony. The crescent encloses a cluster of three moonstones, and these lead down to the jewel's focal point, a chevron-edged inverted teardrop of green chalcedony, the stone of joy, a symbolic confirmation of the mood infusing the whole jewel. The couple's happy union followed two years' determined opposition from Winnie's parents, who had thought their daughter, at twenty, far too young to be married, let alone to a widower almost twice her age and with two sons. For Yvor, aged 10, and Cedric, 8, their new stepmother would in time bring two sisters: Isobel was born in 1914, Marjorie in 1917.

If nature was one source of Wilson's creativity, then – in his design philosophy as explored in *Silverwork and Jewellery* – tradition must be treated as an equally potent source, so long as, like nature, it was interpreted freely through the craftsman's own feelings and instincts. The work of the past and the old documents which enshrined it could be vital resources for the modern metalworker. In his memoirs, Ashbee described how he had learnt his metalworking skills from Cellini's sixteenth century *Treatise on Goldsmithing and Enamelling*. He had translated it himself for publication in 1898. Wilson's personal view of Cellini's art was that it was frequently meretricious and mostly over-rated, but that 'at the same time he was an amazing blackguard, which perhaps accounts for his immortality.'[44]

For him, of all the ancient descriptions of craft practice then known, the eleventh century treatise by the monk Theophilus, *On Diverse Arts*, provided the most inspiring sourcebook, and Chapter XXXIII of *Silverwork and Jewellery*, 'On old work and old methods,' is largely a discussion of the craft insights to be found in this monastic manuscript. He had first read it in Hendrie's translation, but frustrated by the scholar's misreadings of practical details, approached it afresh in the original Latin; it is in his informed translation that extracts of Theophilus's text appear in *Silverwork and Jewellery*. Wilson saw in the medieval craftsman a kindred spirit:

> *This most delightful person knew intimately what he wrote about. And he described his work as only a good workman could, who was at the same time skilled with his pen.... Nothing could be clearer or more practical than this.*[45]

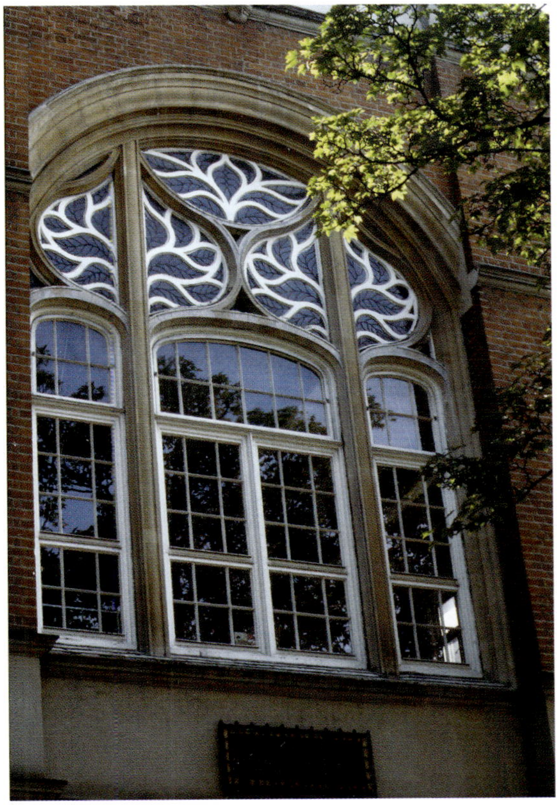

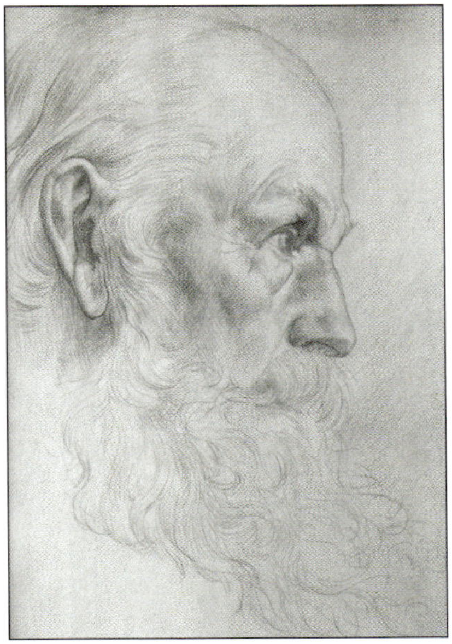

Private Collection

Plate 1. (left) H. Wilson and T.P. Figgis, Library, Ladbroke Grove, London, 1890: window to Lancaster Road.

Plate 2. (above) Wilson's pencil sketch of his father, William Henry Wilson, c. 1902.

Plate 3. (below) Chancel gates, beaten copper with enamel, c. 1890, Holy Trinity Church, Salcombe, Devon.

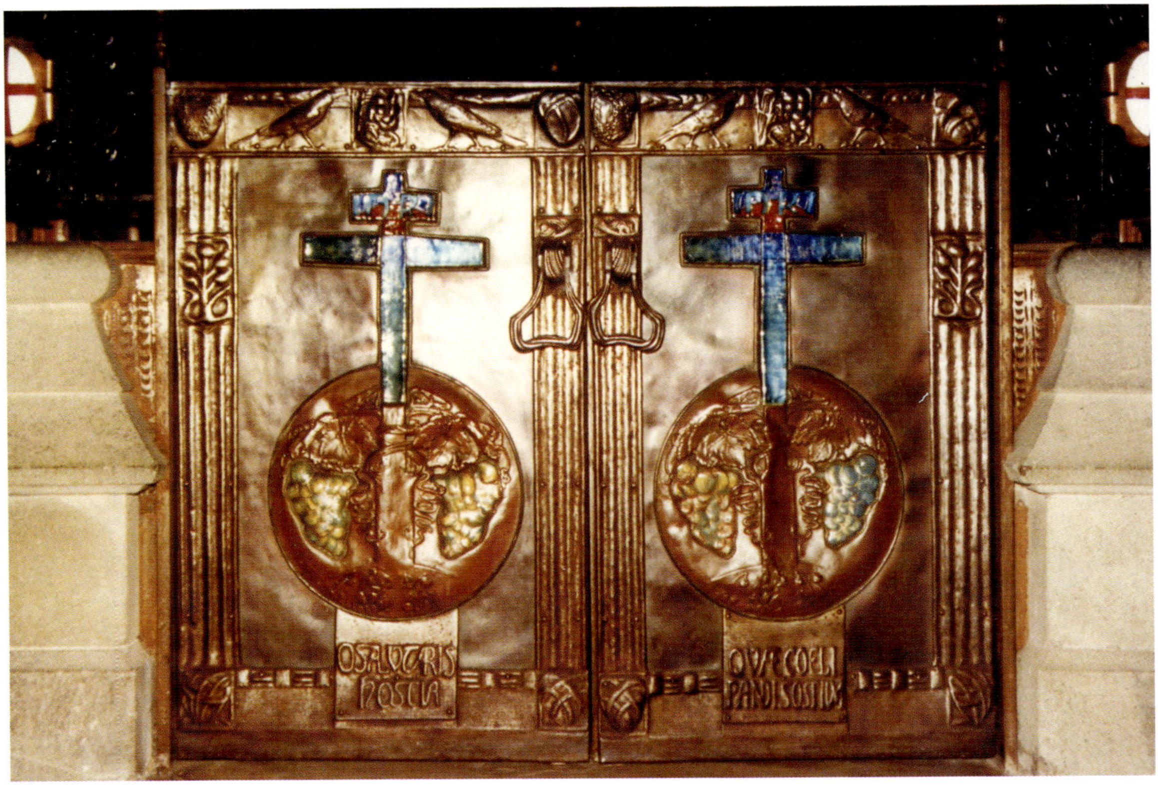

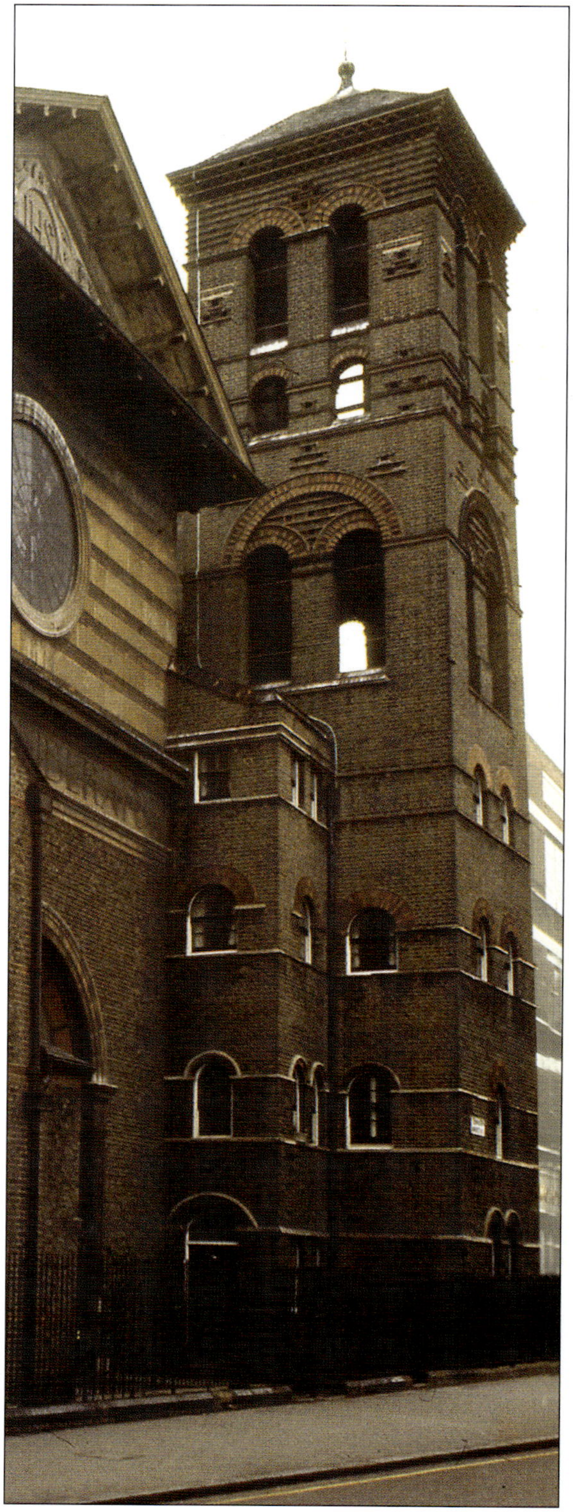

Plate 4. Henry Wilson's campanile and clergy house, added in 1904 to J.D. Sedding's Church of the Holy Redeemer, 1887-8, Exmouth Market, Clerkenwell, London.

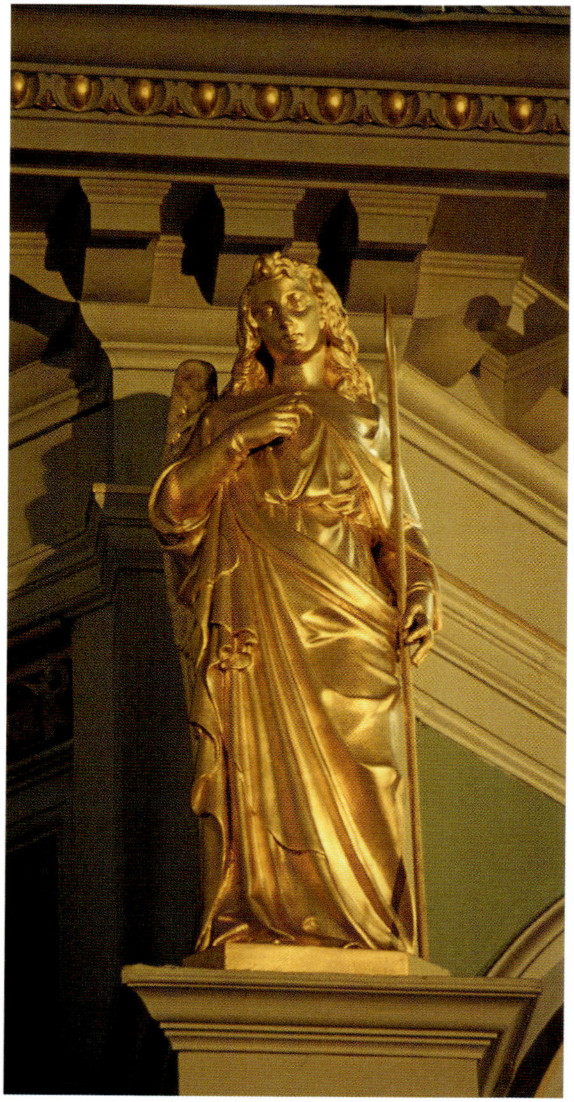

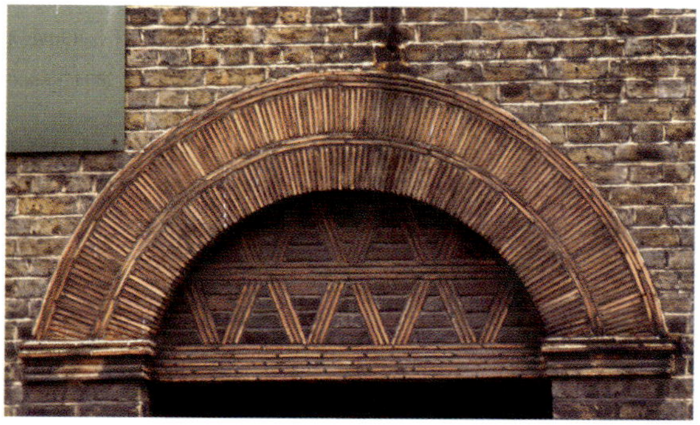

Plate 5. (top) Holy Redeemer, Clerkenwell: one of the gilded plaster angels added by Wilson to the baldacchino.

Plate 6. (above) Holy Redeemer, Clerkenwell: brick and tile detail, exterior door-head of Wilson's Parish Room, 1916.

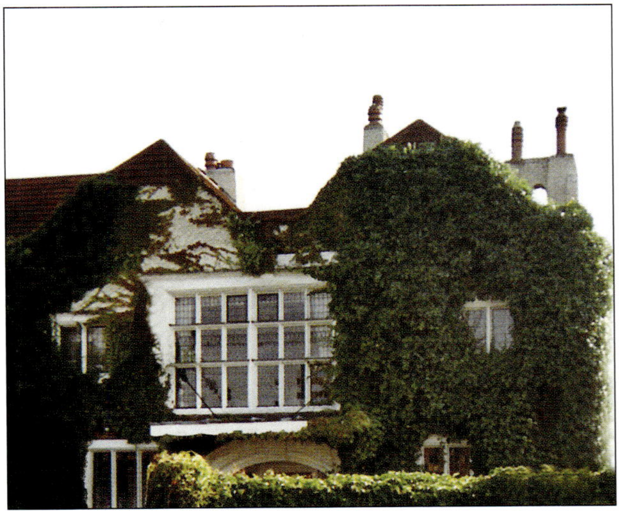

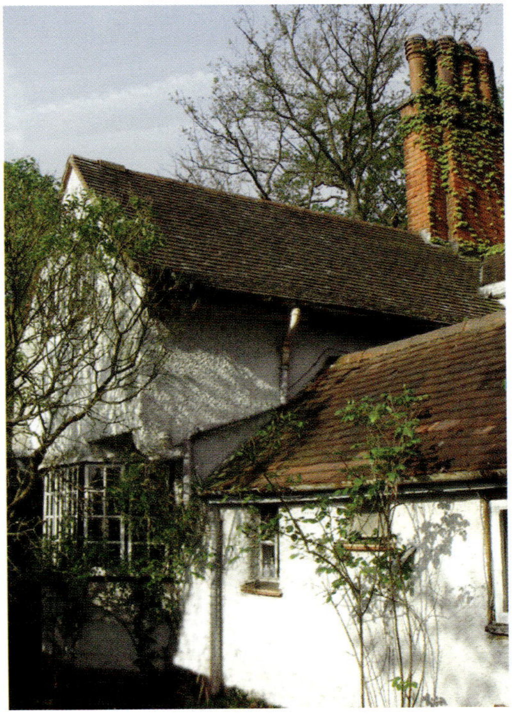

Plate 7. Maybury, Woking, Surrey: Mayhurst House, formerly named Maybury Cottage (dem.): entrance front (above), and Maybury Lodge (right), 1894.

Plate 8. (below) St. Bartholomew's Church, Sydenham: reredos and chancel decoration, carved and painted oak and plaster with silver roundels, 1903-6.

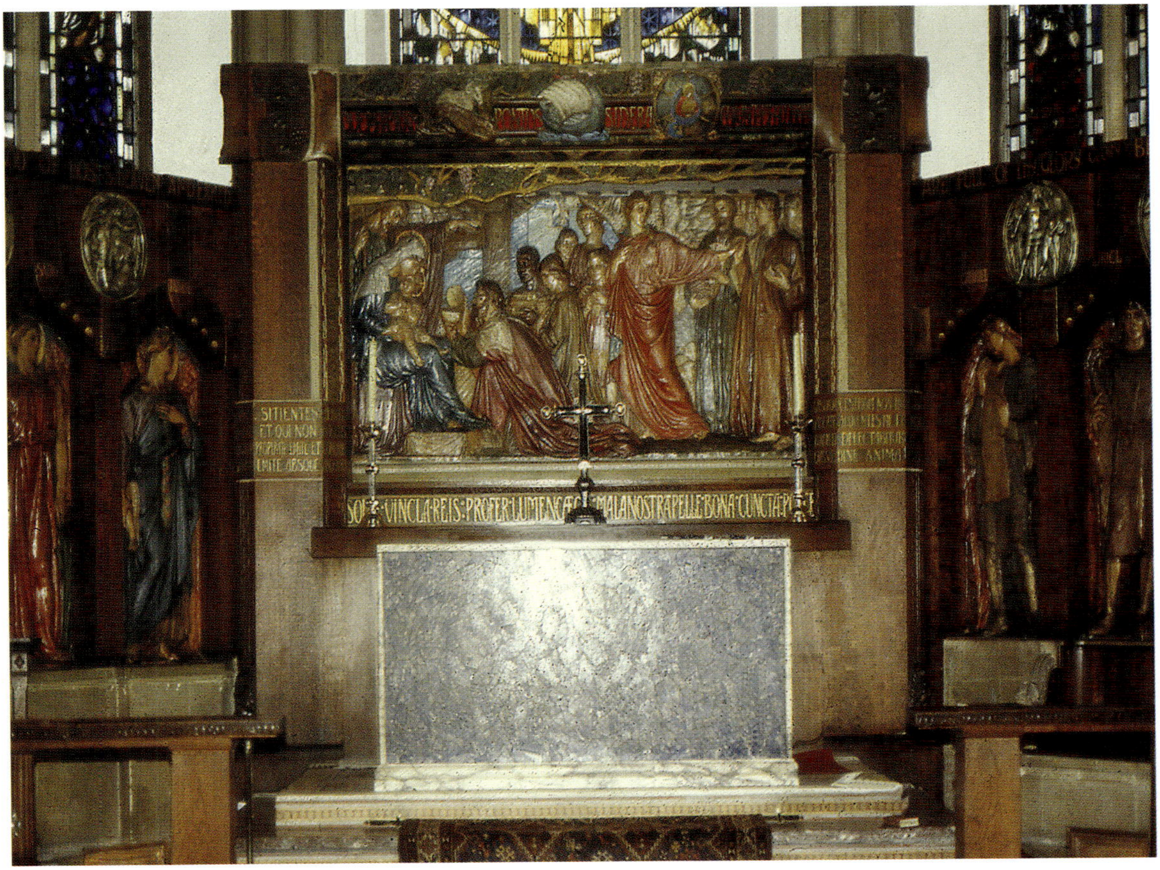

1

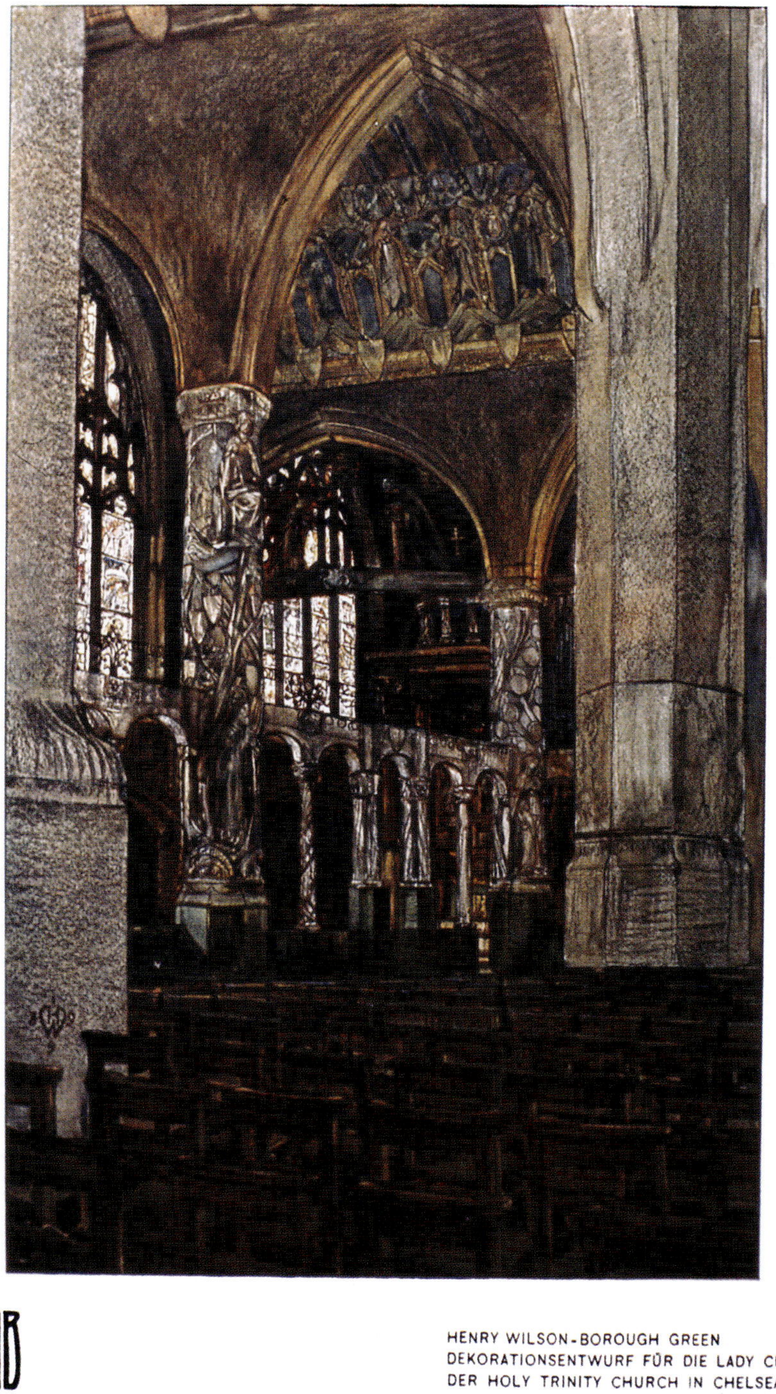

MB
1910

HENRY WILSON-BOROUGH GREEN
DEKORATIONSENTWURF FÜR DIE LADY CHAPEL
DER HOLY TRINITY CHURCH IN CHELSEA

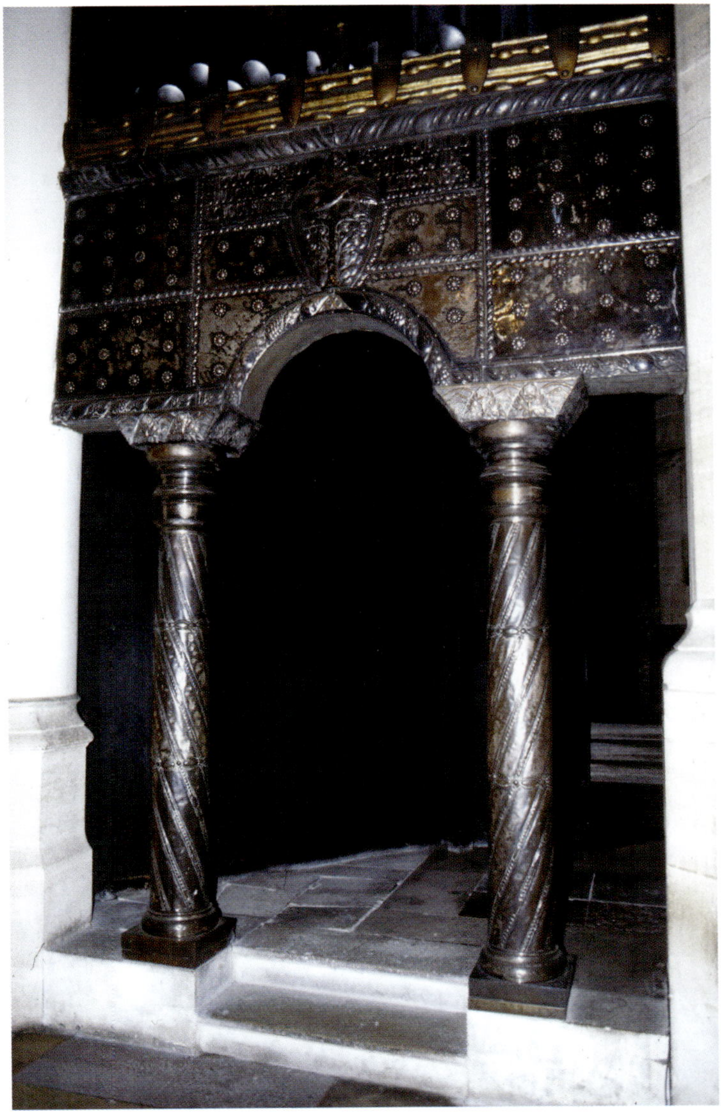

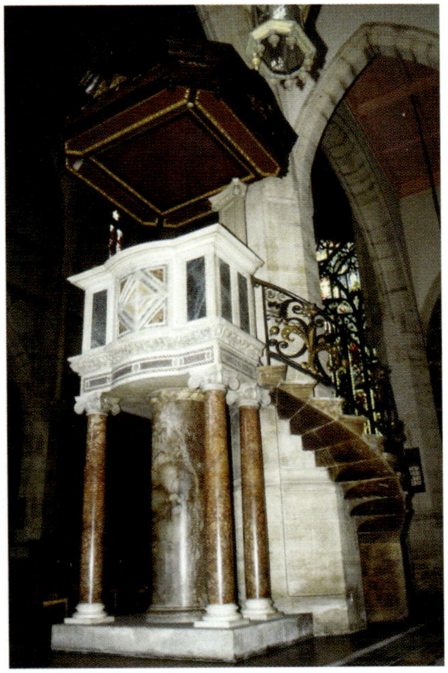

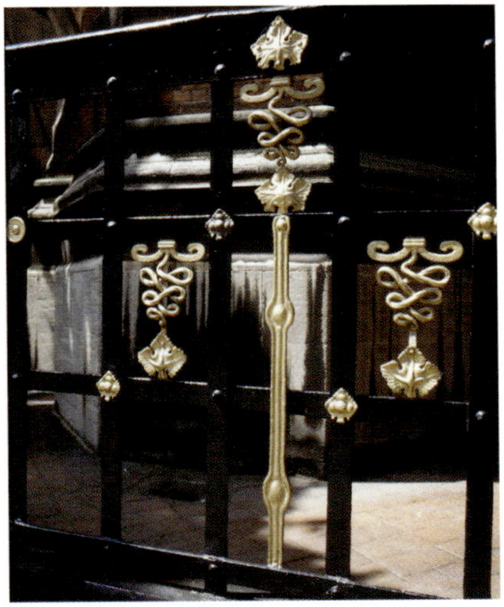

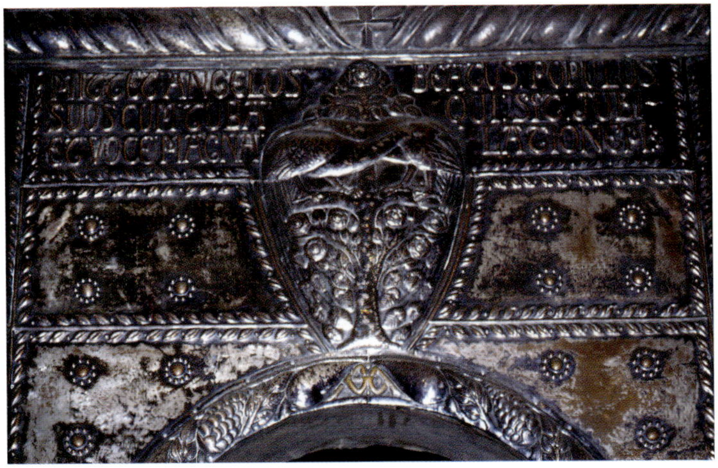

Plate 9. (opposite) Holy Trinity Church, Sloane Street: scheme for Lady Chapel, 'Moderne Bauformen', 1910.

Plate 10. (top left) Holy Trinity, Sloane Street: pillared arch, finished portion of Lady Chapel screen, 1899.

Plate 11. (left) Holy Trinity, Sloane Street, detail of screen: tree, doves and lettering.

Plate 12. (top right) Holy Trinity, Sloane Street: alabaster and marble pulpit, 1891-2.

Plate 13. (above) Holy Trinity, Sloane Street: exterior railings, 1902.

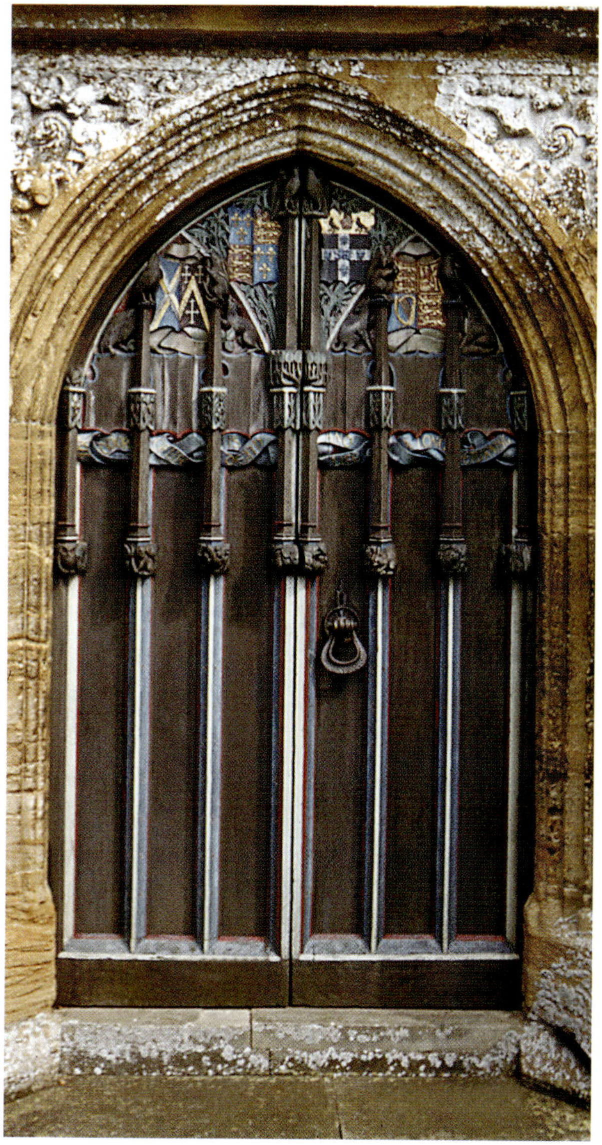

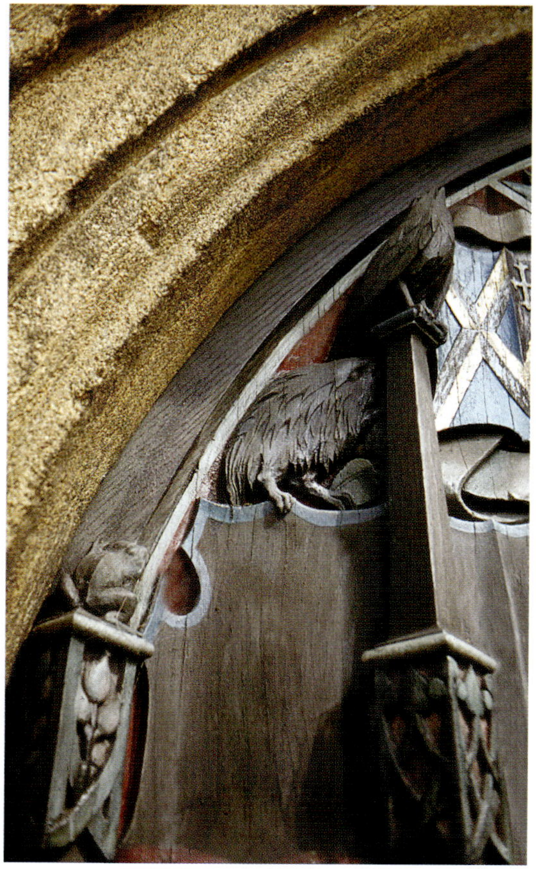

Plate 14. (left and above right) St. Mary's Church, Norton-sub-Hamdon, Somerset: tower door, carved and painted oak, 1894-5; detail: frog, hedgehog, bird.

Plate 15. (below) St. Peter's Church, Ealing, Middlesex: stone carving on chancel cornice, depicting elephant lifting log, c. 1893.

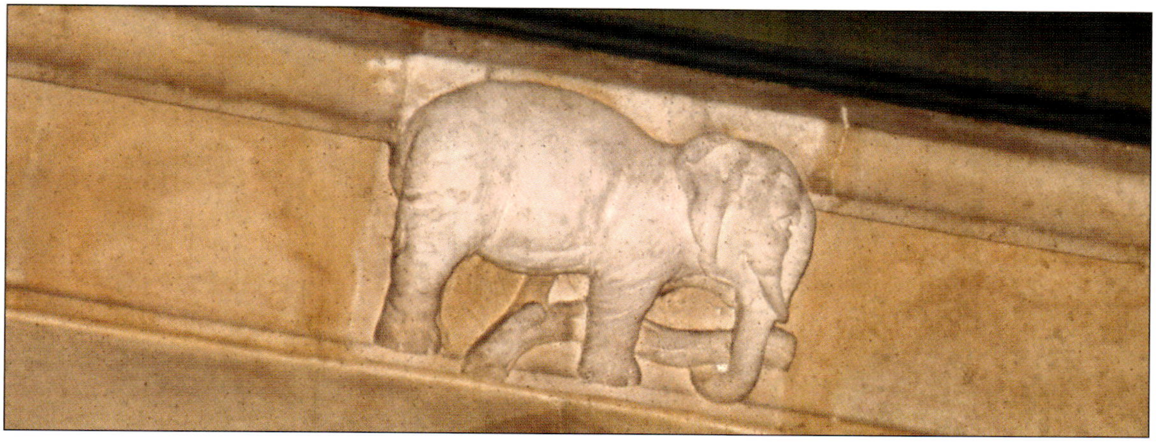

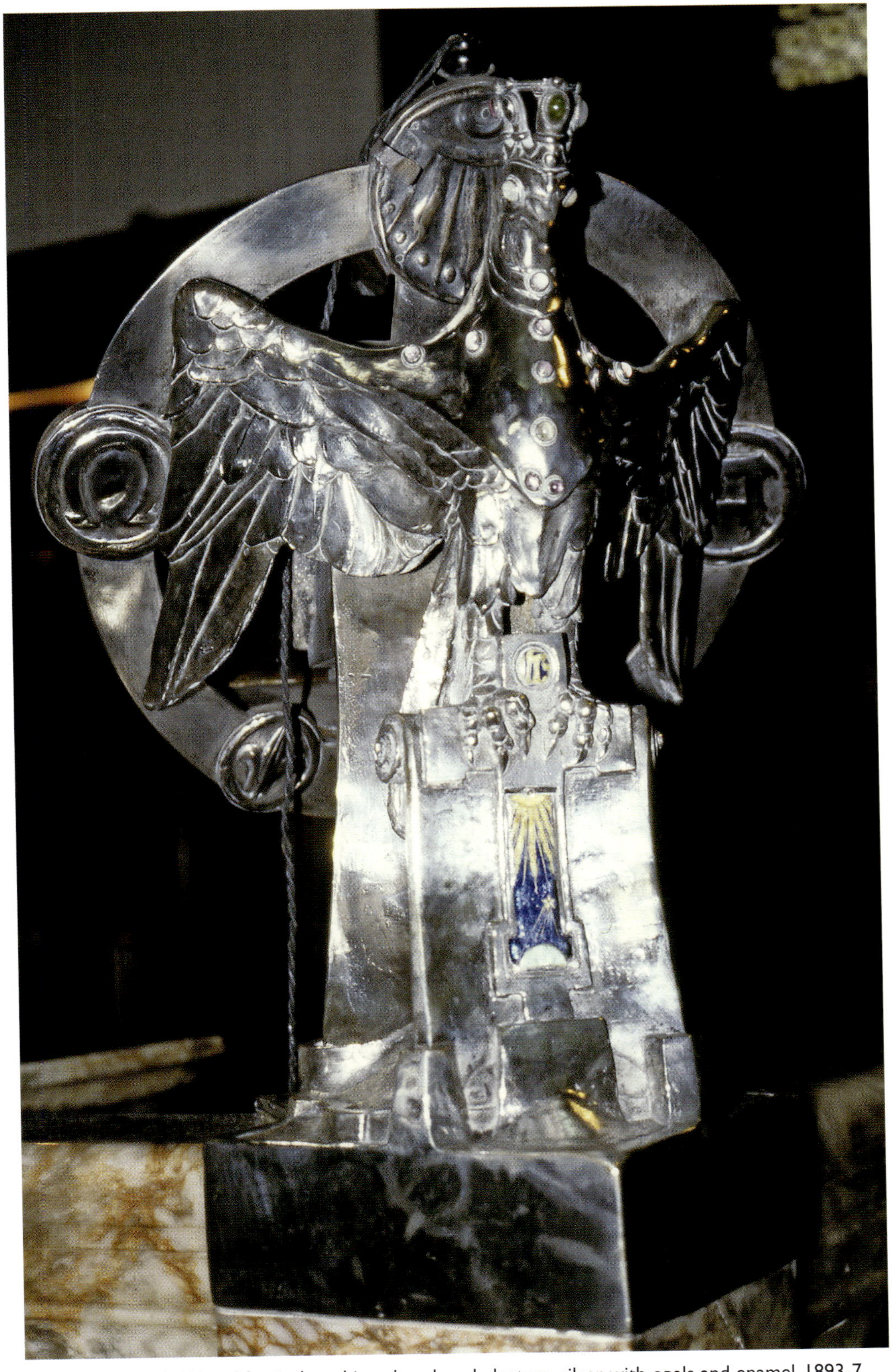

Plate 16. Welbeck Abbey, Nottinghamshire, chapel: eagle lectern, silver with opals and enamel, 1893-7.

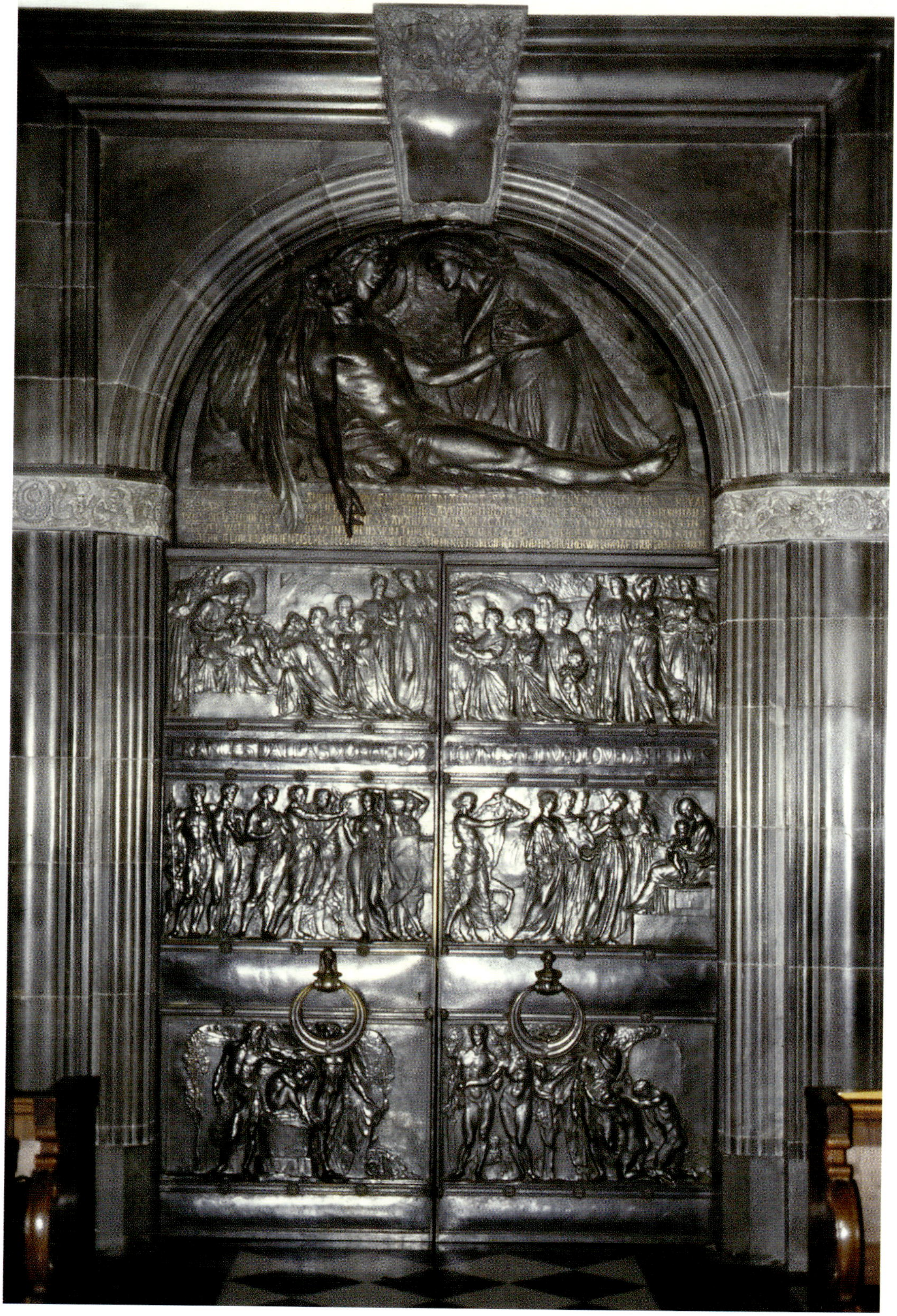

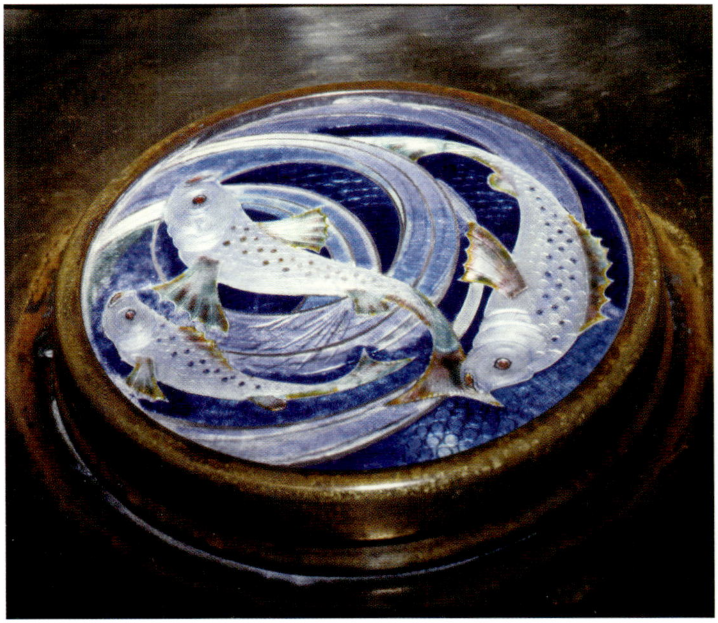

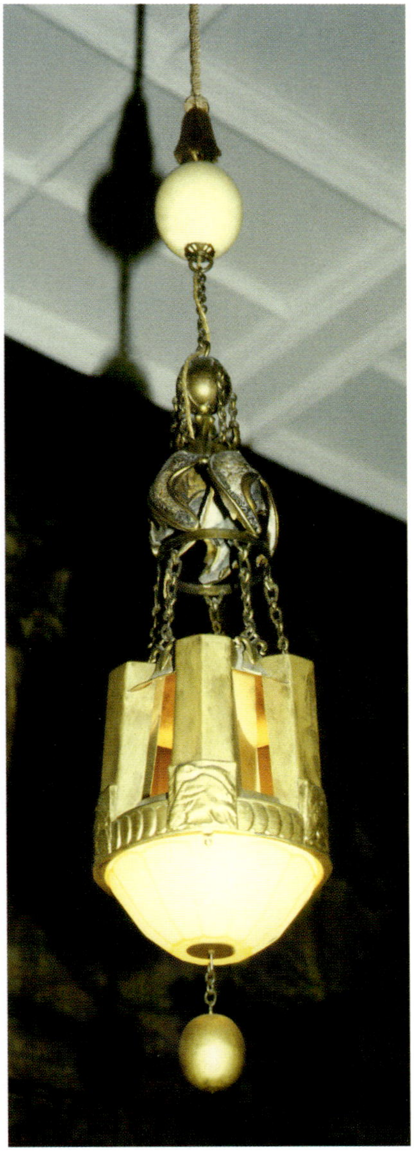

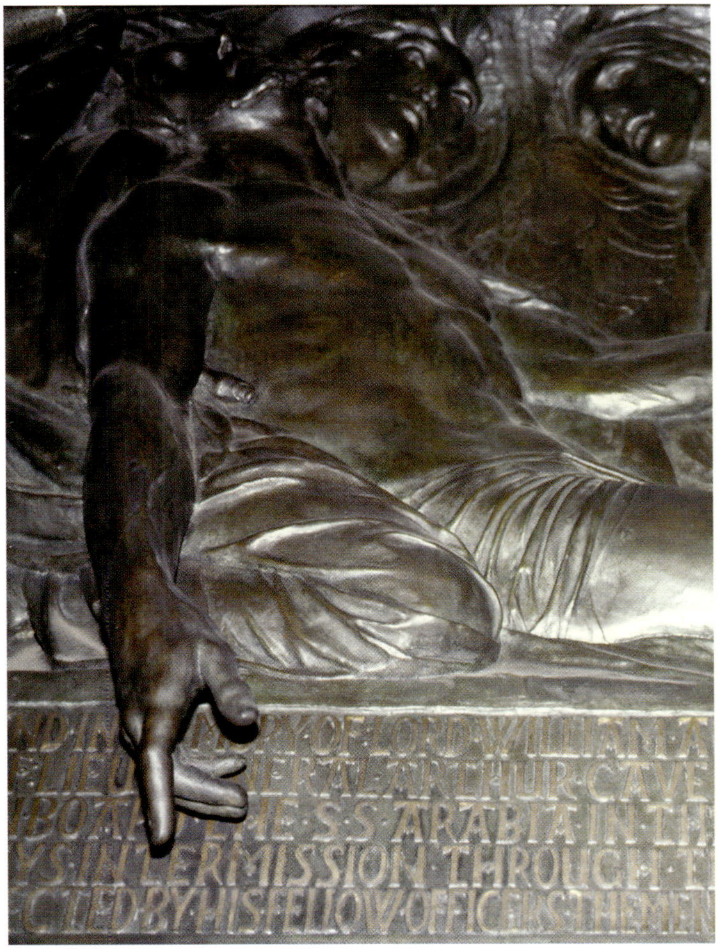

Plate 17. (opposite page) Welbeck Abbey chapel: bronze doors, 1912.

Plate 18. (top left) Welbeck Abbey chapel: enamelled font plug, 1893.

Plate 19. (above) Welbeck Abbey chapel: hanging lamp in aisle, 1893.

Plate 20. (left) Welbeck Abbey chapel: detail of pietà and lettering above doors.

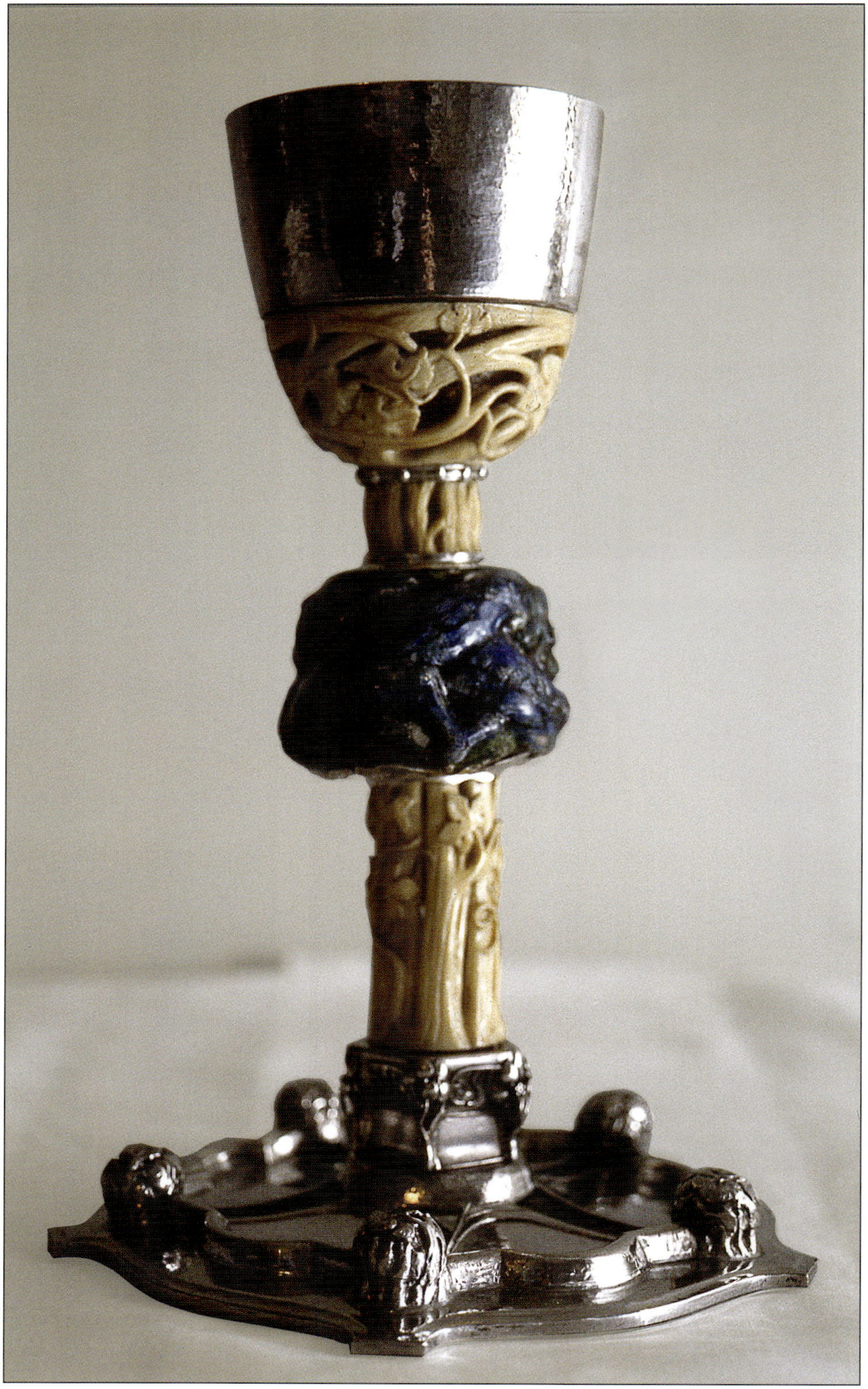

Plate 21. St. Bartholomew's Church, Brighton: communion chalice, silver and ivory with parcel-gilding to bowl and enamel dragon knop, 1898 *(h. 30cm)*.

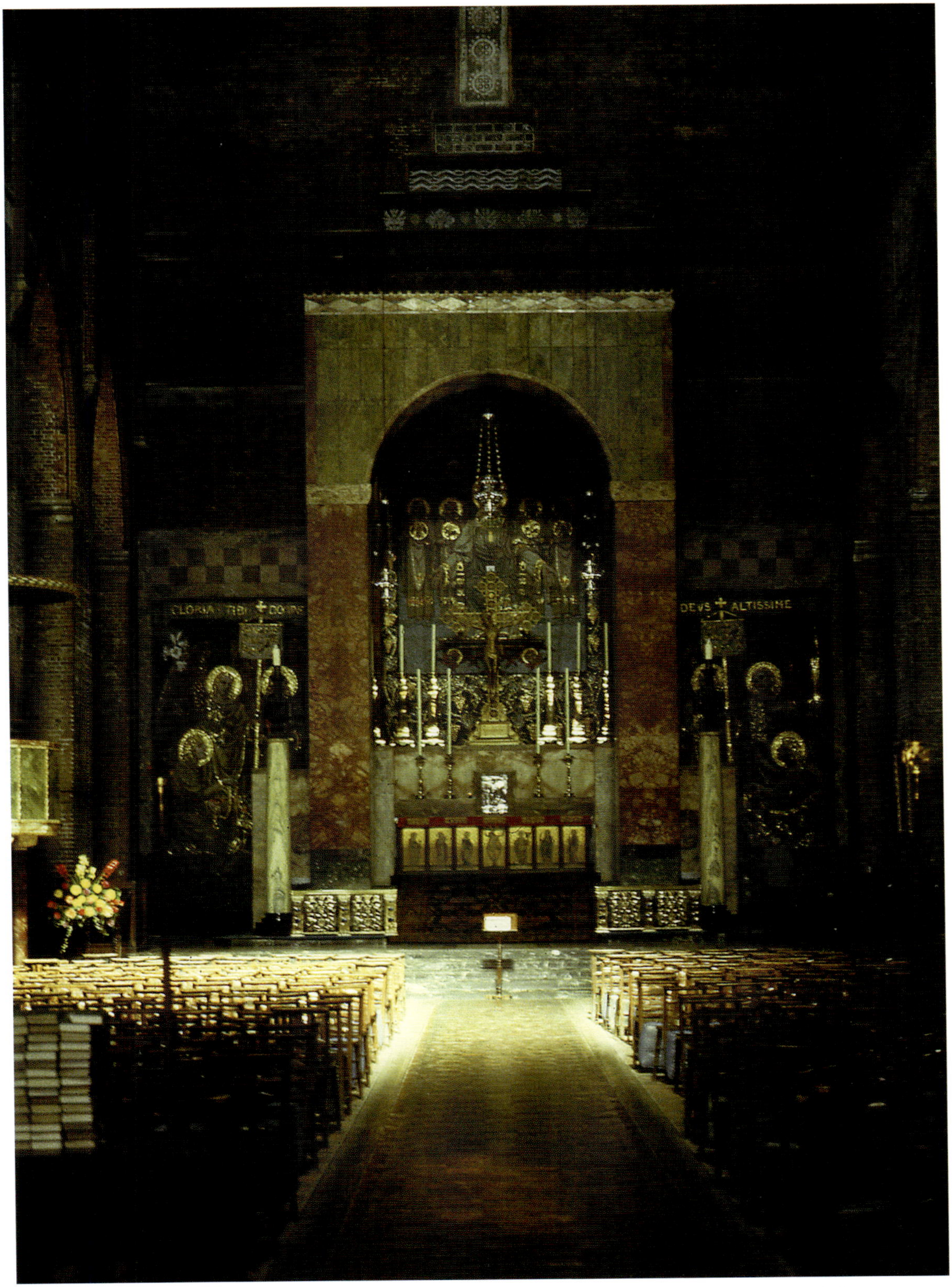

Plate 22. St. Bartholomew's Church, Brighton: interior with Wilson's high altar and baldacchino, 1899-1900.

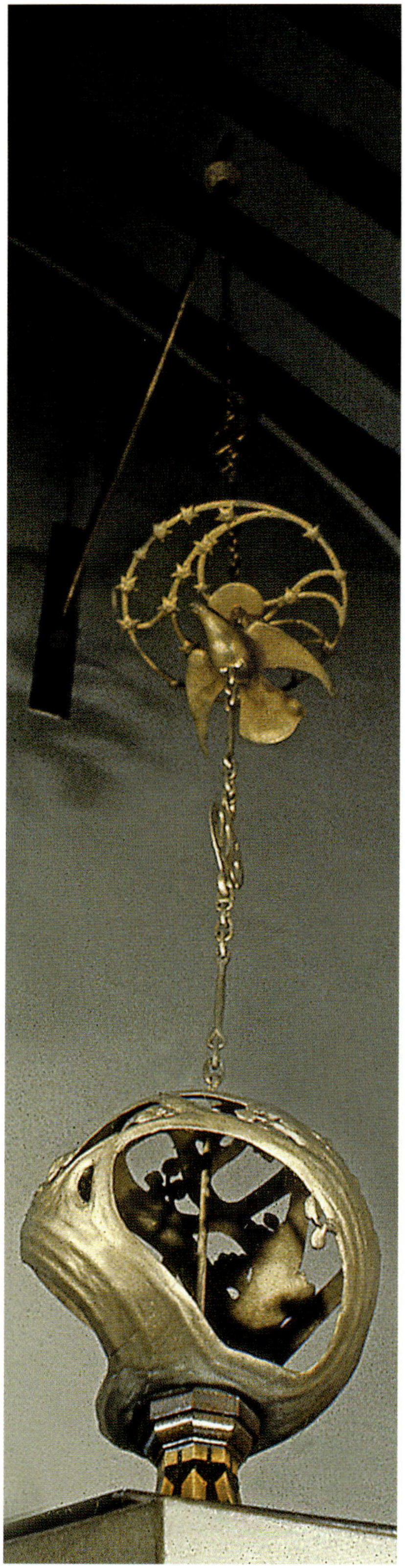

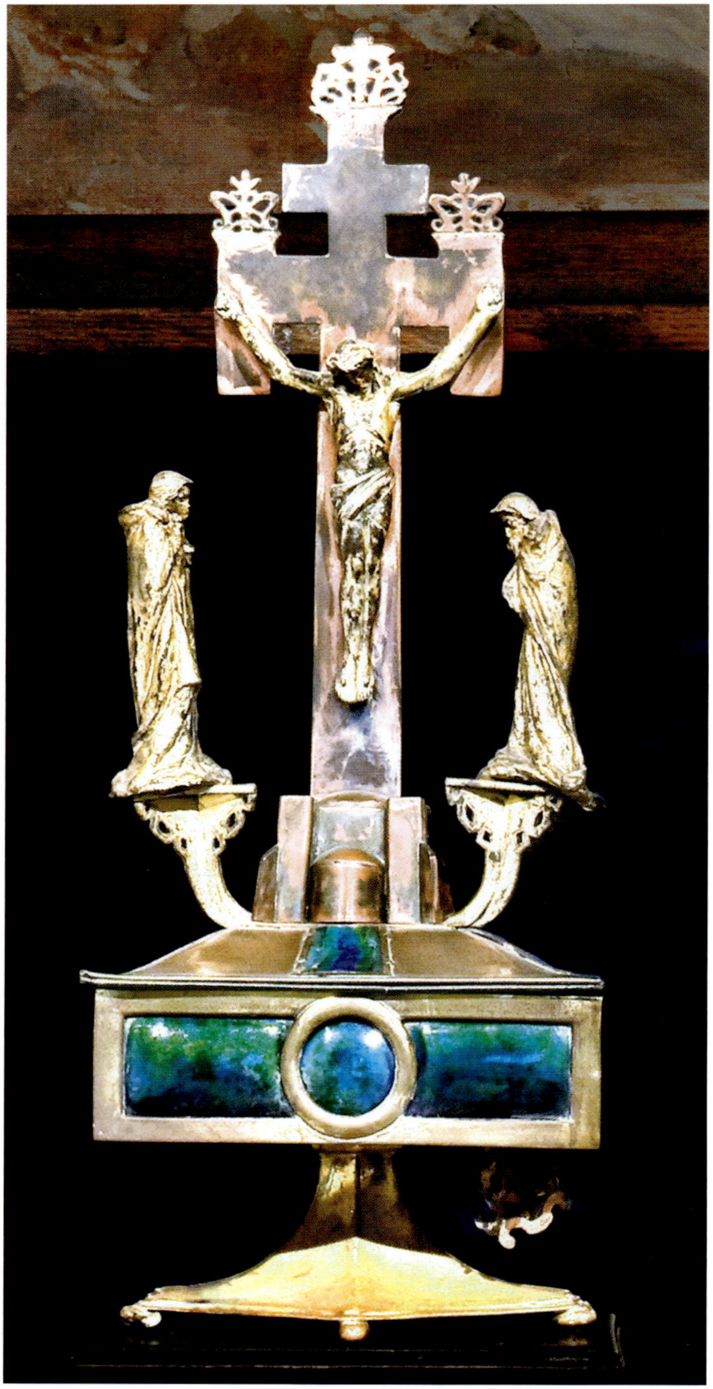

Plate 23. (above) St. Martin's Church, Low Marple, Cheshire: Lady altar cross, silver and enamel, 1896 *(h. 40.5cm).*

Plate 24. (left) St. Martin's Church, Low Marple, Cheshire: gilt-iron chain above ebony and fruitwood veneer font cover, 1900 *(h. of cover to top of openwork knop 66cm w. 80cm).*

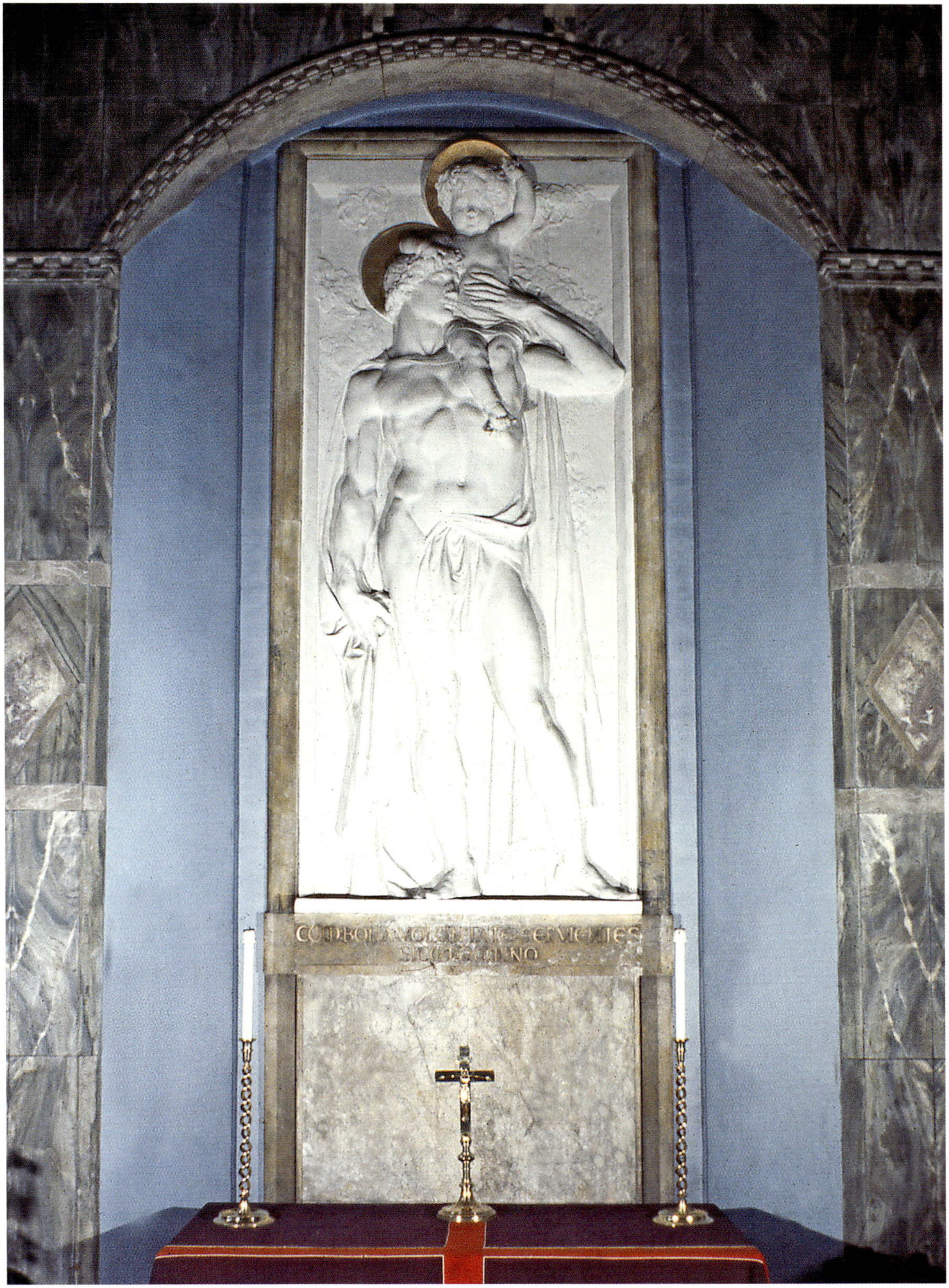

Plate 25. St. Martin's Church, Low Marple, Cheshire: Christopher Chapel, carved plaster with gilding and marble, 1909.

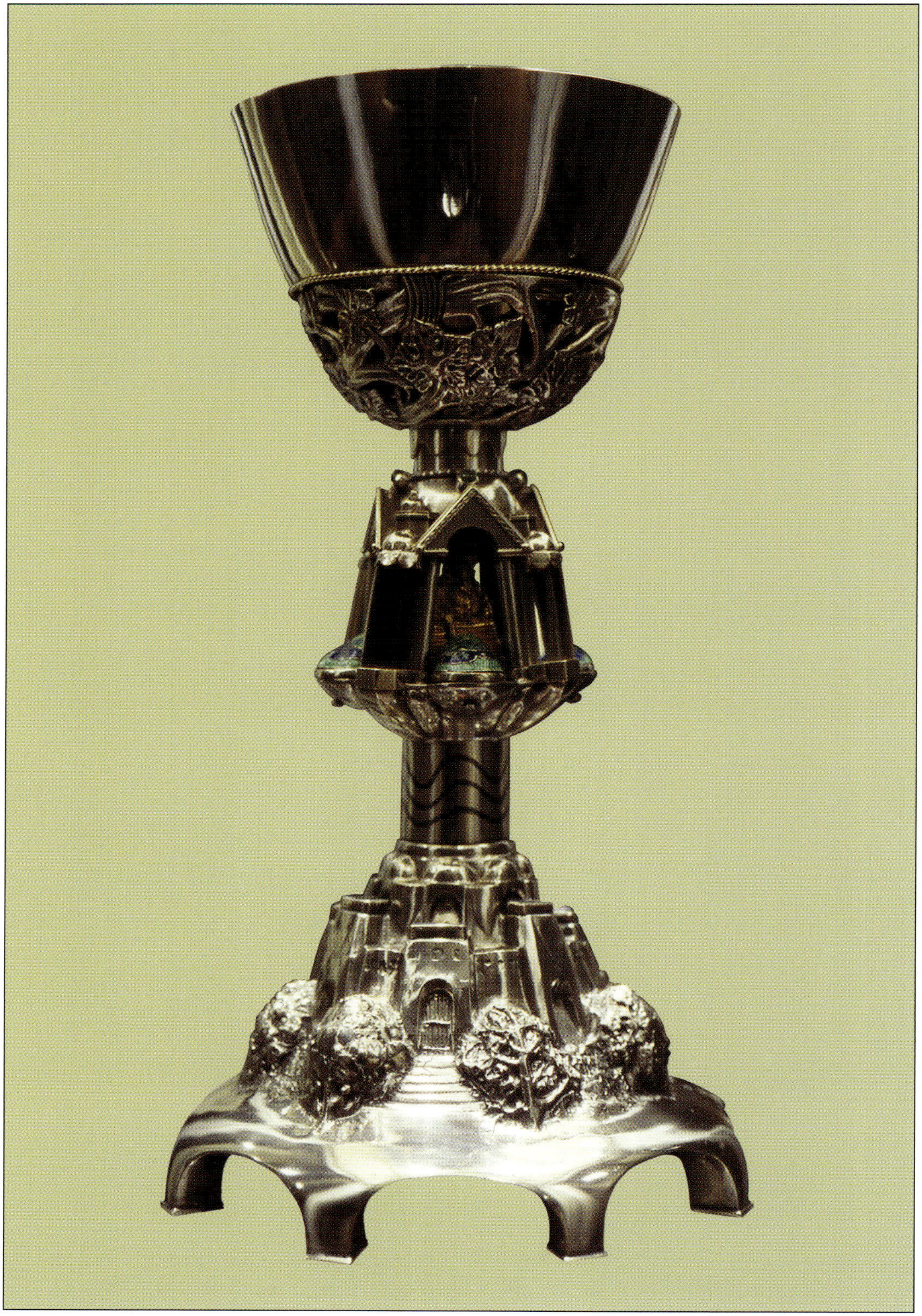

Plate 26. Gloucester Cathedral: communion chalice made by Henry Wilson assisted by Sidney Wiseman and Harry Murphy; silver and parcel-gilt with enamel and niello, 1900 *(h. 27cm)*.

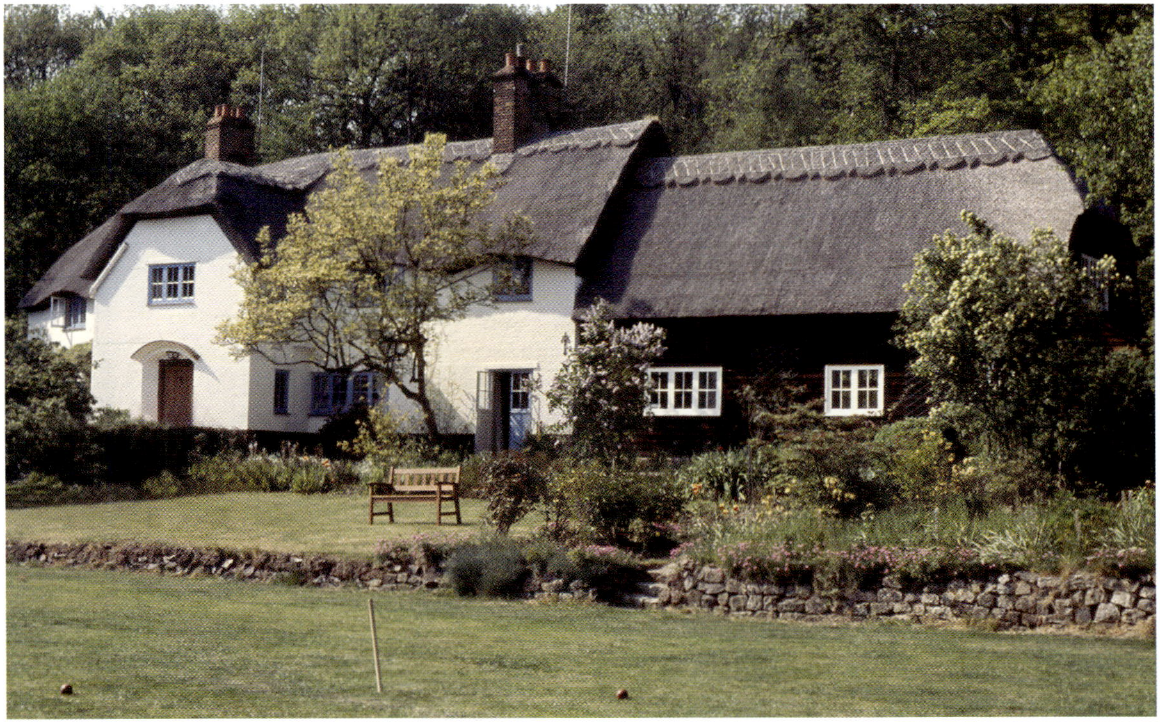

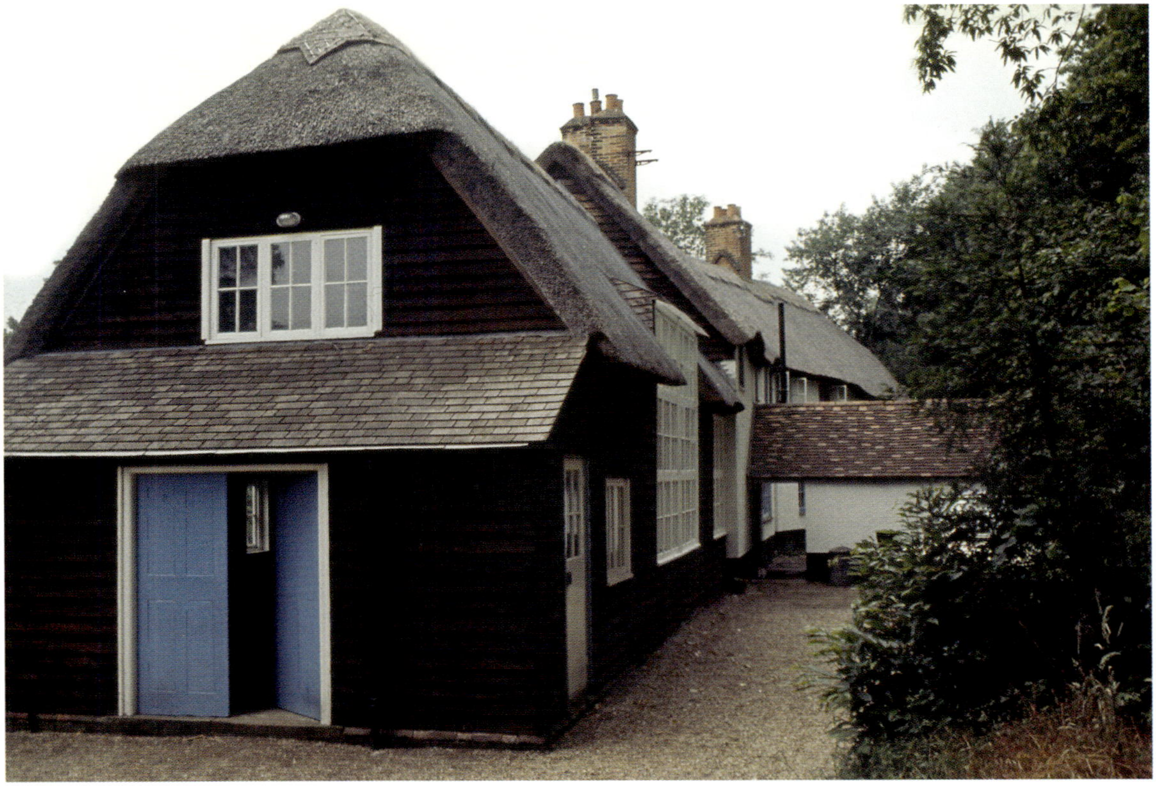

Plate 27. The Thatched House, St. Mary's Platt, Kent, 1902: (top) entrance front and Wilson's studio; (below) back view showing North light to studio.

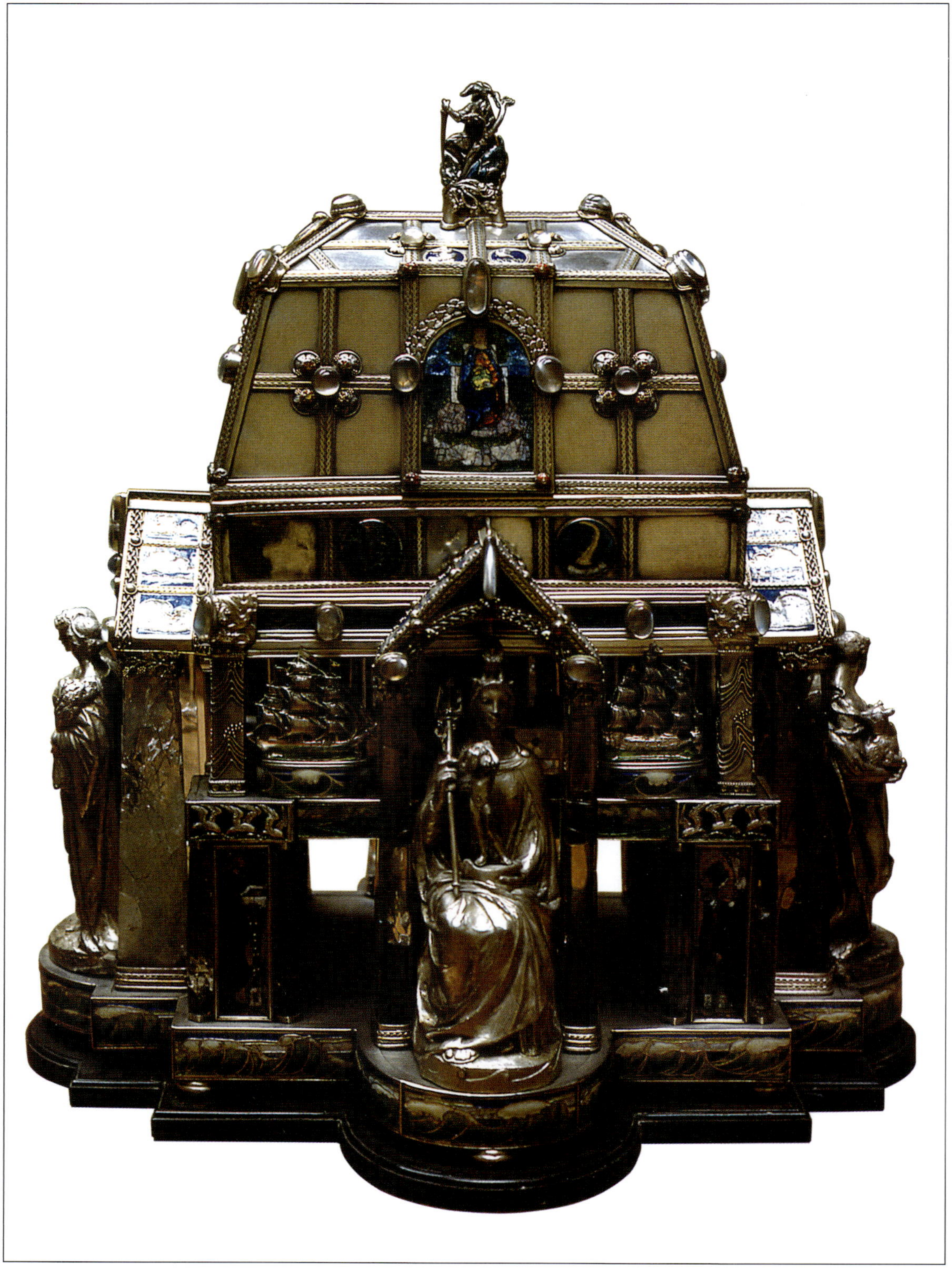

Birmingham Museums and Art Gallery

Plate 28. Chamberlain casket: Britannia with trident, and Commerce on her lap; in the lunette, she is surrounded by infant colonies; silver, enamel, crystal, gemstones, 1902 *(h. 22.5" w. 19.5" d. 16.75")*.

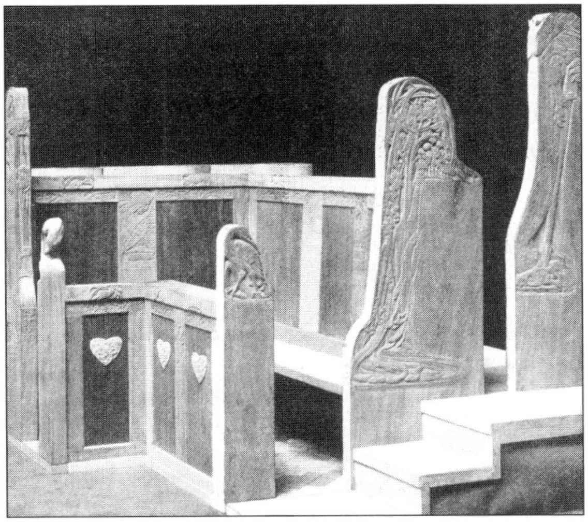

Figure 60. All Hallows' Church, Southwark: oak choir stalls, *Art Journal*, 1896; destroyed in World War II.

Wilson was keen to share the benefits of learning from the methods described in this ancient text, as well as from the processes used by the Etruscans, the Indians, the Japanese and, not least, the Anglo-Saxons: one of his own favourite artefacts was the ninth century gold and enamel Alfred Jewel. In absorbing the past, current practitioners would come closer to the springs of their own inspiration:

Design in the past was the outcome of work. Today the cart is placed before the horse; work is the outcome of design, hence its thin and meagre aspect.[46]

Such meagreness was not to be remedied 'as many may think, by wild struggles after originality' – such a recourse led only to the 'eccentric and the morbid'.[47] Wilson's opinion of the fashionable excesses of Art Nouveau, his target here, comes out in his strictures against unnatural 'curly leaves, coiling branches, wormlike roots and squirming forms'.[48] He admits to having been 'carried along for a while' by the influence of 'New Art:'[49] its forms pervade his earlier commissions, most conspicuously the Ladbroke Grove Library design, or the Marple font cover, or the oak chancel stalls for All Hallows' Church, Southwark, carved with boldly linear trees, flowers and foliage (Fig. 60). These stalls, when first displayed in 1896, had an impact little short of sensational: 'probably nothing in the exhibition', declared the *Studio*, 'has received more attention....'[50] For a while, around the turn of the century, Art Nouveau bore its own seal of approval, despite its often being, as Lethaby said, 'capriciously original', or 'enervating and repulsive'.[51] Within a few years, Wilson's personal disdain for the style, especially in its Continental forms, would be voiced in terms just as severe as Lethaby's – though typically, still with a glimmer of hope:

> *to me it is all slimy, bacterial, microbic. I cannot bear the serpentine spring, the coiling whiplash lines, and all the morbid meanders.... At the same time I know that even the microbe is only an undeveloped angel, and all this neurotic art may lead to ... magnificent creations in the future.*[52]

Wilson was not blind to the benefits Art Nouveau had brought, to architecture in particular; to 'do it justice,' he argued, it

> *brought daylight into architecture. It taught us to appreciate the aesthetic value of large plain surfaces. The experiments we made in 'New Art' strengthened our grip on fundamentals.... It opened our eyes.*[53]

To that degree the style had been a liberating influence, and when designers who had been exploring it rejoined the gently evolving stream of tradition, they had returned refreshed, as 'free men not as slaves'.It was only those who had lingered too long under its spell who had produced 'monstrosities of all kinds'.[54]

Later in his chapter on old work and methods Wilson reflects on the effect traditional Japanese metalwork practices had exerted on him. They presented an all but unknown world to the western student. *Pear skin*, say, or *wood grain*, or *toad's back*: he savours the very names of the complex surface effects Japanese craftsmen had perfected. The observation their work displayed was of an intensity 'not even dreamed of by the Western workman wallowing in the trough of commercialism'.[55]

Inspired by Japanese designs, he suggests using fish as a motif on an enamel pendant, closely observing the way the Japanese draughtsmen made their marks, paying special attention to the 'bony structure of the head and set of the fins'.[56] His work was as good as his word – witness the enamel fish on his Welbeck font plug (resembling those illustrated in his book), and those carved in marble on the font-bases at Welbeck and Norton-sub-Hamdon. When he revised *Silverwork and Jewellery* for its second edition, he included wide-ranging new chapters – his own on design; on gravers and scorpers (illustrated by Charles Jagger, his Royal College student); on raising and niello (with help from his studio assistants Wiseman and Murphy); on card cases (with S. Cowell, who had worked in the Vicarage Gate studio); on Egyptian and Oriental methods (from M.E. Vernier's book) – but the most detailed additions, comprising Chapters XXXIX-XLVI, were those devoted to Japanese metalwork and methods.

The last one, Chapter XLVI, reproduced a lecture, given at Wilson's invitation, at the Central School by Professor Unno Bisei of Tokyo's Imperial Fine Art College, translated by Sakujiro Semoto. In this authentic and inspiring chapter were revealed the many special alloys available, such as *Shibuichi* (copper and silver), and the myriad surface colours that they produce. Various Japanese forms of decoration were introduced, such as *Katakiribori* (engraving), *Hira-Zogwan* (inlay) and *Ukibori* (chasing), with George Jones's illustrations supplementing Professor Unno's own diagrams. A chapter on Japanese patinas describes a demonstration given by Professor T. Kobayshi for Wilson's class at the Royal College; those that follow derive from advanced classes held by the professor for the benefit of Wilson and select pupils.

Wilson's fascination with things Japanese extended far beyond metalwork: he sought to absorb the entire ethos. Consistently 'unusual and interesting,'[57] according to Brown-Morrison, his workshop assistant at Platt, Wilson's conversation often turned to Eastern philosophy or yoga. For a while, he employed a Japanese servant to attend to the daily running of The Thatched House. Even the actor-director Gordon Craig, himself notoriously idiosyncratic, was bemused by this arrangement: 'How are things with you?' he teased, 'Japanese servant and all?'[58]

What most distances *Silverwork and Jewellery* from the standard craftsman's manuals published in England at the beginning of the twentieth century is the debate it opens on individual instinct in the creative process. Scant attention is paid to this in Nelson Dawson's *Goldsmiths' and Jewellers' Work*, published in 1907; rather, he seems to deprecate the 'prophetic' role of the artist, who characteristically

> *is, or should be, a poor talker, and when he does speak it should be rather ... of the technique of the work than its other aspects, which for the purposes of this book are purposely omitted.*[59]

And so, while providing solid information on materials, methods, historical examples, and hallmarking, Dawson restricts his comments on 'design' to a concurrence with Wilson that design and workmanship are indivisible, and to censuring the showiness of commercial metalwares to be seen in the West End. Surprisingly, coming from a former assistant in Wilson's studio, the next significant manual – Herbert Maryon's *Metalwork and Enamelling: a practical guide on Gold and Silversmiths' work* – is almost as non-commital on underlying principles. Techniques that Wilson's book had explained, such as stone-setting, repoussé, casting and enamelling, are revisited; along with Wilson he commends the study of Japanese artefacts; he applauds the celebrated sculptor-jeweller Alfred Gilbert. His warnings against copyism, his praise of nature as a source, and his advocacy of restraint, appropriateness and compositional balance, all these are in the Wilson spirit. But Maryon's lack of engagement with ideas in all their complexity, or on the undefineable mysteries of inspiration, leaves the reader longing for the breadth, depth and, above all, passion of *Silverwork and Jewellery*.

As Wilson had explained in his somewhat laconic interview in the *Art Journal* in 1896, each individual's view of things differs from all others, and is therefore as interesting as its capacity to give us a new viewpoint. In the format of a book, he had room to expand on how a craftsman's awareness of the symbolism of particular materials or motifs may be made to mesh with the practicalities of design.

> *Suppose you have a moonstone which you wish to set. If I were doing it I should probably reason in this way:- 'The moonstone suggests Diana. Her symbol is a stag. The subject shall be a running stag bearing the moon in its antlers'. But this is only one way of looking at it. What is personal to one may be affectation in another, and affected art is bad art. Suppose, however that you choose to do a stag. Make a drawing of [one] running, or standing sidewise with his head thrown back ... .*[60]

exactly, in fact, like that on Wilson's silver repoussé Lady Altar at Brighton, which was completed in the same year as *Silverwork and Jewellery*. Wilson was doubtless aware of such a stag on a sixteenth century gold hat-badge by Albrecht Dürer, in his time as much a goldsmith as painter and engraver. In Wilson's work, the stag is a recurring image: one of the most vivid is on a gold brooch of c. 1906 where the animal, in low relief, rearing slightly, is set within a crystal circlet against a green enamelled background of a tree's foliage.

There, its isolated form created a lyrical and decorative image, but in a gold tiara of the early years in Kent (Plate 36), Wilson endowed a running stag with narrative depth. The tiara with its five symmetrical elements has as its headband a curve of crystal, ringed with green enamel bands using the technique Cromar Watt had admired for its apparently 'flexible' quality. The part-openwork central medallion, set above a blue cloisonné and sapphire-jewelled inverted moon-crescent, shows the kneeling figure of Diana with bow, her hunting horn to her lips. She is flanked by two golden trees which grow from the headband, each set with gems amidst its cloisonné leaves and flowers. The trees spread out to touch openwork roundels, the left-hand one framing a pair of straining and pawing golden hounds, with their quarry in full flight in the right-hand one, the golden antlers of the stag raking its enclosing cloisonné ring (Fig. 61).

The philosophical Chapter XLVIII 'On Design', was new to the second edition. Wilson added it as an acknowledgement that, since its first appearance, *Silverwork and Jewellery* had proved as popular

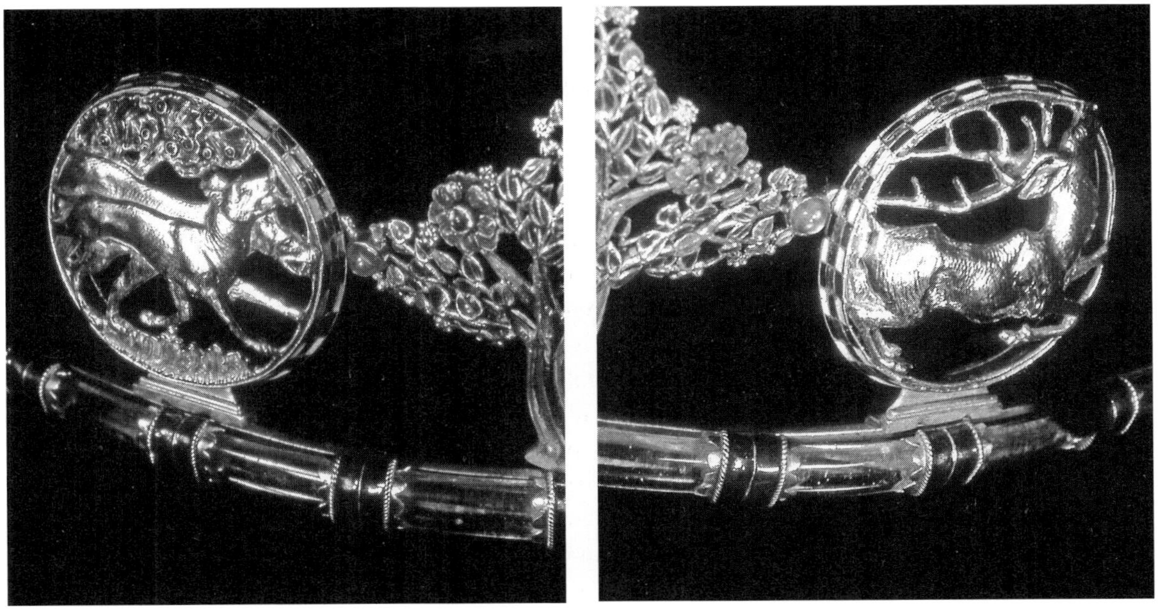

Private Collection

Figure 61. Tiara, gold with enamel and crystal, early1900s: the two outer roundels show (left) hounds in pursuit and (right) stag in flight.

with teachers as with students. Therefore some 'musings'[61] on the individual's design faculty, and how best to train it, seemed appropriate. The indivisibility of design and workmanship is reaffirmed as a prelude to a discussion of one of his greatest preoccupations, the nature of workmanship itself. This topic was important enough for him to have published, in 1912, a paper devoted to it.

All education should be based on it, every ideal directed to it, all life lived for it. And why? Because it means the art of shaping. Because it means creation. It is part of the cosmic process, bound by the same laws that shape the crystals and the clouds.[62]

If workmanship is an aspect of creation, then design is 'a function of vitality',[63] an intrinsic part of simply being alive. And since everyone is an individual, the work each person produces, as long as it is sincere, is bound to be original. Wilson's attitude to the design process, and the words he selects to convey his belief, are demystifying, empowering, and startlingly contemporary.

When we say that a design is original, we mean that more than usual of the worker's life has escaped into [it]. Originality is no rarity, everybody is original. Everybody can design.[64]

The teacher is there to act as facilitator and interpreter, to be the guide and inspirer of students in discovering and communicating their links with the created world. These ideas about the nature of design find their most concentrated and moving expression in Wilson's undated manuscript for a lecture entitled 'The Gates of Wonder'. Its urgency of tone speaks directly to the receptive reader, as it surely would have to its first listeners:

Each mind is a door into a world of infinite possibilities, of infinite beauty, of infinite power; yet most of us spend our lives in ignorance of our own riches. We not only stand with our backs to the door, we lock up the treasure house and throw away the key. There is not a soul in this room but if he could use a tithe of the power wrapped up in his brain would dominate the world by his intelligence and his wisdom; all Art would be possible to him, all Science open to him.... I want you to realise that you can all be great, that you can all be individual, that there is no limit to what you can do if only you will trust yourselves.[65]

In his paper of 1912, 'On Workmanship', Wilson reiterates his sense of the inherited memory, common to all living creatures, as an integral part of the design process: 'The young untravelled bird does not learn, nor is taught the map of the first migration – it remembers'.[66] And it is the idea of inherited memory which occupies most of the remainder of his chapter 'On Design'.

Nothing exists which is not in some sort the embodiment of design, because nothing exists which is not the outcome of memory. The sense of beauty is memory. Love is memory. Design ... is formalised memory; the thought-habit to which each type of organised matter owes its shape. Child and flower, field and fruit ... what are they but the effects of successive recollections, resurgings of being?[67]

From this flows his conviction that 'the worker is a gate of memory', and that design is a form of recapitulation, 'the resounding of an oft-repeated phrase in the cosmic symphony'.[68] The link Wilson claims between every manifestation of life and its forbears owes much to Samuel Butler and his book of 1875, *Unconscious Memory*, which posits the hereditary transmission of acquired behaviour, and the existence of 'living memory'[69] by which a flower seen in the present represents the latest link in a chain of flowers stretching back through time. Wilson's own ideas in this paper bear a striking resemblance to Carl Jung's theory of the collective unconscious, developed in the first decade of the twentieth century and published in 1911, though there is no direct allusion here to Jung's work. Elsewhere, in *Silverwork and Jewellery*, he uses as an 'illustrative parallel' to the design process, the recital he had attended by a famous soprano: she seemed to him to be 'the ghost of an ancestral age', and her voice, though ostensibly individual, 'the cry of clustered millions'.[70]

Again, in 'The Gates of Wonder', Wilson defines the process in a passage in which his characteristically spiritual viewpoint acquires a mystical tinge:

When the magic of Shakespeare sends ... thrills down our spine, it is not the painfully school-educated sense which responds in us, but ... the life of Elizabeth's England still throbbing in our veins. We wind through the mazes of existence, the organism growing simpler with each step backward until we find ourselves with the primordial slime on the shores of the Primal sea. To step beyond this ... is to seek life among the changing atoms. Yet our imagination goes further than this until all being is conceived as a luminous image in the mind of God, and we ourselves faint responsive throbbings to the current of his thought.[71]

In a letter to Edgar Wilson written in 1922, or soon after, from his new studio in S. Cloud outside Paris, Harry included an unusual, and intriguing request to his brother:

I want you to read La Vie après la Mort par Pierre S. Cornillier. Cornillier is a great friend of mine and has told me heaps of interesting things. He took plaster casts of spirit hands. And I'm quite convinced they were spirit hands by the way the casts were made. They could not be faked or produced fraudulently.[72]

The letter itself gives no further details. It is true that there had been a rush of interest in spiritualism in the aftermath of the Great War – but these hands must have been impressively made indeed to convince so consummate a craftsman of their provenance. His openness to the possibility of making contact with the departed may have been triggered by a family tradition. Both his parents had been deeply affected by the loss of his sister Marion when she was four. Since boyhood he had been aware – through his mother's telling of it – of how, a few days after the girl's death, she had seen her, coming down the stairs of the Old School House as if to greet her, smiling and saying 'Don't be sad, Mother, I am so very happy'.

In the years following the publication of *Silverwork and Jewellery* Wilson was appointed to several teaching posts within the metalworking crafts. Already in 1901 he had become part-time Instructor of Goldsmithing at the Royal College, a position he held until 1912. In 1905 he had become visiting Examiner at the Vittoria Street School for Jewellers and Silversmiths, a department of Birmingham Art School, established in 1890 in response to the city's metalworking heritage, initially under Robert Catterson-Smith, and then from 1902, Arthur Gaskin. Painting and illustration were Gaskin's first interest: in the 1890s he had made powerful wood-engravings for the stories of Hans Christian Andersen and the Brothers Grimm, and for the Kelmscott edition of Edmund Spenser's *Shepheardes Calender.* But in 1899 he began a collaboration with his wife Georgina designing and making jewellery and silverwork. They had been fellow students at the Art School, and together, though often with Georgie as chief motivator, they made jewels of gold and silver filigree, invoking delicate natural forms enriched with pale amethysts and mother-of-pearl.

In the atmosphere of the Birmingham school, it was natural that Wilson should become drawn in as both colleague and ally. His position at Vittoria Street entailed frequent visits and the writing of detailed annual reports on the students' work. He continued as Examiner there until 1917, combining his role with a similar position in Goldsmithing at the City and Guilds of London Institute. His reports show him alternating between exalted setting forth of how metalwork should be taught, and the down-to-earth directness he used in his own workshop and public utterances. The role in which Gordon Craig cast him, that of 'practical idealist',[73] sums up perfectly Wilson's ability to combine these two sides: one moment he may be talking of the students' 'precious ... individual, virgin vision', or of 'the air of romance so dear and necessary to the mind of youth';[74]

the next sees him in the guise of pragmatic politician, assuring the authorities that the 'trade of Birmingham could not fail to benefit'[75] by the proper cultivation of such a seedbed of ideas. Adding, to show his eye was on actual studio conditions, 'the work benches must be provided with proper armrests ... and the outsides of the lampshades should be dark green instead of opal'.[76]

Given his experience both of fine metalworking and of up-to-date metalwork instruction, his awareness of declining standards within the craft, and their complacent acceptance by the public, was acute.

> *What are we to think of the state of the goldsmith's art when the drapers and fancy stores, the stationers and the chemists stock their windows with trumpery designs stamped out of silver thinner than paper, or with candlesticks in silver foil filled with plaster? The thing is a disgrace....*[77]

This outburst had been prompted by the shock of his visit to the Franco-British Exhibition of metalwork and jewellery at Shepherds Bush in 1908, in which the 'immense technical and artistic superiority'[78] of the Continental workmen had been all too apparent. Some good, though, came out of his and other practitioners' disappointment – the immediate formation in November 1908 of the Goldsmiths', Silversmiths' and Jewellers' Art Council. Wilson was appointed chairman, and his hopes for it were high. It took the form of a consultative committee under the auspices of the London County Council, its members coming from wholesale and retail backgrounds and from the L.C.C. itself. Its task was to study the existing provisions for teaching silverwork and the allied trades in the L.C.C. schools, and to make recommendations for improvement.

Wilson's own sympathies, embracing all three interests – art, trade and education – represented by the new Council deceived him into assuming there was an established identity of purpose in their aims: good quality work would surely mean good trade figures; good standards in general education would simultaneously raise levels in the artistic crafts; good training in the crafts would enhance education. He had not bargained for the prejudices which emerged on all sides, especially on the part of the representatives of the fashionable retailers, who insisted that only those versed in machine-made design should be employed to teach in L.C.C. schools.

The use of machinery was already widespread in commercial metalworking. Wilson tried to maintain impartiality, and made it clear that he was not against *all* mechanisation. Why, he asked, should someone spend their life making buttons and nails by hand when these can, and should, be made by machines? By this time he was even conceding that die-stamping, which he had purposely left out of *Silverwork and Jewellery*, need not always be inartistic. But just as he had once made a distinction between architecture and 'veneered engineering', now his caveat was against machine products that masqueraded as handcraft. The illusion offered to customers was often blatant. For example, Hutton's, jewellery manufacturers in Sheffield and London, were producing 'hand-made' jewels by machine and thus capitalising on craft's cachet, and Elkington's had their machinery producing hand-made effect vases and mugs, decorated with machine-pressed repoussé.

Sharing Wilson's aversion to factory-produced pseudo-craft, C.R. Ashbee had his own axe to grind about fakery. It was the craft-retailing firm of Liberty's that he had in his sights, specifically over a range of silverware they had carried between 1896 and 1900. Stylistically, these pieces leant heavily on Ashbee's ideas, and, while this might indicate his influence rather than the plagiarism he alleged, particular instances are harder to explain. He claimed, for example, that he had made a silver brooch, exhibited it in his Guild's depot in Brook Street, and within six weeks 'it appeared with 20 others like it in the window of Messrs Nobody and Co. with a label beneath it, *Our exclusive design*'.[79] The reference is unambiguously to Liberty's who, while commissioning distinguished designer-craftsmen like Arthur Gaskin, Archibald Knox and Rex Silver, were also having wares executed by W. & H. Haseler of

Birmingham, whose own productions had obviously taken their cue from the Guild of Handicraft. The crucial difference, and one quite unacceptable to Ashbee, was that the Haseler hollow-wares were invariably spun and their buckles die-stamped, with hammer-marks applied afterwards for effect, a 'modern vice' of which Wilson was utterly dismissive: 'it is more than reprehensible – it is foolish'.[80]

He regarded the gulf between trade and craft as unnecessary and counter-productive. Their interdependence was incontestable – but their fitting together depended on the primacy of craft:

> *Some may say ... 'Craftsmanship is all very well, but it doesn't tell me how to ... increase my output or my profits'. Rightly understood it does do this. Seek true workmanship and these things shall be added....*[81]

A frequent point in his art school reports, and one which he reiterated in his dealings with the new Goldsmiths', Silversmiths' and Jewellers' Art Council, is his disquiet at the gradual leaching away of traditional knowledge among contemporary fine metalworkers: not having learnt the 'grammar' of their craft, they could not fully execute their ideas, and were apt to think that nothing mattered if only they could 'muddle through till Saturday'.[82] Craftsmanship that could truly be called creative was confined to relatively few workshops: that of Arthur Dixon, who had founded the Birmingham Guild of Handicraft for the realisation of designs for silver, silver-plate, copper and brass, and those of Dawson, Ashbee, Cooper, Spenser, and Gaskin, not to mention Wilson's own.

He did, however, recognise encouraging signs in the art schools, in the 'immediate moral, mental and physical improvement' to be seen among the 'shop drudges, the spiritless errand boys and the dullards at the bench'[83] the moment their bosses saw fit to send them to classes at the Central School or Vittoria Street, where they appeared 'reborn ... [and able to] develop ideas, become personalities'.[84] When he turned his attention to the role of the instructors, Wilson insisted that nothing was easier than 'to distort, divert or perhaps destroy'[85] the students' natural insights by imposing extraneous values on them, rather than to unlock and release their individuality. The teacher's real task was to 'train not maim the growing mind'.

Wilson often applied the word 'apprentices' to part-time students on metalwork courses – not just owing to these students being officially apprenticed to trade jewellers. In his practical, but idealistic version of craft training, 'apprentice' denoted a young person learning, if not within a guild system, then at least in a humane art school regime, in which the instructor would be like a master craftsman, providing a living link with age-old craft traditions. Familiarity with traditional methods had once been virtually instinctive; but to the 'poor moderns'[86] of Wilson's time, such habits were fading fast. Still, valuable lessons could be learnt through careful study of historic examples, from a medieval shrine that united 'religion, art, [and] magic';[87] or from the Gold Room at the British Museum, a source of inexhaustible creative insights.

The better to stimulate students' knowledge of traditional techniques and to spark their own inspiration, Wilson proposed that local education boards invite into their schools master craftsmen from countries where tradition still flourished. Sailing through all possible obstacles, he recommends that chosen masters be allocated bench or floor space in craft schools for the unimpeded pursuit of their inherited craft. Like his advocacy of active historical studies, the concept is both unorthodox and intrinsically traditional. His pleasure in contemplating the technical and spiritual possibilities thus presented radiates from his rollcall of trades and their long-established homes:

> *There should be silversmiths from Spain and Mysore. Coppersmiths should come from Benares, workers in brass and pewter from Chota, Nagpore, Madeira and Tanjore. I would have goldsmiths from Madras and Sawantade. From Damascus should come workers in steel and gold, while from Japan I would have cloisonné workers and translucent enamellers, and workers in jade and lacquer from China....*[88]

Far from adopting ready-made educational programmes from continental Europe or America, Wilson's proposal suggests emulation, not imitation. He readily acknowledged that Germany had set an enviable example with its eight technical universities, whose influence was such that 'the largest firm of jewellers in Paris has all its most artistic work done in Leipzig'.[89] While aware of those British voices raised to advocate similar systems, he repudiated the thoughtless parroting that this implied:

> *There are some who say 'Educate our young workmen in the same way as those of France, or Germany or America....' We are assured if that if we adopt similar methods we shall have similar results. But is that so? I think not. French, German and American methods are right because they are the outcome of their respective needs; they cannot ... apply to any other.*[90]

So, then, let the work done on metalworking courses be 'more nearly adapted to national needs'.[91] The old guilds had served the needs of their times and their communities: let the art and technical schools do likewise. If an awareness of the 'mysterious, etheric influence of national life' must be encouraged in the students, one way might be for them to collaborate, with a unifying, 'collective ideal',[92] on civic commissions. In 1911 just such a project came to Wilson's attention – the Freedom Casket, presented on the occasion of his eightieth birthday to the Member for Bordesley, Jesse Collings, outspoken campaigner for the rural poor. His watchword, 'Three acres and a cow', summed up the argument for granting the unemployed the basic means of self-sufficiency – an issue Wilson himself would address in the aftermath of World War I. Collings had been born into a family of agricultural labourers in Devon, and served an apprenticeship to a London ironmonger. By 1885 he had become an intimate of Birmingham's celebrated mayor, Joseph Chamberlain, and the following year saw him join Chamberlain's breakaway Liberal Unionist cabinet. The casket, commissioned by his constituents, was designed by Arthur Gaskin and executed – in time for Wilson's annual Report on the Vittoria Street School of 1912 – by Gaskin's students there, in gold, silver and mother-of-pearl.

Wilson's own opportunity to create a ceremonial casket had arisen nine years before. Politically and geographically, his casket may be linked to Gaskin's presentation piece, one probably being the offshoot of the other. In fact, Wilson would carry out a number of metalwork projects for municipalities and institutions, but the 1902 casket was the earliest; however, not only is it the first of his civic commissions, it is also the most conceptually demanding, and prompts debate in relation to its stance as well as admiration for its splendour as a piece of craft.

In 1902 he had been approached by the Birmingham Constitutional Club to make a ceremonial casket to present to one of the city's most distinguished figures, Joseph Chamberlain, in recognition of his achievements as Colonial Secretary.[93] Its imagery differs profoundly from the arcane, spiritual allusions of Wilson's jewellery. Yet in its variety of workmanship and visual grandeur, it contains, like Elgar's music, something personal, eschewing the jingoism with which such work may be associated, and bringing individual insights to bear on the contemporary world scene.

The first impression may be architectural, a medieval market hall perhaps, its upper room supported on solid corner piers, with a two-storey crystal aedicule projecting from each of its four sides to frame sculpted figures (Plate 28). But as much as Wilson was the architect, so he was the silversmith, and this design is a copious blend of colour and symbolism expressed in that medium. As he himself explained it, the silver casket and its pedestal suggest an ark borne on the seas encircling the British Isles. Jutting from the pedestal's four sides, the aedicules, each like an entrance to a medieval chapel, produce a cruciform plan that evokes the Christian principles governing the British Empire. The columns are of rock crystal, carved with waves to symbolise the oceans of the world, and roofed with intricately carved gables studded with gemstones. For the silverworking

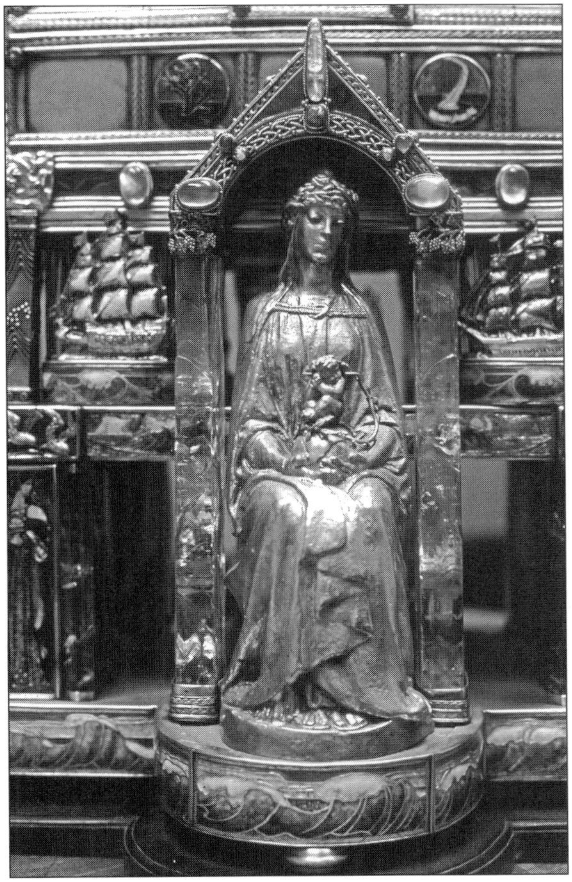

Birmingham Museums and Art Gallery

Figure 62. Chamberlain casket, Peace holds the globe turned to display Africa, with Love sleeping above it, 1902..

and stone-setting process, Wilson was joined by his former studio-assistant Harry Murphy, who was by now master in his own studio. The progress anticipated when they embarked on the job was delayed by problems with getting the crystal cut to Wilson's satisfaction. His letter to the President of the Birmingham Constitutional Club late in the same year, itemises the stone-cutters' shortcomings, and attests to Wilson's perfectionism:

No lapidary in London ... had any experience in the kind of work. I sent it therefore to a foreign firm – German in fact – and after months of delay, I got the columns back with a bill for more than the total amount of the casket! Even then they had to be recut; they were not right in the first instance. Now I have had a good deal of experience with crystal, and know that the charge was absolutely out of all proportion to the value of the work. Still, I have had to pay ... .' [94]

Unlocking the casket's symbolism begins with the silver-gilt figure of Britannia seated on her throne. Having modelled the figure in the studio, Wilson – as he wrote to the Constitutional Club – was let down by two foundries in succession. One was English:

I sent a perfect cast of the figure to a well-known founder. He sent me a replica – imperfect – and returned my original very much damaged....

The other was the trusted French firm of Barbedienne.

Next I sent the work to Paris, to the best founder I could find. Yet though all the other work he has done for me (and that amounts to hundreds of pounds' worth) has been almost perfect, this task he returned to me in an almost unusable condition. [It] had been chased up in the most brutally inartistic way, although I asked to have it returned to me untouched. I have spent days on it, working it up to the effect of the original. [95]

The winged lion on Britannia's helmet, and the trident she holds in her hand, manifest her maritime prowess. On the deck of the miniature ship in her lap stands Commerce bearing on his shoulders a bale of cloth: wool, cotton or worsted were, in 1902, among Britain's chief exports. In the corresponding aedicule on the other side of the pedestal sits Peace (Fig. 62), crowned with an olive-leaf chaplet. The silver globe on her lap has the continent of Africa picked out in gold: the figure of Love slumbering above it represents the newly-signed peace between Britain and the Afrikaans republics of Southern Africa following the Boer War. It would not be long, though, before this imagery would strike a hollow note, not least for the dedicatee: Chamberlain may have won the war, but the Afrikanerdom he had determined to break rallied, precipitating his resignation from office in 1903.

The casket's end aedicules oppose paired female figures – India, cradling an inscribed silver vessel, and Canada, her arms full of wheat to feed the Empire – with two young males, New Zealand carrying a lamb, and Australia, his arms laden with corn and grapes. Wilson's archetypes were modern enough, derived from an imperial idealism common to the radicals and socialists of the time; with excited fascination they sought to assimilate the Empire's diverse cultural and craft traditions. But to a later generation these idealised adolescents seem to hover uneasily between classical and Victorian myth. The Empire had yet to reach its apogee – but the symbolic framework Wilson was using here was already nearing the end of its lifespan.

The freestanding piers supporting the casket's corners contain inset enamel panels of British monarchs bearing tributes, as richly-coloured as Burne-Jones windows, and topped with an enamelled frieze of wheeling seagulls, powerful evocations of arrival and departure for all officials of Empire. In *Silverwork and Jewellery* Wilson had commended them to student jewellers: 'draw [them] with outstretched downward drooping wings. You can see them any day about the bridges on the Thames ... underneath you can place a band of curling waves....'[96] He was as good as his word, enriching the plinth with an enamel ocean and the silver pilasters framing the casket with undulating applied lines scattered with gold 'grains' of seaspray, a motif that would reappear on a silver chafing dish in around 1906.[97] The merchantmen filling the 'windows' were favourites of Wilson's: between 1895 and 1902 he had used them in commissions as diverse as an enamelled silver pendant, a crozier, a hair comb and the Cirencester alms dish.[98] After all, a sailing ship 'is as beautiful a thing as men make nowadays'.[99]

The casket's 'clerestory' displays in painted enamel roundels the English dragon, the Irish thorn, the Scots thistle and the Welsh harp, and its tall lid, like a medieval reliquary with its panels and knots of gems, bears four cloisonné tableaux symbolising Chamberlain's political acts and beliefs. Labour and Capital coming together beneath Love's wings (Plate 29), a scene with the direct appeal of a trade union banner,[100] refers to the Employers' Liability Acts, the first of which Chamberlain steered through Parliament in 1880; Britannia surrounded by infant colonies is set directly above her seated figure (Plate 28); in the third, Love drawing Britain and Ireland together (Plate 30), embodies his opposition to Gladstone's Home Rule, which had prompted him to lead his Radical Unionists out of the Liberal party in 1886; and in the last (Plate 31), Britain spreads her robe around the infant states of the New Commonwealth. Some details of this tableau had been suggested by the nonagerian Sir Charles Nicholson, first speaker of the Sydney House of Representatives and father of Wilson's ally at Sedding's, for whom Wilson's friendship had been, as his widow acknowledged, an 'invaluable influence'.[101] Completing this celebration of a modern empire, the casket is surmounted by a silver and enamel finial forming a vigorous depiction of St. George slaying the dragon – a traditional image, as if to stabilise a course of irreversible transition.

The delivery in 1903 of the finished work, with its glowing colours and intricate symbolism, did not disappoint. Alderman William Kenrick, a former Mayor and MP, and – like his brother-in-law Joseph Chamberlain – a Birmingham businessman, was particularly interested in the casket. As Chairman of the Boards of both the Museum and School of Art he had no hesitation in recommending Wilson for another prestigious local commission in 1905. The city's Water Committee was seeking a suitable gift for their chairman William Lawley Parker, who had recently been granted the Freedom of the City. The casket Wilson was commissioned to make for the occasion, though less stately than Chamberlain's, is all the more eye-catching for its unabashed Art Nouveau lines (Fig. 63).

The chest-like silver casket is panelled, and decorated with gems and painted enamel medallions of lions for Parker's courage, storks suggesting good fortune and goats indicating irrepressible energy;

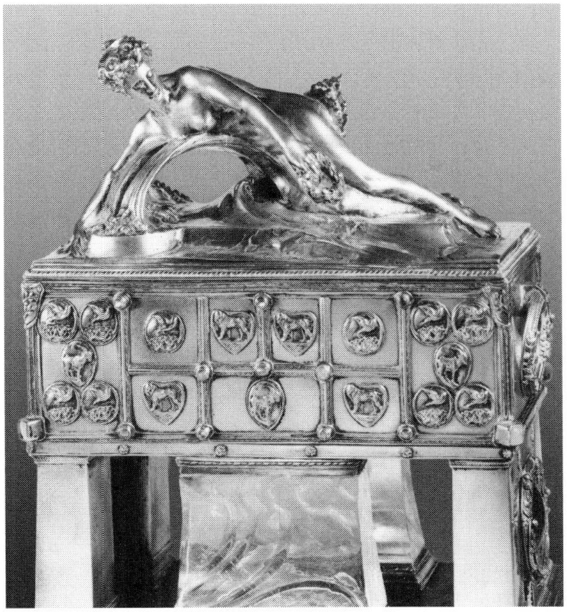

Birmingham Museums and Art Gallery

Figure 63. Edward Lawley Parker Casket, detail showing silver naiad, enamel medallions, crystal blocks (*h.14in, w.13.5in, dia. 7.75in*), 1906.

the four square raked silver columns supporting its corners enclose a void with twin crystal blocks carved in waves, forms which recur on the casket's lid in the most memorable feature of the piece – the silver naiad arching her silver body over the stream to release a garland onto it. Wilson had found the creative combination he had talked about before, where sculpture is emphasised by architectural elements, while *their* formality is mediated by the softening influence of sculpture.

As November 1906 set in, Kenrick wrote querulously to Wilson: the long delay in completing the commission was making him 'feel very uncomfortable.... It was promised for last July'. Besides, he felt 'partly responsible' for the work, 'as it was on my suggestion that it was given to you'.[102] This conveniently overlooked the time spent in considering Wilson's initial designs, revising them, then issuing a new brief. Such delays and changes of plan were by now familiar: the same thing had happened with Wilson's proposed reredos at Sloane Street and, disastrously, over the completion of St. Bartholomew's, Brighton. In relation to the Lawley Parker casket, Wilson's first proposal had been to conjure the dedicatee's birthplace in the mountains of Wales and the source of Birmingham's water supply. Kenrick himself vetoed this as 'far fetched and impracticable'[103] – the very circumstances in which Henry Wilson's creativity was often at its most inspired. Of his original idea, at least Wilson's enamel goats survive.

The 'collective ideal' Wilson had encouraged in his students found practical expression in his own work, in a commission of 1905: he had been asked by the Automobile Club – not yet Royal – to come up with a suitably impressive Tourist Trophy, to be awarded to the winner of the inaugural 208 mile Tourist Race on the Isle of Man (Fig. 64). The event was conceived to foster fast, economical and reliable automobile performance. Wilson approached the director of the Bromsgrove Guild of Applied Art, the sculptor and metalworker, Walter Gilbert, to collaborate with him on the project. The Guild had been formed around eight years previously, among a loose-knit group of West Midlands decorative artists and designers, some associated with the Birmingham Municipal School of Art, others with the Bromsgrove School of Art and Science. By 1900, its eclectic Arts and Crafts style had won acclaim at the Paris International Exhibition, at which it had shown a modern bedroom. Georgina and Arthur Gaskin were linked to the Guild, as was Joseph Hodel, who would later teach metalworking at Liverpool School of Art. Wilson and Gilbert were united in admiring the sculptural mastery of Alfred Gilbert; though unrelated, Walter Gilbert acknowledged the strong influence of his celebrated Victorian namesake.[104]

The Trophy was executed in three stages: a base of four walls, for inscribing the winners names; the plinth, sculpted by Gilbert; and for the upper part, Wilson contributed a fleeting figure of Hermes, messenger of the gods, with heels, helmet and caduceus all winged – an assured twentieth century tribute to Giambologna's 1597 statue of Mercury borne on the breath of the wind, and an apt herald of the first great modern road race.

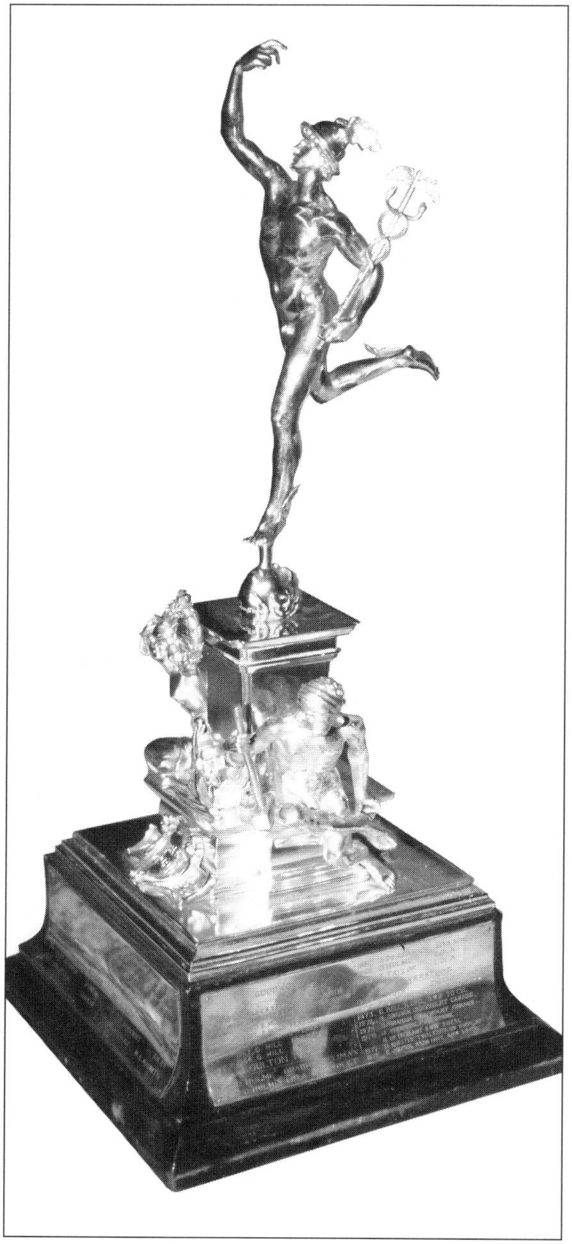

Reproduced by kind permission of the Royal Automobile Club

Figure 64. Tourist Trophy, in collaboration with Walter Gilbert (*h. c. 58cm*); gold Hermes by Wilson, 1905.

Wilson passed his modelled Hermes to Sidney March for casting in 18 carat gold; the same figure was replicated as an independent bronze statuette, and exhibited at the Scottish Arts and Crafts Exhibitions of 1910 and 1912.[105] Gilbert, confronted with the Hermes, admitted being apprehensive about devising a 'worthy' plinth for it.[106] In the event, what he produced was exactly what Wilson himself might have invented. Fame holds a laurel wreath aloft over Industry's achievement, a silver touring car, garlanded with palms. These figures may lack the free-spirited élan of Hermes, but their personification, the product of creative collaboration between the two men, reiterates Wilson's readiness to call on relevant archetypes to serve a changing world. A larger contemporary public image of a car exists – in the 1907 monument in Paris to the automotive designer Levassor[107] – but that in comparison seems flat and immobile. In the image created by Gilbert and Wilson, there is a dynamism, a portant even of Futurism. The award of the Trophy in the spring of 1906 to John Napier, who raced his Arrol-Johnston to victory in six hours nine minutes, was fitting testimony to the rapid changes overtaking both art and automobile design.[108] In 1906 James Cromar Watt suggested his friend Henry Wilson to the Senate of Aberdeen University for the task of executing the MacRitchie Mace (Fig. 65). The mace was to be carried at the inauguration of honorary appointees of the University as a symbol of its authority and heritage. Dr. William Kelly, Professor of Architecture at the University, familiarised Wilson with the underlying symbolical schema, leaving Wilson to resolve the finer points of the design in his own way. In so doing Wilson produced one of his most successful ceremonial pieces. When it was finished, Kelly's response to the individuality of Wilson's vision was half-puzzled admiration: 'I don't think I have got all its mystic suggestions; it is best to leave it so ... .'[109]

Kelly's reference to 'mystic suggestions' suggests why the mace remains evocative where the Chamberlain Casket may seem over-literal. For all its magnificence, the mass of political detail that had to be accomodated in the casket was uncomfortably diverse. In the mace, alongside historic figureheads, Wilson was evoking abstract concepts, loyalty, honour, tradition, within a richly symbolic whole. The haft is ivory, terminating in a large topaz, symbolising faithfulness; eight silver-mounted companion topazes are set around its knop of blue enamel. The four-sided, pinnacled tabernacle at the mace's head enshrines four silver statuettes: King James VI (James I of England) holding the Church in his arms; the Earl Marischal with scrolls of the law; Bishop Elphinstone, the University's founder; and the reigning monarch, King Edward VII.

Despite Kelly's expert tuition, a curious mistake was made in locating each coat of arms beneath its bearer. The red and gold shield of the Keith family, hereditary holders of the office of Earl Marischal, swapped position with that of James VI. When Wilson wrote in March 1907 seeking permission to borrow the mace for that year's Arts and Crafts Exhibition, Kelly readily acquiesced, on condition that whilst the mace was with him, Wilson would re-attach the shields to 'the personages to whom they belong';[110] but somehow, the error remains uncorrected (Fig. 54).

Surmounting the crystal piers between the figures are enamelled symbols of the elements – a tree for earth, foaming waves for water, a silver thunderbolt for fire, a dove for air. One of the four columns is of the unusual yellow form of rock crystal, which, though not intrinsically more valuable, succeeds in imparting a rare preciousness. Symbolic profusion extends to the greenery over them: the oak bough of truth, the thistle of Scotland, the ivy of immortality, and the white rose of innocence. At the mace's summit miniature arches and spires, tipped with spheres of jade for loyalty, are grouped around a crystal column crowned by a silver cross.

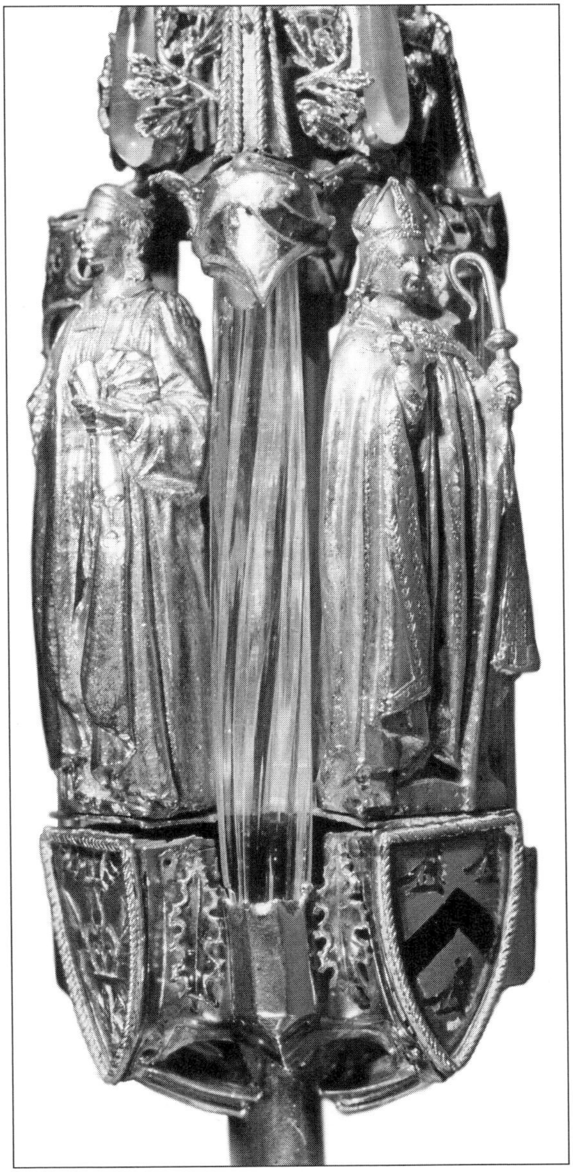

Photograph © University of Aberdeen

Figure 65. Aberdeen University, MacRitchie Mace: silver, detail with crystal and enamel, showing the Earl Marischal holding the Charter, and Bishop Elphinstone, 1906.

Bringing interrelated art forms and messages into the kind of union Wilson achieved here was a complex process. In the MacRitchie Mace their combination seems natural, unforced, almost organic – yet such effortless effects came from hard-won creative experience. Half-humorously, though with underlying seriousness and humility, Wilson summed up the artistic process and the creative trials it entailed in words that highlight some of the most important themes of his character and career:

There is nothing easier than to be an artist. It is all delight, all pleasure. Especially the pain.[111]

CHAPTER SIX

THE ALL–ROUND ARTIST

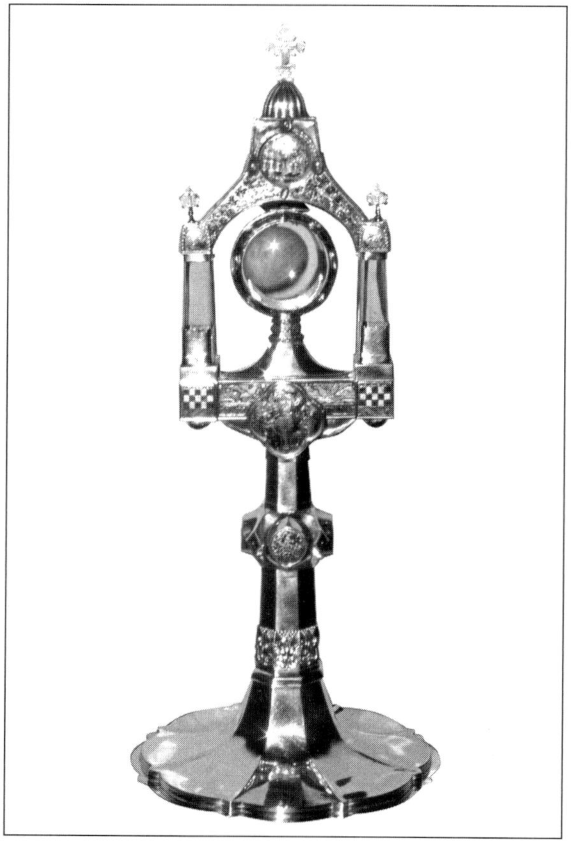

Figure 66. Caldey Abbey monstrance (*h. 61cm*), silver-gilt, enamel, crystal, 1910; transferred to Prinknash Abbey, 1928.

Wilson's move to the country prefigured his distancing himself from professional architecture, but his devotion to architecture in its broadest sense remained undiminished. Incorporating architectural features into particular jewels or pieces of metalwork – always a part of his wide-ranging, architectonic vision – became a means of retaining links with architecture without the need to align himself with the profession *per se*.

In this way, impulses from metalwork and architecture blend instinctively in the silver monstrance he made in 1910 (Fig. 66) for the Benedictine community of the Abbey on the island of Caldey, off the South Pembrokeshire coast.[1] The lightly-ribbed base and eight-sided stem and knop could be those of a silver candlestick, yet the aperture which frames the viewing compartment is like a chancel arch rising from crystal pillars, and its silver-gilt cupola a miniature Byzantine dome. Jewel-like enamel designs – the crucified and risen Christ flanked by doves and set off by bright chequerwork – enrich the threshold of the arch; above, a gable edged with vines encloses a roundel depicting a lamb amidst seven golden candlesticks (Plate 58). Its reverse, with Melchizedek offering sustenance to Abraham,[2] epitomises the liturgical role of the monstrance, whose crystal locket serves to display the wafer of the Eucharist.

Even in the smallest-scale creations of his new workshop, the grouping of masses and figures provides ample evidence of Wilson's continuing engagement with sculptural form, an important component of both Birmingham caskets and Aberdeen mace. Along with such miniaturism, 1904 saw him taking on a metalworking commission on a wholly public scale: to devise and execute new bronze double doors – the second of four such undertakings – for the fifteenth century parish church of St. Mary, Nottingham. Here, architecture could make common cause with architectural sculpture, but there was a personal significance, too, for Harry and his wife, Margaret. The raised and pierced inscription of the transom dedicates the work to one who was part of their lives: 'In loving memory of Francis Morse 1818-1886: father, pastor, friend' – Margaret's father had been vicar at the church from 1864 until the year of his death. She had been born in the vicarage in High Pavement, in November 1869, the fourth of the Morse girls, after Clara, Harriet and Winifred; the youngest, Frances, was born in 1873. Repairs to the porch of St. Mary's were put in hand by her older brother the Rev. Sidney Morse in 1898; the new doors (Plate 57), given by him in their father's memory, were used for the first time on Christmas Day 1905.

These double doors are deeply-panelled and square-headed, leaving the tympanum to reinforce, in a powerful Deposition scene, the theme of their imagery. The steeply-cranked head of the doors' stone arch dictated the form of the sculpture within it, which is balanced around a mandorla-shape. The doors themselves are each divided into ten square segments, two across by five vertically. Their five sculptural panels alternate with five plain ones, each of which has a central roundel framing a rosette, a simple device that rests the eye and accents the 'bronzeness' of the doors. The central pair bear ring-shaped drop-handles, while the panels' intersections are emphasised down the middle of each door by angel bosses.

Wilson outlined his scheme to his sponsors on 23 October 1904, explaining that the sculptural panels – depicting the life and death of Christ seen 'in relation with the Holy Mother' – aim 'by their general treatment' to suggest 'the idea of pity'. The narrative they embody reads from the top left, the Annunciation, where Gabriel 'appears at the Virgin's window in the early morning'. In the next scene, Mary shares her news with her cousin Elizabeth; beneath, is the Nativity. The Adoration of the Magi (Fig. 67) in the tier below recalls the central motif of Wilson's silver Lady Altar in St. Bartholomew's, Brighton, there finely rendered in repoussé. Ralph Cram thought this new bronze version even better: 'in perfection of line composition it is supreme'.[3] The last panel shows the Crucifixion – at the foot of a prophetic cross-shape vine in Eden stand Adam and Eve, heads bowed.

The sequence, though not strict, continues with the Resurrection, which appears at the top of the right-hand door (rather than, as Wilson first intended, as its final panel); in this unusually angular presentation, Christ emerges from the tomb in his grave-clothes, while the Spirit of Life in the form of a dove flies to his breast and 'birds sing overhead'. Beneath, to the left, is the Flight into Egypt; to the right, the Baptism in Jordan. The Entry into Jerusalem (Fig. 68) follows; here, Wilson evokes a reality that defies the scene's frame: Christ rides a donkey through a crowd that extends across – and seemingly *beyond* – the panel itself. In the last scene, the Three Marys at the Sepulchre, Wilson engages the viewer in the shock of the empty tomb with one simple gesture – Christ's mother's hands thrown up in alarm. Throughout the narrative panels, the powerful sense of a story

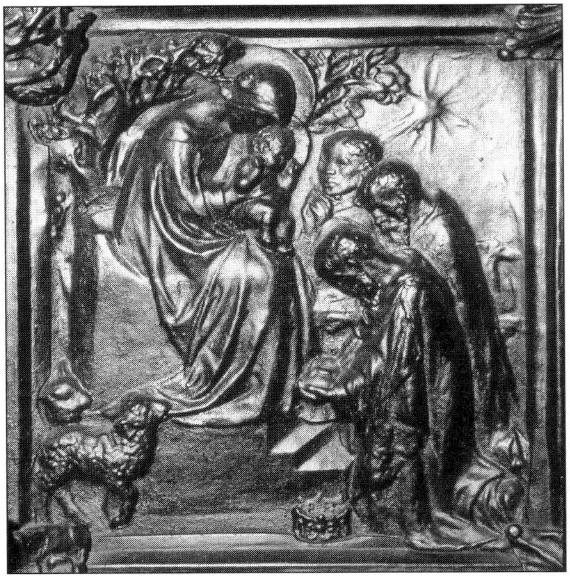

Figure 67. St. Mary's Church, Nottingham: South entrance, bronze door panel depicting Adoration of the Magi, 1904.

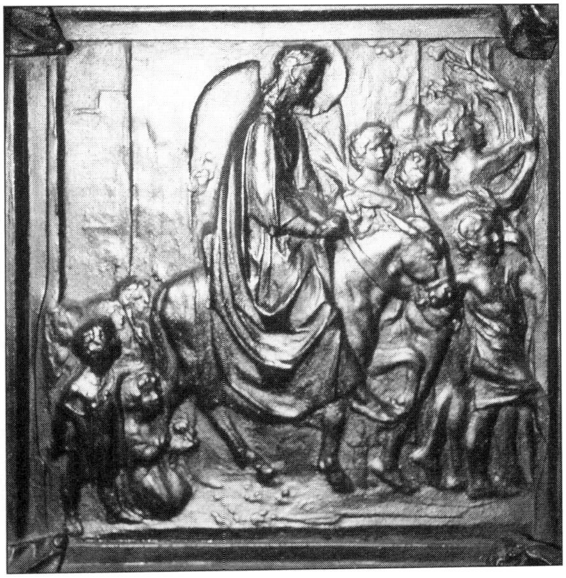

Figure 68. St. Mary's Church, Nottingham: South entrance, bronze door panel showing Entry into Jerusalem, 1904.

unfolding is sustained in fresh symbolism and spontaneous insights. And if that story, told in the panels themselves, does not visibly hinge on the idea of 'pity', Wilson supplies this in abundance with the Deposition tableau in the tympanum.

In his Welbeck pietà of the previous year, Wilson had used the semi-circular format to show Christ lying on the ground, his mother cradling his head, and the third figure, Mary the mother of James, giving comfort. Because of the geometry of the Nottingham arch, the scene becomes concentrated, heightening the sense of catastrophe. Now, just two figures are involved: Mary, seated, and Christ, his broken body held across her lap. Mary's head leans against her son's in the apex of the arch, highlighting the closeness of life and death, a proximity further emphasised as she holds his hand to her lips in a gesture that radiates the intensity of her grief. Her pose, that of a mother consoling her child, stresses the contrast between the joy of Christ's birth and the desolation of his death. Wilson had already used the potent symbolism of the touching of brows – a literal meeting in the midst of parting – in his 1903 Barnes memorial for the medieval church at Somerton, Oxfordshire.[4] There, it appears within a rectangular bronze bas-relief, given an architectural setting by F.W. Pomeroy. In the Nottingham version, the intimacy is all the starker for being in the wasteland outside a city wall, yet the wall is pierced with the Gates of Death and Life. Initially, Wilson had planned to depict a dove 'that enters weary into the one and issues strong-winged from the other', but in the finished doorhead, the Gate of Life is filled with bells pealing in jubilation. This resolution dramatically enhances the power of the whole commission; Cram's verdict on its importance was unequivocal: 'no work of its kind more perfect than this ... has been done since the cinque-cento'.[5]

Wilson's emphasis on the essential links between sculpture and architecture represents only part of his refusal to isolate the crafts from one another. With the same conviction he accentuated links between metalwork and painting, architecture and theatre, jewellery and poetry. All interrelate; all are part of the rich complexity that allows a painterly conception of colour to pervade his treatment of enamel and gems, or a sensitivity to architectural drama to inform his handling of space and emotion. His stage and costume designs give more literal expression to his feeling for theatre. In 1899 he not only collaborated in the staging of *Beauty's Awakening* at the Art Workers' Guild, but also designed the sets for an adaptation, penned for the Stage Society by the English Symbolist Arthur Symons, of an ancient Indian tale, *The Toy Cart*. This, as a contemporary reviewer suggested, derived as much from Wilson's *mise-en-scène* as from Symons's lines:

> *We can only hope that Mr. Wilson will do more work for the stage, for this production showed that he can do as well for it as he has done for the church. The cream of the performance was certain groupings, arrangements of colour, stage pictures.... In 'The Toy Cart' Mr. Wilson gives us Ajanta living and moving. The distinctive joy of the play ... was undoubtedly the joy of the eye....*[6]

That hope, that Wilson would 'do more work for the stage', was fulfilled in 1915 by his scenery and costumes for Lena Ashwell's production of the children's musical *The Starlight Express* at the new Kingsway Theatre. Adapted for the stage by Violet Pearn from the novel by Algernon Blackwood, and with a memorable score by Sir Edward Elgar, the show played from 29 December 1915 to February 1916 to glowing reviews.[7] But there was another project which, if it had progressed beyond long-distance, largely wartime correspondence, could well have established permanent evidence of Wilson's theatrical flair. In a series of letters and postcards exchanged with his friend Gordon Craig between 1913 and 1918, the pivotal topic was an idea for a 'new national theatre'[8] for London. But meeting was impossible: Wilson was in Venice, then in Kent; Craig was domiciled far away in Florence, and the world was at war. In such unpropitious circumstances, the great plan evaporated – and so, with the distance lent by time, Craig alone tends to take the credit for revolutionising

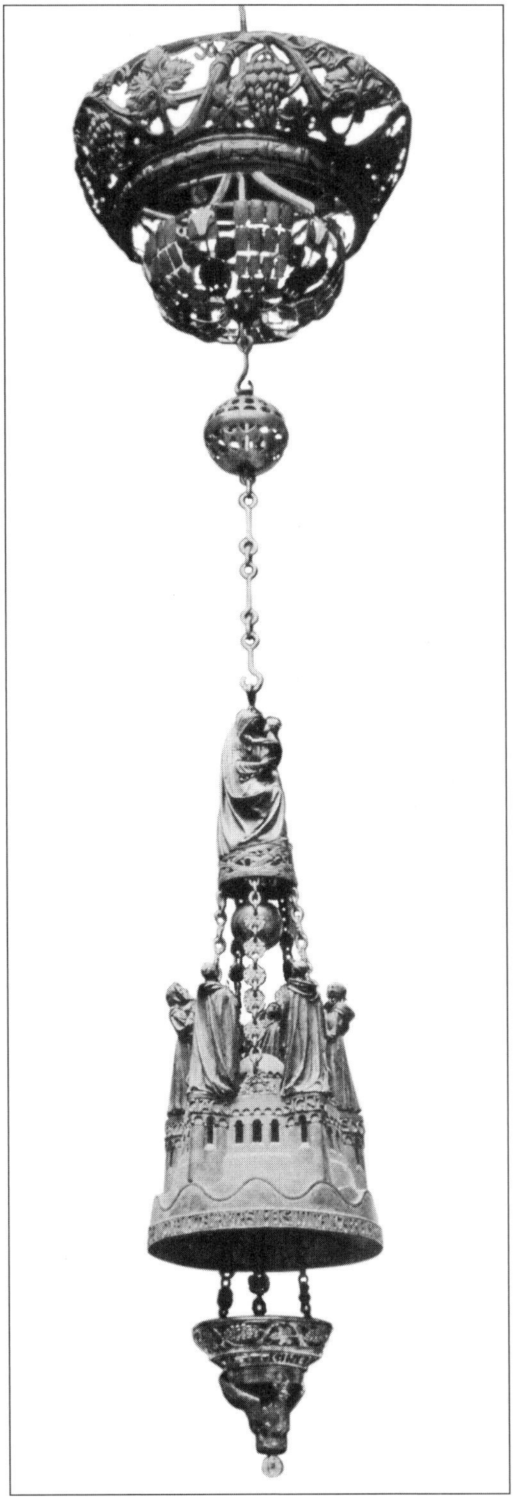

Figure 69. Sanctuary Lamp, commissioned from Wilson for Saragossa Cathedral: bronze, silver, enamel, mother-of-pearl, h. approx. 6m; *The Art Journal*, 1907.

thinking about the future of British theatre.

It was Wilson's sense of the interconnectness of the arts that often led him to transgress their usual compartments. In writing about them, he imbues all with a pervasive symbolism. A deep belief in their underlying oneness is summed up in his description of jewellery's place in his scheme of things:

It touches sculpture on the one hand and painting on the other, giving definiteness to one and concision to the other; while constructive necessities make of it a miniature architecture sparkling with suggestions.[9]

If a single piece of work that emerged from the Platt workshop in those pre-War years may be said to sum up this inter-disciplinary, allusive approach, it is the sensational hanging lamp in bronze and silver for the sanctuary of Saragossa Cathedral (Fig. 69), for which Wilson was privately commissioned in 1907.

From the topmost rim of the bronze vine-trellised corona to the crystal globe beneath the well of the lamp itself, the structure measures some 20*ft*, and comprises five distinct elements: lamp, architectural canopy with saints, Mother and Child, chain with openwork globe, and corona, the latter measuring 5*ft* across. The heads of Mary and her baby mark the mid-point of the vertical sequence, and form its focal point.

The lamp is a bowl of vine-leaves, borne on the upspread wings of a hovering dove; when lit, its suspension chains disappear from sight as they lead upwards into the wide, bell-like mouth of the bronze canopy. Around its rim is the Latin text of the Ave Maria in raised Lombardic capitals. An undulating, sea-like line, reminiscent of that on the font at Brithdir, encircles the walls of its citadel form, beneath twenty-five lancet windows. Each of its five bastions supports a silver robed saint, gazing up to the Virgin and Child.

The upper bowl of the corona, reiterating the vines of the lamp, returns the eye to Mary and Jesus, and the craning heads of the five great saints below, whose names appear in Spanish on the hems of their robes. All have particular significance for Spanish Catholics: James the Apostle of Spain; Ignatius Loyola, the founder of the Jesuit order; the mystic Teresa of Avila; and two pre-eminent founders of preaching orders, Dominic and Francis.

In the event, the would-be donor fell into financial difficulties and was unable to take possession of the lamp, never even having been required (a reminder, perhaps, of Wilson's uncertain business-sense) to secure the work with a deposit. Fortunately, Wilson's great New England advocate Ralph Cram, who had visited Platt to see the lamp prior to writing his 1908 article for *Christian Art*, had mentioned Wilson's work to wealthy Canadian businessman, world-traveller and founder of the Salada Tea Company, Peter C. Larkin. As a result of Cram's words, Larkin paid a visit to Wilson's Kent workshop. A friendship began with him and his son Gerald, which would bear significant fruit in the 1920s; but, in the meantime, the Saragossa lamp made such an impression on Larkin that he bought it on the spot, giving it a fitting home not in Spain, but in St. Thomas's Church, Toronto, where it hangs to this day.[10]

Much depends, in reading the lamp's soaring structure, on the interplay of solid and openwork forms, each illumined by the lamp's own flame and by reflected light within the church, while, as with the Gloucester chalice and Brighton pulpit, Wilson's mastery of proportion and scale finds full expression. Looking up at the lamp-canopy we are tempted to read the turrets as massive architectural features, when in reality, the saints they support are almost twice their height. Again, Wilson uses his already mysterious light-source obliquely, exploiting the quality of light itself to add an extra, intriguing dimension to the work. When the lamp is alight, the citadel's lancet windows reflect the flame below, while the shimmering hemisphere of bronze shields, enamel discs and mother-of-pearl lilies suspended from the corona acts like a baldacchino's inner dome, invoking infinity by means of a half-veiled 'beyond'.[11]

Cram himself fastened on its jewel-like character when describing the lamp in his *Christian Art* article, judging the delineation of the figures as 'crisp as ... some singularly perfect signet ring', and declaring it 'perhaps the most astounding thing visible when I was at the Thatched House'. Before leaving for its permanent home in Canada, however, the lamp had another journey to make: to the 1907 Exposition of Church Art at Aix-la-Chapelle. There it was seen by the Austrian designer Julius Hoffman, who went to great lengths to have it properly photographed for his journal *Der Moderne Stil*.[12] Cram thought it would be impossible for any photograph to convey its 'richness of colour and materials and their imaginative shaping', the very qualities that won such acclaim amongst the exhibition's reviewers.[13]

In the years to come, Larkin's proprietorial admiration for the Saragossa lamp and its fascinating blend of form and meaning would have important implications for its designer. As founding president of a leading tea company, his thoughts turned – with its Boston headquarters in mind – to a project which in the 1920s would entail Wilson working in bronze on a grand scale in Amerca; now, in 1909, Wilson was embarking on another large-scale sculptural design requiring a similarly complex synthesis, creating the work upon which the architect F.W. Troup predicted his fame would ultimately rest.[14] James Harrower, Professor of History at Aberdeen, had raised the question of a suitable memorial – none had survived – to Bishop William Elphinstone, the founder of the University.[15] Two members of a specially convened Elphinstone Committee, Dr. Kelly and James Cromar Watt, had been instrumental in commissioning the MacRitchie Mace in 1906, and its resounding success convinced the remaining seven members, including the University Librarian Dr. Peter Anderson and the Curator of the city's Art Gallery Harry Townend, to approach Wilson with the proposal. This they did, with two key stipulations, one as to its placing, the other as to its iconography. It must fit conveniently within the choir of the University's medieval chapel; and its starting point must be the description in an ancient inventory, of a lost chest-tomb which had been carved with emblematic figures of the Virtues. The only portrait of the Bishop, whose effigy was to rest on top of the new tomb, was a posthumous one, but it was enough to prompt the life-in-death quality that Wilson would conjure up in his design (Plate 60).

Wilson accepted the brief and a year later, in August 1910, outlined his preliminary ideas to the Committee at a meeting in the chapel. Five thousand copies of his proposal and sketch were made by the craft printer Emery Walker to be distributed, with an appeal for donations, amongst graduates and friends of the University. A quarter-size model was commissioned from Wilson and, this having won the Committee's full approval, a completion date of 31 December 1913 was agreed. These preliminaries settled, Wilson was paid the first third of a total fee of £1,500.

Despite meticulous planning, Wilson's completed memorial turned out so much larger than anticipated that a new site had to be found for it in the antechapel. That, too, in time proved cramped, and so in 1945 the tomb was moved to where it now stands – outside, on the paved area opposite the chapel's West doors. As first presented the scheme was for a structure 9'9" long, 6'5" broad and 4'4" high. By the time of its installation, those dimensions had grown to 16' by 10'6" by 6'4"; and the deadline had been exceeded by some thirteen years, the task protracted by illness, war and the logistics of having to work between studios and foundries in Kent, London, Paris and Venice. No doubt a further contributing factor was Wilson's own obsessive perfectionism.[17]

At the heart of the tomb is the recumbent figure of the sixteenth century Bishop laid on a bier whose narrow bronze ends, guarded by freestanding bronze figures – twin angels at the head, twin servitors at the foot – dramatically overfly the tomb's cassone-like stone core. On the two long sides, eight bronze figures, half the scale of the free-standing figures, are arranged in pairs on either side of a crowned and wreathed rosette: this feature, in the work-in-progress photographs, is half-masked by plain shields. Nothing detracts from the primacy of the Bishop on his bier (Plate 60), mitred, coped and sandalled, the long form of his silhouette modelled and cast over-lifesize. However, the quarter-size figures on the sides show how seriously Wilson rose to the challenge set by the University – eight Virtues appear, Contemplation having sprung from his own conviction to join the traditional seven. Vigorous and fully modelled, they actively triumph over eight corresponding Vices that spill over from step to plinth.

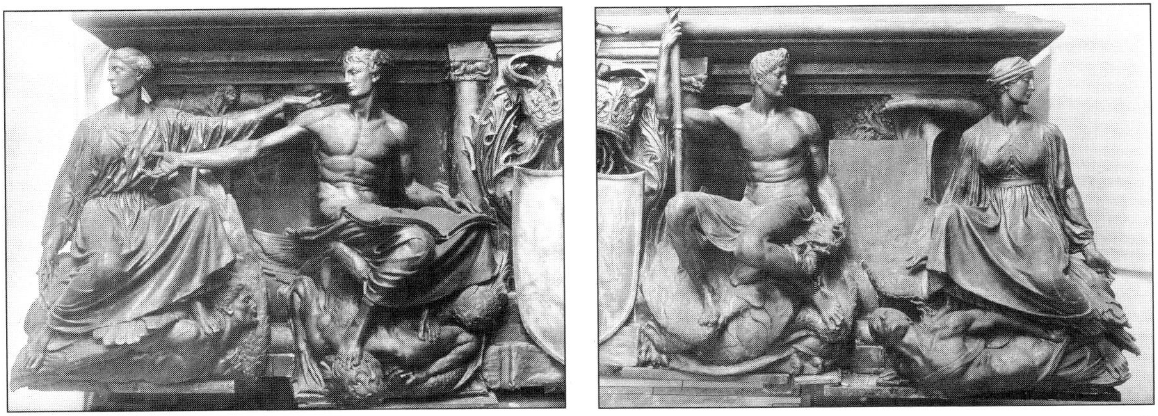

Wilson Archive, Royal College of Art

Figure 70. The Elphinstone Tomb, studio photographs of work-in-progress. North Side: (left) Prudence and Justice quell Rebellion and Injustice; (right) Temperance and Fortitude subdue Licence and Undisciplined Energy.

On the North side (Fig. 70) are Prudence, Justice, Temperance and Fortitude. Prudence, the bringer of order, is identified by the pair of compasses in her right hand. She is seated on the broken-winged Rebellion; with her left hand she reaches out to touch Justice, a book of laws open on his lap and Injustice trapped beneath his feet. The male figure of the third Virtue, Temperance, muzzles the dragon of Licence, while the fourth Virtue, Fortitude, a serene female figure holding an olive branch of peace, sits on the safely-bound Vice of undisciplined Energy.

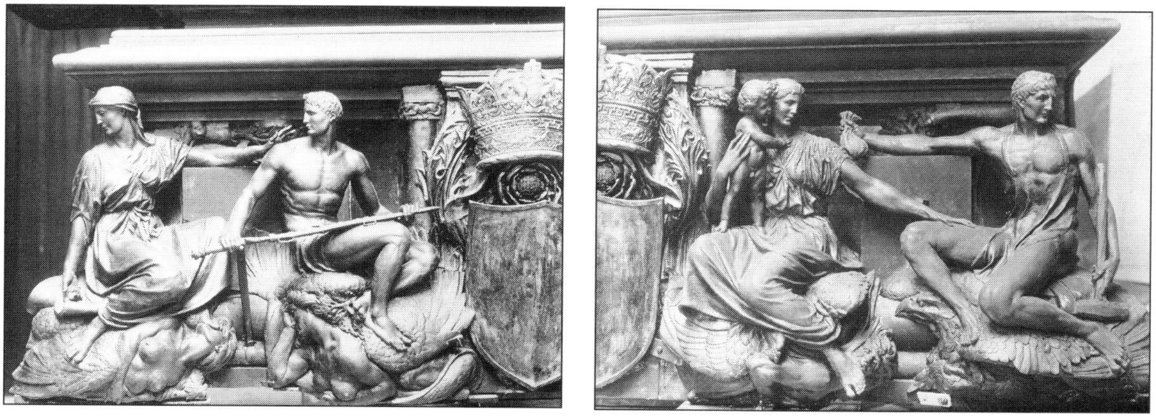

Wilson Archive, Royal College of Art

Figure 71. The Elphinstone Tomb, studio photographs of work-in-progress. South Side: (left) Contemplation and Hope defeat Folly and Despair; (right) Charity and Faith triumph over Self-Love and the Anti-Christ.

On the South side (Fig. 71) are Contemplation, Hope, Charity and Faith. Her foot restraining bare-breasted Folly, Contemplation instructs her neighbour, the youthful Hope, to aim well when he strikes Despair, the heavy-featured Vice crushed beneath him. Biting the heel of the maternal Virtue Charity, is the scaly Vice of Self-Love. With the brooding eagle of the Anti-Christ pinioned beneath him, Faith looks out across the world. The fingers of his left hand touch the haft of his mallet; with his other he brushes the shoulder of Charity with a money-bag: labour and its reward. In Wilson's iconographic scheme, Faith forms the prime emblematic figure among the Virtues, representing the shared 'creative aspect'[17] of the seven other Virtues. By adding Contemplation and the Anti-Christ to the tableau, Wilson has invoked the comforting associations of the number eight: Rebirth and Paradise Regained. And in organising the tomb's diverse forms, a characteristic Wilsonian balance has been struck between sculptural, architectural and iconographic elements. Every nuance tells: the fold of the Bishop's sleeve drooping over the edge of the bier heightens the immediacy of the Founder's solemn rest, in sleep rather than death: 'I didn't want a dead bishop on the tomb', Wilson explained later[18] – while the four standing figures keeping watch at the bier's head and foot mediate between the effigy and the twin octaves of Virtues and Vices, drawing the eye into a deeper reading of the tomb's symbolic messages.

The smaller sections of the figurative scheme were modelled and cast when the deadline still had a good chance of being met. Some details were worked out at Platt, others in the Paris studio Wilson had rented close to Barbedienne, the founder with whom he had established a close and dependable working relationship. But it was in Venice, with its intense artistic heritage, that Wilson felt he could do himself justice as a figure sculptor. Accordingly, he moved the whole family to the city in 1912 – as well as Guthlac, the Wilsons now had three daughters (Fig. 72). He took a studio at 2778 Calle del Forno, S. Maurizio, and carried out the greater part of his modelling there; it would be cast in Munaretti's nearby foundry. It was there that work was continuing, several months beyond the initial deadline, at the outbreak of war in early August 1914. The hostilities were not expected to last long; nevertheless, with their suddenly increased value as scrap, the cast and finished figures were secreted beneath the waters of a canal, and the Wilsons went home to Platt.

Anxiety and illness and the problems of drawing the threads of the project together pushed the work's delivery back to 1926, and raised the cost to the University far above Wilson's 1910 estimate. In their final report the Elphinstone Committee regretted the size of the account – in excess of £2,800 – but also celebrated the tomb's 'nobility and beauty'.[19] What they had acquired for

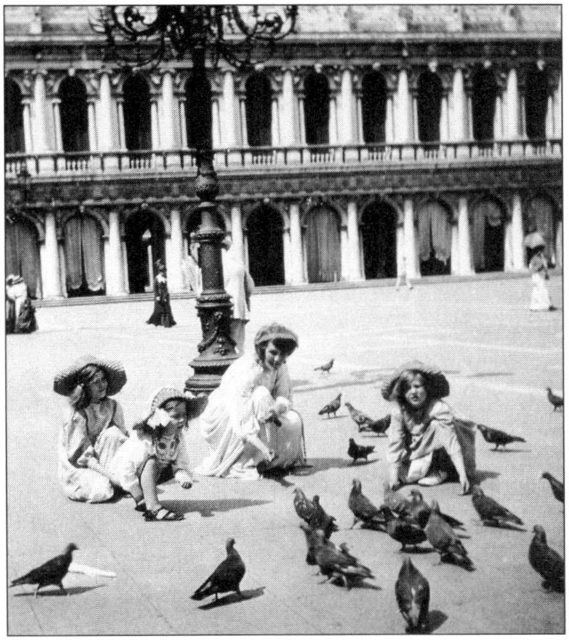

Private Collection

Figure 72. Venice: Margaret Wilson with Fiammetta, Pernel and Dione in St. Mark's Square, c. 1912.

the University was a work demanding in its symbolic complexities and richly satisfying in their sophisticated manipulation. The modelling is consistently eloquent, from the quiet modesty of Prudence to Faith's athletic perfection; the trusting innocence in the baby's clasp of its mother Charity, and the cool elegance of Justice's outstretched arm, constrast with the inspired grotesqueries of the Vices – again the music of Elgar comes to mind, the glorious viciousness of the Demons' Chorus in *The Dream of Gerontius*. Despite the travails of its assembly, and the problematic history of its installation, the tomb never loses the human touch of its story-telling; the delicate fall of drapery, or the fleeting lightness of a hand on a companion's shoulder, repeatedly transcend their bronze solidity.

In the long years of the tomb's gestation, it was the historian Professor Harrower who lent Wilson the backbone of support. He understood Wilson's devotion to the task, and, well-aware of his tendency to overwork, warned him not to take its creative demands too much to heart: 'You mustn't kill yourself over it. It is your own devastating conscience that is the matter ... .'[20] His words eerily anticipate what happened to Wilson under pressure from ongoing projects and their frustration, and from his anguished reactions to news from the Western Front. In Coventry, in March 1915, as he was climbing the scaffolding to inspect the possible siting, high above the city square, of his stone figure sculptures for the then half-built Council House, he was overcome by searing pains. He was narrowly saved from falling, and had to be carried down to ground level in agony. Desperately ill with a stomach ulcer aggravated by exhaustion, he was rushed to hospital, and his contribution to this remarkable building unceremoniously postponed.

The Council House itself was the result of a competition held in 1910 for a town hall and municipal offices. The designated site, south of the parish church of St. Michael, faced Earl Street but presented an irregular space, even after the existing shops and houses had been cleared. Two significant buildings would remain – at its north-eastern corner the Police Department (the product of a similar competition fifteen years before), and the building then serving as the Council Chamber, the fifteenth century St. Mary's Hall, which occupied the central portion. The brief stipulated that the new building take its cue from that ancient Guildhall and the two neighbouring churches, St. Michael's and Holy Trinity. Ruminating on the entries in 1911, *The Builder* quibbled with the terms of the competition, fearing that they had been too prescriptive, and that in consequence, the 130 submissions were 'generally ... disappointing'. For all that, the writer conceded that the winners, the Birmingham architects Edward Garratt and H.W. Simister, had provided bespoke accomodation within elevations which were 'admirable', and that the building demonstrated 'sympathetic knowledge of its chosen manner', collegiate or manorial late Tudor.[21] The required local echoes are effectively combined with features – notably the range of first floor oriels – evidently influenced by one of the most admired late Victorian town halls, T.E. Collcutt's, at Wakefield (1877-80). For the elevations, Runcorn sandstone was deemed a good match for the local stone; for the roofs,

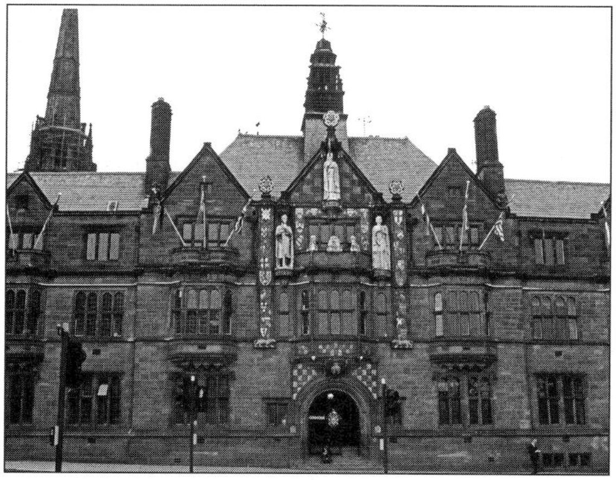

Figure 73. Coventry, the Council House: centrepiece of Earl Street façade with Wilson's sculptures, 1915-26; the spire of St. Michael's Church can be seen to the left.

deliberately paler Cotswold stone slate was chosen. The gabled entrance range (Fig. 73) is crowned with a timber cupola; to the right a square tower turns the corner to Hay Lane. As a late work of the Arts and Crafts in the public domain, what sets Coventry's Council House apart is Wilson's enrichments, both inside and out, though his involvement with the project did not start until early 1915 when, back from Venice, he was brought in by Garratt and briefed by William Grant, Alderman and distinguished local historian, regarding the iconography of the decorative details to be included. It was a blow – not least to Wilson – that its chief architect did not live to see it finished; by then Edward Garratt had been killed in action.[22]

Inside, Wilson took charge of furnishing and embellishing the new first-floor Council Chamber. Outside, he adorned all three storeys of the entrance bay, in due course carving statues in white stone for its three niches. The Hay Lane tower he dressed with the shields of civic office, and carved its four patron saints of the British Isles. Surmounting it, keeping watch over the city, is his statue of St. Michael, with fiery sword and gilded wings. Jutting from the corner of the tower is the cantilevered clock he devised, its spandrels the backswept wings of a golden angel – the original 7' copper dials were replaced with white glass following bomb damage in 1941. Clock and stone figures date from 1924.[23] These, like his other sculptural contributions to the exterior, enhance the building's sense of idealism and history.

When the contractors, Wilcock & Co. of Wolverhampton, started work in September 1912, they predicted two years for completion, at a cost of £64,000. However, with war-time limits on hours and materials, both estimates were exceeded. Some parts of the building were usable in January 1917, but the Chamber not till 1920. Wilson's own work, following his return to health in 1915, began with designs for the Earl Street façade. The blazons of the entrance bay were installed to the architects' design in the following year, with the keystone to the main arch carrying the city's arms, and with carved foliage round the jambs and archivolt to evoke the ancient Forest of Arden. A chequerwork of gold emblems spreads from the spandrels to the skirts of the oriel, while in vertical ribbons of carved, (and, unusually in British stonework of the time) painted and gilded vines, are set twenty-four shields bearing the arms of guilds and dignitaries from Coventry's history in their heraldic colours.[24]

True to Ruskin's dictum that every carving should embody an intellectual meaning, the entire array, including the contributions Wilson would later make in Portland stone, invites contemplation of the city's formative events and characters. In composing his carved 'illustrations', Wilson's thoughts probably turned to E.W. Godwin's Ruskinian-gothic Town Hall in Northampton, which dated from 1860-64 (that is, from the years before Godwin set out on his Anglo-Japanese direction), its arcaded walls studded with sculptures evoking the town's story. Godwin died when Wilson was still in Sedding's office, but his son, Gordon Craig, was one of Wilson's long-standing friends and correspondents. At the Coventry Council House, Wilson created a series of small carved figures spaced round the building at first floor level: Leofric's friend Edward the Confessor; the Black Prince, whose manor of Cheylesmore lay close by; Ranulf, Earl of Chester, founder of both St.

Michael's Church and the annual Coventry fairs; St. Michael again, and St. George, and, at the East corner, Peeping Tom, the young Saxon carpenter who spied on Lady Godiva riding naked through the streets in her bid to shame her husband Leofric into reducing the taxes of his vassals.

Wilson's major sculptures (Plate 32) in white Portland stone, are at second floor level. Earl Leofric of Mercia, the first of these larger figures to be completed, stands to the left of the parapet of the central oriel, leaning authoritatively on his sword. To the right is Godiva, gracefully robed and holding the model of St. Mary's Priory, which she founded with Leofric in 1043. On the parapet between them are smaller figures derived from history and archetype including, on the left, the old man Wisdom. Above the upper window's mullion stands the unifying figure of Justice with sword erect; the openwork lettering identifying all three of the larger figures is picked out in gold at their feet. The delay that plagued their installation was neither of Wilson's making, nor attributable to his 1915 illness. The decision by architects and Council alike to include them was as 'old as the building itself'.[25] Once Wilson had been appointed, monies were set aside, and an order confirmed with him towards the end of the War. But by September 1922, when he informed the council that the figures were almost ready, the allotted sum had been used for other things, and he and his family were about to move permanently to France. The Council House Committee enabled him to be paid from the rates, but thought it best to wait until spring before setting his sculptures in place; Leofric was not lifted into position until 1924, and a further two years passed before Godiva and Justice joined him.

Wilson, meanwhile, had been getting on with furnishing the Council Chamber, the richest of the rooms and the last to be finished prior to the building's official opening by King George and Queen Mary in 1920. Entered from the corridor leading from the grand staircase, it is fully panelled with a public gallery on the South side – part of Wilcock's contract – and mullioned and transomed windows to the North, facing St. Mary's Hall. Their stained glass is by Harvey & Ashby of Birmingham; Godiva occupies the central window, flanked by Edward III, who granted Coventry's charter in 1345, and Henry VI, who gave it city status a century later. The chamber has a high coved ceiling with plaster enrichments by Robert Catterson-Smith. The seating, designed by Wilson, was made by his old associate Micklewright in his Somerset workshop – the craftsman responsible, a dozen years earlier, for the oak pulpit supplied during Wilson's restoration of Lynton church. The main arc of seats of Warwickshire oak inlaid with ebony, is carved with forest boughs; Wilson dignified the Mayor's throne and the ends of the aldermen's benches with figure-carvings, introducing among the Muses – Poetry, Comedy, Tragedy, History – the legendary local ghost, the Veiled Nun of Polesworth.[26]

In its distillation of the core values of craftsmanship, tradition and purposeful design, Coventry Council House is a vivid expression of Arts and Crafts ideals in the second decade of the twentieth century; Wilson's then Presidency of the Arts and Crafts Exhibition Society, a role he filled from 1915 to 1922, was studiously recorded in the programme for the opening ceremony. Significantly, the decorative embellishment of the building's façade, alluding to a venerable civic tradition, coexisted with the most up-to-date facilities of the day: the hollow tile and concrete floors were fireproof, and the Waygood Otis lifts were installed 'with a view to easy working conditions and intercommunication',[27] as befitted a complex, practical building at the heart of a modern municipality.

Wilson's physical collapse at Coventry might have floored a man less tough and resourceful. But his recovery, painful though it was, was driven by a determination which meant that within months he was combining work on the final stages of the Coventry and Elphinstone commissions with important new projects in silverwork and jewellery. Not only that, there were examiner's reports to be written for the art schools, and he was brimming with ideas relating to his Presidency of the Arts and Crafts Exhibition Society; besides which proof of his revived optimism, he was eager to throw himself into plans for post-war reconstruction, and ready to rekindle with Gordon Craig schemes for a National Theatre. Soon, in this way, his career resumed the essentially interleaving course that had shaped it from the moment the Wilsons first arrived in Platt.

Within weeks of their moving in to the Thatched House in 1902, Henry Wilson had accepted a job offered him by the architect Leonard Stokes, who was counting on him to devise inventive sculptural enrichments for the brand-new All Saints' Convent (now Pastoral Centre) at London Colney. This Anglican community, founded in 1851, was a satellite of All Saints' Church, Margaret Street, caring for the sick and elderly and for orphaned children, but within fifty years it had outgrown its London premises. By 1899, Colney Park, a Regency mansion in wooded grounds to the south of St. Albans, had been purchased and demolished, and soon, Stokes's neo-Tudor structure of red and purple brick banded with stone was arising on the site. Arranged around a cloistered garth, it was thoroughly conducive to communal life, to the nursing of patients, to calm reflection. Wilson's carved entablature-frieze to Stokes's entrance was completed in 1903, uniting architecture, sculpture, text and symbol and giving a spiritual focal point to an extraordinary complex of buildings that in 1927 would be further enhanced by Ninian Comper's elegantly pinnacled chapel.

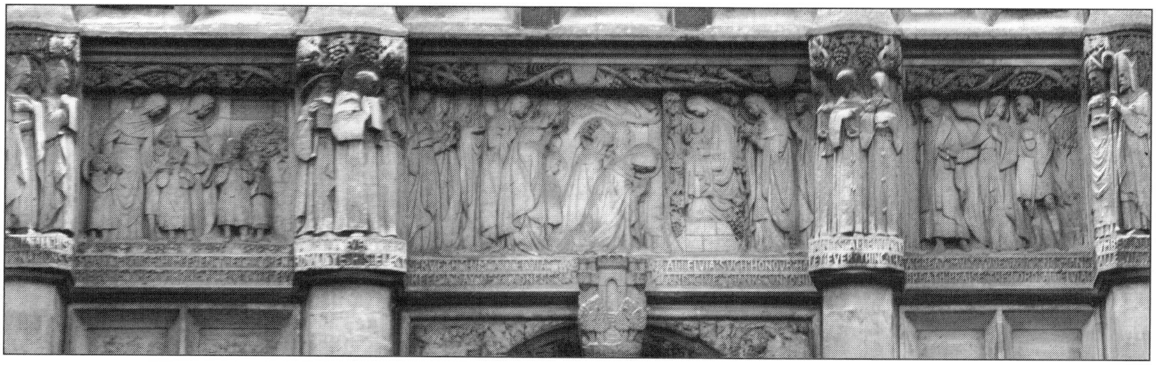

Figure 74. London Colney, All Saints' Convent: Wilson's carved Procession of Saints, Patriarchs and inscription, with keystone depicting Heaven's Gate flanked by Annunciation and Pietà, 1903.

Stokes's gate-tower steps forward of the building line on giant piers. Within these he sets back the entrance wall between smaller rounded piers of stone, two in the corners, two more widely spaced to frame the arch-headed door. The keystone extends into a broad stone entablature four feet high and about twenty-two wide (Fig. 74). This area, along with the flanking spandrels of the door, was reserved for Wilson's design, while high up on the gate-tower, three niches were also available. For these Wilson carved three female saints, Agnes, Mary and Scholastica, sculptures that add further coherence to the façade.

In a continuous band interrupted only by the keystone, the lowest 9" of the entablature bears an inscription from the responses for All Saints' Day: 'Alleluia, all His saints shall praise Him ... let everything that hath breath praise the Lord. Alleluia, amen'. The two lines of raised lettering have a crisp, monoline simplicity reminiscent of Edward Johnston's work as passed down through his pupil Eric Gill, while the words' rhythmic spacing reflects Wilson's characteristic flair for balance and emphasis. The keystone (Fig. 75) is carved with the turreted Gate of Heaven, Lethaby's 'universal temple', with seven stairs leading up to its arched doorway between twin trees in which perch two doves of peace; the 'heavenly spring', the Water of Life, flows from beneath the trees' roots. Wilson continues to enrich familiar Marian iconography with his own potent mythic and mystical archetypes. The left-hand spandrel of the door-arch presents an unusual interpretation of

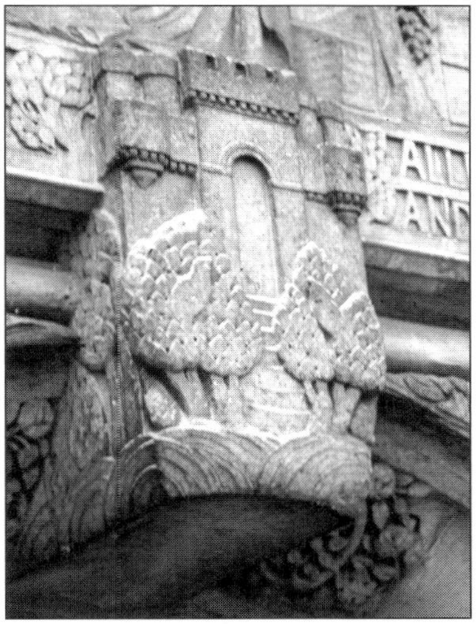

Figure 75. London Colney, All Saints' Convent: keystone with Heaven's Gate.

the Annunciation story, with Mary stretching forward to accept the sleeping baby proffered by an angel, while in the right-hand spandrel, Wilson disturbs the expected format of the pietà by decisively advancing the body of the dead Christ towards the viewer. Further engaging detail appears in his designs for the inside of the head of the arch, which is carved with Christ on one side and Heaven on the other.

In the main sculptural tableau above the Alleluia text, Stokes's rounded piers seem as if cut into to reveal their figures, pairs of patriarch saints – from Patrick and Augustine before the Synod of Whitby, to Dunstan and Benedict after it – crucial in the formation of the English Church. Under a frieze of vines, they frame three panels filled with gentle yet positive human momentum – shepherds and angels approaching from the right, children and their nurses from the left – to where saints special to the Community (Margaret and Edith, the young David and his mother Mordwenna) bow before the Virgin and Child.

The success of Wilson's enrichment of Stokes's building was highlighted when, in 1905, William Reynolds-Stevens, Townsend's collaborator at Great Warley, addressed the Royal Institute of British Architects; his subject was the need for true integration between building and sculpture. It was Wilson's modern, uncluttered approach at London Colney that, in his opinion, set the ideal standard – his sympathetic work there 'really adds a beauty to the building as a whole'.[28]

The sculptures for All Saints kept Wilson's new workshops at Platt not just busy, but at full stretch; indeed, the commission from Stokes had to be dovetailed in with a the reordering of the sanctuary of a South London parish church, St. Bartholomew's, Sydenham. Here, too, the impulses of architecture are interlaced with sculpture and symbolism. Another of Vulliamy's 1820s churches, the building was in Gothic style; in 1857 it had been given a new East end with canted apse. Wilson's task was to reconfigure the altar area up to the high-set windows. Hardwoods would be the principal material, polished and inlaid, or carved in low relief and painted and, in the bands of lettering, gilded. In glimmering contrast to these darker tonalities, Wilson created an altar-frontal from a sheet of blue marble, its surface slightly undulated to reveal its inner luminescence, while pairs of silver repoussé medallions high on the altar-wings harmonise with the silver and ebony of the altar-cross and candlesticks he designed as part of the ensemble.

The reredos (Plate 8) reworks the landscape format of an Adoration he had made when finishing Sedding's Cardiff commission of 1889-90, St. Dyfrig's Church. Under a vine-bower growing from the left margin, Joseph leans over Mary and her baby, looking down on the first of the Kings kneeling with his gift; just right of centre, a red-robed angel turns to beckon, with a sweep of his hand, two hesitant shepherds, from the the right-hand margin. The composition is framed between oak piers and separated from the altar by a supplicating text in Latin, and from the East window by a deep border that has the intricacy and surprise of an illuminated manuscript.[29] The vine-bower continues upwards in two relief bands enclosing more of Wilson's fine, elongated lettering, gold against a scarlet background, and three roundels, carved and painted with lion and lamb, a ship, and guardian of the world, signifying peace, salvation and divine protection. The simple side-wings concentrate the eye on the altar: tall archangels, a third life-size, their heads level with Mary's knee and painted in Burne-Jones colours, occupy the lower niches, while four silver relief roundels depict the Annunciation, the two Marys at the foot of the cross, the expulsion from Eden, and St. Michael tending a garden with sword and spear. The last element to be installed, in 1906, was the oak altar-rail, again adopting vine motifs, and for its balusters, crosses within vine-wreaths.[30]

Involving, as they did, stone, wood-carving and metalwork, the Stokes and Sydenham commissions fully tested the studio and workshops at Platt, as if in preparation for the more comprehensively architectural contract that Wilson signed in 1903. This commission, for the 6th Marquess of Londonderry, would occupy him and his team up to 1910.

Wynyard Hall, a huge neo-classical house near Stockton-on-Tees, is effectively the 'Waterloo Palace' that a grateful nation had sought to give to the victorious Duke of Wellington. It was to be built on the site of his Berkshire seat, Stratfield Saye, which would have been demolished to make way for it. Designed in the 1820s by Benjamin Wyatt, the grandeur of the stately new building had seemed eminently suited to the purpose. However, its blueprint was not to the Duke's liking. The proposed 'palace' was therefore shelved, and plans made instead to aggrandise the existing Stratfield Saye. The drawings for the intended 'palace' were purchased by Wellington's friend and former lieutenant, Lord Stewart, ambitious to augment the Durham coal fortune he had recently acquired through marriage, with which had also come the Georgian mansion, Wynyard Hall, in need of rebuilding after a bad fire. Philip Wyatt reworked his brother Benjamin's 'palace' drawings to incorporate that damaged old edifice, and, paid for by his new and highly successful coaling port of Seaham, Lord Stewart ordered work to proceed at a cost of £102,000.

Included within the house was a Chapel, built out to the West of the new North front, itself resplendent with a six-columned Corinthian porte-cochère. It was fortunate that when a serious fire broke out in the Chapel in 1841 and gutted the Western part of the house, Wyatt's drawings survived; the owner, by then the 3rd Marquess of Londonderry, spent almost £50,000 replicating the original rooms, but with costlier materials: even Disraeli, a guest at Wynyard in the 1840s, felt disconcerted at their lavishness. When the Marquess died in 1854, his widow commemorated him with an equestrian statue by Raffaele Monti in Durham, and a Monument Room adjoining the Western bay of Wynyard Hall's Chapel – a stone catafalque, offset in the space, is surrounded with battle-honours and bears the Marquess's recumbent effigy in bronze, presumably by the same sculptor.

It was the young 6th Marquess, a man with strong views on art and design, who approached Wilson in 1903 with notions of refurbishing the Chapel and Monument Room. In 1888, a third major fire, this time confined to the Chapel, had brought the distinguished Gothic architect James Brooks up from London to see what he could do with the shell. Wilson was now being asked to reinvent 'Brooks's Chapel' (often thus named in his correspondence with the Marquess), to produce a fresh effect. His preliminary drawing (Fig. 76) was published in *Moderne Bauformen* in 1910, and with the work nearing completion, gave an indication of the sumptuousness he achieved with his team at Platt, together with Trask's carpenters, and the glass-maker Louis Davis.[31] The unusual chancel-beam – with its single lily flanked by Mary and the angel of the Annunciation replacing the traditional rood – was omitted, as was a procession of life-size figures in carved plaster for the South wall, exchanged in the finished scheme for grey Italian marble richly-veined with brown. But, if anything, the barrel-vault of the ceiling, latticed rather than coffered and painted deep blue, is more impressive. With panels of vines picked out in silver and gold and armorial shields, and with gilded and chequered ribs, its vibrant colouring gains added harmony by the care with which Davis matched his glass in the small windows to Wilson's scheme. One of Wilson's priorites was (as shown) to move the organ from the window side to a less intrusive site in a new recess in the South wall, and it is with a distinctly Italianate baldacchino, its gold and green mosaic half-dome set on specially imported marble, that Wilson crowns his transformation of Wynyard's sanctuary.

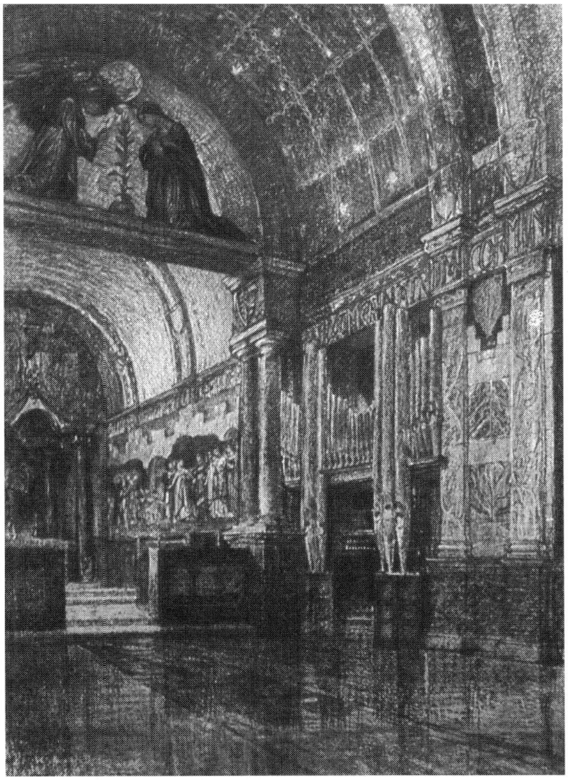

Figure 76. Wynyard Hall, Co. Durham: Wilson's 1903-04 scheme for redecoration of Chapel, *Moderne Bauformen,* 1910.

For whatever reason, the Monument Room, though enthusiastically discussed, was never actually tackled. Wilson was all for moving the catafalque to a central position, and dignifying it with a canopy; his scheme proposed barrel-vaulting the space to match the Chapel, and giving it a 'living' function as a baptistry. To this end, he submitted two sketches to the Marquess, one of a conventional font, the other a life-size bronze angel, standing against the wall with a marble bowl in his extended palms. So bold an interpretation of an otherwise familiar receptacle would have brought that other-wordly aura seen in the Tinling memorial and the Welbeck pietà. The Marquess was much taken with the idea, declining even to consider the more conventional design.[32] However, the contract was terminated without anything being done. The 3rd Marquess's tomb remains, without canopy, in its offset position, under a ceiling by James Lindsay of Sunderland and a skylight by Wailes, recording in its 72 stained-glass panels the campaigns the Marquess had undertaken, but in hues lacking the subtlety of either Wilson's or Davis's work.

In 1909, with the Wynyard commission still a year from completion and work on the Elphinstone Tomb about to start, Wilson returned to St. Martin's Church, Marple to create a new Christopher Chapel in the North aisle. Once again, his skills would unite the impulses of architecture, sculpture and drama. His larger than life-size white plaster figure (Plate 25) seems to break free of the wall behind it. Poised to stride towards us, it recalls in its vital force Rodin's indomitable John the Baptist of 1880. Its effect, emphasised by minimal drapery – cloak and loincloth – is delivered on a scale unprecedented in Wilson's work, while its virtually three-dimensional gestures connect with the viewer through sheer active masculine energy. On seeing it, a fellow member of the International Society of Sculptors, Painters and Gravers wrote to congratulate Wilson, and to 'agree ... that our conception of Christianity needs invigorating with a much more manly presentation of it than we are accustomed to ... .'[33]

With one hand St. Christopher stays his cloak. With the other he steadies the infant Christ sitting on his shoulder. The baby clings to St. Christopher's head with an endearingly child-like clumsiness, captured by Wilson in sketches made of his own children, while with his free hand he points spontaneously out of the enclosing frame. Skilfully exploiting the theatre of space, Wilson has directed our attention beyond the sculpture itself: we must turn round to discover what the child has spotted – Mary his mother, glimpsed, as it were, in a plaster medallion at the top of a nave pier.

The multi-disciplinary nature of Wilson's career was endorsed by the academic world in 1910, when he was adopted as one of that year's candidates for the Slade Professorship of Fine Art at Oxford, an appointment lasting three years. John Ruskin had been the first to occupy the role, from 1869; more recently, H.E. Wooldridge R.A., fresco-painter, stained-glass designer and musician had held it, his tenure twice renewed up to 1904, then Sir Charles Holmes, painter, critic and

Director successively of the National Gallery and the National Portrait Gallery, who served twice. The University's Board of Management had to weigh up supporting statements from distinguished artists and teachers stressing Wilson's range as a thinker and artist, and his authority and attractiveness as a speaker – ideal qualifications for the eight one-hour lectures required, surveying Art and its application from that individual's unique viewpoint.

Richard Norman Shaw, architect and Academician, left no doubt as to Wilson's accomplishments as practical artist and communicator:

> *Trained as an architect (which I may be pardoned for considering the best of all training!) and in which he is a master, his knowledge of the kindred arts of painting and sculpture is also very great.... His feeling for colour is quite exceptional and he has produced many pieces of jewellery and metalwork which appear to me to be unsurpassed in the whole range of modern work.... He would be an invaluable teacher, with broad views on art in its many branches and ample knowledge of all of them. I consider that it would be impossible to find one more qualified to fill the post.*[34]

Equally enthusiastic testimonials came in letters from two veteran painters: William Holman Hunt, a founder with Morris of the Society for the Protection of Ancient Buildings, who recommended Wilson as 'a practical artist in the most extensive sense and a teacher whose sincerity and elevation of ideals are of a rare distinction',[35] and Arthur Hughes, who declared Wilson's facility for conveying his experience of the crafts 'learned, lucid, inspiring and useful'.[36] Edouard Lanteri, head of sculpture at the Royal College, felt his 'eloquent idealism ... could be of great benefit to the nation',[37] while Augustus Spenser, the College's Principal, cast him as a 'man of high artistic ability'[38] who would most worthily fill the vacancy.

Auguste Rodin himself wrote from Paris, that

> *ses idées sur l'art et son éxperience practique basée, ne pourrait qu'être très utile pour l'éducation des jeunes ... et des amateurs qui pourraient assister aux lectures ... .*[39]

while from German-speaking design circles, warm endorsements were sent by Max Schmid, Professor of the History of Art at Aix-la-Chapelle's Technische Hochschule, and by the celebrated author of *Das englische Haus*, Hermann Muthesius.[40]

Wilson's qualifications for the Slade Professorship appeared beyond question. Nevertheless, some of his friends were privately baffled by the prospect, not least Frank Morley Fletcher, Head of Edinburgh School of Art, and, as one of the original teachers at the Central, a trusted colleague:

> *I cannot think of it as a compatible or sane arrangement at all. Do you really mean it, or was it just a freak idea? I cannot imagine you wasting your time over the wives and daughters of Oxford dons.*[41]

Of course, the primary consideration for this particular candidate – Gordon Craig's 'practical idealist'[42] – would have been to turn a receptive audience, privileged or not, into allies in a good cause. But it was a chance he would not be offered. In June the University chose Selwyn Image, designer, illustrator and fellow-Guildsman;[43] and Wilson returned to more familiar bases for the spreading and enactment of his cherished ideas as craftsman, designer and educator. The century had events and challenges in store for design that would far exceed in influence an election to an Oxford professorship.

CHAPTER SEVEN

LEARNING BY LIVING

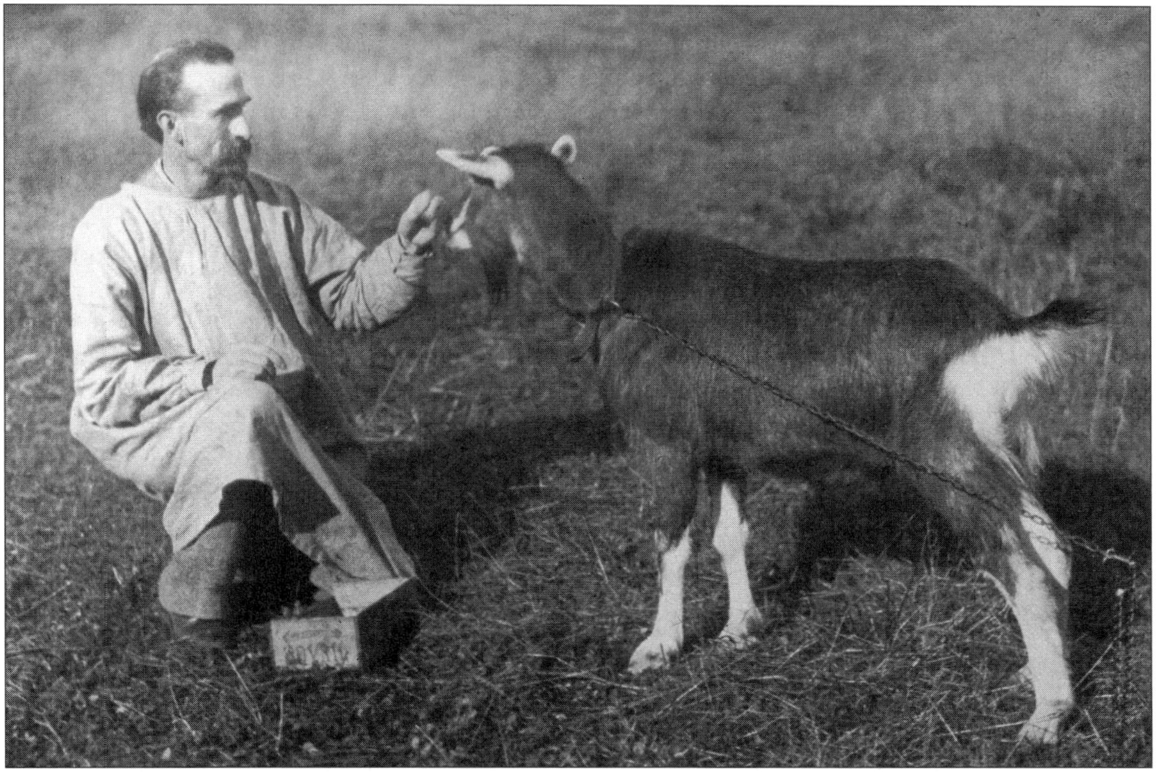

Private Collection

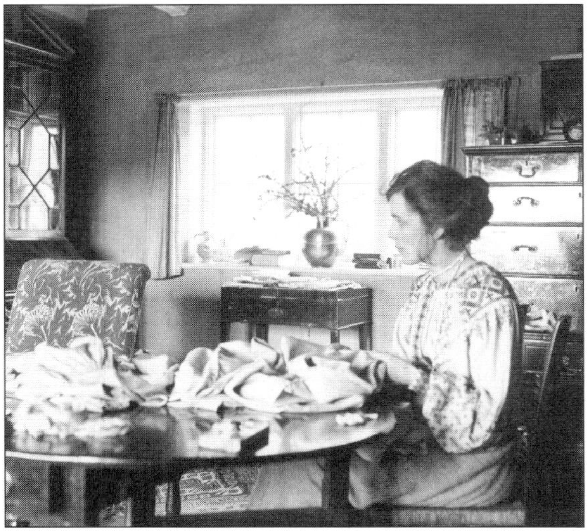

Private Collection

Figure 77. (top) Harry Wilson feeding a goat at The Thatched House, Platt, 1906.

Figure 78. (above) Margaret Wilson sewing at The Thatched House, 1906.

If Henry Wilson may be characterised as a lifelong educator, nowhere is that role more completely exemplified than in the upbringing of the four children he and Margaret brought into the world between 1902 and 1909. Their first child was born in April 1902, a son, Guthlac. His memories of boyhood at The Thatched House would be of the animals, of things being made in the workshops, of his mother's serenity, and his father's endless supply of information and stories. Into this patient and productive ambience were born, between 1904 and 1909, three daughters, Fiammetta, Pernel and Dione. Neither Guthlac nor his sisters attended conventional elementary school. Artistic and erudite, Wilson fully understood the educative value of simple, practical activities, and though himself the son of schoolteachers, his distaste for the usual methods of educating children was intense. His own children would be brought up to shoulder simple tasks in the workshop, to share in the gardening and cooking, and to help with the family's practical menagerie, the Wilsons' goats, rabbits and chickens (Figs. 77, 78). Such activities, together with reading, eurythmics and basic chores, formed their early education – a more far-reaching one, Wilson felt sure, than could ever be imparted in most school classrooms:

> *Even babies can collect eggs, feed fowls, tend rabbits.... There is no task too small to teach great lessons about life, no occupation but gives scope for art, science, or philosophy.*[1]

Wilson's attitude to early learning reflected the deeper consciousness of educational issues that unfolded during the first two decades of the twentieth century. The political, social and economic upheaval dominating the period stimulated a sense of education as a fundamental public service.

The 1902 Education Act had confirmed the role of local authorities as providers of educational facilities; subsequent measures, such as the official recognition in 1912 of the Technical Schools, and the passing of the Fisher Education Act in 1918, ensured closer links between education and industry. At the same time came a growing recognition of the ethical aspects of education. Both Friedrich Froebel (whose theories were well-known to Wilson, not least from talking to Isobel, his Froebel-trained sister-in-law), and Maria Montessori insisted that the development of the individual's character was every bit as important as academic achievement. Their views were endorsed by the New Education movement, which flourished in Britain between 1890 and 1914, and the New Ideals in Education Conferences, at which Wilson himself was to make some distinguished appearances,[2] and embraced by the Arts and Crafts groups whose members – designers, architects, and craftsmen like Crane, Lethaby, Gaskin and Wilson – played important roles within the educational establishment.

Throughout his discussions of education, the breadth of Wilson's interpretation of the word is evident. He refused to see it as some special activity artificially confined to particular age groups and to strictly 'useful' subject areas; rather, in common with other progressive educationalists, he took the view that education was quite simply an integral aspect of being alive. 'Whether we will or no,' he wrote,

> *life insists upon educating us, and by following her ways we may learn with less pain ... than if we follow systems which leave life too much in the background. Properly considered, education should result in the extension of consciousness and the absorption of the self in the wider consciousness of the community.*[3]

Life in modern industrialised society, however, could seem positively inimical to such an educational process:

> *Walk through any large industrial town and study the faces of the people passing by. Nine out of ten will be suffering from some kind of mental or moral suppression....*[4]

He argued that the palpable benefits industry had brought – machine-aided manufacture, railways, the internal combustion engine, aerial transport (which for Wilson still included airships) – could only represent real value where the workforce was happily and fairly employed rather than subsisting as virtual slaves of the process, and if the benefits of what was being produced were available to all, not just to sectional interests. Writing in 1916, he could discern few positive signs. His bleak image of the urban landscape echoes scenes that Dickens described some sixty years earlier.

> *Down a long slope stretched rows of low, mean hovels of raw-beef brick, with grimy gardens, stunted trees ... struggling for existence in the poisoned soil. Evil-smelling grog shops at every corner, and a grimy corrugated-tin mission church made the more hideous by decay and flapping posters. Butchers' shops and bluebottles, ...*

gasometers, squabbling children, mangy dogs yawning on dirty doorsteps, sardine tins and frightened cats.... And then the voices [of] the ... pitiable women, and the waste paper, and the garbage, and the empty beer bottles, and the broken palings, and the washing, the unseemly, patched and pitiful washing.[5]

In such a context, any compassionate ideology that education might profess was conspicuously failing; instead of education influencing industry, industry was corrupting education. The effect of 'false industrial ideals' seemed all-pervasive: everything, including teaching, had to be 'done by system' which, Wilson maintained, had succeeded in 'industrialising teaching, but not helping education'.[6]

Whenever he focuses on the problems of contemporary education, he invariably returns to discussing the same faculty that had shaped his entire attitude to life: creativity. He cites the author of *Erewhon*: 'The essence of effective education is expressed in Samuel Butler's memorable phrase "Don't learn to do, but learn in doing".'[7] Butler's maxim is at the heart of Wilson's *Silverwork and Jewellery*, and is woven into all his later writings: 'The Value of Learning by Doing', 'The Suppression of the Creative Instinct', 'The Creative Impulse ... in Education'.[8] Had the Slade Professorship come his way, it's not hard to guess what his lectures would have been about.

All four Wilson children inherited his convictions. The careers of the first two, Guthlac and Fiametta, were cut tragically short. Guthlac, born in 1902, seems the embodiment of his father's belief that 'As early man's hand grew more skilful, so his mind became more active'.[9] To a man who held that manual aptitude expanded mental capacity, it seemed perfectly feasible to trace a direct link from the competent use of tools to mathematics, physics, engineering and beyond, to astro-physics, astronomy and philosophy. Harry and Margaret had named their son after the Fenland hermit-saint of Saxon times, attractive to them for his rapport with the wild creatures that shared his solitary life at Crowland. Like his siblings, Guthlac mastered the rudiments of handcraft in the Platt workshops, eventually opting to become a civil engineer – a calling not unknown in the family, with his uncle Harold Morse already established in the profession in Birmingham, while grandfather Wilson had given up the prospect only after being persuaded to go into teaching. An expert in concrete design, by his forties Guthlac was acting as consultant on the Festival Hall on London's South Bank – alongside Leslie Martin and his team of L.C.C. architects under the general direction of Robert Matthew – to design the structure of the roof's shell-vault. No doubt it was through Guthlac that Professor Martin discovered the fifty-year-old Liverpool Cathedral competition entry – the radical scheme with concrete ripple-vault submitted by Lethaby and Wilson – that he would include in his lectures in the Cambridge Architecture School. Guthlac Wilson specialised in bridge design, and it was while making surveys for a new bridge in Tanganyika (Tanzania) in 1953 that he met his death in a plane crash, aged 51.

Guthlac's first sister, Fiammetta Giulietta Francesca, acquired this romantic string of names through her parents' acknowledgement of the country of her birth: they were staying in Italy in 1904. Encouraged by Grace Christie, whose *Embroidery and Tapestry Weaving* appeared in the Artistic Craft series alongside *Silverwork and Jewellery*, Fiammetta had, as a girl, set up her first loom at The Thatched House, and grew to be a skilled weaver. However, having contracted sleepy sickness (*encephalitis lethargica*) during one of the epidemics that swept through Europe after 1917, she was never strong. In the 1930s, she moved to the New Forest, where she worked for four years within a small community of artistic weavers. Frequent appointments at London hospitals meant leaving Hampshire for a flat in Westminster. She died in August 1940 in her 37th year, but already her work had won her recognition as Master of the Guild of Weavers, Spinners and Dyers.[10]

The last two Wilson girls showed a natural feeling for music. Pernel Imogen Yolande, her naming drawing on chivalric sources and the Symbolist poets, was born in 1906; her aptitude flourished in a family receptive to Dalcroze's theories of teaching music, and would form the foundation of her career as a professional violinist. Her sister, Dione Narona Margarita, was born, like Fiametta, under Italian skies: by the time of her birth in 1909, Wilson had installed the entire family in Venice while he worked on the Elphinstone commission. She would find a different, though no less passionately engaged form of creative expression. Her early vocation was as a cellist, but she left her course at the Paris Conservatoire when her father's health began to fail in 1928, and, inspired by her early experiences of cooking for the family at The Thatched House, she qualified as a Cordon Bleu chef. On moving to London, she became a freelance caterer whose clients included the Prince of Wales and the Archbishop of Canterbury, before starting her own restaurant in Sloane Street. When the Blitz made business impossible she moved to Manhattan and opened The Cordon Bleu restaurant and cookery school in 1942; here, her famous lunchtime demonstrations of omelette-making never failed to draw a crowd. In the post-war years she had her own show on CBS television and, with her quintessentially English accent and arresting presence, became one of the first celebrity chefs, placing fine cuisine on a par with music; she would later marry the influential Modernist architect Colin Lucas.[11]

Keenly observant of the progress of his own children, Wilson was decisive as to where education was going wrong at all levels – it was artificial, over-disciplined and over-regulated, at the expense of individuality and self-expression. It should release the learner's own powers and allow the individual to be the 'pupil of his own soul'.[12] To refer to the stultifying system of drilling and directing that his generation called education was, in his view, a gross misnomer. To a great extent his analysis was accurate. Between the end of the nineteenth century and the Great War the elementary syllabus was dominated almost exclusively by the three Rs and religious instruction, and the teacher's authority was unquestionable. To be sure, there were moments of relaxation in the regime – once a week there might be an art class when coloured chalks, watercolour blocks and crayons were brought out, and the best work displayed on the walls – yet even during such nominally liberal creative pursuits those who were naturally left-handed were routinely constrained to work with their right hand. Wilson's 1916 portrayal of a typical class, though deliberately provocative in a Blakean way, is not without a strong element of truth:

> *The bright cherub, all instinct and impulse, is set down in a schoolroom of oppressive plainness. Everything is contrived to make knowledge repulsive. Emotion makes movement, and movement intensifies emotion. For that reason children are settled at desks. They are spoonfed from textbooks written specially for children in a special language – the language of drivel, piffle and poppycock. They are set tasks more-or-less dissociated from … actual life. No account is taken of differences of character. Individual enthusiasm is supplanted by a kind of machine-made alertness … .*[13]

The system condemns itself in a seemingly innocuous statement, on which Wilson pounces:

> *The whole essential falsity of our modern idea of school is expressed in the sacrosanct valediction of the headmaster, '… you are now leaving school to enter real life'.*[14]

As a son of the schoolhouse, Wilson must often have found himself caught in debates about current educational trends, especially when, after retiring, his father was free to help with some of his commissions. The younger Wilson was bound to gravitate towards educational pressure groups which reflected his own developing outlook in relation to 'real-life' teaching. One such was the Parents' National Education Union, formed in 1887 to promote the progressive theories of Charlotte Mason, notably her belief that in drawing out a child's physical confidence and intellectual and moral individuality, nature, art, movement and books all had equal roles to play. In its earliest years, the P.N.E.U. established the Charlotte Mason College at Ambleside, one of the country's first

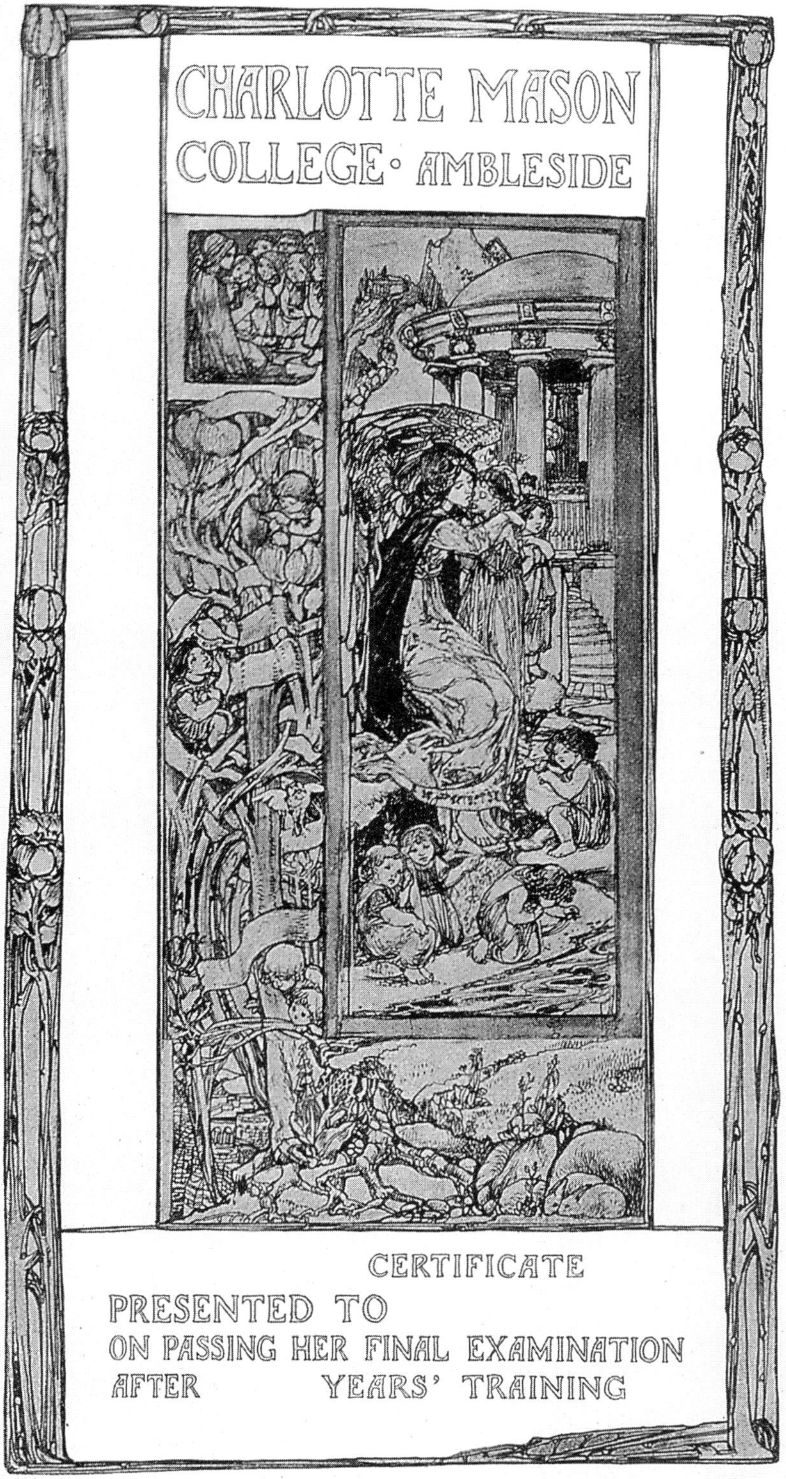

Ambleside Museum

Figure 79. Henry Wilson: leaving certificate for Charlotte Mason College, Ambleside, 1895 (*h. 45cm w. 28cm*).

teacher training colleges, attracting female students aged from 17 to their early 20s, with a 'Practicing School' for 4-16 year olds attached. In 1895 it approached Wilson to design a graphic document with few precedents, a leaving certificate; the symbolic schema he arrived at (Fig. 79) stands as much for his own evolving educational vision as for that of the college itself. In its characteristic treatment of figures and lettering, it is also a telling model of his marrying of text and sculpture in church commissions such as those at Brighton or Sydenham. His accompanying notes provide a clear signal of his distance from most of the methods then in use in elementary and secondary schools:

The subject is education. The stream of figures represents the river of mental life flowing from beneath the ... temple of the spirit. Above the altar is a lamp, typifying the source of life. The dome symbolises the heavens. The top of the mountain passes beyond the picture to suggest that the highest peak is unattainable. Psyche, clothed with knowledge, embraces a child to suggest that love is the inspiring agent of education.... On a little beach, children are playing with insects, plants and animals to suggest that in play each child gives not only a clue to its character, but also indices of the right way of educating that individual.[15]

In 1916, with the benefit of some twenty years' pondering the issues, and with his own young family fully engaged in their singular paths of 'learning by living', Wilson was ideally placed to speak at the New Ideals in Education Conference. These, by now, annual conferences had begun in 1914, when the prospectus had outlined the promoters' conviction that a 'new spirit' was stirring in education. This spirit was rooted in a 'reverence for the pupil's individuality' and in the conviction that this grows best 'in an atmosphere of freedom'.[16] From the handful of delegates at the first meeting, attendance would increase to over four hundred by 1919. A different theme was chosen for each year's gathering, and a report published, in which every lecture appeared in print.

For the 1916 Conference, whose overall theme was the role of the crafts in education, Wilson presented a paper on 'Craft Education for the Young'. In this he crystallised his views about education in twin propositions: education 'is not the acquisition of knowledge but the enlargement of consciousness'; and the character of any civilisation is revealed through the environment it creates for itself. Thus, the art, literature and architecture of Greece, Rome, Byzantium and the medieval world demonstrated those societies' rich 'response to stimulus'. Their counterparts in the twentieth century made unflattering comparisons.

Today we have the advertising hoarding, government by posters, the sky sign, the daily press. We have musical comedy in place of the mysteries. As a substitute for St. Francis we have Mr. Charles Chaplin.[17]

As he contemplated society on the brink of cultural crisis from which only humanistic education could save it, he insisted that

There never was a time when the socialisation of power, knowledge, skill, love, opportunity, was more necessary than the present. How shall we secure this? What would be desireable is the linking up of the essentials in the three outstanding movements in education: the Montessori system, the Dalcroze system, and the craft method.[18]

It was in the course of his wide-ranging reading that Wilson had encountered the Montessori approach; it was at the New Ideals in Education Conferences that he was to come into direct contact with its followers. In the thirty years since Maria Montessori had opened her first Children's Houses in Rome in the 1880s, her ideas had attracted an international following. Like Froebel before her, she stressed the need for free expression and self-education, and emphasised that *learning* was secondary to *doing*; but, disagreeing with Froebel's overriding emphasisis on development within the group, Montessori's concentration was on the individual. Her method defended the child's right to develop mental, and hence moral, resources through sensory awareness. This process, which she termed 'scientific pedagogy',[19] relied in its early stages on recognition and classification, for which she devised simple wooden blocks and metal shapes to be arranged according to their size and colour. In its fullest realisation, Montessorian 'training for practical life'[20] included serving meals, gardening, reading, writing and modelling in clay.

Ideally, Montessori maintained, during all of the lessons the personality of the teacher 'should disappear',[21] leaving the pupils free to develop their own identities – an attitude Wilson consistently upheld in his own teaching – and like him, she felt uncomfortable with the conditions in most orthodox schools, where children were 'restricted by the desk and by material prizes and punishments'.[22] In her schools, rows of desks were replaced with tables and chairs and wicker armchairs, and the children were allowed free access to the garden. Rewards and penalties were discarded in favour of those means that might best release each child's 'inner force'.[23]

Striking similarities already existed between Wilson's attitudes and Montessori's methods, and he quickly perceived the merits of her approach, applauding the way she had restored 'the natural method to teaching, and brought happiness to hundreds of young creatures....'[24] Nevertheless, he took issue with some aspects of her thinking, fearing that the habitual use of shape-and-size equipment 'tended too much to mechanism'.[25] Most significantly, he disagreed with the Montessorian inclination to marginalise children's imaginative capacities until the age of eight: stories based on make-believe were not allowed in the Montessorian regime, on the grounds that they encouraged a separation between the imaginative and reasoning faculties. He made this divergence clear in 1908, in his capacity of adjudicator at an exhibition of children's art. Turning to the teachers listening to his comments, he implored them to acknowledge the essentially childlike elements within children, rather than to try and make them into little adults:

> *All that the teacher can do is to keep the children surrounded by beautiful and natural things, to see that they acquire some form of craft, to encourage the instincts of play and memory – and do his utmost to keep their imagination fed with stories and fairy-tales.*[26]

By the second decade of the century, the Montessori system had been joined in the attention of progressive educationalists, Wilson included, with the theories of a Swiss music teacher. Emile-Jacques Dalcroze, who had brought an educational team to London in 1912 to help promote his ideas. Where conventional practice was bound hand and foot to learning by rote, Dalcroze based his system on the platonic precept that grace of movement and harmony of living – in other words morality – derived from a student's recognition of rhythm and consonance:

> *Life is a rhythm, ... a succession of multiple units, forming an invisible whole. Individuality may also be regarded as a rhythm, for the combination of its faculties constitutes an entity.*[27]

Enlarging on this principle, Dalcroze explained that the structure of music resides in its beats, and that it was by them that early forms of dance – rhythmic movement expressing the dancer's own emotions – were governed. These rhythms could be stored in the living resonators within the human nervous and muscular system, and be reproduced, modified or combined at will. Wilson shared Dalcroze's conviction that rhythmic training could only refine the individual's powers of perception and enhance concentration. With such faith in the deep-seated benefits of music, Wilson enthusiastically encouraged the devotion his middle daughter, Pernel, began at an early age to show to the musical arts.

That encouragement was richly repaid: in adult life 'Pernie' won international fame as the violinist Orrea Pernel (another performer had a similar name to her own real one), acclaimed for

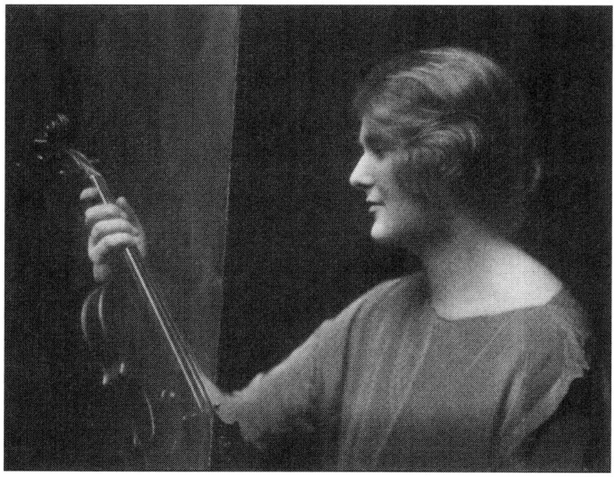

Figure 80. Orrea Pernel: detail from programme for a violin recital, with Kathleen Long (pianoforte) and Gerald Moore (accompanist), Grotrian Hall, 11 November, 1929.

the calm, intuitive quality of her performances. Having studied at the Paris Conservatoire, she was the first Briton to win a Premier Prix. The string quartet she formed with friends from the Society of Women Musicians, including Winifred Copperwheat and Priaux Rainier, played to appreciative London audiences for three years. It was in 1928, under the baton of Dr. Malcolm Sargent, that she made her debut at the Wigmore Hall; her repertoire grew to include Bach and Mozart, Brahms and Delius, Bartok and Webern and, throughout the 1930s, she was a regular soloist at the Queen's Hall Promenade Concert under Sir Henry Wood. She played Sibelius's music before the composer himself, and collaborated with the exiled Pablo Casals at his festivals at Prades. In the 1950s she became the resident soloist with the Boston Symphony Orchestra – living in the city where, in the 1920s, her father had created one of his finest sets of bronze doors – and established a string quartet at Bennington College, Vermont, where she taught for many years before returning to England in 1968 to become a regular contributor to the BBC's Third Programme concerts and a teacher at William Glock's Dartington Summer Schools.[28] Her pupils testified to her patient, inspirational approach: compare the tributes paid to her father by the students and the craftsmen he had helped direct.

Wilson had disputed Montessori's relative neglect of the child's imaginative faculties; to his mind, the Dalcroze method also had its limitations, in relation to the practicalities of life. Yet these shortcomings could be addressed by instilling elements of a third system, the one he himself advocated above all others – craft training. He reserved his fullest encomium of the 'wonderful educative powers' of the craft system for his address to the New Ideals Conference of 1916:

> *When mind and activity are joined the work thus produced is the channel by which the worker receives wisdom. Craft training is indeed the the ladder of humanity, with power not only to [improve] education but also in time to transform industry and to regenerate … society.*[29]

The teaching of the crafts, he urged, must play a far greater part in elementary and secondary school syllabuses than it had so far. It was true that the conditions for manual training had been broadened by the Board of Education in 1910 to encompass a wider range of ages and skills, and to allow the inclusion of these skills within the normal curriculum. This created opportunities for some boys to learn the rudiments of wood or metalworking. Such measures marked a significant improvement on the stipulations of 1890, which stated that manual training would be provided outside school hours, and only for boys over 11. Despite these reforms, however, manual training was offered on utilitarian grounds alone, with the aim merely of supplying industrial and commercial workmen to fortify the nation's material wealth.

For Wilson, the craft system had advantages that went far beyond such formal, measurable benefits, in allowing children to explore their individuality, in promoting concentration, in encouraging broad-mindedness, in developing the important attribute of mental flexibility. He summed up these benefits with particular vividness in his 1916 conference address:

Even children whose bent is predominantly intellectual ... should be encouraged to take up creative work, because a mind without any outlet is apt to become doctrinaire and dangerous. Had Lenin, for example, a single creative hobby I should have more hope for Russia ... .[30]

Furthermore, the pursuit of a craft necessarily entailed spirituality, since in the creative process 'we make knowledge as well as things'. The impact of such 'spiritual training' could not be overestimated; in the future, 'that will be seen as the real significance of the Arts and Crafts movement'.[31]

In Wilson's opinion, the spiritual training implicit in the practice of craft was the essence of love, and so stood for religion in its deepest, purest sense. This philosophy lends vital insight into the iconography of his designs, which habitually blends astrology, pagan myth, and alchemical symbols with Christian signs (prime examples being Brighton's Lady Altar, or the Welbeck lamps), as if to stress the oneness of all religious impulse. Predictably, he was dismissive of that brand of religion with which the average school day began. To him, such empty ritual represented 'at best, a spiritual narcotic'. On the other hand, '*laborare est orare*, and creative passion, work concentration, is only another form of the mystic's ecstasy which is the essence of religion, and that is why the suppression of the creative impulse is perhaps the greatest evil ... '.[32]

He had no time for religion as a palliative to the meanness of industrial existence; the outrage he felt at the thought amounted to barely suppressed contempt.

The industrialists in the House of Commons had the effrontery recently [1914] to suggest that workers need more religion, forgetting that you cannot breed saints in a pigsty, nor expect a man to be religious if you destroy his creative manhood. All the arts are religion, and craftsmanship is a living creed. But stew mankind in factories and hovels, and the hell-broth of revolution is the right and inevitable result.[33]

If Wilson can be said to have formulated an ideal of education, then it was one that brings together the essentials of the Montessori, Dalcroze and craft systems, then throws in a final locking-piece, gardening and husbandry. He had noted with approval Montessori's identification of plant-growing as a species of 'auto-education',[34] encouraging observation, patience and harmony with nature. Characteristically, when he described his preferred system of education to the 1916 Conference, he did so in story form, a sort of *News from Nowhere* reverie, itself a deliberate rebuttal of Montessorian strictures against 'make-believe'. The imaginary scene he sets is specifically calculated to emphasise the indivisibility of school and work.

Once in a dream I found myself passing through a village in a hilly, well-wooded and watered country. The fields were dotted with delightful dwellings which seemed to have crystallised naturally out of the soil. Each house had a large workshop attached, and I saw smiths, weavers, metalworkers, carpenters at work. In some I saw young learners under the care of a workman absorbed in simple task suited to their powers.[35]

The sight recalls the environs of Wilson's own home at Platt and its workshops, with his assistants – and children – at work within. As he walks on, the scene shifts:

Entering a lofty room with an arched roof and high windows I found it full of children of all ages seated facing a stage [which], hung with beautiful draperies from the village looms, figured the enchanted chamber, wherein on a low couch a lovely child lay asleep. Her long hair flooded the pillow and she was covered with a rich cloth sewn all over with birds and trees and woodland creatures. The stage, accessories and costumes were all done by the scholars as lessons. They were giving the masque of 'Beauty's Awakening', the product of far-off Victorian days. It appeared they did such things at frequent intervals, aided by the artists and workers around them ... .[36]

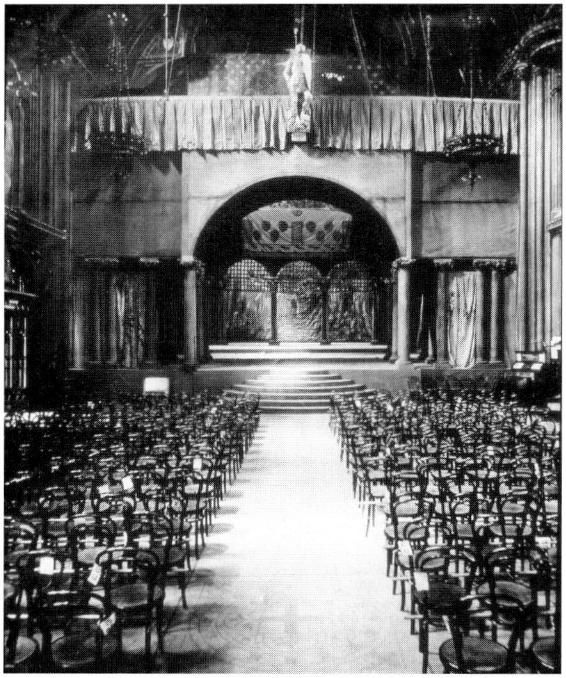

Art Workers' Guild

Figure 81. Guildhall, City of London: Wilson's set for the Art Workers' Guild masque 'Beauty's Awakening', 1899.

This vista, with pupils making their own theatrical props aided by the 'workers and artists around them', echoes conditions at The Thatched House, as recalled by Pernie in her account of the young Wilsons' daily tasks in the workshop which, while help was always at hand, 'we had to carry out ourselves';[37] the 'woodland coverlet' can only be a direct reminiscence of Margaret Wilson's accomplished needlework.

The allusion to *Beauty's Awakening* referred to an actual event in Queen Victoria's penultimate summer: *Beauty's Awakening: a masque of winter and of spring* had been presented on 27 June 1899 before the Lord Mayor of London and his Council – and on subseqent nights for two further audiences – in the Guildhall, by a band of Brothers of the Art Workers' Guild, Ashbee, Walter Crane, Selwyn Image, Townsend, Christopher Whall and Wilson, to a script by Wilson, Whall and Crane. Its elaborate props and costumes had been Wilson's, while his stage set had transformed the 'lofty' space in the Byzantine style he had used to furnish St. Bartholomew's Church, Brighton, starting in the previous year (Fig. 81). The real Masque's idealistic, and apparantly innocent, story-line had carried, for its select audience, a subversive sting. The target had been the spoliation of London by successive Mayors and their Corporations, abetted by leading industrialists and charlatan architects pandering to commercial interests. It had embodied hopes for greater social, spiritual and artistic awareness that might allow London to walk with Athens, Venice, Florence and Nuremburg in the Procession of Fair Cities. Fayremonde, the Beauty of the title, the Spirit of All Things Beautiful, had been portrayed exquisitely gowned, asleep under the spell cast upon her by Industry, the attendants at her couch seven motionless Spirits, embodying Ruskin's Seven Lamps of Architecture as described in that seminal volume of half a century before – at the time, at Brantwood, just down the road from Ambleside, its ailing author had still a year to live. Fayremonde's saviour was Trueheart, champion of the Crafts, who entered her tapestried chamber to wake her with a kiss, cue for the Guild chorus to sing 'Wake, sweet one, and make me wise'.[38]

The self-same words are woven by Wilson into the visionary fable with which he regaled the 1916 Conference, though there they are chanted by children dressed as dancing 'leaves'. Back in 1899, Wilson, ever the diplomatist of Brithdir, had sought to spell out the Guild's message without raising hackles, but its import had come through loud and clear: Trueheart's kiss broke the spell cast on Fayremonde by Victorian industry, the attendants at her couch (designed for that production, like her gown, by Wilson) embodied the Seven Lamps, their costumes by Wilson and Whall, their names borrowed straight from Ruskin: Sacrifice, Truth, Beauty, Power, Life, Memory, Obedience.

The message reiterated in Wilson's 1916 dream-journey is similarly transparent – work and education naturally pollinate one another, through the process of work and through the knowledge that work reveals. The quarries he passed along the way had masons' yards adjoining them 'wherein there seemed to be classes for masonry and geology ...', these bringing him to the secondary stage of his vision of education. In conventional terms, 'elementary' denoted the 4-11 age group and 'secondary' 11-16, but Wilson was loathe to make such distinctions; after all, the class in his dream included 'children of *all* ages', and, as he explained elsewhere in a paper on secondary education, 'there should be no age limit. All should be free to come and study at any time'.[39] A better definition of 'secondary' education might be supplied by the functions it performs, these being more advanced and closer to everyday life. Quite simply, 'love, music, knowledge, begin their higher evolution in the secondary schools, which would become the apprentice schools of every trade'.[40]

As for the next stage in the learning process, the art and technical schools, these should be reservoirs of art and experience. Wilson was all too aware of their shortcomings in the real world. Their modern facilities meant that they were sometimes almost *too* well equipped: staff and students alike were prone to rely overmuch on machine-aided techniques, and on concepts being *taught* at the expense of creative discovery. Such regimes, he had noted as early as 1906, were producing 'respectable but dull' students working on unedifying or irrelevant projects, while the atmosphere was often artificial in another sense also, being too focused on the polemical 'idea of art'.[41]

The rationale for many of these criticisms was self-evident: it was quite possible for full-time art and design students, on general courses in the 1890s and early 1900s, to avoid handwork altogether. Instead, the design classes that formed the bulk of each student's course were confined to drawing programmes slanted towards the Board of Education's examinations – design in *outline*, design from *casts*, design using *natural forms* – and were complemented by theoretical lectures on the principles and history of styles. Wilson, subjected to such a regime as a student at Kidderminster a quarter of a century before, denounced these courses as 'saturated' with drawing to the detriment of 'simple workmanship',[42] and their unproductive nature was widely condemned, notably by Walter Crane, the first Principal of the Royal College of Art.

Such disapproval surely contributed to a spirit of change which, between 1900 and 1914, would effect a revolution in the art schools. Reinvigorated, they would emerge with the dual character of art and trade schools, serving three categories of student – those working for the Board of Education's qualifications in art teaching, fine art students, and vocational students sent on day or evening-release by local trades associations to improve their skills in a given craft. While the schools' main structure was planned around the first category, several principals were edging towards a recognition of the third category as their main priority. For example, the Head of Leicester School of Art, Wilson's fellow-Guildsman and friend B.J. Fletcher, could by 1916 state categorically and that his institution's chief purpose was 'to help the trades, and to localise and develop skilled workmanship. It is with the worker-craftsman and employers that the school is mainly concerned.' Wilson's old Kidderminster School of Art had been thoroughly brought into the twentieth century under R.B. Dawson, who felt able to speak for his fellow-Heads in observing 'Every school is now free to develop on the lines best suited to its local industry'.[43]

In this emerging movement, the pioneering role of the Birmingham Municipal School of Art stands out. Edward R. Taylor served as Principal from the 1880s until 1903; under him the sterile emphasis on drawing gave way to real work in real materials, and in 1893 extra workshops were added to the existing studio accommodation on the Margaret Street site. Close links were forged with the 'Birmingham Group' – talented ex-students working in an Arts and Crafts style, some even being appointed to the staff. In 1890, at the prompting of Birmingham Jewellers' and Silversmiths' Association, it had opened a second site in Vittoria Street as the School for Jewellers and Silversmiths, which, for all that it was a trade school, quickly became infused under Robert Catterson-Smith with the same practical ideals as those of the main School. Taylor had actively coaxed this noted Arts and Crafts designer from London to Vittoria Street, and when he retired

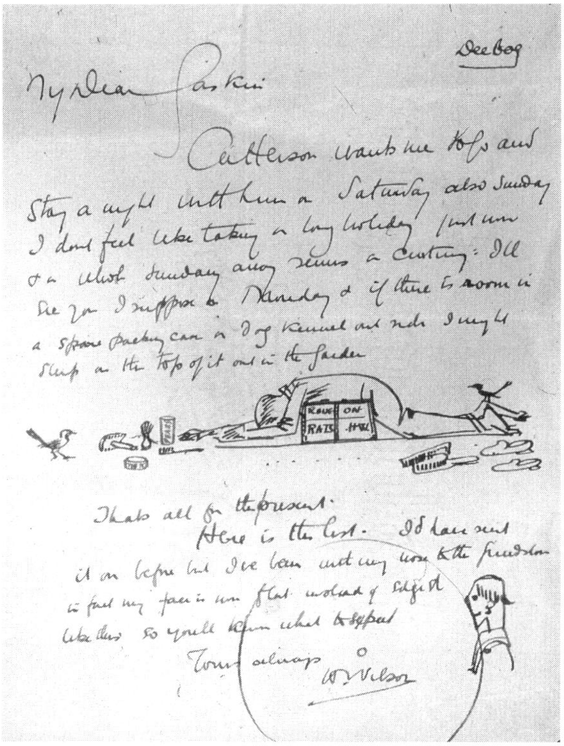
My dear Gaskin
Catterson wants me to go and stay a night with him on Saturday also Sunday
I don't feel like taking a long holiday just now
& a whole Sunday away seems a century: I'll
see you I suppose on Monday & if there is room in
a spare packing case or dog kennel outside I might
sleep on the top of it out in the garden

That's all for the present.
Here is the list. I'd have sent
it on before but I've been out very soon to the foundry
to find my face is now flat instead of [illegible]
like this so you'll know what to expect
Yours always
H Wilson

Private Collection

Figure 82. Note to Arthur Gaskin, 6 Dec.1909, from a busy Wilson about his Vittoria St. class. Transcript in Ch. notes.[44]

ten years later, Catterson-Smith was his natural successor as Principal. The vacancy as Vittoria Street's Director was taken by Arthur Gaskin, a former student and by now an influential member of the Birmingham Group; and it was under him that Wilson came to officiate as Examiner between 1905 and 1917 (Fig. 82).

Amongst the art schools founded in the capital from the 1890s into the new century – including Camberwell, Hammersmith, Westminster and Lambeth – under the aegis of the London County Council, the Central School of Arts and Crafts was indubitably the flagship. Henry Wilson taught there under first, W.R. Lethaby, then Fred Burridge, from its foundation in 1896 until 1911. Like Birmingham, the Central emphased its craft bias: Wilson's own life classes were seen as part of a training in craftsmanship, and all Lethaby's initial staff were active practitioners or designers, Since the Art Workers' Guild had established its role as the catalyst of the craft revival in education, most were also Guildsmen, each passing on their particular skills and insights: Catterson-Smith, designing for textiles and other media; Halsey Ricardo, architecture; Douglas Cockerell, bookbinding; Edward Johnston, letter-form and calligraphy; Christopher Whall, stained glass; and F.W. Troup, casting in lead. With this expertise in the teaching force, no wonder that in 1901, the year of Lethaby's departure, Hermann Muthesius could write of the Central as 'probably the best organised contemporary art school'.[45]

Wilson shared the ideals that inspired Lethaby's headship and permeated the Central School's syllabus. Both men saw craft as the union of hand and brain; both nurtured the survival of living traditions; both believed in the existence within each individual of instinctive knowledge of how to design. And when Lethaby left to become principal of the Royal College of Art in 1901, Wilson followed him there, though keeping a toehold at the Central.

The Royal College's founding principal, Walter Crane, himself a member of the Art Workers' Guild, had from the outset established Guildsmen on his staff – Alexander Fisher for enamelling, Cobden-Sanderson for bookbinding, Joseph Pennell for illustration, J.S. Sparrow for stained glass. Through a programme of craft demonstrations, students gained direct contact with tools and materials, and were encouraged to be aware both of their own individuality and of the relevance of what they were doing.

In 1901 the Board of Education reorganised the Royal College into the four schools which would provide the model for the provincial colleges – Design under the new Principal, Lethaby, Sculpture under Edouard Lanteri, Painting under Gerald Moira, Architecture under Beresford Pite. All four were members of the Art Workers' Guild, as were most of the teachers they appointed. Thus Wilson, acting from 1901 until 1912 as goldsmithing instructor, would have been working alongside such fellow Guildsmen as Christopher Whall, teaching stained glass, Edward Johnston, demonstrating calligraphy, George Jack, instructor in woodcarving, and Frank Short, who gave classes in etching and lithography.

Before Wilson's career in formal teaching drew to its close in 1915-17, further important changes would be made within the schools of art and design, notably when in 1915, that elaborate hierachy of prizes and scholarships, the National Competition, established by Henry Cole in 1852 to reward proficiency in various branches of art, was finally abandoned. Wilson's reaction does not survive, but given his earlier comments, it would surely have been good riddance to a system that had condoned a kind of institutionalised bribery and competitiveness without stimulating the student's innate need to produce good work for its own sake.

In his role as an educator, Wilson had always sought to liberate the creative powers which he constantly saw striving for expression, even in children at elementary level. His hope was that in time, and at more advanced levels, these powers would produce not only a 'new scheme of symbolism' but also, develop into 'a fresh tradition'[46]- a hope which had special relevance in the changing world of the early twentieth century. He identified potential ways of stimulating this new tradition: by cultivating, for example, the students' sense of social responsibility. This idea reflects an objective he had articulated in his Examiner's reports, that students might become involved in municipal commissions. In a lecture on art and advertising given during the second year of the Great War, he advocated collaboration between students and their municipalities to raise standards for posters and public hoardings.

As usual his cross-disciplinary idealism is clear; he detected, in the very process of selling goods, the opportunity for rich creative expression. The concept is familiar today, some of the best advertising campaigns making only the most oblique reference to the product being promoted; at the time of Wilson's talk, the approach was brand-new. If it was 'by no means essential' *literally* to depict the object being advertised, then the possibilities were countless, and 'imaginative subjects, local history, legend even, might be utilised – the text only would proclaim the purpose of the panel'.[47] This understanding of subtle understatement foreshadowed the poster campaigns of Shell, of London Transport, of the railway companies, with artists like McKnight Kauffer and F. Gregory Brown powerfully, even poignantly, evoking the attractions of London or a region's scenery and resorts.[48]

It was an area with which he was well-enough acquainted to relish and discuss, through his brother Patten's work in illustration and commercial art. Patten's designs reinforced Harry's faith in the well-presented message. His Art Nouveau and Arthurian illustrations featuring in *The Builder* in the 1890s brought Patten Wilson some acclaim, and may even have influenced the drawing style of the P.N.E.U. certificate (Fig. 79); later, he created an effective brochure for a charity concert season in aid of Boer War veterans, and by 1912 he was illustrating books for The Bodley Head. Amongst these was M.D. Haviland's *Wild Life on the Wing*, for which he provided eight full-page and fifty small line drawings that elicited his sensitivity and lightness of touch in a whole range of avian subjects, from swooping herons to starlings jostling for position on a telegraph wire. Married since 1900 to Alice Harding and settled in Isleworth, Patten's family grew to include a son, Aldred, and a daughter, Joan. In 1924 he devised a distinctive design for the Ministry of Labour's humble unemployment stamp by setting the Board of Trade's galleon above the Royal insignia, and in the same year he created the design of the 7d National Insurance stamp. The first of these was lodged with the printer Emery Walker under Henry's name, for billing purposes, perhaps, or simply convenience; the National Insurance stamp, with its crown, mortar, bouquet of herbs and the apothecary's twisting serpent, achieves a fluency of symbolic language reminiscent of his brother's jewellery.[49]

If imaginative advertising hoardings could 'appeal through beauty, raise civic pride, and provide valuable training for students in colour schemes, media, design and methods',[50] then the town planning movement, still in its infancy, must in Wilson's opinion, yield even greater opportunities for civic authorities and students to cooperate. Since Ebenezer Howard had introduced the idea in his 1898 book, Garden Cities – and suburbs – had become a reality in Letchworth, Hampstead and Port Sunlight. Considering their visual freshness, Wilson at once perceived the scope for improving existing environments. With the locality's requirements lending relevance and vitality, each scheme might harness the skills being taught in the art and technical schools. He gave an example to show what he meant –

> *Trafalgar Square might be transformed from a desert of dust and waste paper sprinkled by unruly fountains into a green and flowered pleasance with the story of London running round its walls and an artists' way, statue bordered, running up the centre....*[51]

The students and teachers in the art and technical schools were, he felt, ideally suited to the task of enhancing the urban environment 'under the direction of some outstanding personality in Architecture, Sculpture or Decoration.' The students were bound to benefit: 'we have only to see Lanteri's groups [at the Royal College] to realise their interest in such work and its value in education.'[52]

Another of Wilson's suggestions for sparking 'fresh traditions' was that art and technical schools should work to improve everyday product design. His approving reference in a joint art school report to 'the movement towards better design in the objects of ordinary use'[53] anticipates the stance of the Design and Industries Association, founded in the year of his report, 1915, to promote good design at an affordable price. Curiously, despite Lethaby being among its promulgators, Wilson himself never joined, though its aims ran parallel with distinct strands in his own thought. He was quite sure that the 'thousand and one objects used in daily life,' from pottery, garments, rugs and furniture right up to cars, trains and aeroplanes, were properly within the province of the professional designer, and by taking these areas seriously 'the [art] school would become in truth what it is in theory, a meeting ground for the Artist, Workman and Manufacturer.'[54]

Crucially linked to 'objects of ordinary use' was the concept of mass production. Far from shrinking from the idea Wilson welcomed its arrival, and vigorously rebutted the charge that 'mechanic-artists' producing cheap goods on a large scale were somehow operating on a lower level than the 'real' artist craftsmen: 'I look forward to the beginning in our technical schools of a new order of beauty, a new species of craft, a new field for energy....'[55]

Such an option for the schools was the natural corollary of his wish to cure their common fundamental flaw – their isolation from the real world. Exasperated by this detachment, he had gone so far as to argue in his paper of 1906, 'The Value of Learning by Doing', that in their existing form art schools should be abolished, and the Board of Education itself be done away with. In the ethos he was proposing, art schools would be transformed into workshops presided over by 'first rate workmen.' Rather than prizes, the students, working in the capacity of paid apprentices, would receive incremental pay rises and certificates of skill. The technical schools, too, would be updated to train mechanic-artists, eager to gain technical and artistic competence in useful, modern trades. Wilson's perspective, controversial in its stance and radical in its implications, preceded C. R. Ashbee's book *Should we stop teaching art*, with its similar propositions, by some five years. Like Wilson, Ashbee saw the art schools confined by an artificial, self-propagating system, turning out students fit only to teach, and so proposed their wholesale conversion – with state support – into mechanised workshops researching and developing products relevant to modern society.[56]

The parallels between Wilson's template for the art and technical schools of the future and his image of the guild system of the past are striking. Indeed, his belief that the teachers should ensure constant contact between students and manufacturers, and undertake to circulate lists amongst prospective employers 'giving the chief qualifications, training and capacity of each student and details of character and parentage',[57] was an earnest, if slightly contrived, attempt to make each school more akin to the old 'craft family',[58] where such information would have accrued naturally.

Whilst he never assumed that art and technical schools could replace real workshop training, and resented unscrupulous firms exploiting them as 'free substitutes'[59] for the apprenticeship system, he nevertheless admitted in 1911 that an art school course or training at a day technical school 'might yet be considered as a part of the period of apprenticeship'.[60] In whatever discipline, the all-important proviso should be the relevance to the outside world of the skills the students were learning. He was keen that young craftsmen and mechanic-artists be taught to adapt their creativity and expertise to the specific needs of their future occupation, just like the old guild-apprentices, and was much encouraged by seeing this actually occur in the schools where he himself was working:

> *It is in the production of such a race that the schools of Birmingham are now engaged. They, and the County Council art schools and the technical institutes of London are our hope for the future.*[61]

For a man like Harry Wilson, whose entire life had been devoted to creative work, the outbreak of the Great War was catastrophic. It was the utter antithesis of everything he held dear, the total denial of the future he had thought possible in the years up to 1914. Its destruction and death, witnessed or reported on a more terrible scale than in any previous war, confirmed and exceeded his worst fears. He had often sought to demonstrate how crucially the fabric of modern existence, education included, had been sapped by the intrinsically unnatural, anti-social and damaging lifestyles engendered by industrial society. Writing in 1915, it was plain to him that this, the first truly industrialised war, must be identified as a component and ultimate corollary of the same pattern.

> *We have evolved a system which teaches science without art producing the ugly, art without science producing the useless, medicine apart from psychology resulting in the abstract, politics apart from ethics resulting in the sordid and futile. Thus instead of learning to live we have systems of education and modes of existence ultimately divided from productive life. The main avenues of expression are barred, craft is foiled, and we see the youth of the world charging through the one gate left open to them, the gate of death.*[62]

His condemnation of the prevailing educational and social climate is systematic and irrefutable. But there is no triumph in Wilson's tone; only an empty and horrified sense of vindication. If the reckless stampede of modern industry, egged on by the '*ignis fatuus* of profit', must be blamed for making the conditions in which the present 'morass of war'[63] was possible, then there was no doubt that it had been nourished by 'a gradual process of miseducation, a total failure to educate the world [as] to what is Education, what is real work, [and] what ... humanity as a whole should strive for'.[64]

Still worse than that pre-War failure of understanding was to be the incomprehension that followed this War to End All Wars. 'Even now,' he wrote almost disbelievingly in 1919, 'after years of the bloodiest slaughter, men are still talking of war as the solution, ... studying to produce more murderous gases, more diabolical bombing machines. At this very moment a Committee is sitting at the Hague to decide on the conduct of future wars.'[65] His faith in the League of Nations with its short-term political strategies, rather than larger humanitarian ones, was limited.

> *The settling of boundary disputes is not enough.... Before they can find a way of peace they must seek to bring a new spirit into industry and education. The root evils of war – false education, false economics and false industry – must be extirpated....*

If it was to succeed in the long term, Wilson had a prophetic role for it: 'The League must become an education authority, ... a new economic and industrial brotherhood'.[66]

At about the age at which thousands of young soldiers had been meeting their deaths on the battlefields of northern France, Harry Wilson had himself been passing through that identical region, on excited architectural forays with Gimson and other assistants in Sedding's office; he was naturally deeply shaken by the news that Sedding's son, George, had died on 23 October 1915 of wounds received in action there. His work both as teacher and Guildsman would bring Wilson into contact with many who had had first-hand experience of this war that compounded the efforts of industry, engineering and chemistry. His conversations during his visits to disabled ex-servicemen's craft exhibitions affected him profoundly. Some of the testimonies left him lost for a reply:

> *A young soldier who had been through the whole war from 1914 onwards said to me 'I don't know if you will be shocked, but this war has made me a conscientious objector and a pacifist'.*[67]

Struggling to identify any remotely positive effects of the War, he acknowledged that it had at least enabled, indeed forced, people to take stock of the educational, industrial and social systems they had been constructing before it began. Only occasionally could he muster enough optimism to sound convincing.

> *Devastating wars have invariably been followed by periods of great creative activity. The desire for vitality in art, sincerity in the theatre, emotion in music, simplicity in life, the Arts and Crafts, the Garden City companies, the socialist movement, the Housing and Town Planning enterprises – are witnesses to the indestructable vitality of the human ideal.... Some recent art movements bear witness to the divine irresponsibility of creative force. We must not condemn but welcome the Post-Impressionists, the Cubists, the Orphists, the Futurists and the Vorticists [with their] slightly aggressive Blast.*[68]

The energy of such movements remained valid to Wilson – he himself would make his own translation of the Futurist Manifesto – but there is palpable irony in his endorsement of the Italian provocateurs' dynamism: they drew much of their inspiration, like the Vorticists, from the very War that took a dreadful toll of some of their leading lights. On the whole, as he insisted with his habitual clarity, the mealy-mouthed consolations offered by some commentators were futile:

> *It is of no avail to point to the ...fine physique of the survivors, to claim the habits of comradeship, obedience and sacrifice as gifts of war. These gifts are procurable by means less hateful, less wasteful, less bloody... .*[69]

... in other words, the crafts, 'rightly directed industry',[70] and productive agriculture.

His 'bitter and burning thoughts'[71] about the War were painful to articulate, but the memorials he would subsequently design show his feelings about the physical and emotional swathe it had cut eloquently enough. Two stained glass windows, for instance, mark particular aspects of loss. One, the East window of Holy Trinity church, Fareham, sets two brothers' deaths within the unfolding experience of family bereavement: the figure of St. Helen stands before the True Cross, with two angels. The design had been commissioned in 1910 by Miss Helena Tylor, to go hand in hand with the chancel commissioned from Wilson – settled by this time in Venice, and working on the Elphinstone Tomb – by her brother-in-law, the church's vicar, the Rev. C.L. Arnold.[72] The window was her own memorial, ordered in anticipation of her death which came in 1913, and was installed with an inscription in her memory. When the vicar's two sons, her nephews, fell in France in 1916 and 1918, Reverend Arnold had Wilson revise its dedication to include their names. The other, for the church of St. John the Baptist, West Ashton, Wiltshire (Plate 59), addresses the notion of sacrifice. Commissioned by Walter Long of Rood Ashton, it was made to Wilson's design by Powell & Sons in 1919. Its unveiling and blessing took place on 30 November that year, in a service attended by Viscount French and the Primate of Ireland, their presence emphasising the gravity of its theme. For the ceremony of dedication Wilson prepared notes on its iconography. A youthful, unbearded Christ stoops in blessing and welcome above a kneeling soldier; at its apex hover the dove of peace and 'the [four] angels of the winds'. The young man is wearing armour, but his helmet and sword lie on the ground, his days of fighting – and dying – for his country over. By translating his uniform from a modern into a mythic realm, Wilson was seeking to make the message timeless; the rich illumination of the design, and its abstract upward movement, enhance the sense of reconciliation, while the inscription, 'In memory of our gallant sons who fell in the Great War', spoke for all the parishioners. Yet for a visitor unaware of his declared wish to invoke a universal theme, the design may present a troubling dichotomy – Wilson the man who understands the trauma of war, and Wilson the artist, who typically relies on archetype.[73]

In the years after 1918, war memorials were created by Wilson in several forms. The Surrey village of Limpsfield Chart commissioned one of his last buildings, a Memorial Hall, in tribute to its lost sons, to be sited next to Blomfield's 1895 church of St. Andrew-on-the-Chart. Although it was demolished in 1950, the rest of Wilson's commemorative work for the village survives inside the church: the coloured bas-relief reredos, a version of those he made for Cardiff and Sydenham, was installed in 1918. The memorial commissioned that year for the church of the Holy Redeemer, Clerkenwell, already home to some of his major designs, took the shape of a mortuary chamber: on either side of arched walnut doors, an unadorned roll of the War dead stands silent witness to the parish's grief.

The remorselessness of war would surely have filled his thoughts when in 1920 Wilson completed a wall plaque commemorating a soldier of the Great War at St. Giles's, Stoke Poges, Buckinghamshire, given that some twenty years before, in the same church, his lancet window, with a gold-armoured Archangel Michael standing on a slain dragon, had been installed to honour a victim of the Boer War.[74] In 1922 Wilson's work again marked the relentless cost of war when, at the request of Mary Harvey, he adjusted the inscription in his mosaic in the sanctuary of Holy Trinity church, Fareham, to add to the original dedicatee, Thomas Harvey, the name of his son Kenneth, who had died of wounds received in action at Ypres.

In the Hertfordshire churchyard of Much Hadham, Wilson had designed a pillared stone crucifix in 1916 for the grave of Frederick Norman. In 1921, he was asked to design a suitable public War Memorial on land given by Frederick Norman's eldest son, Montagu, later Lord, Norman. Each of the forty-three local men killed in the conflict was more-or-less known to his fellow villagers. Wilson's 15' obelisk of Somerset Hamstone, surmounted by a rose-garlanded Latin cross, was unveiled by Viscount Hampden in January 1921; it would form a focal point for the whole community, a dignified testimony to a shared sense of loss.[75]

Two of Wilson's memorials give vivid figurative expression to the losses of war. In 1924 he returned to St. Martin's Church, Marple, to design a bronze wall-panel in bas-relief of Christ receiving into Heaven the kneeling figure of a young man. Behind Christ stands the armour-clad St. George, while angels and cherubs congregate beneath a canopy of vines. In the bottom right-hand corner, 'Henry Wilson' is delineated with rare clarity, the name's distinctness, on the work of a designer who seldom claimed personal authorship, suggesting the intensity of his feelings.

In terms of scale, the second is at the other extreme. While his many war memorials show Wilson's readiness to fulfil small or individual commissions, at Tonbridge School, Kent, he took on the challenge of truly architectural monument-making. The commission, for the ante-chapel, was completed in 1919, though as a result of a serious fire in September 1988 his work survives only in incomplete form. The fire prompted the wholesale remodelling of the chapel itself. As

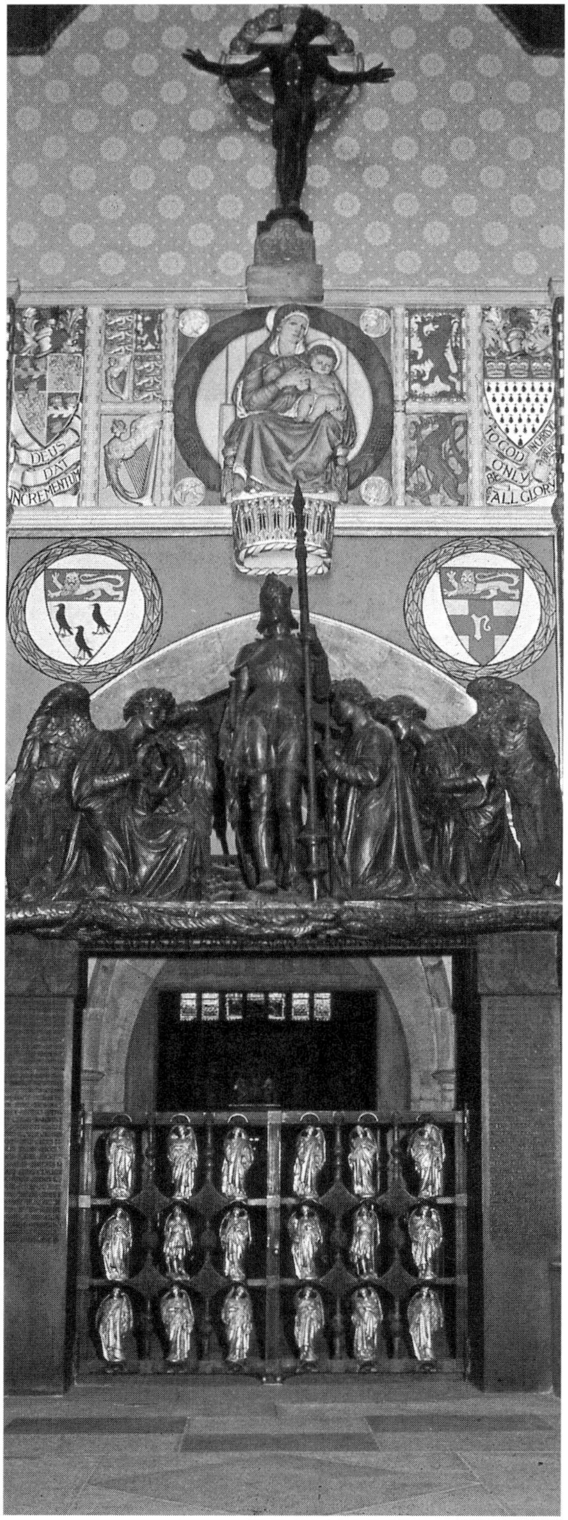

Figure 83. Memorial Gates, Tonbridge School chapel: bronze with gilt angels as installed, prior to 1988 fire, 1919.

designed, his Gate of Remembrance (Fig. 83), commemorating the 415 former pupils and three masters who died in the Great War, led into the chapel. For Wilson, such a commission, in a school of all places, was an acute reminder of the links he had traced between education and war; the fact that his brother Edgar's two sons were pupils at the school would inevitably have sharpened his unease. Yvor and Cedric had started as day pupils, living nearby with their grandfather – Wilson's father – and step-grandmother at Boughton Monchelsea, while Edgar and Winnie were in the Middle East. The paired gates themseves were lost in the fire: each comprised an openwork grid framing nine gilded angels, while the tall bronze jambs still bear the serried names of the fallen.

But it was the bronze figure group, set high above the angel gates, that made the major visual impact and, having survived the blaze, continues to exert a powerful sense of drama. It was modelled at Platt and cast in Paris by Barbedienne. At its centre stands the armour-clad St. George, his hand resting on the hilt of his sword. Beside him kneels a robed youth holding a sheathed sword – a gesture of peace recalling Wilson's Boer War memorial at Walmsgate – while twin angels, wings outspread, bear wreaths, emblems of honour. The spandrels display the arms of Canterbury and Rochester; between them a golden coronet both crowns St. George and forms a throne for the Virgin and child in the roundel above, carved in bas-relief, painted and gilded, and flanked with the arms of the School and its Patrons, the Skinners' Company. Above the Virgin's inclined head was set the polished basalt figure of a boyish Christ, descending from the cross. This, the original version of Clerkenwell's Eyre Memorial, appears in a context where youth is painfully relevant. The depiction of St. George, the holy figures, and the wreaths of honour would have satisfied the most ardent claims of patriotism and faith, when on the 10th October 1925, the commission was unveiled by Major General William Ironside and blessed by the Bishop of Birmingham. Yet with a force that outstrips any post-war rhetoric which the design might call up, is Christ's purity of outline: the figure connects in its vulnerability with deeper streams of spiritual and creative hope.

Later in the 1920s an American journalist commiserated with Wilson, guessing that he must have found the numerous war memorials he had created 'harrowing' things to do. The reply he received took him aback, but perfectly epitomised Wilson's idealism as to what design could achieve: 'No, oh no ...', Wilson explained, he *liked* to do them – but not 'boys in khaki, and guns, and all that'; rather, 'everything ... was symbolic, trying to bring out the meaning of it all, and the beauty, and interpret so that people might understand, and be comforted'.[76] Quietly concluding the interview, he seemed to be looking forward; as he freely acknowledged, all of life's old assumptions had been destroyed by the War:

The whole world outlook has changed. Nothing can be as it was before.[77]

And so, for all the sincerity of feeling he poured into commemoration, Wilson would staunchly maintain that

the best memorial for those who have died will be to make a new birth possible. We must believe in the infinite perfectability of human kind, in its boundless recuperative powers – and refuse to despair.[78]

In keeping with this unflagging, ever-practical idealism, once hostilities were over, Wilson turned his energies to the greatest imperative peace presented: reconstruction. In particular, he was anxious to consolidate any improvements he had detected in education before 1914. The War seemed to have confirmed everything Wilson had ever believed about education: its basis should be regional, occupational, individual. Above all, it should be *creative.* Syllabuses must meet the practical, and the innately spiritual, needs of the everyday world. Here the advice of Art Workers' Guild members would be invaluable:

Professor Lethaby's book on cottage crafts, Mr. W.A.S. Benson's ... on elementary woodwork, and Mr. George Jack's on 'Carving and Simple Furniture' are all full of helpful suggestions. Beds, shelves, chairs and tables could all be made by any boy or girl of average ability ... .[79]

The prospect of post-war reconstruction added decisive new impetus to that long-held wish of his to give a craft bias to education at all levels. Confirming the debt owed by industry to the patient craftsman, Wilson reminded the education authorities how the crafts could help rebuild Europe's wrecked economy.

Mechanical industry draws its inspiration from the handicrafts and depends on them for its continuance. The motor industry, particularly in France, grew out of the manifold improvements ... of French handymen in small shops. In like manner grew the aeroplane industry ... .[80]

Watching the streams of men coming home from the Front, many disabled, all emotionally exhausted, and, despite the welcome awaiting them, most with all sense of purpose knocked out of them, served to intensify Wilson's views on the importance of craft training.

In a paper he presented to the Ministries of Pensions, Labour and Reconstruction on behalf of the Art Workers' Guild in 1918, at the end of his year as Master, he reminded his listeners how the healing value of the crafts had been endorsed by the medical profession. He drew their notice to the resolution just passed at the Inter-Allied Conference in Paris, which urged that in re-education, 'psycho-therapeutics unite with physic-therapeutics', and that the 'psycho-therapeutic value of technical work' be recognised. Wilson apologised for the 'highly technical language' (for so it must have sounded when post-traumatic stress and occupational therapy were yet to be fully acknowledged), but assured his audience that 'it would be difficult to express this cardinal point with greater brevity or truth'.[81] His own experiences and observations gave clear support to the theory – a case in point was the 1917 Disabled Servicemen's exhibition:

> *Men without any previous training have produced all the admirable work in the present exhibition.... Their bodies have been maimed, often beyond recognition. Yet they offer us this flower of beauty which has healed them as it grew.*[82]

It offered an inkling that casualties of war might be rehabilitated, through the crafts, in much the same way as those of industry – like the consumptive Bradford clerk whom Wilson had encountered years before, who within months of learning metalwork, had almost miraculously recovered and was now earning a good wage in a trade he enjoyed.

Taking stock in typically sanguine mood, Wilson set the problems caused by the War alongside the solutions ex-servicemen could supply. Against 'depleted industries and labour scarcity' he set 'thousands of workers returning from the trenches'. Against 'our deserted villages' he set 'men waiting to be settled and trained by those who have made British handicraft world famous'. Against food shortages he set 'new possibilities of culture'.[83]

Since becoming Chairman, in 1918, of the Committee on Handicraft Training (one of a group of bodies set up by the Ministry of Labour to consider post-War training in the trades), he had been devoting considerable thought to the first of these problem areas, industry. His suspicions of it remained strong, even where it seemed to have a benign face:

> *... the Levers and the Cadburys and the Rowntrees ... have built garden cities for their workers ... who live in quasi-independence in attractive surroundings, with nurses and reading rooms, ... but when we are told ... that these things are done as a good business proposition, ... then we see that however well cared for, the worker is still a cog in the machine and not a complete individual.*[84]

He therefore insisted in his report to the Committee that industry should be communalised, for the benefit everyone, not just a few. This precondition made him guarded in his admiration for designated workers' settlements such as Port Sunlight (established near Liverpool in 1888 for the employees of Lever's Cheshire soap factory), and New Earswick near York (the model village commissioned from Parker and Unwin in 1901 by Joseph Rowntree for his cocoa factory workers), both of which might, with some justice, be criticised for their paternalism. However, Wilson's sceptical views regarding Bournville (the housing project begun in 1895 outside Birmingham by the confectioner Cadbury) were misplaced: Bournville had been envisaged as a model suburb for artisans, irrespective of their place of employment; true to the Cadbury strain of philanthropism, no such exclusive qualifications for residency applied, even if, in the event, most of the inhabitants were part of Cadbury's workforce. Still, the cautious note struck by Wilson rings true, while his ambition that the rewards of industry be shared is both radical and conforms to his broad social idealism.

Nevertheless, the concept of an independent garden city appealed to him far more than any development with the whiff of a 'tied' township. Ebenezer Howard's 1898 book *Tomorrow: the peaceful path to real reform* had been the first to propose the idea of semi-rural 'green belt' communities linked to, yet separate from, large industrial centres. Howard took the idea further in his *Garden Cities of Tomorrow* of 1902. But pleasant as planned settlements like Parker and Unwin's Letchworth (1904) and Hampstead Garden Suburb (1907) may have seemed, they failed to confront, head-on, the issue that Wilson was struggling with, capitalist industry in relation to its workforce. In the wake of war, therefore, he doggedly continued to argue for an essentially socialised vision.

The second problematic issue Wilson had observed, the country's moribund villages, was a crucial element in what he termed 'the coming battle of reconstruction'.[85] On the one hand there was large-scale industrial production. On the other there was small-scale craft production, the 'best of all means' to restore disabled men to active life, the 'nuclei of new industries', and potential 'centres of national revitalisation'.[86] He was not being infeasibly partial in his support of the crafts. With the rapid expansion of the aircraft industry and the simultaneous contraction of the luxury market, many displaced craftsmen had found employment in that growing sector. In 1914 the aeroplane was a novelty, but by November 1918 more than 55,000 had been produced by British workers in centres like Filton (Bristol), Brooklands (Weybridge), Norwich, Farnborough and Hendon, firmly establishing the new industry. The provision of specialised components such as altimeters and airspeed indicators relied largely on traditional skills of watchmakers and jewellers, and in this fast-changing field, the profusion of handmade prototype parts for experimental aircraft (from which jigs and dies for mass production could be made) was enormous.

In some alarm, he compared the scanty post-War preparations to make the crafts accessible to the returning men with the provisions made in the large scale industries to absorb great numbers of them, and recommended establishing a network of workshops run by craftsmen, arranged in numerous 'work-centres'.[87] These would constitute small communities engaged in one craft (or two linked) where such crafts related to the region's industrial tradition; in a textile district, for example, weaving and the manufacture of looms. To begin with, these could be financed by local or municipal aid but, in time, Wilson expected them to become self-supporting. Local advisory committees of master craftsmen, artists, workmen and manufacturers would be attached to each one. He likened these committees to the Consultative Committees established by the L.C.C., with which he himself had worked at the turn of the century in his art school teaching and examining.

Wilson's ideal of 'work-centres' irresistibly brings to mind the German and Austrian Werkstätten, clusters of craft workshops founded around cities such as Munich, Dresden, Berlin and Vienna in the same years that the L.C.C. had been creating its art schools, the 1890s and early 1900s. Adopting a Secessionist or Jugendstil manner, they had taken the British Arts and Crafts movement as their model. But by 1907, craft ideology had been transformed into mass-produceable, universal standards of design, and the powerful early-twentieth century design force, the Deutscher Werkbund, had been born. Within it major figures from art, design, architecture and manufacturing had been united, just as Wilson was advocating in post-War Britain. Furthermore, if the existing educational institutions played their part, 'education, creative activity and national life would effectively knit together'.[88]

The craft or industrial settlements Wilson envisaged would consist of productive workshops and associated dwellings, which led him to a linked topic of huge national concern – Homes fit for Heroes, or, put more prosaically, housing. The schoolchildren in his 1916 dream-journey had been receiving education through the process of constructing their own stage set. Similarly, Wilson imagined demobilised servicemen learning useful skills in the course of building much-needed new communities. Implicit in the skills the men would thereby gain was the reinvigoration of neglected crafts: 'the arts of the smith, founder, modeller, plasterer, metalworker, potter and glassworker ... could [all] be revived ... .'[89]

Sometimes the men would be erecting new houses, sometimes restoring derelict ones. Here, Wilson's preoccupations echo Ashbee's decision of 1902 to settle the Guild of Handicraft in the Gloucestershire Cotswolds, where it flourished until 1914. At Chipping Campden, his Guild members had established a range of workshops in previously dilapidated cottages, revitalised some failing crafts such as lead glazed window-making, and established their own school in a disused malthouse, open, like the school in Wilson's vision, to adults as well as children. Its syllabus, equally unorthodox, included drama, gardening, carpentry and an awareness of the 'duties of the citizen'.[90]

If realised, Wilson's own scheme for a craft village, drawn up in 1917, would at last have brought to life the imaginary community he had been dreaming of since the 1890s. But so, too, would it have extended into a post-War world ideas which had been explored at Chipping Campden. Wilson described his scheme in a closely argued manifesto for what he named the Association of Architecture, Building and Handicraft.[91]

The Association's primary aim was simple – to assist 'the organisation and development of the hand craft movement'.[92] The original membership it attracted comprised leading architects, artists and craftsmen. The architecturally-trained craftsmen Sidney Barnsley and Ernest Gimson were amongst the first to offer their support. Other notable figures followed, including such old colleagues as the architects R.S. Weir (until 1914 R. Weir Schultz) and F.W. Troup, also the builder G.H. Lupton, veteran embroidress and textile designer May Morris, the glass-smiths Alfred and Louise Powell, and Wilson's long-standing friends, the stained-glass maker Christopher Whall and the fine metalworker and jeweller J.P. Cooper. Further individuals expressed interest in the Association's aims – the upshot being that Augustus John was invited to teach wall painting, George Jack to take charge of carving and mosaics, Ethel Mairet to establish facilities for spinning, weaving and dyeing, Eric Gill to instruct in sculpture and letter-cutting, and Harold Ellis in husbandry – and all this before a plot had been found to set the enterprise down on. By the time of writing his manifesto Wilson had won an impressive range of supporters from the fields of architecture, building, plaster- and leadwork, pottery, artistic glazing, toymaking, furniture, needlework, jewellery, copper, brass and wrought ironwork, and gold and silversmithing.

The village was to be established in the Cotswolds, where it could acquire enough land to be self-supporting, 'close to the present workshops'[93] of some of the proposed directors – meaning Gimson and Barnsley. Gimson himself had already bought land locally with a view to creating a craft community, and it seems likely that, predicting the conviction and energy his old friend would bring to the enterprise, he now amalgamated his plans with Wilson's. It was proposed that during the building of the village, and later, when it became fully productive, each director should organise workshops in their particular area of expertise. The governing officials would be practicing designers: W.R. Lethaby was the Association's proposed President (Earl Ferrers filling the role of Vice-President), the printer St. John Hornby would become Treasurer, and Wilson, as well as playing a part in the architecture, metalwork and jewellery workshops, would be Chairman.

The Association's aim of nurturing the crafts was expressed through its five fundamental commitments. Its first was to encourage the influence of the crafts by embracing architecture, its second to further each member's work. Thirdly, and crucially, came the commitment to enhance the role of craft in industry through the expedient of establishing new workshops 'making in quantity things of common use at prices within the range of average incomes, and building a village for 200 handworkers for this purpose'.[94] Fourth came the intention of setting up 'affiliated centres' further afield so as to 'stimulate the growth of a national tradition'.[95] Finally came the forward-looking aim of assuring the Association's future by training pupils and apprentices in workshops attached to the village school, and in an advanced craft school.

However idealistic the concept, this was no vague, uncosted scheme; the initial funds would be raised from debentures and the sale of shares, and the directors of the workshops would receive small salaries and a percentage of the profits of the work executed under their direction. The whole scheme could be launched with capital of £115,000. This was enough to lay roads, infrastructures and services, to make a start on erecting – or converting – 100 workmen's cottages, four larger houses, a workers' hostel, and workshops (these absorbing members' current workshops where appropriate), and to build the village hall, the showhouse, the shop, the school and the inn, as well as ensuring the village's water supply.

Nor was the scheme's proposed future an unwordly, uncommercial one. To support its aim of promoting the crafts in modern life, the Association itself was to be promoted using current methods of advertising. Catalogues of all repetition work would be issued, and the Association's views publicised in a series of essays. These would include extracts from some of the most influential writings of Ruskin and William Morris, with the addition of new discussions of 'Architecture in Relation to Building' by Weir and Powell, 'Sculpture' by Eric Gill, 'Painting' by Augustus John, and 'Handicraft' by Lethaby, who promised his thoughts on 'The Modern Town', and on 'The Uses of Machinery'. May Morris offered her 'Story of the Handicraft Movement', and Clutton Brock his 'Philosophy of the Handicraft Movement'. 'Village Agriculture' by Christopher Turnor and 'The Modern Village' by H.C. Fairfax-Cholmeley would also be featured. Wilson himself was polishing up his 'Future of the Handicraft Movement', along with reprints of some of his earlier lectures.

An essentially modern awareness of the power of publicity was implicit in the decision to exhibit at every future Arts and Crafts Exhibition Society show. In those rare years when none were held, the Association would mount its own display in its London headquarters. An up-to-date note was struck in its confident proposals for its first exhibition. This, declared the manifesto, would comprise 'a large and comprehensive show' of 'useful things at moderate prices'. It would include four fully furnished rooms, and various scale models. These would represent a London shop designed by Lethaby, a memorial by Wilson, a domed church by Sidney Barnsley and George Jack, a painted room by the Powells, and a hall for a women's institute by the unusual team of Augustus John and Ernest Gimson. In the most decisively cliché-breaking project of all these models, at least in terms of the traditional old Arts and Crafts rubric, was a factory in ferro-concrete by F.W. Troup in collaboration with the Association's consulting engineer.

Wilson's involvement with the Association of Architecture, Building and Handicraft embodied heartfelt aspirations to recast the crafts in an early-twentieth century mould. But neither his plan for a fully-fledged craft village nor his idea of affiliated settlements were to reach fruition. The venture's demise came suddenly, in August 1919, when, at the untimely age of 55, Gimson died. His old friend Barnsley was not one for large schemes like this and before long, with others of his fellow travellers dropping out, Wilson's project foundered. Nevertheless, many of the scheme's ideals would find optimistic expression in his subsequent career. Aspects of his vision for the crafts in modern life would be embodied in the major post-war Arts and Crafts exhibitions he organised in the later stages of his Presidency of the Arts and Crafts Exhibition Society, which he held from 1915 to 1922. Something of his vision for the intelligent design of the 'thousand and one everyday items' he had mentioned found expression in the British Institute of Industrial Art, which he would help establish in 1920. His continuing involvement in education appeared in his work as teacher and Examiner throughout the 1920s and in his stance as enthusiatic commentator for the rest of his life.

Meanwhile, there remained the third post-war problem Wilson had highlighted in his 1918 report to the Ministry, along with dehumanised industry and disused villages: food shortages. Urgent questions were being asked about how to re-establish agriculture, in steep decline since the War. In fact, the issue had opened up 'the whole rural problem'.[96] In Wilson's analysis, though, problem turns into possibility. The training and afflictions which ex-servicemen had undergone during the War had given many 'a dislike of the office, of super-urbanised industry' – and 'a desire to revert to some more healthy, active occupation is known to be almost universal'.[97] For such individuals, the kind of life offered by running a smallholding was ideal. Rather than competing with large farms, Wilson suggested that these new smallholders concentrate on a specific branch of farming and supplement whatever they produced with paid employment in one of the re-established rural crafts.

He examined this concept of the 'dual occupation'[98] from an urban angle too. As in many of the comparisons he made between Britain's and continental Europe's moves towards reconstruction, progress abroad seemed more advanced. All the same, he was glad to see positive steps being taken at home:

> *The movement ... to develop urban allotments is of the greatest importance. Not only have many millions of pounds worth of vegetables been produced where they are most needed, ... but the men themselves have earnt an important sense of independence.*[99]

Motivated by a sad and angry yet indefatigable energy, Wilson was prepared to offer every assistance to the government. He assured it that the creative intelligence of the Arts and Crafts organisations was at its disposal in setting up craft villages like the one he himself had planned. Disappointingly, despite his confidence, the London-based Arts and Crafts groups fell short of Wilson's faith in them. In 1917, the year Wilson became Master of the Art Workers' Guild (Fig. 84), the government had actually sought the Guild's help in forming a concerted policy of teaching the arts and crafts to demobilised servicemen. However, as Ashbee explained, the prospect was overwhelming and the Guildsmen felt too daunted to respond.

> *It was a question of livelihood, and workshops and tradition. How were we, on whom the burden had fallen, to hold things together? [Were we] strong enough and representative enough?*[100]

Looking back in the shadow of Wilson's death, Ashbee suggested that his plans for re-education via reconstruction had been somewhat immature, as nobody could possibly have comprehended the War's full repercussions in terms of national and psychological upheaval. Yet with an unmistakeable 'if only' tone to his words, he expressed his certainty that the ideas behind such educative reconstruction had the potential to work, with so impassioned a man as Harry Wilson behind them:

> *We who could have helped him were scattered over the face of the earth by war. The work fell into the wrong hands and failed. Yet we know he could have done it.*[101]

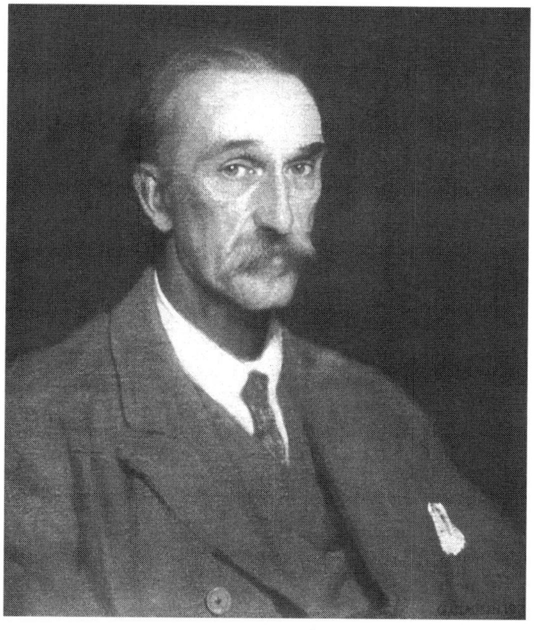

Art Workers' Guild

Figure 84. Portrait of Henry Wilson as Master of the Art Workers' Guild, painted by George Clausen, 1917.

CHAPTER EIGHT

PUBLIC FACE OF THE ARTS AND CRAFTS

In the debates that preoccupied the schools of art and design during the early years of the twentieth century, Wilson would invariably be fighting the same corner as his old friend Lethaby, the Principal of the Central School. One important issue, though, divided them: the role that should be taken by the Design and Industries Association. Lethaby was indeed the Association's 'godfather'[1] – the word used by Hamilton Temple Smith, his fellow founder-member on the first committee of 1915, to describe his involvement. Yet Wilson, despite sharing so many of Lethaby's – and the Association's – ideals, never could see his way to becoming a member.

To him, the problem was this. The Association stood for collaboration between craft and industry – a praiseworthy aim, he would have been the first to agree, but one that also struck him as unsustainable: the craft element would all too soon fall prey to industrial interests. So unequal a union could hardly inspire British industry with the 'new spirit of truth and beauty'[2] projected by the Association. The motives of the craftsmen who had joined it seemed sensible enough. They professed themselves willing to 'compromise with machinery' if by so doing they could 'raise the standards of design in production'.[3] Wilson fully understood the impulse for compromise of this kind. It was an impulse born partly of the immediate effects of the War, partly of the need (as he saw it) to match the leadership in product design established in pre-war Germany, where the rapport between designers and manufacturers was much closer than in Britain. There was a time when he himself had favoured such a compromise, but on reflection he realised that its eventual outcome would be the extinction of the craftsman. Now, therefore, instead of compromise, Wilson turned to a more fundamental solution, through a close examination of industry and how it organised itself. The words that surfaced have a manifesto-like ring whose radical force makes the Design and Industries Association's programme seem quiescent.

The Design and Industries Association was inaugurated with a great flourish in the press, and the promoters no doubt expect great things of it. It may be premature to pass judgement upon it. But I doubt it. I am not saying this because I do not wish the movement well. I have no objection to the policy which is described as the 'thin end of the wedge'. But a time comes when tact and compromise are no longer effective, and the only thing to do is to prepare for revolution.[4]

'Revolution' signified nothing less than the systematic reorganisation of industry on the basis of fairness and co-operation: when the War ended Wilson would be advocating the creation of a network of craft villages where these two elements would be thoroughly embodied. It was not enough to focus on machine production as the sole factor at stake in forging an entente between craft and industry: what had actually made the Arts and Crafts keep their distance from industry was the catalogue of insidious commercial abuses pervading the industrial system which craftsmen, simply by joining forces with it, had scant hope of curbing. He knew, for example, how little compunction certain West End jewellers felt about pirating original designs, and his paper issued a sharp warning to the craft designer of the lion's den he or she may be about to step into:

Mere buying and selling not only seems to undermine a man's morality, but seems to make him stupid. Salesmen are particularly so. As one compelled for a time to work to their dictates I may state that I can only recall one who seemed to have any intelligence at all.[5]

Wilson does not name this exception to the rule. One possibility is an understanding contact at Hayward & Co., for whom he had carried out a commission in 1889 for a wallpaper and frieze; or he may have meant a buyer for Jeffrey & Co., a sympathetic firm accustomed to dealing with Arts and Crafts designers. He had designed a wallpaper for them in 1893 that captured the flowing dynamics of Art Nouveau in trees and leaves, small flowers and nesting birds – it featured that year as an illustration in the *Studio* (II p. 22) – and he would include their wares in the international shows he would soon be organising on behalf of the A.C.E.S. Generally, though, Wilson's transactions with trade reps were frustrating: he recalled with disdain a salesman from an unnamed manufacturer who had asked him to design a chimney-piece, omitting to give him the dimensions since 'the sale' had not yet been clinched, but which in any case were deemed 'unnecessary'.[6]

Unscrupulous manufacturers relied less on their ability to deliver a proper solution to need than on their 'grip on human weakness and their ability to manipulate prices'. Plain, simple goods, say chairs or chests, could be rapidly cobbled together for the mass market, and carried relatively little profit, while more elaborate, often pretentiously decorated items, commercially produced, could be sold at cynically inflated prices. This inevitably put craftsmen at a disadvantage, making it impossible for them to sell at a profit well-made, useful pieces to a public conditioned to equate value with the degree of decoration. Craftsmen would be expected to charge less for items which were outwardly modest, even if palpably better made. Ironically, therefore, despite the movement's commitment to sane, sound, beautiful practicality, the greatest success of the Arts and Crafts was bound to come in the luxury market; regardless of their attempts to sell their work in ordinary shops, dedicated craftsmen had been forced to use galleries and other specialist outlets scarcely associated with everyday goods.

To illustrate his reservations about its ability to reform such abuses, Wilson took up two apparently minor yet revealing points voiced at the Association's inaugural meeting.

> *One speaker urged that the thing to do was to enlist the ... large retail buyers on their side, because the taste of the public was in their hands. Another dampened the enthusiasm of the designers by affirming that manufacturers could not consent to the names of their designers becoming public property because it would set up competition among manufacturers for their services ... .*[7]

As for buyers in commercial outlets being fit arbiters of public taste,

> *They are men entirely devoid of culture, without conviction in matters of taste who trifle with the interests of the arts. They back fashion as other men back horses. So long as the direction of industry is in their hands it will flounder....*[8]

He was well aware of the danger implicit in the other point too, about artists remaining obscure. Craftsmen would not in the least mind staying anonymous if that allowed them to get on and produce worthwhile work for a broader public. But the inherent risk of such a stance was their loss of independence, and with it the integrity of a personal style. His wariness about craftsmen being subsumed by commerce was visibly demonstrated in the layout of the Arts and Crafts Exhibition Society's 1916 show, of which he himself was overall organiser. In it, the Design and Industries Association was given a small room to itself where, significantly, each exhibit bore the manufacturer's name and, alongside it, that of its designer. As it happened, the same meeting of the Society in July 1916 at which the decision was made thus to identify the individual work, received with shock Lethaby's resignation, as of then, from both Presidency and membership. This act unambiguously signalled his disenchantment with the old Society – and effectively proclaimed his endorsement of the aims of the fledgling D.I.A..

The 1916 show therefore marked a turning point in the professional relationship between Wilson and Lethaby, and for Wilson himself, a watershed in his career as an exhibition designer, reinforcing, through the way he set about organising displays, his role as a practical philosopher of craft and craftsmanship. Curating such shows had by now become a major theme of his work. But while admitting a need to publicise the crafts in general, he was also intent on finding intelligent, engaging, accessible formats through which to convey their full meaning. He understood the limitations of displaying craft exhibits as arbitrary *objets,* with random, if seductive, appeal, when in fact they represented products of profound social and individual consciousness. And so, while it was vital to proselytise for the crafts in order to combat public apathy and ignorance, it was also important to discover cohesive modes of presenting them. Wilson's acknowledged mastery of exhibition design played a crucial part in heightening public awareness of the crafts throughout the War years. More than that, in the series of exhibitions he organised at home and abroad, he succeeded in promoting a vision of the crafts' full creative, educational and humanising potential.

For all the faith in the archetypal 'beyond' that so often characterised his work, he had little time for the deliberate mystification of the design process. Not himself drawn to working in this particular field, Wilson readily conceded the need for rational design capable of production on a large scale, just as Ernest Gimson had urged the rightness of letting 'machinery be honest, and make its machine buildings and machine furniture'.[9] Lethaby's 1915 definition of art as 'the well doing of what needs doing'[10] had his blessing too – with the one proviso that 'needs' applied not just to functional necessities, but equally to spiritual and symbolic ones.

It was his niggling impatience with the way the Exhibition Society carried out its remit that had prompted his resignation from it at the end of 1909. Now, in 1915, just when Lethaby was moving on from the Society to give the D.I.A. his full support and attention, Wilson found himself re-enlisting in the A.C.E.S. as better representing his own evolving views. Funtionalism versus craftsmanship – a parting of the ways between two old allies – and, as if to emphasise his continuing commitment to craft practice, 1915 was also when Wilson began work on a processional cross for Durham Cathedral, a piece which indeed gave expression to human spiritual and symbolic needs while simultaneously fulfilling its appropriate ritual function (Fig. 85).

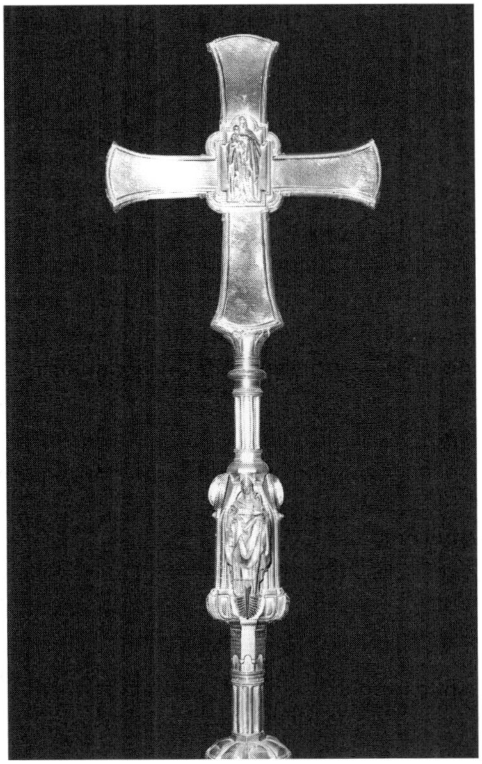

Durham Cathedral

Figure 85. Durham Cathedral: processional cross, silver with topaz and aquamarine, 1917.

It was commissioned by Theresa, Marchioness of Londonderry, in memory of her husband the Sixth Marquess, who had died in February 1915. Given his long association with the Londonderrys, begun in 1903 through his work on their private chapel at Wynyard, Wilson was her first choice. Like the Elphinstone Tomb, his Durham cross drew on precedent: he found inspiration for its distinctive outline in the medieval cross unearthed within the Cathedral, when the tomb of Cuthbert, the Cathedral's patron saint, was being excavated in the 1820s. On the elaborate silver knop of the new cross, the figures of Cuthbert and Bede would stand back to back, each at the helm of a boat, the vehicle for the spreading of Northumbrian Christianity, and with resonances of Noah's Ark. Set between them, a large topaz evoked the Light of Heaven, and an aquamarine symbolised the faith's journey across the seas. The arms of the cross are smooth polished silver with repoussé panels at its heart displaying, on the one side, the Virgin and Child, on the other, St. Helena – Helen was the middle name of the Marchioness – who was not only the mother of the 'British' emperor Constantine, but also revered for finding the True Cross in Jerusalem. In completing the work, Wilson encrypted a second compliment to its commissioner, making the stem of the cross spring from a lily, both the emblem of purity and the Marchioness's own favourite flower. The knop was removed in 1962, making the cross far lighter to carry.[11]

Despite his irritation with the ostrich-like attitudes manifested at times by the Arts and Crafts Exhibition Society, Wilson never lost faith in the ideals embraced by the movement itself, nor in the positive benefits of exhibiting its members' work. When he had resigned from the Society in 1910, it had been because 'it wasn't constructive' and represented merely 'a collection of isolated artists lamely following a banner whose meaning they'd forgotten'.[12] Such a conclusion was reached in a critique of the Society's 1912 show, the last to be held under Crane's faltering leadership. The deficit the display threw the A.C.E.S. into only aggravated a sense of its flagging energy and loss of purpose. The ill-assorted arrangement of objects, in serried ranks within display cases set out in perfunctory rows, dissipated any originality that might light up particular exhibits. The *Studio*'s correspondent surely spoke for many, Wilson included, when he wrote: 'here is skilled craftsmanship, but no great designer leads the way into fresh fields of invention'.[13]

The bad press the 1912 exhibition attracted had rocked the membership. The two-year period of self-examination that ensued was brought to a sudden end by an event that would have far-reaching consequences for the status of creative design, as well as for the Arts and Crafts movement itself. It occurred not in Britain but in the Rhineland, and galvanised the theory and practice of design throughout Europe and beyond. Those forward-thinking members of the Exhibition Society who, in 1914, took the opportunity to visit the Deutscher Werkbund's exhibition in Cologne, found themselves confronted with the freshness and integrity that had once characterised their own output. The British craftsmen and educators who attended included Harold Stabler, Ambrose Heal, Cecil Brewer and Harry Peach. They were stirred by what they saw, whether at the product-design scale of Richard Riemerschmid's mass-produced Typenmöbel modular furniture, or at the challenging industrial scale of Walter Gropius's brick, black steel and glass Fagus shoe-last factory. Although some exhibits upheld the cherished ideals of tradition and independent craftsmanship, it was the radical elements in the show that most impressed the British contingent, who recrossed the North Sea with an answer to the Deutscher Werkbund – the Design and Industries Association – taking shape in their minds.

While the sidestep of these key members from the Arts and Crafts fold may not have fatally undermined the movement, it was a severe psychological blow, and exarcerbated a declining sense of solidarity and relevance among the core faithful. Yet on those left behind in the A.C.E.S. the realignment of the defectors with the more favourable elements in commerce and industry also had a surprisingly energising effect, in forcing determined traditionalists to confront the issues of self-renewal and the need for a vigour of outlook equivalent to that to be seen in the Werkbund.

Wilson was not among those who travelled to Cologne, but he studied every report of the exhibition in depth, and made it his business to absorb the impact of 'that most significant society'.[14] He couldn't help admiring the Werkbund's commitment to quality in design (the 'Qualität' constantly reiterated in its early writings), as well as the energy of its approach to designing. This vigour could be discerned in 'two of its wonderful modern buildings, grain elevators in Montreal and Fort William,' selected by Wilson for special praise from the Werkbund's illustrated yearbooks: 'they look like enchanted castles, stark, grim, and beautiful....'[15] Here, it has to be said, his analogy with fantastic medieval castles sets him two generations back from Le Corbusier's Machine Age advocacy of grand lakeside silos and ocean liners; this is the imagery of his old master J.D. Sedding's Cornish world, lyrically recalled. Nevertheless, the heroic mechanisation of the contemporary scene was tempting him, visually at first, and then philosophically, to yield to the inherent thrill of modernity.

With his concern for the public face of the Arts and Crafts, and his commitment to group displays, Wilson was acutely aware of the Werkbund's committed approach towards organising exhibitions. The contrast between the practical, indeed opportunistic, endorsement of the Werkbund and its aims by German regional and state government, and the British government's relative indifference to good design, was inescapable:

> *The Werkbund has spent large sums on schemes of decoration in its exhibitions ... to show the manufacturers and public that quality of material and beauty of design are important considerations, not only from the point of view of gain, but also from that of National and Individual welfare. So successful were they that in 1914 they induced the City of Cologne to grant an exhibition site and £25,000 towards expenses....*[16]

The differences in national attitude were all the more galling in view of the Werkbund's clear debt to British design, one which could be traced back a good twenty years to the first confident blooming of the Domestic Revival in English architecture and the associated arts. It was in the autumn of 1896 that the Prussian Board of Trade had delegated the architect and civil servant Hermann Muthesius to travel the length and breadth of Britain and report on the technical advances in ordinary life that he found there, his remit embracing architecture, industry and transport. Muthesius was an ideal and perceptive observer; his survey complete, he returned home in 1903 and filed an influential report. His own special interests, domestic architecture and the Arts and Crafts movement, would find independent expression in his book *Das Englische Haus*, published two years later in 1905.

In his absence, the Sezession movement had been gathering strength in Austria and Germany; from 1897 its associated workshops – Werkstätten – were being established in Munich, Dresden, Hellerau, Berlin and Hanover. English Arts and Crafts designers were invited to participate in Sezession exhibitions, while Josef Hoffman, head of the workshops launched in Vienna in 1903, acknowledged that they had taken as their model Ashbee's Guild of Handicraft. Muthesius himself had, as early as 1897, written up the Guild for the journal *Dekorative Kunst*; and as soon as other commitments allowed, in June 1907, he took the step that would fuse the creative impulses of the Werkstätten with national aspirations for good quality, mass-produced design: he set up the Deutscher Werkbund. Even in the midst of hostilities – 1916 – Wilson was recording the pre-War force of the Werkbund:

> *Springing out of the efforts of a few artists who sought to raise the quality of German manufactures by basing their efforts on ... the methods of Morris and the English Arts and Crafts, the Werkbund has become a powerful organisation with the openly avowed intention of capturing the world market for German wares....*[17]

Wilson did not mince his words as he warmed to his theme:

> *Foreigners who study ... these matters say 'we are enormously interested in your decorative art because there you undoubtedly lead the world.' Germany has recognised that. Before the War she was actually in the habit of sending commissioners over here to crib our ideas and buy up our artists and craftsmen.*[18]

Muthesius, he is saying, is in the business of state-sponsored plagiarism. The German success only emphasised the relative feebleness of British manufacturers and of all those whose business was visual communication. The response to some work by Edward Johnston, who was about to develop from master calligrapher into the originator of fonts that would become the foundation of twentieth century typographic practice, was a case in point. Wilson hardly knew whether to laugh or rage at the almost farcical cycle of innovation being spurned at source:

The Germans came, studied Johnston's designs and methods, ... completely reorganised their own fonts, and were soon selling to our printers the very types they had refused at the hands of their own countryman.... The Americans then copied these German types and sold them here. English printers are now buying American copies of German copies of the original English type. And in every branch of endeavour – furniture, textiles, wallpapers, cretonnes, jewellery, interior decoration – our manufactures have been buying inferior German copies of English artists' productions....[19]

Driven by a conviction that nothing could be satisfactorily designed by one hand and translated by another, Johnston's excursions into typography up to the moment Wilson was writing had been limited to commissions such as a Gothic face for the private Cranach Press of the celebrated anglophile Count Harry Kessler. It was in this year, however, 1916, that his legendary display face for London Transport was launched with immediate, and revolutionary, effect. But Wilson's indignation over German designers stealing a march was not misplaced: it was Johnston's calligraphy, given wide currency in Germany, which had prompted print and display designers, brought up on the black-letter face, to ditch it for the candour of Roman letter-form and Johnston's thorough reappraisals of it. In reacting to the injustice done to his old colleague, Wilson may be guilty of conflating Johnston's prolific calligraphic practice with his emergent career as typographer, but his indignation stands.

It was little wonder, then, that his enthusiasm for the Werkbund was more circumspect than that expressed by the Committee of the D.I.A., if to imitate it was simply to perpetuate the pattern of one nation appropriating design solutions from its neighbour. This stance was entirely consistent with the premium he set on intellectual and artistic individuality, though, ironically, it has its exact counterpart in the internal arguments that took place within the Werkbund itself between 1911 and 1914. On one side stood Hermann Muthesius, advocating the promotion of German products in world markets through high-quality, standardised design; on the other, stood the Belgian architect-designer Henri Van de Velde who, seeing in mass-production a materialistic denial of creativity, robustly asserted his mistrust of it: 'So long as there are artists within the Werkbund,' he claimed, 'they will protest against standardisation.... The artist is essentially a passionate individualist'.[20] Van de Velde had an articulate ally in the socialist reformer Friedrich Naumann, who in its 1913 Yearbook urged the Werkbund to resist endorsing any one single style or principle of production, since taste was a matter of personal choice. Wilson quoted Naumann in 1916 with the delight of discovering shared ideas:

If you treat a worker like scum, his work will be scum. The German art and craft movement sets the ... spiritual and material conditions of the worker in the first line. Our ... school system must be reorganised to produce practical ability. Artistic enterprise cannot succeed unless the workers are able to regard the business as their own. Work must not be done for material advantage but for its own sake. [Imaginative] work saturated with character alone creates commercial value.[21]

The real message the Werkbund had for Britain was radical and clear. A mere lobbying body like the Design and Industries Association was no substitute for the plain duty of the government to subvent and promote the British Arts and Crafts, its productions and its creative spirits: 'German states ... subsidised the Werkbund; why should not our state give us, its [the Werkbund's] parents, a subsidy?' demanded Wilson.[22]

The crisis of confidence and inspiration in the Arts and Crafts after the debacle of the 1912 A.C.E.S. show had led to the formation of the Design and Industries Association, but also to a resurgence of the movement at large. If that London exhibition is taken as his starting point, the course that Wilson chose to steer out of the impasse becomes clearer. Typically, he drew his own

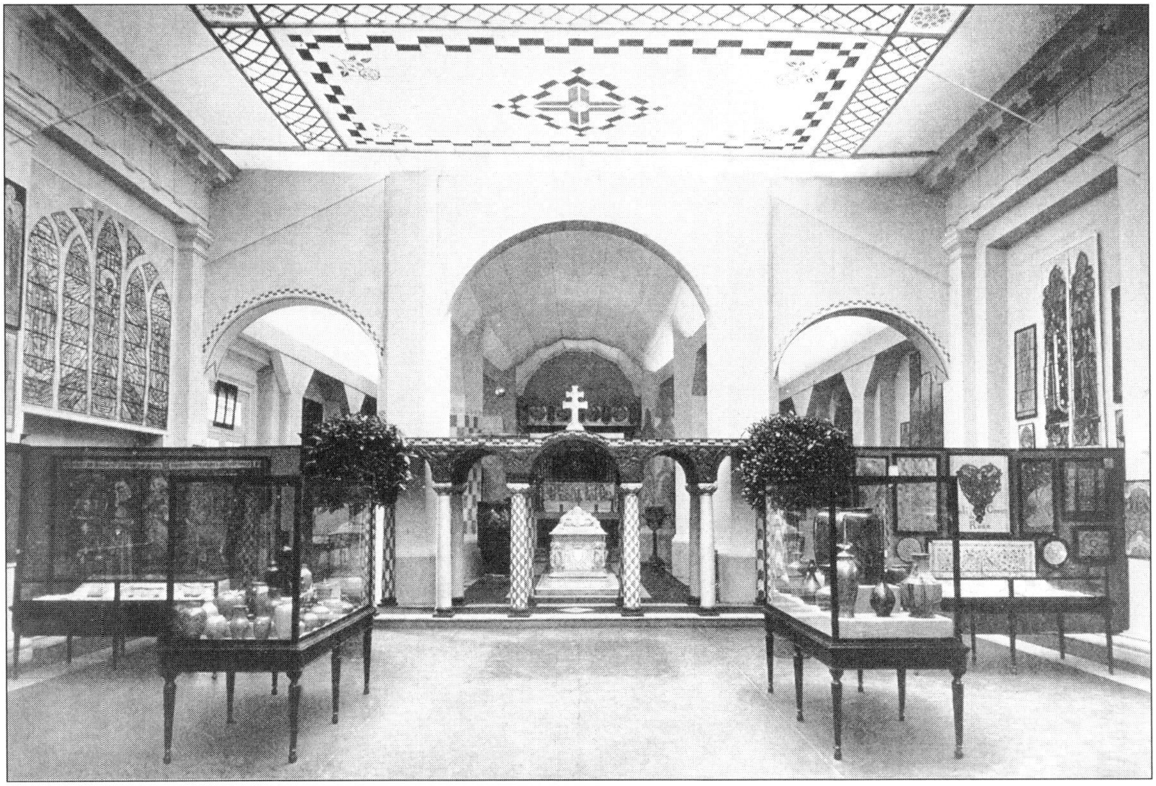

Figure 86. Ghent International Exhibition: A.C.E.S. gallery, looking towards the 'temple crafts'. *Studio*, 1913, Vol. 60.

charts. He had already declared his position on education, and set the watchword for the future: innovation, but innovation *within tradition*. The same watchword governed his involvement in the three subsequent Arts and Crafts-based exhibitions – for which he partly or totally shouldered responsibility – and in particular, his organisation of the displays.

First came the 1913 International Exposition in Ghent, in which Britain, represented by the Arts and Crafts Exhibition Society, occupied a complete gallery (Fig. 86). A wholly British display followed in Paris in 1914, showcasing recent Arts and Crafts design; then, biggest and best, came the Society's 1916 show at Burlington House. This, the eleventh and most ambitious of the A.C.E.S. exhibitions, was entirely selected and arranged by Wilson, who, having rejoined the Society in 1915, had succeeded Crane as President.

At Ghent, with some exceptions, the works presented in the British Section (a mixture of retrospective and contemporary pieces) was essentially a repeat of the previous year's London show (Fig. 86). Yet the exhibits that in 1912 had sparked no enthusiasm, now found themselves hailed in the *Studio* as 'one of the most complete and important collections of modern British art ever presented',[23] and the Royal Society of Arts thought the display more interesting than 'any recent exhibition of modern English craftwork held at home or on the Continent'.[24] This comprehensive reappraisal was the result of one crucial factor – the presence of Wilson as organiser and animateur. With his history of resignation and sudden reaffiliation five years later, Wilson was still regarded as something of an outsider to the Exhibition Society, but his equivocal position equipped him better than most amongst the unquestioning membership to understand and clarify the issues. At a stroke, he transformed the haphazardness of 1912 into something cogent and purposeful.

In the Ghent display he took control of the 'scenic architecture'[25] to ensure that the setting and layout was given the same careful consideration as the exhibits themselves. In his contribution to the catalogue, the preceding President, Walter Crane, was generous in his acknowledgement of the innovations of the *mise-en-scène*: 'Owing to the skill and invention of Mr. Wilson we have been able for the first time to unite various examples of the Arts and Crafts in a more co-ordinated relationship than hitherto'.[26] Since Muthesius had noted in 1902 that

> *... a complete room has never been shown at any of the London Arts and Crafts Exhibitions, it has always been a question of individual pieces and the usual Arts and Crafts trivia.... That any serious art must concern itself with the room as a whole seems to be clear everywhere except in London....*[27]

It had taken eleven years for London to grasp the point; now, thanks to Wilson, it was grasped.

In its upholders' disposition to display objects regardless of setting, Muthesius had detected the backwardness of the Arts and Crafts in Britain, which to him had advanced little since the death of William Morris. He was thus able to identify 'the room as a work of art' as a European phenomenon. In its command of the wholeness of interior space, the Scottish partnership of Margaret Macdonald and Charles Rennie Mackintosh was seemingly unique among British designers in breathing pan-European air untried by adherents of the craft revival in Britain. However, when Wilson put his mind to the layout and selection of the three exhibitions mounted between 1913 and 1916, it was not in the quest for mere aesthetic consistency based on style or image. From Ghent onwards, the setting he sought to create for the chosen exhibits was one based primarily on intellectual coherence.

As soon as the London exhibition closed in 1912, he busied himself with organising the Ghent project. His own current commissions, from the relatively simple crucifix memorial to the 24-year-old Margaret Skrine in the churchyard at Itchen Stoke, Hampshire, to the complex and demanding Elphinstone Tomb in Aberdeen for which, the following year, he would take his whole family off to Venice, kept his feet firmly on the ground. Nevertheless, no sooner had he taken charge of the arrangements for Ghent than he submitted an incisive report to his Committee, recommending a rational, readable and inventive layout that, while leaving 'nothing to chance', avoided the 'merely mechanial or alphabetic'. Significantly, he gave a cautious nod towards commercial production:

> *It has occurred to me to suggest a logical scheme for Ghent, based on the natural evolution of the arts & crafts, and on their relation to life itself. So arranged, the Exhibition might be of ... great educative value, and open the way to new developments in industry.*[28]

Wilson's Ghent layout revived something unexpected, the expansive, challenging symbolism of the Guild's masque of Beauty's Awakening, from the far-off Jubilee year. He exploited the rectangular space of the gallery to present in sequence the 'conditions of a fruitful life' – play, worship, home, learning, occupational training, complete with a performance-stage. Play, the realm where Apollo presided, filled one end, Worship, Zeus's sphere, the other (Fig. 86a).

Along the entire length of the North side of the gallery were grouped exhibits relating to home, school and household – the domains of Hera, Hermes and Ares. Included among them were the leading names in contemporary British craft-printing and book production: Graily Hewitt, Allan Vigers, Edward Johnston of course, Douglas Cockerell and Cobden-Sanderson. Illustration was represented by Jessie King, Walter Crane and Frank Morley Fletcher. Ceramicists and glass-makers included Bernard Moore, Alfred Powell, Howson Taylor, the Martin Brothers and Powell & Sons, while Jeffrey & Co. showed handprinted wallpapers. What pulled this section together visually and gave it focus was the furniture supplied by Ernest Gimson, Morris & Co, and Heal's, adroitly stationed in the space by Wilson.

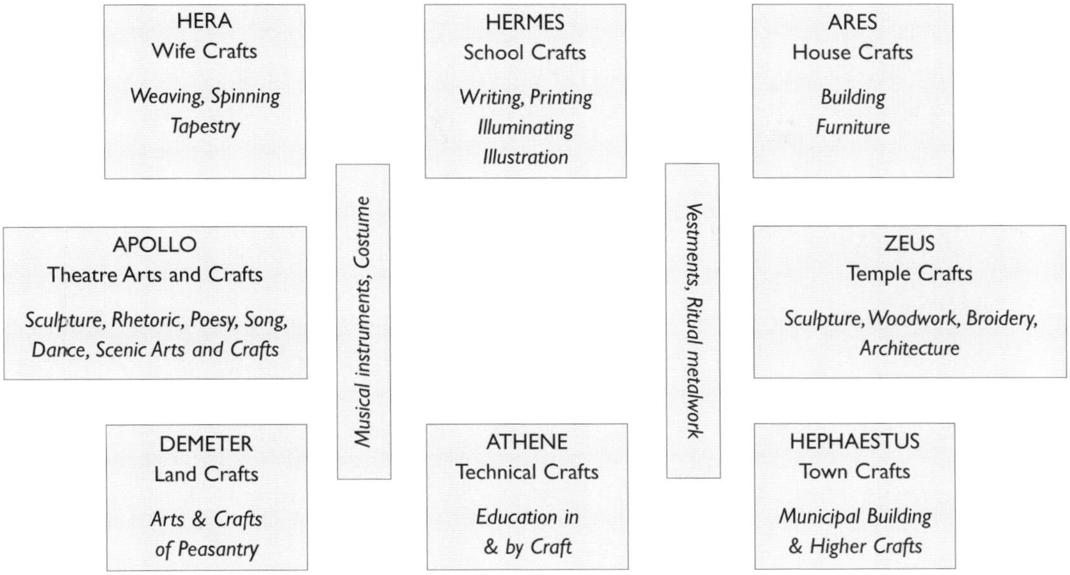

Figure 86a. Wilson's floor plan for the Ghent Exhibition, 1913.

Facing this sequence across the gallery were exhibits relating to town planning, agriculture and craft-education, in sections allotted to Hephaestus, Demeter and Athene – it was she who gave a place to domestic and secular metalwork and jewellery, with plate by Omar Ramsden and Alwyn Carr, tableware by Stabler, Paul Cooper's shagreen caskets, enamels by Alexander Fisher, Nelson Dawson's artistic metalware, and jewels by Arthur Gaskin. Here, too, was a chance for Wilson to present some of his own jewellery and fine metalwork: the Chamberlain Casket, the silver chafing dish with the thread-spinning classical nude as its finial (Plate 53), and twenty-two pieces of jewellery, including the Diana tiara with its crystal and enamel headband, forming a breathtaking array of skill and beauty.

Wilson's Ghent layout scrapped the usual static mode of exposition which had tended to suggest that the exhibits were self-absorbed and segregated one from another, in favour of a sense of movement typical of life's complementary activities.

> *Land crafts leads to Music (who thinks of Apollo will see why). Music leads to the Theatre, which through costume and subject brings us to the school … and the house … .*[29]

Thus one display led continuously to the next, encapsulating all aspects of the 'fruitful life', while the central space was transformed into a garden, a quiet area featuring sculpture by George Frampton, Alfred Drury and Gilbert Bayes, and murals by Gerald Moira and the late Sir Edward Burne-Jones.

If his work had made a sensational appearance amongst that of eminent contemporaries in Athene's realm, in Zeus's domain Wilson was the moving spirit – no single British designer had, since the turn of the century, so excelled in the 'temple crafts'. The area he allotted to these at Ghent was divided from the main hall both physically – by three arches and a Byzantine-inspired chancel screen, made for him by Trask and enriched with modelled zodiac signs by J.P. Cooper – and visually, by the spatial volumes Wilson had created within it, all enhanced by the modulated lighting. If the screen was recognisably by the hand that had finished Holy Trinity, Sloane Street and furnished St.

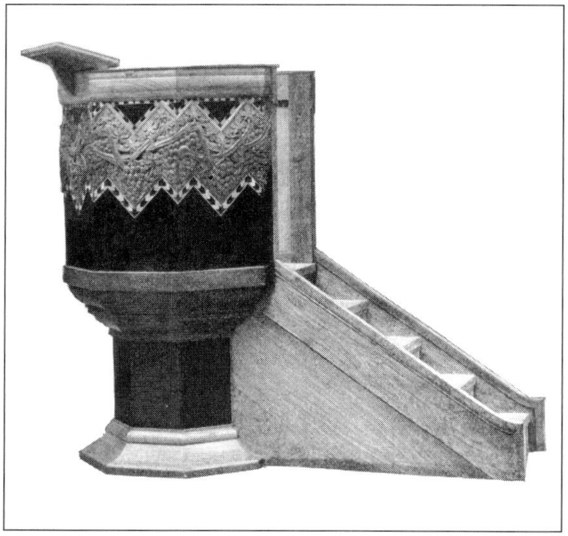

Figure 87. H. Wilson: pulpit, oak inlaid with ebony, shown at Ghent Exhibition, illustrated in the *Studio*, Vol. 29, 1903.

Bartholomew's, Brighton, the space beyond it, with its Byzantine vault and crisp detail, showed what Wilson had still to give to architecture. The Journal of the Royal Society of Arts admired 'Sir Goscombe John's impressive monument to Lord Salisbury, a vigorous wrought iron lectern by Mr. Edward Spenser, some unusual altar rails by Mr. Reynolds Stevens ...';[30] but the setting Wilson had created for these exhibits, his 'temporary church', had an immense, defining impact. Within the space were five further pieces made or designed by him, including the sturdy oak and ebony pulpit[31] with his own ebullient zigzag decoration, made for him by Trask in 1903 (Fig. 87) for the restoration, by Edmund Sedding Jr., of St. Wyllow's Church, Lanteglos-by-Fowey, Cornwall. The reredos in Ghent's 'temporary church' had figures modelled by Wilson, and he collaborated with George Sedding, JD's son, on an altar panel made in repoussé copper by Conrad Dressler to Wilson's designs; this was neatly complemented by his 1906 plaster bas-relief panel for Sloane Street of Christ and the little children. But what instantly announced Wilson's mastery here was his Caldey Abbey monstrance (Plate 58), with its pure crystal compartment and intricately enamelled caligraphic texts.

The overall organisation at Ghent also attracted critical notice. The reviewers spotted at once that the exhibition encompassed something novel, a distinctly fresh way of presentation. They latched on to the way Wilson had worked things out, and how each section took its place within the scheme as an entity. They were comfortable with his use of classical deities to differentiate its thematic areas, though this, along with the naming of some of the categories – broidery, poesy – is the most dated aspect of the scheme. The twelve gods were inexorably showing their age: in an accelerating world, the calm predictability that they enshrined would soon be shattered by war.

As to what the British section at Ghent achieved, the press was generally positive, the *Studio* declaring it 'a very great success'.[32] However, as the Royal Society of Arts correspondent lighted on the one flaw that Wilson, in recasting and reorchestrating a collection of exhibits he had inherited from the 1912 London show, could not conceal – despite offerings from Powell & Sons, Jeffrey & Co., Warners, Pilkington's and Heal's, the manufacturers were not adequately represented. Given that he had not selected the spread of the objects from scratch, and taking into account his caveats about mingling craftworks with industrial products, the balance in favour of craft was probably about right in Wilson's eyes: industry was indeed represented, but within appropriate limits.

If Wilson had been an unknown quantity before, or if there had been whispers among Society members as to his commitment, the Ghent project unmistakeably established him as a resourceful and creative exhibition designer, while confirming his growing critical reputation in Europe as an architect-craftsman. His name had been established in the Aix-la-Chapelle (Aachen) Exhibition of Church Art six years earlier, and boosted in the award made to him in 1909 of the coveted German National Medal, a remarkable occurrence in the case of a foreign artist. His contribution to the Aix exhibition amounted, in effect, to a retrospective of Henry Wilson's best independent church work, such as the widely-praised lamp for Saragossa Cathedral and the pietà for Welbeck Abbey, but most influentially, his perspective drawings of church interiors whether executed – the Lady Chapel at Sloane Street, the baldacchino for St. Bartholomew's, Brighton, and Clerkenwell's high altar – or unbuilt, like his monumental scheme to complete St. Augustine's, Highgate.

The German National Medal came in response to his submitting the Gloucester Cathedral chalice and his drawings for the proposed East end of St. Bartholomew's, Brighton to the 1909 International Exhibition of Church Art in Düsseldorf. In 1912 it was the turn of Brussels to hold an exhibition of Religious Art. Naturally, Wilson, was invited to participate, and two aspects of his craft – and art – caught the Belgian public's imagination: the technical expertise of the Saragossa lamp and the Caldey Abbey monstrance, and the brilliant suggestiveness of the architectural watercolours, all contributed to marking him out as a 'great architect-decorator'. [33]

Further strength was added to Wilson's European fame as the look and feel of his work began to be conveyed through the pages of *Moderne Bauformen*, the prestigious and internationally influential German design and architecture periodical published from 1902. Its founding editor, Julius Hoffman, was already aware of Wilson's highly individual attitudes through reports of Arts and Crafts Exhibition Society events, and through his articles and lectures; but it was as a direct result of the Aix exhibition that Hoffman approached him with a view to reproducing some of his schemes within the magazine's pages. Between 1909 and 1911 he chose a series of the most striking and dramatic of Wilson's drawings for such crucial exposure. Writing from Stuttgart, Hoffman contracted that *Moderne Bauformen* would pay him five guineas an illustration;[34] between them they agreed a selection including the haunting perspective for the West end of St. Augustine's, Highgate, the spectacular fittings (and his proposed extension) for St. Bartholomew's, Brighton, the sanctuary rail for Holy Trinity, Sloane Street, the Lady Chapel at St. Martin's, Marple, and his chapel and monument room proposal for Wynyard Hall. *Moderne Bauformen* reproduced Wilson's designs in full colour to powerful effect, and in this form his work and reputation reached a Europe-wide audience.[35]

Following Ghent, the next important European exhibition organised on its behalf by Wilson, in Paris in 1914, provided further reassurance of his faith in the fundamental values of the Arts and Crafts Exhibition Society. Initially, the terms of the French government's invitation would have secured the transfer of the Ghent display to Paris *en bloc*. However, the considerably larger exhibition space afforded by the Louvre's Pavillon de Marsan persuaded the Exhibition Committee – it comprised representatives from the Board of Trade and the A.C.E.S., chaired by the Director of the Victoria and Albert Museum – to ask Wilson to devise a new scheme incorporating additional works.[36]

The Committee immediately re-appointed him as Chairman of the Hanging Committee, which, with members like May Morris, Walter Crane, Robert Anning Bell and Douglas Cockerell retained much of the old ideological ardour of the Arts and Crafts. The sternly meticulous eye for craftsmanship that governed their selection of the additional material excluded anything startlingly innovative, and gave the contents of the Paris exhibition its sense of dynamic stasis; not so Wilson's setting for the show. It embodied in vibrant form his will to reinvigorate the movement without compromising its fundamental beliefs. For a start, he 'completely metamorphosed'[37] the main gallery, reducing the daunting loftiness of the glass-roofed hall with a linen velarium, or canopy. This, decorated with signs of the zodiac, not only corrected the scale for the viewer, but also lent an intriguing 'golden light'[38] to the interior and the exhibits.

At one end of the pavilion he placed the altar, reredos and pulpit which had featured at Ghent. Needing to tame the bulk of a dozen giant pilasters on the long sides of the gallery, he drafted in twelve of Christopher Whall's cartoons, made for his Lady Chapel windows in Gloucester Cathedral. Whall – a member of the Hanging Committee – joined Wilson in Paris and helped him install the show. The pairs of free-standing piers at either end of the main space were likewise given over to Whall cartoons, his depictions of the Four Elements for the West window of Upton-on-Severn church. Wilson's 'sanctuary' space achieved contextual enrichment over Ghent, with Whall again a key contributor: two more window cartoons set above altar and reredos, this time for his glass at Canterbury, then the addition of a work of his in three dimensions, the full-scale plaster maquette for a somewhat Wilsonian altar cross.[39]

As for the main space, despite being focused round Wilson's own great work-in-progress, the life-size modello for the Elphinstone Tomb for Aberdeen University, the flavour was by no means uniquely ecclesiastical: there was also much secular sculpture, and a wider spectrum of craft furniture than the space at Ghent had permitted. The form of the pavilion itself gave Wilson an opportunity to bring subtle drama and intimacy to the display of jewellery and silverware. The semi-circular screen of columns opposite the 'sanctuary' gave onto an enigmatic dark space, where skilful electric illumination enhanced the exhibits' preciousness.

The impact of Wilson's special display won immediate approval from the *Studio*'s correspondent, who applauded the fineness of Phoebe Traquair's and Harold Stabler's enamelling, as well as J.P. Cooper's 'fascinating' silverwork[40] and several exhibits by Wilson himself: the mysteriousness and concentration of the setting also worked on the larger scale, to the benefit of the Gloucester chalice, the MacRitchie mace, and the chafing dish with the thread-spinning classical nude, as well as creating a glinting, alluring ambience for some thirty of his jewels – brooches, buckles, necklaces, haircombs, and, most dazzling of all, the tiara commissioned for Lady Llewellyn Smith's presentation at Court in 1904.

Made of gold and with a headband of crystal, the tiara shows a superbly imperious Apollo, his right arm raised in a dramatic flourish, a lyre held in his left hand (Fig. 88), poised within a gold circlet flanked by lions. At the sides are upswept wings of cast gold. A detachable roundel at the back is designed to hold three ostrich feathers. The line of the crystal headband, itself banded with enamel, is echoed in blue-green enamel and pierced gold, and embellished at its sides and centre with clusters of crystal, pearl and semi-precious stones. In the years following its commission, Wilson and Lady Llewellyn Smith's husband,

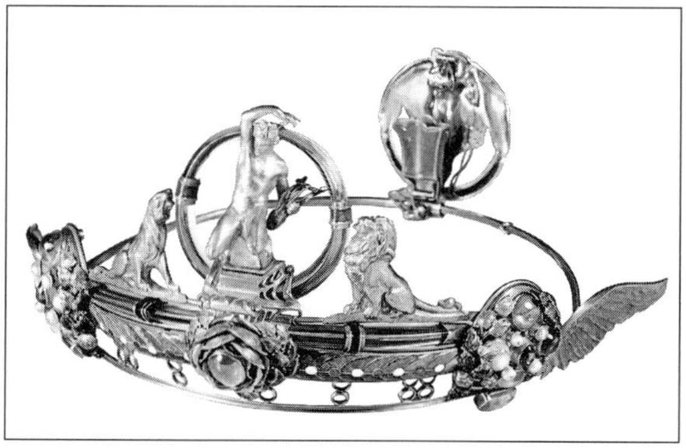

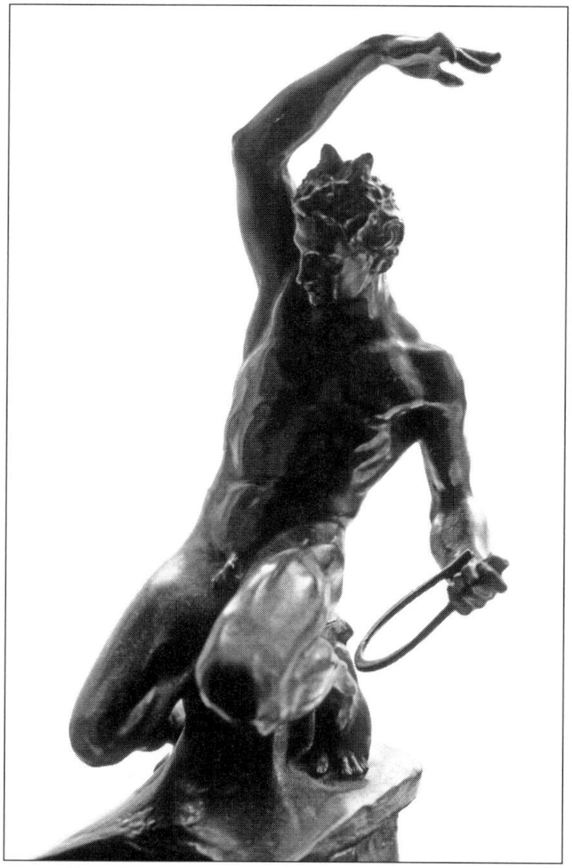

Figure 88. (above) Apollo: bronze statuette (h. 38cm), study made by Wilson for the central figure crowning (top) the Lady Llewellyn Smith tiara, 1904.

Hubert, would work together in a variety of contexts: the latter, as Permanent Secretary to the Board of Trade from 1907 to 1919, was instrumental in financing British displays abroad, the A.C.E.S. Paris show of 1914 marking the mid-point of his tenure. In matters of education and technical training he saw eye-to-eye with Wilson. A lecturer in the 1880s for the Toynbee Trust, he served for four years as Secretary of the National Association of Technical Education from 1888, and sat on the Royal Commision on Secondary Education for the year 1894-95. In 1920, he would become the first Chairman of the British Institute of Industrial Art, of which Wilson was a founder member. Later, in 1925, he chaired the editorial committee that compiled the official report on that year's Paris Exposition.

Aside from the main space in the Pavillon de Marsan there were additional smaller rooms along the South side which, without need for major reinterpretation, lent themselves perfectly, one for each, to craft displays: glassware, ceramics, needlework, book production – with the Vale, Doves and Arden Presses represented – and a review of the multifarious output of the groundbreaking craft firm Morris & Co.

In its acclaim of the superlative workmanship of individual exhibits, the press was unanimous, and there was general agreement on the originality of Wilson's setting. However, some complaints were raised, the most common concerning the dearth of stylistic innovation. Even if not manifestly retrospective, the exhibits seemed to cling to the past. One commentator regretted the omission of famous names:

> *One or two rooms by Baillie Scott ... would have been interesting, or by C.R. Mackintosh, whose work has had a wider influence on the Continent than ... any of the moderns represented, yet does not figure here beyond one small drawing. Mr. Voysey has a very modest exhibit, and George Walton, E.L. Lutyens, Walter Cave, George Logan etc. show nothing ... .* [41]

Here, the *Studio*'s reviewer seems intent on rekindling that magic Muthesian moment fifteen years before, when British interior design was eagerly devoured in the pages of that very magazine and perhaps achieved its greatest international éclat. There was something decidedly out-of-touch about this critic's comments. By 1914, with his thriving practice in pleasant pebbledashed or half-timbered houses in the Home Counties, Baillie Scott would hardly be submitting portable pieces or experimental rooms to international expositions. Mackintosh had some design initiatives in him yet, but with the final phase of the Glasgow School of Art complete, no arresting new work was crying out for exhibition. George Walton, mentioned in early reviews, was by this time immersed in routine architectural work and had faded from sight. Edwin Lutyens, a scene-setting architectural presence since 1899 was preoccupied, Herbert Baker meanwhile having become his uneasy collaborator, with New Delhi; while the furniture designers Cave and Logan were never more than minor figures.

The truth was that mainstream Arts and Crafts designers such as May Morris, Cockerell and Johnston, into whose orbit Wilson had returned, had kept faith with the authentic ideals of the Arts and Crafts, and accusations that the style had lost momentum or become old-fashioned were chiefly journalistic ones: what grumbles like the *Studio*'s pinpointed was that while fashion and journalism demand change, the character of the Arts and Crafts had not changed. In this context, Wilson's championship of the movement preserves a sense of its honest, lasting value.

More serious than this hankering after change, however, was the inescapable lack of co-operation between craftmen and manufacturers. As one critic remarked, such wilful separatism would have struck even first generation Arts and Craftsmen as outdated:

> *William Morris, with all his love of handwork, was happy to design wallpaper and cretonnes but the twentieth century artist-craftsman apparently can only be interested in work he can execute entirely by himself....* [42]

But the debate this comment might have set off was never to be fully engaged; the Paris Exhibition had scarcely opened when war broke out, and the displays were hastily dismantled and dispersed. Wilson had been given neither a clean slate nor sole responsibility in choosing the exhibits for a show which, in the event, had been so ominously forestalled. But in the future, when he had a freer hand in the selection process, a more open-minded attitude would emerge; and Wilson's own recognition of the role of ethical commerce would be confirmed by the next major Arts and Crafts show held in London two years later, even if here too, the primary values of craftsmanship and tradition remained the keynotes of the show.

In March 1916, the Government established a Reconstruction Committee, its remit to set the country on the road to recovery once the years of war, still far from over, were ended. Well-intentioned, though often inconclusive, research was initiated to ascertain and act on those areas most in need of improvement: training, trade, education, agriculture, and to ensure that any available help was properly directed. Wilson's own activities in the name of reconstruction – a cause whose importance he felt to the centre of his being – were undertaken in a positive, practical mood; for all its devastation the War had created a melting pot, an openness on the part of government in assessing what ought to be done next. This would be the framework of Wilson's endeavours, and those of other Arts and Crafts activists; as early as July 1916, a dedicated sense of mission informed the Arts and Crafts Exhibition Society's press announcement of its eleventh show, to be held at the Royal Academy between October and December. The list of exhibitors was open to 'all craftsmen, whether members of the society or not', the aim of the event to give a 'constructive' demonstration of Britain's creative potential. Its form was to be based on the 'successful experiments'[43] in Ghent and Paris, but on an even more ambitious scale.

As well as holding a permanent position in the recently formed Ministry of Reconstruction, Wilson was now President of the A.C.E.S. The misgivings of the membership had been reconciled, and a substantial majority had voted for him. In a circular to them Wilson expressed his intentions more precisely. By 1916 he had greater influence than ever, not just in devising the setting of the exhibition, but also in selecting the exhibits. In this way the 1916 exhibition may be closely identified with his own views.

In keeping with his powerful emotions about the War, Wilson predictably defined the show as a chance to stress the crafts' vital role in reconstruction. Furthermore, he was intent on clarifying his and the Society's views on the relationship between craft and industry: the crafts must come *first*. With that proviso, Wilson and the members he represented were not against seeking commercial success. He enlarged his argument with a quick glance at continental Europe, where craft workshops and training schemes were, even in the conditions of 1916, receiving state support. But, he warned, 'mistakes' were being made, by relying too much on machinery and on the ideas of 'other countries' – a knowing phrase, all but spelling out Britain. By contrast, the forthcoming London exhibition would reveal a reassuringly 'British quality ... subtle, elusive, but easily recognisable everywhere'.[44]

This was the first time anything so openly utilitarian as a large-scale exhibition of the Arts and Crafts had appeared at the Royal Academy. The importance of this bridgehead was keenly felt by Wilson, and he urged his A.C.E.S. membership to make the show 'worthy'[45] of the venue. The journey to these hallowed galleries had been a long one. In 1888, the year the Academy had hosted the first congress of the National Association for the Advancement of Art, Walter Crane had urged the necessity of the practical work of the artist-craftsman forming part of the associated exhibition; his plea was turned down. In his candidature for the Slade Professorship in 1911, Wilson had stood, in effect, as the Arts and Crafts representative, with the hope of infiltrating and informing an influential if largely indifferent institution. But the year 1916 had delivered a stroke of luck to the proponents of Arts and Crafts in the person of the President of the Royal Academy who was an advocate of the applied arts, the neo-Grecian painter Sir Edward Poynter; the meeting of minds between the newly-elected P.R.A. and Wilson the craftsman-idealist was instantaneous, and at last the time had come for the doors of Burlington House to open wide to those endeavours.

Pacing out the galleries of this formerly unassailable stronghold in the summer of that year, Wilson began the work of organising and designing his third major exhibition of national crafts in four years. An exhibition presented here, in a venue incomparably more prestigious than the New Gallery in Grafton Street where the Society's shows were normally held, was bound to draw in a new range of visitors, in numbers far exceeding those of the usual devotees. Beside the general public, the audience Wilson was angling for included those influential elements in society which he had targeted in his art school role: those with political clout, teachers, industrialists, retailers. As he hospitably put it in his introduction for the catalogue, 'the official world, the world of education, and the world of trade and manufactures are invited to flock to Burlington House ...'.[46]

And so they did. The Academy show gave the Society its highest-ever attendance figures, while the strangeness of finding the Arts and Crafts within those 'once sacred precincts'[47] left pundits incredulous: 'a miracle has been worked',[48] wrote one. By including the 'official world' Wilson was acknowledging that the message of the exhibition had to strike home to public authorities and municipalities. It was for their benefit in particular that the first thing every visitor would encounter, on climbing the steps from the courtyard and entering the Academy, was a model of a 'redesigned and glorified'[49] Trafalgar Square, a place for which Wilson had long nursed a vision: witness his earlier call to the authorities of the capital to join with London's art schools to improve this increasingly sorry site. In his eyes, it also presented an opportunity for the productive interdependence of architects, sculptors, artists and the elected bodies. In the event, of course, it was doomed to remain a traffic-bound battleground until the early years of the new millenium, well after cities like Birmingham, Sheffield and Manchester had recreated their central squares as truly civic spaces.

The 'world of education' to which Wilson reached out in his introductory remarks included not just the heads of training institutions and educational authorities, but also the student body. That the capabilities of those learning their craft were to be openly acknowledged was part of Wilson's credo, and in the finished show a whole room was dedicated to embroidery by students from the Royal College of Art, another to jewellery and stained glass by students from the Birmingham School of Art. When it came to the construction required to create the *mise-en-scène* of the entire exhibition, this was entrusted to students from four institutions: the Central School, the Westminster Technical Institute, and the Camberwell and Leicester Schools of Art, as a means of getting artists, designers and students working together on a real task – Wilson's ideal training method. The educational bias of the exhibition was to be enhanced by public lectures on topics ranging from the zodiac in art to architectural sculpture and stage design, these proving so popular as to be 'often crowded to inconvenience'.[50]

To the 'world of trade and manufacturers' the exhibition's appeal, Wilson insisted, must lie in its emphasis on the crafts as the 'most potent means of ... national reconstruction',[51] with the implication that craftsmen could be full participants in the nation's commercial and industrial prosperity.

From the moment the eleventh Arts and Crafts Society's show opened, it was apparent that the transformation Wilson had effected in the galleries was a crucial factor in how visitors absorbed its message. The layout – in his words, the 'chief aspect'[52] of the exhibition – received considerable attention. The *Studio* pronounced 'Mr. Wilson's plan bolder than anything that has been carried out before'; in none of the preceding Arts and Crafts exhibitions in London had there been evidence of 'any general scheme'.[53] Yet the link with the shows in Ghent and Paris was clear; reporting back to its American readership, *The Nation* succintly declared, 'Up until then [the Society] had made little

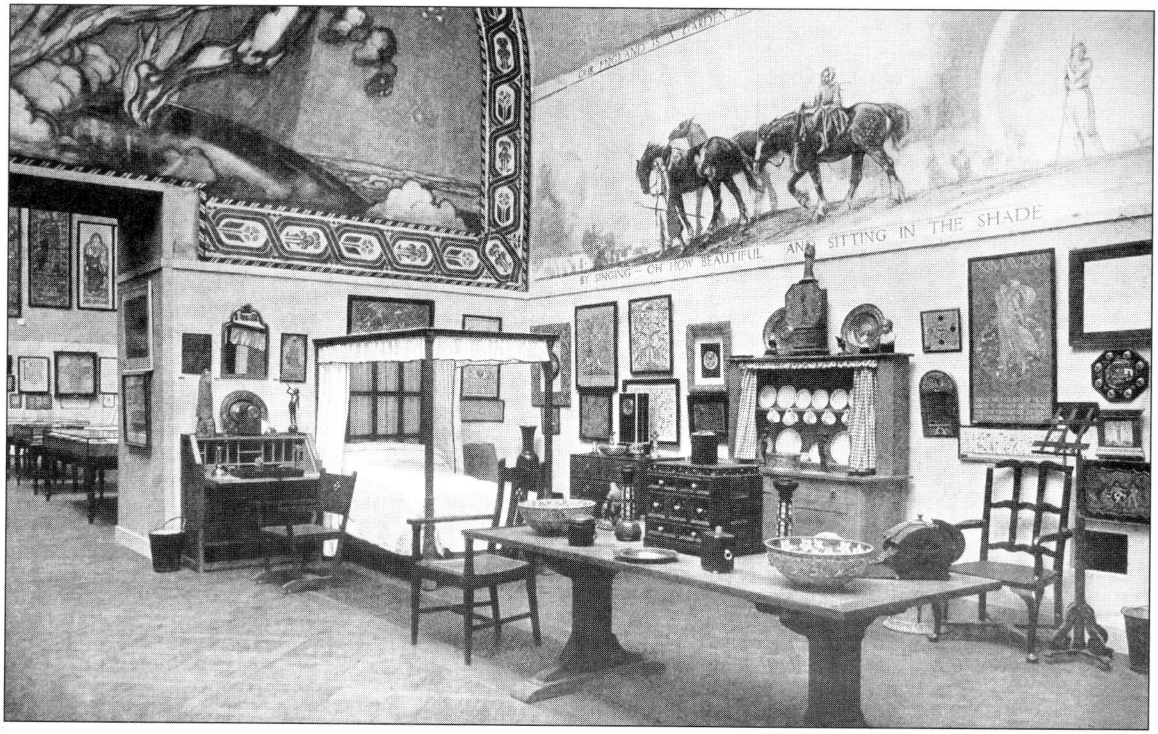

Figure 89. A.C.E.S. 11th Exhibition, Burlington House: Civic Hall, or "Hall of Heroes", designed by H. Wilson, constructional work by F.W. Troup. *Studio,* 1916, Vol. 69.

effort to do more than show what they had to show',[54] while his visit to the Academy convinced the correspondent of the Royal Society of Arts of something that the visitors to all three overseas shows had surmised all along, that 'Mr. Wilson is a real genius in the conception of exhibitions of this kind'.[55]

The first gallery was retrospective, containing work by Morris and his contemporaries. That it was the only room wholly finished by the opening date formed a sharp reminder of the wartime restrictions imposed on building materials and night-work.

The second gallery contained textiles. Two working looms gave continuous demonstrations of craft weaving; at one of these presided, for the duration of the exhibition, a confident Miss Fiammetta Wilson, already a talented weaver at the age of twelve.

The third and largest gallery became a Civic Hall (Fig. 89), its high vault concealed by a linen canopy, its overall mood Byzantine. Wilson had commissioned for its four wall-bays monumental paintings on patriotic and uplifting themes from each of four artists, Harold Speed, Walter Bayes, Sidney Lee and Gerald Moira[56] – hence the name coined for it among the members of the Society and soon adopted by the general public, the "Hall of Heroes". Wilson also contributed a painting of his own to this room, a Madonna and saints, and filled the apsidal end of the gallery with figure-sculpture in two tiers: below, a quartet of Scottish saints from the set Stirling Lee was in the process of carving in alabaster for St. Andrew's Chapel in Westminster Cathedral;[57] and again, above, his own plaster maquette for the Madonna and Child that would, some three years later, take its place above his Memorial Gates in the Chapel of Tonbridge School.

The names given to the fourth and fifth galleries were thoroughly in tune with Wilson's outlook: Domus I and Domus II. They concentrated on how the Arts and Crafts could serve the house and home, with exhibits ranging from embroidery to furniture. Several smaller adjoining rooms were given over to complete room settings, outstandingly a bedroom designed by A.H. Christie and F.W. Troup. Of the three remaining, one each was designed by the Women's Guild of Arts, by Ernest Gimson in collaboration with May Morris, and the last, with its plain household wares and light fabrics, was contributed by the Design and Industries Association.

The sixth gallery or University Room was allocated to examples of fine printing in the form of books and illustrations, laid out in cases or mounted and wall-hung. At one end was William Rothenstein's frieze of a University Graduation Day, wittily counterpointed on the facing wall by Augustus John's fresh and vibrant *Galway Peasants*. The seventh gallery became the Municipal Hall, dedicated to the crafts of everyday life. Here, paintings by Charles Sims, George Clausen and Maurice Greiffenhagen gave vivid, empathetic portrayals of ordinary life, as in Clausen's studies of the English rural landscape and its inhabitants. Below, in display cases was a choice selection of domestic pottery and glassware.

The area where a regular visitor to the Royal Academy might have expected to find watercolours and prints had been converted into five galleries separately showing off lithography, drawings, stained glass, toys and, finally, jewellery and metalwork. Wilson had naturally contributed to the drawings section, and his talents were also in evidence in the jewellery and metalwork room, where his work kept company with pieces by Stabler, Gaskin, Cooper, Ashbee, Spencer and Fisher. The display case assigned to Wilson was a treasury of over thirty pieces of his most characteristic jewellery, from pendants, brooches, necklaces, buckles and bracelets, to a coronet and, as in the 1914 show at the Pavillon de Marsan, the Apollo tiara, justly acclaimed as one of the best pieces of jewellery on display, the figure 'distinguished in expression' and its workmanship 'perfect'.[58] Another commentator found it 'very ingenious and dignified' and especially striking amongst the rest of his jewellery,[59] though all was 'excellent in workmanship and uncommon in design'.[60] Not only that, but singled out from the display of practical metalwork were sweetmeat dishes and silver spoons by Wilson, a chalice, and, 'worthy of special notice, ... his beautiful [thread-spinning classical nude] chafing dish'.[61]

Before leaving the exhibition, there remained for the visitor one crowning spatial experience: the Ecclesiastic Gallery. Here, Wilson's team had contrived four apsidal chapels, fitted out under the guidance of Charles Spooner, Reginald Hallward, Louis Davis or Wilson himself. His own space permitted him to exhibit personal work, both in progress and recently completed: the centrepiece was a bronze hanging lantern on a scale to match the plaster maquette for the bronze doors for St. Mary's, Nottingham. Nearby was set a panel made and modelled with his friend the architect Arthur Grove for E.S. Prior's startling new church of St. Osmund at Parkstone; beside it stood a further set of entrance doors, designed by Wilson and modelled in plaster by Richard Garbe, and one of those architectural, semi-sculptural conceits so typical of Wilson's allegorical cast of mind, a Pantheon of the Five Dominions, made by L.A. Turner from the drawings of the Scottish arch-Byzantinist Robert Schultz Weir. From Wilson's space alone, the interested visitor would walk out into the daylight of Piccadilly with a mindful of thoughts on the crafts and a sense of this unique artistry within them.

Most reviewers of the 1916 exhibition were quick to admire its layout and range, for which Wilson was given full credit. The high standard of craftsmanship also won generous praise. Yet concealed in the approbation of the show as a whole, was disquiet to do with Arts and Crafts ideology from the earliest years of the twentieth century onward. There was evidence, or so it seemed, of a general inability on the part of the craftsman-designer to stand back and take a critical overview of the item being made: the workmanship 'is irreproachable, but [often] the labour is misspent for lack of thought – of architectonic design'.[62] A dichotomy was noted, too, in the exhibits' tendency to veer from plainness to over-elaboration. On one hand craftsmen were making pieces so sturdy as to suggest 'they still think of us as ideal peasants'.[63] On the other, the use of surface patterning was at times fussy to the point of aggravation. The ubiquitous chequered edging (of which Wilson, of course, was one of the chief exponents) seemed to be 'bursting out ... all over...'.[64]

It is easy to imagine how cluttered the overall effect might have seemed, for the comment strikes a chord even from this distance; it would assuredly have been amplified by actually being there. Furthermore, despite its sense of civic pride and the acknowledged need to incorporate the crafts into real life, several observers found it impossible to ignore an inclination to hark backwards. This air of nostalgia hovering over the enterprise was briskly enapsulated in the *Burlington Magazine*: 'Courage is lacking in this exhibition – courage to recognise that Morris, Crane and Burne-Jones, great as they were in their time, belong to a bygone age'.[65]

One of its most trenchant assessments came from *The Nation*, a magazine with a reputation for wit and independence. No surprise if the American correspondent of an American publication seemed largely immune to the specifically English quality Wilson was aiming to promote. From his transatlantic perspective, it all had 'the air of a bazaar', although the Design and Industry Association's display seemed 'promising'. The only exhibits undiminished by the positively 'gloomy,' canopy-filtered light were the Brangwyn lithographs 'made for the London Underground', while the otherwise 'good lines' of Wilson's structural adaptations in the Hall of Heroes were too reminiscent of an 'old basilica' to be called original. Some pieces received short shrift: Sims's, Moira's and Wilson's own pictures, for example, were condemned as banal, while the artefacts *en masse* comprised the 'usual' Arts and Crafts display, where 'even the bedspread must have its inscription'.[66]

Welcome relief was offered by the plainly furnished, white-curtained bedroom by Christie and Troup. Amidst the works of devout Arts and Crafters struggling ideologically, aesthetically and emotionally with the challenges of the new century, it was like a glimpse of the future. Further such portants were visible in the D.I.A.'s room. Here were earthenware pickle and tobacco jars, affordable bedroom wares and bright cotton fabrics made at the Bentinck Mills, near Bolton – all everyday objects, capable of mass-production. Wilson had invited the Association to display its work 'in order to suggest the unity which should exist between the products of industry and the works of the craftsman'.[67] Its members were all for taking a large room, and this was what Harold Stabler had requested on the their behalf.[68] The final decision was Wilson's, but with heavy demands on space, together with his own predilections, the room they were eventually allotted was small and cramped. Consequently, partly from expedience, partly, as they themselves graciously put it, so as to make their point about bold design 'more forcefully',[69] the focus in their display was thrown largely on their ceramic wares.

Wilson's instincts about the timing and venue of the 1916 exhibition were well-founded. His conviction that the crafts would survive to counteract the destruction of war was manifest in the creativity on show at the Academy; at the same time, the crafts' appearance within the bastions of the Fine Arts implied that at long last some sort of equal footing had been achieved. However, Wilson's desire to improve industry via the crafts remained in some degree equivocal. The point about the need to co-operate with industrial production came across, but only sporadically. All in all, with its inherent hand-made bias and its lukewarm attitude to the Design and Industries Association, the exhibition might be seen less as a reaffirmation or fresh start than as the swansong of the Arts and Crafts movement. From now on, the artist-craftsman was on his own, strategically and continuously reassessing his place in an ever-industrialising world. As a reporter for the Royal Society of Arts remarked, it was all too easy to imagine a manufacturer going round the displays, and at the end asking 'All this is very beautiful, but where do I come in?'[70]

CHAPTER NINE

ARTS AND CRAFTS IN A MODERN WORLD

Though Henry Wilson would end the 1920s in self-chosen emigration, at work in his Paris studio on the sculptural project that would crown his creative life, he began the decade as a key figure in London design circles. As such, his decision about where to place his loyalties regarding design in relation to commerce would create a considerable stir. Part of the trouble, as he saw it, with the Design and Industries Association, was that the 'and' in its title, with its tacit sense of equality, had in effect been transformed into 'for'. If he was right, the craftsmen-designers within it would sooner or later be sacrificed to commercial imperatives: it might just as well acknowledge the fact, and drop any illusions about meaningful collaboration. On the other hand, the British Institute of Industrial Art, which Wilson was instrumental in launching in 1920, seemed to demonstrate different priorities. Its identity was emphatically British, and far from eschewing *Art* – as the D.I.A. had done on the grounds that the word implied 'a mystery only understood by artists'[1] – art was part of the B.I.I.A.'s mission statement. Besides, the Institute's official status gave Wilson hope in its potential for doing genuinely influential work. In other respects the two bodies were closely allied and, indeed, until 1924 were unofficially linked, both in the exchange of advice as well as in their shared doctrine that good design was *appropriate* design.

In 1919, as conditions of war receded, the Ministry of Reconstruction had issued its pamphlet 'Art and Industry', arguing that without wholesale improvements in the design standards of industrially produced goods, Britain would be swiftly outstripped by post-War competitors. Wilson's work for the Ministry continued well beyond the Armistice with lectures and articles concentrating on the rehabilitation of returning troops. His voice can be heard distinctly in that 1919 pamphlet, both in characteristic turns of phrase and argument, and in the insistence that art is indispensible to life: he quotes from Sedding's 1883 lecture that art must relate to everyone, and strengthens the assertion with Ruskin's words of 1852 to the manufacturers of Bradford, alerting them to their duty to 'form the market as much as to supply it'. In the continuing craft-versus-industry debate, rehearsals of such past clarion-calls would be familiar to readers of the D.I.A. Journal;[2] what carried weight in 1919 was the Ministry's adoption of the theme and its backing of the formation of a British Institute of Industrial Art. This recommendation would be one of the Ministry's parting initiatives; as early as 1917 the home front was reacting against it as intrusive, over-prescriptive, too closely identified with the conditions of war – and in June 1919 it was closed down; other emergency ministries, such as Munitions, followed soon after.

Within eight months, the British Institute of Industrial Art had been established by the Board of Trade in conjunction with the Board of Education, and with advice from the Royal Society of Arts, the Art Workers' Guild, the Arts and Crafts Exhibition Society and the Design and Industries Association. Its declared aims were 'to raise the standard of work produced by British designers, craftsmen and manufacturers, and to stimulate demand for such work'.[3] The new Institute acknowledged a special debt to the Arts and Crafts exhibitions, not least the Ghent and Paris shows. As it happened, its aims tallied with a plan then crystallising at the V&A. Personified in Cecil Harcourt Smith, its Director from 1909 to 1924, the museum's attitude to acquiring contemporary work was ambivalent: such a collection should be built up, but preferably not in the museum itself. While he agreed that the state should promote art as applied to manufacture, and appreciated that the museum's remit, established under Cole, was to show and stimulate the best in design and workmanship, the area was alien to him personally. His aversion to making the museum look as though it was advertising stirred memories of the 'Donaldson affair' – the quandary that had arisen when a Bond Street dealer had offered the museum some Art Nouveau pieces he had purchased at the Paris Exposition of 1900: these, considered too unrepresentative and unproven to accept, were finally taken, but consigned to the Bethnal Green branch. As for acquiring modern industrial art, Harcourt Smith proposed creating a separate institute for the purpose, adjacent to the V&A. Events overtook his plan in the form of the B.I.I.A. – a government agency, its role embraced the selection of suitable modern objects to be displayed, by agreement, in the museum's North Court.

The B.I.I.A.'s first Council of nine Governors included F.V. Burridge (Lethaby's successor at the Central School), the architect F.W. Troup, and Wilson himself; the man appointed Director was Major Henry Longden, Arts and Crafts ironmaster and Guildsman, only recently out of uniform. The Treasury financed the B.I.I.A.'s own exhibition gallery in Knightsbridge, together with a programme of short exhibitions at the V&A; the three temporary shows of industrial products and handcraft it held there in 1920 formed the basis of a permanent collection to be exhibited under its name at the museum. The title of the inaugural display in the Knightsbridge gallery, 'Modern Crafts and Manufactures', underlined the Institute's policy of using careful labelling to differentiate items 'mechanically produced' from the 'works of individuals' – the very antithesis of the approach of the D.I.A, which on principle gave few credits to specific craftsmen.

Sharing the Knightsbridge address was the B.I.I.A's Information Bureau, Longden's special responsibility; through a system of telephone and personal appointments, it acted both as an agency for the sale of craftsmen's work, and as a 'labour exchange' for designers, recalling Wilson's earlier proposal that art schools should help find placements for students by circulating their details to potential employers; it also issued pamphlets on practical and artistic topics such as 'Public Departments and Industrial Art' and 'The Art of Training the Middleman'.

Because of the prevailing post-War slump the Treasury grant to the B.I.I.A. did not continue beyond 1921. Thereafter, despite its official status, it had to rely on private donations. The Knightsbridge gallery was given up, though its informational role and exhibition programme were unaffected. In 1922 the Institute mounted displays in Birmingham, Bradford, Huddersfield and Leicester. That year's exhibition at the V&A, 'Present Day Industrial Art', provided something of a showcase for the Wilson family – Henry showed a two-handled copper bowl, a pair of copper and silver candlesticks, and a case of jewellery, while Fiammetta exhibited scarves handwoven in silk.

Meanwhile, his commitment to the B.I.I.A. and its rolling exhibition programme unabated, Wilson's designs for twin angel musicians in stained glass were being installed in a permanent site, filling the existing pair of roundels that lit the organ loft (Plate 62) of the Georgian resort church of St. Mary's, Weymouth. On a field of brilliant blues and warm golds and browns bordered with chevrons, the angels, each with delicately pink-tipped wings, play their instruments – the one a traditional lyre, the other, a violin. The visual assurance of this second angel resonates with the child breathing inspiration into the father: the years 1921 and 1922 were when the Wilsons' teenage daughter Pernel was starting to reveal the depth of her talent as a concert violinist.

The makers of the Weymouth windows, Powell & Sons, were represented in the Institute's 1923 exhibition, 'Industrial Art Today'; other familiar names included the ceramics firm Doulton's, while new names came from the crop of up-and-coming artist-craftsmen who sold through the Rowley Gallery in Kensington Church Street, such as the textile designer Marion Dorn and her American-born graphic artist husband Edward McKnight Kauffer, with their shared belief in the enrichment of life through art. Wilson's work appeared in the form of jewellery, including the plique-à-jour Cupid clasp, and furniture, made to his design by W.E. Micklewright – an oak-framed couch[4] and an oak chest whose twelve carved zodiac panels (Fig. 90) vividly anticipate the

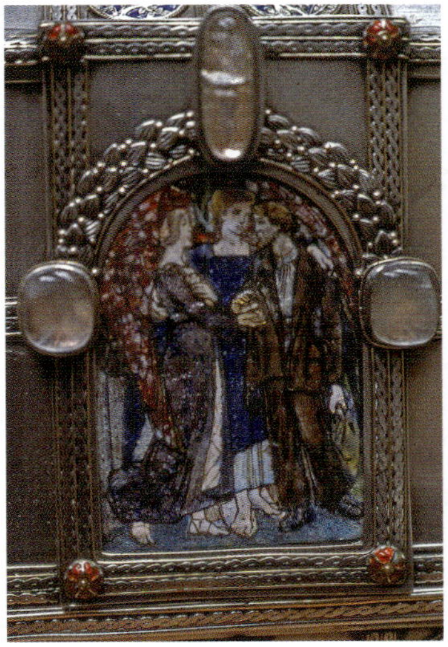

Plate 29. Chamberlain casket, silver enamel lunette: Britannia unites Labour and Capital.

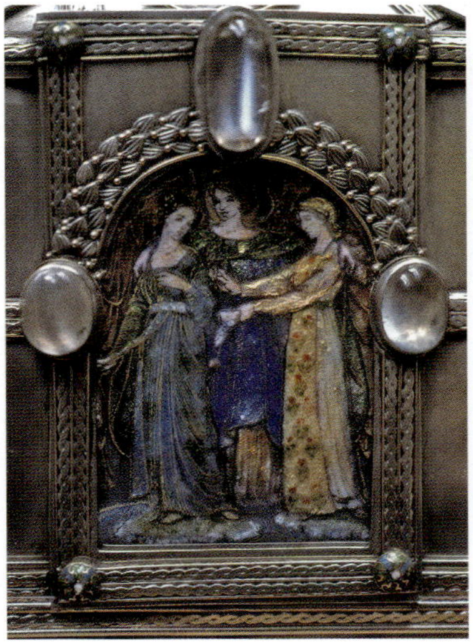

Plate 30. Chamberlain casket, silver enamel lunette: Britannia offers sisterhood to Ireland.

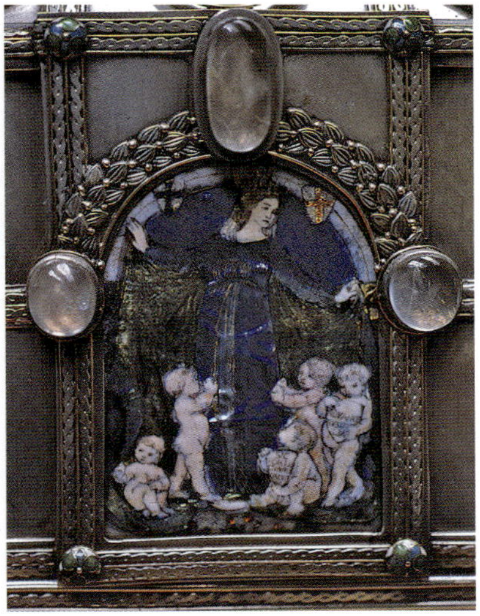

Plate 31. Chamberlain casket, silver enamel lunette: Britainnia draws her cloak around the New Commonwealth states.

Birmingham Museums and Art Gallery

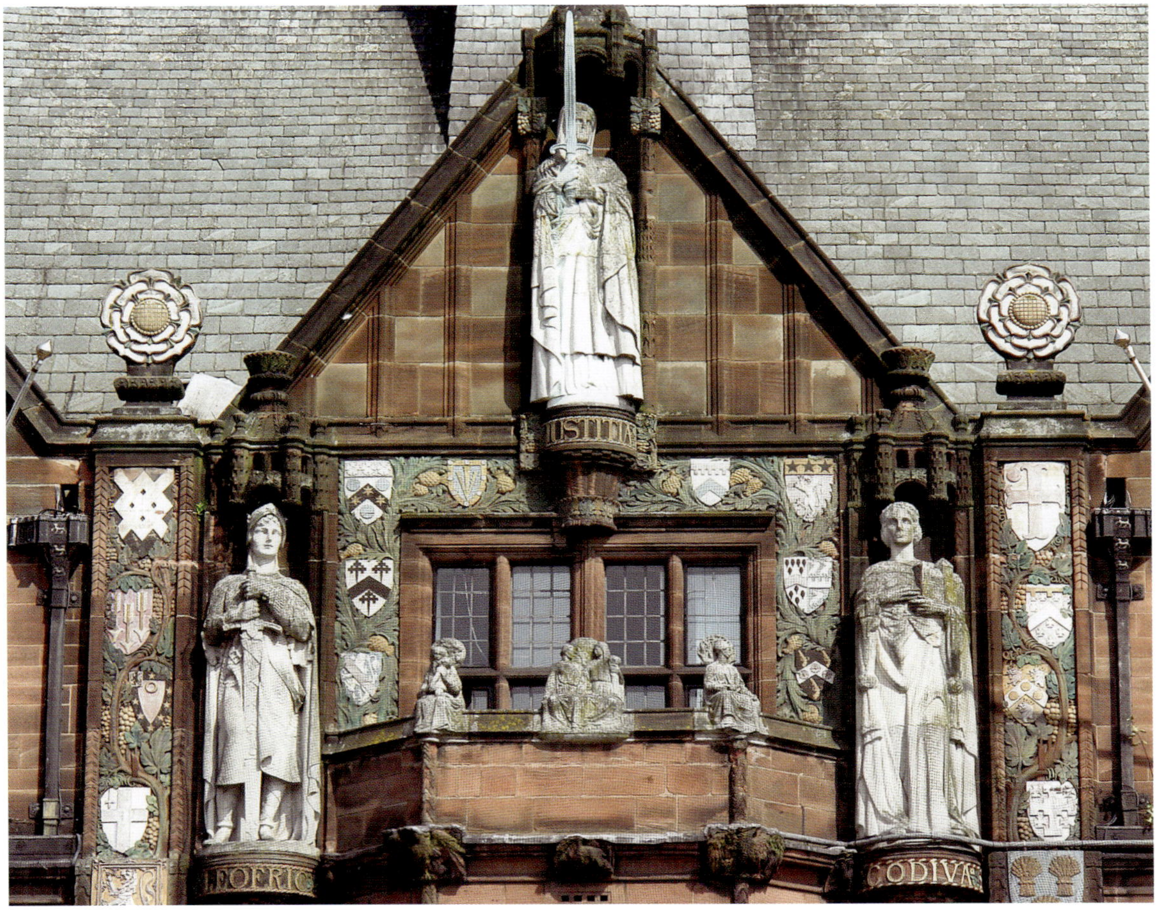

Plate 32. The Council House, Coventry: central gable with Wilson's sculptures in Portland stone, installed 1915-27: Leofric and Godiva with emblematic and historical figures around window-ledge and Justice presiding over them all.

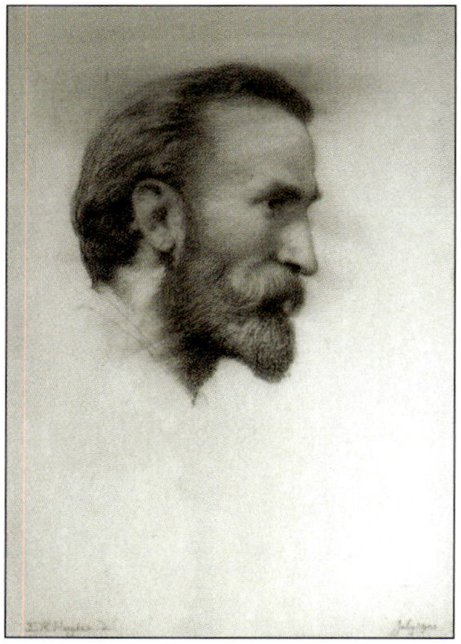

Private Collection

Plate 33. Henry Wilson in 1901, pencil portrait by E.R. Hughes *(40x30cm)*.

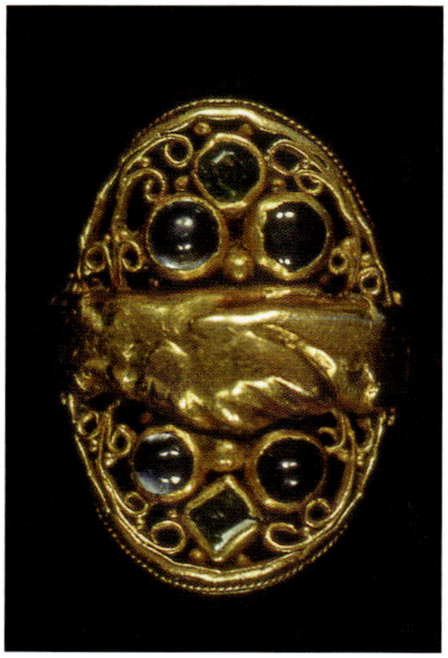

Private Collection

Plate 34. Wilson's gold engagement ring for Margaret Morse, clasped hands set with sapphires and emeralds c. 1899.

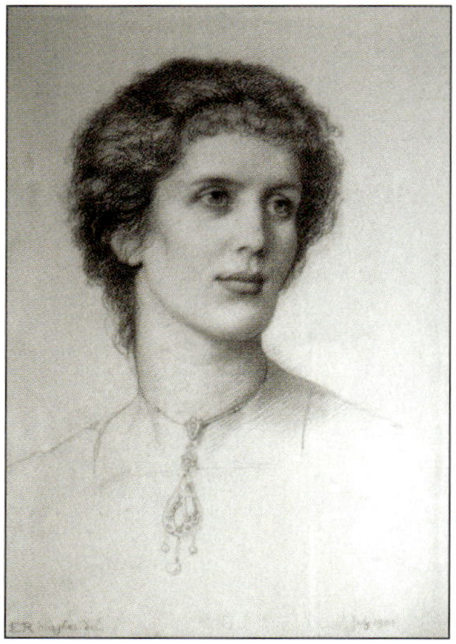

Private Collection

Plate 35. Margaret Wilson by E.R. Hughes, 1901 *(40x30cm)*; her necklace with pendant and jewelled drops typifies Wilson's work of the e. 1900s.

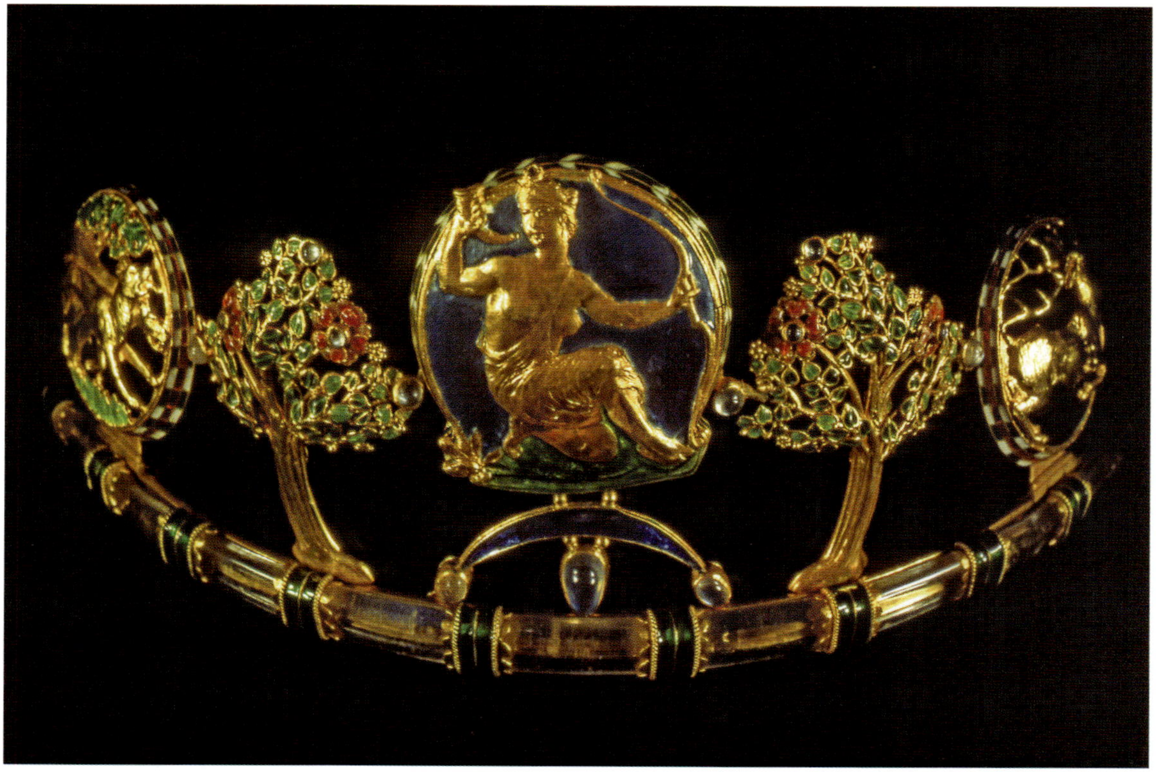

Private Collection

Plate 36. (above) Tiara, gold with crystal and enamel, set with sapphires and semi-precious stones, early 1900s: Diana sounds her hunting horn, her hounds chase a stag in a jewelled forest *(h. 5.8cm dia. 19.5cm)*.

Plate 37. (opposite) Rambling rose locket, silver enamel set with amethysts and emeralds on chain of silver with wound-wire and cloisonné beads, early1900s *(locket h. 4.5cm w. 3.5cm, necklace l. approx. 70cm)*.

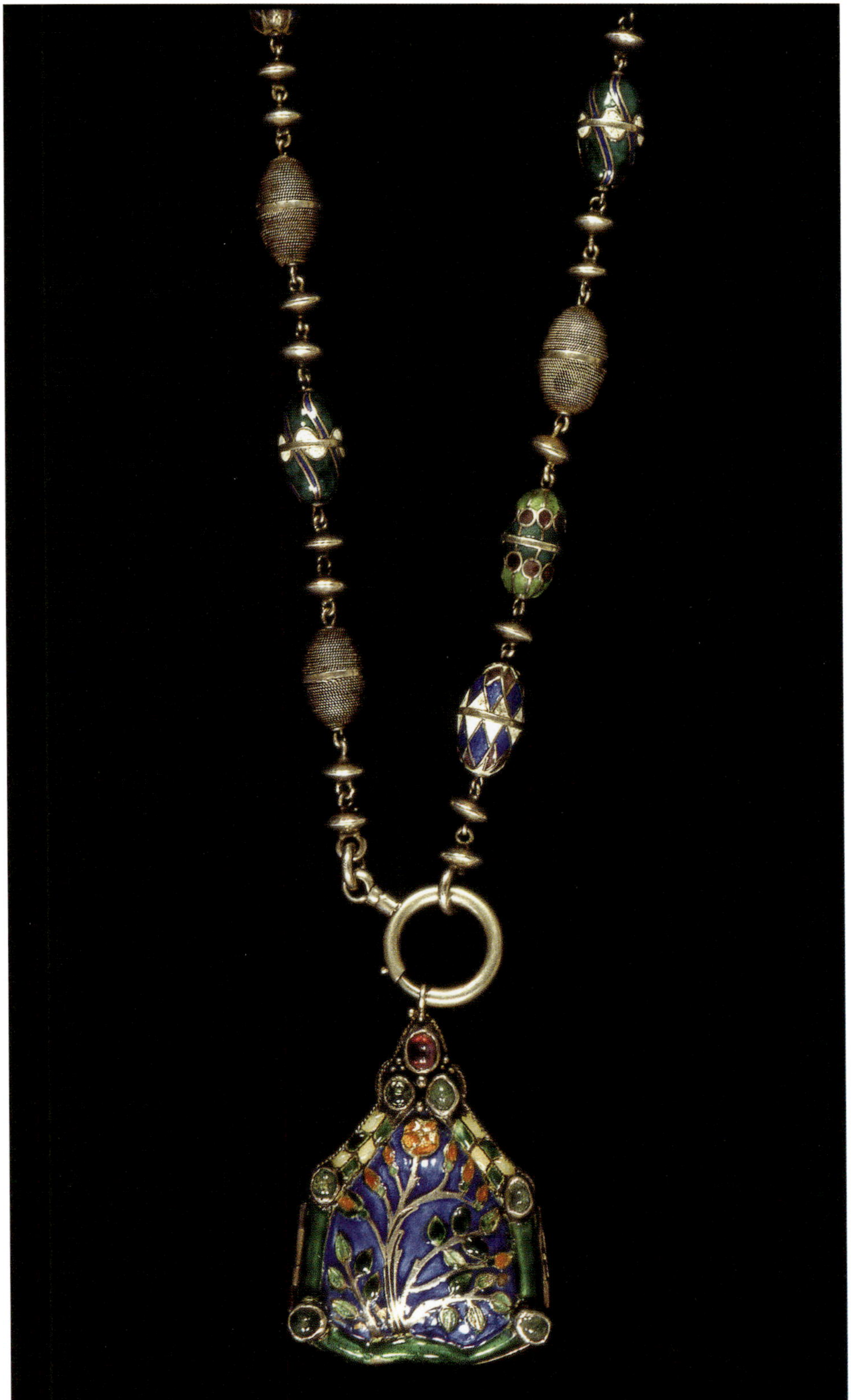

Private Collection

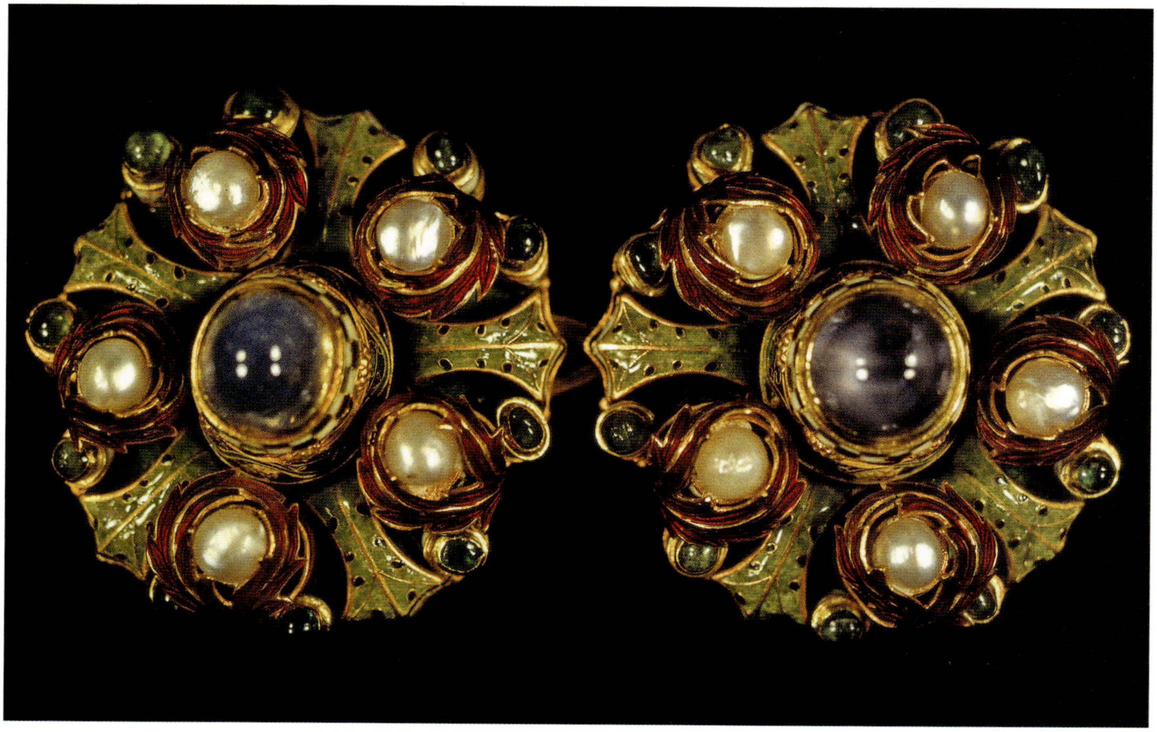

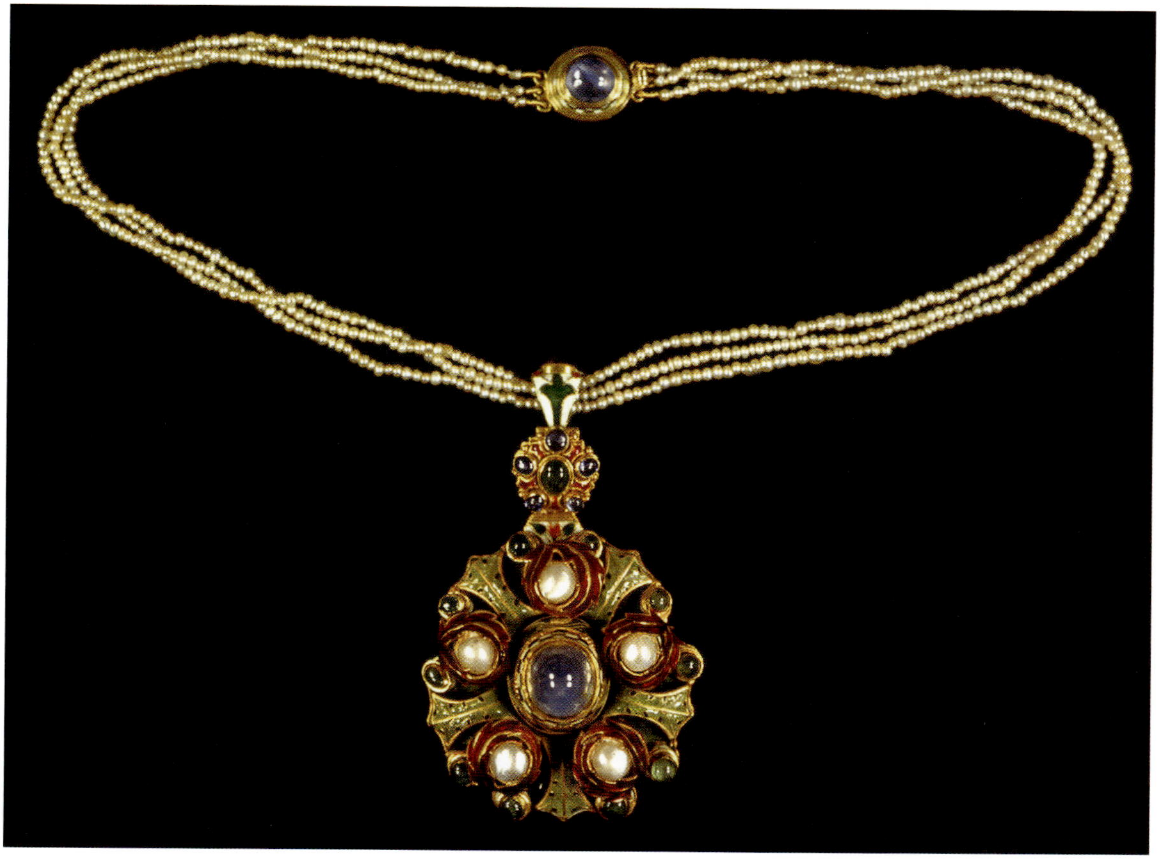

Private Collection

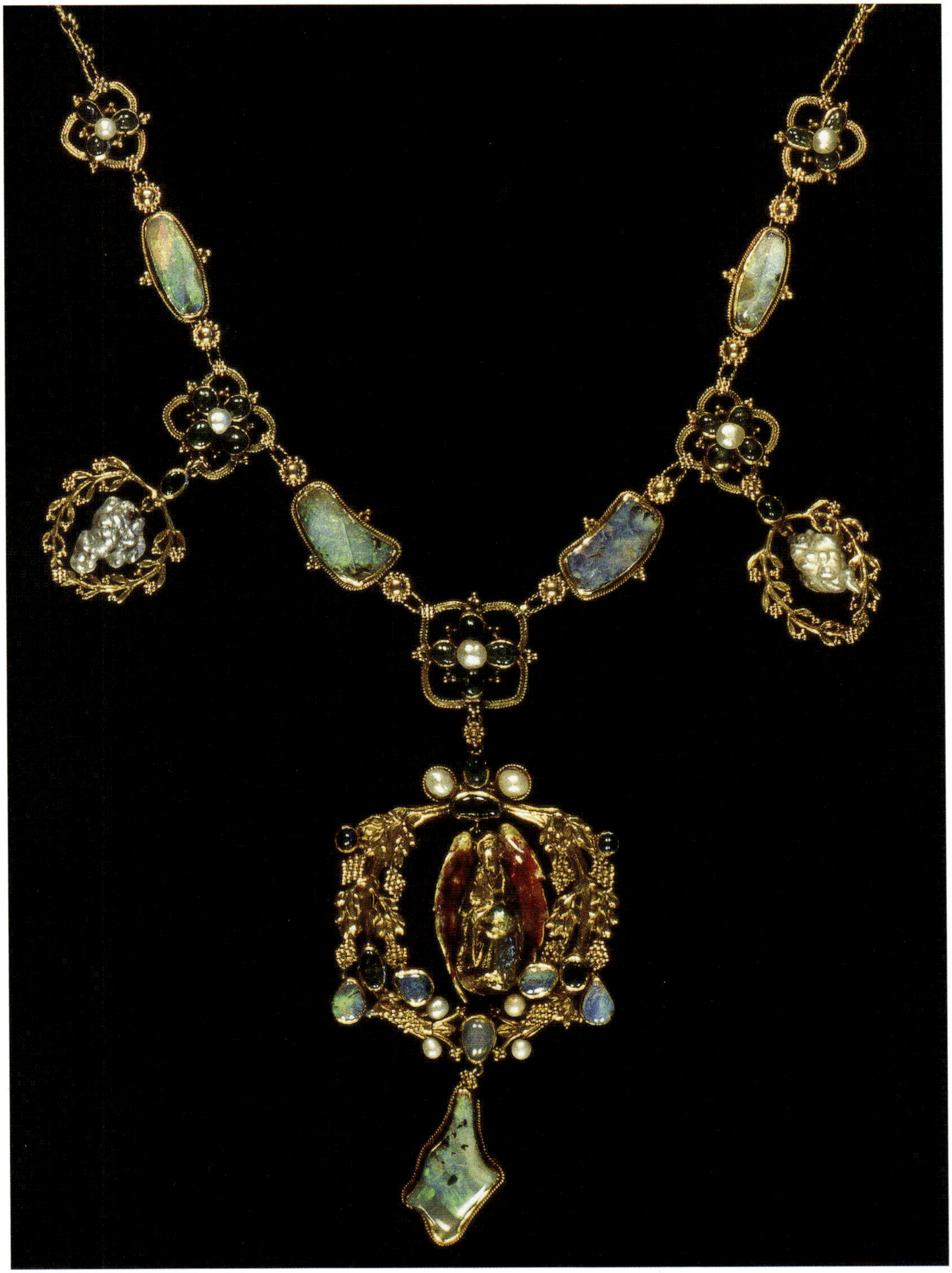

Private Collection

Plate 38. (opposite top) Gold enamel buckle, c. 1905: pearls and emerald-tipped leaves encircle cabuchon sapphires, *(each half dia. 5cm)*.

Plate 39. (opposite) One half of buckle has a decorated gold loop which unfolds to create a pendant.

Plate 40. (above) Gold necklace *(l. 38cm)* and angel pendant *(h. 9cm, w. 3.8cm)*, 1905: the angel, with red enamel wings, floats in a wreath of vines set with semi-precious stones.

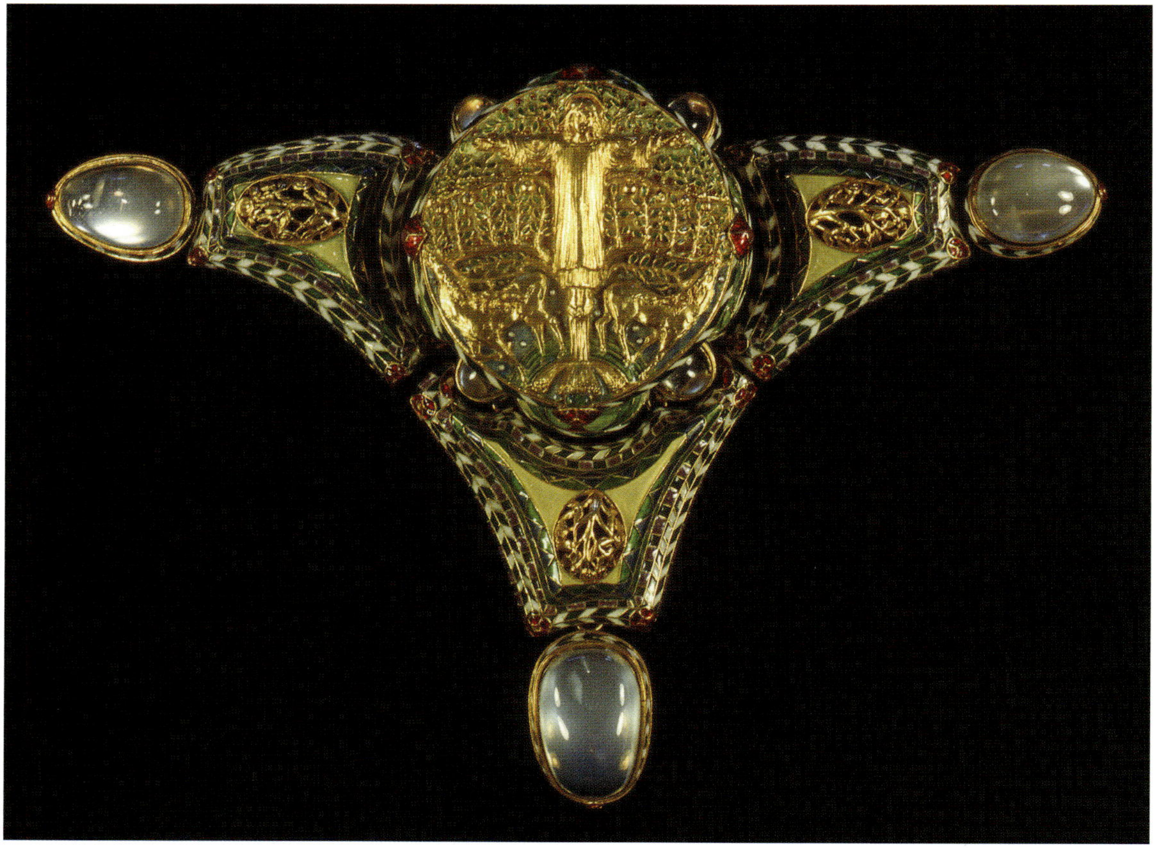

Plate 41. Gold morse, 1910: tripartite form enriched with enamel and semi-precious gems, with three large moonstones at tips and central repoussé figure of robed Christ between two harts *(h. 11cm w. 15.6cm d. 2cm).*

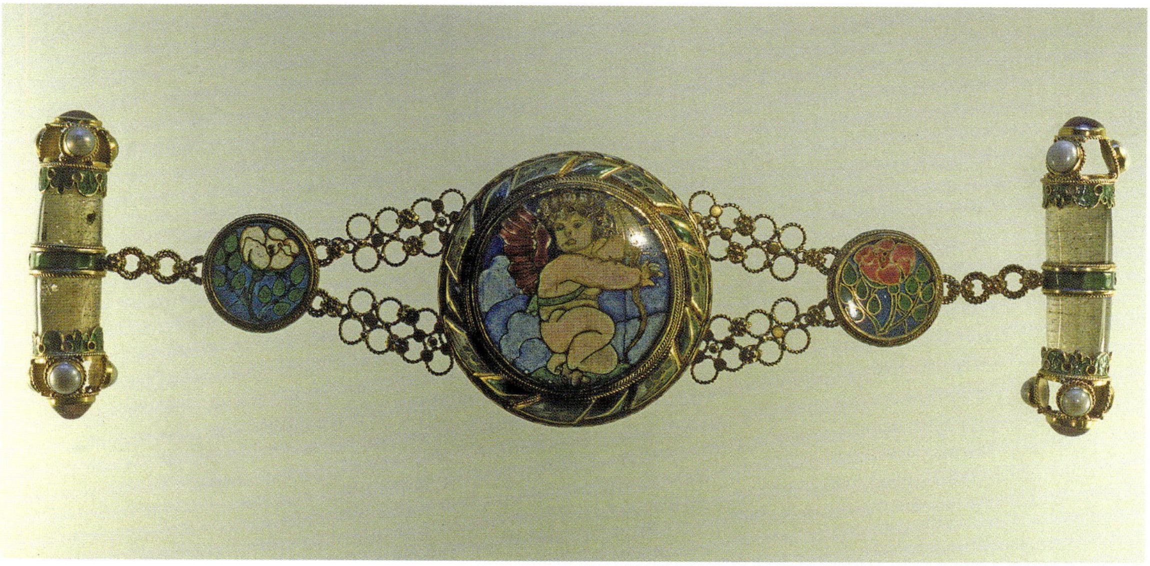

Plate 42. Cupid cloak clasp, early1900s: gold with plique-à-jour roundels and crystal rods enriched with semi-precious stones *(span about 17.5cm).*

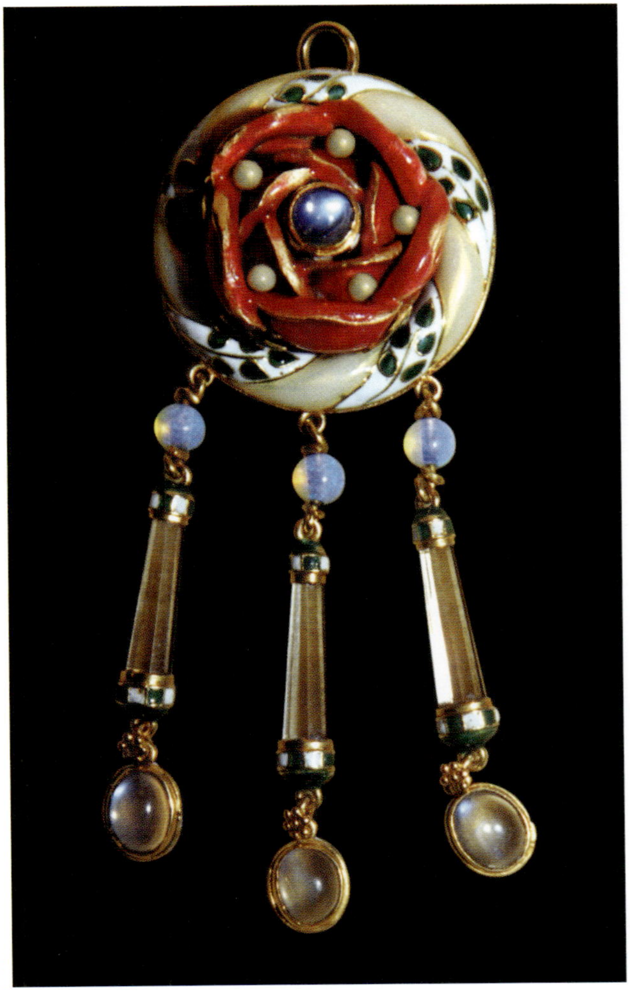

Private Collection

Plate 43. (above) Gold enamel rose brooch, c. 1912: with five pearl dewdrops and crystal, cloisonné and moonstone rods, three pearls to right digitally restored *(h. 6cm w. 2.5cm)*.

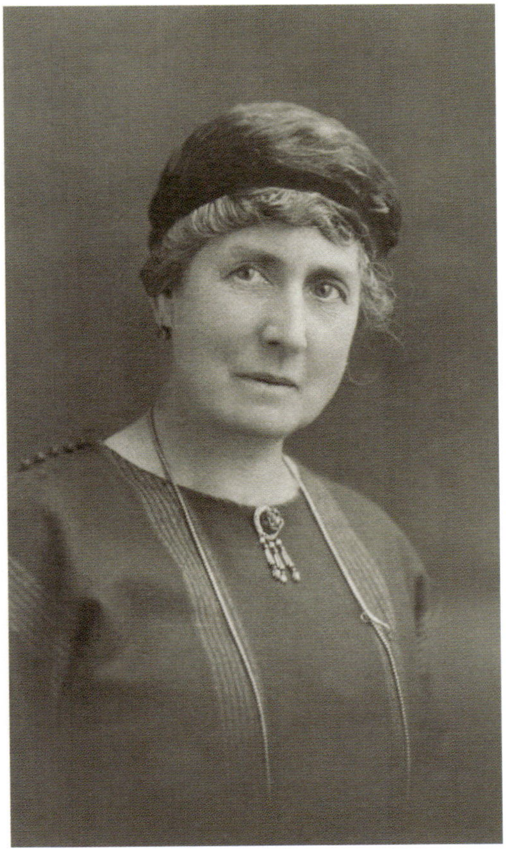

Plate 44. (top right) Edgar Wilson's mother-in-law Alice, recipient of the gold enamel and crystal rose brooch.

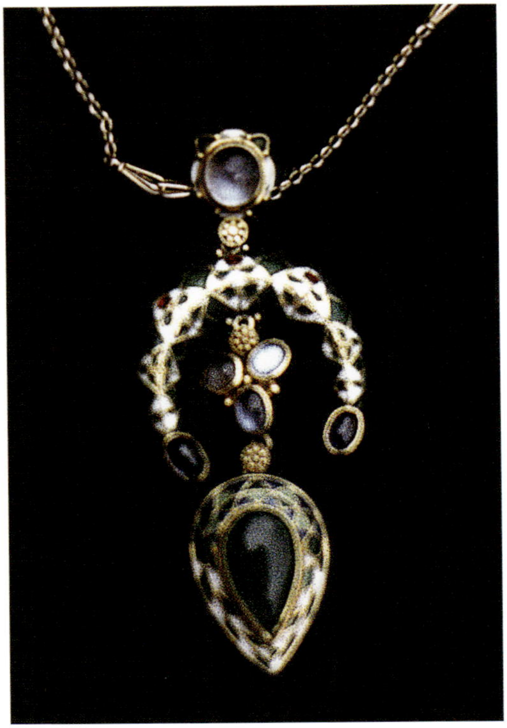

Private Collection

Plate 45. (bottom right) Gold pendant, 1912; inverted crescent in green and white enamel with calcedony teardrop, Edgar's wedding gift to his first wife Isobel Cooper *(approx. h. 5cm)*.

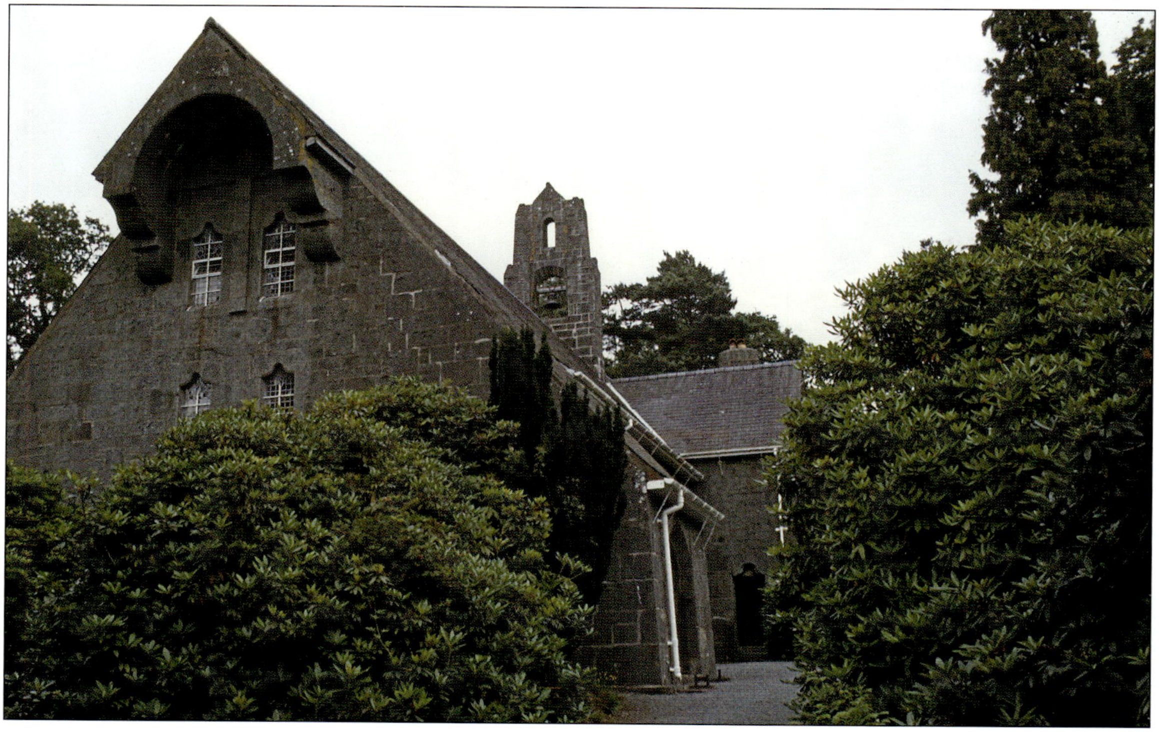

Plate 46. St. Mark's Church, Brithdir, Gwynedd, 1895-98.

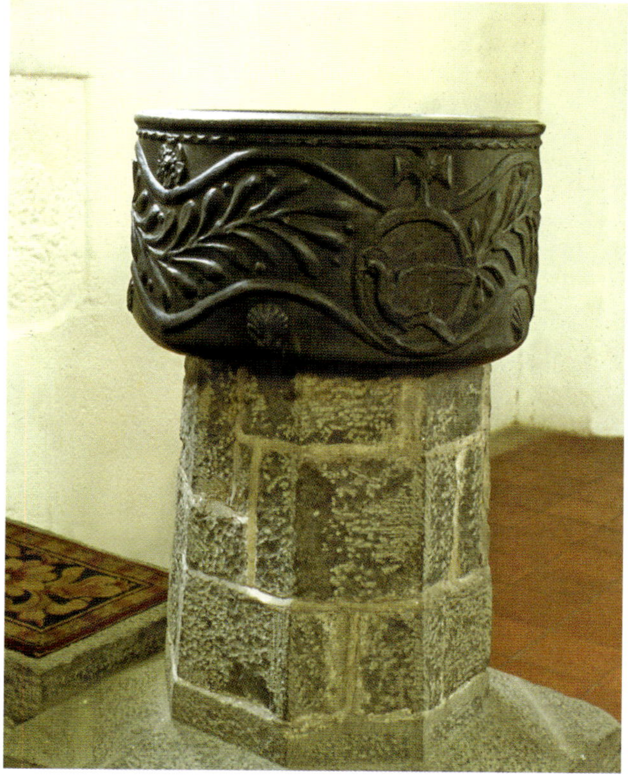

Plate 47. St. Mark's, Brithdir: font with bowl of flat-cast 'bent round' lead on ashlar stem.

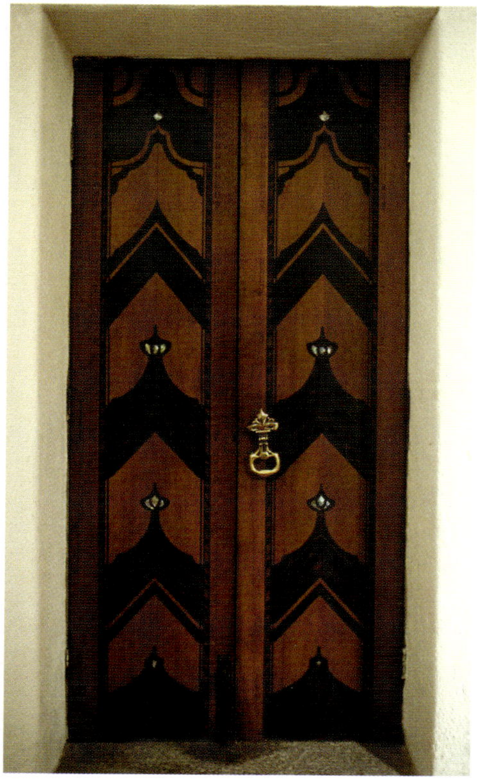

Plate 48. St. Mark's, Brithdir: inner face of doors with teak and ebony chevrons and nacre insets.

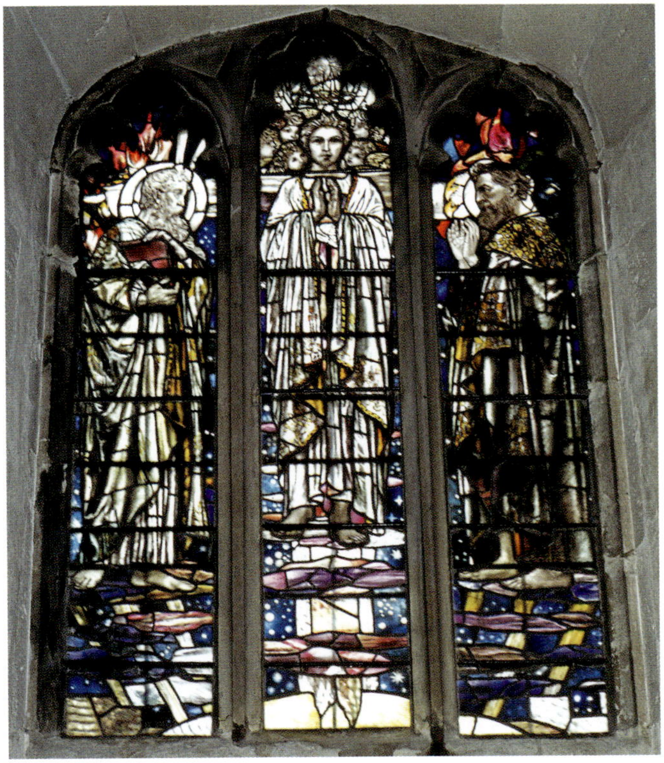

Plate 49. St. Mary's Church, Kemsing, Kent: traditional forms in Wilson's Transfiguration window give way to abstraction, 1905.

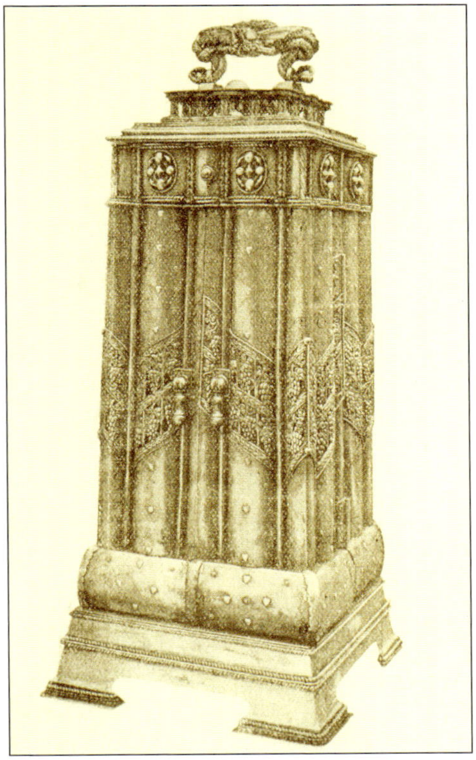

Plate 50. Steel travelling case for Tourist Trophy, 1905, from *Automobile Club Journal*, 30 May 1907.

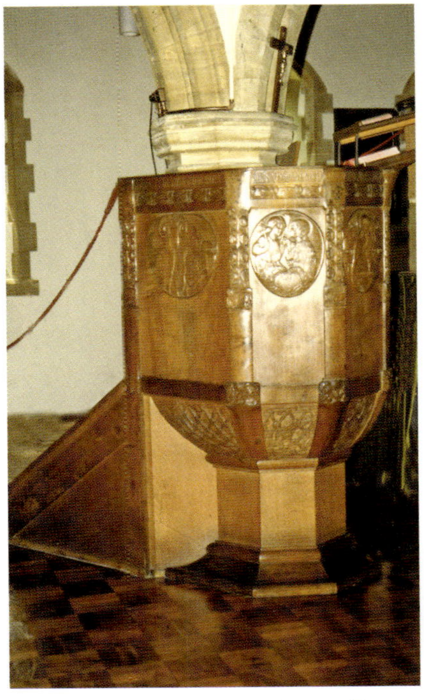

Plate 51. St. Mary's Church, Lynton, Devon: carved oak pulpit, 1906.

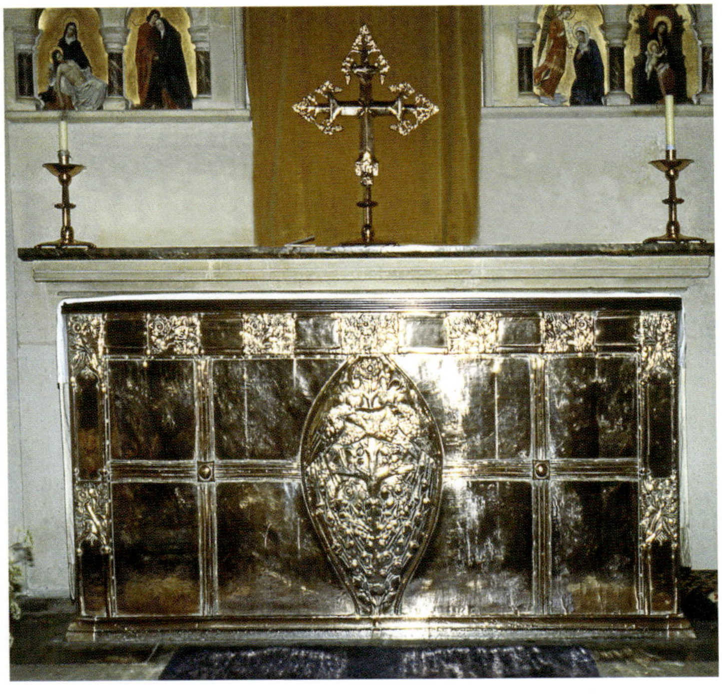

Plate 52. St. Mary's Church, Lynton, Devon: Lady Chapel altar frontal in beaten copper, with cross and candlesticks, 1905-7.

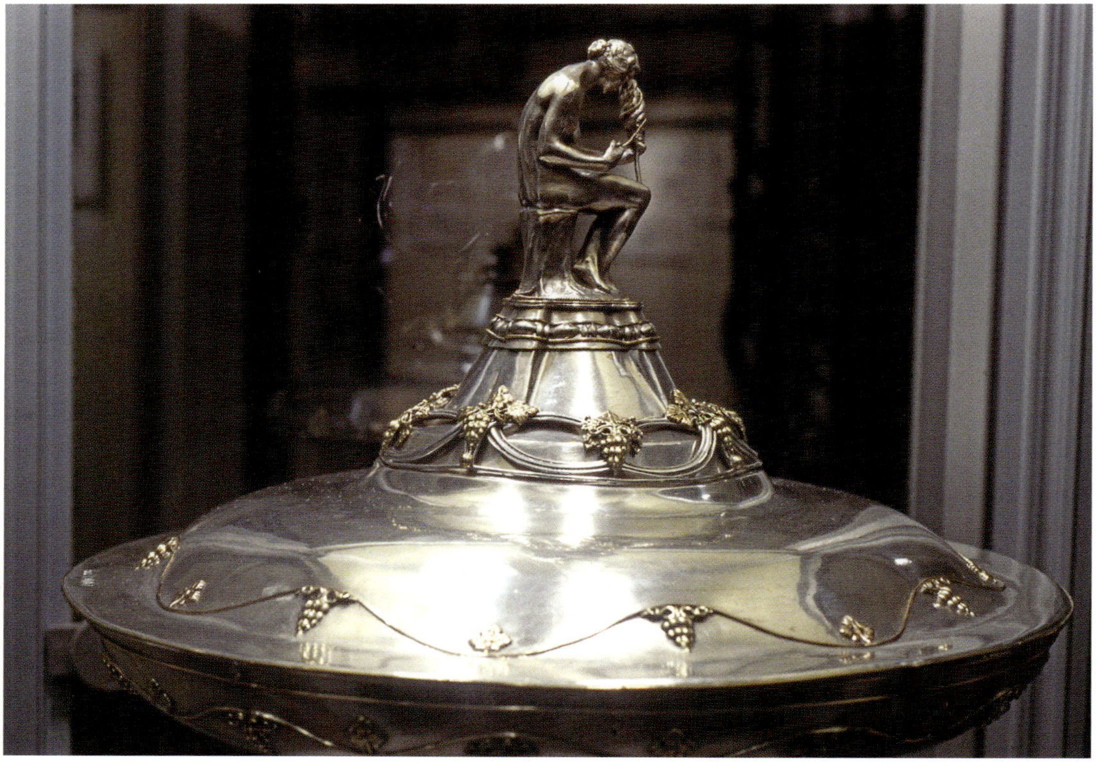

Victoria and Albert Museum

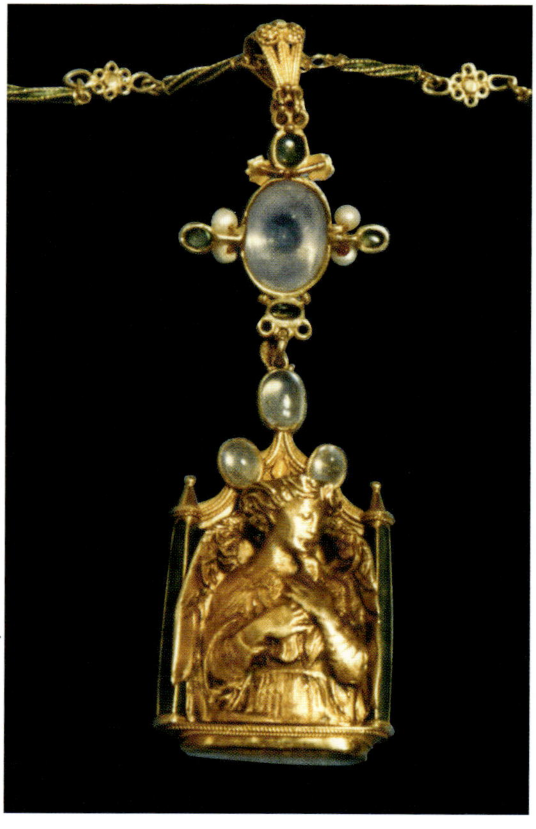

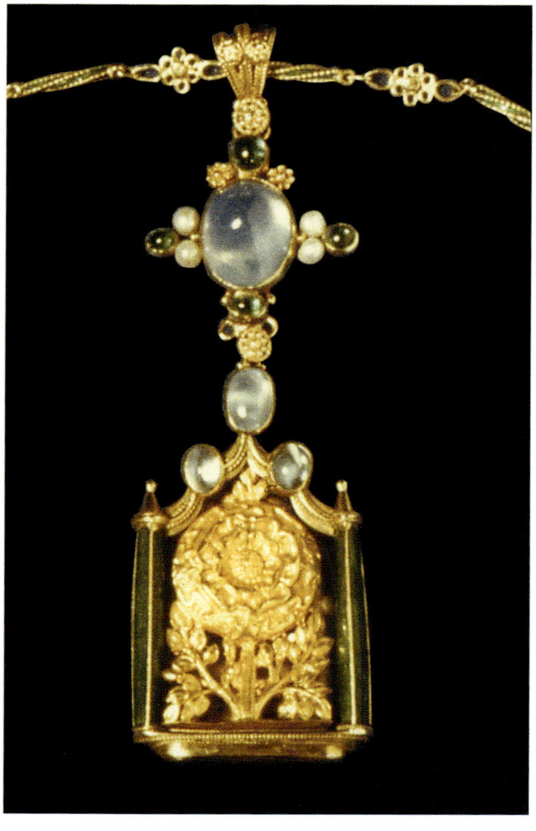

Cheltenham Art Gallery & Museum

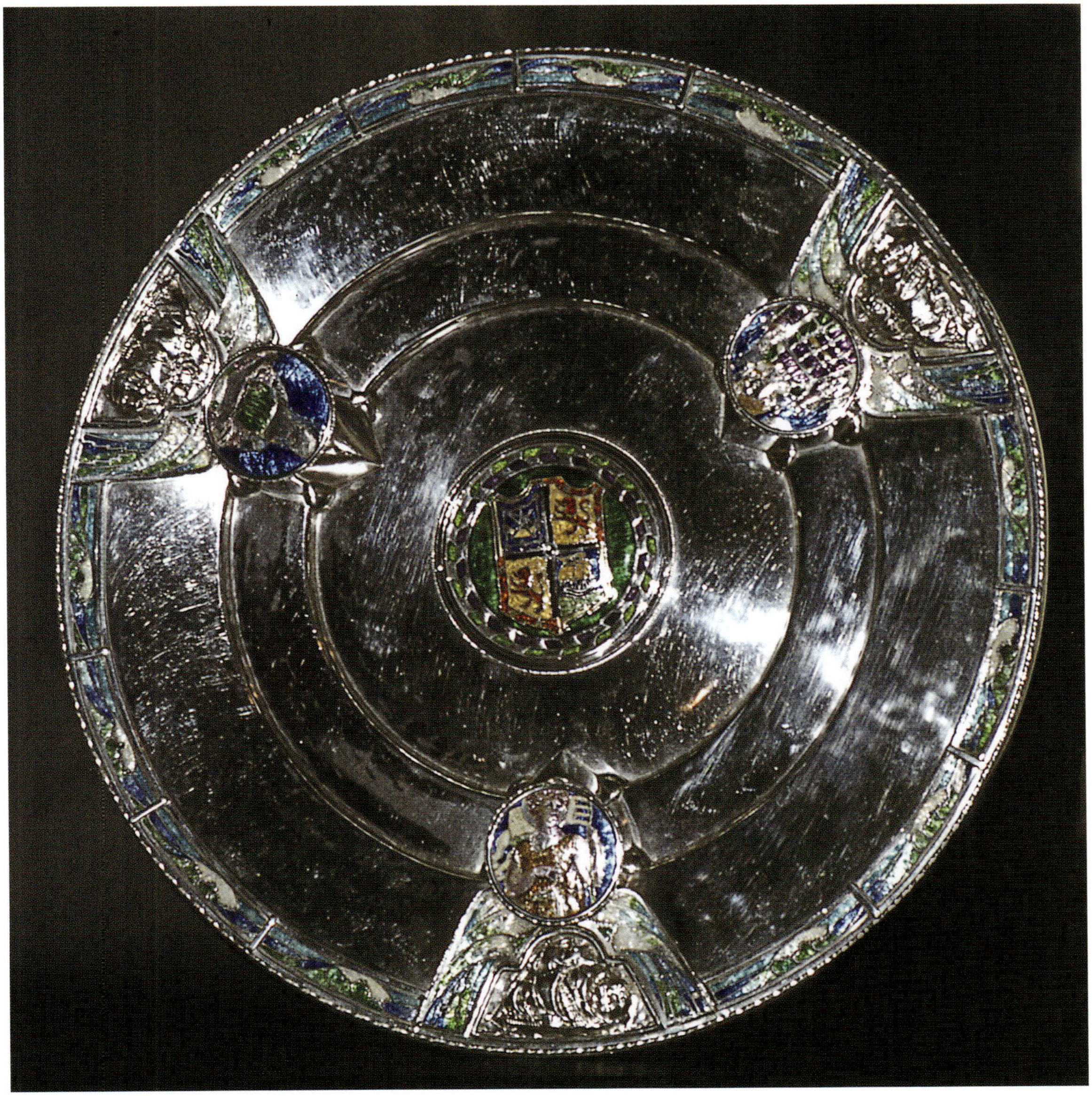

Plate 56. St. John's Church, Cirencester, Gloucs.: silver enamel alms dish, 1902 *(dia. 40.5cm).*

Plate 53. (opposite top) Chafing dish cover, silver and gold with embossed, cast and applied decoration: the finial depicts classical female nude spinning thread, HW monogram appears on base, London hallmark 1908 *(h. with stand 29 cm, dia. 28.3cm).*

Plate 54. (opposite left) Gold pendant, 1905: cast plaque depicting angel and dove set between green enamel columns and enriched with opals, emeralds and pearls *(approx. h. 8.5cm w. 2.7cm).*

Plate 55. (opposite right) Obverse of gold pendant, cast plaque showing sprigged Tudor rose.

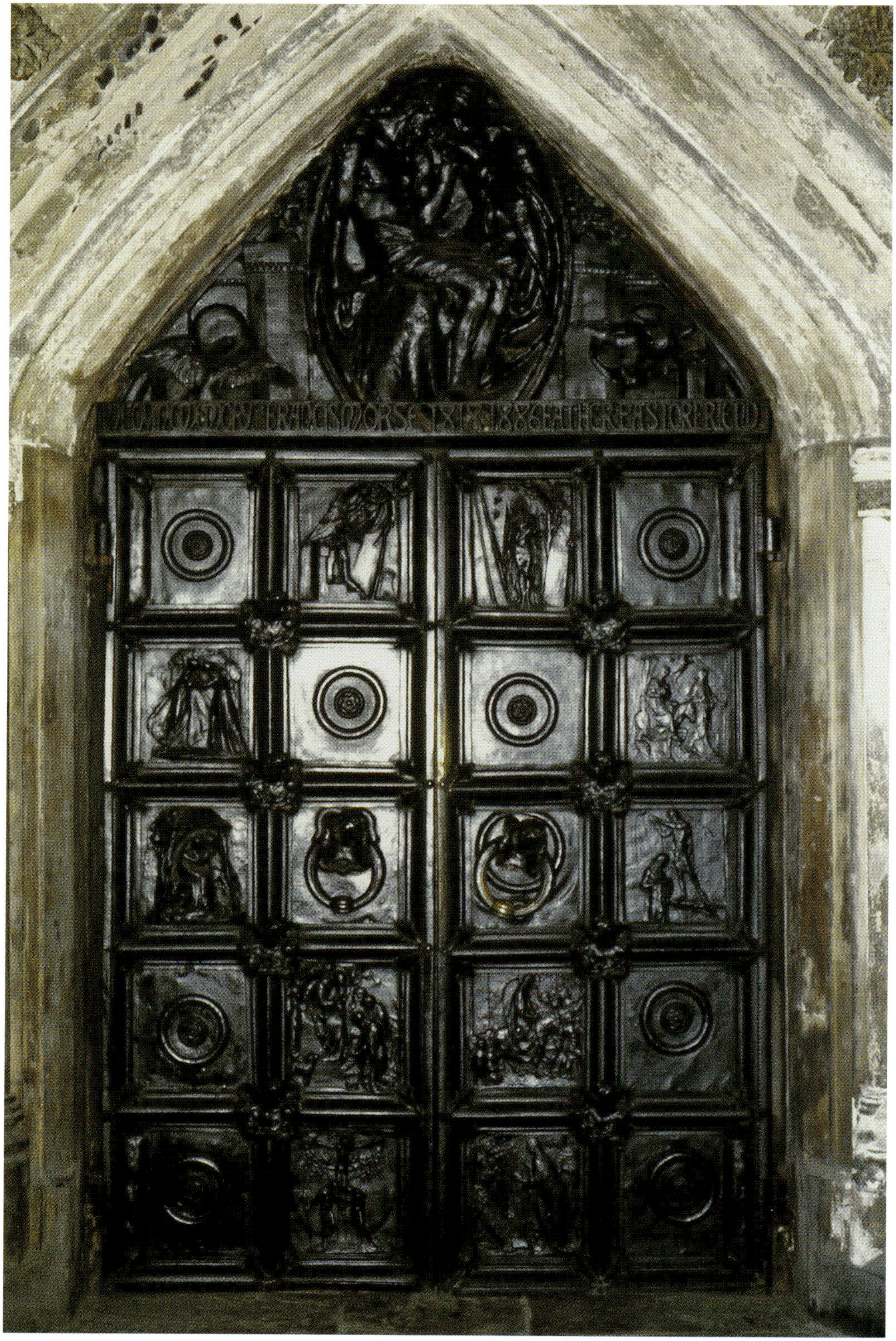

Plate 57. St. Mary's Church, Nottingham: South doors, given in memory of Margaret Wilson's father, the Rev. Francis Morse, bronze, 1904.

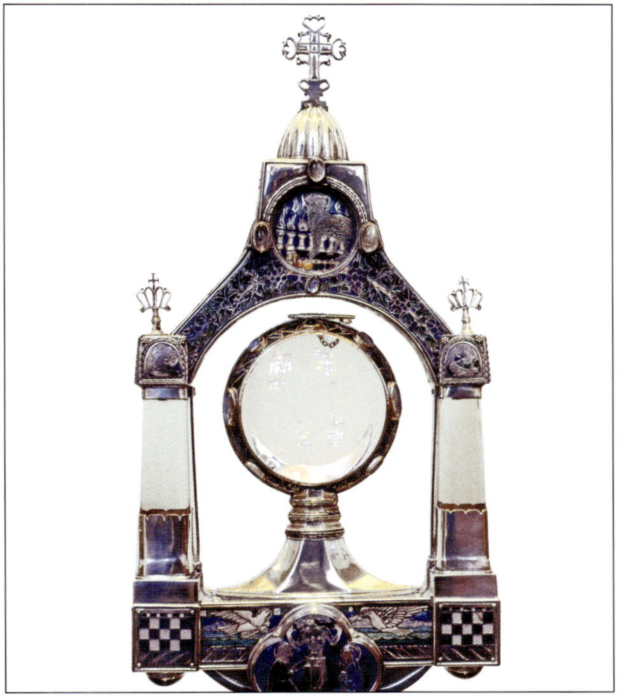

Plate 58. Monstrance for Caldey Abbey, silver, enamel, crystal, gemstones, 1910: detail of corona and crystal compartment.

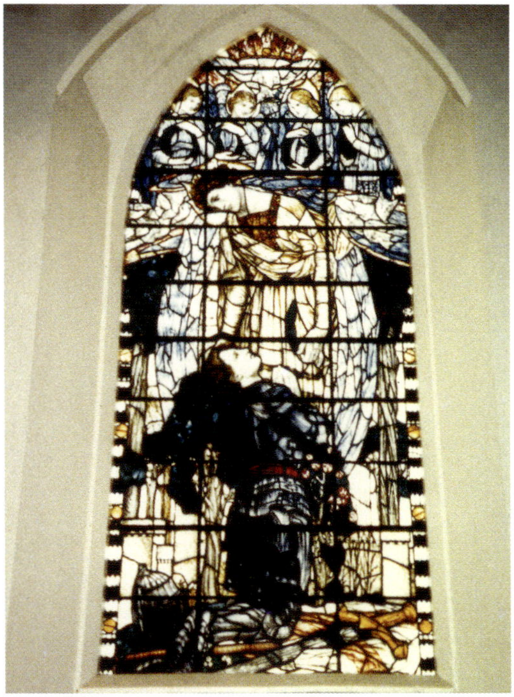

Plate 59. Church of St. John the Baptist, West Ashton, Wiltshire: Long Memorial window, 1919.

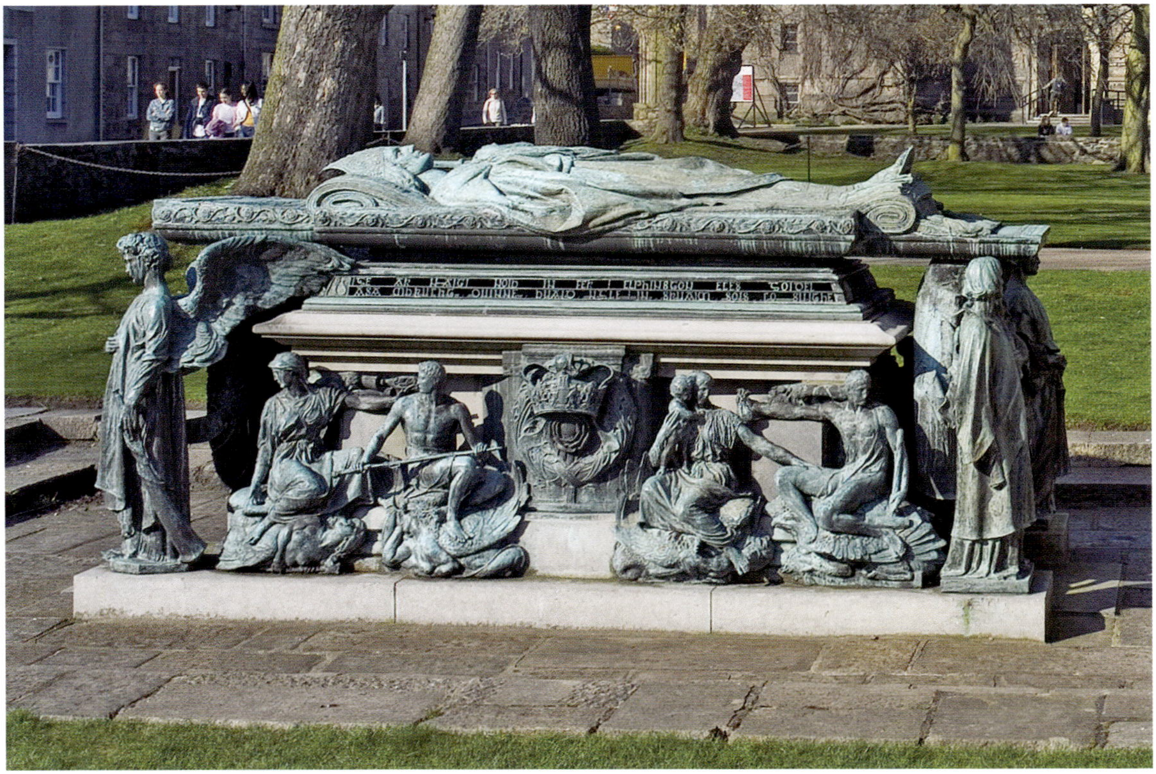

Plate 60. King's College, University of Aberdeen: Elphinstone Tomb, 1910-26, South side, sandstone and bronze.

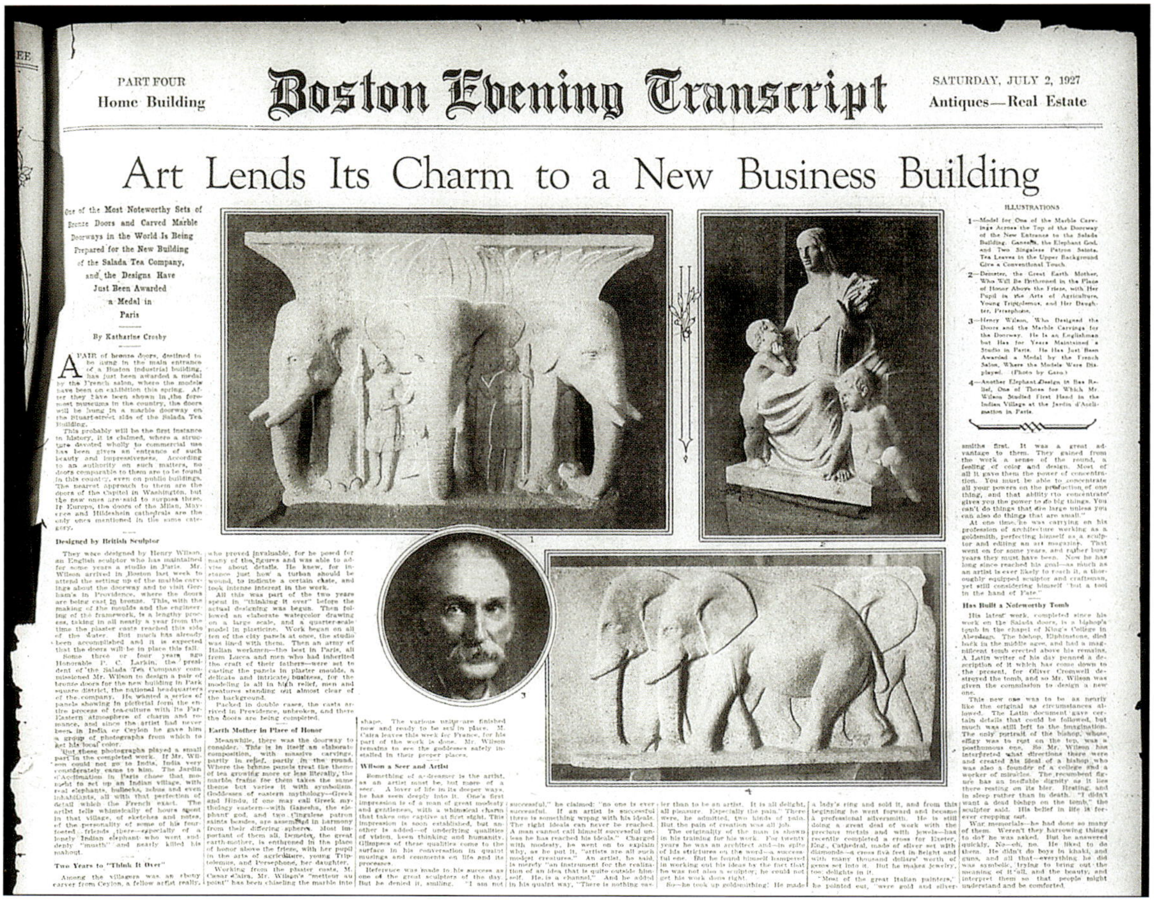

PART FOUR
Home Building

Boston Evening Transcript

SATURDAY, JULY 2, 1927
Antiques—Real Estate

Art Lends Its Charm to a New Business Building

One of the Most Noteworthy Sets of Bronze Doors and Carved Marble Doorways in the World Is Being Prepared for the New Building of the Salada Tea Company, and the Designs Have Just Been Awarded a Medal in Paris

By Katharine Crosby

A PAIR of bronze doors, destined to be hung in the main entrance of a Boston industrial building, has just been awarded a medal by the French salon, where the models have been on exhibition this spring. After they have been shown in the foremost museums in the country, the doors will be hung in a marble doorway on the Stuart-street side of the Salada Tea Building.

This probably will be the first instance in history, it is claimed, where a structure devoted wholly to commercial use has been given an entrance of such beauty and impressiveness. According to an authority on such matters, no doors comparable to them are to be found in this country, even on public buildings. The nearest approach to them are the doors of the Capitol in Washington, but the new ones are said to surpass these. In Europe, the doors of the Milan, Mayence and Hildesheim cathedrals are the only ones mentioned in the same category.

Designed by British Sculptor

They were designed by Henry Wilson, an English sculptor who has maintained for some years a studio in Paris. Mr. Wilson arrived in Boston last week to attend the setting up of the marble carvings about the doorway and to visit Gorham's in Providence, where the doors are being cast in bronze. This, with the making of the moulds and the engineering of the framework, is a lengthy process, taking in all nearly a year from the time the plaster casts reached this side of the water. But much has already been accomplished and it is expected that the doors will be in place this fall.

Some three or four years ago Honorable P. C. Larkin, the president of the Salada Tea Company commissioned Mr. Wilson to design a pair of bronze doors for the new building in Park square district, the national headquarters of the company. He wanted a series of panels showing in pictorial form the entire process of tea-culture with its Far-Eastern atmosphere of charm and romance, and since the artist had never been in India or Ceylon he gave him a group of photographs from which to get his local color.

But these photographs played a small part in the completed work. If Mr. Wilson could not go to India, India very considerately came to him. The Jardin d'Acclimation in Paris chose that moment to set up an Indian village, with real elephants, bullocks, zebus and even inhabitants, all with that perfection of detail which the French exact. The artist tells whimsically of hours spent in that village, of sketches and notes, of the personality of some of his four-footed friends there—especially of a lonely Indian elephant who went suddenly "musth" and nearly killed his mahout.

Two Years to "Think It Over"

Among the villagers was an ebony carver from Ceylon, a fellow artist really, who proved invaluable, for he posed for many of the figures and was able to advise about details. He knew, for instance just how a turban should be wound, to indicate a certain caste, and took intense interest in the work.

All this was part of the two years spent in "thinking it over" before the actual designing was begun. Then followed an elaborate watercolor drawing on a large scale, and a quarter-scale model in plasticine. Work began on all ten of the sixty panels at once, the studio was lined with them. Then an army of Italian workmen—the best in Paris, all from Lucca and men who had inherited the craft of their fathers—were set to casting the panels in plaster moulds, a delicate and intricate business, for the modeling is all in high relief, men and creatures standing out almost clear of the background.

Packed in double cases, the casts arrived in Providence, unbroken, and there the doors are being completed.

Earth Mother in Place of Honor

Meanwhile, there was the doorway to consider. This is in itself an elaborate composition, with massive carvings, partly in relief, partly in the round. Where the bronze panels treat the theme of tea growing more or less literally, the marble frame for them takes the same theme but varies it with symbolism. Goddesses of eastern mythology—Greek and Hindu, if one may call Greek mythology eastern—with Ganesha, the elephant god, and two Cingalese patron saints besides, are assembled in harmony from their differing spheres. Most important of them all, Demeter, the great earth-mother, is enthroned in the place of honor above the frieze, with her pupil in the arts of agriculture, young Triptolemus, and Persephone, her daughter.

Working from the plaster casts, M. Cesar Caira, Mr. Wilson's "metteur au point" has been chiseling the marble into shape. The various units are finished now and ready to be set in place. M. Caira leaves this week for France, for his part of the work is done. Mr. Wilson remains to see the goddesses safely installed in their proper places.

Wilson a Seer and Artist

Something of a dreamer is the artist, as an artist must be, but more of a seer. A lover of life in its deeper ways, he has seen deeply into it. One's first impression is of a man of great modesty and gentleness, with a whimsical charm that takes one captive at first sight. This impression is soon established, but another is added—of underlying qualities of vision, keen thinking and humanity. Glimpses of these qualities come to the surface in his conversation in quaint musings and comments on life and its processes.

Reference was made to his success as one of the great sculptors of the day. But he denied it, smiling. "I am not successful," he claimed: "no one is ever successful. If an artist is successful there is something wrong with his ideals. The right ideals can never be reached. A man cannot call himself successful unless he has reached his ideals." Charged with modesty, he went on to explain why, as he put it, "artists are all such modest creatures." An artist, he said, is merely "an instrument for the realization of an idea that is quite outside himself. He is a channel." And he added in his quaint way, "There is nothing easier than to be an artist. It is all delight, all pleasure. Especially the pain." There were, he admitted, two kinds of pain. But the pain of creation was all joy.

The originality of the man is shown in his training for his work. For twenty years he was an architect and—in spite of his strictures on the word—a successful one. But he found himself hampered in working out his ideas by the fact that he was not also a sculptor; he could not get his work done right.

So—he took up goldsmithing! He made a lady's ring and sold it, and from this beginning he went forward and became a professional silversmith. He is still doing a great deal of work with the precious metals and with jewels—has recently completed a cross for Exeter, Eng., Cathedral, made of silver set with diamonds—a cross five feet in height and with many thousand dollars' worth of gems set into it. But he makes jewelry, too; delights in it.

"Most of the great Italian painters," he pointed out, "were gold and silversmiths first. It was a great advantage to them. They gained from the work a sense of the round, a feeling of color and design. Most of all it gave them the power of concentration. You must be able to concentrate all your powers on the production of one thing, and that ability to concentrate gives you the power to do big things. You can't do things that are large unless you can also do things that are small."

At one time he was carrying on his profession of architecture working as a goldsmith, perfecting himself as a sculptor and editing an art magazine. That went on for some years, and rather busy years they must have been. Now he has long since reached his goal—as much as an artist is ever likely to reach it, a thoroughly equipped sculptor and craftsman, yet still considering himself "but a tool in the hand of Fate."

Has Built a Noteworthy Tomb

His latest work, completed since his work on the Salada doors, is a bishop's tomb in the chapel of King's College in Aberdeen. The bishop, Elphinstone, died back in the middle ages, and had a magnificent tomb erected above his remains. A Latin writer of his day penned a description of it which has come down to the present, for Oliver Cromwell destroyed the tomb, and so Mr. Wilson was given the commission to design a new one.

This new one was to be as nearly like the original as circumstances allowed. The Latin document gave certain details that could be followed, but much was still left to the imagination. The only portrait of the bishop, whose effigy was to rest on the top, was a posthumous one. So Mr. Wilson has interpreted what directions there were and created his ideal of a bishop who was also a founder of a college and a worker of miracles. The recumbent figure has an ineffable dignity as it lies there resting on its bier. Resting, and in sleep rather than in death. "I didn't want a dead bishop on the tomb," the sculptor said. His belief in life is forever cropping out.

War memorials—he had done so many of them. Weren't they harrowing things to do? he was asked. But he answered quickly, No—oh, no. He liked to do them. He didn't do boys in khaki, and guns, and all that—everything he did was symbolic, trying to bring out the meaning of it all, and the beauty, and interpret them so that people might understand and be comforted.

ILLUSTRATIONS

1—Model for One of the Marble Carvings Across the Top of the Doorway of the New Entrance to the Salada Building. Ganesha, the Elephant God, and Two Singalese Patron Saints. Tea Leaves in the Upper Background Give a Conventional Touch.

2—Demeter, the Great Earth Mother, Who Will Be Enthroned in the Place of Honor Above the Frieze, with Her Pupil in the Arts of Agriculture, Young Triptolemus, and Her Daughter, Persephone.

3—Henry Wilson, Who Designed the Doors and the Marble Carvings for the Doorway. He Is an Englishman but Has for Years Maintained a Studio in Paris. He Has Just Been Awarded a Medal by the French Salon, Where the Models Were Displayed. (Photo by Gaza.)

4—Another Elephant Design in Bas Relief, One of Those for Which Mr. Wilson Studied First Hand in the Indian Village at the Jardin d'Acclimation in Paris.

Plate 61. *Boston Evening Transcript*, July 2, 1927: the Salada Tea Company doors reviewed before installation.

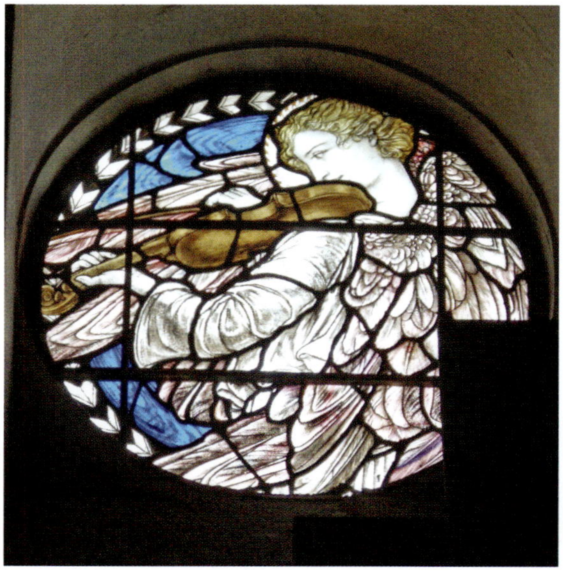

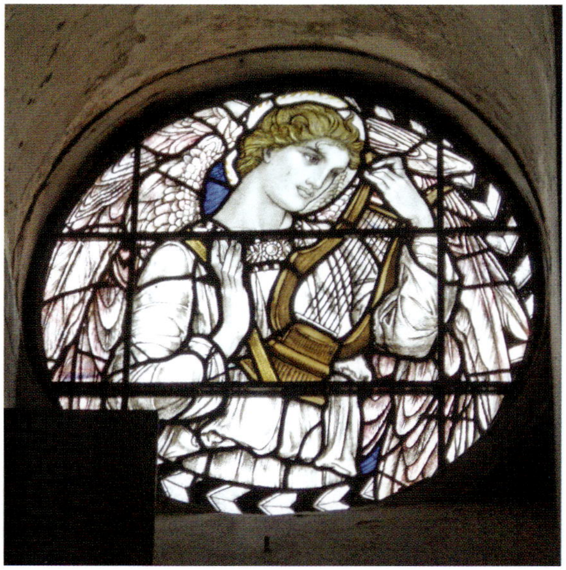

Plate 62. St. Mary's Church, Weymouth, Dorset: Wilson's stained glass angel-musicians lighting organ-loft, 1922-1923.

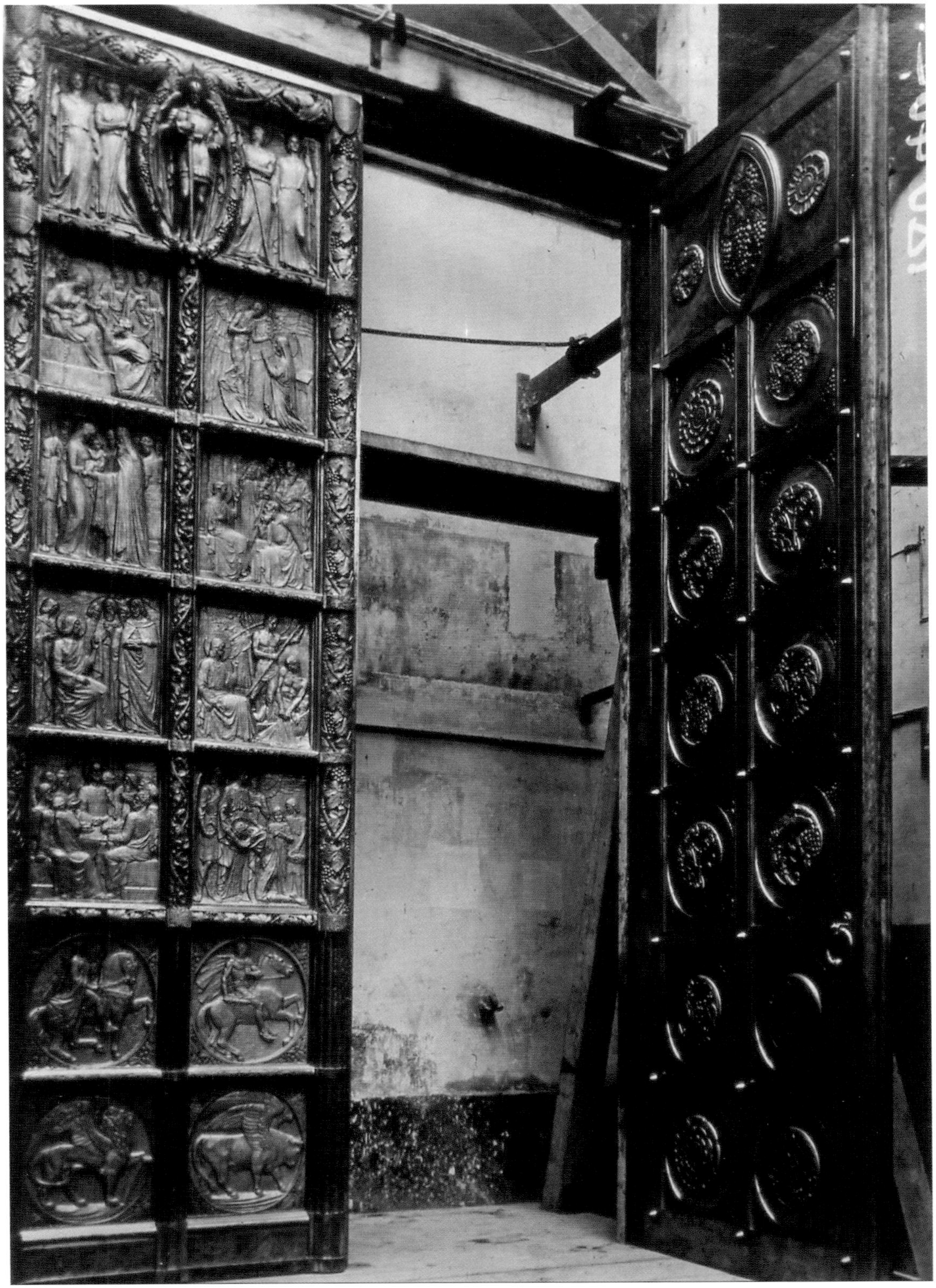

Wilson Archive Royal College of Art

Plate 63. Cathedral of St. John the Divine, New York, West doors: New Testament valves at assembly stage in Barbedienne's foundry, open to show the inside face, 1934.

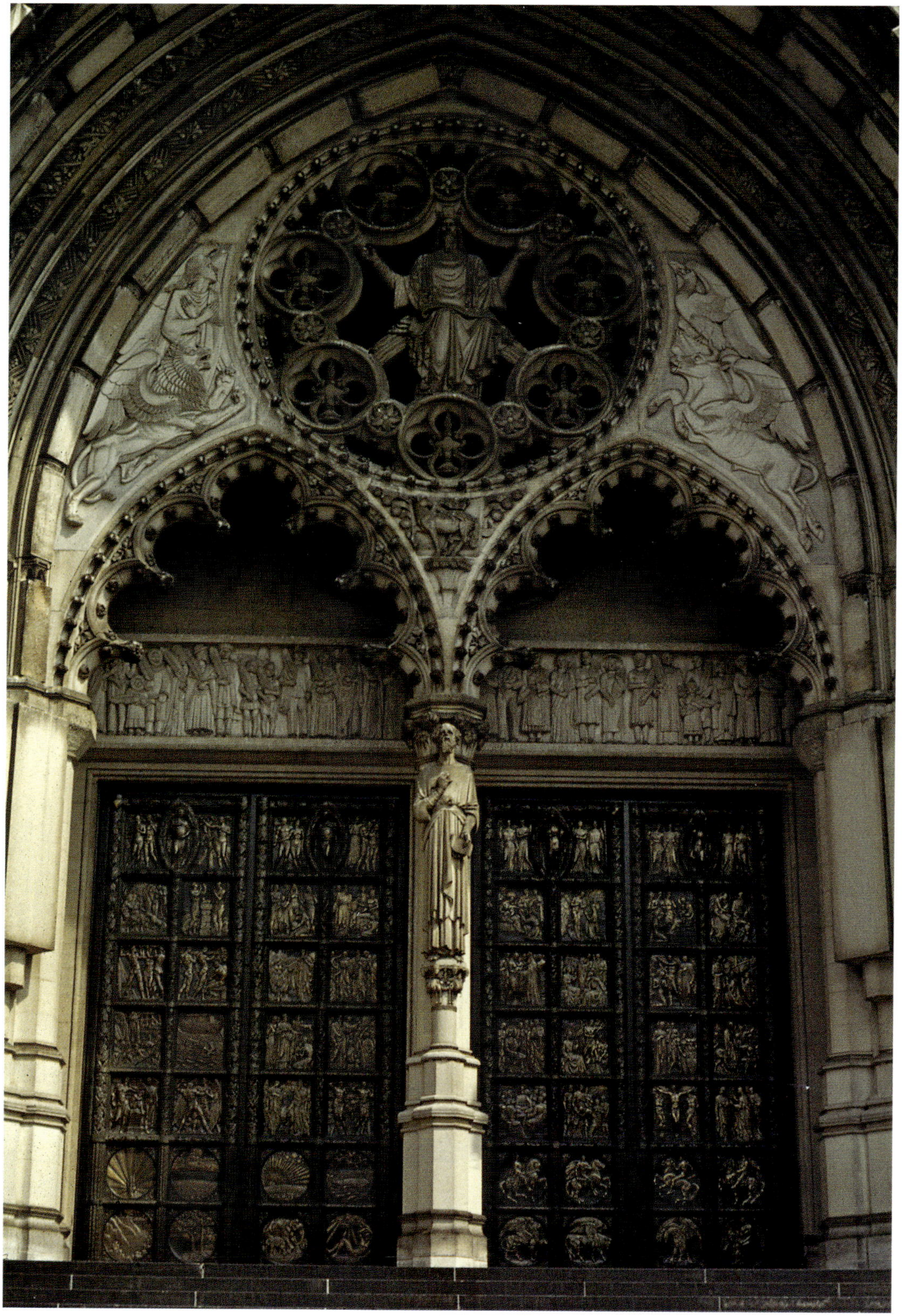

Plate 64. Cathedral of St. John the Divine, New York: West doors, 1927-31; seen here regilded in the 1970s.

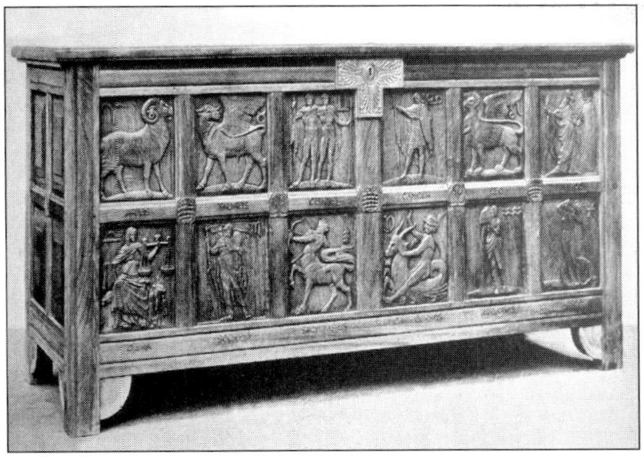

Figure 90. Panelled carved zodiac chest in English oak, designed by Henry Wilson, made by W.E. Micklewright, illustrated in the *Studio*, Vol. 86 1923.

sculptural treatment of the two great projects in bronze of his last decade.

That same year the Institute mounted an exhibition in Bradford, opened by Wilson. His speech underlined the B.I.I.A.'s determination to 'persuade the industrial world that the arts can do something for industry'.[5] With an eloquence recalling Ruskin's in the same city seventy years before, he anatomised the inevitable rift between the artist-craftsman and Bradford's factory system. Art could never thrive while 'human beings, half-alive, are summoned by the hateful hooter in the morning' then 'wait again for its sound at night.'[6] Nor could the dearth of good quality design be remedied by the simple expedient of factory owners recruiting token artists into their workforce, though – reading between his lines – that was Wilson's sceptical view of what the D.I.A. was advocating. In the post-War confusion, he was seeking a new approach within industry, where artistic principles would be assimilated into the manufacturing process, production methods reorganised, and profits shared by others rather than 'the shareholders alone'.[7] Characteristically, he had ventured outside the bounds of design theory and into the realm of up-to-date philosophical thinking:

> *That revolution in thought ... was but the expression in science of the new principle of human relativity which we were beginning to discover. This budding consciousness means that all our industrial methods and work relationships must change, and ... the arts and crafts take their due place in the scheme of national life.*[8]

Wilson's faith in what the B.I.I.A. could do was implicit in its constitutional aim of fostering good design allied to value for money. In this it foreshadowed the influential Gorell Report, issued by the Board of Trade in 1932. Though its own terms were strictly industry-based, that report would propose strategies comparable to those espoused by the Institute: periodical regional shows, a permanent Standing Exhibition, facilities for visitors to purchase exhibits on temporary display, encouragement for industry to collaborate with artists, and improved standards in art education. It sought, like the B.I.I.A., to enhance the taste of designers, manufacturers, distributors and the public, and at the same time, to create opportunities for enlightened purchasers of moderate means.

Despite the B.I.I.A.'s flying start, its activities would, through the 1920s, be gradually but thoroughly curtailed. Yet its 1929 exhibition, 'Industrial Art for the Slender Purse', in name and aim a clear precursor of Gorell, proved its most important; its theme – that 'beautiful things need not be costly'[9] – was especially pertinent, given the frequent criticism levelled at the Design and Industries Association for recommending 'almost entirely costly things'.[10]

'Slender Purse' addressed itself primarily to the practical householder: not only was the first section divided into familiar product classifications – furniture, building crafts, domestic textiles, pottery, glassware, metalwork, book production – but the B.I.I.A. had taken the bold step of attaching price tags to each exhibit. The next section, effectively the B.I.I.A's pledge to quality, comprised the Institute's own Permanent Collection of objects designed for use. Wilson was not represented in the earlier temporary section, but in recognition of the importance of the display, the permanent section had been strengthened by five purchases from him – two bronze figures, an enamelled gold and emerald pendant depicting Syrinx, a gold and crystal hair ornament, and a silver plique-à-jour cloak clasp.

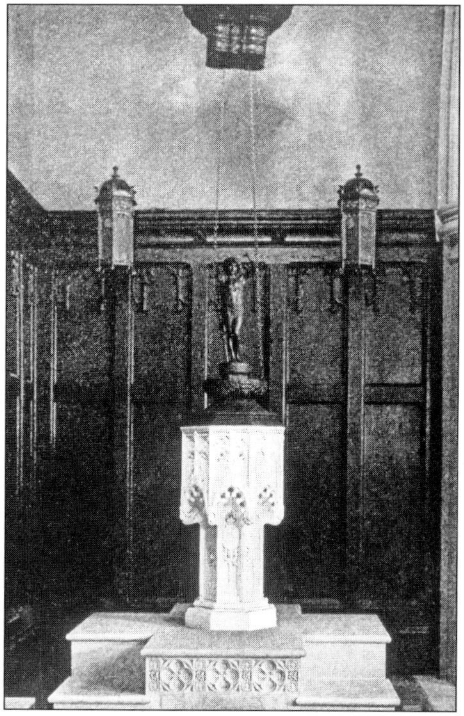

Figure 91. St. James's Church, Roxbury, Mass.: font by Goodhue, font cover by Wilson, *The Architectural Record* (NY) XXIV January 1911.

But it was the third component of the 'Slender Purse' show that most strongly underwrote its innovative thrust, the Margaret Bulley Collection of everyday product design, which consisted of household objects from beer bottles and custard dishes to tables and textiles, rethought or designed from scratch by avant-garde Russian, French and Italian designers. Contemporary British design was represented by Roger Fry's Omega Workshops, whose work had always been spurned by the D.I.A. Exciting and dynamic wares of this kind may have been seen by visitors to the famous 1925 Paris Exposition, but for novices the Bulley collection formed a new and arresting spectacle. Not even 'Slender Purse', however, could replenish the B.I.I.A.'s funds, and the Institute finally closed in 1934, donating its collections, mainly textiles, to the Victoria and Albert Museum.

One of the chief benefits to Wilson of his situation after the Great War was the chance to contemplate new creative projects, and to evaluate in practice his extended 'theory of relativity' through which the crafts achieved harmonious terms with commerce. A transatlantic commission of 1922, received at about the time the Wilsons chose to uproot themselves, after twenty years on and off, from the Thatched House, and move to France, offered a full-scale test of Wilson's theory: a set of sculpted bronze doors for the Stuart Street headquarters in Boston, Mass., of the leading tea importer, the Salada Tea Company. The catalyst of Wilson's commission was his great New England enthusiast Ralph Adams Cram, who was to play an ever greater part in Wilson's creative life. It had been Cram who, in the early years of the century, had brought Wilson to the attention of Salada's founding President, Canadian businessman Peter C. Larkin, the 'Tea King of America'. In 1907, with Cram's introduction, Larkin had visited the Wilsons at Platt, inspecting photographs of the bronze doors for St. Mary's Church, Nottingham, and admiring the narrative impetus and symbolism of the designs.

Once back in New England, Larkin made a point of visiting the eighteenth-century church of St. James, Roxbury, with the font cover and two hanging lamps that Cram, staying at Platt in October 1906, had arranged for Wilson to create in fulfilment of a commission from T.A. Forsyth, who wished to commemorate his late sister (Fig. 91). Cram himself had recently designed a new baptistry for the church in his typical free Late Gothic style; Goodhue, a partner in the firm, designed the font, but it was Wilson's work that Larkin was especially interested in seeing. The cover for the font, characteristically ingenious and expressive, captivated him instantly.

Suspended from the baptistry ceiling, a copper globe with hollow tempietto beneath is attached by twin chains to the font-cover below. Edged by a stepped border, it curves smoothly upwards from the marble font-bowl's white rim to meet a broad wreath of vines and text; passing beyond this tier it sweeps steeply up again to form a plinth, a preaching stage, for the bronze figure of John the Baptist. Commanding the space between the chains, unencumbered but for cross-staff and loincloth, his youth and poise recall Donatello's David. The chain-mechanism housed above him allows the whole structure, measuring 3' from font-rim to the top of the Baptist's head, to be wound effortlessly upwards to reveal the font-bowl.[11]

This visit to Roxbury settled Larkin's thoughts about the Salada project; he wrote forthwith to Wilson, formally requesting him to commence work on bronze doors for the company. In Wilson's hands these would display a complete sculptural illustration of the story of tea from its planting to the beginning of its journey to the households of America. Salada Tea was already a brand-leader before the War, and Larkin's son, Gerald, was fully primed to assume its Presidency. Delayed by his War service, he did not assume the role until 1922; meanwhile his father's own political and diplomatic interests were expanding, and would culminate in his appointment as Canadian High Commissioner in London. Under Gerald's leadership, Salada became the third largest supplier of tea in the world. Heir to his father's love of art as well as business – he would commission Sir Giles Gilbert Scott in the 1950s for Toronto University's Trinity College Chapel, endowing it with some $8 million – the younger Larkin took on the Salada doors project with enthusiasm. For Larkin, the name Salada provided a romantic, if anecdotal, link with a particular tea estate in Ceylon. For Wilson, there was no such connection: his completion in 1907 of a commission for two communion cups for St. Andrew's Church in Poona (the modern Pune), was as close as he had come to India, let alone Ceylon. Nevertheless, the photographic dossier Peter Larkin had sent him on his acceptance of the job allowed him to envisage the sights and working rhythms of the tea gardens, and to translate the story they revealed into drawings and modelled panels.

And he was about to receive help, in an unexpected form, from the city which the Wilsons were shortly to make their adopted home. His Salada research, the younger childrens' education, and the process of resigning his seven-year presidency of the Arts and Crafts Exhibition Society, were preoccupying Wilson as he and Margaret set about packing up Platt for Paris in 1922. They were convinced internationalists, but the immediate spur to moving was 13-year-old Dione gaining a place at the Conservatoire – where Pernel had been studying the violin since the previous year – on the strength of her cello playing.

The Wilsons' home, until April 1929, was 4 rue Jules Simon, Boulogne-sur-Seine; they then moved to 11 bis rue Alfred-Laurant, where they would remain until 1931. Here, on one of their periodical trips home from the Middle East, Edgar and Winnie Wilson broke their journey to visit them. Edgar told his brother how he had persuaded his company to be the first to use diesel tugs on the Tigris; Harry talked about liners and skyscrapers, and took them off to see 'work in progress'. This entailed more of journey than it would have done at Platt. In Kent, his studio was built onto the house, and the workshops were a step across the yard. In Paris, domestic and workspaces were more distinct, and his studio in S. Cloud was a bridge away from home, over the Seine at 1 rue Feudon, Quai Président Carnot; it was here that the Salada commission would take shape, as well as Wilson's next American commission, which would prove to be his last work.

It was during the Wilsons' second summer in the French capital that an extraordinarily-timed event took place which relegated Larkin's documentary photographs to a supplementary role. Between 1922 and 1924, in an imaginative cultural exchange, the Subcontinent paid Paris a visit: a living Indian village and its inhabitants established themselves in the Jardin d'Acclimation, complete with working bullocks, elephants and zebus. This was an authentic, changing settlement going about its daily life. Its typical buildings and routines fascinated French and international visitors alike, who came to soak up its ambience. Wilson was a ceaseless observer for the duration of its stay, filling his sketchbooks with images and memoranda, and befriending an ebony carver from Ceylon, who became his self-appointed consultant, sitting for figure studies and giving advice of a kind hardly available to Larkin on the minutiae of dress and caste. It was precisely this kind of information that enabled Wilson to fulfil the terms of the contract that Larkin had prepared, outlining the doors' technical requirements and the fees payable on completion.

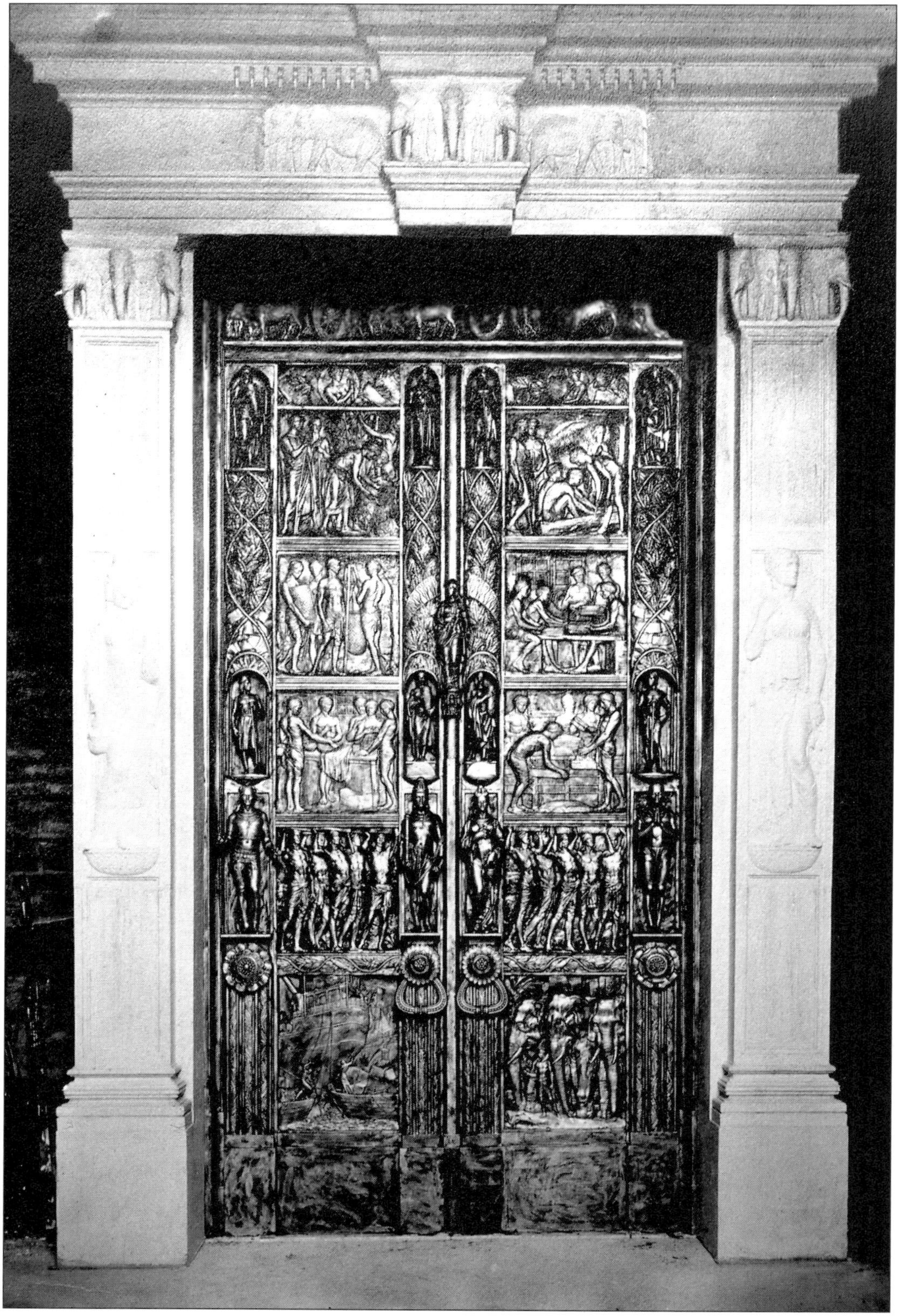

Wilson Archive, Royal College of Art

Figure 92. Salada Tea Company doors: workshop photograph reproduced in the *Boston Herald,* 5 February 1928.

That he should choose to recreate Hindu and Singhalese life in terms of the Graeco-Renaissance tradition of bas-relief modelling and create a genuine cross-cultural blend was typical of Wilson's immersion in the worlds his imagery inhabited. His first submission to Larkin was a comprehensive layout sketch in watercolour. Having received his patron's assent, he then created his proposed doors at one-quarter scale in the newly-invented material Plasticine, cohesive, transportable and infinitely malleable. Sketches and maquettes were dispatched to Boston for approval, which was given without hesitation. Work was put in hand at once, modelling the ten-panel series at full-size, in the traditional material of clay. In time, they lined every wall of Wilson's studio in S. Cloud. Once complete and refined in every detail, Wilson sought out the best mould-makers in Paris, Italian craftsmen from Lucca, to produce perfect plaster casts for the bronze doors and their overpanel, as well as of his full-scale models for the figurative elements of the doorcase which he had modelled life-size, for translation into marble. It was with quiet confidence that Wilson arranged for these casts, safe in their double packing cases, to be shipped to Boston, where Larkin attended their arrival in person, supervising the sending on of those containing the plaster doors and overpanel to the foundry Cram had recommended, the Gorham Company of Providence, Rhode Island (Fig. 92).

The Boston doors tell their story in *boustrophedon*, or plough-turn, sequence, zigzagging from top to bottom. The top right panel begins the narrative with the clearing of the ground; its neighbour to the left shows the tending and harvesting of the young tea shoots. Immediately below, the crop is weighed, then, on the right, comes the sifting of the leaves. In the third panel down, the tea is being sorted and graded, then, on the left, packed. Down one panel, porters form a frieze-like procession crossing to the right from one door to the other as they carry laden tea-chests to elephants waiting in the bottom right-hand panel. In the last scene, bottom left, the valuable cargo is hoisted into ships bound for Salada's Boston warehouses. The bronze overpanel is a tableau of oxcarts and bearers, making their way from right to left – their steady, resolute gait perhaps seeding the boustrophen sequence in Wilson's mind.

Tea bushes in flower, tied in sheaves, frame the upper panels, topped and tailed with shallow niches, each containing the standing figure of a plantation worker in full relief, workmen on the hinge sides, women tea-pickers forming the central pairs. The lower panels are bordered with neo-classical reeding, topped with rosettes, those at the centre masking the mountings of the twin doorhandles. Immediately above, and on a scale exceeding that of the porters they frame and the niche figures of the upper border, are four emanations of Vishnu, each separately cast; these include the two patron deities of Hindu Ceylon – Sundara Murthi Swami and Appar Swami. On a similar scale, set at two-thirds height amidst a halo of foliage and stook-bindings over the doors' closure, presides a female deity, drawn not from indigenous myth

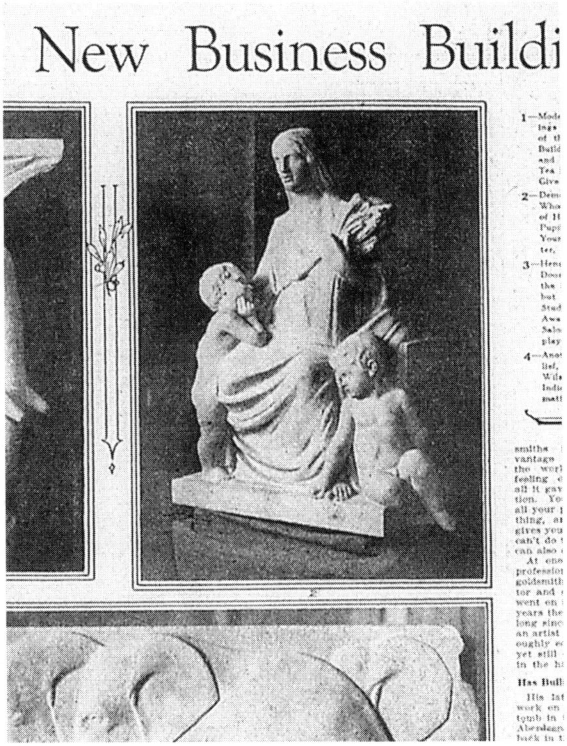

Figure 93. Marble figure group above entablature of Salada doors, *Boston Evening Transcript*, 2 July 1927.

but from the Mediterranean world: Artemis, goddess of the classical woodlands. She provides the focal point, but throughout, Wilson varies the density of his storytelling to allow some panels, like the tea-weighing, a Flaxmanesque openness, while filling others, notably the frieze of porters, with Rodin-like physicality.

The doors' extreme richness contrasts with the cool white marble sheerness of the doorcase to create an impressively harmonious whole. In the carved elements, the mix of Graeco-Roman and Indian iconographies remains as paradoxical and convincing as that in the cast work, whether in the matching of goddesses from either world – the love-goddess Kwannon to the left, Persephone, goddess of regeneration, to the right – occupying the low-relief mid-panel of each pilaster, or in Wilson's deft substitution of elephant trunks for the volutes of his capitals. Trios of these stately beasts, embodying the wisdom of Ganesha, also share the entablature and its keystone; but it is with a return to his own traditions (Fig. 93) that he binds his portal to the façade of the building: a flowing-tressed Demeter, the earth mother, cradling a sheaf of corn, sits with her infant daughter Persephone and her pupil, Treptolemus, at her knees. While the doors and bronze fittings were being cast in Rhode Island, a workspace was created within the Salada building itself for preparing the marble elements. There was ample room – indeed, so capacious were these headquarters that one area would serve as a temporary repository for the furniture and china that prominent Liberal supporter Peter Larkin was amassing for the party leader's official residence. It was Caesar Caira, Wilson's *metteur au point*, who carried out the carving in marble to the plaster maquettes of the figures, animals, and decorative details; his work was completed in readiness for Wilson's own arrival in Boston in July 1927 to direct the raising of the portal and the hanging of the doors.

As soon as the Salada composition was installed, American reviewers hastened to point out the rarity of such a liaison between art and business, one acclaiming it as 'probably the first instance in history where a structure devoted wholly to commercial use has been given an entrance of such beauty.' He omitted to mention the aesthetic success of Louis Sullivan's business and commercial buildings in Chicago, with their funtional integration of architecture and sculptural embellishment, but justly accentuated the interdependence Wilson's work had upheld between two different yet equally necessary branches of life. When the article (Plate 61) 'Art lends its charm to a new business building'[12] reached Wilson, he wrote at once to Edgar in Teheran:

> *They have treated me very well in Boston, and gave me half a page in the Boston Transcript ... and the most hair-curling review you can possibly imagine. The doors allowed me to pay off my bank overdraft and have a good substantial balance so for the first time in many years I am free of that burden. And it was a burden. I feel quite lightheaded to think that at last I am a free man....*[13]

Paris was similarly responsive to the Salada doors; the full-size plaster models – some 16' in height – were exhibited with Larkin's blessing at the 1927 Salon, where they won for Wilson the highest distinction open to a non-native exhibitor, the Médaille d'Argent de la Société des Artistes Français. Following the Salon, Larkin gave permission for the models to be displayed in some of America's foremost museums, enjoying the recognition they, and by association, the company, attracted. Today, Salada has been subsumed within a larger foodstuffs conglomerate and its Boston headquarters is a multi-office building; but the doors survive intact in Stuart Street, telling the story of tea to each passer-by who pauses to inspect them.[14]

Wilson was energised by America and by the novel vistas opening before him. The late 1920s were giving him a chance to reappraise modernism and reaffirm his welcoming attitude to it, a stance he had first professed some ten years earlier in his 1917 paper on New Schools in Art, to which he had appended his own translation of Marinetti's Futurist Manifesto. In his discourse, Wilson hailed art movements like the Cubists, the Vorticists and the Orphists not only for their pioneering spirit, but also for the healthy aeration their subversive humour gave society:

They have been described as one third each of youthful exuberance, public leg-pulling, and genuine artistic experiment. This last ... is enough to justify our attention. Traditional methods are invaluable but they take little account of the ever-widening range of perception, emotion and expression of artist and public alike.[15]

In thus saluting some of the most significant recent art movements, he seemed to be acknowledging that his own era was passing. It is as if he has recognised that the traditional approach that had informed his lifelong vision was no longer enough: its stake in a suddenly transient world was diminishing. How could anything which had applied to life before the War be relevant now? What insights could forms and ideas inherited from the past offer this fragmented new century? In registering the limitations of age-old responses, Wilson was placing himself on the side of those who kept their minds open to new artistic expression. In the same address he allowed himself a little gentle satire at the expense of those who chose not to engage with the present:

"Good gracious, Mary, No. 20, Venus – her bust – two blancmange moulds without jam, on top of a rice pudding. Has the artist never...."
"Ssssh! darling, people will hear you".
"... and that half pound of candles slipping out of a bag at her side; whatever is it?"
"I expect its her hand" said Mary.
"Well I never.... How funny artists are.... I'm so glad Tom is a stockbroker...."[16]

Wilson's persona as champion and standard-bearer of British art and design held its own contradictions, though. In public pronouncements Wilson berated the narrow-mindedness of the art and design establishment. But when it came to the design and decoration of Britain's pavilion at the 1925 Exposition Internationale des Arts Décoratifs et Industriels Modernes, an exhibition whose very title indicated a zest for modernity and industrial production, his approach seemed positively anachronistic. In his own perception he might be, but in his practice he shied away from actually becoming, an exponent of the 'ever-widening' expression he had observed in the New Schools, and despite the exhibition organisers' directive that each country's offering should break free from tradition, his instinct was to rely on familiar forms. Given Wilson's faith in educated intuition, along with his other artistic mantras – stylistic continuity, a sense of racial identity, design as a symbolic language – he produced for the Paris display exactly what might have been predicted of Wilson the practitioner, devotee of the old earth-rooted crafts.

The 1925 Exposition was the biggest, most important display of decorative art ever held – yet British firms seemed half-hearted in their response. Their attitude stemmed partly from its timing, so soon after the effort and expense of the British Empire Exhibition the previous year at Wembley; and from the knowledge that British goods had never been particularly popular in France. The Wembley display had had a different emphasis, decorative objects playing a comparatively minor role, with more weight being laid on scientific, mechanical and agricultural items, and on exhibits calculated to feed national pride in Empire: ethnic handicrafts, regional produce, samples of richly-grained timbers captivating enough to trigger a craze for exotic veneers. In the planning process for Wembley, Wilson had represented the crafts and decorative arts on its Art Council, and two of his own works had featured in the exhibition's Palace of Art – the octagonal oak pulpit seen at Ghent in 1913, and the tall silver memorial cup (Fig. 95) commissioned as a tribute to Sir Kenneth Anderson, first Chairman of the Council of the D.I.A., its stem enriched with galleons in low-relief and its finial with St. George slaying the dragon. The piece, forming one of the plates in the illustrated souvenir of the show, signalled the friendly tolerance subsisting between Wilson and the Association, but its manner of execution, and its iconography, struck a retrospective, elegaic note. More significant than any individual item, however, was a feature directly attributable to the D.I.A.'s influence: the high standard of signage throughout the exhibition, heralding subsequent display practice and forming a milestone in post-War typographic design.

If the nature of the Empire Exhibition had sidelined Wilson, preparations for Paris in 1925 had him working at full stretch. He was appointed to the British contingent's Paris Committee, and in that capacity liaised both with its London-based Art Council and with the Board of Trade, which was funding the British Pavilion. It was a modest grant, and although it soon became plain that the resultant pavilion would be too small to house a truly representative selection of British products, the Board of Trade declined to finance more space, rented or purpose-built.

This first great post-War embodiment of the French love of the grand commercial manifestation filled the twin footprints, linked on either side of the Seine by the Pont Alexandre III, of the famous exhibition of 1900. Every tree on the site had to be preserved, and each pavilion was to be surrounded by gardens, complete with fountains fed by the Seine. Underpinned by a desire to raise morale, the French exhibition committee stipulated that the displays must be representative of contemporary life, and should contain nothing directly copied from any decorative style of the past, except where the design reflected national characteristics. If the British pavilion seemed to fly in the face of the agenda of the exhibition at large, it was that proviso that allowed it to give rein to an incipient historicism. The official requirement for 'œvres d'une inspiration nouvelle et d'une originalité reélle' had not excluded the development of existing forms, but the work of the other exhibitors, especially France (which occupied around two-thirds of the entire site), left the British committee feeling that 'real originality' had too often been taken to mean 'novelty' at all costs. Such an interpretation, it warned, risked giving undue importance to 'experimental departures'[17] from the norm.

With its riverside location prompting allusions to the nation's maritime heritage, the British Pavilion (Fig. 94) would take the form of a stylised ship, with four tapering columns rising above the roof evoking masts. At the back rose a church-like glazed lantern, which served both as a fanciful light-scoop for the interior and added a quasi-cinematic levity to the elevations. A weather-vane, a Wilsonian galleon in full sail, crowned the spire. Evidently the glass cupola, with its hints of Mackintosh, was thought sufficiently unusual to satisfy the French hosts' demand for novelty. The Pavilion substantially observed the exhibition's stipulations, which stated that every building must be low in height and temporary. Most, like this one, were of plaster on a timber armature. In all other respects – in taking on a young architectural firm's pavilion design, organising its interior layout, and adding decorative motifs to its exterior – Wilson remained true to his own inspirational sources

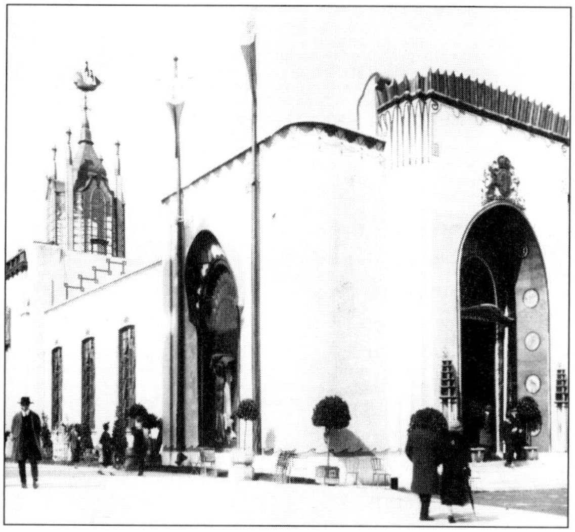
Figure 94. Easton and Robertson, with Henry Wilson:the British Pavilion, Exposition des Arts Décoratifs et Industriels Modernes, Paris 1925 *Introductory Survey 1927.*[18]

Economy of construction was a vital factor for all the Exposition's participants in view of the depleted post-Armistice resources of France and most of the other twenty-two invited countries, which included all the European states except Germany and Norway. Surprisingly to some, considering its crucial intervention in 1917, the United States was absent too, declining to take part on the grounds that its quintessential contribution to modern design (a few distinctive early pieces by Paul Frankl, Donald Deskey, Kem Weber and their peers aside) was non-portable: its architecture.

The mood and manner of the British Pavilion – mass played off against delicate detail, touched by an underlying symbolism, and with heraldic embellishments – signal Wilson's close involvement from the outset. Intrinsic to that involvement was the sympathetic bond he forged with the young would-be modernists Murray Easton and Howard Robertson, who, for its design, found themselves drawing on sources that they, and most of their affiliation except Oliver Hill, would soon reject. Robertson and Easton had already worked on French soil, at Le Touquet, just before the War. In their long partnership they would come to represent established modernism, a safe choice for faculty and office buildings, including, in the 1930s, Robertson's Shell Centre in London's Strand, with its imposing Deco styling.

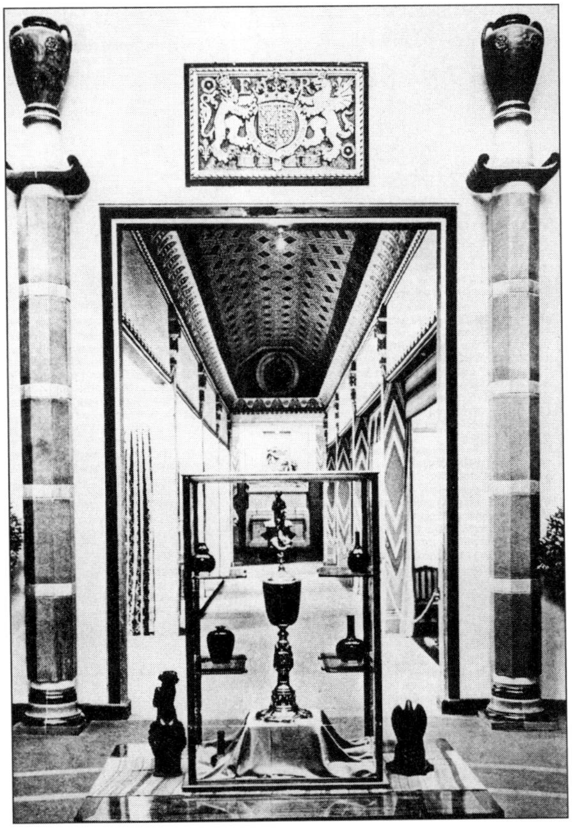

Figure 95. Easton and Robertson, with Henry Wilson: British Pavilion, Exposition des Arts Décoratifs et Industriels Modernes, Paris 1925, main interior space with the Kenneth Anderson memorial cup in foreground.[19]

Inside, Wilson decorated the wagon ceiling with diamond coffering, and the walls with brightly painted chevrons (Fig. 95). On the far wall hung a coloured plaster Virgin and Child, a replica of the tondo above the Tonbridge School memorial gates which, given the shape of the gallery, lent the space the overtones of a nave. In fact, only one of its sub-divisions was devoted to religious work: the Ecclesiastical section. Here was an array of Wilson's most impressive sacred commissions – plaster casts of his recumbent Bishop Elphinstone, the Marple wall panel, and four panels from the Nottingham doors, as well as a jewelled silver crozier, its crook embellished with a galleon and cherubs playing in the waves. His design sequence was well-defined and methodical, though it failed to create the thrill sparked by the Ghent show twelve years earlier – but that had been craft-based, a genre that his setting skills fully complemented, and had taken place in world as yet untouched by world war.

While acknowledging some worthy offerings from craft and commerce, the *Studio* regretted the preponderance of 'period' styles and pale colours, and the meagreness of the printing and carpet exhibits; the glass (including that by Powell & Sons) was judged mediocre, the commercial ceramics unadventurous, and the studio pottery, which might be expected to be daring, lacking in boldness. Later, when the Department of Overseas Trade published its official review of the exhibition, it reiterated those shortcomings: some important pottery firms were missing; the virtual absence of posters belied the considerable achievements of British artists in the field; the furniture, metalwork and glassware were, quite simply, 'very far from being representative'.[20]

Entering the British pavilion through its 'prow', the first display visitors saw was Exhibits lent by Private Collectors, an eclectic collection of virtuoso work, including two Wilson pieces, the silver cherub chafing dish, and the Kenneth Anderson memorial cup (Fig. 95). Metalwork and Jewellery featured four of his silver boxes, as well as a stunning range of jewels, from brooches and earrings to the gold morse of 1910; by now a regular feature on the exhibition circuit, their technical brilliance remained unsurpassed. Sharing the space were items by leading metalworkers – Cooper, Ramsden, Stabler – and retailers such as Garrard & Co., each presenting their current range. Furniture included pieces by Waring & Gillow and Heal's, but nothing by Wilson, though a further example of his work was seen in a watercolour sketch in the Architecture room. A woven silk scarf and an evening wrap by Fiammetta Wilson appeared in the Textiles display which, by and large, tended towards the chintzy, muted and floral, though Foxton's captured a contemporary mood in finely-drawn cotton fabrics patterned with small geometrical repeats.

Wilson designated four alcoves off the main space as room settings, each by a leading contemporary furnisher. In his area Gordon Russell created a nursery; Heal's furnished theirs as a bedroom in plain yet attractive light oak. Rallying to the exposition's international importance, Wilson sought to present quality home-grown work, whether from long-established firms or from younger enterprises like the Poole Pottery. The Pilkington Tile and Pottery Company's innovative matt glazes sat easily alongside their renowned Royal Lancastrian lustre-ware, whose origins went back to the early days of the business, when Walter Crane and Lewis Day had been its advisors. There were wallpapers devised, like the chintzes, to go with 'period' settings, a couple even reworking William Morris patterns; yet there were also painted wall panels in which Frank Brangwyn had nudged still-life portrayals of fruit and flowers in the direction of European expressionism. Despite taking some steps into modernity, however, the British exhibits seemed intent on preserving tradition and avoiding extremes – the critical parameters, instinctively endorsed by Wilson, of British design in general; after all, hadn't he always maintained that each country must use its native character and traditions to find its own design solutions?

Interpreting the exact sense of the exposition's entry stipulations had perplexed the British contingent from the start, raising issues that were still being debated in the Survey compiled by the Department of Overseas Trade some two years after the event. Even in so late a post-mortem, it seemed crucial in the Department's eyes to assess how representative Britain's participation had been, and what lessons might be learnt – not least, the need for dispassionate self-examination. The Survey took account of the economic, political and psychological world changes stemming from the War, as well as the impact of recent social, technical and scientific developments. Yet many products and buildings in this international gathering must, it concluded, be regarded as 'exhibition pieces', never meant for ordinary use. Furthermore, while the show was, as a whole, 'saturated' with modern inspiration, the 'more extreme phases and fashions of "Modernism"' were relatively few. The most 'marked impress'[21] of that style had been in the exhibits sent by Russia, a country where revolution had meant a complete break with the past; it was evident, too, within the architecture throughout the show. In this discipline a general striving for simplicity was detected, and some impressive examples of collaboration between architect and craftsman, especially in the Grand Palais, with its majestic staircase by Charles Letrosne graced by, the Survey noted with patriotic pride, a set of murals by Anning Bell. The absense of America was regretted as much as Germany's and, while expressing approval for the event's international range, the Survey also recorded how Britain's exhibits, for all their excellent craftsmanship, conveyed a 'comparative dullness, and aloofness' from foreign influences.[22]

Accompanying this broad review came individual Reports by experts on specific subject areas – on glassware by A. Marriott Powell, on architecture by H.C. Bradshaw, on textiles by Sir Frank

Warner and A.F. Kendrick, and on metalwork, by Wilson himself. Contemplating the 'variety, vitality, [and] radiant promise' of the Exposition in general, he commended the 'very great strides' taken in silver and metalwork in particular. Like several other Reports, Wilson's mentioned a spirit of collaboration – the 'nurse of progress'[23] – pervading the show, as well as a 'passion' for structural awareness: '... construction! construction! is everywhere' he exclaimed. Even where it became 'too evident [and] produced boniness', it was 'always interesting, as bones are', and anyway, in time, it would be 'taken up into the rhythm of design [and] subordinated to general form'.[24] He also took the opportunity to highlight the contrast between the conditions under which British craftsmen were labouring and those in France, where encouragement and subsidies, from either government or individuals, had freed the designers' creativity; to judge from their displays, he added, they had had 'the time of their lives'.[25]

One such individual, characterised by Wilson as 'perhaps the most famous smith in the world', was Edgar Brandt, whose lavish metalwork screen in the Salle des Ambassadeurs appealed greatly to the English craftsman, with its complex blending of construction, materials and innovative techniques. By adopting the new process of autogenous soldering, Brandt had overcome the usual structural limitations and the screen, built up of copper, brass and iron, had attained an effect comparable to 'a kind of larger jewellery'.[26] His series of doors in the maison Ruhlmann, and his grilles for the Porte d'Honneur replicating work originally made for American clients, won Wilson's acclaim for having arrived 'at a kind of natural gothic, which is very beautiful'. Wilson also singled out Claudius Linossier's vases of beaten copper decorated with electro-damascene; it was 'impossible to describe the richness of the effects M. Linossier [has achieved] by the marriage of copper [with] oxidised and matt silver' in designs inspired by, yet avoiding any 'slavish copying' of, Mycenean artefacts recently excavated in the ruins of Knossos.[27]

Among the jewels, Wilson noted pieces that were 'more ingenious than happy', but welcomed current experiments with materials and methods; he observed with forbearance such unconventional jewellery as that he came across in the Catalan pavilion, which struck him as 'very curious, very ugly, very foolish, but interesting'. He even found a 'cubist crucifix'.[28] Several examples of miniature Oriental carved stones used as centrepieces of jewels intrigued him, as did the interest shown in unusual or semi-precious components, from ivory, glass, crystal, lapis lazuli and malachite to ebony and other tropical woods; all these announced that 'a living tradition of romantic materials is being built up'. Again, he was glad to see an ardent if over-insistent awareness of structure, and admired the 'production of beautiful shapes by the skilled use of the hammer', which gave rise to a 'rich play of light and shade on the polished surfaces'[29] of vases and tea and coffee pots, especially those that were octagonal or polygonal in plan.

For Wilson, the 1925 Exposition, and assembling the British display for it, had been an experience unlike the previous large-scale displays he had organised. There, his mission had been to restore a sense of energy to useful and decorative craft-based design whose visual message had grown stale. But in Paris he found himself operating in a very different context: here Britain's contribution stood alongside the most up-to-date design of Europe and of half the world. Unswayed by the caprices of fashion, he quickly sensed the potential that ran through the Exposition, its in-with-the-New ethos. Though not represented in Paris, the Weimar Bauhaus had been in existence since April 1919; Wilson had watched its evolution from the vantage points of The Thatched House and the family's Venetian lodgings in the Calle del Forno. He voiced a commonly held view in deploring the 'unfortunate void'[30] left by Germany's absence from the Paris show, but whatever the outcome for his own country's design practice and manufactures, the pan-European in him rejoiced in the spirit of renewal that he had absorbed among the pavilions, minutes from the family's new home.

In his own summary, Sir Hubert Llewellyn Smith, Chairman of the Department of Overseas Trade Survey Committee, carried on claiming that the British pavilion had been both new and original, with 'no precedent'.[31] That assertion must have seemed strained: other buildings on the site had shunned historical allusion for authentic modernism, like Pierre Patout's entrance gate on the Place de la Concorde, with its ten square towers or, even more significantly, the Pavillon de l'Esprit Nouveau, with its bands of horizontal windows, its plain white render, its interpenetrating cubist spaces proclaiming the invented name under which its author, the Swiss architect Pierre Jeanneret, stepped onto the modernist stage – Le Corbusier. French critics were not alone in decrying the British pavilion's aura of nostalgia, which Wilson's heraldic echoes did little to dispel. These, apt for Coventry's Council House with its blazons and Tudor roses, patron saints and statues of Justice and Wisdom, struck many in 1925 Paris as old world and irrelevant.

The year 1927, the publication date of the Department's Exposition Survey, illustrated something of the divergent paths to be seen within British design, with the D.I.A. struggling to asssemble a convincing cross-section of 'modern' commercial pottery, metalwork and textiles for the Leipzig Fair, and Wilson attending the Salon to receive the silver medal for his Boston doors. The Fair would run from early March to the end of August, Britain's representation, by the D.I.A.'s own admission, worthy but dull in comparison with the European contributions. Best in the British section were domestic ceramics, and the 'Modern Textiles' exhibit, including some printed fabrics by Alec Walker and Paul Nash, and there were a couple of Eric Gill bas-reliefs. The significant distance between the D.I.A. and Wilson inevitably meant that his flair for bringing visual coherence to such a display was absent: the commentary in the Association's Quarterly Journal of September that year could not help but note the show's 'miscellaneous' air, and the way the space was 'cut up' by glass cases.[32]

By July, as the Werkbund's Weissenhof estate was about to open in Stuttgart, Wilson was in New York, on the point of embarking on his largest-ever work of architectural sculpture – work that would draw him away forever from the exhibition circuit. Like Ashbee before him he was exhilarated by the atmosphere of the place. From the comfort of the Arts Club, where Cram had got him temporary membership, he sent Edgar his responses to the supreme modernist metropolis, throwing in some good news of his own:

> *... I find New York very exciting with its noise and rush and skyscrapers. The latter are particularly fine and impressive.... I'm sailing for Europe on 5th of August on the Grasse. Not so fine of course as the Ile de France. I shall be glad to get back because I want to be at work. I have just been given another £3,000 job....*[33]

Work, or affinities with certain locations, had led Wilson over thirty years from Kensington to Kent, then to Venice to concentrate on the Elphinstone Tomb, and from there back to The Thatched House for the duration of the war. The move to Paris in 1922, prompted by his second musical daughter Dione's acceptance at the Conservatoire to pursue her cello studies, coincided providentially with the arrival in Paris of the Indian village that would inform his Salada designs. Now, at 63, paid in full for the Boston doors, he was at last liberated from the financial worries that had accompanied his working life. The fee assured by the New York commission would subsequently comprise a large proportion of Harry Wilson's estate: in his will, written at Platt in 1903, witnessed by the family's cook and nurse – both, reflecting the Wilsons' internationalist outlook, being Scandinavian – and administered by Pernel thirty-one years later, the sum to be disposed was £4,483-12-4d net.[34]

That summer of 1927, as he sailed for his meeting with Cram, he went with the satisfaction of seeing his children thriving in their chosen careers. Guthlac was now 25 and an established civil engineer; Fiammetta, at 23, was a noted craft weaver, and the 21-year-old Pernel was well on her way to becoming a world-class violinist under her stage name Orrea Pernel. Even Dione, recognising that her talent as a cellist fell far short of Pernie's intuitive gifts, and aware that money concerns might rekindle the chronic exhaustion her father had suffered some twelve years earlier during the Coventry commission, was settled: she had abandoned her musical studies in favour of her abundant culinary gifts, setting up at the age of 18 as a high-class professional caterer. Within the immediate family, then, an ideal balance had been achieved; less so, between Harry's two brothers. It was a constant worry to him that Patten's early potential as an illustrator had never quite been fulfilled, and that his ventures into commercial design were so intermittent. By now, divorced from Alice, remarried to Florence, and living in a flat in south London, he was glad of occasional financial help from his youngest brother Edgar, the successful shipping manager. Edgar recalled the time when he and Harry had between them purchased a pony and trap for their father, by then in his 70s, infirm, and increasingly reliant on their stepmother, Bessie: it was no use expecting their brother to contribute, as 'Pat was always poor'. In their interest in art, Patten and Harry were finely attuned, but in perseverence and determination, Harry was closer to Edgar. Indeed, that cheerful letter about the '£3,000 job' could only have been sent to one brother; in the other's household it may inadvertantly have caused upset.

As for the 'job', no wonder Wilson was enthusiastic to start – it was to make the bronze West doors for the world's biggest cathedral, then slowly approaching completion: the Episcopalian Cathedral Church of St. John the Divine on Amsterdam Avenue, in Manhattan. Of all Wilson's works they are the most conspicuously sited, and constitute a work of religious art on a truly architectural scale, each pair measuring 18 feet by 12 across, and weighing six tons. The task of concentrating the narrative and and symbolism of the Christian revelation within these massive and powerfully-crafted doors would fill all the working hours of his final years.

Once again, the initial proposal had been made by Ralph Adams Cram, senior partner of what was by now Cram & Ferguson, consulting architects to the Cathedral, whose appointment had followed a series of disagreements between the Cathedral's Trustees and Heins & LaFarge, winners of the original competition of 1888 to build it. Heins had died in 1907, and after construction had progressed from the choir to the crossing, the authorities decided not to renew LaFarge's contract, engaging Cram, Goodhue and Ferguson in 1911 to complete the nave. Back in 1907, Ralph Cram had arranged for photographs of Wilson's ecclesiastical work to be exhibited at the American Institute of Architects,[35] reviewing the display for the Boston journal *Christian Art* in the following year; Cram personally had recommended Wilson for the font-cover commission for St. James's Church, Roxbury, Mass., and encouraged P.C. Larkin of Salada Tea Company fame to visit Platt in 1907, where the idea for the company's doors was born.

Early in 1928 Cram travelled to Europe ostensibly to interview prospective designers for the Cathedral's 'Golden Doors' which, even before the question of the sculptor had been raised, had been prized as an idea by Trustees and sponsors though never – in regard of the gold surface – by the Bishop, William Manning, by the foundry, nor, indeed, by Wilson himself. Cram had by now intimated to the Bishop that Wilson was his man for the commission, and had proposed the Salada doors to him as an exemplar. Once in Paris, he went straight to Wilson's studio, and afterwards wrote a measured letter to Manning from his hotel:

> *After careful study, I am persuaded in my own mind that the sculptor who should be given this work is Henry Wilson, an Englishman by birth (he is nearly as old as I), and now resident in Paris. He was trained as an architect under the great John D. Sedding, who was the architect who most inspired me when I began work in ecclesiastical architecture. Yesterday I went to his studio in St. Cloud, to see the work he is now doing, including the full-size casts of the great bronze doors just completed for a building in Boston.*

Though not as large as those we shall require for the cathedral, they are very large and really magnificent. I am perfectly sure that there is no other sculptor who's genious fits in so perfectly with this ... type of work; of course those of the cathedral would be considerably different in design, much simpler,... and more architectural, but the quality is, I think, right.[36]

Cram's respectful advice to the Bishop would prove crucial not only in the choice of Wilson as sculptor, but also in determining the iconographic sequence, especially in the Old Testament diptych. His role as as the driving force behind the project is apparent in his letter to Manning:

I suggest for these great 'Golden Doors', in one pair, twenty-four panels epitomising the Old Testament, and for the other pair, twenty-four panels epitomising the New Testament, the first to give scenes from the Creation to St. John the Baptist, the second one from the Announciation to the Ascension.[37]

Wilson was thinking along the same lines himself: an episodic interpretation of familiar scriptural sources seemed best suited to a New World setting where, he rightly surmised, pragmatism would be favoured over the ethereal, indefinable allusions he had used in earlier British commissions. Spoken and unspoken, there existed a working rapport between Cram and Wilson that had only strengthened since their first meeting twenty-one years before. 'I should like very much' – Cram continued to the Bishop – 'to begin tentatively with Mr. Wilson ...' and

to have him prepare a sketch for these doors. This would not mean that the commission was given to him definitively, but only that he would be asked to submit a scheme for the consideration of yourself and the trustees.... I should like to do this while I am here, in order that we might talk it over together, and so work the design out to our mutual satisfaction.[38]

The client commissioning the doors was a powerful commercial sponsor, the Metropolitan Life Insurance Company, whose Field Force of agents throughout America and Canada had been pondering the options for a suitably impressive commemoration of their late president, Haley Fiske. It had been agreed that this should take the form of a contribution to the rising fabric of St. John the Divine. The company's initial idea had been for a Fiske Memorial rose window in the as yet unbuilt South transept; but this scheme was dropped in favour of the 'Golden Doors', for which Cram had already provided the architectural context in his own preferred Gothic manner. Since Heins & LaFarge had used a Byzantine style, it was necessary to subsume their portions within the vast new structure Cram was creating. The choir and sanctuary were accordingly revaulted, and the nave, originally intended to bring the Cathedral's East-West dimension to 520', lengthened by a further 80'. The façade Cram's West front presented to Wilson was Early English, a central stone pier, yet to be carved, supporting paired arches whose emphatic cusps fly free of the shadows they cast. Above them, a circular openwork stone roundel was carved with Christ in Majesty within the orbit of seven quatrefoiled 'wheels', while the door frame and lintel frieze remained, for the time being, untouched Indiana limestone blanks.[39]

By June 1928 Wilson had completed his first pencil study of the narrative arrangement of the doors and despatched it to the Cathedral Trustees. Without delay, they informed Metropolitan Life's new president, Frederick H. Ecker: 'The doors are colossal in size', they wrote, excitedly. 'We want them to be one of the greatest works of art in the world'.[40] On seeing the sketch design, the Haley Fiske Memorial Committee was equally expectant. Cram, writing to the the Cathedral Bursar, stressed that these were early days, all the more so since the commission had yet to be officially awarded:

As a sketch, ... it is about the lovliest thing I have ever seen. Of course, modifications would have to be made if Wilson had the contract....[41]

His practiced eye was already seeeing possible improvements and simplifications to the bronze rails and stiles framing the sculpted panels. By April 1929 Wilson had sent his adjustments and Cram could furnish Bishop Manning with a revised estimate and measurements. Inclusive of Cram & Ferguson's 6% commission, it came to $84,800, comprising $50,500 for Wilson's design and models, and $29,500 for casting.

Having won the approbation of both sponsor and Cathedral, Wilson could hardly wait to get on with the work. He recognised the magnitude of the task, and sensed the possibility of 'the other side'[42] claiming him before its completion. Back in his studio in S. Cloud, he began work at once, distilling his designs and re-engaging some of the Boston team of specialist mould-makers, adept at precisely this type of project and in tune with his dedicated workshop procedures. The Salada doors had reinforced Wilson's facility for fluent, sculptural storytelling, and refined his architectural expertise in handling change and contrast. The New York commission demanded of him a new mastery of monumental scale, and all the old skills – the emblematic artist, the jeweller and, in making the panels readable in such rich surroundings, the stage and exhibition designer – that among all the artist-craftsmen of the time combined, perhaps, in Henry Wilson alone.

These were, of course, the self-same qualities that Cram would have expected of their collaboration. What he could not have foreseen was the patience and fortitude that would be required of his old friend over the next four years. He had not allowed for the Sinclair factor. Donald Sinclair, Metropolitan Life's Murray Hill district office manager and energetic, if ever prudent, chairman of the Fiske Memorial Committee, had advised the Bishop to seek testimonials on Wilson – one came from Peter Larkin[43] of the Salada Tea Company, another from an English patron, Lord Dulverton, a member of the Wills family. In 1916, Dulverton had bought the Gloucestershire mansion Batsford Park from Lord Redesdale; this George & Peto house, dating from 1888, had required some alterations to suit its new owner. These adjustments, carried out by Wilson in 1919, had been so sensitively devised as to make Dulverton one of his warmest advocates.[44]

In other New York quarters, Wilson's credentials were beyond question, and needed no such external advocacy. Early on in their friendship, Cram had asserted in his *Christian Art* article that Wilson's talents should be used 'for the Church in America while the power is yet with him',[45] and now there was not only tangible evidence of that power in his 'wonderful bronze doors' for Salada, but also the *Boston Herald*'s claim, unintentionally prescient in the cicumstances, proclaiming that 'the doors of the Milan, Mayence [Mainz] and Hildesheim cathedrals are the only ones that can be considered to excel them in any way'. Writing to Edgar from S. Cloud in July 1928, five months after its appearance, Wilson was obviously revelling in the praise, adding dryly, 'there was a very good photograph of myself also, so I am becoming famous over there if not in England'.[46]

The testimonials served to eliminate any possible doubt as to Wilson's aptitude for creating an entrance of suitable drama and dignity for the Cathedral. Sinclair, however, despite all assurances, and his own protestation in a letter of 24 July 1929 that 'we are eager for the work to commence as speedily as possible', was not prepared to release any preliminary funds to Wilson without a definitive, signed agreement. Cram & Ferguson's partner charged with managing the commission, Chester N. Godfrey, poured out his exasperation at Sinclair's excessive caution to the Bishop in a letter of January 31, 1930 – it had left Wilson without cash to carry the work substantially forward, even though he had been devoting himself to it since early 1928:

While we sympathise with Mr. Sinclair's desire to safeguard the interests of the donors, there are certain conditions and customs that can hardly be overcome by contractual requirements. It is necessary to recognize that we are dealing with an artist, and it is his ability and talent that is being purchased. It would, of course, be a serious situation should the sculptor die before the work is finished, but [we] look upon this as a risk that must be taken and know of no reasonable way to safeguard against it.... We are prompted to write to you this morning ... because of a letter just received from Mr. Wilson, stating that he is going on with the work, as he had supposed this to be your wish. If there is any doubt whatsoever in your mind that Mr. Wilson should be so permitted pending ... contract forms, will you kindly let us know immediately, so we can cable him to stop. We are certain that this would be a very serious blow to him, and also [to] the Cathedral.... As has been pointed out, he is no longer a young man and a very considerable amount of time has already elapsed since he started the work.[47]

Sinclair was also keen that the doors be made in the United States, rather than France, as Wilson wished, despite Godfrey's warning that pursuing such an option would only complicate matters:

As far as we are concerned we should have no objection whatsoever to having the doors built in this country, but undoubtedly this proceedure would make a very considerable addition to the proposed contract with Mr. Wilson if not in voiding it altogether....[48]

At last, on 12 February 1930, a contract calculated to satisfy all parties was drawn up between Henry Wilson and Cram & Ferguson. Addressed to Wilson, it specified that

you are to furnish all materials and labor and make and finish full size models for two pairs of bronze doors for the central entrance of the west front of the Cathedral of St John the Divine New York, all as shown by drawing S.17, with simplified stiles and rails in accordance with detail drawings; inside of doors to be paneled and ornamented. All to be completed to the satisfaction of the Architects. Detail drawings showing both sides of both sets of doors are to be submitted for the approval of the Architects, the Bishop and Trustees of the Cathedral before the work begins.

The work is to include a memorial inscription, the text of which shall be furnished by the Owner.

You are to obtain the exact measurements of the existing stone work before beginning the models, to insure absolute accuracy....

All models must be submitted to the Architects for approval ... before final castings are made. The work is to include furnishing of ... models suitable for ... making bronze castings. These models are to be delivered free of all duty or transportation charges at such point in the United States or France as the Owner may direct.

Work is to be started at once and completed as early as possible.

You are to keep all this work, including models and castings, covered by insurance payable to the Owner or yourself, ... until the bronze castings are made.

The amount to be paid to you for all models ... is the sum of FIFTY THOUSAND FIVE HUNDRED DOLLARS ($50,500.00), of which amount $7,500.00 is to be paid when this contract is signed by the Sculptor and the Owner; $7,500.00 more is to be paid when the models for one door are completed; $7,500.00 more is to be paid when all models are completed and accepted by the Architects; $15,000.00 more is to be paid when all models are delivered complete at point directed; and the balance, namely $13,000.00 is to be paid within sixty days thereafter.[49]

This document was designed to set out a clear basis on which to proceed, or rather, to bring the paperwork into line with what had been accomplished by Wilson over the preceding two years; however, as the work progressed, so the legal and financial difficulties proliferated. His initial elation was quickly dimmed by the interminable delays that came to haunt the project, none of which he had any power to prevent. The contract of 12 February 1930 had been an attempt to formulate a binding agreement – a hopeful development, Wilson having worked for so long on the project without proper payment.[50] But Sinclair's letter to the Bishop later that year, railing against paying anything at all until the whole job was complete, did not bode well.[51]

In an attempt to ease matters, the Dean of the Cathedral, Milo Gates, tried to soothe an 'extremely solicitous' Sinclair by guaranteeing, on behalf of the Bishop and Trustees, that the contract to erect the doors 'entirely protects you....'[52] Yet Sinclair's hesitation persisted through another year; at the beginning of March 1931 the Bishop, in a letter to Lord Dulverton, confessed that he was 'grieved at the difficulty and embarrassment' caused to Wilson. Persuaded that the contracts would be signed 'in a few days', he explained that 'the Dean is today cabling $500 to Mr. Wilson in anticipation of that action'.[53] Cram's letters to Dean Gates grew more and more agitated – in the absence of fees reaching his old friend, he himself had stepped in to help:

> *I simply cannot stand this situation with regard to the delay in payment, consequent to the inexcusable delays on the part of Sinclair in signing the contract. I know something about Wilson's condition and that of his wife, and the thing is so much on my nerves that it gives me insomnia. When I spoke to you some months ago about this, telling you that we had already sent $2,000 from our own account, you said, I think, that you yourself would be willing to do something along the same lines. I now ask you point blank if you can send him a thousand dollars at once. My own bank account is too low to permit my [sending] it myself without borrowing, and naturally I don't like to resort to this extremity. Can you let me know, if possible by Saturday of this week, whether a thousand dollars can be found for him in New York?*[54]

Wilson's immediate financial predicament in November 1930 was resolved through Cram's generosity and with a small advance from the Cathedral Trustees; not enough, however, to remedy his real difficulties. At the beginning of February 1931, he was moved to 'beg the kind help' of the Bishop in person. Desperate to move South to Menton because of a sudden decline in Margaret's health, and as concerned for the foundry's cashflow problems (he had recruited Barbedienne on signing the contract) as for his own, he stated the plain facts:

> *My Lord, I don't know the true American style of address so I put this formal one. I am writing now to ask if you will be so kind as to arrange to send me my first payment. I have signed the contract in which there was nothing about waiting until Barbedienne had signed. As to Barbedienne, he simply wants the usual Parisian methods of payment, [the installments arranged] more equitably, instead of delaying any payment.... till the first door is finished. As he points out, by the time the first door is done the second must be nearly ready if he is to finish by the time specified. The delay in the first payment is very serious for me. I have already spent more than $2,500, to do which I have had to borrow money and pay interest. The work is nearly done, but it will have to stop if the Treasury does not pay me what has long been overdue.*[55]

Dean Gates himself, mulling over the choice of foundry, and fully aware that the Haley Fiske Memorial Fund was 'distinctly limited'[56] to the agreed fee of $84,800, had voiced his concerns about Wilson's preferred firm. From the start, Wilson had shown a commitment to the Parisian family business which he knew and respected. Its credentials for translating the plaster versions of the doors into bronze were impeccable: it was to the younger Barbedienne, Emile Gustave Leblanc, that Rodin had entrusted some of his most important work, while Wilson himself had used the foundry for the

Chamberlain casket, the Welbeck doors, and the memorial gates for Tonbridge School. Barbedienne had inherited the business from his uncle Ferdinand in 1892, soon clinching exclusive twenty-year contracts to cast *Eternal Spring* and *The Kiss*, and, in 1895, making the first bronze version of the *Burghers of Calais*. Leblanc Barbedienne undertook to oversee the New York castings in person, bringing experience and an up-to-date outlook to the project.[57] Mindful, however, of Sinclair's advice that the Memorial Committee should seek prices from other foundries, Dean Gates asked Wilson to cable him the designs early in 1930, so that estimates could be sought 'from Gorham' – where the Salada doors had been cast – 'or other bronze founders here....'[58]

At this point, a new worry was brought to the attention of both Wilson and the Cathedral authorities: the import tax status of the doors, were they to be cast in Europe. Should they be classified as art or utility artefacts? If they fell on the utilitarian side of the line (doors unarguably serving a useful purpose), the Cathedral could be liable for charges it had not budgeted for; if, on the other hand, they were classified as works of art, they would be exempt. As far as Wilson was concerned, this was for the Bishop and the Trustees to resolve: he himself was entirely, and equally, preoccupied with the exigencies of their design and execution, and with Margaret's welfare. With the doors, he had demanding technicalities to address regarding their structural specifications and their manufacture and assembly. Each valve consisted of an interior face coming from the cast with all mouldings and decorations complete, and an exterior one cast without its ornamentation, which would be cast separately and riveted onto an electrically welded steel frame. For the exterior, the ornamentation comprised a total of fourteen panels, along with cast decorative sections covering the frame.

In their final form, the stiles and outer frames of the doors stand proud of the panels, growing from reeded piers at the base to become linear wreaths of vines. The upper corners are enriched with twelve shields bearing the signs of the zodiac. Each 4'6" wide valve is symmetrically arranged, two panels across, seven high. This grid format varies only in the top tier, where flanking panels meet around a vesica, a pointed ellipse of foliage, to form a continuous frieze.

Wilson made the pair of valves to the left of the central stone pier a visual summation of the Old Testament (Fig. 96), their upper tiers forming an evolving narrative set in Eden. The story begins in the frieze with Adam and Eve inhabiting the garden, followed by the temptation of Eve, then of Adam; finally, heads bowed, the couple follow the path indicated by the Archangel, out of Paradise. Two figures interrupt the scene, the angels of the sun and moon, reminders of Wilson's propensity for mingling orthodox imagery with an idiosyncratic iconography all his own. They gain extra immediacy from being rendered in higher relief than the characters in Eden, while the curve of their frames imparts a sense of movement to the whole sequence.

In the panels beneath, the sequence of Old Testament stories, each delineated like a picture in its frame, extends downwards to the fluted piers, with emblematic roundels filling the two lowest tiers. The eight biblical images of the left-hand valve start with Adam naming the animals, a complex scene whose fecundity contrasts with the stark simplicity of the next, where Adam's second son, Abel, sacrifices the first lamb of their flock, while his older brother Cain looks jealously on. The straining, naked figures that dominate the panels of the next tier – constructing the Tower of Babel, building the Ark – evoke physical labour; the viewer senses the noise of the building-site and the sweat of toiling human forms. In the tier below, the animals enter the Ark, with elephants and giraffes waiting to board, leopards and antelopes climbing the gangplank, a quizzical chimpanzee sitting in the corner. This scene, brimming with incident and humour, leads to the emptiness of the Ark afloat on the flood: Noah's land-seeking dove flies out over a calm ocean, its surface broken only by flying-fish, Wilson filling the lower expanse of the tableau so as to emphasise the vastness of the seas and the vessel's isolation. Anxiety meets energy in the next tier down: Abraham, on the point of sacrificing his son Isaac, with an angel intervening in the nick of time; and Jacob wrestling with an angel, the fierce struggle of the figures infused with the muscular neoclassicism of Marple's walking St. Christopher of 1909.

The panels on the companion door of the Old Testament pair get underway with the story of Moses: Pharaoh's daughter watching her handmaid gather up the baby boy from the Nile's edge, then Moses, a grown man, in Pharaoh's palace, pleading for the Israelites' freedom to leave Egypt. The princess, clad in headdress and diaphanous robes, fanned by the servant at her shoulder, has the symmetry of a sarcophagus, while the might of the Pharaoh, in profile as if in a tomb painting, is accentuated by the slave cowering beside the throne. Stillness permeates the twin scenes of Moses's desert journey: the amazing sight of the Burning Bush, and the poisonous serpent miraculously turned into a staff. In the next tier, at the foot of Mount Sinai, Wilson juxtaposes the despair and rage of Moses at the Israelites' faithless worship of the Golden Calf, with his joy at striking living water from the dry rock. The narrative panels end with another Wilsonian angel, invisible to Balaam but clear to his donkey, which turns obediently away; and bring us to the Promised Land: a stave slung with vine-clusters carried home across the shoulders of two half-stripped vineyard workers, an image of plenty that recalls the Salada doors.

In the lowest two tiers of all four doors, square panels give way to roundels. To complete his Old Testament doors Wilson reinterprets the story of Creation in a series of emblematic discs, in deliberate contrast with the modelling of the narrative panels. The sequence starts with a Deco sunburst – God's hand creating light. As a secular modernist icon, the motif had pervaded the 1925 Paris Exposition on a scale ranging from the entire façade of the Galeries Lafayette pavilion down to the smallest printed fabric; Wilson, alert to its ancient pedigree in Egypt and the recent archaeological finds at Luxor, would have enjoyed its proximity to Pharaoh's daughter. With his steep bank of rainclouds hanging above the sea-covered rim of the world, Wilson conjures up the creation of water within a vast universal geometry; then the birth of sun, moon and stars evokes a shimmering, visionary firmament – Wilson as jeweller in bronze. Last in the upper tier come the birds of the air, great whales swimming below them. Beneath the creation of light, a line of precipices announces the emergence of land from water, Wilson providing a rocky foreground like the Manhattan waterfront imagined from an aerial viewpoint. The trees and plants of the following day are those of Wilson's tiaras or altar frontals, while the animals of the next roundel are prodigious, diverse and emblematic: the prowling lion, the elephant safeguarding its calf, the snake slithering across the foreground. Finally, God's hand reappears in a cloud to create man; from it shower down rays of life to rouse the naked Adam from sleep – if Blake had designed in bronze he would have recognised a fellow spirit at work here.

Early in 1930, the embodying in bronze of this first set of signs and wonders, as well as their as yet incomplete successors, was at last entrusted to Leblanc Barbedienne who, both to signal his eagerness to the Trustees and in anticipation of being awarded the contract, had had special sheds built in his yard at 30 Boulevard Poissonnière (Plate 63). According to Barbedienne's contract, initialled by Cram in March, he was to

> *furnish all materials and labor and make, finish and erect complete two pairs of bronze doors for the central entrance ... in accordance with detail drawings. Inside of doors to be paneled and ornamented ... [and] completed with bronze frames with substantial and easy working hinges, locks, etc. Full size working models will be furnished to you ... made by Henry Wilson, ... and will be suitable for use in making bronze castings. They will be delivered at your shop free of transportation charges. [All] to be of best quality cast statuary bronze. Modeling ... shall be done with the greatest delicacy and refinement and the chasing after [casting] to produce the very finest possible finish. All exposed portions of all bronze work are to be heavily gold plated by the nitrate mercury process.... Work is to be started at once and completed on or before July 31 1932.*

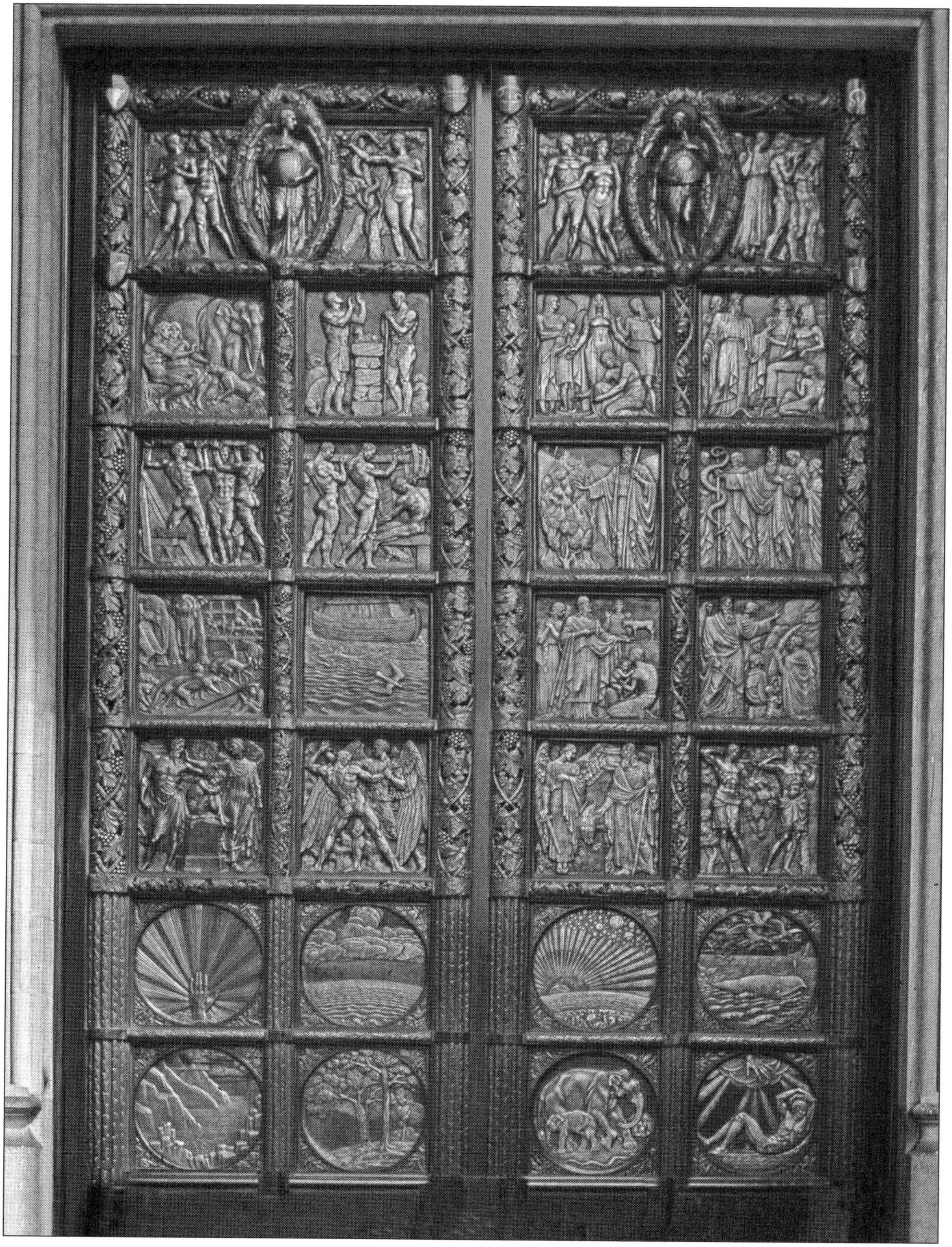

Figure 96. Cathedral of St. John the Divine, New York, Henry Wilson, West Doors, designed and modelled 1927-32, cast 1930-34, installed 1936: the Old Testament valves.

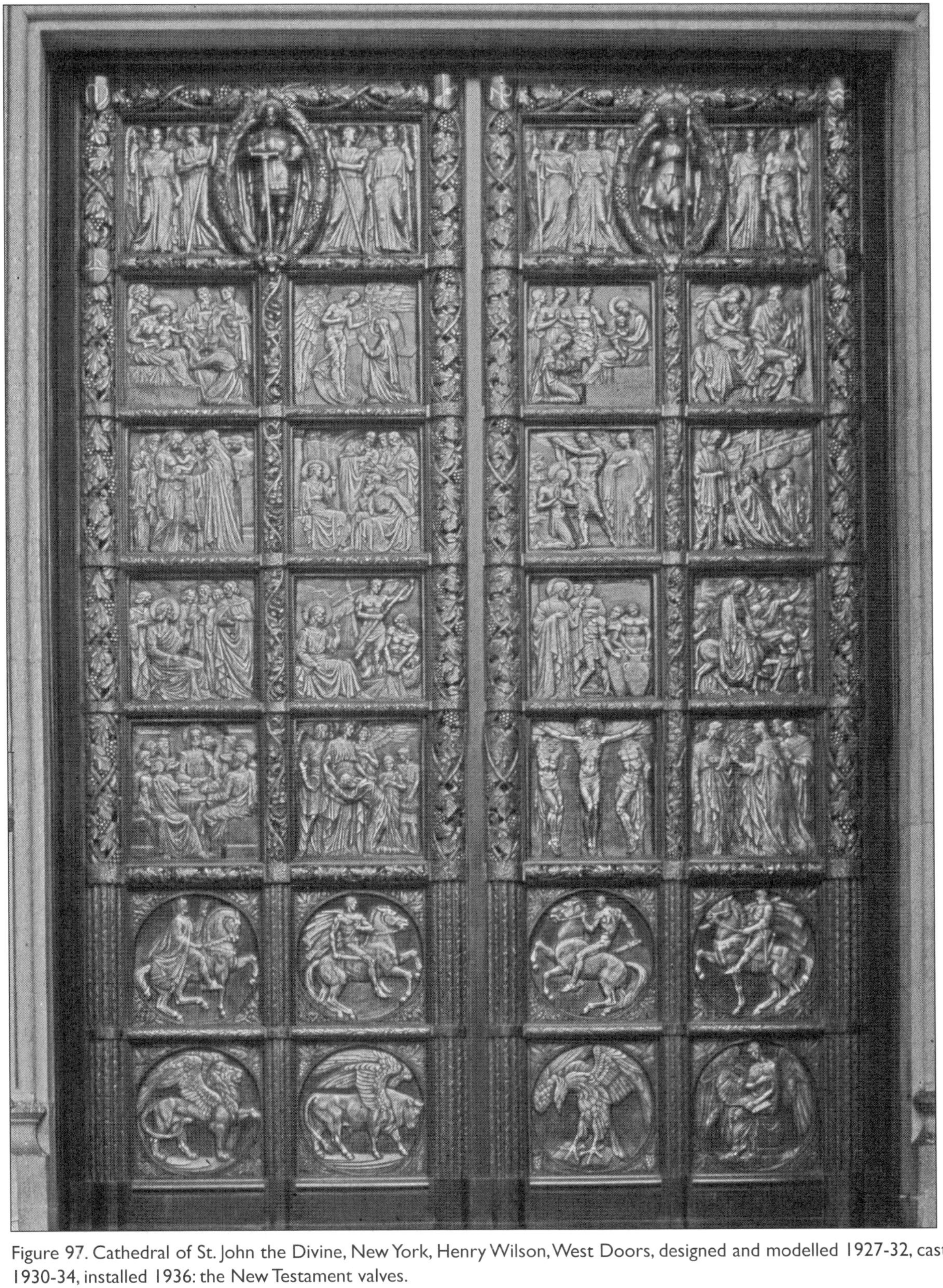

Figure 97. Cathedral of St. John the Divine, New York, Henry Wilson, West Doors, designed and modelled 1927-32, cast 1930-34, installed 1936: the New Testament valves.

On the issue of gilding, the architect, Trustees and sponsors had won out over the sculptor and Bishop Manning. As with Wilson's contract, the fees were specified and timetabled – a total of $29,000.00, inclusive of 'customs duties, taxes and all other charges', would be 'made by check on a New York bank'; of this, $7,500.00 would be paid on completion of the first pair of doors, $7,500.00 more when all were complete in the workshop, a further $7,500.00 when the doors were delivered to the Cathedral, and the balance of $7,500.00 thirty days after the doors had been installed and found satisfactory.[59] The signing of the contracts meant that, finally, the fees owed to Wilson could start to flow – so long as the Cathedral was willing to guarantee the full cost of the work. Ralph Cram's letter to Manning in November 1930 reads like a sigh of relief:

> *I am vastly relieved to learn this morning ... that Mr. Sinclair has at last agreed to an arrangement whereby the contracts for the Golden Doors, now held up for something over a year and a half, can be signed. It appears that the only possible delay may be due to Judge Finch postponing still further the preparation of the guarantee the Cathedral gives to Mr. Sinclair that the doors can be erected for $84,800.*[60]

Edward R. Finch, Associate Justice of the Supreme Court of New York, was to review these initial agreements made by Cram with Wilson and Barbedienne, and to adjust them as necessary to block any possible loopholes; Wilson signed his revised contract on 13 Jan 1931 at the British Consulate in Paris. It was countersigned on 25 March by Bishop Manning in New York, together with an equivalent document in respect of Barbedienne, while Judge Finch prepared the guarantee. In so doing, he made it clear that, in legal terms, the course that the Cathedral Architect and the Fiske Memorial Committee had taken to date was unsafe, in that it exposed all parties to risk:

> *In my opinion, solely because of the fact that the sculptor has performed work for approximately two years under the verbal authorisation of Mr. Cram, who as our architect might be held to have such authority from us, the best way out now for the Cathedral is to sign the contracts with the sculptor and with Barbedienne. This will, of course, impose the obligation on the Cathedral of paying ... for this work up to the time that the final installments are due.... [This] outcome is not satisfactory, but seems to me the best that can be done under the existing facts.*[61]

The contracts were at long last signed, the guarantee was in place, and it really did seem that from now on there would be no more delays. The problems still to beset the doors and their installation could scarcely be imagined, but for the 68-year-old Wilson they were for others to solve: in finishing all his models for the panels and frames of both pairs of doors and getting them to Barbedienne by June 1932, he had fulfilled his part. In December that year, by which time most of the Old Testament panels had been cast, the architect Jacques Gréber, Cram & Ferguson's representative in Paris, despatched his assistant to inspect the doors at Barbedienne's. Adrien Dumas duly reported on their quality and thoroughness:

> *... all the casting work so far is very remarkable; practically no chiselling will be necessary. All the delicacies of the plaster models both in figures and ornaments are remarkably well designed and I do not think that the casting work could have been better executed.*[62]

A particular reason for Dumas' visit was to broach – on Cram's and the Trustees' behalf – the matter of gilding the Golden Doors, using the nitrate mercury process. Barbedienne recoiled at the notion, feeling sure that such a surface would 'soon become black and ugly'. If the doors *must* be gold, then gold leaf would be the better bet, though both he and Dumas were aware of the disadvantage that the necessary base of at least two coats of size would impair the fine detail. As a permanent, dependable alternative to gilding he therefore proposed for Cram's consideration a 'very soft green Pompeian patina', as altogether 'more suitable for this style of sculpture and casting'.[63]

Their conversation also tackled the issue of the time needed to complete the work, which, after the delay in finalising the contracts, was already running some months behind schedule; Barbedienne assured Dumas that the two Old Testament valves would be assembled by the end of 1933, the outstanding work consisting chiefly of the bronze frame. The New Testament valves were as yet only one quarter cast, though the plaster models for them were ready and waiting.

In Wilson's New Testament doors (Fig. 97), groups of angels fill the upper friezes; Saints Michael and Gabriel occupy the twin vesicas. Below them Wilson unfolds the life of Christ. In the visit of the Magi, in portraying the child with hand outstretched, he referred to the composition in his 1896 chapel doors at Welbeck. Alongside, staged with the simple force of a mystery play, is the Annunciation. One tier down is the circumcision, beside the scene of Jesus in the temple: the listeners' rapt attention heightens the incongruousness of a mere youth expounding scripture to his elders. In the next tier, Christ's outlining of their commission to the disciples, leads on to Wilson's account of the miraculous draught of fishes, with the apostle at the gunwale opposite Jesus struggling to haul aboard a net pulsing with life. For the Last Supper, Wilson's positioning of the table so overtly at the front of the panel practically invites the viewer to join in, and, by a similar device in the next panel, to become a quiet observer in the scene with the angels comforting Jesus as, kneeling, he faces up to impending death.

The corresponding New Testament door begins with contiguous panels, the adoration of the shepherds and the flight into Egypt, which had Wilson consulting his sketchbooks for the working drawings for the 1904 bronze doors at St. Mary's, Nottingham. The next three scenes – the baptism of Jesus in Jordan, the calling of Peter, and, known at once by its giant clay jars, the wedding in Cana, where water was turned into wine – were all worked out especially for New York. Nottingham provided the scheme for the entry into Jerusalem, with Christ's donkey threading its slow way through a cheering crowd. Wilson reserves his greatest dramatic contrast for the lowest tier. His unflinching portrayal of the Crucifixion, with Christ's cross square to the viewer and the other two angled back and inwards, recalls in its grim finality the sombreness of the 1896 watercolour sketch for a new sculpted West front for St. Augustine's, Highgate, while developing the composition of the Lady Altar crucifix for St. Bartholomew's, Brighton, of five years later. But Wilson finishes with a hope not fully comprehended: the astonishment of the three softly-robed Marys as, in the garden of the tomb, they encounter the living Jesus. Wilson captures the scene, as if in a snapshot, with a sense of half-arrested movement.

As in their counterparts to the left of the central stone pier, the lower panels of the New Testament doors are composed of eight roundels. Here, the iconic task was suggested by the Cathedral's dedication – to St. John the Divine, and his vision on Patmos, as recounted in the book of Revelation, of the four horsemen of the Apocalypse. These harbingers of the Day of Judgement fill the first tier with authority and strength; and to bring the work, and the viewer's reading, to a conclusion, Wilson needed only to revisit drawings made in the course of his commission of 1923 for the 9'-tall silver processional cross for St. Matthew's, Westminster.[64] For this he had created in relief the emblematic winged creatures, man, lion, bull, eagle, that stand for the four canonical gospels. For Wilson, though, one of them, St. Mark's winged lion, went much further back – to his first independent church commission for Brithdir in 1895, where he had worked it into the foundation plaque. At St. John the Divine, it is perhaps the proud lion of St. Mark at the doors' bottom left-hand corner, modelled by Wilson in 1932 and cast by Barbedienne's men in 1933, that stands as signature to the whole colossal undertaking.

The finished casts of the New York doors had had one preliminary public outing, appropriately for Wilson and Barbedienne at the 1931 Salon, where their expressive and exquisite modelling, allied to sheer scale, made them a sensation. Wilson's creative energy spread onto their reverse planes, on which he lavished his skills in intricate low-relief work whose finish could withstand the severest scrutiny: released from the demands of narrative and theology, his pleasure in abstract pattern-making set rounds-within-squares and wove twigs, and birds, berries and roses into borders and sprays like the natural motifs in his silverwork and jewellery. It was here, destined to face Eastwards towards the High Altar of the Cathedral, that Wilson positioned the commemorative inscriptions, on a level at which they could be read without difficulty, beside the heavy drop-handles whose design he had scaled up from those on the Welbeck Chapel doors. One bore the doors' dedication to Haley Fiske for his life and work, the other the Trustees' acknowledgement of the generosity of Metropolitan Life as donor.[65]

At the Salon, the opportunity was taken to photograph the doors for Cram's records; Dumas secured the loan of the prints to help him monitor their progress through the foundry. In February 1931, knowing he was being watched with impatience from New York, and feeling anxieties of his own at having to proceed as the Depression tightened its grip, Barbedienne sought assurance from Dean Gates:

> *Since several months the world is disturbed by a financial crisis which has no precedent, values as steady as the pound sterling are depreciated and the British government is obliged to abandon the purity in gold. This situation compels us to confirm ... by letter that the price of $29.5000, [the] amount of our contract of 25 Feb 1931, is well in dollars gold....*[66]

Wilson's concerns, as his contribution to the doors drew to an end, were as much with caring for Margaret as with the fees he was due. All too conscious, as the winter of 1930-31 set in, of the uncomfortable situation persistently late payment had placed the Wilsons in, Cram reminded the Bishop of their plight.

> *I happen to know, as you do, that Wilson thinks he is old and is certainly not strong, while at present his wife is ill, and unless he had some money at once he could not get her out of the abominable Paris climate down to Menton.*[67]

However advanced Margaret and Harry's preparations may have been to withdraw to the warm South, there was one more visit to make – to England, to see family and friends, and to seek medical attention for Margaret before taking up permanent residence in Menton. They made the journey in the summer of 1931. But all further plans had to be abandoned when Margaret was taken seriously ill. She died in London on 26 August, and it fell to Harry to organise her burial, on 30 August 1931; it naturally took place in the churchyard of St. Mary's, Platt, and Wilson returned alone to the rue Feudon. In the studio, working on through the year, he completed the models for the second set of Cathedral doors, putting the finishing touches to them in the summer of 1932.

By now, though, Wilson's own health had begun to fail, weakened by grief and work, and undermined by the fact that his fees for the Cathedral doors had still not been settled in full. With only $42,500 of his bill paid, he wasted no further time and quit Paris for Menton.[68] It would be months before Cram sought to resume their correspondence. Unsure of exactly where a letter might find him, he sent copies of his letter of July 1933 to S. Cloud, and to the most likely hotel in Menton. One aim in writing was to keep Wilson informed of continuing worries in New York.

Barbedienne is certainly making the slowest kind of progress on the Golden Doors, much to the irritation of the Cathedral authorities. They have asked explicitly that we obtain a detailed statement of the dates on which the various models were delivered to [him]. Can you furnish such a list? It is long since I have heard from you and I am not sure just where you are at the present so I am sending a copy of this letter to the Hotel Splendid. I certainly hope by this time you have made an appreciable recovery in point of health. Always yours, Ralph.[69]

Its recipient in Menton will have been in no doubt that he was being used as a lever to move the work on, especially since, in his December report to the architects, Dumas had insisted that while he was 'rushing' Barbedienne as much as he could, the suspicion lingered 'that having executed a good deal of the work [he] did not push it as fast as he could'. The Dean had consulted Chester Godfrey on this very topic in the spring of 1933, his letter striking a weary note:

I wish your representative in Paris would do something to hurry up Barbedienne. If I am not mistaken they are exactly a year behind in their contract. Unfortunately their contract has no teeth in it so I suppose there is nothing we can do....[70]

Godfrey took this up at once, using his letter to Barbedienne to confirm their decision regarding the surface finish of the doors:

... the sample of gold plated bronze (re-your letter of 30 Jan 1933 termed 'dorure a l'or pur') is received and approved. Please do your very best with this plating and give it the treatment that will result in great durability. The owners are becoming extremely anxious to have these doors completed and installed.[71]

Settled now in Menton, and indeed, at the Hotel Splendid, Wilson was little inclined to join in the fuss, even though his own final payment depended on the foundry's completion of the doors. Writing to Cram, he brought the patience and understanding of a practical craftsman to the debate. His note was short, but made his views on the door's surface finish clear to his friend, who remained firmly, and, for Wilson, inexplicably, committed to their gold-plating.

My dear Ralph, It is indeed a long while since I heard from you. Barbedienne isn't really being slow. There is a great deal to do to the doors, it is the chasing which takes the longest time, and that cannot be hurried. They had the last door in plaster on June 2nd 1932 ... [and] all the framework for the second door. They had all the panels beforehand. Have you heard any more about the gilding? ... Hope you will have the doors you want, although personally I prefer patina, but there is something noble about gilt bronze whatever one may say ..[72]

The letter itself had been typed by Pernel: her father had burnt his last strength on the doors, and now, tired and frail, he had laid aside his pen with his tools. About the doors there was nothing more for him to say or do. As it turned out, the 'gilt bronze' of the doors behaved far from nobly, though that tortuous history was one which would not involve him. Barbedienne bit his lip over his preferred Pompeian green patina, carried out the Consultant Architect's instructions, and in the course of 1933, saw the doors gilded using the foundry's innovative 'dorure à l'or pur' process. He was counting on this new technique to cope with the challenges of New York's 'sea air'.[73] Furthermore, he reassured Dumas, having shown itself proof against tarnishing by incense smoke in a wide range of ecclesiastical ornaments, this gilt-bronze surface should be able to withstand the traffic fumes in Manhattan's atmosphere. Unlike the old nitrate process which involved mercury, Barbedienne's 'galvanoplastic' method submerged the pieces of cast bronze for six to seven hours in a bath of 'cyanore d'or',[74] through which a low voltage current was passed. If it had a drawback, it was to produce random highlights, but these could be toned down later using ordinary oil paints.

It was with this new galvanoplastic gilding that the doors arrived in New York aboard the S.S. Manhattan on 27 November 1935,[75] seventeen months adrift of Gréber's estimate to Cram of their being finished and installed by June 1934. Their passage from France had been arranged by the New York customs brokers and forwarders R.F. Downing & Co., who took care to remind the Dean that, as agreed in March 1931, their duty-free entry was dependant on the carrier who collected them from the dockside furnishing a letter of presentation addressed to the Cathedral by the donors, and a letter of acceptance from the Cathedral in return. These documents would serve to confirm the doors' status as works of art constituting a public monument, rather than as utilitarian objects attracting import duty.[76]

In addition to outlining their iconography, noting salient points about their designer and his 'unique ... genius', and commending their manufacturer's 'outstanding' craftsmanship, the souvenir booklet, issued by the Cathedral within appropriately gold-tinted covers, confidently announced that 'the bronze doors are entirely gold-plated, the first time the treatment has been used in this connection'.[77] But from the moment of their installation, at 11a.m. on the bitterly cold morning of Wednesday 22 January 1936, their ultra-modern gilding began to fall prey not simply to the expected air pollution, but also to the hazard of temperature extremes. In truth, from the outset, the Golden Doors presented a disappointingly mottled appearance, which soon deteriorated yet further. The specialist firm employed to remedy their shabby, patchwork look tried washing them, but to little effect – advice was even offered that they would best be painted battleship grey. In 1941, Bishop Manning took the drastic decision to have the gold removed altogether, using the 'experimental' technique of sandblasting, and, except for a period in the 1970s when the relief panels were regilded as if in emulation of Ghiberti's doors in Florence (Plate 64), the natural bronze that Wilson had always favoured was reinstated.[78]

But all these subsequent vicissitudes were well beyond the reach of their designer and maker. Wilson had died in Menton on 7 March 1934. Ralph Cram was vacationing in Bermuda at the time, and was only made aware of his death on returning to the office; a letter followed from Pernel, dated 9 August, informing him more personally of the 'tragic event'. He replied at once, telling of his 'distress and grief', and recalling some cherished memories of her father.

> *I had known him for many years; I think at least 30. I knew of him first indirectly through the exquisite things he did for Holy Trinity Sloane Street London, when he was associated with John D. Sedding. Then, when Mrs. Cram and I went down to see him in Kent. You were there at the time, were you not, as a small child? From then on I counted him as one of the nearest and most sympathetic friends I had. His death makes a vacancy in my life that no one else can quite fill.*[79]

His letter contained reassuring advice concerning the Cathedral's final payment to Wilson's estate, and ended with a simple yet moving verdict on the doors. 'I have seen portions of them at Barbedienne's place in Paris', he wrote, 'and I have no doubt whatever that they will be the finest sculptured doors ever produced during the last three centuries'.

Bishop Manning's dedicatory address was given on 2 February 1936 to a congregation that included Chester N. Godfrey (representing Cram & Ferguson) and Frederick H. Ecker (President of the Metropolitan Life Insurance Company), but, ironically, not Donald Sinclair, who had died in 1933. The Bishop greeted the new doors as the 'maturity and crowning achievement of Mr. Wilson's career.'[80] It was a fitting verdict: they stand as the summit of a life's work and thought, surpassing Wilson's earlier consecrated doors at Welbeck and Nottingham in the complexity and precision of their composition and modelling, while broadening the expressive range of their secular prototypes at Boston by harnessing conceptual and spiritual dimensions. Above all, they extend the validity of narrative into a fractured age that thought it had no room for narrative sculpture. The effect of this remarkable Cathedral entrance is one of awe and anticipation; the size of the doors is humbling, while their ordered variety sparks an irresistible compulsion to explore and 'read' them, like an invitingly detailed picture or a great illuminated book.

Throughout the long years of friendship with Cram, Wilson's career had never ceased evolving, its pathways continuously interweaving. His efforts as activist on behalf of an ideal, as publicist, exhibition animateur and champion of the British Institute of Industrial Art, were resourceful, forward-looking and unstinting. But it was as artist-craftsman, with the enduring aim, at whatever scale of endeavour, to create works of art that engaged with purposefully symbolic themes, that he made his most powerful and lasting impact. An observation Ashbee made about the unity within diversity of Wilson's artistic vision may be used equally well to focus on a brooch, the decorative interior schemes, or the West doors of St. John the Divine: in his old fellow-Guildsman's estimation, Henry Wilson came 'nearer than any Englishman to those Florentine jewellers who had their little shops on the Ponte Vecchio, and turned to necklaces, frescoes, or cathedrals indiscriminately'.[81] Wilson himself surely put his finger on the spirit of intuition underlying his own approach and achievements when, in the preface to the second edition of *Silverwork and Jewellery*, he wrote of those accomplished artists 'to whom nothing is secret, by whom nothing is withheld, and in whose souls the creative fire burns with unfading lustre'.[82]

EPILOGUE

'THE ARCH-INDIVIDUALIST'

Wilson would not have been in the least surprised, at any time in his career, to open a letter addressed to him in the conventional manner, then discover a message beginning 'Dear Peter'... He would have smiled, knowing that it came from one of a select few with whom he shared a deep and special bond. Partly, like its biblical counterpart, the designation implied a rock-like steadfastness; but chiefly, to them, it meant someone who held the Keys of the Kingdom – not to heaven, perhaps, but to memory and meaning. A letter with a Yorkshire postmark arrived for him at Platt in July 1906 starting in this way; it was from Emily, widow of Howard Stables, vicar of Far Headingley, concerning the altar cross she had commissioned for St. Chad's Church.[1] At the time Wilson was designing her late husband's gravestone in the churchyard, and would later undertake Stables' most splendid memorial, the copper and marble pulpit of Ripon Cathedral. Ralph Cram entered the circle soon afterwards – in artistic and spiritual terms he was on the same wavelength as Wilson, and habitually used the code-name, receiving letters signed 'Peter'[2] in return. 'Dear Peter' is how James Miller begins his note to Wilson about a new appointment at the Royal College. Chiding him for his reserve, Miller urges him to set down exactly, 'in black and white', what he wants in terms of title, hours and remuneration, for '... remember, there is only *one* Wilson'.[3]

In formal dealings then, and to the general public, he was Henry Wilson; to friends and family he was Harry – except for brother Edgar, who was in on the soubriquet: in a letter of 1928, relishing the privacy it implies, Wilson writes of some 'vague' ideas for stained glass, 'a very good lunch with Cooper' and longing to see 'son Guthlac', before signing himself 'Yours affectionately, P.'[2] The very existence of this trinity of names must modify Miller's 'one' Wilson, while also providing an effective reminder of Wilson's scepticism about categories, about labelling something as if that designation were entire and absolute. In his 1898 tribute to Sedding, he had been glad to describe his beloved master's work as the 'despair' of the 'classifying bookmaker,'[4] words that seem prophetically autobiographical. And as for definitions – well, these, Wilson warned, must never be taken too seriously:

> *Definitions are apt to be like Mother Hubbard. They open empty cupboards. Even when the bone is there it becomes the bone of contention.*[5]

This caveat is reassuring when considering the 'defining' aspects of Wilson's own career. There is no doubting the individuality of his creative vision, though it is tempting to pick out the roles with which he is most readily identified – as designer-craftsman, and especially, as jeweller and silversmith. Perhaps fewer know and treasure him as an architect. But such partial descriptions can never do justice to his many-sided creativity. Wilson was a designer in the broadest sense, a maker of thoughts as well as things. He comfortably embraced roles from opposite ends of the creative spectrum, from architect to enameller, from sensitive craftsman to empassioned writer and speaker. And critically, each of these roles profoundly shaped all the others: his buildings, like his sculptures, capture fine shades of feeling; jewels embody their own intricate architecture; lectures are crafted as carefully as decorative schemes.

Wilson remained active in each of his chosen spheres right up to the end of his career. He had never quite given up the idea of publishing the 'special work' on his jewellery Julius Hoffman had mooted soon after organising the Wilson illustrations for *Moderne Bauformen*: Wilson's jewels had 'greatly attracted his attention' and a volume about them was sure to be popular, *Silverwork and*

Jewellery having 'sold so well'.[6] Meanwhile, the Salada doors won their silver medal in the 1927 Paris Salon and the New York doors were acclaimed at that of 1931. By then, Wilson and his wife, both in their sixties, and with all four children following their chosen paths, were anxious to leave Paris behind, for the sake of Margaret's health: the South was beckoning.

Viewed from northern Europe, the benevolent climate of the Riviera seemed to grow in appeal: Harry and Margaret longed for its sunlight and restorative air. With its red-tiled roofs, set amidst olive and orange groves between the Alpes Maritimes and the sea, Menton had a medieval simplicity about it. Its terraced setting put Wilson in mind of his Brithdir commission of the 1890s; he had remarked at the time that St. Mark's, on its Welsh hillside, recalled those little churches 'just south of the Alps'. Besides, situated on the warm Mediterranean coast, the place shared the ethos of both France and Italy, countries to which both husband and wife felt instinctively drawn; in their conversations, they pronounced its name the Italian way, 'Mentone'.

By 1931, Margaret's condition had worsened. She was suffering from cancer, whose inexorable progress they could only hope to delay. The Wilsons decided to return to London for Margaret to receive the most up-to-date therapy then available, at the Radium Hospital in Fitzjohn's Avenue, but it was of no avail. Her death there, in Hampstead, in the late summer was a loss from which Wilson never fully recovered. As Frances Troup said, 'her death clouded the remainder of his life'.[7] Margaret was laid to rest in the chuchyard of St. Mary's, Platt, on 30 August 1931, her grave marked by a slab carved simply with name and dates. Its plainness made a poignant contrast with the memorial Wilson had created many years earlier for the same churchyard: in the workshops at The Thatched House, he had carved playful squirrels on the gravestone of the young son of a local family.[8]

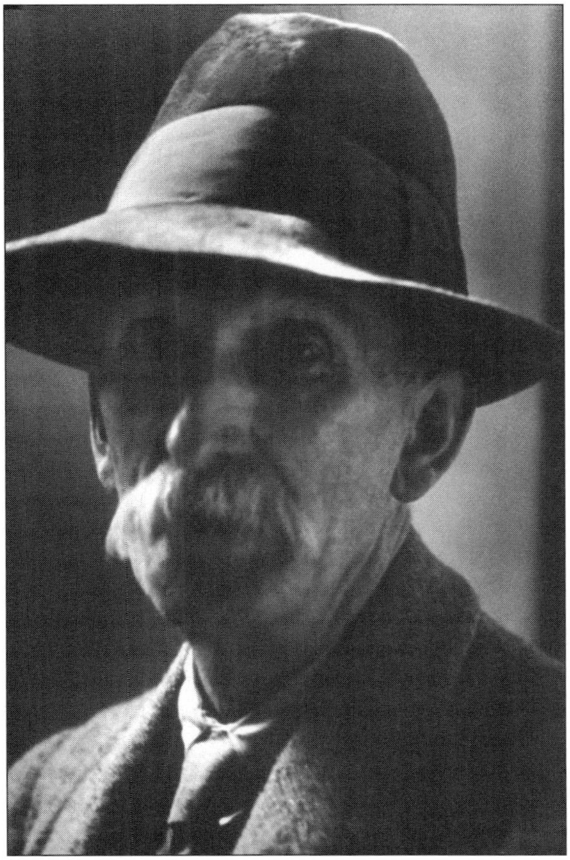

Private Collection

Figure 98. Henry Wilson in his late sixties.

After Margaret's funeral Wilson returned to S.Cloud, to clear the house and studio before making his solitary way to Menton. It was to the Hotel Splendid that he initially retreated, and it was there that he received Cram's letter in July 1933. Within weeks he had moved on to the quiet of the Hotel l'Amaurite for the final year of his life. The shock of bereavement accelerated his decline. Troubled with the frailties of old age, including the onset of Parkinson's disease, everything but reading had become more-or-less impossible for him: drawing was difficult, writing out of the question. Knowing that the New York doors were about to be realised sustained him for the next months. His own part of the task – the plaster models – had been finished in June 1932, but the final bronze casts were completed only shortly before his death, which came on 7 March 1934, five days before his seventieth birthday. The correspondence between the solicitors Morse & Co. of Aldersgate, London, acting for the Wilson estate, and the Cathedral of St. John the Divine, New York, lasted well beyond that date. The process of getting the money owed for the job paid dragged on until 1936 – the year, in fact, of the Golden Doors' dedication.[9]

Ashbee was right when he described Wilson as an 'arch-individualist' who was bound to be 'agin the world'.[10] He shared in many movements of the day and can be seen in many different ways, for just as his expertise eludes tidy delineation, so does his style. Recognisable stylistic and ideological threads emerge, including those of the Arts and Crafts movement and Art Nouveau. But to each he added something more: under his hand idiosyncracies of scale, unexpected fusions, and an allusive, spiritual and poetic dimension interlink to produce an effect which is uniquely, irreducibly Wilsonian.

The most familiar attitudes dominating the Arts and Crafts approach to design are ingrained in Wilson's work. His regard for tradition, for example, and a talent for bringing originality from it, is seen constantly in his reinterpretation of old forms. This forging of the known into something new was central to the movement, and exactly describes Ashbee's silver, Barnsley's furniture, Gimson's plasterwork, Lethaby's architecture. The impulse informs Wilson's own multifarious creativity, drawing on sources perhaps more arcane than those in common use but, mysteriously, appealing to an even deeper psychological reality. Indefinably remembered forms and methods were implicit in his use of traditionally-trained workmen, and in his desire to see age-old techniques resurrected. Jewellery processes like graining or painted enamel were reinvented for his caskets, lockets, buckles and brooches; the long-disused medium of flat-cast lead was revived for the font at Brithdir; repoussé metal sheathing, practically forgotten for generations, became one of his favourite decorative methods, adding Art Nouveau accents to his interiors and furnishings – almost, as in some of Mackintosh's or Townsend's or Reynolds-Stevens's decorative schemes, the sense of forbidden materials. It was as if Wilson had made real the technique Burne-Jones had visualised for King Cophetua's throne, or for the canopy above the sleeping Arthur in Avalon.

Over this apparently revivalist territory hangs a potential charge against the craft renaissance of the early twentieth century, of espousing mere stylistic nostalgia. The accusation was firmly rebutted by Hermann Muthesius. As an informed and discerning critic who was both authoritative and, significantly, there at the time, his judgment is invaluable. Numerous artists – he named Voysey, Nelson Dawson, Alexander Fisher, George Frampton, Charles Ricketts, and Ashbee – having once climbed on the shoulders of Morris, had confidently abandoned historical echoes to create a tradition 'of their own'. They were the 'representatives of a genuinely new style of artistic handicraft'. Wilson is placed firmly amongst them, but even so, is made exceptional: quite simply, as Muthesius said, his 'high artistic sensibility ... far outshines'[11] the rest.

The verdict is both generous and deserved. Through bold compositional invention and brilliant manipulation of sophisticated symbol-systems Wilson had created his own style. Forms of nature were a familiar, in effect, an almost necessary, theme of the Arts and Crafts; in Wilson's work they gained new and vivid freshness. Nature came naturally to his designs, both formally and through his chosen materials – semi-precious, unostentatious, redolent of symbolic value. Preferring to sketch directly from the natural world, the images he distilled from it vie for space, often at odd angles amidst the jottings in his notebooks, in a creative stream, like the small line-drawings within the text of *Silverwork and*

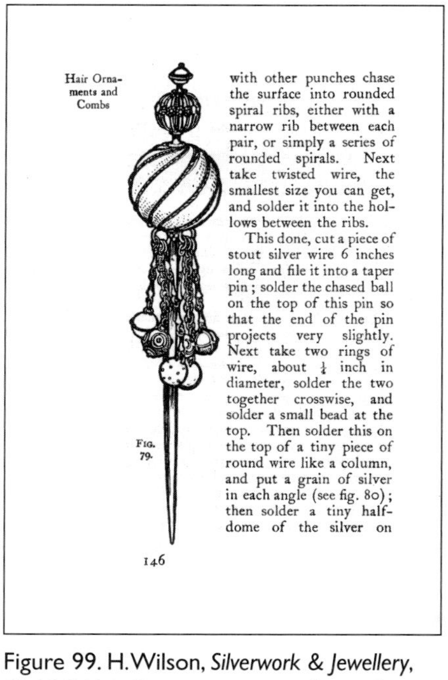
Hair Ornaments and Combs

with other punches chase the surface into rounded spiral ribs, either with a narrow rib between each pair, or simply a series of rounded spirals. Next take twisted wire, the smallest size you can get, and solder it into the hollows between the ribs.

This done, cut a piece of stout silver wire 6 inches long and file it into a taper pin; solder the chased ball on the top of this pin so that the end of the pin projects very slightly. Next take two rings of wire, about ¼ inch in diameter, solder the two together crosswise, and solder a small bead at the top. Then solder this on the top of a tiny piece of round wire like a column, and put a grain of silver in each angle (see fig. 80); then solder a tiny half-dome of the silver on

Fig. 79.

146

Figure 99. H. Wilson, *Silverwork & Jewellery, Ch. XVII Hair Ornaments*: a typical page layout.

Jewellery (Fig. 99), while in his sketchbooks ground-plans, architectural details, and studies for human or angelic forms proliferate, across double-page spreads if need be. Such guileless visual records formed his personal commonplace-books of design, aiding and abetting his imagination, flowing as easily as the ideas he penned beside them in his quick, unaffected handwriting.

Meanwhile his practical, often virtuoso, skills testified to a typically Arts and Crafts reverence for personal inspiration. But in Wilson's case this come with the strict proviso that it shun self-indulgent egotism which, he warned, leads 'to the asylum'[12] – an allusion, perhaps, to the loss through dementia of the younger George Gilbert Scott, a great talent from Sedding's generation.

The Arts and Crafts ideal of forming communities of craftsmen shines through Wilson's invitations to distinguished artists like Pomeroy and Powell, Christopher Whall, and his former protégé John Paul Cooper, to join in his archi-decorative projects from Welbeck to Wynyard. The same creative fellowship was intrinsic to his own workshops deep in the Kent countryside, and found expression in his plans for a complete craft village, though these were never pursued after the family moved to France. Productive collaboration was fundamental to the status he believed the crafts deserved, even – or *especially* – within industrial society. Such inclusivity shapes his every discussion of education, where his determined stress on the crucial links between craft, design and industry had led Robert Catterson-Smith, his former colleague at Birmingham School of Art, excitedly to concede how close his views came to 'revolution'.[13]

At the same time, a sensitivity to line, the most fundamental ingredient of the Art Nouveau style, flowed from his early association with the sweeping curves of Gothic architecture. His sympathetic translation of the sinuous, growing forms of nature, and his repertoire of surface effects from repoussé to inlay, in materials from marble to mosaic, irresistibly suggest the expressive terminology of the New Art – sumptuous, exuberant, inventive, organic. His metalwork often invites such descriptions: the Sloane Street railings, the Brighton chalice, Marple's font cover, the Lawley Parker casket all these easily fit Art Nouveau's stylistic criteria. His jewellery, with its profusion of natural forms, glowing colours and rich textures, shares the dynamic delicacy of the best of the style. In architecture the stylistic correlations are just as pronounced, as in the swirling tracery in the west window of St. Clement's, Bournemouth. Indeed, the original Ladbroke Grove Library competion drawings have been hailed as the first work of Art Nouveau in Europe,[14] though any such claim for the finished building was inevitably forfeited in its pared-down construction.

Yet Wilson's stylistic affinities with Art Nouveau, though striking, were selective. He recognised the virtues of the style, and was quick to acknowledge it as a potentially liberating force. He admired the success of 'the wonderful and wholly admirable Horta'[15] at combining structure, ornament and natural forms. He applauded the thoughtful approach of Van de Velde with his structural and functional honesty. Both designers, like Wilson, had used their architectural insights to create coherent frameworks for their formal ideas. But however much their styles might overlap with those of their European contemporaries, Arts and Crafts loyalists including Wilson were hostile to the excesses of Art Nouveau. He never specifically identified himself with the style, and it was predictable that later on he should have denounced it for the superficial 'monstrosities' its unthinking imitators produced. Given his stylistic independence and inveterate dislike of style without purpose, the prospect of aligning himself with what had degenerated into a banal fashion would have been anathema.

He himself had always used visual impact to direct attention to a design's underlying message, and his own versions of Art Nouveau were tempered with decorative restraint; crucially, too, they were mingled with other influences. Such was the case with his copper-sheathed pulpit for the Cathedral of Leeds and its district, St. Wilfrid's, Ripon. Dating from more-or-less midway through his career it is an impressive, characteristically symbolic design, and even in so bright and thronged an interior, capable of shocking at first sight. But this is the shock of recognition, like that felt when chancing upon his church at Brithdir, which strikes the finder with a recognition of its thought-through rightness, and a dawning sense of who it must be by.

Financed through the bequest of Howard Stables, vicar of Far Headingley, whose headstone his widow Emily had commissioned the previous year, the new pulpit was given the go-ahead in 1907. Busy with other work, Wilson did not begin the real task of designing it until 1910. It was finally installed by Charles Trask in 1913. Without actually imitating Gothic details it is unmistakeably Gothic in spirit, and subtly accords with the lines of the cathedral itself; its plan-form of semi-circular bays projecting from each of its four flat sides echoes the section of the nave pier against which it stands. In keeping with his ambition to restore neglected crafts, Wilson had already produced groundbreaking examples of sheathing in beaten metal – at Salcombe, Brighton, and Brithdir. These, together with his earlier work under Sedding, guaranteed a renewed interest in the gentler effects of metal overlay which, having been overshadowed during the Renaissance by casting in bronze, were in danger of being lost forever. With its softly gleaming hammered surfaces embellished with repoussé vines and figures, the Ripon pulpit (Figs. 100 and 101) sustains that precious sense of rediscovery. At the exposed corners of the bowl stand founding saints of early English Christianity: Cuthbert of Durham, Chad of Lichfield,

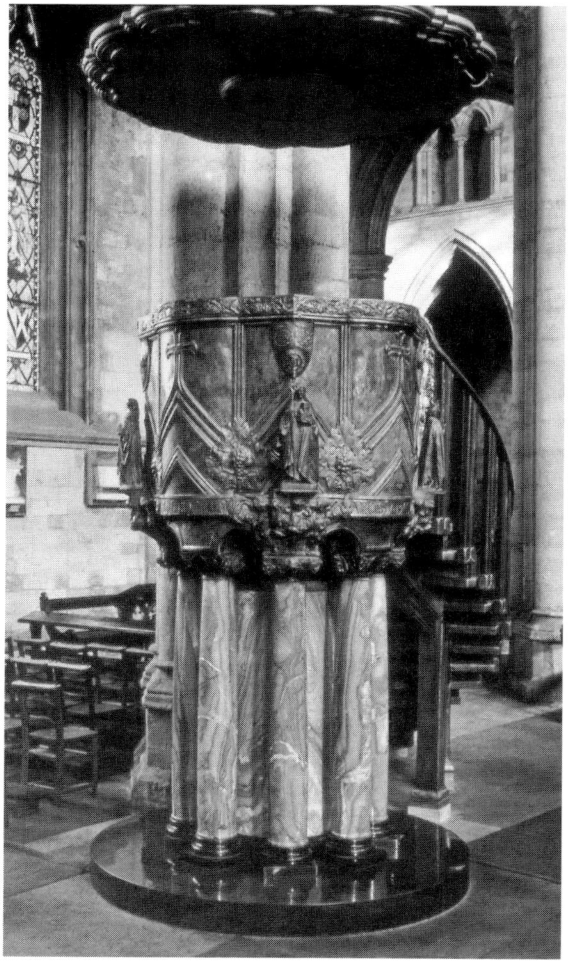

Wilson Archive, Royal College of Art

Figure 100. Cathedral of St. Wilfrid, Ripon: Henry Wilson, pulpit in bronze, copper, marble, timber, 1910-13.

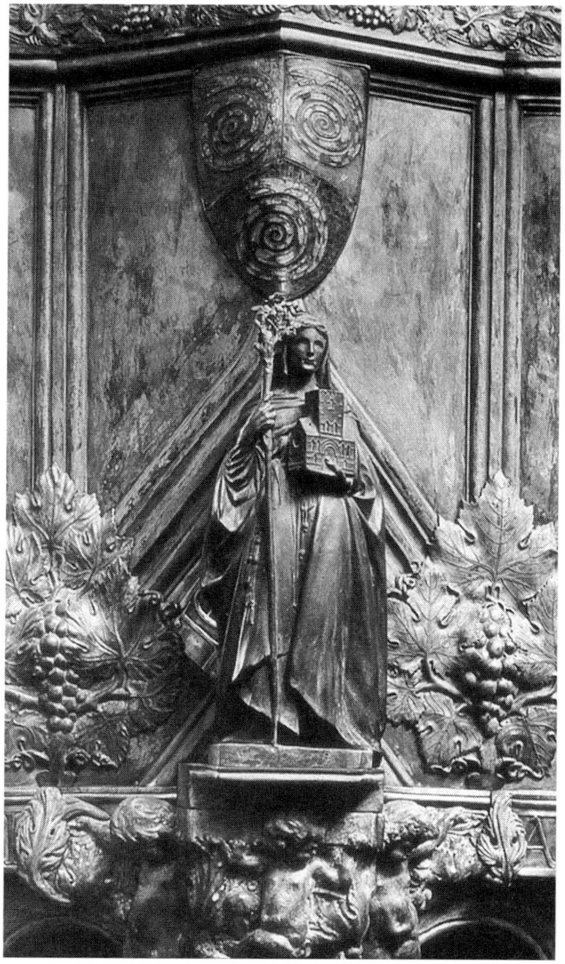

Figure 101. Ripon Cathedral pulpit: bronze detail showing St. Hilda of Whitby.

Ethelreda of Ely and Hilda of Whitby. Above each are the arms of their diocese, while beneath them are child angels – the Cardinal Virtues – entwined with curling vine leaves. A bold zig-zag band recalling that of the Lanteglos pulpit of 1903 encircles the bowl; its course is ingeniously followed by a raised inscription (traversing the pulpit's door, disappearing then re-emerging from behind the saints) that records Howard Stables's generosity. Set on a round plinth of black Belgian marble, the ring of supporting pillars of cream Cippolino marble is battered inwards and yoked together at capital height by shadowy copper-sheathed arches to give a feeling of mass and authority to the pulpit-bowl – the sense of which, as an enclosed vessel, is enhanced by the way the open treads of the stair wind up from behind, and round, the adjacent nave pier. The stair's rail, its rectilinear, hollow-box section emphasising its resolute, curved ascent, seems in its own way to share the modernist impulse of Gropius. The one element missing from this quintessential work is Wilson's blue-painted sounding-board, evoking the sky and integral to the pulpit's symbolism. It went missing in the 1920s, when a Jacobean tester, retrieved from the Deanery after years of service as a table, replaced it.

During the planning stage, Canon Danks, to whom Wilson addressed his correspondence about the pulpit, advised him not to worry about checking its every detail with the Cathedral authorities: far better, Danks confided, to let the final design 'spring on them whole like a tiger from its lair'.[16] Locked into the very heart of the building, where the nave meets the crossing, its blend of symbol and tradition, evocative forms and finely-crafted finish, continues to create just such an impact.

In fulfilling the dual claims of tradition and craft most of Wilson's designs seem at first sight anything but 'Modern': it would be impossible, for instance, to apply the term to the classical personae of the 1905 Tourist Trophy, and yet, ironically, what they permit the piece to celebrate is an essentially modern preoccupation, speed. On the other hand, despite his wish to sustain the currency of old forms, Wilson played a crucial role in the free design movement at the turn of nineteenth and twentieth centuries, an initiative which, aided by protagonists as diverse as Lethaby, Ashbee, Voysey and Mackintosh, would release design from dogmatic period imitation. The strangeness and originality of Wilson's scheme for St. Andrew's, Boscombe bears witness to his bold sense of innovation. So too, did his leading role in the proposal submitted by the Lethaby/Wilson team to the 1902 Liverpool Cathedral competition, a radical scheme in reinforced concrete that epitomises the pioneering spirit surging through British architecture at that moment, and attests to Wilson's flair as a form-builder on a monumental scale. Never likely to sway those then passing judgement, its honeycombed, loofah-shaped belfry, with the brio of Norman Foster's St. Mary Axe tower, remains an astonishing invention. The same openness to the new is evident in Wilson's support for the British Institute of Industral Art which welcomed both craftsmanship *and* industrial production. It was felt again in his admiration for the refreshing vigour of the Werkbund, in his thrill at the New York skyline, in the praise that he, like Le Corbusier, bestowed on the lines of modern ships – and in his recognition of the 1925 Paris Exposition as

> *partly realised prophesy. The germination of new ideas was visible everywhere. What intrigues one is what the ... oaks will be like which will surely spring from this acorn.*[17]

For all his faith in tradition, his outlook still belonged firmly to the present:

> *No-one in his senses wants to bring back the thirteenth or any other century. The opportunities, the wonder and promise of the present century are greater than all.*[18]

An arresting, perhaps unexpected parallel, may be drawn between Wilson's creative vision and that of modern art. In 1919, discussing recent art movements, Wilson acknowledged the common ground they shared with his own attitude to visual expression: 'no great art is ever realistic in the sense of literal accuracy'.[19] Given his recognition of the infinite complexity of humanity's emotional responses, he was bound to feel with the Symbolist painter Maurice Chabas[20] that 'the greatest error of the times' was to try to understand life simply through what was 'perceptible by our five senses'. A quality as elusive as the 'fleeting loveliness of a dream', for example, could be communicated only by symbol or synthesis. The 'heroic' attempts being made by the new schools of art to capture 'transitory moments of insight' by stripping away the 'details by which the world recognises things'[21] earned his sincere respect. Theirs was an approach which, though finding very different forms of expression from those he typically chose, reflected something of his own attitude: 'For myself, I can only say that what I draw is not what I see, and what I see I don't know how to draw'.[22] Most importantly, he knew that it was his systematic store of *ideas* which lay at the core of his originality:

Ideas are the only wealth. Creative energy is the only real estate.[23]

According to those who knew him, two distinct levels co-existed within Wilson's personality. The first impression he gave was of great modesty, of gentleness, of charm. But soon would emerge another – of vision, of astuteness, and of an intense, idealistic humanity. A short letter he wrote to his sister-in-law Winnie in March 1922, encompasses both. It begins chattily enough, acknowledging a thoughtful gift:

It was most awfully kind of you to remember my birthday. I had almost forgotten all about it, and would have done had not Margaret and the children reminded me. The cheese is delicious.... Quite a royal lunch therefore ...[24]

but soon opens into wider, shared concerns:

I do wish we could get our mean disorderly disgraceful and discredited government to do something human and helpful for the starving Russian children. It makes ones blood boil to think of our officials one & all....[25]

For Wilson it was entirely natural that a note of thanks should digress into thoughts on the aftermath of the Russian Revolution and Lloyd George's ineffectual coalition. As usual, there are no watertight compartments.

These same distinct levels are just as clearly visible in his designs as they were in his character. Initially a jewel, or a sculpture, or a building may impress with its colour, its craftsmanship, its sense of spontaneity. Any single piece can combine aspects of the Arts and Crafts, Art Nouveau, free Gothic, or the neo-Byzantine, and its message, told through archetype and symbol, may be embodied in richly allusive forms and materials. But beneath its outward expression lies the inspiration by which disparate elements are moulded into complex, vital entities. For all his craftsmanship and stylistic audacity, Wilson consistently maintained that it was the deeper emotions and thought processes which had contributed to a design, rather than their material testimony, that were truly impressive.

Man's greatest achievement is not the Parthenon, nor Rheims cathedral, nor the Taj, but his own brain. That is man's chef d'oevre.[26]

The intriguing, haunting quality of Wilson's work stems ultimately from a readiness to defy so-called correctness. Always present is the possibility of diverging from the orthodox to add a further dimension. The Elphinstone Tomb is rooted in the tradition of the Seven Virtues but, with the extra emblematic dimension Wilson awarded it, assumes the existence of eight. Jewels transcend craft and beauty to reveal intricate stories and significances. Within Wilson's cross-disciplinary overview, the chemistry of thought and feeling constantly produces curious, unexpected turns of design.

For Wilson, real individuality meant far more than simple ego; in fact, it was the egotistic component of personality, self-regarding and over-important, that was responsible 'for half the trouble in life'.[27] Instead, he embraced a mysterious, spiritual conception of the self, seeing every individual as the different expression of a hidden power. Each artist is merely an instrument, a tool in the hands of fate, realising ideas that 'are quite outside himself'.[28] Wilson was an influential and internationally regarded designer; but then, his modesty was apparent to all who knew him. Such a man, at the end of a long and largely fulfilled life, could declare

> *I am not successful; if an artist is successful there is something wrong with his ideals. The right ideals can never be reached.*[29]

His modesty was matched by his idealism, and a profound belief in 'the infinite perfectability of mankind'.[30] A faith in human insight flooded his designs, and a confidence in humanity's inclination for good never ceased to inform his thinking. That inexhaustible optimism would surface in the darkest days of world conflagration. In October 1915 he was in correspondence with George Bernard Shaw, seeking his support for craft teaching in their war-torn world. He caught the usually sanguine Irishman in the depths of disillusion, demanding of Wilson 'what's the use of preaching occupational education when it's impossible? I have shot my bolt about education'.[31] Wilson's stance resounded with an unwavering, practical energy. Conceding that England was 'slow to take ideas,' he insisted that plans for peacetime schemes were 'beginning to germinate', but would need 'constant tending' if they were to survive.[32] With three years yet to go before Armistice Day, the words ring with Wilson's tireless trust in human potential. Let this affecting aphorism, scrawled hurriedly in one of his notebooks, speak for the spirit of Wilson's entire life and career:

> *It is not the thing you have done that has value, but what you are going to do; not the thing you possess, but that you desire; not what you are, but what you hope to be that matters.*[33]

HENRY WILSON 1864-1934 – GAZETTEER

GAZETTEER

ENGLAND

BUCKINGHAMSHIRE

Stoke Poges: St. Giles's Church: Boer War memorial window in sanctuary depicting St. Michael and commemorating Frederick Alhusen, 1900; oval marble plaque in memory of Samuel Hickson for N. wall of chancel, 1920.

CHESHIRE

Low Marple: St. Martin's Church (by J.D. Sedding 1869-70): Lady Chapel and furnishings (altar cross and candlesticks, wafer box, altar rail) 1895-96; font cover and chain, 1900; N. aisle and Christopher Chapel, 1909; bronze bas-relief Great War memorial, 1924.
Brooklands: St. Mary's Church: wrought iron screen, 1907.

CORNWALL

Lanteglos-by-Fowey: St. Wyllow's Church: restoration and pulpit of oak inlaid with ebony, 1903.
Launceston: Church of St. Mary Magdalene: restoration; new choir stalls, 1892-94.

CUMBRIA

Ambleside: Charlotte Mason College leaving certificate, 1895 (coll. Ambleside Museum).

DEVON

Holbeton: Completion of Sedding's restoration, including altar rail, choir stalls, 1892.
Ilfracombe: Holy Trinity Church: vestry and lychgate, 1894.
Kenton: All Saints' Church: silver-sheathed cross on rood (originally for high altar, Exeter Cathedral) and small silver diamond-set companion cross, 1923.
Lynton: St. Mary's Church: proposal for tower exhibited R.A. 1892; addition of vestry and lychgate, 1892-3; rebuilding of nave and N. aisle, 1893-4; decoration of chancel, 1905; decoration and furnishing Lady Chapel, 1905-7; carved oak pulpit and lectern, 1905.
Salcombe: Holy Trinity Church: copper and enamel chancel gates, 1889-90. (Chancel to James Ball's 1844 church added by J.D. Sedding, 1889-90).
Shaldon: St. Peter's Church (by Edmund Sedding Jr., 1893-1902): altar rail with kneeling angels (originally for St. Martin's Church, Marple), installed in Lady Chapel, 1905.

DORSET

Weymouth: St. Mary's Church (built by James Hamilton 1815-17): paired circular stained glass windows, 1922 and 1923, either side of bell-tower and opening into organ loft, each depicting an angel, one playing a violin, the other a lute; glazed by James Powell & Son, in whose order books they appear as Job No. 5829 and 6149 (V&A Archive of Art & Design).

CO. DURHAM

Durham Cathedral: Processional cross made for Marchioness of Londonderry in memory of 6th Marquess, 1917.
Wynyard Hall: Decoration commissioned by 6th Marquess of Londonderry for private chapel, 1903-10; scheme of decoration (not executed) for monument room, c.1906.

GLOUCESTERSHIRE

Batsford Park: Alterations to house prior to 1st Lord Dulverton taking up residence, 1919.
Cirencester: Church of St. John the Baptist: silver and enamel alms dish, 1902.
Gloucester Cathedral: Marble and brass memorial tablet in S. transept to Canon Evan Evans, 1891; bronze and marble monument in N. aisle to Canon Edward Tinling, 1898; chalice, 1900; clockface in N. transept, c.1900.
Knowle: Completion of J.D. Sedding's 1890 Industrial Schools; refectory 1904.
Prinknash Abbey: Silver, enamel and crystal monstrance, 1910 (commissioned for Caldey Abbey), transferred to Prinknash in 1928.

HENRY WILSON 1864-1934 – GAZETTEER

HAMPSHIRE

Boscombe: Unpremiated competition entry for new church of St. Andrew, 1895 (ill. *The Builder* 4 January, 1896 p. 16).
Bournemouth: St. Clement's Church: West tower, 1889-93, in completion of Sedding's church of 1871-73.
Parkstone: St. Osmund's Church (begun by Livesay 1904; completed 1913-16 by E.S. Prior assisted by Arthur Grove): chancel screen in collaboration with Bainbridge Reynolds, 1914.
Fareham: Holy Trinity Church: mosaic over Lady Chapel altar, 1910-13 (installed 1922, painted over c. 1955); stained glass memorial window E. wall commemorating Helena Tylor and her two nephews, commissioned 1910, dedication revised 1918.
Itchen Stoke: Marble and bronze churchyard memorial to Margaret Skrine, 1913, commissioned by her father John Skrine, vicar of St. Peter-in-the-East, Oxford.

HERTFORDSHIRE

Much Hadham: Church of St. Andrew and the Holy Cross: grave with crucifix in churchyard for Frederick Norman, 1916; possible collaboration with Gaskin on altar cross, c. 1905; village war memorial, 1921.
Pitstone: St. Mary's Church: completion of Seddings's restoration; stained glass in S. aisle lancets; E window dedicated to Rev. Charles Hutchinson, 1891-93.
London Colney: Sculptural decoration, 1903, for façade of All Saints' Convent (built by Leonard Stokes, 1899-1903).

KENT

Kemsing: Church of St. Mary the Virgin: Collet and Skarratt gravestones in churchyard, 1905-22; Transfiguration window given by Dame Antonia Collet in memory of Sir Mark Wilks Collet, 1905; bronze bas-relief in baptistry depicting Virgin and Child set on green marble, 1922.
St. Mary's Platt: The Thatched House (the Wilson family home), 1902; St. Mary's Church: headstone in churchyard with squirrel carvings for grave of Percival Turner, 1904; memorial wall-plaque inside church to Rev. George Billing, 1907; gravestone for Margaret Wilson in churchyard annexe, 1931.
Tonbridge School: Gate of Remembrance in chapel, 1919 (damaged by fire 1988; partially reinstated against wall).
West Wickham: St. John's churchyard: headstone for the grave of J.D. Sedding and his wife Rose, 1891.

LANCASHIRE

Ardwick: St. Matthew's Church: altar cross and proposed processional cross, 1906-7.
Liverpool Cathedral Competition: Unpremiated design, 1902, submitted jointly with W.R. Lethaby, in collaboration with Robert Weir Schultz, F.W. Troup, Stirling Lee, Halsey Ricardo, Christopher Whall.
Rawtenstall: St. Mary's Church: unspecified fittings, 1907 (untraced).

LINCOLNSHIRE

Langworth: St. Hugh's Church, reconstructed 1960, originally commissioned by Frances, Duchess of Portland in 1901 as the private chapel of Walmsgate Hall, Burwell, in memory of her brother, Haliburton Dallas-Yorke.
Stamford: St. Mary's Church: completion during 1890s of Sedding's restoration.

LONDON

Kensington and Chelsea: Holy Trinity Church, Sloane Street, by J.D. Sedding and Henry Wilson, 1888-90. Completion and later additions by Wilson: gilt panels on chancel gates, 1891; pulpit, 1891-92; Lady Chapel and its surrounding screen and altar cross, 1899; organ screen (executed by Nelson Dawson), 1899; exterior railings, 1902; saints over choir stalls, 1904-05; plaster medallions in chancel spandrels, 1904; baptistry panel, 1907; flanking figures and arched entrance to N. chapel, c.1920.

Holy Trinity Church, Brompton Road: plaster relief in chancel, 1906.
Free Public Library, Ladbroke Grove, with T.P. Figgis, 1890.
Clerkenwell: Church of the Holy Redeemer, Exmouth Market, by J.D. Sedding, 1887-88: angels on baldacchino, c. 1891; completion of E. end, 1894; clergy house and campanile, 1904-5; decoration of Lady Chapel, 1907-09; font, 1908; parish room, 1915-16; All Souls' Chapel, 1921-22, with pietà in memory of Arthur Gladstone Shaw, d.26/6/1921; mortuary chamber, 1918; Poyntz memorial, 1925; Eyre memorial, 1927.
Finsbury: Completion to Sedding's design of Children's Hospital, Mark Street, 1893.
Highgate: St. Augustine's Church: nave completed to Sedding's design with some modifications, and addition of Lady Chapel with iron screen, 1893-95; unpremiated design for W. front, 1896 (Ill. *The Builder* 12 September 1896 p. 212), rejected in favour of 1912 design by J.H. Gibbons.
Holborn: St. Alban's Church: memorial tablet, c. 1892 to J.D. Sedding and his wife Rose, with enamel portraits by F.W. Pomeroy.
Lambeth: Memorial brass to Lettice Sarah Verney, with decorative border incorporating the words Dominus Illuminatum Mea, dedicated and installed 11 November 1908 in chapel (this enlarged and equipped with organ using funds from her father) of the Lady Margaret Hall Settlement, 129-133 Kennington Road (leased from Walcot Ed. Fdn). A student of L.M. Hall, Oxford 1894-97, she worked for the Settlement from October 1902 until her d.7 June, 1908. Spent six months a year working in the library and six months with the Invalid Children's Aid Association, providing accomodation for delicate children in cottages near her home, Claydon House, Winslow, Bucks.
Southwark: All Hallow's Church, Pepper Street: rood and choir stalls, 1896 (destroyed in World War II).
Stepney: St. Augustine's Church, Settle Street: mortuary chapel, parish hall, vestries 1897 (destroyed in World War II).
Sydenham: St. Bartholomew's Church: carved and painted reredos with repoussé medallions; altar cross and candlesticks 1903-05; oak altar rail, 1906.
Westminster: St. Matthew's Church: processional cross made for Anglo-Catholic Conference, 1923.

MIDDLESEX

Ealing: Completion of J.D. Sedding's commission for St. Peter's Church 1889-93: 'the work done may be entirely attributed to Wilson ...' (see C.A. Nicholson *Jnl RIBA* 14 April 1934).
Yiewsley: St. Matthew's Church: altar cross and candlesticks, 1898.

NORFOLK

Norwich Cathedral: Proposal with E. S. Prior for sculpted ciborium for Lady Chapel, 1915.

NORTHAMPTONSHIRE

Chipping Warden: Church of St. Peter and St. Paul: bronze eagle lectern, 1902.

NOTTINGHAMSHIRE

Welbeck Abbey: Completion and development of Sedding's 1889 commission by 6th Duke of Portland to convert Robert Smythson's riding school into Chapel and Library, 1893-1912: altar cross, eagle lectern, hanging lamps, font, 1893; baptistry gates, 1896; bronze chapel doors with pietà in memory of William Bentinck, 1903; completion of Sedding's altar frontal, 1890-93; library fireplace and inglenook, 1893; bronze plaque recording creation of library and chapel from former riding school, 1912; panelled entrance hall, 'dragon' landing with fireplace (in collaboration with F.W. Pomeroy); 'Virgins' Wing' print gallery with murals by Whall, plaster by Davis, 1897; Lion Gates, 1892.

Nottingham: St. Mary's Church: S. doors with bronze pietà, 1904- 5, dedicated to Wilson's father-in-law, Francis Morse.

OXFORDSHIRE

Somerton: St. James' Church: Barnes memorial in bronze and alabaster (in collaboration with F.W. Pomeroy), 1896-1903.

Oxford: Church of St. Peter-in-the East: sculpture of Virgin and Child, 1913, commissioned as gift to Glenalmond School chapel, Perthshire by Rev. J.H. Skrine, given to this church instead (untraced; see Ch. 8 n. 17).

SOMERSET

Bristol: Industrial Schools, Knowle 1890-96: completed by Wilson largely to Sedding's designs. Later additions: interior plasterwork, and refectory, 1904-06.

Charlton Adam: Church of St. Peter & St. Paul: restoration work including repairs to pulpit, 1892.

Norton-sub-Hamdon: St. Mary's Church: restoration of tower and W. end including tower screen, font, carved and painted exterior tower door, 1895; stained glass window for fiftieth wedding anniversary of Charles and Susan Trask, 1904.

Winsford: St. Mary's Church: completion of Sedding's restoration, 1891; Sedding died at the vicarage 7 April 1891.

SURREY

Richmond: Church of St. John the Divine (by Lewis Vulliamy 1831-36): following addition of Arthur Grove's 1905 chancel, Wilson made plaster bas-relief of the boy Jesus in Children's Corner, 1908-10; silver tabernacle, c. 1910.

Limpsfield Chart: Church of St. Andrew-on-the-Chart (by Reginald Blomfield, 1895): carved and coloured reredos, 1918; parish hall, 1918 (demolished 1950).

Woking: Maybury: House and Lodge, 1894, for Miss Graham, the Duchess of Portland's aunt (former converted into Mayhurst House Residential Care Home, 9 Mayhurst Avenue, dem. 2002; Lodge remains as 1 East Hill).

HENRY WILSON 1864-1934 – GAZETTEER

SUSSEX

Brighton: St. Bartholomew's Church (by Edmund Scott 1872-74): chalice and scheme for E. end extension, 1898; baldacchino, 1899-1900; Lady Altar, 1902; altar rail, 1905; pulpit, West gallery, 1906; choir stalls, 1907; giant standard candlesticks, font, 1908; statue of St. Bartholomew for West front, 1909.

WARWICKSHIRE

Birmingham: Chamberlain Casket, 1903 and Edward Lawley Parker Casket, 1906 (both in Birmingham Museum); altar candlesticks (untraced) for Birmingham Cathedral, c.1906 (ill. R.A. Cram's 1908 article in *Christian Art*).

Coventry: Sculptural embellishments for façade of Council House and clocktower, 1915-26; clockface, 1924; Council Chamber seating, 1917.

WILTSHIRE

South Marston: Church of St. Mary Magdalene: reredos, 1886.

Malmesbury: Design (unex.) for Hunting Lodge, exhibited Royal Academy, 1892 (ill. *The Builder* 1892 p. 395).

West Ashton: Church of St. John the Evangelist: memorial window, E. end, 1918-19.

YORKSHIRE

Far Headingley: St. Chad's Church: gravestone for Rev. W.H. Stables, 1906.

Ripon: Cathedral pulpit, 1913.

WALES

CARDIFF

Cardiff: St. Dyfrig's Church (by J.D. Sedding 1889-90): reredos, interior colouring, 1889-90.

GWYNEDD

Brithdir: St. Mark's, 1895-98.

PEMBROKESHIRE

Caldey Abbey,: Monstrance, 1910; transferred in 1928 to Prinknash Abbey, Gloucestershire.

SCOTLAND

ABERDEENSHIRE

Aberdeen University: MacRitchie Mace, 1907; Elphinstone Tomb, 1909-26 (intended for choir of King's College chapel, relocated 1945 to present site outside W. door).

LANARKSHIRE

Douglas Castle: Decoration of chapel, 1894-96 (dem. 1956).

STIRLINGSHIRE

Kippen Church: By William Stirling Jnr. & Snr. 1823-27, chancel by Reginald Fairlie 1924-28: bronze relief in chancel *Youth with the Cup of Life in his Hand* commissioned c. 1925 by Sir D.Y. Cameron (whose own works here include banner, S. wall of chancel); further works commissioned by Cameron for this church include silver vases and an alms dish by Edward Spencer of the Artificers' Guild, stained glass showing Faith, Hope and Charity by Herbert Hendrie, bronzes by Alfred Gilbert – *Charity* in baptistry, *St. Elizabeth and Virgin Mary* in Prayer Chapel – and a hanging lamp by Robert Lorimer in Prayer Chapel (a trial-cast for one in the Thistle Chapel, St. Giles's Cathedral).

HENRY WILSON 1864-1934 – GAZETTEER

OUTSIDE UK

USA

NEW YORK

New York City: Cathedral of St. John the Divine: West doors, 1927-32.

MASSACHUSETTS

Roxbury: St. James's Church: font cover, 1907, given by Thomas A. Forsyth in memory of his sister Margaret; transferred 1968 to St. Luke's Home for Convalescents (lost in 1970s).
Boston: Entrance doors for Salada Tea Co. head office, 330 Stuart Street, 1922-27.

CANADA

BRITISH COLUMBIA

Victoria: Unpremiated design for Christ Church Cathedral, 1893 (ill. *The Builder* 28 Oct 1893, *Academy Architecture* 1893).

ONTARIO

Toronto: St. Thomas's Church: votive lamp, 1907 (intended for Saragossa Cathedral, Spain); standing sanctuary lamp, 1906-7.

INDIA

Pune (Poona)**:** St. Andrew's Church, Solapur Road: two communion cups, 1907 (church now disused, cups untraced).

HENRY WILSON 1864-1934 - **CHRONOLOGY**

CHRONOLOGY

1864
Born 12 March, 91 Red Rock Street, West Derby, Liverpool.

1866
Family moves to Old School House, Cleobury Mortimer, Shropshire.

c. 1880
Student, Kidderminster School of Art.

c. 1882
Assistant to E.J. Shrewsbury, Maidenhead, Berks.

1884
'Improver' with John Oldrid Scott, London.

1886
Assistant to John Belcher, London.
Reredos, St. Mary Magdalene Church, South Marston, Wiltshire.

1888
Chief assistant to J.D. Sedding (d.1891) at 447 Oxford Street, London.

1887-88
Church of the Holy Redeemer, Clerkenwell, London, by J.D. Sedding.
Later additions by Wilson:
completion of E. end 1894,
clergy house and campanile 1904-05,
decoration of Lady Chapel 1907-09,
font 1908,
parish room 1915-16,
mortuary chamber 1918,
All Souls' Chapel 1921,
Poyntz memorial 1925,
Eyre memorial 1927.

1888-90
Holy Trinity Church, Sloane Street, London, by J.D. Sedding and Wilson.
Later additions by Wilson:
gilt panels on chancel gates 1891,
pulpit 1891-92,
Lady Chapel 1899,
organ screen 1899 (exec. by Nelson Dawson),
exterior railings 1902,
carved medallions in chancel spandrels 1904,
series of saints above choir-stalls 1904-05,
baptistry panel 1907.

1889-90
Chancel gates, Holy Trinity Church, Salcombe, Devon (chancel by Sedding).

1889-90
Reredos and interior colouring, St. Dyfrig's, Cardiff (built by Sedding in 1889).

1889-93
Tower, St. Clement's Church, Bournemouth (church by Sedding 1871-73).
St. Peter's church, Ealing, London. Sedding commission, which 'may be entirely attributed to Wilson' (C.A. Nicholson).

1890-91
Winning entry (with T.P. Figgis) in competition for Free Public Library, Ladbroke Grove, London.

1890-96
Industrial Schools, Knowle, Bristol: completed by Wilson to Sedding's designs. Refectory added by Wilson 1904. Chapel by G.F. Bodley 1900.

1891
d. of J.D. Sedding, 7 April.
Gravestone for J.D. Sedding and his wife Rose, St. John's churchyard, West Wickham, Kent.

1891-93
Restoration, with new E. window dedicated to C.R. Hutchinson, and stained glass in S. aisle, St. Mary's church, Pitstone, Buckinghamshire.

1892
Restoration, Church of St. Peter and St. Paul, Charlton Adam, Somerset.
Proposed Hunting Lodge, Malmesbury, Wiltshire.
Member of Art Workers' Guild from 8 January; elected to Committee 1898; Master 1917.
c. 1892-93 Rebuilding of nave and N. aisle St. Mary's Church, Lynton, Devon; proposal for new tower; addition of vestry and lychgate.
Later additions by Wilson:
decoration of chancel c. 1905; decoration and fittings for Lady Chapel completed 1905-07.

1892-94
Restoration, Church of St. Mary Magdalene, Launceston, Cornwall.

1893
Entry for competition for new cathedral, Victoria, B.C.

1893-95
Completion (largely to Sedding's designs) of nave, St. Augustine's Church, Highgate, London; addition and decoration of Lady Chapel.

HENRY WILSON 1864-1934 – **CHRONOLOGY**

Later proposal by Wilson:
new W. end elevation, 1896 (completed instead to design by J.H. Gibbon 1912).

1893-1912
Decoration of private chapel, library, staircase and print gallery, and proposal for Lion Gates, Welbeck Abbey, Worksop, Nottinghamshire, commission from 6th Duke of Portland.

1894
New vestries and lychgate, Holy Trinity Church, Ilfracombe, Devon.
House and Lodge, The Ridge, Maybury, Woking, Surrey, for Miss Graham, aunt of the Duchess of Portland (house dem. 2002).

1894-95
Restoration of W. end, St. Mary's Church, Norton-sub-Hamdon, Somerset, including tower door, tower screen and font.
Later addition by Wilson:
E. window, S. chapel, dedicated to Charles and Susan Trask.

1894-96
Decoration of chapel, Douglas Castle, Lanarkshire, commissioned by 12th Earl of Home (Castle and chapel dem. 1956).

1895
Competition entry for new church of St. Andrew, Boscombe, Hampshire.

1895-96
Lady Chapel and furnishings, St. Martin's Church, Marple, Cheshire. (Church by Sedding 1878).
Later additions by Wilson:
font cover 1900,
N. aisle and Christopher chapel 1909,
bronze relief war memorial 1924.

1895-98
St. Mark's Church, Brithdir, Merionethshire.

1896
Rood and choir stalls, All Hallows' Church, Pepper Street, Southwark (destroyed by bombing in World War Two).

1896-1901
Editor of The Architectural Review.

1896-1911
Teacher of Life Drawing, Central School of Arts and Crafts.

1897
Moves to 17, Vicarage Gate, Kensington. Partnership with Alexander Fisher until 1899.
Mortuary chapel, parish hall and vestries, St. Augustine's Church, Settle Street, Stepney (destroyed by bombing in World War Two).

1898
Altar cross and candlesticks, St. Matthew's Church, Yiewsley, Middlesex.
Tinling Memorial, Gloucester Cathedral.
Later work for Cathedral:
tablet in S. transept, to Canon Evans (d. 1891),
clock, north transept c. 1900,
chalice 1900.

1898-1910
Furnishings for St. Bartholomew's Church, Brighton, West Sussex (church by Edmund Scott 1872-4):
chalice; scheme for E. end extension 1898,
baldacchino 1899-1900,
Lady altar 1902,
pulpit 1906,
choir stalls 1907,
font 1908,
statue of St. Bartholomew for W. front 1909,
scheme for E. end rejected 1910.

1899-1925
Member of Council of International Society of Painters and Gravers.

1901
Married 1 August to Margaret Ellinor Morse, Savoy Chapel, London.
Private chapel, Walmsgate Hall, Lincolnshire (reconstructed 1960 as St. Hugh's Church, Langworth).

1901-06
Chancel decoration, St. Bartholomew's Church, Sydenham, London.

1901-12
Instructor of Goldsmithing, Royal College of Art.

1902
Moves to Kent.
Completes building of own home, The Thatched House, St. Mary's Platt, Kent, including studio and workshops.
Birth of Guthlac 12 April (d. 29 March 1953).
Liverpool Cathedral Competition; joint entry with W.R. Lethaby, F.W. Troup, R. Weir Schultz and Stirling Lee.
Alms dish, St. John's Church, Cirencester, Glos.
Bronze eagle lectern, Church of St. Peter and St. Paul, Chipping Warden, Northants.

1902-03
Silverwork and Jewellery: a textbook for students and workers in metal (completed Nov. 1902, pub. in Artistic Crafts series ed. W.R. Lethaby), John Hogg 1903.
Chamberlain Casket, commissioned by Birmingham Constitutional Club to present to Joseph Camberlain MP.

1903
Restoration; pulpit, St. Wyllow's Church, Lanteglos-by-Fowey, Cornwall.

1903-10
Decoration of façade, All Saints' Convent, (now Pastoral Centre) London Colney, Hertfordshire.(Built by Leonard Stokes 1899-1903).
Decoration of chapel (partly executed) and of monument room (not executed), Wynyard Park, Billingham, Co. Durham, for Marquess of Londonderry.

1904
Gravestone of Percival Turner, churchyard of St. Mary's Church, Platt, Kent.

1904-05
Bronze doors and pietà, St. Mary's Church, Nottingham (pietà design reused in Barnes memorial, St. James's Church, Somerton, Oxfordshire).
Birth of Fiammetta 3 February (d. 7 Aug 1940).

1905
Tourist Trophy, Automobile Club. (A.C., Pall Mall, London).

1905-06
Edward Lawley Parker casket, commissioned by Birmingham Corporation Water Committee.

1905-17
Examiner in Metalwork, Vittoria Street School for Jewellers and Silversmiths, Birmingham School of Art.

1905-22
Gravestones for Collet and Scarratt families in churchyard of St. Mary the Virgin, Kent; inside church, bronze relief beside font and Transfiguration window in S. wall.

1906
Registers maker's mark 7 May, London Assay Office: two versions of HW *monogram recorded, these varying chiefly in size, and used according to scale of piece to be marked*

HENRY WILSON 1864-1934 - **CHRONOLOGY**

Plaster relief, sanctuary, Holy Trinity Church, Brompton Road, London.
Birth of Pernel (stage name Orrea Pernel) 9 July (d. 23 February 1993).
Silver chafing dish with cherub finial (Goldsmiths' Hall).
Altar cross, St. Chad's Church, Far Headingley, Leeds; gravestone in churchyard for W.H. Stables.

1906-07
Altar and processional cross, St. Matthew's Church, Ardwick, Manchester.

1907
MacRitchie mace for Students' Representative Council, Aberdeen University.
Font cover, St. James's Church, Roxbury, Mass. commissioned by Ralph Adams Cram.
Votive lamp, commissioned for Saragossa Cathedral (now in St. John's Church, Huron Street, Toronto, Canada).
Wrought-iron screen, Brooklands Church, Cheshire.
Work displayed at Aix-la-Chapelle (Aachen) Exhibition of Church Art.
Brass memorial plaque to Rev. G. Billing, St. Mary's Church, Platt, Kent.

1908
Silver chafing dish with nude woman finial (Victoria & Albert Museum).
Wall plaque memorial to Lettice Sarah Verney, in chapel of Lady Margaret Hall Settlement, 129-31 Kennington Road (lost).
Wall plaque in memory of Rev. George Billing, N. wall St. Mary's Church, Platt, Kent; also here in churchyard: carved headstone for Percival Turner (1904) and in churchyard annexe, gravestone of Margaret Wilson (1931).
Chairman of L.C.C. Consultative Committee on teaching Goldsmiths' Work and Jewellery.

1909
Stained glass roundels showing angel musicians, St. Mary's Church, Weymouth, Dorset commissioned by Mary Hanbury, installed 1922 and 1923.
Düsseldorf Exhibition of Christian Art: award of German National Gold Medal for work shown, including scheme for extension of St. Bartholomew's, and Brighton and Gloucester chalices.
Birth of Dione 10 October (d. 18 December 1972).

HENRY WILSON 1864-1934 – **CHRONOLOGY**

1909-26
Elphinstone Tomb, Aberdeen University.

1910
Monstrance for Caldey Abbey (given to Prinknash Abbey 1928).
Application for Slade Professorship, Oxford University.
Leaves Arts & Crafts Exhibition Society (until1915).

1910-13
Mosaic reredos (installed 1922, plastered over in 1950s), and stained glass E. window (completed c. 1918) in memory of Mary Tylor and her two nephews, Holy Trinity Church, Fareham, Hampshire.

1912
Work displayed at Exhibition of Religious Art, Salon de Bruxelles.
Moves to 2778 Calle del Forno, Venice (until 1914).

1913
Memorial to Margaret Skrine, Itchen Stoke churchyard, Hampshire.
Pulpit, Ripon Cathedral.
Exhibition of Arts and Crafts, Ghent International.

1914
Exhibition of British Arts and Crafts, Pavillon de Marsan, Paris.
Moves back to The Thatched House, Platt (until 1922).

1915
Processional cross, Durham Cathedral.

1915-c. 26
Exterior sculptures, clock and furnishing of council chamber, Council House, Coventry, Warwickshire.

1915-22
President of the Arts and Crafts Exhibition Society.

1916
Gravestone for Frederick Norman, in St. Andrew's churchyard, Much Hadham, Hertfordshire; village war memorial, 1921.
11th Exhibition of Arts and Crafts Exhibition Society, Burlington House, London.

1917
Master, Art Workers' Guild.

1918
Reredos, Church of St. Andrew-on-the-Chart, Limpsfield Chart, Surrey, and memorial hall (latter dem.).

1918-19
East window, Church of St. John the Evangelist, West Ashton, Wiltshire.
Memorial Gate, Tonbridge School, Kent (following fire in chapel 1988, parts salvaged and reinstalled against wall).

1920
Member of Council of Governors, British Institute of Industrial Art.
Memorial plaque, N. wall of chancel, St. Giles's Church, Stoke Poges, Buckinghamshire.

1922
Moves to Paris, 4 rue Jules Simon, later to 11 bis rue Alphons Laurent. Studio at 1 rue Feudon, Quai Président Carnot.

1922-27
Bronze doors, Salada Tea Company headquarters, 330 Stuart Street, Boston, Mass.

1923
Silver-sheathed cross (originally for high altar, Exeter Cathedral) on rood beam, All Saints' Church, Kenton, Devon, commissioned with small companion cross (the latter retained by Cathedral).
Processional cross, St. Matthew's Church, Westminster.

1925
British Pavilion, Exposition International des Arts Décoratifs et Industriels Modernes, Paris.

1927
Silver medal awarded for Salada doors by Société des Artistes Français at Paris Salon.

1927-32
Bronze doors, Cathedral of St. John the Divine, New York (cast by Leblanc Barbedienne, Paris, 1930-34, installed and dedicated, 1936).

1931
Death of Margaret Wilson 26 August.
Moves to Hotel Splendid, then to Hotel l'Amaurite, Menton, France.
Gravestone of Margaret Wilson, churchyard annexe, St. Mary's Church, Platt, Kent.

1934
Dies 7 March at Hotel l'Amaurite.

HENRY WILSON 1864-1934 - **BIBLIOGRAPHY**

SELECT BIBLIOGRAPHY

Isabelle Anscombe and Charlotte Gere
Arts and Crafts in Britain and America (Academy Editions London, 1978).

Paul Atterbury and John Betjeman
Arts and Crafts to Art Deco: Harry Murphy (Antique Collectors' Club, 2005).

Nicholas Bullock
Building the Postwar World (Routlege, 2002).

Alan Crawford
C.R. Ashbee: architect, designer and romantic socialist (Yale University Press, 1985).

Elizabeth Cumming and Wendy Kaplan
The Arts and Crafts Movement (Thames and Hudson, 1991; 1995).

Peter Davey
Arts and Crafts Architecture: the search for earthly Paradise (Architectural Press, 1980).

Roger Dixon and Stefan Muthesius
Victorian Architecture (Thames & Hudson, 1978).

Charlotte Gere and Geoffrey Munn
Artists' Jewellery: Pre-Raphaelite to Arts and Crafts (Antique Collectors' Club, 1989).

Peter Hinks
Twentieth Century British Jewellery 1900-1980 (Faber and Faber, 1983).

Graham Hughes
Modern Jewelry: An International Survey 1890-1963 (Studio Books London, 1963).

N. Natasha Kuzmanovic
John Paul Cooper: Designer and Craftsman of the Arts and Crafts Movement (Sutton Publishing, 1999).

Lionel Lambourne
Utopian Craftsmen: The Arts and Crafts Movement from the Cotswolds to Chicago (Astragal Books London, 1980; Van Nostrand Reinhold Co., 1982).

Fiona MacCarthy
All Things Bright and Beautiful: Design in Britain 1830 to today (George Allen and Unwin, 1974).

Gillian Naylor
The Arts and Crafts Movement (Studio Vista London, 1971; 1980).

Frank Scarlett and Marjorie Townley
Arts Décoratifs 1925: A personal recollection of the Paris Exhibition (Academy Editions, 1975).

Alistair Service
Edwardian Architecture: a handbook to building design 1890-1914 (Thames and Hudson, 1977).

Douglas Shand Tucci
Church Building in Boston 1720-1970, with an introduction to the work of Ralph Adams Cram and the Boston Gothicists (Rumford Press, Concord, MA, 1974).

Douglas Shand Tucci
Ralph Adams Cram: Life and Architecture, vol. 1 Boston Bohemia 1881-1900 (University of Massachussetts Press, Amhurst, MA, 1995).

A. Symondsen & S. Bucknall
Sir Ninian Comper (Spire, 2006).

Giles Worsley
The British Stable (Yale University Press, 2004)

CATALOGUES

Sylvia Backmeyer & Theresa Gronberg (ed.)
W.R. Lethaby 1857-1931: Architecture, Design and Education (Lund Humphries, 1984).

Annette Carruthers
Ernest Gimson and the Cotswold Group of Craftsmen: A catalogue of works by Ernest Gimson, Ernest and Sidney Barnsley and Peter Waals in the collections of Leicestershire Museums, 1979).

Alan Crawford (ed.)
By Hammer and Hand: the Arts and Crafts Movement in Birmingham (Birmingham Museums and Art Gallery, 1984).

Charlotte Gere and Geoffrey Munn
Artists' Jewellery (Wartski, London 1989).

Ian Hamerton
W.A.S. Benson: Arts and Crafts luminary and

pioneer of Modern Design (Antique Collectors' Club, 2005).

Peter Howell
Victorian Churches (RIBA 1979).

Beauty's Awakening: centenary exhibition of the Art Workers' Guild 1884-1984 (Brighton Museum, 1984).

Victorian Church Art (Victoria and Albert Museum, 1971).

ARTICLES

Ian Allen (ed.)
'Henry Wilson and St. Mark's Brithdir' Open University A305, 1980 (Microfiche, RIBA).

'Arts and Crafts Loyalist',
Julian Browning. *Country Life* 12 Sept. 1974.

'Alien Styles in Harmony',
Mary Corbett Harris. *Country Life* 16 Sept. 1976.

'Henry Wilson's Welsh Church',
Cyndy Manton. *Fad or Function* (Design Council, 1978).

'Byzantium in Brighton: furnishings of St. Bartholomew's church', Nicholas Taylor. *Architectural Review* April 1966.

CONTEMPORARY PERIODICALS

Studio; *The Architectural Review*; *The Builder*; *The Architect*

COLLECTIONS

Wilson Archive, Royal College of Art

Orrea Pernel, Biographical Note, National Art Library

HENRY WILSON 1864-1934 - **BIBLIOGRAPHY**

The Life and Times of Edgar Augustus Wilson: an autobiography, British Library

Victoria & Albert Museum: Jewellery and Silverwork Collections, also Prints and Drawings Collection, Art & Design Archive

Drawings Collection, RIBA at V&A

Cheltenham Art Gallery & Museum

Hull Grundy Bequest, Fitzwilliam Museum, Cambridge

Birmingham Museums and Art Gallery

Goldsmiths' Hall

Glasgow Museum

ABBREVIATIONS

A.A.B.H.
Association of Architecture Building and Handicraft

A.C.E.S.
Arts and Crafts Exhibition Society

AR
The Architectural Review

A.W.G.
Art Workers' Guild

B.I.I.A.
British Institute of Industrial Art

D.I.A.
Design and Industries Association

RA
Royal Academy

RCA
Royal College of Art

RIBA
Royal Institute of British Architects

RIBADC
RIBA Drawings Collection at V&A

THE WILSON FAMILY TREE

William Henry WILSON
born 11 Jul 1834 - Snodland, Kent
died 29 Jul 1914 - W. Malling, Kent

m(i) **Clara Louisa BROADLEY**
born 17 Dec 1836 - Huddersfield
married 1 Jul 1863 - Kirkheaton
died 16 May 1898 - Sudbury, Mdx

m(ii) **Elizabeth Mary WELDON**
born 6 Jun 1869 - Snodland, Kent
married Aug 1904 - Trotterscliffe, Kent
died 21 Apr 1930 - St. Albans, Herts.

Harry

Marion
born 29 Oct 1865
died 9 Jul 1870

Theodore
born 16 Jul 1867
died 28 Sep 1867

Patten
born 23 Mar 1869
married(i) 16 Jun 1900
Alice HARDING
St. George's Church, Hanover Square, London
married(ii) 31 Mar 1921
Florence FACEY
Hither Green Wesleyan Church
died 22 Jan 1934 - London

Edgar Augustus
born 14 Apr 1873
married(i) 13 Apr 1901
Isabel May CLARK
Christchurch, Streatham
married(ii) 10 Dec 1912
Winifred COOPER
American Presbyterian Church, Iran
died 13 Feb 1954 - St. Albans

HARRY'S DESCENDENTS

Harry WILSON = **Margaret Elinor MORSE**

Harry WILSON
born 12 Mar 1864 - 91 Red Rock Street, Liverpool
married 1 Aug 1901 - Savoy Chapel, London
died 7 Mar 1934 - Hotel l'Amaurite, Menton

Margaret Elinor MORSE
born 21 Nov 1869 - High Pavement, Nottingham
married 1 Aug 1901 - Savoy Chapel, London
died 26 Aug 1931 - Hampstead, London

Guthlac
born 21 Apr 1902
died 29 Mar 1953

Fiammetta
born 3 Feb 1904
died 7 Aug 1940

Pernel
born 9 Aug 1906
died 23 Feb 1993

Dione
born 10 Oct 1909
died 18 Dec 1972

THE OTHER HENRY WILSON (1849-99)

Investigating the life of Henry Wilson – the Wilson of Brithdir and Brighton, of Welbeck and Aberdeen, the consummate sculptor, silversmith and jeweller, the eloquent writer, teacher and Arts and Craftsman whose work is so memorably represented both in the UK and the US – reveals another nineteenth-century architect named Henry Wilson. It might be regretted that the JD-trained Henry Wilson ever departed from his real name, Harry; and that, in a generation when middle names were common, neither had a second initial. Again fuelling potential confusion, the *other* Henry Wilson had his office in London in the 1890s, though in Gray's Inn rather than Kensington. It is unlikely that Harry was aware of the short and largely unrecorded career of his semi-namesake; but his using Henry as an alternative (if inadvertently shared) forename forms a curious reminder of his aversion to pigeon-holing.

'Gray's Inn' Wilson was born in 1849, and was married and widowed by 1882. Following his wife's death he lived with the family of her brother Henry Stall, also an architect, at 'Crowhurst', Uxbridge Road, subsequently moving to 'Hawkhurst,' Muswell Hill. His London work included the Clergy House c. 1891 attached to George Gilbert Scott's church of St. Matthew, in Great Peter Street, Westminster, where remarkably the paths of Henry and Harry would converge – if separated by some 33 years – when Harry, in 1923, made his processional cross for St. Matthew's; a further 'Gray's Inn' Wilson commission, a brick-built Hall, dating from the early 1890s, was completed for the Mission of the Good Shepherd, St. Matthew Street (destroyed in the Blitz). However, his most substantial work was outside London: the Hospital of St. Cross, Barby Road, Rugby. Its attribution by Sir Nicholaus Pevsner in his *Buildings of Warwickshire* to H. Wilson is not wrong, but he was referring (knowingly or not) to this *other* Henry Wilson. The solid red brick building of 1882-84 in late Gothic domestic style, with black brick patterns and Bath stone dressings, reflects the Butterfieldian architecture of the nearby Rugby School. The neat, careful signature on its plans is patently not the free-flowing one to be seen in the drawings of Harry Wilson, who, aged around 18 at the time of the Hospital's commission, had only just left Kidderminster School of Art, and was embarking on his first professional position, a two-year stint as assistant in the Maidenhead office of E.J. Shrewsbury. Originally comprising three wards accommodating 31 patients and with the latest operating theatres and convalescent rooms, the Hospital was endowed by a wealthy local benefactor, the former Manchester sharedealer R.H. Wood. With its various modern extensions, it functions still as a local hospital.

'Gray's Inn' Wilson's final commission was for a meeting house and domestic quarters in Dartmouth Street, Westminster, for the Society of St. John the Evangelist. In anticipation, this strict, aescetic brotherhood had purchased the existing houses at numbers 13-15. A fourth, at 12 or 16, was acquired soon after. In his office at 8 Gray's Inn Square, Wilson calculated the conversions and demolitions that would be needed, tailoring his designs to fit the limited site available. His proposals were printed in miniature for distribution to potential donors. It was only then that the Society raised serious objections to the whole idea: belatedly, they had recognised the unsuitablity of the site, its being too cramped and, given its proximity to the Imperial Theatre, entirely inimicable to prayer and meditation.

'Gray's Inn' Wilson died suddenly on 23 June 1899 at work in his office, wrestling with the Society's misgivings about the project. The Dartmouth Street dilemma was left for the architect who took over his practice – Edward Burgess of 6 South Square, Gray's Inn – to resolve. In the end, nothing new was built on the site; the Society purchased another one at 22 Great College Street, and Burgess's design for St. Edmund's House was completed for it there in 1904.

B.F.L. Clarke. *Parish Churches of London* (1966) p. 187-8

National Probate Calendars to Wills and Administrations.

St. Matthew's, Westminster 1851-1951 (1947; City of Westminster Archives Centre)

Rugby Advertiser, 23 December 1882, 10 July 1884.

Rugby Past and Present. Rev. W.O. Wait (1893, Frost & Sons, Rugby).

Rugby News and District Observer (Bazaar Supplement) 15 October 1898.

Kelly's Directory of Birmingham, Staffs, Warwicks and Worcs 1884.

Illustrated Rugby Family Almanack 1887.

Cowley Evangelist 1897-1904 (London).

NOTES

INTRODUCTION
'PERHAPS THE GREATEST ARTIST OF THE LOT.'

1. H. Wilson. *Silverwork and Jewellery* Ch. XIX p. 176. The edition used throughout is the 1978 Pitman/Taplinger facsimile reprint of the 1912 second edition of *Silverwork and Jewellery: a text-book for students and metal by H. Wilson. With diagrams by the author and other illustrations. Second edition, with new sections done in collaboration with Professor Unno Bisei of the Imperial Fine Art college, Tokyo.* While all records agree on the date of this second edition, a discrepancy may appear regarding that of the first. The title page of the John Hogg edition shows the date 1903, and its publication in January that year is confirmed by both the British Library's General Retrospective Catalogue and Whitaker's Cumulative Book List, although some sources cite 1902. The discrepancy stems partly from Troup's recalling, and recording in his obituary on Wilson for *Jnl RIBA*, his friend's finishing the book in the autumn of 1902, and partly from successive printers assuming that the book's first publication date matched that of the Author's Preface, dated in the first John Hogg edition November 1902. The Editor's Preface lends credence to the assumption, being dated November 1902, although Lethaby's editorial remarks were penned early on as a general opening for each of the many titles in the Artistic Crafts Series of Technical Handbooks, including Wilson's.
2. C.R. Ashbee. *Ashbee Memoirs* (1938) Vol.1 The Guild Idea p. 115 (V&A Library).
3. C.R. Ashbee. *Masters of the Art Workers' Guild from the beginning till 1934.* p. 315-6 (AWG m/s).
4. H. Muthesius. *The English House* (1904-5) trans. J. Seligman (1979) p. 45.
5. H. Wilson. 'Some considerations of John Sedding's work'. AR I 1897-8 p. 237.
6. H. Wilson. 'The Work of Sir Edward Burne-Jones' (i). AR I 1896 p. 17.
7. H. Wilson. *Silverwork and Jewellery* (1903) Ch. I Introduction p. 28.
8. H. Wilson. *The Economic Problem in the Moveable Arts.* (Wilson Archive RCA).
9. C.R. Ashbee. *Masters of the Art Workers' Guild from the beginning till 1934.* p. 315-6 (AWG m/s).
10. C.R. Ashbee. *Ashbee Memoirs* (1938) (V&A Library). In his fuller *Journal* for September 1902 (King's College Library, Cambridge) Ashbee includes Cecil Brewer (1871-1918).
11. C.A. Nicholson. Obituary: H. Wilson. *Jnl RIBA* 14 April 1934.
12. H. Wilson. 'The Town Planning Movement.' (c. 1916; Wilson Archive RCA).
13. D.S. MacColl. Letter to the Editors with editorial reply. AR CII 1947 p. 142-4.
14. H. Wilson. Lecture given at Montreux: 'How are we going to give a new heart to humanity?' c. 1912; and 'The Arts and Crafts Movement' c. 1918 (Wilson Archive RCA).
15. Review of 'Silverwork and Jewellery' (Second Edition). *Architectural Review* XXXII 1912 p. 111-12.
16. H. Wilson. *Address to Goldsmiths', Silversmiths', Jewellers' and Allied Trades' Art Council at the presentation of prizes to workmen and apprentices at Goldsmiths' Hall 1908.* Printed in *The Watchmaker,* January 1909 (Wilson Archive RCA).
17. Letter from James Cromar Watt, 71 Dee Street, Aberdeen. 21 August 1906. (Wilson Archive RCA).
18. Letter from C. Whall. 20 August 1915. (Wilson Archive RCA). The letter continues 'He has great ideas of doing things in a widespread way, but he puts workers off – they say Look at his work!' His skills comprised only rudimentary ones in modelling.
19. H. Wilson. Letter to Edgar Wilson from 1 rue Feudon, Quai President Carnot, S. Cloud. (Wilson Archive RCA).
20. Brown-Morrison. Letter to M. Beasley, March 1959. (Coll. D. Ottewill, Portsmouth).
21. H. Wilson. 'Notes on Collet Memorial' (V. E. Bowden, church historian, Kemsing). The tomb was commissioned by Dame Antonia Collet and her son Mark as a memorial to her husband Sir Mark Wilks Collet (1816-1905) and to members of the Skarratt family, who were related to them by marriage; with its memorial cross it forms part of a group of monuments (Drawings Collection PA529/9). Wilson explains that the tomb, which consists of 'a hollow stone slab (like an altar)' is set on four bronze pillars which represent the 'fourfold nature of humanity: Body, Soul, Spirit and Ether'. The stag on each pillar represents the soul, regeneration, Diana and the moon. The rose bush around the edge of the slab is an emblem of 'existence within existence', and the birds' nests in its branches, of human life. On each side is a shield symbolising the elements – the olive tree of earth, a ship for air, a wave for water, and a phoenix, fire.
    Inside the church are two further works by Wilson: an oval bronze bas-relief of the Virgin and Child c. 1922, intended, but found unsuitable, for Dame Antonia's grave which is situated outside, next to Sir Mark's; and a three-light stained glass window (c. 1905) commissioned by Dame Antonia in memory of her husband. Located in the South wall, it was glazed by Whall and depicts the Transfiguration (Plate 49). Christ is at the centre, crowned with thorns and with child angels above. In profile to the left is the figure of Moses holding a book, based on a sketch made by Wilson of his father (Plate 2); the saint to the right was modelled on Lord Norman of St. Clere as a young man. Wilson's portrayal of his father was reused for the bas-relief of Isaiah in one of the spandrels of the nave arches at Holy Trinity, Sloane Street c. 1904-05.
22. H. Wilson. *Silverwork and Jewellery* Ch. XI p. 93.
23. Letter from Frances Gibson, The White House, Lansdowne Road, Aldershot 13 December 1906. (Wilson Archive RCA).
24. Brown-Morrison. Letter to M. Beasley, March 1959. (Coll. D. Ottewill, Portsmouth).
25. E.D. Sedding in *St. Bartholomew's Parish Magazine,* September 1952. St. Bartholomew's church, Brighton.
26. H. Wilson. *De Quelques Caracteres de la Renaissance de l'art du Jouilleur en Angleterre,* 1914. (Wilson Archive RCA).
27. H. Wilson. 'The Gates of Wonder'. Undated lecture. (Wilson Archive RCA).

28. Letter from W.R. Lethaby, 111 Inverness Terrace, London 15 June 1917 (Wilson Archive RCA).
29. Letter from E. Gimson. 15 June 1917 (Wilson Archive RCA).
30. H. Wilson. On Workmanship (1912) pub. J. Hogg. (Wilson Archive RCA).
31. H. Brown-Morrison. Letter to M. Beasley, March 1959. (Coll. D. Ottewill, Portsmouth).

CHAPTER 1
FIRST INFLUENCES

1. In legal documents relating to his birth, marriage and death, Harry is given as his only forename, these incidentally revealing his whereabouts at different stages of his life, for instance his residence in the precinct of the Savoy at the time of his wedding (qualifying it to be held in the Chapel Royal), his address at the time of his father's retirement in 1892, and in 1894, with his move to Hindes Road. Harry appears on his will, 4 Blackburn Road, West Hampstead being given as his last address in England (the house he built in Kent in 1902 having been sold c. 1922). A few catalogue entries list him as Harry Wilson, as with the exhibition of his chalice for St. Bartholomew's, Brighton at the Royal Academy in 1899. In later life, Harry became still rarer, though it appears in the Durham Cathedral Bank Report in relation to his processional cross of 1917.
2. Sir William died in 1714, but it took almost twenty five years to get the building of the Lacon Childe school underway on its elevated site off Viols Walk, East of St. Mary's church. Both of Street's buildings used the rubble sandstone of Shropshire vernacular building with cut-stone dressings. The school buildings survive as private houses.
3. H. Wilson. Biographical Note 1910. (Wilson Papers, V&A Library).
4. P. Wilson. Illustrations for Sir Lancelot. *The Builder* 4 January 1896 p. 14.
5. Patten (b. 1869) died in 1934. Edgar (b. 1873) died in 1954. Theodore died in infancy in 1867. Their sister, Marion (b. 1865) died in 1870. Wilson's father (1834-1914) had trained as a teacher at Edinburgh Episcopal Training College; his mother Clara Louisa (née Broadley, 1836-1898), an orphan of one of the Yorkshire Broadleys, was a trained schoolmistress.
6. H. Wilson. Biographical Note 1910. (Wilson Papers, V&A Library).
7. Obituary: E.J. Shrewsbury *The Builder* 14 March 1924. See also *The Maidenhead Advertiser* 12 March 1924. For personal recollections on Shrewsbury, see *The Maidenhead Advertiser* 27 August and 3 September 1941. In his obituary on Wilson in *The Times* 12 March 1934, Pite inadvertantly has Wilson being articled to 'Mr. Squirhill, an architect of Maidenhead, where he distinguished himself as a swimmer.' The only recorded architect of that name is a Daniel Goodman Squirhill (1809-1863) of Leamington Spa. Pite's misapprehension of Wilson's father being a 'country clergyman who kept a school at Cleobury Mortimer, in Herefordshire' suggests something of the household's demeanour.

8. Obituary: J.O. Scott. *The Builder* 6 June 1913 p. 650.
9. The bishop's throne was Scott's design, made in 1903 by R. Bridgeman of Lichfield; Scott also designed the Dean's mace, the brass eagle lectern and two organ cases.
10. Presentation of RIBA Gold Medal. Belcher's reply *Jnl RIBA* 29 June 1907 p. 573.
11. Ibid.
12. Ibid.
13. Report on St. Mary Magdalene Church, South Marston, Wiltshire, submitted by J. Belcher FRIBA RA, to the Church Commissioners 2 December 1884. Reprinted in *The North Wiltshire Herald* 9 July 1886.
14. Ibid.
15. B. Pite. 'Design in Drawings' AR I 1896 p. 250.
16. Obituary: B. Pite. *Jnl RIBA* 23 December 1934.
17. W.R. Lethaby and H. Swainson *The Church of Sancta Sophia, Constantinople* (1894); R.W. Schultz 'Byzantine Art' AR I 1896-7.
18. M. Macartney. Obituary: J. Belcher. *Jnl RIBA* 22 November 1913 p. 77.
19. C.A. Nicholson. Obituary: J. Belcher. *Jnl RIBA* 6 December 1913 p. 79. Both Nicholson and Macartney refer to the scheme as Belcher's design for a 'church in Maida Vale' or 'Maida Hill'.
20. Ill. R. Macleod *Charles Rennie Mackintosh* (1968) p. 30.
21. 3rd Arts and Crafts Exhibition Society Catalogue (1890) no. 150, illustrated in *The Architect* 16 January 1891. See also sketch by T. Raffles Davison *The Architect* vol. 45 p. 41, its paired side columns probably casualties of the cuts. The frieze, shown *in situ* (GN/186 Kensington and Chelsea Public Libraries neg. archive) was lost, presumed destroyed.
22. The site itself, including the old Notting Hill library, had already been purchased for £4,150, and was unaffected by the new building budget. The first set of 'Reductions' required by the Commissioners for Public Libraries was recorded in the Minutes of 15 January 1890.
23. The more severe 'Reductions' Figgis presented to the Commissioners on 1 April 1890 meant that items that he and Wilson had chosen for quality and aesthetic effect had had to be given up, as with the largest saving – 'Bath Stone in lieu of Doulting, less value of carving £144-0-0'. This 'practical' alternative scheme was well underway when the original scheme was published in June in *The Architect*.
24. Though less well-known than Gladstone (who was Prime Minister in 1886 and 1892-94), Sir John Lubbock, MP for Maidstone 1870-80 and, after 1900, the 1st Lord Avebury, would have been an obvious choice for the ceremony, given his introduction of the Public Libraries Act and his own publications on the natural sciences. During his decade in Parliament he guided into law bills including the Open Spaces Act, the Wild Birds Protection Act, and several regulating shop hours. For a time, by popular assent, August Bank Holiday was nicknamed 'St. Lubbock's Day'.

CHAPTER 2
SEDDING AND HIS IMPACT

1. The idea of Wilson as a continuum of Sedding echoes that which Wilson himself noted regarding Sedding and his dead

brother, in 'Some considerations of John Sedding's work' AR III 1897 p. 241: 'Edmund's ideals and influence survived and had a new existence in the spirit of his brother John'.

2. J.D. Sedding. *Garden-craft Old and New* (1891). This 'charming interior' by Wilson is quoted in the Introduction by E.F. Russell, the vicar of St. Alban's, Holborn, where Sedding was churchwarden 1876-1888.
3. H. Wilson. 'A memorial to the late J.D. Sedding'. Published by the Architectural Association 1892 p. 11.
4. J.D. Sedding quoted in H. Wilson and J.P. Cooper, 'The work of J.D. Sedding' (i) AR III 1897 p. 37. Their six articles on Sedding's work appeared in *The Architectural Review* III (1897) and IV (1898).
5. Ibid.
6. H. Wilson and J.P. Cooper. 'The work of J. D. Sedding' (ii) AR III 1897 p. 70. Wilson described Ruskin's advice to Sedding in his 'Concerning Drawing' AR V 1899 p. 193: 'When Sedding was in debate as to what course of study would best fit him for his work, he wrote to Ruskin ... and received a delightful letter in which he urged Sedding to take up a craft and nature study. Ruskin took great interest in his work and gave him invaluable help and criticism'.
7. G.E. Street. 'On the true principles of Pointed Architecture and the possibilities of its Development'. (1852).
8. H. Wilson and J.P. Cooper. 'The work of J.D. Sedding' (i) AR III 1897 p. 35.
9. H. Wilson. 'Some considerations of John Sedding's work' AR III 1897 p. 241.
10. H. Wilson and J.P. Cooper. 'The work of J.D. Sedding' (ii) AR III 1897 p. 72.
11. Wilson attended the SPAB committee as a visitor on 28 April 1892 along with C.C. Winmill (SPAB Minute Books). On 19 May 1892 Sydney Cockerell's diary (BM Add. MSS 52629) records 'Antiscrape Committee. Webb, Hebb, Jack, Fletcher, Walker, Kershaw and Wilson. [Fairfax]-Cholmeley, Hallam Murray, Dr. Burgess, Purdon Clarke and Mr. Constable as visitors, the last four to discuss the preservation of Indian monuments. Supper afterwards with Webb, Walker, Wilson, Cholmeley, Jack and Cobden-Sanderson'.
12. W.R. Lethaby, with A.H. Powell and F.L. Griggs. *Ernest Gimson: his Life and Work* (1924) pp. 3-4. Lethaby enlarges his contention that the SPAB was a real school of 'practical building', by defining this as 'architecture with all the whims which we usually call "design" left out. Architecture should mean solid realities, not paper promises ... [in it], 'Gimson's love for old buildings deepened into a passionate reverence, and he came to see that ancient architecture was an essence and reality, not a "style"...'
13. Philip Webb. *Notes on the repair of ancient buildings*. (London, SPAB, 1903) p. 17: 'where modern work is essential, ... it should be simple and unpretentious, of good material and workmanship, and frankly the production of the present day.' This stance only took effect in the SPAB from the early 1890s. Gimson's comments about Sedding's restorations in North Somerset show his unease: 'It is poor old JD who [was] responsible for the spoiling of all the churches. He did Porlock, Selworthy, Bossington, and a host of others. Thank goodnesss they were done after my time with him. I shouldn't like to have made the drawings for Porlock chancel'. (Letter from Ernest Gimson 27 July 1891, Cheltenham Art Gallery).
14. H. Wilson and J.P. Cooper. 'The work of J.D. Sedding' (ii) AR III 1897 p. 72.
15. Ibid.
16. H. Wilson. *A memorial to the late J.D. Sedding*. Published by the Architectural Association 1892.
17. J.D. Sedding. *Garden-craft Old and New* (1891) Ch. 1 p. 17.
18. H. Wilson and J.P. Cooper. 'The work of J. D. Sedding' (iii) AR III 1897 p. 128-9. see also pl. 5 and 6 in the Architectural Association's *In Memoriam. J.D. Sedding* (1892) Preface by H. Wilson.
19. Ibid.
20. Ibid.
21. Ibid.
22. J.D. Sedding. *Art and Handicraft* (1893) Ch.1 'On the study of English Architecture' p. 17.
23. H. Wilson and J.P. Cooper. 'The work of J.D. Sedding' (vi) AR IV 1898 p. 33.
24. H. Wilson and J.P. Cooper. 'The work of J.D. Sedding' (i) AR 1897 p. 35.
25. E.W. Mountford, in discussion at the Architectural Association following a paper by Wilson on Sedding and his influence. *The Builder* 5 December 1891 p. 424.
26. In *Art and Handicraft* (1893) Ch. 6 'Expression in Architecture', Sedding extols Wren's sense of geometry and the religious expressiveness it achieves. For him, Wren exemplified the fact that some architects 'speak best out of their heads', others from their hearts. see also Lethaby's 'Architecture as Structural Geometry' *The Builder* CXXXVI 1929 p. 52: 'geometry is an idea, a principle, an enthusiasm' underlying architecture.
27. J.D. Sedding in *The Sign* 1920 p. 76. Frescoes appear in G.C. Horsley's interior perspective of 1888. (Drawings Coll. RIBA).
28. W. Pater. *Holy Redeemer Church Chronicle* August 1893. See also *The Illustrated London News* 3 November 1888.
29. H. Wilson. *Holy Redeemer Chronicle* August 1893. See also *The Builder* 7 July 1887: 'the style and arrangement of the church are admirably suited for a modern church'.
30. H. Wilson and J.P. Cooper. 'The work of J.D. Sedding' (i) AR III p. 35.
31. *Holy Redeemer Herald* April 1928. Wilson supplied the bronze plaque to Fr. Poyntz in the same year, 1927.
32. H. Wilson and J.P. Cooper. 'The work of J.D. Sedding' (vi) AR IV 1898 p. 38.
33. H. Wilson and J.P. Cooper. 'The work of J.D. Sedding' (iii) AR III 1897 p. 133.
34. W.R. Lethaby. Obituary: J.D. Sedding. *The Builder* 1891 p. 270. Wilson's 'Concerning drawing – a plea for discontent' AR V 1899 p. 184, warns architects against being exclusively dependant on architectural drawings as a way of getting builders to construct a building. The article is illustrated with watercolour sketches by Sedding of plants and architectural details.
35. H. Sumner. 'An Appreciation of J.D. Sedding' AR IV 1898 p.74.
36. C. Whall. 'An Appreciation of J.D. Sedding' AR IV 1898 p.36.

37. H. Wilson and J.P. Cooper. 'The work of J.D. Sedding' (i) AR III 1897 p.35.
38. C. Whall. 'An Appreciation of J.D. Sedding' AR IV 1898 p.36.
39. H. Wilson and J.P. Cooper. 'The work of J.D. Sedding (ii) AR III 1897 p.72.
40. H. Wilson and J.P. Cooper. 'The work of J.D. Sedding (vi) AR IV 1898 p.33.
41. H. Wilson. *A memorial to the late J.D. Sedding*. Published by the Architectural Association 1892.
42. J.D. Sedding quoted in W.R. Lethaby, Obituary: J.D. Sedding. *The Builder* 1891 p. 270
43. H. Wilson and J.P. Cooper. 'The work of J.D. Sedding' (iv) AR III 1897 p. 188.
44. H. Wilson and J.P. Cooper. 'The work of J.D. Sedding' (vi) AR IV 1898 p. 33.
45. AR VI 1899 p. 152.
46. Sedding's brother Edmund was still more musical – he was the organist at St. Mary, Soho and published several collections of carols and hymns, including 'Nine Ancient Christmas Carols' (1860), 'Five hymns of ye Holy Eastern Church' (1864) and 'Sun of my Soul' (1864).
47. Sedding's drawing 'Bay of Nave Arcade, New Church, Sloane Street' was exhibited at the Arts and Crafts Exhibition Society show of 1889.
48. Specific claims of the authorship of works in the post-Sedding years never preoccupied Wilson, as was clear in his completion of Sedding projects from Clerkenwell to Marple. The assumption that the pulpit was by Wilson is a logical one, its being completed well after Sedding's death, viz. Amery and Cruikshank's attribution of it to Wilson in AR July 1974 p. 43. A series of illustrations in the Architectural Illustration Society (2nd series) No. 356-61 and 365-6, and in *The Architect* vol.45 1891 show the interior, the chancel gates, the pulpit, the exterior of the church (pre-Wilson's railings) and a plan of the church, all under Sedding's name.
49. *Holy Trinity Sloane Street: 1828-1953* by F.H. Spicer. Armstead's name appears on Sedding's drawing of a nave bay in *The Builder* 12 October 1889 as maker of the carved medallions from models by Wilson, that of Isaiah being based on sketches made by Wilson of his father.
50. 'Notes on watercolour scheme of decoration for Lady Chapel shown Royal Academy'. AR VI June-Dec 1899 p.15.
51. Wilson's proposed Lady Chapel illustrated AR 1898 pl. XXIV and *Moderne Bauformen* 1910 Heft 1. The chapel walls' original gold and brown patterning can be detected in a photograph c. 1900 (RIBA Photographic Coll.) and in M. Richardson, *Architects of the Arts and Crafts Movement* (1983) p. 70. The patterns (which extended to other parts of the church) were plastered over and whitewashed c. 1920 by F.C. Eden, this task forming one of his priorities on becoming church architect; according to Spicer, he found the gilt and rough plaster on the walls 'slighty vulgar', and in any case it was beginning to deteriorate. He thought the Lady Chapel the least satisfying part of the church, 'complicated and restless' in its effect and recommended its simplification and enrichment by 'the removal of what is tawdry and unworthy'. Wilson's organ screen (see below) made a 'very uncomfortable' background for the Lady Altar, producing a 'mere unintelligible jumble'; he proposed hanging a curtain of green and gold between the baldacchino columns to hide the organ.
52. 6th Arts and Crafts Exhibition Society Catalogue (1899) no. 255.
53. *The Builder* 14 October 1899.
54. H. Wilson *The Builder* 22 September 1894 p. 207. The reredos was illustrated *in situ* in *Academy Architecture* 1894 (1692) p. 40, with Armstead's lectern. As Wilson said in *The Builder*, his design was 'not intended to be in any way final, but to be used as a suggestion, a guide to future efforts'. His Elevation (1693) appeared on p. 41.
55. *The Builder* 22 September 1894 p. 207.
56. H. Wilson and J.P. Cooper. 'The work of J.D. Sedding' (vi) AR IV 1898 p. 33. A similar comment, about William Morris, serves to emphasise the practical and ideological obstacles both met: 'It is not the graceful and charming designs which flowed so readily from Morris' facile hand ... which will place [him amongst] the most honoured English artist craftsmen, but more his teaching....' *Studio* vol. 9 1896 p. 134.
57. H. Wilson. *A memorial to the late J.D. Sedding*. Published by the Architectural Association 1892.
58. J.D. Sedding quoted in W.R. Lethaby, Obituary: J.D. Sedding. *The Builder* 1891 p. 270. Below the crucifix is the inscription 'In loving memory of John D. Sedding of The Croft, West Wickham, who died April 7 1891 and of Rose Catherine Sedding, who died April 15 1891. Shew thy servants thy work and their children thy glory'. Wilson was also commissioned to make a memorial to Sedding for St. Alban's Holborn, where he had been a churchwarden. This memorial, of 1894, situated near the font, was of Devonshire marble, again commemorated both husband and wife. Its design and modelling were by Wilson, with firegilded bronze medallion portraits by F.W. Pomeroy of Fortitude and Mercy, angels and two hearts entwined in roses. It survived World War II but subsequently disappeared.
59. Quoted in H. Wilson and J. P. Cooper, 'The work of J.D. Sedding' (v) *The Architectural Review* III 1897 p. 236.
60. J.D. Sedding. See also n. 35 above.

CHAPTER 3
LIFE AFTER SEDDING

1. Ernest Barnsley (1863-1926) and Ernest Gimson (1864-1919) established a craft workshop with Sidney Barnsley (1865-1926) at Pinbury, then c. 1900 at Sapperton, Gloucestershire. Their working relationship ended acrimoniously c. 1905, Barnsley returning to architecture. His buildings include his own cottage in Sapperton, Coates Manor, Northamptonshire, Sapperton village hall (1909), and Rodmarton Manor and cottages (1909-26) near Cirencester (finished after his death in January 1926 by Sidney Barnsley, before his own death in September). Gimson's buildings around Leicester include The White House, Clarendon Park, (1897) for Arthur Gimson; Stoneywell Cottage, Ulverscroft (1898-9) for his brother Sydney; his own house, The Leasowes, Sapperton (1901); Rockyfield cottage, Markfield (1908); cottages and village hall, Kelmscott, Oxfordshire

(1914-28). In hand at the time of his death was Bedales School, Petersfield, Hampshire. Its library was completed by Sidney Barnsley, whose own buildings included St. Sophia's, Lower Kingswood, Surrey (1891) and the Gyde Almshouses, Painswick, Gloucestershire (1913).

2. As well as collaborating on decorative schemes, Alfred Powell (1865-1960) worked with his wife Louise decorating pottery, and taught china painting at the Central School of Arts and Crafts 1906-07.

3. The Welsh work of Arthur Grove (1870-1929) included the restoration of St. David's and a new girls' school in Merthyr Tydfil, Glamorganshire (1903); restoration of church and addition of parish room, Llanvaches, Monmouthshire (1908); chancel improvements and font, Cadoxton, Glamorganshire (1909).

4. Charles A. Nicholson, later Sir Charles (1849-1924), was in partnership with H.C. Corlette 1895-1914. Amongst his buildings are St. Matthew's, Charlston, Torquay (1896); St. Alban's, Westcliffe-on-Sea, Essex (1898-1908); St. Augustine's, Grimsby, Lincolnshire (1911); St. Paul's, Yelverton, Devon (1913-14). Yiewsley commission ill. *Academy Architecture* 1896; *Recent Ecclesiastical Architecture* 1920. Wilson's cross and candlesticks can be seen in interior view AR V 1898-9.

5. Christopher Whitworth Whall (1849-1924) was the son of the vicar of Thurning, Northamptonshire. His sketches for 'The Elements' were published in *The Builder*, May 11, 1889 (nos. 212, 213, 216).

6. Undated letter to Wilson from Gordon Craig (Wilson Archive RCA). Their friendship led to Cooper's commission to make alterations to Ellen Terry's home at Smallhythe, Kent.

7. Francis Cooper, quoted in J. Farleigh *The Creative Craftsman* (1950) p. 147-8.

8. At the 1916 Arts and Crafts Exhibition, Grove exhibited a screen for the chapel at St. Osmund's, Poole, and is listed, alongside Prior, as the joint architect of the church, Catalogue No. 166. Wilson appears as one of the craftsmen who collaborated with him on the screen, contributing to its modelled panel. MacDonald Gill painted it, and F. Stuttig executed its gilding and carving.

9. His own words, quoted in *Ernest Gimson* p. 14 (Leicestershire Museums, 1978). See also n. 11 below.

10. H. Wilson. 'Federated Workshops' 1918 (Wilson Archive RCA). In September 1918 Gimson was formulating plans for a craft village, about two miles from Sapperton, see letter from Gimson to Sir Sydney Cockerel 20 September 1918 (Leicester Record Office DE1763/16). His plans were more an expansion of his own working methods than a pursuit of the broad concepts Wilson was confronting.

11. A sign of his divergence from architecture was Gimson's involvement in 1890 in the formation of Kenton & Co., furniture designers and makers, along with W.R. Lethaby, S. Barnsley, R. Blomfield, Colonel Mallet and M. Macartney. Despite its high-quality work and a successful exhibition in 1891 at Barnard's Inn (the premises of the Art Workers' Guild), the venture was poorly financed and closed in 1892.

12. S. Barnsley and R.W. Schultz. *The Monastery of St. Luke of Stiris in Phocis; and dependant Monastery of St. Nicholas-in-the-Fields, near Skripon, in Boetia* (1901).

13. R.W. Schultz. 'Byzantine Architecture' AR I 1896.

14. W.R. Lethaby and H. Swainson. *The Church of S. Sophia, Constantinople: a study of Byzantine building* (Macmillan, 1894).

15. H. Wilson. 'On architecture' (undated m/s, Wilson Archive RCA).

16. H. Wilson. Introduction: *Garden-craft Old and New*, J. D. Sedding (1891).

17. W.R. Lethaby. *Architecture, Mysticism and Myth* (1891). Introductory, p. 3.

18. Ibid.

19. 6th Arts and Crafts Exhibition Society Catalogue (1899) no. 260 Processional cross. Designed by W.R. Lethaby and H. Wilson.

20. E. Gimson, 12 October 1915. (Wilson Archive, RCA). 'Ossington Street' alludes to number 19 in this Notting Hill street, where Gimson lodged from 1887-88 and 1890. It is unclear who Cook was. The 'walk across the Park' refers to Hyde Park; W.R. Butler, a member of Sedding's office and a close friend of Gimson's, makes frequent appearances in Leicester Museums' Collection of Gimson's letters. 'Meredith' – Edward William Meredith – was born in London in 1872, and was living at 18 Greystones Avenue, Sheffield at the time of his death c. 1949. Articled to Sedding from 1890, he completed his articles with Wilson in 1895, becoming assistant in offices in Southampton and Torquay 1895-1898. He took up independent practice in 1898, then began working for Everard & Pick, architects, civil and mining engineers and surveyors, in existence 1875-1955. The firm' s full name was Pick, Everard, Keay and Gimson (see Leicestershire, Leicester and Rutland Record Office). From 1901-04 Meredith worked with Walter Brierley, the so-called 'Lutyens of the North', at Demaine & Brierley, York, then, from 1904, for the Sheffield City Architect, becoming a Licentiate of the RIBA in 1911. The obituary of 'Finch' – Henry William Finch (1869-1942) – appeared in *The Builder* vol. 162, 23 Jan 1942 p.78; the office that he made available to Wilson and Cooper from April 1896 to minimise the disruption of moving to Kensington was at 121 East Street Buildings, Manchester Square (see also Ch. 4 n. 21). 'Longden', Major Henry Longden, was master of ironworkers Longden & Co., whose London office was below Sedding's at 447 Oxford Street; 'JD' was the familiar yet respectful soubriquet by which Sedding's assistants knew their master. Typically, Wilson's own recollections would culminate in a reference to his old boss: 'All feel it is him who gave us what insight we have'. (*Garden-craft Old and New*, J.D. Sedding, Introduction by H. Wilson).

21. Roof and seating were renewed, and the floor relaid; Wilson completed the restoration after Sedding's death.

22. The east window bears the dedication 'To the glory of God and in memory of the Rev. Charles Ring Hutchinson, vicar of this parish for 26 years, this window is erected July AD 1893.' Plans for the restoration of St. Mary's had been drawn up in Sedding's lifetime, and were approved by J.O. Scott, who deemed them 'satisfactory'. An appeal for £800 was submitted to the Oxford Diocesan Church Building Society by the Rev. Frank Heath in 1891. (Dept. of Western Manuscripts, Bodleian Library, Oxford). Completed in 1893

the work comprised the restoration of roofs on chancel, side chapel and vestry; cleaning down and making good rendering of walls; relaying vestry floor; removal of defective stone dressings to E. window and to 5 stained glass windows; providing a new oak hanging cupboard and a new oak S. door. It came to a total of £1,200, the excess being met by Rt. Hon. Earl Brownlow, and was carried out by the Ashridge Estate. Wilson was sensitive throughout to the church's exceptionally interesting old fabric, including its twelfth century 'Aylesbury' font, its chancel of 1230 with medieval floor tiles, its N aisle of 1300, and, in a chancel arch pillar, a fourteenth century brass of the wife of Sir John Neyrnut, one of the earliest of a woman in England.

23. The dedication inside the lychgate at Holy Trinity, Ilfracombe reads 'To the glory of God and in memory of John Mill Chanter for 51 years vicar of this parish 1836 - 1887'. Kingsley's *Westwood Ho!* was published in 1855, *The Water Babies* in 1863.

24. The commission to restore St. Mary's, Lynton (executed 1892-1906) had been given to Sedding and Wilson, but Sedding died before work began. Wilson's scheme for a new tower (unexecuted) and that for the lychgate (built 1893) were exhibited at the Royal Academy in 1892, pub. *The Builder* 22 Oct. 1892, and *Academy Architecture* 1892 no. 1788 p. 40. While his scheme for the new tower was rejected, wall paintings by him inside the church were painted over. (see n. 29 below).

25. *The Builder* 22 Oct 1892 p. 321.

26. The urgency of completing the interior of the church was reflected in a letter to Wilson from the Rev. W.E. Cox, The Rectory, Lynton 20 March 1905: 'Pullen ... has been ill, but I do hope we shall see him ... within the next few days or we shall never have the painting finished by Easter.' In the same letter the vicar asked about Wilson's progress with the Lady Altar: 'how is the work getting on? Will it all be finished *well* before Easter?' (Wilson Archive RCA). The new chancel window was made by A.L. Moore.

27. Letter to Wilson from the Rev. W.E. Cox, 16 December 1905. (Wilson Archive RCA). Cox's enthusiasm for the speedy completion of the Lady Chapel is felt in his letter to Wilson of March 1906: 'You do not say anything ... about the drawings of the altar etc. I am applying for a faculty & really must have the drawings to lay before the Vestry. Please send them immediately and show the scale....' By 16 June 1906 the vicar had changed his mind: 'I have decided to sit tight & let matters rest about the faculty. One has not heard any objection to the altar; indeed it is very much approved of, and I question ... if the Chancellor ... can prove that it is illegal'. (Wilson Archive RCA). The pendant-cross, whose openwork motifs echo the vines and grapes of Lynton's altar cross, hangs from two fine chains beneath a baroque pearl, suspended from a tiny pillared temple. ill. L.Lambourne op cit pl. 112

28. Letter to Wilson from the Rev. W.E. Cox, The Rectory, Lynton 18 November 1907. (Wilson Archive RCA).

29. The cost of the glazing clearly caused some concern: 'I have at last settled the matter with Shrigley and Hunt – with a cheque for £70-4-0 – it seemed the only way to avoid friction. I quite agree with you Messrs. Shrigley and Hunt were seriously at fault for not communicating with Mr. Jones as to the price'. (Letter to Wilson from the Rev. W.E. Cox 16 Dec 1905; Wilson Archive RCA).

30. Wilson's tower proposal had been abandoned, but work by him inside the church was lost to redecoration – the north aisle's E wall once bore wall paintings by him. He sent his bill for the work to the Building and Decorating Committee in January 1907: 'To preparing 2 large cartoons of the decoration of the East Wall in colours. To preparing sundry foliage details of the ornaments and inscription £12-12-0. To two visits of inspection and superintendence, time spent in starting the work, selecting colours and settling the details of the ornament £12-12-0 = £25-4-0.' On 25 January 1907, the Rev. Cox sought to clarify the amount due: 'I enclose a cheque for £25-4-0. I believe there is still a sum for the two sketches of the E end & proposed E window, but I remember you said there would be a deduction from these if ... the decoration and windows were carried out. Will the sum be any less now that part of the scheme for the decoration has been carried out?' On 18 November 1907 Cox wrote again with 'your cheque to the value of £18-14-0 which will make matters right between us as follows: £25-0-0 less discount £6-6-0 = £18-14-0'. (Wilson Archive RCA).

31. Wilson's memorial window (made by Shrigley and Hunt) shows in its central light the seated figure of Pity, with the dedication 'To the glory of God and in thanksgiving of Charles and Susan Trask of this parish for the 50th year of their marriage October 10th 1904'. The side lights show full-length figures representing Life and Work. Costing some £50, it was paid for by Trask, but the petition to install this 'East Window of the Chapel of our Lady of Pity' was challenged soon after its submission by the vicar, Guy Fitzmaurice, on 11 August 1904, to the Consistery Court of the Diocese of Bath and Wells, enclosing Wilson's description: 'Life as a young, serene woman, clasps Love to her, and folds him in her orange robe, which is the symbol ... of Venus the life-giver.... Pity bears an orb with a rose tree having six roses, and a fallen rosebud upon the ground ... to shew that his spirit has put off the body. Labour offers the result of his harvest for there can be no love without work and no work without love. Pity sits with her head amid the stars in a blue vault.... Life is in a golden robe to signify the golden date....' The faculty was blocked by Chadwick Healey, Chancellor of the Court, pending certain changes – his letter to the vicar on 7 September insisted that 'the words "Our Lady of Pity" should be struck out, and the description "north" or "south" chapel added as may be. Note: Lest the central figure be confused with the Virgin Mary the nimbus on the figure of Pity should be removed'. The changes were duly made, but not without Trask, and presumably Wilson, resenting the interference. Trask's letter of 13 September to the Court office captures their mood: 'Courtfield, Norton-sub-Hamdon. Dear Sir, I enclose the petition for the stained glass window, altered as required. Some few years ago I got an old will from the Record Office which spoke of the South Chapel in our Church as "the Chapel of our Lady Pity" and of one on the North side as the Chapel of St. Saviour. These names

are part of the History of our church and I should have thought Mr. Chadwick Healey would have too much regard for the History of the County to ask me to extinguish the proper name of this Chapel. "Our Lady of Pity" has a far greater meaning than that of "the Virgin Mary" and should not be mistaken for it, and would not be but by ignorant people – or fanatical persons, who are the less to be respected' (Somerset Record Office).

32. H. Wilson. AR I 1896-7 p. 164. 'Every stone has settled into vital connection with the whole structure. The weathered surfaces, the abraded edges ... have acquired in the course of time an accidental beauty inimitable by man.... All this can be saved without danger.' The apprehension felt by objectors, like Wilson, to the gable's being dismantled and reassembled had been fuelled by memories of the 1883-6 scheme of Pearson and others to rebuild the Cathedral's central Norman tower, which had caused huge controversy; it would have meant reconstructing the tower in two stages (to ensure unity of design, two – E and W – Norman arches would have been recreated at the crossing at the expense of the two existing 14c ones; then a further arcaded stage was to be added, plus a 13c-style 360' spire). The plan was finally reined in on the grounds of cost, and the old tower, carefully dismantled stone by stone and with the crossing piers made good, was reinstated and secured exactly as it had been. See also Antony Quiney, *J.L. Pearson* (Yale, 1979) pp. 186-8; 194-8.
33. H. Wilson. 'The Pre-Raphaelite School in relation to the revival of Design and Handicraft'. Lecture delivered at New Gallery, 7 Nov. 1899. Printed in *The Times*, 15 Nov. 1899.
34. Ibid.
35. H. Wilson. *Silverwork and Jewellery* (1903) Ch. 1 'Introduction' p. 28. see also Ch. V 'Instinct'.
36. H. Wilson. 'The work of Sir Edward Burne-Jones' (i) AR I 1896 p. 177. Wilson's views on instinctive recognition find parallels in Lethaby's book: 'Behind every style ... there is an earlier style in which the germ of every form is to be found.' *Architecture, Mysticism and Myth* 1891 p. 2, and in early 20c Jungian theories on archetype and shared primitive experience.
37. The window was glazed by Powell to designs by Henry Holliday.
38. The vicar called Sedding's plan 'more English and dignified' (*St. Clement's Church Banner* April 1892), though E.F. Russell in *A little book about St. Clement's* called it 'the most beautiful tower of modern times'; C.A. Nicholson in his Obituary on Wilson, *Jnl RIBA* 14 April 1934, thought it 'probably the best building he ever designed and carried out.'
39. H. Wilson. 'The work of Sir Edward Burne-Jones' (i) AR I 1896 p. 274-5.
40. H. Wilson. 'A Plea for Imagination and Poetry in Architecture' (undated m/s, pre-1910. Wilson Archive, RCA).
41. H. Wilson. 'The work of Sir Edward Burne-Jones' (ii) AR 1896 p. 324.
42. H. Wilson. *Arts and Crafts in their relation to Architecture. A paper read before the Architectural Association* 11 Nov. 1898, published 1898 p. 12; reprinted in *The Builder* Nov. 1898.
43. *The Builder* 1889 vol. 57 p. 359; *The Architect* 1890. The design for St. Peter's was selected from three entrants in a limited competition.
44. C.A. Nicholson. Obituary: H. Wilson. *Jnl RIBA* 14 April 1934. 'In the case of St. Peter's new church at Ealing ... Sedding had left only the scantiest of notes, and the work done may be attibuted entirely to Wilson'. The Rev. Petty's account of the founding of the church (dated 9 Mar 1894 in the Vestry Book), clarifying the circumstances surrounding the creation of the church, recorded Wilson as Sedding's successor, 'responsible for supervision of building, details and tracery of W window.' His account was printed in *St. Peter's Parish Magazine*, March 1894. F.W. Troup's list of Wilson's 'more important architectural works' appeared in his Obituary for Wilson *Jnl RIBA* 24 March 1934. As such, St. Peter's appears in Alastair Service's entry for Wilson in *Edwardian Architecture* p. 212. In *The Buildings of England: London 3: North West* (1991) p. 167 it is described by Bridget Terry and Nicholas Pevsner as having been 'designed by J.D. Sedding, who died in 1991: executed in 1892-3 by his partner, Henry Wilson'.
45. *New and Old*. Architect's Report 1889. St. Peter's Vestry.
46. *Ibid*
47. V&A Dept. of Prints and Drawings.
48. *New and Old*. Architect's Report 1889. St. Peter's Vestry.
49. W.R. Lethaby. *Architecture, Mysticism and Myth* (1891) Introductory p. 1.
50. 5th Arts and Crafts Exhibition Catalogue 1896 No. 552: 'Door, beaten brass. By H. Wilson and W.H. Wilson.' Other exhibits by Wilson included the casts for the Welbeck baptistry gates (with F.W. Pomeroy), altar cross and wafer box for St. Martin's, Marple, a chalice in silver and bronze, a further altar cross, chancel stalls for All Hallows' Church, Southwark (destroyed in WWII), a bronze lectern (with Pomeroy), and the title page for a magazine (probably *The Architectural Review*). When on 31 May 1893 they attended the official opening of the Ealing church – the ceremony, recorded on Wilson's cornerstone, being performed by Queen Victoria's third daughter Princess Christian – both Wilson and Joseph Dorey believed that they would be called upon within the next 10 years to complete the E end of the church with an ambulatory; this again was never executed.
51. *The Builder* 28 Oct 1893 p. 320. The design is illustrated here and in *Academy Architecture* 1893, and in C.A. Nicholson and H.C. Corlette's 'Modern Church Building' *Jnl RIBA* 23 Feb. 1907 p. 279. Plan appears on p. 249.
52. Ibid.
53. C. Whall. 'An Appreciation of J. D. Sedding'. *Academy Architecture* IV 1898 p. 34. Shaw's comment is quoted by Sir John Betjeman in his *Plea for Holy Trinity Church* (Church Literature Association, 1974).
54. B.F.L. Clarke. *Anglican Cathedrals outside the British Isles* (1958) p. 72. 'New and Old was a magnificent design ... Duomo and Hope were admired, but the winning design was Fides by Keith and Evers of Victoria.'
55. Ill. *The British Architect* 17 May 1895.
56. Ill. *The Builder* 4 January 1896.
57. H. Wilson. 'The work of Sir Edward Burne-Jones'. (iii) AR I 1896 p. 277-8.
58. H. Wilson. 'Concerning Drawing: a plea for discontent'. AR

V 1898 p. 191-3.

59. Henry Wilson's time working in a bronze foundry is recorded in his Biographical Note 1910 (V&A Library). No details are given of when or where this work took place; for potential locations see Ch. 4 n. 19.
60. H. Wilson. 'On the Real Impediments to British Architecture'. AR VIII 1900 p. 37
61. Letter from Wilson, The Thatched House, St. Mary's Platt to Professor Patrick Geddes June 1906. Wilson opens with a rebuttal of Geddes's opinion of the talents of Baillie Scott: 'I demurred, with a huge mental shout, at the inclusion of Baillie Scott among those worthy of admiration. The very plan you admired – and justly – was cribbed – lifted – and spoiled. It originally sprang from the fertile brain of E.S. Prior'. Later Wilson alludes to Lorimer's mother in terms which he might easily have applied to his own: 'so perfect a creature, the very miracle of sweet intelligence conjoined with perfect intuition & every other gift needed in a mother'. (Geddes Papers, University of Strathclyde, Glasgow, pressmark TGed 9/650)
62. H. Wilson. 'Concerning Drawing: a plea for discontent'. AR V 1898 p. 191-3.
63. Ibid.
64. H. Wilson. 'On the Real Impediments to British Architecture'. AR VIII 1900 p. 37
65. H. Wilson. 'A Plea for Imagination ...' (see n. 38 above).
66. Ibid.
67. Ibid.
68. H. Wilson. 'Arts and Crafts in their relation ... '(see n. 40 above).
69. H. Wilson. 'Concerning Drawing ...' p. 184. (see n. 53 above).
70. H. Wilson. 'On the Real Impediments ... ' (see n. 55 above).
71. B. Pite. Obituary: H. Wilson. *The Times* 12 March 1934.
72. Lethaby states 'the world tree rises in the centre of the earth, its branches forming the several heavens'. *Architecture, Mysticism and Myth* (1891) p. 11. The significance of the seven stars is explained in Ch. VI 'The planetary spheres', where Lethaby explores the mystical implications of the number seven (p. 122).
73. Sedding's design illustrated in *The Building News* 30 January 1885. Wilson's scheme was illustrated in *The Builder* 12 September 1896 p. 212.
74. Townsend's Cliff Towers was illustrated in the *Studio* 1898 Vol. 13 p. 239, and in *The Builder* 1898 Vol. 75 pp. 230 and 343.
75. *The Builder* 12 September 1896 p. 212.
76. Gibbon's design was illustrated in *Building News* 12 January 1912.
77. H. Wilson. 'The work of Sir Edward Burne-Jones' (iii) AR I 1896 p. 277-8.
78. Wilson's conception of architecture a 'music' art with the architect as a 'composer in charge of a thousand living instruments' underscores his vision of the ideal building; this depiction unites two passages from his 'The work of Sir Edward Burne-Jones' (iii) AR I 1896 p. 277-8, and 'Nineteenth Century Church Building' AR III 1898 p. 50. Each feature – pillared porch, doors sheathed on beaten metal, pale windows, frescoed walls, coloured roof timbers, marble dado, baldacchino, silver altar – appears at some time in Wilson's own buildings. Many phrases – 'pavements like the sea', 'ceilings like the sky' – echo those in Lethaby's *Architecture, Mysticism and Myth*. A design by Wilson for a 'visionary' church interior on the scale of St. Bartholomew's appears in a 50'x28' charcoal sketch (Drawings Coll. RIBA): large free-standing sanctuary columns support figure groups (Adam and Eve to one side, the Expulsion to the other); suspended from the ceiling between them is a boat inscribed Arca Salutis.
79. Ibid.
80. A copy of a photograph of the exterior of the chapel is held by Royal Commission on the Ancient and Historical Monuments of Scotland, Edinburgh; it was made in 1973 from the original in the collection of the Earl of Home, together with others showing the chapel's interior and decorative details. See Lanarkshire, Douglas Castle Drawings NMRS ref LA/869 (interior with unimpeded view of hanging lamps), LA/871, LA/870, LA/808/27. Copies of photographs of the Castle itself are also in NMRS ref LA/88 and ( )a/3882. A photograph of the original architectural drawing for the chapel was made in 1980, see Lanarkshire, Douglas Castle Drawings (Inventory 36 RHP 24719); labelled 'New Chapel Hall etc', it shows Longditudinal Section looking South and Transverse Section looking West, March 188( ),' last digit illegible. 'Wardrop & Reid' 188( ) is on the back; the National Register of Archives gives the date 1888. George Henderson's involvement seems to comprise *additions* to the Chapel (Obit. *Scotsman* 29 March 1905).
81. *The Builder* 28 March 1896 p. 39, ill. showing general interior view of chapel, reredos, organ case, frieze by Pomeroy, window by C. Whall, ceiling design also Whall; and *Academy Architecture* 1894 ill. 1699 (design for reredos and altar rail). See also *The Builder* 28 March 1896 p. 278: 'New steps and floor have been added to the chancel, and the latter divided from the nave by a pair of marble columns. The oak and inlay work, the reredos and organ case were all admirably done by Messrs. Trask, the marble work with equal skill by Mr. Davison.'
82. Ibid.
83. Ibid.
84. Listed 3rd Arts and Crafts Exhibition Catalogue 1890 no. 278. *The Beauties of Sherwood Forest* by Sissons (3rd ed. 1896) refers to the altar as 'the joint design of Mr. Sedding and Mr. Wilson', reprinted in *Welbeck Abbey: Treasures* by D. Bradbury (ed.).
85. W.R. Lethaby. *Architecture, Mysticism and Myth* Ch. VIII 'The Golden Gates of the Sun' p. 179-80. The eagle reappears, though in plainer form, in Wilson's 1902 bronze lectern at Chipping Warden church, Northamptonshire, given in memory of their parents, George and Catherine Douglas, by their children. The Douglas family were prominent in the parish, and represented a long line of churchwardens. Restorations and changes were made to the church 1901-5.
86. W.R. Lethaby. *Architecture, Mysticism and Myth* Ch. IX 'The Symbol of Creation' p. 265 and p. 269.
87. This 'temple' resembles Lethaby's 'perfect temple ... standing at the centre of the world ... its walls built foursquare with

HENRY WILSON 1864-1934 – **CHAPTER THREE**

the walls of heaven', *Architecture, Mysticism and Myth* Ch. III 'Four Square'.

88. Listed (with Wilson's altar cross, and lectern) in 4th Arts and Crafts Exhibition Society Catalogue 1893 no. 276. Its inscription reads ' ... to the glory of God and in memory of the baptism of their eldest son May 1893 this font is offered by Arthur 6th Duke of Portland and Winifred his wife.... '

89. Wilson's limestone slab for the grave of the Rev. Walter Howard Stables is inscribed '... waiting for the manifestation of the Son of God here resteth the body of Walter Howard Stables, vicar of St. Chad's Far Headingley 1896-1906 died 28th September 1906 aged 45 years.... ' A similar run-on format is used for the circular text at the head of the stone '... I will bless the Lord at all times....' A cross extends the length of the gravestone's chamfered surface, with the words 'Per ardua stabilis' at its midway point. Its Celtic-style lettering recalls that on the panelling at Norton-sub-Hamdon, Somerset. Both commissions were carried out to Wilson's specifications by Charles Trask and Sons, whose estimate for the Leeds gravestone, dated 24 August 1909, amounted to £55 'for providing and working out of the best selected Irish limestone (grey) the curbs etc in accordance with your designs and particulars received, delivered and fixed complete on cement foundations at Headingley Leeds. We have taken for the inscription motto, as shewn on one side on chamfer – also for the outer inscription to the four sides of the curbs, the lettering to be deeply sunk as shewn'. (Wilson Archive RCA). A year after the Rev. Stables' death his widow Emily commissioned an altar cross from Wilson for the church. Executed in oak, brass finials cap each arm and brass sunrays radiate from the centre. The ogee base is oak edged in brass, with a shield (like one on Wilson's Ripon pulpit) showing a cross enamelled half red and half white and wreathed in brass foliage set with three cherub masks.

90. 5th Arts and Crafts Exhibition Society Catalogue (1896) no. 84 and 85: 'Casts for bronze gates for the baptistry, Welbeck Chapel. Designed by H. Wilson, executed and exhibited by F.W. Pomeroy', ill. *Studio* IX 1896 p. 262. The dedication, on the inward face of the gates beside the tailpiece of hinge with heart-shaped motif, records: 'These gates are dedicated to the glory of God and in loving memory of Augusta Mary Baroness Bolsover who passed away August 7 1893 by her sons Henry Cavendish Bentinck, William Cavendish Bentinck, Charles Cavendish Bentinck, her daughter Ottoline Cavendish Bentinck, her stepson Arthur, 6th Duke of Portland 1896'. The walls of the baptistry were to be decorated with murals by Whall, just visible in Wilson's sketch of the chapel doors *Annual Architectural Review* 1893 p. 110. These murals were never executed, but in 1897 Whall painted others, in the quadrant corridor, or Print Gallery: their pale colours are in marked contrast to those c. 1845, depicting Dawn and Dusk, on the ceiling of the old riding school, which he would have seen during the Welbeck project. Painted on stretched canvas panels, these vivid skyscapes remain, unseen, in the roof space above the chapel and library.

91. *Studio* IX 1896 p. 130.

92. H. Wilson. *Silverwork and Jewellery* Ch. XXXIX p. 321: 'All who have seen Japanese gold-and silversmiths ... must have been impressed not only by the simplicity of [their] methods, but also by the ... skill with which [these] are employed.' see Ch. V below.

93. Nottinghamshire County Record Office: Portland Papers DD/P6/19/2/1, 10 sheets of foolscap paper comprising a carbon copy of transcriptions of 'Letters passing between Henry Wilson Esq and J.W. Stevens re: the Bronzework for the Chapel Doors at Welbeck Abbey, and for the inscription Tablet(s) for the Library'. Their correspondence dates from 20 April 1909-12 May 1912.

94. Ibid.

95. Ibid.

96. Ibid.

97. The only clash between Wilson and his patron arose over the bronze tablet, which is set into the right-hand side of the Library's entrance archway and whose Latin inscription records the transformation in 1893 of Smythson's riding school into chapel and library. So impatient did the Duke become that he threatened on 2 January 1911 to get it carried out elsewhere 'unless it can be completed within the next few weeks'. Wilson protested that there had been no avoidable delay, and on 14 March assured him that the tablet, having been 'cast in bronze ... will be silvered shortly and I will forward it at once.' The Duke decided against silvering, but on 11 Dec. 1911 Stevens warned that 'His Grace is not at all pleased with the long delay.' The Duke's irritation grew when Wilson, noticing 'concealed defects in the casting,' proposed sending the offending tablet to Welbeck anyway, while having a second cast made to replace it later. Stevens wrote on 14 Dec. 1911 asking Wilson to send the 'perfect casting only,' but, on 3 January 1912, after consulting the Duke, wrote again, insisting that the 'casting *you have* be sent *at once.*' Wilson explained on 5 January that it had only been to avert disappointment arising from there being no tablet at all that he had proposed sending the imperfect cast, adding 'it is not so defective as you think – it only is not quite perfect to the expert'. Two months later on 5 May 1912 Stevens noted that it was only as a result of Wilson's spotting flaws in the cast that the issue had flared up in the first place, and requested that he would 'kindly send the present casting so that it may at once be tried in position'. It was this cast which was installed, its 'defects' comprising some barely noticeable bubbles in the surface of the bronze background.

98. Completed c. 1906, with the dedication: 'To the glory of God and in loving memory Lord William Augustus Cavendish Bentinck, K.D.S.O. Major X Royal Hussars and second son of Lieutenant General Arthur Cavendish+Baroness Bolsover, born January 3 1865 died suddenly on board the S.S. Arabia in the Suez Canal on his way to India November 5 1903. He served without a day's intermission throughout the whole course of the Boer War 1899-1901 in South Africa. This monument is erected by his fellow officers, the men of his regiment and his brother William Arthur 6th Duke of Portland K.G.' A maquette of the pietà was shown at the International Society's Exhibition in Bradford, ill. *Studio* XXXVI 1905-6 p. 25 and at the Arts and Crafts Exhibition, Ghent (1913). An early design for the chapel doors appeared in *Annual Architectural Review* 1893 p. 110, an organ, rather than a pietà, over them. It was

anticipated that here, rather than at the E end of the chapel (its final site) the instrument would be heard equally well in chapel and library. In this sketch the doors also differ from those made; instead of the regular, rectilinear effect, the upper panels include a roundel showing, to the left, Virgin and Child, to the right, Christ the King. These roundels feature in letters between Wilson and Mr. Stevens (Wilson's of 10 January 1911 refers to 'the small circular panels', another of 14 November 1911 reports 'only the handles and the small circular panels remain to be completed'. In the published design, instead of the pietà, is a relief of Christ in Glory.

99. Ill. *The Builder* 23 September 1893. See also *Academy Architecture* 1893 p. 41 and H. Muthesius *The English House* (1904-5; trans. Seligman 1979) p. 46 fig. 86. A further screen design appeared in 1900 with Wilson's 'columned screen for a billiard room for Cranfield Esq.' (RIBA Drawings Coll. PA530/8).
100. 4th Arts and Crafts Exhibition Society Catalogue 1893 no. 176.
101. *Studio* II 1893 p. 15.
102. This oak staircase was to be decorated with plaster reliefs by Louis Davis but these were never executed. See AR VI 1896; ill. *Academy Architecture* (1st series) and in *Annual Architectural Review* 1897. The external architecture of the wing, its casements piercing the long curve of sheer rendered wall, owes nothing to the Abbey's own 18c forbears; the almost Oriental metal roof of the Virgins' wing is hung with pale diamond-scales, enriched with crestings and drained by fiercely-angled rainwater-goods, while its outline rings a distant bell in Wilson's unbuilt tower for Lynton church (see n. 23 above).
103. Further work carried out by Wilson at Welbeck included an Entrance Lodge, his scheme appearing in *Annual Architectural Review* 1892 p.63 and subsequently built as the Lion Gates on the B6005 Ollerton road. See Ch. 4 below.
104. H. Wilson. 'Arts and Crafts in their relation ... ' 1898 p. 16 (see n. 42 above).
105. H. Wilson. 'A Plea ... '(see n. 40 above).
106. Ibid.

CHAPTER 4
CREATIVE TRANSITION

1. D.S. MacColl. *Confessions of a Keeper* (1931) Ch. 1 p. 14. MacColl, an artist himself, was sympathetic to the Arts and Crafts, writing occasional articles on art and architecture for *The Architectural Review*.
2. H. Wilson. 'Nineteenth Century Church Building' *The Architectural Review* III 1897 p. 49.
3. H. Wilson. 'Architects, Sculptors and Monuments' *Manchester Guardian* 19 August 1916.
4. Cardiff City Hall was by Lanchester, Stewart and Rickards, Hull Central Library by Wills and Anderson, Bradford's Cartwright Library by Simpson and Milner-Allen, and the Imperial College of Science, Kensington by Aston Webb, the architect of the Royal Naval College, Dartmouth of the same year, 1899.
5. H. Wilson. AR VIII p. 3. The Old Bailey designs were published in *The British Architect* 27 July 1900 and in *The Architectural Revew* VIII 1900 p.3 and XXI p. 136-52.
6. D.S. MacColl and C. Nicholson. AR CII 1947 p. 142.
7. 5th Arts and Crafts Exhibition Catalogue no. 602 'Titlepage for a magazine'.
8. Articles which indicate the flavour of the *Review* under Wilson's editorship include 'Byzantine Art' by R. Weir Schultz (I); 'The Renaissance of the Art of Enamelling' by A. Fisher (IV); 'The Chapel of St. Peter the Martyr, Milan' by A. Melani (VIII); 'Architecture on the Stage' by J.A. Marshall (VIII), and Wilson's own – on Burne-Jones (1-III), on Sedding (jointly with J.P. Cooper) (III-IV), 'T.A. Jackson's restoration of St. Mary's, Oxford' (IV), and 'Persian Art' (IX).
9. H. Wilson. Retiring article as Editor. AR (IX) 1900-1 p. 250.
10. Brown-Morrison. Letter to M. Beasley, March 1959. Coll. D. Ottewill, Portsmouth. In their articles on Sedding, Wilson and Cooper reach a similar verdict on his views on business: 'Architecture to him was an art first, and as little of a business as possible'. AR III 1896-7 p. 133.
11. The gatehouse for Welbeck Abbey appeared in *Academy Architecture* X1VV p. 234. The proposed 'Hunting Lodge at Malmesbury' (1892) was illustrated in *Academy Architecture* (1892) 1693 p. 25 (plan p. 147), and listed in *The Architect* Vol. 48 p. 169. See also *The Builder* 21 May 1892 p. 395: 'This sketchy well-executed watercolour shows a stone house of quiet domestic architecture.... There is character in the management of the octagon bay ... and the chimneys have a quaintness all their own.'
Maybury Cottage (as Wilson's commission was known), standing on Pembroke Hill, is shown on the 1896 Ordnance Survey map as a House with a Lodge. By 1901, C.A. Pope was the owner and H.W. Crickmay the tenant; in 1912, the main property, then owned by H. Fearon, was renamed Mayhurst. This was echoed in the names of the adjacent roads, built when the grounds of Wilson's main building were sold for the 'development of newly erected houses and bungalows, for occupation in 1955, at Mayhurst, East Hill, Woking' (Surrey History Centre Archive). The addresses of the House and its Lodge were redesignated as 9 Mayhurst Avenue/1 East Hill. With its subsequent additions, the House became Mayhurst House Residential Care Home, while the Lodge (retaining in its name the 'Maybury' of the original commission) remains a separate private dwelling, since extended. When the Care Home was demolished in 2002 it was replaced by Mayhouse Mews.
For Wilson's design for cottage near Welwyn, Hertfordshire, see RIBA Drawings Collection PA530/10(1-3).
For his own house at St. Mary's Platt (1902) see below.
12. Ibid.
13. Ibid.
14. Ibid.
15. Harry Wilson first appears in the register of electors for 1892 in Sheepcote Road, the number 2 appearing in the register for 1893. Early numbering was consecutive, there being houses on one side only. As development grew, No. 2 became No 4. It was demolished in 1962, and Victoria Hall built on the site. Wilson himself moved to nearby Hindes Road in 1894, where he stayed until at least 1897.
16. H. Wilson. 'The Economic Problem in Architecture' (undated m/s, post 1914). (Wilson Archive, RCA).

HENRY WILSON 1864-1934 – **CHAPTER FOUR**

17. *The Arts and Crafts in relation to Architecture* (1898) p. 1.
18. A. Griffith to Wilson, August 1915. Wilson's reply of August 1915 is undated (Wilson Archive RCA).
19. D.S. MacColl and C. Nicholson. AR CII 1947 p. 142.
20. The Industrial Schools, or House of Charity, (later St. Agnes' Retreat) was built for a community of Anglican nuns, the Sisters of Charity. The design of 1890 (ill. *The Builder* June 1890) was altered in execution after Sedding's death, the sculptural embellishments being omitted, and the chapel built to a new design by G.F. Bodley. However, the laundry was erected as planned, its functional design being praised by Wilson in his article on Sedding in *The Architectural Review*. Sedding's design ill. in *Victorian Architecture* (1978) by R. Dixon and S. Muthesius p. 26 and in *Bristol: an architectural history* by A. Gomme, M. Jenner and B. Little (1979) p. 396. Also ill. is Wilson's fireplace in S range. A typescript *Bristol: street index of buildings of architectural interest* by A. Gomme in Bristol Central Library acknowledges the 'notable' Wilson interiors and fireplace. Wilson's sketch for the quadrangle ill. *The Architect* 22 May 1891 Vol. 45 p. 311, and in *The Architectural Illustration Society (2nd series)* pl. 362. An interior view of Wilson's refectory ill. *The Builder* 22 October 1904. See also Clare Crick, *Victorian Buildings of Bristol*.
21. C. A. Nicholson. Obituary: H. Wilson. *Jnl RIBA* 14 April 1934.
22. H. Wilson and J.P. Cooper. 'The Work of J.D. Sedding' (vi) AR IV 1898 p. 33. Examples of Sedding's metalwork appear in the catalogue of *Victorian Church Art* (V&A 1971) p. 120 ff. Both Lethaby and Wilson note that when Sedding came to London in 1875, his architectural commissions were few. Only in the 1880s would architecture practically monopolise his time. See W.R. Lethaby 'A Note on the artistic life and work of John D. Sedding' in *The Builder* 10 October 1891 p. 271, and Henry Wilson 'John Sedding, his life and work' in *British Architect* 1 January 1892 p. 16.
23. H. Wilson. Biographical Note 1910, Victoria and Albert Library. This note does not specify when Wilson worked in the bronze foundry. The brief biographical notes in the RIBA Drawings Collection confirm only that it was after he had 'completed most of Sedding's unfinished commissions'. It is unlikely to have constituted Wilson's sole occupation, given his known commissions. In speculating where it might have been, convenience might suggest a firm in London, one perhaps recommended by Henry Longden – Wilson's familiarity with foundry work in general was assured by his contact over many years with Longden, whose foundry was in Sheffield but whose London office was adjacent to the Sedding/Wilson practice in Oxford Street (see also Ch. 3 n. 49). If not in London, it is possible Wilson's foundry experience was at Munaretti's in Venice: his presence in the city in 1910 is confirmed by Mrs. Mary Harvey of Fareham visiting him there, to discuss her commission for a mosaic in Holy Trinity church, Fareham (see n. 87 below). However, the reference to his gaining foundry experience after finishing Sedding's outstanding commissions suggests a date within a few years of 1891, making another candidate more feasible: Singers of Frome, Somerset. A bronze lectern in the 1896 ACES display (ill. Marianne Tidcombe, *The Doves Bindery*) was captioned 'Modelled by Frederick W. Pomeroy and H. Wilson. Cast by J.W. Singer & Sons'. This firm was known both for its links with distinguished scuptors and for its high quality work.
24. Ibid.
25. H. Wilson. Letter to Mrs. L. Tooth 27 December 1897. Brithdir Collection, Merioneth Historical and Record Society Vol.8 1979-80. To ease the move Wilson briefly shared an office in Manchester Square with J.P. Cooper and H.W. Finch. See also Ch.3 n. 19.
26. J. Farleigh. *The Creative Craftsman* (1950) Ch. 10 p. 149.
27. Ill. AR V 1898 pl. iv. The beaten bronze tabernacle is illustrated in AR IV (Supplement, 2nd series) 1898.
28. Colorossi later worked for J.P. Cooper and for his son, Francis Cooper (b. 1906). Luigi Movio was the father of the better known Latino Movio, a silver chaser working independently 1892-1905. He registered his mark at Goldsmiths' Hall in 1894. From 1907-8 he worked for Holland, Adwinkle and Slater.
29. Sedding's chancel was added to Holy Trinity, Salcombe in 1889-90, together with the small chapel in the north-east corner, the vestries in the south-east corner, the organ space above, and his brass altar cross and candlesticks. (*Victorian Church Art* no. M4; V&A 1971). For the scheme to enlarge the church, see *The Builder* 13 December 1890 and *The Architect* Vol. 44 1890 p. 97. Sedding's 'Design for Salcombe church, Devon' appears in the article 'Attainable Ideals' in AR VI p. 149. Wilson's chancel gates bear the inscription 'To the Glory of God and to the memory of C. and T. Turner and their 20 years' work for music of the church'.
30. Wilson's scheme for Marple's Lady Chapel ill. *Academy Architecture* 1896 p. 31 and in *The Builder* 10 October 1896 p. 290. See also RIBADC. It was modified in execution by the substitution of a chevron-patterned wooden altar rail for the marble one illustrated. The angels kneeling at its entrance were used instead on the altar rail at St. Peter's, Shaldon, Devon, built 1893-1902 by J.D. Sedding's nephew, Edmund.
31. W.R. Lethaby. *Architecture, Mysticism and Myth* (1891) Ch. III 'Foursquare' p. 53. 'A four-square enclosure stands at the top of the world mountain, where the polar column stands and whence issue the four rivers. From the thought of such an enclosure we get, Lenormat states, one word *Paradise*'.
32. *Studio* IX 1896 p. 130. A case in the West Gallery of the 5th Arts and Crafts Exhibition Society show held the Marple altar cross, wafer box and candlesticks (Cat. no. 179 a-d).
33. Version with dove appears in the collection of Wilson's sketchbooks in V&A. Spencer Carey Curtis (1865-1945), who assisted on the wafer box, was articled to Wilson 1896-99. Having completed his articles, he served in the Boer War, returning to London in 1902. In 1904 he was proposed as ARIBA by T.P. Figgis, H. Hall and J. Slater, and in 1920 as FRIBA by Charles Nicholson. He practiced in London until 1910, designing large Cape Dutch Revival houses after Herbert Baker's in South Africa. He later settled in Guernsey, building Arts and Crafts style houses.
34. H. Wilson. Biographical Note (1910) V&A Library: 'Orcagna, Leonardo and the Pisani were my ideals.' Wilson cited a retable by Andrea Orcagna (1308-68), sculptor, painter, architect and member of both the Painters' and the Stonemasons' Guilds of Florence, in his lecture *Arts*

HENRY WILSON 1864-1934 – **CHAPTER FOUR**

and Crafts in their relation to Architecture (pub. as a booklet by the Architectural Association in 1898). His multi-talented ideal was again borne out by Leonardo (1452-1519) who, in a letter to the Duke of Milan, described himself as a complete artist and craftsman, able to construct buildings, to sculpt in marble, bronze and clay, and to paint 'as much as anyone'. The works of Niccolo Pisano (1220-84) and his son Giovanni (1245-1314) include four great pulpits: Niccolo's in the Baptistry at Pisa and a jointly-made one in Siena Cathedral are illustrated in Wilson's booklet (see above). The International Society of Sculptors, Painters and Gravers ('the International'), founded in 1898, aimed to show the finest art of the day, irrespective of nationality. The venue for the first two shows was the former Princes Skating Rink, Knightsbridge; after displays in Europe (1902) and America (1903), exhibitions took place at the New Gallery, at the Grosvenor Gallery, and once, finally, at the Royal Academy. Whistler was the Society's first president with work in its opening show, which included art by Rodin, Klimt, Manet, Fantin-Latour, Toulouse-Lautrec, Guthrie, Anning Bell and J.J. Shannon. By 1899, its international flavour had faded, though under Rodin's presidency (1903-17) its role as a forum for modern art revived. (see P. Athill, 'The International Society of Painters, Sculptors and Gravers' *Burlington Magazine* vol. CXXVII no. 282 Jan. 1985).

35. H. Wilson. 'The Creative Impulse and its place in Education'. (undated m/s c. 1922, Wilson Archive RCA). Much of this paper duplicates a lecture given by Wilson at the 1918 New Ideals in Education Conference, there being renamed then printed as *Education and the Handicrafts*. (Wilson Archive RCA). The phrase 'the building arts' appears in 'Nineteenth Century Church Building' AR III 1897-8 p. 49 and in 'Some Considerations of J.D. Sedding's Work' AR III 1897-8 p. 238.
36. J.D. Sedding. *Art and Handicraft* (1893) Ch. V 'Expression in Architecture'.
37. H. Wilson. 'Architects, Sculptors and Monuments'. *Manchester Guardian* 17 August 1916.
38. Ibid.
39. H. Wilson. Letter to Mrs. Tooth 21 June 1895. The Wilson/Tooth letters are in the Brithdir Collection (ref. 2/M/149/7), Archifdy Dolgellau, Gwynedd, reprinted in an edition by I. Allen for the Merioneth Historical and Record Society Vol 8 1979-80.
40. H. Wilson. Letter to Mrs. Tooth. 28 August 1895.
41. C.H.B. Quennell won, in 1895, two awards: the National Gold Medal for Architectural Design, and the RIBA Silver Medal. He set up his own practice in 1896, specialising in domestic architecture.
42. H. Wilson. Letter to Mrs. Tooth. 22 October 1895.
43. H.L. North later practiced from Llanfairfechan. See I. Allen, PhD thesis Liverpool University.
44. H. Wilson. Letter to Mrs. Tooth 13 July 1895.
45. H. Wilson. Letter to Mrs. Tooth 1 August 1895.
46. H. Wilson. Letter to Mrs. Tooth 5 March 1897.
47. H. Wilson. Letter to Mrs. Tooth 29 February 1896.
48. H. Wilson. Letter to Mrs. Tooth 21 June 1895.
49. H. Wilson. Letter to Mrs. Tooth 29 September 1895.
50. H. Wilson. Letter to Mrs. Tooth. 1 November 1897. Wilson staked out the site on 12 and 13 September 1895. See also his letter of 13 July 1895: 'I propose not to use the assorted slates generally in use ... but to select myself from the quarry ... to produce a building which should harmonise continually with its surroundings.'
51. H. Wilson. Letter to Mrs. Tooth 30 October 1896.
52. H. Wilson. Letter to Mrs. Tooth 21 June 1895.
53. H. Wilson. 'Some Considerations of J.D. Sedding's Work' AR III 1997-8 p. 240.
54. H. Wilson. Letter to Mrs. Tooth 8 June 1896.
55. H. Wilson. Letter to Mrs. Tooth 14 July 1896. The 'house in Lincolnshire' was probably Walmsgate Hall (see below and n. 93).
56. H. Wilson. 'The Work of Sir Edward Burne-Jones' (ii) AR III 1896-7 p. 232.
57. H. Wilson. Letter to Mrs. Tooth 9 August 1898. Pullen and two assistants had recently been colouring the inside of a church for Wilson 'near Chester', perhaps St. Martin's, Marple. Pullen sent his bill for the Brithdir job on 27 Sept. 1898: 'Sidney Pullen, Decorative Painter, 24, Barrington Road, Brixton, S.W. St. Mark's Church, Brithdir. To sundry decorative distemper work throughout, including scaffolding, fares and expenses £52 – 11 – 0'. Wilson noted the relationship between a building and its decoration in 'The Work of Sir Edward Burne-Jones' (ii) AR I 1896-7: 'The ideas of permanence and mass associated with a building are themselves the most potent influences upon the painter who essays to decorate it.'
58. H. Wilson. Letter to Mrs. Tooth 19 February 1896.
59. H. Wilson. Letter to Mrs. Tooth 26 August 1897.
60. H. Wilson. Letter to Mrs. Tooth 15 March 1898. see also Letter to Mrs. Tooth 21 June 1895: 'I have been so much interested in [the work] that I have spent more time on it than usual.'
61. H. Wilson. Letter to Mrs. Tooth 12 August 1896.
62. H. Wilson. Letter to Mrs. Tooth 15 March 1898. He continues 'The altar will assert itself and be the key to the whole church by the richness of the design. The pulpit was kept simple for that very reason.... When it has taken on the dark rich colour that copper always does the effect will be very solemn and splendid.'
63. H. Wilson. Letter to Mrs. Tooth 27 December 1897.
64. H. Wilson. Letter to Mrs. Tooth 15 March 1898.
65. H. Wilson. Letter to Mrs. Tooth 14 September 1898. See also his letter of 21 June 1895: 'A rood would seem to work well and I should like to get it done.... I have been sorely tempted to put columns and mouldings, but quite apart from my invincible dislike of any copying of medieval details I felt that the site and nature of the building forbade any work of that nature'.
66. H. Wilson. Letter to Mrs. Tooth 9 November 1897.
67. H. Wilson. 'The Gates of Wonder'. (undated m/s Wilson Archive RCA). See also letter from Wilson to Mrs. Tooth 20 December 1897 about the oak altar rail: 'I have made it more solid than usual because the common rail is so flimsy it imparts an air of weakness to the whole church. The common brass ones are not one quarter as good looking, and have the disadvantage of needing constant cleaning.'
68. H. Wilson. Letter to Mrs. Tooth 21 September 1895. In a

letter of 29 September he explained that since the plaque was not as big as he had first intended, he would have preferred another site: 'Instead of fixing it in the centre of the W. wall, it might on account of its smaller size be fixed in the porch ... the bronze plate would then be visible to all ... who cared to sit [there]'. The inscription gives 10 October 1895 as the date it was installed, 'to the glory of God and the beloved memory of Charles Tooth, priest MA'.

69. W.R. Lethaby's *Leadwork* (1893) p. 148 expresses the wish that the craft may enjoy a revival: 'The capabilities of lead have been sufficiently proved by more than two thousand years of artistic manipulation. That someone may again take up this fine craft ... as an artist and original worker, expressing only himself – this has been my chief hope in preparing this little book'. The article in *The Builder* appeared on 31 March 1900 p. 320. Troup's comments were made in Lecture XII, 'External Leadwork' which appeared in a book edited by R. Davison *The Arts Connected with Building* (1909).
70. H. Wilson. Letter to Mrs. Tooth 1 June 1896.
71. H. Wilson. Letter to Mrs. Tooth 15 March 1898.
72. H. Wilson. Letter to Mrs. Tooth 6 October 1898.
73. H. Wilson. Letter to Mrs. Tooth 15 March 1898.
74. Ibid.
75. H. Wilson. 'The Architecture of Monuments' (undated m/s Wilson Archive RCA).
76. Ibid.
77. The lettering on the base of the memorial is arranged in two panels: 'In loving memory of Edward Douglas Tinling, for 30 years Canon of this Cathedral and inspector of schools. Born 2 Dec 1815; died 2 Dec 1897'.
78. H. Wilson. 'The Work of Sir Edward Burne-Jones' (i) AR I 1896 p. 177.
79. H. Wilson. Address on teaching and the value of learning by doing, delivered at the Vittoria Street School, Birmingham 1904-6. (Wilson Archive RCA).
80. Wilson's initial sketch of an astrological clock (undated) has hands and two outer rings like Gloucester's, but in the central panel is a female saint and Mercury as a medieval knight (RIBA Drawings Coll). The Treasurer's Accounts of Gloucester Cathedral for 1898-9 record the beginning of Wilson's commission: 'Work and material in preparation for new clock £72'. Dent's attendance – the start of their long-term supervision of the clock – is recorded in the same account: 'examining clock and chimes £2-10'. The replacement of the rod and gear mechanism by an electric motor is described in the *Gloucester Journal* Oct 12 1985 (coll. Stainburn & Taylor Architects, Ledbury).
The wooden plaque beneath the clock is inscribed 'To the glory of God again in memory of Barholomew Price DD FRS FRAS. Born May 14 1818 Died Dec 29 1898 Canon of Gloucester Master of Pembroke for 45 years Sedlian Professor of Natural Philosophy in the University of Oxford'. The marble and brass memorial tablet Wilson made in 1891 in the south transept is inscribed 'In loving memory of Evan Evans, Master of Pembroke College and Canon of this Cathedral for 27 years. He fell asleep in Jesus Nov. 23rd 1891. The souls of the righteous are in the hands of God'.
81. The dish was commissioned by Canon John Sinclair, vicar of St. John's 1898-1908. Measuring 16" across, its central enamel panel bears the arms of the Sinclair family, whose background was naval. At intervals around the rim are three decorative panels, each enclosed in a triangular border of enamel, whose blue-green colour suggests the sea and whose pointed form evokes a Gothic archway. Each contains a silver sailing ship, reiterating those on the Sinclair arms. At the apex of each are circular enamel portraits: St. John the Baptist, patron saint of the church, St. Lawrence with the gridiron of his martyrdom, and St. Katherine, tortured on a spiked wheel and beheaded for her faith. Each portrait rests on a range of miniature silver mountains suggesting the heavenly foothills. The outermost rim of the dish is wave-patterned blue-green enamel. Its underside is inscribed with details of its commission. See Cat. *Victorian Church Art* V&A 1971. An undated sketch in the Wilson Archive shows a typical ship motif.
82. Henry Wagner (1792-1870) arranged for the completion of Sir Charles Barry's parish church of St. Peter (1824-8), as well as commissioning several new churches for the town. His son Arthur (1824-1902) commissioned St. Paul's, West Street by R.C. Carpenter (1848; additions 1861 by G.F. Bodley); St. Mary and St. Mary Magdalene, Bread Sreet by G.F. Bodley (1862, dem. 1950); The Annunciation, Washington Street by W. Dancy (1864; additions 1881 by Edmund Scott); St. Martin's, Lewes Road (1872-5) by G. Somers Clarke; the Resurrection, Russell Street by R.C. Carpenter (1877). See *The Wagners of Brighton* by A. Wagner (1959); *Some Brighton Churches* (1922), *Seven Churches* (1947) and *Wagner of Brighton* (1949) by H.H. Maughan; *The Wagners of Brighton* (1983) by A. Wagner and A. Dale; 'Wagnerian High Church' by N. Taylor in AR March 1965, reprinted in A. Service (ed) *Edwardian Architecture and its Origins* (1975).
Edmund Scott (1828-95) built Wagner's rural retreat at Buxted, West Sussex, with its church of St. Mary (1885-86), whose design is based on the symbolism of sevens. Scott's other churches include St. Andrew, Portslade (1863), St. James, Brighton (1874-5, dem.) and chancel (1878-9) for Christ Church, Eastbourne; St. Saviour, Preston (1885, with F.T. Cawford, succeded to firm 1895).
83. Residents living at the west end of the 'barn' (see *Church of St. Bartholomew Brighton*, R.J.G. Holmes 1975 p.7) were most inconvenienced by smoke in their homes; they were soon mollified when Arthur Wagner bought the houses then let them back to them at reduced rents. These nicknames apart, St. Bartholomew's became in *The Brighton Herald* 'The Wagner Folly, a frowning mass of bricks ... a tall bully ... '; Sir John Betjeman called it the 'cathedral' of the area's High Church revivalism. (see Holmes p. 3). Its clergy shared a propensity for the 'morning Opera' type of worship first used at Arthur Wagner's own church, St. Paul's (see *St. Martin's Brighton* by M.J. Leppard and K.H. Hackman p. 5). The term 'London, Brighton & South Coast Religion' (Maughan, *Seven Churches* p. vi) was the obvious one to apply to the large churches springing up along the south coast c. 1870-80 to embrace post-Tracterian ritual, including Christ Church, St. Leonard's-on-Sea, St. Peter's, Folkestone and Sedding's and Wilson's own St. Clement's, Bournemouth

– all drew large congregations from wide catchment areas linked by the new railway lines. The outspoken reactions that St. Bartholomew's always provoked ensured its fame far and wide: as Maughan remarked in *Seven Churches* p. 9: '... no church in the provinces, scarcely even in London itself, has attained wider fame; even in remote colonnial settlements, there are faces which light up at the mention of St. Bartholomew's Brighton'.

84. The division of the rivers of Eden occurs in Genesis Ch. 2 v.10: 'And a river went out of Eden to water the garden; and from thence it was parted, and became into four heads....' Wilson's inclusion of the source of the waters of Paradise (making a total of five streams on his chalice) shows him exploiting this biblical text for compsitional ends. (see also *Victorian Church Art* no. M.15, V&A 1971). The chalice is unmarked, but its underside is inscribed with a cross and the words 'given to the Church by the Ward of C.B.S. 1898 A.M.D.G'. It was displayed at the Royal Academy in the year after its completion: 'Harry Wilson 1899, no 1694. Design for Chalice, St. Bartholomew's Church Brighton'.See A. Graves *Royal Academy Exhibitors* vol. viii 1906 p.307. See also *Victorian and Edwardian Decorative Arts* 1952 no. Z.14, V&A; *Sources of Twentieth Century Design* (1960-1 Council of Europe Ex, Paris) no. 1326; *Beauty's Awakening: centenary exhibition of the Art Workers' Guild 1884-1984* no. 433 (Brighton Museum 1984).

85. H. Wilson. 'Nineteenth Century Church Building' AR III 1897 p. 49.

86. H. Hamilton Maughan. *Seven Churches* (1947) p.11.

87. H. Wilson. 'The Work of Sir Edward Burne-Jones.' (iii) AR 1897-8 p. 278.

88. W.R. Lethaby. *Architecture, Mysticism and Myth* (1891) Ch. III 'Foursquare' p. 53. *St. Bartholomew's Magazine* of May 1906 recorded that an anonymous donor's gift had enabled further work on the sanctuary, including 'the filling in of the spandrels of the Baldacchino with mosaic, the erection of marble steps to the Altar, the marble paving, and ... a marble Pulpit'. The steps and the baldacchino were dedicated on 14 October, that month's magazine noting that the steps leading up from nave are of Belgian marble, with a central section of Swiss green marble, the altar steps being black with a 5' broad strip of red 'giving the effect of a carpet'. In the top step is a 'large plaque of magnificent blue lapus lazuli [whose centre] is set with a circular piece of rich green marble quarried in Devonshire ... we can say with confidence that the Sanctuary ... is one of the most beautiful in the South of England.'

89. The high altar, of oak and dating from 1874, was made by S. Bell, with seven painted panels depicting the crucified Christ, Our Lady, St. Joseph, St. Peter, St. John, St. Bartholomew, and St. Paul. Bell also designed the large crucifix on the east wall, of painted and incised on encaustic tiles. Wilson's tabernacle shows the crowned figure of 'perpetual youth, ever ... sustained by the true Vine' (*Jubilee Book: St. Bartholomew* 1924), with the words 'Ego sum vitas vera' and 'Mane in Me.'

90. 'she was one of the most regular communicants: in all weathers, & under all circumstances she would always be found in her place in church ... the new altar is the work of Mr. Henry Wilson of London, & we venture to think that it is a unique specimen of that artist's excellent work. The following description may be of interest to our readers. The Altar is in beaten copper plated with silver, the largest portion being of Sheffield Plate. The subject is the Epiphany. The panel in the centre is encircled by a wreath of vine to symbolise the True Vine; round the panel are grouped the seven planets circling ... round the Central Sun of Righteousness.' (*Chichester Diocesan Gazette* 1902). Four years later Wilson received a letter of complaint from Louisa's widower: 'I was down at St. Bartholomew's last week and was told that you were much disturbed by the state of the memorial altar you ... put up for me to my wife's memory. They told me that you considered the front on each side of the centre had not been sufficiently plated hence its bad colour *quite yellow*. They tell me that they have cleaned it from time to time according to your instructions (using chlorate of silver paste). I should be glad to have your opinion as to *what had better be done ... considering what it cost.*' (letter from Thorncliffe Gilpin, 10 Cheyne Walk, Chelsea, 12 November 1906; Wilson Archive RCA)

91. Whall's carved oak crucifix (now in the William Morris Gallery), was shown at the 1888 Arts and Crafts Exhibition Society, and at their 1914 show at the Louvre. Wilson would have been familiar with this design, which hung in Whall's home.

92. H. Wilson. 'The Work of Sir Edward Burne-Jones' (ii) AR I 1896-7 p. 230. 'Vista is of fundamental importance in a building. But how many Architects take the trouble to ... show the infinite by the finite, to make a beyond by building a barrier?' Wilson used the same argument, unsuccessfully, when defending his proposed reredos at Holy Trinity, Sloane Street.

93. Ill. *Moderne Bauformen* XIII 1909 Heft 65. See also P. Howell, *Victorian Churches* (RIBA) p. 61-3.

94. H. Wilson. Letter to Churchwarden, St. Bartholomew's, 28 May 1909. (Wilson Archive RCA). Wilson goes on to mention a statue of St. Christopher and two candelabra (these subsequently made by Barkentin and Krall), and 'the statue of St. Bartholomew' which he himself carved for the exterior over the E. door – in one hand the saint holds a knife (the instrument by which he had been flayed alive), in the other is a model of his church (the indestructable nature of faith). The attention Wilson paid in this letter to different but related pieces of work reflects his wish to secure the essential 'unity of purpose and design'; he argued that 'those who have ... no practical experience of such work do not realise the time necessary.... I have explained this many times to Mr. Cocks, but doubtless parochial duties have obliterated these facts from his mind. Mr. Edwin A. Abbey R.A., Mr. Norman Shaw R.A., Mr. J. Belcher R.A., the Duke of Portland, the Marquess of Londonderry ... & many others will all be willing to testify that my work is work of value, & done with interest, sincerity & even tenacity of purpose ... & with some degree of artistic success'.

95. Ibid.

96. Ibid.

97. Wilson was commissioned to add a chancel and sanctuary to Holy Trinity, Fareham in 1910-13. In 1910 Mrs. Mary

Harvey visited him in Venice, and ordered the mosaic for the east wall, above his alabaster altar. This mosaic, for which Wilson designed a pierced and gilded frame of vines, was installed at Mrs. Harvey's expense in 1922. The parochial church council of 31 August 1922 recorded Mrs. Harvey's gift with its dedication: 'To the glory of God and in loving memory of Thomas Henry Harvey of Blackbrook Grove who died April 15th 1915 and his only son Kenneth, Lieutenant Royal Field Artillery who was mortally wounded in action at Ypres Sept. 26th 1915'. According to the recollections of some elderly parishioners, neither the Harvey family nor its Italian craftsman were entirely pleased with this mosaic, but it was not until the late 1950s that it was covered over. Wilson's sketch for the mosaic is in the Hampshire Record Office. The chancel screen is dedicated to the memory of Mrs. Harvey herself. For Wilson's memorial stained glass east window for the church see Ch. 7 below.

98. N. Taylor. 'Byzantium in Brighton' AR CXXXIX 1966 p. 174 (see n. 74 above). The underside of the gallery is lined in red and white alabaster, together with the back wall. The architect and designer Charles Spooner, an admirer of Wilson's work, later made a copy of this pulpit for his own church of St. Bartholomew, Ipswich.
99. 'Raphael warns Adam and Eve' and 'The Archangel Michael foretelling the Crucifixion' formed illustrations in the edition of *Paradise Lost* that William Blake made for Thomas Butts c. 1808. Wilson's description of the impact Westminster Abbey had on Blake reflects his own response to Gothic architecture: 'Those spirit haunted aisles were to influence his whole life. Architecture had become a religion to him; the Abbey itself a symbol of the Holy Kingdom'. H. Wilson, 'The Pre-Raphaelite Movement and its influence on the Arts and Crafts' 1899. (unpub. m/s, Wilson Archive RCA). The pulpit was installed on 23 December 1906, and pieces of the old wooden pulpit sold to parishioners.
100. Wilson had originally intended to keep the organ at the East end, where the pulpit is situated. A drawing in the RIBA Drawings Collection dated 1898 shows a large organ loft, whose frame had been built in 1901, but which was declared out of proportion and rejected by Wilson. The small pulpit shown in front of it was never made. see AR III: Supplement on the Arts & Crafts at the Royal Academy 3 May 1898; and *Moderne Bauformen* VIII 1909 Heft 64. Wilson's design for the flooring for the organ gallery (RIBA Drawings Collection PA529/14) is dated 1900.
101. H. Wilson. 'The Pre-Raphaelite Movement and its influence on the Arts and Crafts', 1899 (unpub. m/s Wilson Archive RCA).
102. W.R. Lethaby. *Architecture, Mysticism and Myth* (1891) Ch. VI 'The planetary spheres' p. 124-7. The temple evokes the Holy of Holies at the centre of Jerusalem. The centre itself had mystic and ritual connotations (op. cit. p. 87). Lethaby describes the four rivers of Paradise flowing from beneath the temple (op. cit. p. 127), the water flowing from beneath the central rock was 'the source of all fresh water on earth' (op. cit. p. 90). In addition to featuring at the Exhibition of Christian Art, Dusseldorf in 1909, the chalice appeared in the 1914 Exposition des Arts Décoratifs de Grande Bretagne et d'Irlande in Paris (see illustrated catalogue p. 94 no. 1054. NB the decoration of knop is wrongly attributed to the paten). See also *Copy or Creation*, Goldsmith's Hall 1967 no. E. 19; *Victorian Church Art* (1971, no. M17); *W.R. Lethaby: Architecture, Design, Education*, at Central School of Art and Design 1984 (cat. no. 87). Wilson's drawings in the V&A Print Room include a similar chalice (E. 669 (358)-1955), and another a sketch shows a battlemented base, like that of the Gloucester chalice, dated 20 Feb 99.
103. Ibid.
104. Ibid.
105. Letter from Mrs. Dallas-Yorke, Walmsgate, 30 November 1905 (Wilson Archive RCA). The altar is of plain marble slabs.
106. W.R. Lethaby. *Architecture, Mysticism and Myth* (1891) Ch. IX 'Pavements like the sea' p. 208.
107. Letter to Wilson from Mrs. Dallas-Yorke, Walmsgate, 27 August 1905 (Wilson Archive RCA).
108. C.R. Ashbee, recounting Janet Ashbee's comments. *Ashbee Memoirs* Vol. 1. 9 May 1899 p. 118.
109. Letter from Mrs. Dallas-Yorke, Walmsgate, 30 November 1905 (Wilson Archive RCA). The altar is of plain marble slabs.
110. Letter to Wilson from Mrs. Dallas-Yorke, Walmsgate, 19 December 1905 (Wilson Archive RCA).
111. 6th Arts and Crafts Exhibition Society Catalogue (1899) no. 227. 'Chalice veil. Designed by Henry Wilson. Executed and exhibited by Miss M. Morse.' After the Wilsons' move to France, Margaret took up painting, one of her works being published in the *Studio*, 1923 vol. 86 p. 330: Margaret E. Wilson, 'Miniature'. A panelled chest by Henry also appeared, p. 265. Another of her paintings appeared posthumously in the *Studio*, 1949 vol. 137 p. 191: Margaret E. Wilson, 'Strand on the Green'.
112. Letter from Jessie (wife of Harry) Murphy, 'Falhalla', St. Mary's Platt, Kent to M. Beasley. Coll. D. Ottewill. The Murphys' house was built by Curtis and Caine in 1914.
113. Orrea Pernel. Reminiscences. Wilson Papers, V&A Library.
114. H. Wilson. 'The art of a nation is the expression of its moral condition'. (typewritten m/s, 1914-18. Wilson Archive RCA). For all its discreetly-added 21st century amenities, Orrea Pernel, Dione Lucas (née Wilson), indeed Henry Wilson himself, would still know the house: its essentially local and modest character remains unchanged.
115. Ralph A. Cram, the Gothic-inspired American architect, with whom Wilson became friendly in the early 1900s, was a member of the American Institute of Architects and of the Architectural Association of London. He was also a fellow of the Boston Society of Architects. His article on the work of Henry Wilson for the Boston magazine *Christian Art* Vol. II no.6 March 1908 p. 261-73 discusses many of his major works. (see Ch. 9 below).
116. H. Wilson. 'The Architecture of Monuments' (undated m/s, Wilson Archive RCA).
117. Brown-Morrison. Letter to M. Beasley February 1957. Collection D. Ottewill.
118. Prior's collaboration with designers and craftsmen is exemplified again by a proposal he was working on with Wilson in the 1890s for a ciborium with sculpted

decoration for Norwich Cathedral.

119. Lewis Vulliamy (1791-1871) and his son George John Vulliamy (1817-1886) both practiced in London. In addition to adding the chancel, Grove also built the parish hall 1910-11.
120. Ibid.
121. P. Grove. Conversations with N. Taylor 1965. (typewritten m/s, RIBA Drawings Collection RAN/8/B/11). This claim is used without demur in M. Richardson *Architects of the Arts and Crafts Movement* (1983) p. 74.
122. C.A. Nicholson. Obituary: H. Wilson. *Jnl. RIBA* 14 April 1934.
123. The Southwell Diocesan Magazine (Feb. 1905) Vol. XVIII p.34 has 'Mr. H. Wilson of London (sic)' as the designer of the doors for St. Mary's, Nottingham.
124. H. Wilson. 'The art of a nation....' See n. 101 above.

CHAPTER 5: **FOCUS ON THE METALWORKING ARTS**

1. Fred Miller. 'Some gold, silver and coppersmiths'. *The Art Journal* 1896 p. 345-9.
2. *New York Sun* 21 October 1899.
3. H. Wilson. 'Goldsmiths' work and Jewellery'. (undated m/s; Wilson Archive RCA). The creative logic that led Wilson into fine metalworking provoked a delighted incredulity from an American journalist reviewing his career in the 1920s. '... he was an architect and – in spite of his strictures on the word – successful. But he found himself hampered in working out his ideas by the fact that he was not also a sculptor; he could not get his work done right. So – he took up goldsmithing!' (*Boston Transcript* 2 July 1927).
4. H. Wilson. *Address to the Goldsmiths', Silversmiths', Jewellers' and Allied Trades' Art Council at the presentation of prizes to workmen and apprentices for essays upon the applied arts at the Franco-British Exhibition at Goldsmiths' Hall*, 8 December 1908, printed in *The Watchmaker, Jeweller, Silversmith and Optician* January 1909.
5. R.A. Cram. 'The Work of Henry Wilson', op cit p. 270-2.
6. H. Wilson. *Silverwork and Jewellery* Ch.1 Introduction p. 28-9.
7. In the collection of Cheltenham Art Gallery and Museum. The Artificers' Guild had been established 4 years before by Nelson Dawson with a workshop employee Edward Spencer, and acquired in 1903 by Montague Fordham (a former director of the Birmingham Guild of Handicraft), who moved it from Chiswick to the Fordham Gallery, Maddox Street. J.P. Cooper created many pieces for it; his style, combining with that of Spencer, established a recognisable Guild look. It closed in 1942.
8. Wilson's sketches for the ring appear along with a Lethaby drawing for it in an album of Wilson's designs (V&A Prints and Drawings). The ring itself, its hoop struck with Wilson's monogram, is in the collection of Victoria and Albert Museum. A version of this idea appeared in Wilson's gold and brass ring of 1903-06, in which he depicted a Byzantine church whose dome is formed by a chalcedony. (Coll. Fitzwilliam Museum, Cambridge). Parallels with Wilson's Gothic church ring are seen in a Liberty ring design (V&A Prints and Drawings), and in a ring of 1899-1901 for May Morris by Charles Ricketts (ill. C. Gere *Victorian Jewellery Design* pl. 70a).
9. C.R. Ashbee. *Modern English Silverwork* 1909 (new ed. A. Crawford and S. Bury, 1974) p. 6.
10. W.R. Lethaby. *Architecture* 1911 p. 248-9. As well as prefiguring Berg's 1913 *Jahrhunderthalle*, the Liverpool proposal formed a precursor of the plastic forms of the Amsterdam architects of the early 1920s, such as Theo van der Vijdeveld's Volkstheater. Lethaby's words were prophetic, too, in the context of Liverpool itself, where Sir Frederick Gibberd's circular Roman Catholic cathedral – its principal materials steel, glass and concrete – was consecrated in 1967.
11. R.S. Weir in 'W.R. Lethaby 1857-1931: a symposium in honour of his centenary'. *Jnl RIBA* April 1957.
12. Ibid.
13. *The Builder* LXXXIII 1902 p. 70.
14. *Building News* LXXXIII 1902 p. 102. The models and plans are now in the collection of V&A. See also *Victorian Church Art* (1971) op cit.
15. To judge from Margaret Macdonald Mackintosh writing to Anna Muthesius in September or November 1902, Bodley was unimpressed with the overall standard of the entries for the competition: 'It is as you say a great pity about the Cathedral but only what one must expect. In architecture, originality is a crime – especially to those who can themselves only be copyists. We heard from a cousin of Mr. Bodley's that "He had the greatest difficulty in selecting any of the designs sent in – they are all so bad" – a funny opinion when one thinks that amongst those designs were those of H. Wilson, Leonard Stokes, Beresford Pite – not to mention *one* highly thought of – However he is still alive & kicking and serenely thinking of what he will do next.' (Muthesius papers, Werkbund Archiv, Berlin; copy in Hunterian Art Gallery, University of Glasgow). A letter of 23 January 1903 from C.R. Mackintosh to Hermann Muthesius requested him to forward an enclosed letter to Wilson. Mackintosh was hit hard by the outcome of the Liverpool competition, and asked Muthesius to have a word with Norman Shaw about it. It might be surmised that in that enclosed letter Mackintosh shared his anger with Wilson, perhaps even suggesting their making a joint protest. (ibid).
16. H. Wilson. *Silverwork and Jewellery*. Author's Preface to first ed. (p. xiii).
17. H. Wilson. *Silverwork and Jewellery*. Author's Preface to first ed. (p. xx).
18. H. Wilson. *Silverwork and Jewellery*. Author's Preface to first ed. (p. xiii).
19. H. Wilson. *Silverwork and Jewellery.* Ch. VII Hammerwork p. 61-2.
20. H. Wilson. *Silverwork and Jewellery.* Author's Preface to first ed. (p. xiv-xv).
21. Ibid.
22. H. Wilson. *Silverwork and Jewellery.* Ch. IX Spoons p. 79-82.
23. H. Wilson. *Silverwork and Jewellery.* Author's Preface to first ed. (p. xiv-xv).
24. 'Decorative and Industrial Art at the Glasgow International Exhibition'. 5th notice. *Art Journal* 1901 p. 328.
25. H. Wilson. *Silverwork and Jewellery.* Ch. II, heading p. 29. see also 'The study of methods ... is absolutely the most fruitful

HENRY WILSON 1864-1934 – **CHAPTER FIVE**

source of ideas. The hand and brain work together'. (*S&J* Ch. I p. 26); and 'Suggestions of decorative treatment ... constantly arise while the work is in progess. The behaviour of the metal is more instructive than any teacher' (*S&J* Ch.VI Repoussé Work p. 50); and 'Design is the language you learn from your work, and as your skill in handiwork grows, so will your power of design' (*S&J* Ch. XIX Gold Work p. 175-6.).

26. Orrea Pernel. Reminiscences. Wilson Papers, V&A Library.
27. In a letter to R.C. Norman in 1957, Lady Collet remarks on the silversmithing skills Dione had acquired 'during her father's lifetime. I have two silver spoons she made for me'. Wilson completed his gravestones in Kemsing churchyard for Lady Collet between 1905 and 1922. (see above, Introduction).
28. H. Wilson. *Silverwork and Jewellery* Ch. II Materials p. 29-32; see also pp. 213, 232, 241, 377 etc.
29. A. Vallance. 'Modern British Jewellery and Fans'. *Studio* (Special Winter Number) 1901-2 p. 2.
30. H. Wilson *Silverwork and Jewellery* see n. 6 above.
31. A. Vallance. 'Modern British Jewellery and Fans'. *Studio* (Special Winter Number) 1901-2 p. 2.
32. H. Wilson. *Silverwork and Jewellery* Ch. XIV Necklaces p. 113-7.
33. H. Wilson. *Silverwork and Jewellery* Ch.VII Hammerwork p. 60. The morse was shown in the Arts and Crafts Exhibitions at Ghent (1913) and Paris (1914), the Wilson Memorial Exhibition at the Beaux Arts Gallery, London (1949), and in the Victorian Church Art Exhibition (1971-2) at the V&A, where it is on permanent loan.
34. H. Wilson *Silverwork and Jewellery* see n. 6 above.
35. Letter to Wilson from James Cromar Watt, 21 August 1906, 71 Dee Street, Aberdeen. (Wilson Archive RCA). A chalice by Cromar Watt is illustrated in 'Scottish Arts and Crafts' *Art Journal* 1907 p. 317: 'Chalice, silver parcel gilt set with pearls, carbuncles and enamel panels'.
36. Ibid.
37. H. Wilson. *Silverwork and Jewellery* Ch. XVII Hair ornaments p. 152.
38. H. Wilson. *Silverwork and Jewellery* Ch. XIII Rings p. 111.
39. H. Wilson. *Silverwork and Jewellery* Ch. XIV Necklaces p. 126-7.
40. William Morris. 'The Lesser Arts of Life' (Address to SPAB, 1882), reprinted in *William Morris: prose, verse, lectures and essays* ed 1948 p. 496; also 'The Decorative Arts in relation to modern life and progress', delivered before Trades' Guild of Learning, 4 Dec. 1877.
41. H. Wilson. *Silverwork and Jewellery* Ch. XLV Necklaces p. 122-3.
42. H. Wilson. *Silverwork and Jewellery* Ch.VII Hammerwork p. 61-2. (Private Collection).
43. Of the five pearls, two on left remain fixed in place: Plate 43 enhanced to show original design.
44. H. Wilson. *Silverwork and Jewellery* Ch. XXXIII On Old Work and Old Methods. p. 263 (f/n).
45. H. Wilson. *Silverwork and Jewellery* Ch. XXXIII On Old Work and Old Methods. pp. 266 & 270. The Hendrie Theophilus was published by Murray.
46. H. Wilson. *Silverwork and Jewellery* Ch. XXXIII On Old Work and Old Methods. p. 275-6.
47. Ibid.
48. H. Wilson. *Silverwork and Jewellery* Ch. XIV Necklaces p. 124. see also. Ch. XVI Pendants p. 138 'Avoid grotesque or extraordinary forms'.
49. H. Wilson. 'The Arts and Crafts Movement' lecture, 1918. (Wilson Archive RCA).
50. *Studio* IX 1896 p. 130. The stalls were displayed at the 5th Arts and Crafts Exhibition 1896, no. 251 'Chancel stalls from designs by H. Wilson, executed by Charles Lask (sic) and Co., with the assistance of J. Parkin'. The review explains that their colour and form together 'secure the desired effect of variety, coupled with severe restraint', but still questions 'the wisdom of employing subtle plains of relief in any variegated material ... for the exquisite delicacy of the carving can hardly be appreciated ... owing to the grain of the wood'. G.G.Scott's All Hallows' church was bombed in WWII, and the stalls destroyed, along with Wilson's rood (which had appeared in *The Builder* 15 June 1895) and decorative panel for the Boys' desk, which he had designed c. 1892 (see RIBA Drawings Coll. PA528/17). This was Wilson's earliest depiction of St. George, others following in 1909 in the round stained glass window commissioned by Mary Hanbury for the upper wall dividing entrance hall and nave within St. Mary's church, Weymouth, in 1918 on the Tonbridge memorial gate, and in 1924 for the Sir Kenneth Anderson memorial cup shown at the Wembley exhibition (qv: Ch.9), and featured in the Illustrated Souvenir of the Palace of Arts, British Empire Exhibition 1924, p.159.
51. W.R. Lethaby Editor's Preface in H. Wilson. *Silverwork and Jewellery*.
52. H. Wilson. *Silverwork and Jewellery* Ch.VII Hammerwork p. 61-2.
53. H. Wilson. 'The Arts and Crafts Movement' lecture, 1918. (Wilson Archive RCA).
54. Ibid.
55. H. Wilson. *Silverwork and Jewellery* Ch. XXXIII On Old Work and Old Methods. p. 275-6.
56. H. Wilson. *Silverwork and Jewellery* Ch.VII Hammerwork p. 61-2.
57. Brown-Morrison. op cit. See above, Introduction.
58. Gordon Craig. Undated letter to H. Wilson. (Wilson Archive RCA). Wilson himself also added the chapter on box-making.
59. Nelson Dawson *Goldsmiths' and Jewellers' Work* (1907).
60. H. Wilson. *Silverwork and Jewellery* Ch. XV Brooches p. 131-2.
61. H. Wilson. *Silverwork and Jewellery* Ch. XLVIII On Design p. 414.
62. H. Wilson's *On Workmanship* was published in 1912 by John Hogg. This essay draws on sources ranging from Arthurian literature and Persian legend to Chinese and Greek mythology in its discussion of the topic which typefies Wilson's thought – inherited racial memory.
63. H. Wilson. *Silverwork and Jewellery* Ch. XLVIII On Design p. 414.
64. Ibid.
65. H. Wilson. 'The Gates of Wonder' (undated m/s Wilson Archive RCA).
66. H. Wilson's *On Workmanship* was published in 1912 by John Hogg. This essay draws on sources ranging from Arthurian

HENRY WILSON 1864-1934 – **CHAPTER FIVE**

literature and Persian legend to Chinese and Greek mythology in its discussion of the topic which typefies Wilson's thought – inherited racial memory.

67. H. Wilson. *Silverwork and Jewellery* Ch. XLVIII On Design p. 416-7.
68. H. Wilson. *Silverwork and Jewellery* Ch. XLVIII On Design p. 418-21.
69. Samuel Butler's *Unconscious Memory* was published c. 1875 by A. Fifield. Wilson's regard for Butler's works is evident in his many references to them in his own writings; *Erewhon* (1872), interested him as an essay on utopia. See also H. Wilson, letter to Dr. Garnett 1 April 1911: 'The pioneer in this as in so many matters was the late Samuel Butler in *Erewhon* and *Erewhon Revisited*. The chapters on machinery are so stimulating, so illuminating, that I go to them again and again for joy and comfort and life.' (Wilson Archive RCA).
70. H. Wilson. *Silverwork and Jewellery* Ch. XLVIII On Design p. 418-21.
71. H. Wilson. 'The Gates of Wonder' (undated m/s Wilson Archive RCA).
72. H. Wilson. Letter to Edgar Wilson (undated letter, Wilson Archive RCA).
73. Letter to Wilson from Gordon Craig, Arena Goldini, Florence. August 1915. (Wilson Archive RCA).
74. H. Wilson. Birmingham Municipal School of Art: Vittoria Street School for Silversmiths and Jewellers. General Report of the Examiner for the year ended 5th Dec. 1905. (Wilson Archive RCA).
75. H. Wilson. Birmingham Municpal School of Art: Vittoria Street School for Silversmiths and Jewellers. General Report of the Examiner for the year ended 5th Dec. 1906. (Wilson Archive RCA).
76. H. Wilson. Report of the Consultative Committee on Goldsmiths, Silversmiths, Jewellers and Allied Trades to the Polytechnics and Evening Schools Sub-Committee. (undated m/s Wilson Archive RCA).
77. H. Wilson. *Address at Goldsmiths' Hall* 1908 (see n. 4 above). Wilson's apprehension about how thoroughly the use of machinery had infiltrated the manufacture of jewellery is borne out in 'Some Examples of Modern English Jewellery,' in the *Studio* vol. 60 1914 p. 265: 'a whole army of workers is employed in cities such as London and Birmingham where the manufacture of jewellery is carried on as a highly organised branch of industry. And in this industry like most others ... the use of machinery is extensive, especially ... for the cheaper grades'.
78. Letter from H. Wilson, The Thatched House, Platt, 1 March 1909 to Lord Henry Bentinck. (Wilson Archive RCA).
79. C.R. Ashbee. *Craftsmanship in Competitive Industry* (1908) p. 96-7.
80. H. Wilson. *Silverwork and Jewellery* Ch. IX Spoons p. 86.
81. See n. 77 above.
82. Ibid.
83. See n. 78 above.
84. See n. 77 above.
85. H. Wilson. Birmingham Municipal School of Art: Vittoria Street School for Silversmiths and Jewellers. General Report of the Examiner for the year ended 5th Dec. 1905. (Wilson Archive RCA).
86. H. Wilson. 'Goldsmiths' Work'. (undated m/s Wilson Archive RCA).
87. H. Wilson. 'Goldsmiths' Work and Jewellery'. (undated m/s Wilson Archive RCA).
88. H. Wilson. *Silverwork and Jewellery* Ch. VII Hammerwork p. 61-2.
89. H. Wilson. Birmingham Municipal School of Art: Vittoria Street School for Jewellers and Silversmiths. General Report of the Examiner for the year ended 5th Dec. 1908. (Wilson Archive RCA).
90. See n. 77 above.
91. H. Wilson. Confidential Report to the Consultative Committee on Goldsmiths, Silversmiths, Jewellers and Allied Trades on the entry of boys into the Day Silversmithing School held at L.C.C. Central School of Arts and Crafts. April 1911. (Wilson Archive RCA).
92. H. Wilson. Birmingham Municipal School of Art: Vittoria Street School for Jewellers and Silversmiths. General Report of the Examiner for the year ended October 1912. Rough Draft sent from 2678 Calle del Forno, S. Maurizio, Venice (Wilson Archive RCA).
93. Chamberlain, Birmingham-born, had originally worked for a firm of screw manufacturers. He rose to become the city's mayor 1873-5, its MP 1876-1910, and Colonial Secretary 1895-1903. The commission's dedication to him is inscribed in the silver latticework that forms the division between casket and pedestal. Surrounding it are four enamel roundels for the British Isles, each portraying a girl wreathed in her national plant – the rose of England, the shamrock of Ireland, the thistle of Scotland, the leek of Wales. The casket sits on top between the four apexes of the pedestal niches.
94. Letter from H. Wilson, Platt, to Sir John Holder 4 Nov. 1902 (Birmingham Museum). 'Harry Murphy: Goldsmith, enameller & artistic metalworker, 5 Kenton Street, Russell Square. 8 Sept. 1904. Total Chamberlain casket £52-14-7.' (Wilson Archive RCA).
95. Ibid.
96. H. Wilson. *Silverwork and Jewellery* Ch. XVI Pendants p. 143.
97. The graining technique is explained in *Silverwork and Jewellery* Ch. XVI Pendants p. 142. The legs of the chafing dish are visually intriguing in tapering towards their tops. A silver band with a raised chevron pattern encircles each at its base. Silver trees fill the spaces between them, enclosing the spirit burner. An undulating line punctuated with stamped vine leaves and grapes is applied to dish and lid, the latter with a finial comprising four leaves enclosing a cherub (Coll. Goldsmiths' Hall). Another dish, c. 1908, has as its finial a nude goddess spinning thread. (Coll. V&A).
98. Wilson's silver and enamel pendant (c. 1895; ill. C. Gere *Victorian Jewellery Design* pl 85a & b, and I. Anscombe and C. Gere *Arts and Crafts in Britain and America* p. 140), is in the collection of the Hessisches Landes-Museum, Darmstadt. Its working sketch is in the Drawings Collection, V&A. The crook of the crozier (c. 1900) is bronze, enriched with enamel and semi-precious stones, and encloses a silver ship. (Ex. and ill. *Victorian Church Art* M18, 1971), and L. Lambourne *Utopian Craftsmen* p. 98). The hair comb (c.1902) is ill. I. Anscombe and C. Gere op cit p. 148. For the Cirencester alms dish see above Ch. 4 n. 73.

99. H. Wilson *Silverwork and Jewellery* Ch. XVI Pendants p. 139.
100. The first two Employers' Liability Acts (allowing employees to be compensated for injuries suffered at work) were passed in 1880 when Chamberlain was President of the Board of Trade, a post he held 1880-05. A third followed in 1893.
101. Wilson's acquaintance with Sir Charles Nicholson (1808-1903) had grown through his long friendship since the Sedding years with his son, Charles (1849-1924). A distinguished politician and educationalist, Sir Charles had trained as a doctor in his native Yorkshire, but emigrated to Sydney, Australia in 1834, where he praticed for ten years. Entering politics, he was elected to the New South Wales Legislative Council in 1843, becoming its first Speaker 1847-1855. A co-founder of Sydney University, he served as its Vice Chancellor 1854-60. He was created baronet 1859. On his return to England in 1862, he settled at The Grange, Totteridge, Hertfordshire. Wilson designed his tomb c. 1911 in the churchyard of St. Andrew's, whose Vicarage (1892) is by his son, Wilson's contemporary, Charles Nicholson. Sir Charles's widow wrote to Wilson, recalling the influence he had had on her husband and delighting in a statuette of St. Joan on horseback which she had purchased from him, undated letter from Sarah E. Nicholson, St. Mawes, West Malvern (Wilson Archive RCA). This figure was exhibited at the Ghent International Exhibition 1913. Present whereabouts unknown.
102. Letter to Wilson from William Kenrick 2 November 1906. (Wilson Archive RCA).
103. Ibid.
104. Alan Crawford suggests in *By Hammer and Hand: The Arts and Crafts movement in Birmingham* (Birmingham Museum and Art Gallery, 1984 p. 32) that the Bromsgrove Guild began c. 1897 as a loose association of artist-craftsmen associated with the Birmingham Municipal School of Art. In *The Bromsgrove Guild: an Illustrated History* ed. Quintin Watt (The Bromsgrove Society, 1999 p. 9), it is characterised as the brain-child of Walter Gilbert, closely associated with the Bromsgrove School of Art and Science, and began on 26 November 1898. It would appear that its organisation, encompassing designers, makers and employees was always loosely defined. Walter Gilbert was no relation to Alfred, the sculptor of the same name. See Richard Dorment *Alfred Gilbert* (Yale 1985 p. 298).
105. Letter to Wilson from Frank Morley Fletcher, 23 George Square, Edinburgh 18 March 1910: 'We have had your little Hermes here in our exhibition [of the Scottish Arts and Crafts Society] during the last fortnight.' On 31 October 1912 Douglas Strachan, Hillcrest, Morningside, Edinburgh wrote to Wilson about his own version of: 'I have been asked to lend the little Hermes of which I am the happy possessor. Have I your consent? And if so, what title do you want given to it?' (Wilson Archive RCA).
106. *The Automobile Club Journal and Motor Union Gazette,* 24 May 1906 p. 605-06. (R.A.C., Pall Mall, London).
107. Camille Lefèbre's Monument to Levassor, Porte Maillot, Paris was erected in 1907 to commemorate the 1895 road race from Paris to Bordeaux and back, which had been won by the engineer Emile Levassor in his Panhard-Levassor 5.
108. The Arrol-Johnston completed the course in 6 hours 9 minutes at an average speed of 33.9 mph. In second place was Percy Northey driving a Rolls Royce at 33.6 mph, taking 6 hours 11 minutes. To transport the trophy from the Club's Pall Mall headquarters to the annual Tourist Race (1914 a 600-mile two-day event), Wilson made a steel case (Plate 50). Architectural in conception, his description of making it mingles terms pertaining to architecture and to metalwork: 'A mild steel sheet was beaten down into a cast iron mould with mallets, punches and hammers to give the fluted sides.... The design of the pierced work was then made, and the curved surfaces decorated by repoussé and chasing with the vine pattern.... The columns were made of twisted wire [to suggest] ... carved and chased columns.... The base was built up of sheet metal and decorated with twisted wire work in the form of rich-looking mouldings. The gallery of decorated panels was next made....' The inside of the casket is described as 'a sort of shrine'. During its travels this carrying case was lost; the only record of it is an engraving in the May 1906 edition of the Club's *Journal.*
109. Letter to H. Wilson from William Kelly, 62 Rubislawden North, Aberdeen 12 Feb. 1907 (Wilson Archive RCA). The value of the Mace – £200 – is pencilled in (perhaps for insurance purposes, or as a guide for other potential clients) in the V&A's copy of the catalogue of the Paris Arts and Crafts Exhibition of 1914.
110. Letter from H. Wilson to William Kelly, 62 Rubislawden North, Aberdeen, March 1907 (Wilson Archive RCA).
111. 2 July issue of *Boston Evening Transcript,* 1927. In the newspaper a small misprint makes the last word 'job'; Wilson would have enjoyed the unintended truth this error contained.

CHAPTER 6
THE ALL-ROUND ARTIST

1. The monstrance, with Wilson's maker's mark on its base, was taken from Caldey to Prinknash Abbey, Gloucestershire in 1928. It was displayed at the Ghent International Exhibition of 1913 (British Section p. 189 no. 1051); *Victorian and Edwardian Decorative Arts* (V&A 1952 no. 215); *Copy or Creation* (Goldsmiths' Hall 1967 no. E20); *Victorian Church Art* (V&A 1971 no. M.20).
2. Genesis 14.18 'And Melchizedek King of Salem brought forth bread and wine: and he was the priest of the most high God'.
3. R.A. Cram. 'The work of Henry Wilson'. op cit p. 261-73. Illustrations of the doors and selected panels appear within Cram's critique. For Wilson's collaborations with Cram, see below Ch. VII. For Wilson's description of the doors see St. Mary's Archive Coll., Nottinghamshire Archives Office.
4. See Oxfordshire Record Office Doc. Ref. ORO/Par. Somerton/d.4. The pietà was commissioned from Wilson in 1896 in memory of William Barnes of Exeter (1817-1892), by his son, the Rev. George Edward Barnes, for whom William Barnes had bought the patronage of the church: George was vicar there 1875-1923. Wilson asked Pomeroy to carve the alabaster capitals of its Devonshire marble columns, the shield, the mantelling above, and the corbels – Blakean masks of youth and age – beside the bronze inscription. Pomeroy sent his invoice, from Wentworth

HENRY WILSON 1864-1934 – **CHAPTER SIX**

Studios, Manresa Road, S.W., on 2 Feb. 1896, for £17 – 10 – 0; a note of 8 Jan. 1924 records that Mr. Phillips of Burlison & Grylls painted the Long and Barnes shield for £10 – 10 – 0. Wilson was paid in 1903: 'Paid H. Wilson Esq. Architect for bronze "Pieta" to above & bronze inscription £40 – 0 – 0'.

This original, rectangular version omits the turrets of the holy city seen in the Nottingham pietà. The bronze inscription beneath it gives detailed information on the life of its dedicatee: 'This window & monument were erected in memory of William Barnes of Great Dunyard, Exeter, Esquire, Patron of the living of Somerton 1875-1892, son of Samuel Barnes (6th son of Ralph Barnes Archdeacon of Totnes) and Juliana Speke Barnes (daughter of William Speke Esq. of Jordans, Somerset). Born 25th Jan 1817, married, July 2nd 1840 at Great Haseley Church, Lucy (a. 7th July 1850) daughter of Walter Long Esq. of Preshaw, Hants & Great Haseley, Oxon. and the Lady Mary Carnegie (eldest daughter of William 5th Earl of Northesk) died 21st Jan. 1892, buried at Clyst St Mary, Devon'. The 'window' is Whall's 1892 three-light stained glass window in the N. aisle of the Lady Chapel; commissioned by Barnes's children it cost £75. Its N. light depicts St. Paul – William Barnes' birthday, 25 Jan., coincided with St. Paul's conversion. The centre light shows the resurrection and the sleeping centurion. The S. light depicts James, the patron saint of the church. Christ's tomb extends across the width of the window. Its dedicatee is inscribed with 1 Corinthians XV 4 at the base of the N. and S. lights.

Wilson's work at Somerton church included the angel- and foliage-carved choir stalls of 1892, these, as George Barnes's notes explain, were 'devised by Mr. H. Wilson pupil and successor to Mr. Sedding'. A further note explains 'these are entirely new, made of oak, beautifully carved by the firm of Charles Trask & Sons of Norton, near Ilminster. The 2 old ends of the "Return Stalls" have been preserved in the new stalls....' Designs by Sedding himself appeared in the oak altar rails and lectern, also carved by Trask. Trask's work was itemised in the Chancel Account, and paid Aug. 19 1892 by G.E. Barnes: it amounted to £210.0.0, on which Wilson received 5% (£10) commission.

5. R.A. Cram. 'The work of Henry Wilson'. op cit p. 261-73. Illustrations of the doors and selected panels appear within Cram's critique. For Wilson's collaborations with Cram, see below Ch. VII. For Wilson's description of the doors see St. Mary's Archive Coll., Nottinghamshire Archives Office.
6. *The Toy Cart* review. (Press cutting, Wilson Archive RCA). 'Ajanta' relates to some Indian frescoes owned by Lady Herrington.
7. Lena Ashwell OBE (1872-1957), daughter of Commander Charles Ashwell Pocock, was born on board a training ship on the Tyne. The family emigrated when she was eight to Toronto where she studied singing, but in 1891, after moving to London, Ellen Terry (Gordon Craig's mother) advised her to abandon music for the stage. By 1900 she had become a leading figure in the British acting world, appearing at the Lyceum, the Haymarket, the Criterion and Drury Lane, where in 1903 she acted in *Dante* opposite Sir Henry Irving. She repeated some of her roles in America in 1906-07. Back in London she leased a theatre which she reopened as the Kingsway, where she produced and acted in many successful plays. After *The Starlight Express* she relinquished management in favour of her Lena Ashwell Concerts at the Front (1914-20) and helping the Actresses' Franchise League. Later, with the assistance of the Mayor of Stepney, Clement Attlee, she started the Once-a-Week Players to provide good, accessible entertainment. Amongst the several books she wrote on the theatre, is her autobiography *Myself a Player.*
8. Undated postcard to H. Wilson from Gordon Craig. (Wilson Archive RCA).
9. H. Wilson. 'Goldsmiths' Work and Jewellery'. (undated m/s, Wilson Archive RCA). The poetic associations intrinsic to Wilson's creativity are inherent in very words he chose to express his thoughts. His pleasure at he kinship of language and craft is clear in his showing how goldsmithing terminology informs poetic diction, where 'words gleam like gems, phrases flash like polished metal', the 'sky [is] sapphire' and 'the mead set with dew'.
10. Letter to Robert Morris from Gerald Larkin, Salada Tea Company, Boston, Mass. 26 February 1957 (coll. D. Ottewill). The lamp hangs in the baptistry. Some discrepancies exist regarding its commission and intended home: in a letter dating from the 1950s, Wilson's former workshop assistant Brown-Morrison writes of 'a very big sanctuary lamp being made for Saragossa Cathedral, bronze, wrought and enamelled and cast figures' (coll. D. Ottewill); Cram's article in *Christian Art* (1908) also identifies it as being 'for Saragossa cathedral' (p. 264-6). However, a letter from Wilson's daughter Orrea Pernel recalls a 'bronze hanging lamp originally made for a convent in Saragossa, Spain, which was bought by the Director of the Salada Tea Company and now hangs in a very chilly looking chapel, within St. Thomas's, Toronto, Canada' (coll. D. Ottewill). The 1993 Centennial Book of St. Thomas's records (p. 302) that 'Larkin gave many beautiful items, one of which was the Sanctuary Lamp in the Baptistry originally intended for a Portuguese monastery.' In his letter to Morris, Larkin went on to say that in the Lady Chapel of the same church there was also a 'standing sanctuary lamp of Wilson's ... made up of crystal, ivory and silver' and that he himself had 'one or two things of his' at his home at 8 Castle Frank Road, Toronto.
11. See also Wilson's comments in relation to his proposed reredos for Holy Trinity, Sloane Street, by which he was intending to produce a sense of the 'beyond'. See above Ch. 2 n. 42: 'By these means only can mystery be obtained ...' and Ch. 4 n. 84: '... how many Architects make a beyond by building a barrier?'
12. Letter to H. Wilson from Julius Hoffman, *Verlag fur Kunst und Kunstgewerbe*, Stuttgart, Nov. 1907 (Wilson Archive RCA).
13. R.E.D. Sketchley. 'Metalwork and Jewellery', *The Art Journal* 1907 pp. 165-78. Unlike the photograph which illustrates this article and shows the work as it appeared during the Aix-la-Chapelle [Aachen] exhibition, the lamp later had a four-branched bracket just above the saints, effectively spacing the chains as they pass them before reaching the Mother and Child. Each branch curls upwards and outwards to terminate in an open-work heart-shaped leaf, point

HENRY WILSON 1864-1934 – **CHAPTER SIX**

uppermost and bearing the face of a cherub. The reason for the discrepancy is unclear, perhaps to give better visibility.

14. F.W. Troup. Henry Wilson: Obituary. *Journaln RIBA* 24 March 1934.
15. William Elphinstone, Bishop of Aberdeen, founded the university under the authority of a papal bull of 1495 which had been obtained by James IV of Scotland. The university's original name was King's College. A second college, the Marischal College, (founded in 1593 by George Keith, 5th Earl Marischal) was joined with it in 1860 to form the present University of Aberdeen.
16. The difference between the proposed and actual dimensions are given in the Business Committee's Report 21 April 1928 (Elphinstone Archive, Aberdeen University Library m/s V701/1). In his obituary on Wilson, Troup interpreted the tomb's unplanned size as a virtue, and maintained that its new (though as it happened, temporary) site in the antechapel was better anyway.
17. H. Wilson. Memorandum to Elphinstone Committee June 1915 (Elphinstone Archive, Aberdeen University Library m/s 2054).
18. 'Art lends its charm ...' *Boston Transcript* 2 July 1927.
19. Final Report, Elphinstone Committee 1929 (Elphinstone Archive, Aberdeen University Library m/s V701/1). In deference to the Bishop's original black marble gravestone, Wilson gave his tomb a plinth of black Tournai marble, but in 1945, when the tomb was moved outside, it was placed on a plain granite base. Entrusted with refurbishing the old gravestone inside the chapel, Wilson made no attempt to repair the general wear and tear time had inflicted on the old slab. However, since it was probably not precisely on the burial site of Bishop Elphinstone, he had it shifted two feet to the east to bring it into alignment with the major axis of the chapel. The firm of architectural craftsmen MacDonald Creswick Ltd. of Edinburgh was employed to construct a bronze setting for it and to raise it to a height of three feet on brick piers.
20. Letter to Wilson from J. Harrower, Langham Hotel, London 12 April 1915. (Wilson Archive RCA). Wilson's tendency to work too hard was well-known to his closest associates; the Rev. J.H. Skrine (who had commissioned the Itchen Stoke grave) alluded to this characteristic when reluctantly alerting him to some problems besetting that work: 'Your overwork and illness make us compunctious at having to bother you with the shortcomings – or latecomings – of Trask. I daresay "now we shan't be long", though yesterday the new coping stone had not arrived and the carver could not get on at the graving. The bronzes had not come either'. Letter to Wilson from Skrine 2 September 1913 (Wilson Archive RCA). See above Ch. 8 n. 17.
21. *The Builder* 28 April 1911 p. 524-6. The elevations to Earl Street, St. Mary Street, Bayley Lane and Hay Lane, ground and first floor plans, and sections of the building show the firm's full name Garratt, Simister, Buckland and Farmer. G.A.T. Middleton's review praises the convenience of the accommodation, noting that 'the East (sic) Street front gives access to well-lighted hall and staircase'; yet complained that some areas were 'imperfectly lighted', some corridors had 'blind ends' and the gables of the main front needed 'more breadth and quiet'. The earlier town hall and municipal offices competition from which the police offices had resulted featured in *The Builder's Journal* 16 July 1895. That competition had stipulated that the winning design should be able 'to be easily erected in blocks, the Police Department being the first proposed to be built'. The entry by 'Leofric the Saxon'(the pseudonym of local architect Harry Quick) was judged the winner by Sir Charles Barry, but after these offices had been built, the rest of Quick's design was abandoned and a fresh competition announced.
22. The opening by the Duke of York (the future George VI, this being his first appearance since assuming the dukedom), was on 11 June 1920. The programme listed all the firms and individuals represented in the building (see Opening Ceremony Programme, Coll. Coventry Archivist, 39022/C1a), including, for the Marble Work – Jenkins & Son, Torquay; Heating – Ashwell & Nesbit, Leicester; Electrical Lighting – Burbury & Co., Coventry; Electrical Fittings – Smith & Ansell, Birmingham; Furniture – Wilcock & Co., Wolverhampton, Maple & Co., London and The Midland Educational Co., Birmingham). Roses representing York and Lancaster were added either side of the main door for the event. The Duke used a ceremonial key, addressed the council in their new Chamber and unveiled a memorial to the war dead (see Archive Supplement, 4 December 1976, *Coventry Evening Telegraph*).
23. During its installation, St. Michael was often mistaken for a German eagle, an emblem inevitably uppermost in the public's mind. (*Coventry Herald* 1916, Local History Collection reference JN 725.13). The clock was by John Smith of Derby. During renovations in 1959-60 to repair bomb damage, its copper dials (each weighing 3cwt.) were replaced and its oak embellishments removed.
24. The city arms, comprising an elephant, castle and mountain cat, was the first embellishment to be added; they extend into the porch itself, with the arms of historical figures associated with Coventry. Alderman William Grant's involvement in selecting the blazons for the façade is recorded in the *Coventry Herald*'s article 'History in Stone' (Local History Collection reference JN 725.13); see also 'The Old Council House' (Information Bulletin 52, January 1977 p. 1-3).
25. The slowly turning wheels of local bureaucracy, specifically of the Council House Committee, were reported over several years. Bewildering delays were recorded, see *Midland Daily Telegraph* 25 March 1919, and the *Coventry Evening Standard*, where on 13 July 1923, after noting that Wilson's sculptures had featured from the start, doubts were raised as to whether Justice was a sufficiently 'local' figure, and a preference expressed for St. Mary, to whom Leofric's and Godiva's priory had been dedicated.
26. The stained glass throughout the Council House is by Harvey & Ashby of Birmingham, a relatively small firm whose work was of good quality. Ernest Harvey (the brother of W.A. Harvey, architect of Bournville garden suburb) attended Birmingham School of Art in the 1890s, as probably did his partner Ashby. Their designs reflect the Burne-Jones style typical of Birmingham work at the time; at Coventry their cartoons were probably based on drawings by and discussions with the architects, possibly in

consultation with Wilson. More commercial firms such as Hardman of Birmingham would have had little in common with Garratt & Simister, Catterson-Smith or Wilson. The rest of the Council House's windows and leaded lights were by Hope & Sons of Birmingham, who supplied windows with the glass already fitted. The individuals depicted in the Council Chamber's stained glass (see Civic Affairs, February 1968) were relevant to the city's story, while those in Wilson's carved bench ends, are allegorical rather than historical, with the exception of the Veiled Nun. The story of this spectral figure involves Robert de Marmyon, to whom King William had granted the castle of Tamworth and adjacent lands. Marmyon had expelled the nuns from Polesworth Abbey, which fell within his estate, to Oldbury, four miles away. A year later, St. Edith appeared to him as a veiled nun, crozier in hand. She warned him that unless he restored the abbey to her successors, he would suffer eternal damnation. To reinforce this threat, she struck him with the crozier before vanishing, and so, with Sir Walter de Somerville, he rode to Oldbury, begged the nuns' pardon and brought them back to Polesworth.

27. See n. 22 above.
28. Archetypes including the heavenly spring and the temple as described in W.R. Lethaby's *Architecture, Mysticism and Myth* pp. 70, 76 had been thoroughly absorbed into Wilson's creative lexicon by the time of the All Saints commission; his approach suggests a modern slant, as in the semi-circular fanlight with its iron grid and single leaf motifs, which recalls the vines and grapes in his organ screen of 1899 at Holy Trinity, Sloane Street. W. Reynolds-Stephens's appeal for properly considered architectural sculpture, citing Wilson's at London Colney as the ideal, followed an address by Stirling Lee. *Jnl. RIBA* 1905 Vol. 12 p. 507.
29. Using medieval Latin forms the text reads 'Quem terra pontus sidera colunt et adorant solve vincla reis profer lumeneais melanstrapelle bona cuncta posce.' (You whom earth, sea and stars worship and adore, loose prisoners' chains, bring forth light from darkness and bestow all good things). Wilson had been given permission for simple fretwork over the reredos, but had developed the idea further than the Rev. Holme had anticipated: 'I was surprised to find your carpenter has put boards at the top of the reredos. The sanctuary is already dark, and these take away further from the light. If I had seen them before they were fixed I should not have agreed to them.' (Wilson Archive RCA). Gold lettering either side of the reredos sets out verses from Isaiah 55.
30. Soon after the altar rail was installed the Rev. Holme had further cause to complain, and wrote from The Parsonage, Sydenham, on 25 April 1907 (Wilson Archive RCA) about one of the balusters having developed 'a serious crack.' Perhaps Wilson did not share the vicar's alarm, and saw the crack as natural ageing; or perhaps the church, having already queried Wilson's fees exceeding his estimates, was unwilling to pay to have it rectified. In any case, the crack remains clearly visible.
31. RIBA Drawings Collection X16/18. See also *Moderne Bauformen* ix 1910.
32. This alternative design had an oak cover with a kneeling angel as its knop; this the Marquess dismissed as 'a crouching figure on top of the font'. Letter to Wilson from Wynyard, Stockton-on-Tees 28 September 1906 (Wilson Archive RCA).
33. Letter to Wilson from B. Hawker, 2 Princes Gate, London 25 January 1915 (Wilson Archive RCA). Beneath St. Christopher is a plain grey marble panel with a dedication to Miss M.A. Hudson, an early benefactress of St. Martin's. In front is an altar with a small brass crucifix and pair of twisted brass candlesticks like those Wilson had made for his Clerkenwell Lady Altar. A letter to Wilson from the Rev. W.R. Hickson indicates that Wilson originally meant to add a marble pavement and rail in front of the Christopher Chapel altar, but the idea was dropped for lack of space. The chapel was dedicated by Bishop Jayne on 24 July 1909.
34. Letter to Oxford University from Norman Shaw R.A., 6 Ellerdale Road, Hampstead, 14 March 1910 (Wilson Archive RCA).
35. Letter to Oxford University from W. Holman Hunt, 18 Melbury Road, London, 3 March 1910 (Wilson Archive RCA).
36. Letter to Oxford University from Arthur Hughes, Eastside House, Kew Green, 28 March 1910 (Wilson Archive RCA).
37. Letter to Wilson from E. Lanteri, Royal College of Art 16 March 1910 (Wilson Archive RCA). Lanteri took over the teaching post of Jules Dalou at the Royal College in 1881. He devoted himself to teaching and sculpture, and in 1910 completed his three-volume *Modelling: a Guide for Teachers and Students*, for which Rodin wrote the preface. Lanteri's recommending Wilson for the Slade Professorship was based not only on Wilson's work at the Royal College, but also on the experience of collaborating with him on the Brompton plaque: his receipt of 5 June 1906 records £35 paid him by Wilson in respect of this work (Wilson Archive RCA).
38. Undated letter to Oxford University from Augustus Spenser (Wilson Archive RCA).
39. 'His ideas on art and his practical experience could not help but be very useful for the education of young people ... and of amateurs who would be able to attend his lectures.' Undated letter to Oxford University from Auguste Rodin, 77 rue de Varenne, Paris (Wilson Archive RCA).
40. Max Schmid's letter was sent from the Technische Hochschule, Aix-la-Chapelle 10 April 1910; Hermann Muthesius's is dated 25 April 1910 (Wilson Archive RCA).
41. Letter to Wilson from Frank Morley Fletcher 18 March 1910 (Wilson Archive RCA). Morley Fletcher taught wood cut at the Central School: his *Woodblock Printing* appeared alongside Wilson's *Silverwork and Jewellery* in the Artistic Crafts series. Examples of his work were shown at the Ghent Exhibition in 1913.
42. Gordon Craig: see above Ch. 5 n. 56
43. An Oxford and Slade School graduate, Image had initially trained as a curate, serving for four years at St. Anne's, Soho. On his dismissal from that living in 1882, he joined A.H. Mackmurdo in founding the Century Guild, designing the title page for its quarterly magazine *The Hobby Horse.* While concentrating on graphics, he also designed stained glass and mosaics for the church of St. Mary Magdalene, Mortahoe, Devon, and embroideries for the Royal School

of Needlework. He was Master of the Art Workers' Guild in 1900, and was Slade Professor at Oxford until 1916, when the post was frozen for the war.

CHAPTER 7
LEARNING BY LIVING

1. H. Wilson. 'Craft Education for the Young: an address delivered at the Conference on New Ideals in Education' Oxford, 31 July 1916. (Wilson Archive RCA). In its printed form the lecture was renamed *The Value and Importance of Handicraft in Education.*
2. Conferences were held annually between 1914 and 1923. Wilson had direct acquaintance with Froebel's theories through his brother Edgar's first wife, Isabel. Although they had first met when she had been sent to nurse his mother Clara Wilson in her last illness, Isabel Wilson was a Froebel-trained governess; she died in 1904, three years after her marriage to Edgar.
3. H. Wilson. 'On Education: Definitions'.
4. H. Wilson. 'The Suppression of the Creative Instinct' 1915 (Wilson Archive RCA).
5. H. Wilson. 'Craft Education for the Young' (see n. 1 above).
6. H. Wilson. 'The Suppression of the Creative Instinct' (see n. 4 above).
7. Letter from Wilson on behalf of ACES to the University of Oxford, 1917 (Wilson Archive RCA).
8. The timespan of these lectures indicates the importance of 'creativity' in Wilson's thinking: 'The Value and Importance of ...' (1906; Wilson Archive RCA), 'The Suppression of ... ' (1915; Wilson Archive RCA), 'The Creative Impulse ... ' (c. 1922; Wilson Archive RCA).
9. H. Wilson. 'The Value of Learning by Doing' (1906, Wilson Archive RCA).
10. While Guthlac had been born on 21 April 1902 at The Thatched House, at the time of Fiammetta's birth (3 Feb. 1904), the Wilsons were in Italy, Wilson renewing his inspiration for his ongoing chapel at Wynyard. Mrs. Christie's book (1906) led on to her editorship of the periodicals *Embroidery* (from 1908) and *Needle and Thread* (from 1914). Margaret Wilson shared her interest in needlework, while Grace Christie's husband, Archibald H. Christie, was co-editor with Lethaby of the Artistic Craft series of handbooks. Fiammetta's London address was 10 Westminster Mansions. She died in West End Hospital 7 August 1940 of complications following an operation and post-encephalitis. Her 'sleepy sickness' was a manifestation of a post-war European viral disease (as distinct from sleeping sickness, or *trypanosomis africanus*, the tropical disease transmitted through the bite of a tstetse fly). Sufferers who survived the brain inflammation of its acute phase made a remarkably complete recovery, though others, like Fiammetta, never regained their former vigour.
11. Dione was born 10 Oct. 1909. Along with reading, writing and metalcraft, she had cello lessons, and showed a particular talent from her early years for helping in the family kitchen. Her London restaurant, Au Petit Cordon Bleu, opened at 29 Sloane Street in 1933, when she started taking pupils in cookery, including Lady Halifax, Lady Inchcape and the Marquise de Tallyrand. Prior to this, her first venture, a freelance catering business, had flourished with clients including Lord Sandwich and Lady Beecham, while the special meal that she prepared for the Prince of Wales – a particular lobster dish – enhanced her fame. Her greatest success came after leaving London for New York in 1940, with her husband – the English Modernist architect Colin Lucas (1906-1988), renowned for his dramatic, flat-roofed reinforced concrete houses, most notably 66, Frognal, Hampstead (1938), built during his time in the '30s as part of Connell, Ward & Lucas – and two sons. In 1942 she opened The Cordon Bleu restaurant and school at 117 East 60th Street, and several showbusiness stars enrolled, including Joan Fontaine and Harold Lloyd. Her early TV appearances were filmed in the restaurant's kitchen for Columbia, but later they were transferred to the central studio of CBS and finally, in 1950, to the studios of ABC, where she presented four daytime programmes a week and an evening series for men. Her book, *The Dione Wilson Lucas Cookery Book*, appeared in 1950, and she often featured in magazines such as *Life* 4 April 1949, *The New Yorker* 28 May 1949, and the *New York World Telegraph* 18 March 1953. She attributed her success to her adherence to traditional French cookery, her respect for fresh ingredients, and to never stinting on time. Her scorn for the 'jiffy dinner' was implacable. From all accounts her audiences were entranced by the confidence and charm of this 5'5" figure with her coppery hair coiled in a bun at the back of her head, and by the sense of authority she exuded as she moved around her TV kitchen, sampling dishes with the occasional clipped comment 'veddy good, indeed.' Her self-possession was observed during a live TV broadcast when a towering Baked Alaska would not fit into the oven: unperturbed, she simply spooned brandy over it and set it alight.
12. H. Wilson. 'The Suppression of the Creative Instinct' (see n. 4 above).
13. H. Wilson. 'Craft Education for the Young' (see n. 1 above).
14. H. Wilson. 'The Town Planning Movement' (c. 1916, Wilson Archive RCA).
15. H. Wilson. 'Some general remarks on the design of the Charlotte Mason certificate'. (Handwritten notes c. 1895, Wilson Archive RCA). The Charlotte Mason College (formerly the House of Education) was founded in 1892; the certificate is in the collection of Ambleside Museum.
16. Quoted in *Educational Experiments in England* by A. Woods (1920) Ch. 2 p. 35.
17. H. Wilson. 'Craft Education for the Young' (see n. 1 above).
18. H. Wilson. 'Craft Education for the Young' (see n. 1 above).
19. M. Montessori. *The Montessori Method* (1912) Ch. III p. 68-70.
20. Ibid. Ch. VII p. 119.
21. Ibid. Ch. VI p. 116 et seq.
22. Ibid. Ch. I p. 21-6.
23. Ibid. Ch. I p. 21-6.
24. H. Wilson. 'On Education' (see n. 3 above).
25. H. Wilson. 'Craft Education for the Young' (see n. 1 above).
26. H. Wilson. 'Discussion of an exhibition of children's drawings', 20 May 1908 (Wilson Archive RCA).
27. E-J. Dalcroze. *Rhythm, Music and Education* (trans. H.F.

HENRY WILSON 1864-1934 – **CHAPTER SEVEN**

Rubinstein, 1921) p. 238.

28. On her return from America Orrea Pernel (b. 9 July 1906) resumed her appearances at the Proms and taught at five Summer Schools at Dartington – an establishment whose unorthodox educational stance her father would surely have admired. She continued into her late seventies to give master classes and lessons to individual students. One, a member of the Lindsay Quartet, purchased the Stradivarius violin she had played for most of her career. She retained her Amati until selling that, too, to another professional violinist, ensuring, as she wished, that it remain in use. She retired to Bideford, Devon, spending the rest of her life residing alongside the family of Dione's son, Mark Lucas. Her favourite piece of jewellery, which she often wore, was the rambling rose locket. This and several other Wilson jewels such as the moonstone buckle/pendant were bequeathed by her to the V&A. Obit. *The Independent*, 27 Feb. 1993.
29. H. Wilson. 'Craft Education for the Young' (see n. 1 above).
30. H. Wilson. 'Craft Education for the Young' (see n. 1 above).
31. H. Wilson. 'On Reconstruction' (c. 1920, Wilson Archive RCA).
32. H. Wilson. 'Craft Education for the Young' (see n. 1 above).
33. H. Wilson. 'Life and Labour', written for the *Arts and Crafts Journal* 1914.
34. M. Montessori. opus cit Ch. X p. 157. This claim for auto-education was reinforced in Wilson's 1916 paper 'Craft Education for the Young' by the theories of the American psychologist Dr. Stanley Hall, who maintained that 'keeping pets, tilling the soil, mastering simple ... crafts lay the best foundation for intellectual careers'.
35. H. Wilson. 'Craft Education for the Young' (see n. 1 above).
36. H. Wilson. 'Craft Education for the Young' (see n. 1 above).
37. Orrea Pernel. Reminiscences. Wilson Papers (V&A).
38. 'Beauty's Awakening' ran for three consecutive evenings. It was described by Walter Crane, the originator of the idea of composing a masque, in *An Artist's Reminiscences* (1907), and in C.R. Ashbee's *Memoirs*. The *Studio* (Summer Number) 1899 included Wilson's illustrations of the stage, the plan of the Guildhall and the capital of a column. Also Lethaby's drawing of the ivory throne. The original drawings and script are in the collections of the Art Workers' Guild. Sketches of architectural details are in the collections of RIBA and V&A.
39. H. Wilson. 'The problems of secondary education' (undated m/s Wilson Archive RCA).
40. Ibid.
41. H. Wilson. Birmingham Municipal School of Art: Vittoria Street School for Jewellers and Silversmiths, General Report of Examiner for year ended 5 Dec. 1906. (Wilson Archive RCA).
42. H. Wilson. 'The Value of Learning by Doing' (see n. 11 above).
43. C. Holme (ed.) *Arts and Crafts: a review of the work in the leading art schools* (London 1916) pp. 105, 101.
44. Transcript of Letter to Arthur Gaskin: Dec 6 09. My Dear Gaskin, Catterson wants me to go & stay a night with him on Sat. also Sun. I don't feel like taking a long holiday just now & a whole Sunday away seems a century. I'll see you I suppose on Monday & if there is room in a spare packing case or dog kennel outside I might sleep on the top of it out in the garden. That's all for the moment. Here is the list. I'd have sent it on before but I've been with my nose to the grindstone & find my face is flat instead of edged like this so you'll know what to expect. Yours always H. Wilson.
45. H. Muthesius. *Die Krisis in Kunstgewerbe* (Leipzig, 1901) quoted in N. Pevsner *Academies of Art* (London, 1940) p. 265.
46. H. Wilson. Report on the Work of the Design Classes in the Schools of Edinburgh, Glasgow and Aberdeen, 1915. (Wilson Archive RCA).
47. H. Wilson. 'Art and Advertisement' (c. 1915, Wilson Archive RCA).
48. Edward McKnight Kauffer's London Transport posters *Winter Sales are best reached by Underground* date from 1921. He had designed posters with rural themes for the London General Omnibus Company, such as *The North Downs* (1915) with its abstract representation of downland in shades of green and brown, and *Reigate* (1916) seen from a hilltop, with silhouetted trees and blue hills in the distance. F. Gregory Brown's 1916 poster for the L.G.O.'s route 84 to St. Albans showed in his pared down style farm buildings, a haystack and the outline of a tree, while his *Dorking by Motor Bus* (1920) portrays a quiet country scene with dark, leafy trees in the foreground and a green hill beyond. The same atmospheric style that made advertising copy superfluous appeared in the work of other commissioned artists, such as Robert Gibbings's depiction of the botanical gardens in *Wisley* (1922) with its calm lake and black trees, or *Summer Outings by Private Bus* by L.B. Black (1926), with couples alighting from their open-topped bus for a picnic. The effect such posters produced is encapsulated in *London Memories: Kew Gardens* by Fred Taylor (1918), where imagery alone creates a mood so potent as to have made this Underground poster the official choice to send out to the troops.
49. Patten's Design for Panel in a Frieze, a woman smelling a flower amidst the curving lines of the plant's foliage, was well-received in *The Builder* 2 Nov 1895 p. 310. An equally sensuous mood infused his natualistic design in *The Builder* 5 Jan 1895 vol. 68 p. 10, while a castle's arcaded courtyard provides the setting for his drawing 'Sir Launcelot ... there him thought was a fair place to fight in', *The Builder* 4 Jan. 1896 vol. 70 p. 14. In 1900 Patten designed notices and invitations for the *Daily Telegraph* Transvaal War Fund – one showed 'the last corporal', his resolve implicit in his defensive yet determined stance. Other designs were for charitable bodies set up to help former soldiers; in his view these men had become discarded commodities for whom society had no further use. His illustrations for Agnes Herbert's *The Moose* (1912) are closely observed studies of the natural world, while his *Wildlife on the Wing* illustrations of 1913 evoke the habits and character of the species depicted, like Iolar the falcon and Shacaim the redwing. The reason for the 'stamp' appearing in Walker's archive labelled Henry Wilson (information for which I am indebted to Alan Crawford) could be due to the brothers having collaborated on it, or simply to convenience, both explanations being stylistically and historically plausible: evidence of the job itself exists in family papers re-Patten.
50. H. Wilson. 'Art and Advertisement' (see n. 41 above).

51. H. Wilson. 'The City Beautiful': address to King's College, 26 July 1915 (Wilson Archive RCA).
52. Ibid.
53. H. Wilson. Report on the work of the Design Classes in the Schools ... (see n. 40 above).
54. H. Wilson. Report on the work of the Design Classes in the Schools ... (see n. 46 above).
55. H. Wilson. Letter from The Thatched House, Platt to Dr. Garrett 1 April 1911 (Wilson Archive RCA). Dr. William Garrett, a physicist, was Chairman of the Technical Education Board.
56. H. Wilson 'The Value of Learning by Doing' (1906, Wilson Archive RCA). C.R. Ashbee's *Should we stop teaching art* was published in 1911.
57. H. Wilson. Confidential Report of the Consultative Committeee on Goldsmiths', Silversmiths', Jewellers' and Allied Trades on the entry of boys into the Day Silversmithing School held at L.C.C. Central School of Arts and Crafts, April 1911.(Wilson Archive RCA).
58. Ibid.
59. H. Wilson. 'Goldsmiths' Work and Jewellery' (undated m/s Wilson Archive RCA).
60. See n. 56 above.
61. H. Wilson. Birmingham Municipal School of Art: Vittoria Street School for Jewellers and Silversmiths General Report of the Examiner for the year ended Dec. 1911.
62. H. Wilson. Address to L.C.C. 5 Jan 1915 (Wilson Archive RCA).
63. H. Wilson. 'Brightening of Human Life': address by Wilson on his opening the B.I.I.A. Exhibition, Cartwright Memorial Hall, Bradford. *Yorkshire Daily Observer*, 3 Dec. 1922.
64. H. Wilson. 'On Reconstruction' (Wilson Archive RCA).
65. Ibid.
66. Ibid.
67. H. Wilson. 'Education and the Handicrafts' 1918 was largely reused as 'The Creative Impulse and its place in Education c. 1922 (Wilson Archive RCA). See also 'Report on the exhibition of wounded and discharged sailors' and soldiers' work organised by the Womens' Guild of Arts': 'If I could put into words all the bitter and burning thoughts which this exhibition brings to mind, the reader would not know whether to weep ... or rejoice.' (undated m/s c.1918). Wilson Archive RCA). George Sedding had been born in Bloomsbury May 13, 1882. In 1915 he was repatriated and died in Hampshire at the age of 33.
68. H. Wilson. Address delivered at a meeting of King's College called to consider the possibility of the correlation of existing artistic, educational and social activities (19 July 1915, Wilson Archive RCA).
69. See n. 65 above.
70. H. Wilson. Address delivered at ameeting of King's College called to consider the possibility of the correlation of existing artists, educational and social activities (19 July 1915, Wilson Archive RCA)
71. H. Wilson. 'Report on the exhibition of wounded and discharged sailors' and soldiers' work organised by the Women's Guild of Arts' (Wilson Archive RCA). See n. 65 above.
72. The Rev. Charles Lowther Arnold was vicar of Holy Trinity 1902-23. Alban Charles Phileas Arnold, 2nd Lieutenant 11th Batallion Royal Fusiliers, was killed in the battle of the Somme 7 July 1916 aged 23. Edward Gladwin Arnold, Lieutenant 232nd Army Brigade, Royal Field Artillery, died aged 26 on 21 March 1918 at Pozières. St. Helena, the central figure of Wilson's window, was the mother of Constantine, the founder of the Holy Roman Empire. According to tradition she located the cross used for Christ's crucifixion in a cave beneath what became the Church of the Holy Sepulchre in Jerusalem. Her namesake Helena Tylor who commissioned the window, was the granddaughter of Sir Henry Thompson, who paid for the building of the church to Thomas Ellis Owen's design in 1832. It was enlarged with the addition of the chancel and a new vestry commissioned from Wilson 1910-13. Miss Tylor put her royal connections (her mother having attended Queen Victoria) to good effect when she invited Princesses Henry of Battenburg and Ina of Spain to open a bazaar in aid of these additions. Repositioning the east window to the west end was achieved in 1913. Wilson's original sketch (see Hampshire Record Office) is signed H. Wilson, 2678 Calle del Forno, S. Mauricio, Venezia. The dedication appears at the foot of the second and fourth of the five lunettes: 'To the glory of God and in loving remembrance of Alberta Helena Louise Tylor who entered into rest June 10th 1913'. In the event, this wording was simplified and extended to record the deaths of Miss Tylor's nephews. Around the central area containing the figure group Wilson sketched cherubs, stars, and, to the left and right, 'nebuly' and 'the walled garden'. Beneath St. Helena a cartouche displays the words 'But far be it from me to glory save in the cross'. The east wall surrounding the window was decorated with painted designs, but no trace remains. The window's possible maker, J.H.M. Bonnor, was an architect, sculptor, and craftsman in stained glass, mosaic and jewellery, which he taught at Camberwell School of Arts and Crafts. Born in Wales in 1875, he worked for architects Young and Hall, later joining the architects' department of the L.C.C. and running evening classes at the Central School. He joined the Artificers' Guild c. 1904, starting his own workshop 1908. He died in New York 29 January 1917 while designing decorations for the New Parliament House, Ottawa. (for Bonnor's work see the *Studio* XXIX 5 Mar 1920).
73. The inscription on the sill beneath the window reads 'In memory of our gallant sons who fell in the Great War 1914-19 this window is erected by the parishioners of West Ashton'. Following Wilson's instructions, Powell tried to make the window 'as much like old jewelled glass as possible'. Wilson's description of the window's symbolism (held at the church) explains that in his right hand Christ is holding a wreath, or crown of peace; with his left he blesses the new-born spirit of the young man who has made 'the supreme sacrifice'. Above are the four angels of the 'winds of the spirit'. The holy dove descends with an olive wreath. Behind the angels an arch is formed by a flock of birds, 'typifying the flight of souls to their rest and rebirth'. Below are the ramparts of the holy city; on the earth is the flag of St. George with the sword and helmet of righteousness.

HENRY WILSON 1864-1934 – **CHAPTER SEVEN**

Behind the young man is the English oak and rose; nearby 'grows the true vine'. Only a small part survives of Rood Ashton, the ancestral home of the Long family; this 18th century this red brick manor house, built for its wealthy mercantile owners, commanded a park with vistas to the Bristol Channel, until the family lost its fortune in the Wall Street crash. The church of St John the Baptist (1846) was by diocesan architects T.H. Wyatt and J.R. Brandon.

74. Surmounted by his regimental emblem, the inscription on an oval marble tablet to Samuel Einem Hickson explains that he was a 'Lieutenant. 2nd Battn. loyal North Lancashire Regt. the grandson of the late Revd. Vernon Blake for 35 years vicar of this parish, who was killed at Tanga in German East Africa whilst leading his men with great gallantry on November 4th 1914. Aged 21 years. Erected in loving memory by his stepmother.' A letter from Wilson to the vicar of St. Giles, Stoke Poges, 22 January 1920, alluding to the design of his 'memorial plaque' is in the collection of the Council for Places of Worship. Wilson's earlier work for St. Giles's church, his single light sanctuary window of 1899, commemorates Boer War victim Frederick Alhusen: the victorious and protective figure of Michael holds a child and staff. It was probably made by the glassmaker Benjamin Nelson, one of Christopher Whall's pupils at the Central School. Its dedication appears at the bottom of the design: 'To the glory of God for his mercies vouchsafed to the memory of Frederick Henry Alhusen captain of 9th Royal Lancers during the South African war 1899, this window is erected by his sister Margaret.' The Alhusen family lived in the village for generations until the late 1930s, in the house now called Stoke Court, a building closely associated with the poet Thomas Gray whose 'Elegy written in a Country Churchyard' was composed c. 1770 under the yew tree opposite the the southwest door of St. Giles's: the poet's mother and aunt lived in the house, and he himself often stayed there.

75. In addition to Frederick Henry Norman's grave (situated in churchyard, to the east of the chancel), Wilson may also have participated in the design of the silver altar cross inside the church. It was made in Birmingham c. 1905 when he was Examiner at Vittoria Street, while Gaskin was its Director. Wilson's village war memorial, whose dedication on 2 January 1921 attracted 600 people, comprises a Latin cross with an octagonal shaft set on a 9'3" square pedestal; on its central face is the inscription: 'To the memory of the men of this parish who gave their lives in the Great War 1914-18'; on the three remaining faces are carved the names of the 43 men who died. Its site, just S of the northern entrance to Moor Park Place, had been given by Captain Montagu Collet Norman DSO (later Lord Norman), whose military decoration had been awarded in 1900 for his service in the Boer War; by the time Viscount Hampden unveiled the Much Hadham memorial, he had been governor of the Bank of England for a year. The installation of the obelisk, with diaper-patterned paving in flint and brick on its three steps, was entrusted to Wilson's old associate W. Micklewhite of Stoke-under-Ham, Yeovil, and executed by G. L. Thurgood & Son, employing mostly ex-servicemen for the work. The cost of the memorial was 'upwards of £800' (*Hertfordshire Mercury* 8 Jan 1921).

76. Tonbridge gate is included in C. F. Kernot's *British Public School War Memorials* (1927). Sketches in RIBADC. Wilson's comments on designing memorials appear in *Boston Evening Transcript* 2 July 1927. 'Art lends its charm....'

77. H. Wilson. Report on the design classes in the schools of Edinburgh, Glasgow and Aberdeen 1915 (Wilson Archive RCA).

78. H. Wilson. 'The City Beautiful' (see n. 51 above).

79. H. Wilson. 'The Creative Impulse and its place in Education' c. 1922 (Wilson Archive RCA). W.R. Lethaby's writing on 'cottage crafts' is probably a reference to his *Simple Furniture*, which appeared as *Cabinet Making in Plain Handicrafts* (1892) and was reissued in 1922 as one of the Dryad leaflets. W.A.S. Benson's writings would include his *Elements of Handicraft and Design* (1893) and his *Rudiments of Handicraft* (1919). George Jack's 'carving and simple furniture' is an allusion to his *Woodcarving – design and workmanship*, which was published in the Artistic Craft Series in 1903.

80. H. Wilson. 'Crafts in Education and Reconstruction' was included in *Handicrafts* (John Hogg 1919) p. 10-17.

81. H. Wilson. 'Some Provisional Suggestions on the Training of Wounded and Disabled Soldiers and Sailors, submitted to His Majesty's Ministries of Labour, Pensions and Reconstruction' by the Art Workers' Guild and the Arts and Crafts Exhibition Society, 1 Hare Court, E.C., 1918.(Wilson Archive RCA).

82. H. Wilson. 'Report on the exhibition of work of wounded and discharged sailors' and soldiers' work organised by the Women's Guild of Arts' (see n. 50 above; see also 'The Creative Impulse and its place in Education' c. 1922 (see n. 8 above): 'Dr. H. Munro found a consumptive clerk in a Bradford cellar. Rejected by every hospital as incurable, given six months to live, the man was devoured by anxiety for his wife and children. Finding he longed to use his hands in craft work, Dr. Munro procured tools, materials and instruction, and in a short time the man recovered, and is earning good wages as a metalworker. Mental creation brings physical regeneration.'

83. H. Wilson. 'The Handicrafts in Re-education' (undated m/s c. 1918. Wilson Archive RCA).

84. H. Wilson. 'Federated Workshops' delivered before the Art Workers' Guild (1918, Wilson Archive RCA).

85. Ibid.

86. H. Wilson. 'Report on the National Importance of Handicraft Training' (1919, Wilson Archive RCA).

87. H. Wilson. 'Report on the exhibition of the work of wounded sailors and soldiers' (see n. 65 above).

88. H. Wilson. 'The Handicrafts in Re-education' (see n. 69 above).

89. Ibid

90. C.R. Ashbee. *Craftsmanship in Competitive Industry* (1908, Essex House) p. 194.

91. H. Wilson. Manifesto of the Association of Architecture, Building and Handicraft. 9 July 1917 (Wilson Archive RCA).

92. Ibid.

93. Ibid.

94. Ibid.

95. Ibid.

96. H. Wilson. 'Federated Workshops' (see n. 82 above).
97. H. Wilson. 'Report on the National Importance of Handicraft Training' (see n. 84 above).
98. H. Wilson. 'Report on the National Importance of Handicraft Training' (see n. 84 above).
99. H. Wilson. 'Report on the National Importance of Handicraft Training' (see n. 84 above).
100. C.R. Ashbee. 'Masters of the Art Workers' Guild from the beginning to 1934' p. 315-6. (m/s in collection of Art Workers' Guild).
101. Ibid.

CHAPTER 8
PUBLIC FACE OF THE ARTS AND CRAFTS

1. Hamilton Temple Smith, quoted in F. MacCarthy, *All Things Bright and Beautiful* (1972) p. 72.
2. D.I.A. Journal III 1917.
3. H. Wilson. 'The Economic Problem in the Movable Arts' c. 1918 (Wilson Archive RCA). See also Epilogue n.13.
4. Ibid.
5. Ibid.
6. Ibid.
7. Ibid.
8. Ibid.
9. W.R. Lethaby and others, *Ernest Gimson: his Life and Work* (1924) p. 14.
10. W.R. Lethaby, 'Art and Workmanship', in *The Imprint* no.1.(Imprint Publishing Co., London 1913). Reprinted as D.I.A.'s second pamphlet.
11. The fluted column leading down from the cross to a silver-studded ebony staff is of Sheffield plate. On the knop a Latin inscription records the presentation of the cross to the Cathedral on Christmas Day 1917. The final part of its wording – attributed to the embattled Constantine on seeing an apparition of the cross in the clouds – In hoc signo vinco (With this sign I conquer), stresses the symbolic value of the cross. For some years, for comfort's sake, the top portion of the cross only was routinely borne on a simple staff. The Cathedral Architect G.G. Pace provided a more complete solution when in 1962, during its restoration, he redesigned the cross by removing the boat knop altogether and substituting a new shaft with a decorative silver socket into which the cross fits directly.
12. H. Wilson quoted by C.R. Ashbee in *Masters of the Art Workers' Guild from the beginning to 1934* p. 315-6; see also Walter Crane, letter to Wilson 29 December 1909, regretting that despite his 'artistic kinship with us' [ACES] he could not be induced 'to remain' (Wilson Archive RCA). Wilson's resignation, submitted in the last days of 1909 became effective in the New Year.
13. *Studio* vol. 57 1912 p. 293. Further parts of this review appear on p. 290 and in vol. 58 1913 p. 21.
14. H. Wilson. Notes relating to the 1916 Burlington House Exhibition, Notebook 5 (Wilson Archive RCA).
15. H. Van de Velde. *Die Form* (vii) 1932 p. 316.
16. H. Wilson. 'The Art of a Nation' 1914-18 (Wilson Archive RCA).
17. Ibid.
18. Ibid.
19. H. Wilson. Notes relating to the 1916 Burlington House Exhibition, Notebook 5 (Wilson Archive RCA).
20. H. Van de Velde. *Die Form* (vii) 1932 p. 316.
21. H. Wilson. 'The Art of a Nation' 1914-18 (Wilson Archive RCA).
22. H. Wilson. *Daily News* 1916 (Wilson Archive RCA).
23. *Studio* vol. 60 1913 p. 78.
24. *Jnl RSA* 5 September 1913 p. 938.
25. W.A.S. Benson. 'The Aims of the Arts and Crafts Exhibition Society', in *Handicrafts* (1919) by members of the Arts and Crafts Exhibition Society p. 124-5.
26. Ghent International Exhibition 1913. Catalogue of the British Section. Foreword by W. Crane p. xxii. Muthesius's comments appear in his article on C.R. Mackintosh and Margaret Macdonald in *Dekorative Kunst* 9 March 1902 p. 194.
27. Ibid.
28. H. Wilson. Catalogue of Ghent International Exhibition. (V&A). The Hampshire grave, its execution entrusted by Wilson during his stay in Venice to Trask, was for Margaret Skrine. It had been commissioned by John Skrine, the incumbent at St. Peter-in-the-East, Oxford; his letter to Wilson from 4 South Parks Road, Oxford, 2 September 1913 notes the balancing act Wilson had to perform between his design and exhibition commitments: 'We often pictured you in Ghent, but did not guess how much of work – and of interest – was falling to your lot'. (Wilson Archive RCA). A carved stone crucifix set within a kerbstone with coping stones carved with the parable from John X; its pedestal bore bronze-framed marble tablets carved on the North side with 'To the glory of God and in the fair memory of Margaret Susanna Skrine beloved twin daughter of John Huntley Skrine DD and Mary his wife'; on West side: 'Born June 4 1883 Betrothed September 4 1907 Changed her life December 4 1907; on S. and E. sides: 'A maiden knight to me is given such hope I know not fear'; and a stanza from the Land of Zion: 'Bone Pastor, Papus vere Tu nos pasce nos tuere Tu nos bona fac videre In terra viventium'. (Good Shepherd, true Pope, feed us, watch us, give us to see good things in the land of the living). Beneath the figure of Christ were words suggested by Wilson himself, Mary Skrine expressing particular satisfaction with them in her letter of 18 October 1913: 'See how your "I am the door" has harmonised it all'. The grave was consecrated a few days before Skrine's letter of 5 September 1913: 'I can do no justice to the joy we take in its beauty. But the greatest of [it] is the thought that while bronze and marble stand there, there will stand for any dweller or passer-by the most profound and uplifting of parables in a tongue ... the wayfaring man can read. And I am sure I name there the reward of your art that you will covet most.' In his letter of 7 September 1913 he comments on the design: 'How you have got the wind of the spirit into that blown banner! And how human and cherishing is the Christ! It is not possible to tell you how happy I was those two days in Itchen Stoke churchyard.'
Skrine's delight with the grave eclipsed the irritation voiced in his letter of 24 October 1913 re-the late delivery of the

HENRY WILSON 1864-1934 – **CHAPTER EIGHT**

bronzes, and Trask's bill – the carving on the kerbstone was unsatisfactory, the stone having cracked. Skrine refused to pay for the task to be redone, and Wilson had to persuade Trask to bear the cost of the replacement. The new stone amounted to £1-12-8; the carver for the inscription was paid £10-3-10, and the expense of 'Sending a man to fix the bronzes ... as directed' was also Trask's.
None of this lessened Skrine's regard for Wilson, however; he already had in his possession a statue depicting the Virgin and Child. It had been meant for the Scottish public school where Skrine had been headmaster 1899-1902 – Glenalmond, Perthshire – but as he said in his letters to Wilson of 5 and 7 September 1913, it presented him with a dilemma: 'If I write again upon the Virgin Birth I shall go to [your statue] for inspiration. It is all full of lovely new meaning to me. We took off the lid and looked: then let Lawrence nail [it] down again and brought it straight home. There is a new churchwarden going to Glenalmond ... [but] we could not bring ourselves to part with it. So having begged Our Lady to come into our poor house, it becomes henceforward her shrine. In plain words, we mean to keep her ourselves!' (Wilson Archive RCA). The statue was left by him to his Oxford church, which was subsequently incorporated into St Edmund's Hall library; the statue remains untraced.

29. Ibid.
30. *Jnl. RSA* 5 September 1913 p. 938. Wilson had advised Edmund Sedding (JD's nephew) on the restoration of this Cornish church, as well as designing its pulpit.
31. This pulpit had already been exhibited in 7th Arts and Crafts Exhibition in 1903. Ill. *Studio* vol. 29 1903 p. 22.
32. *Studio* vol. 60 1913 p. 78.
33. *Studio* vol. 60 1913 p. 81.
34. Letters from Julius Hoffman, Verlag für Kunst und Kunstgewerbe, Stuttgart, 11 November and 21 November 1907 to Wilson (Wilson Archive RCA). *Moderne Bauformen: Monatshefte fur Architektur und Raumkunst* continued to publish discussions and illustrations of notable 20th century architecture and interior design from 1902 to 1944.
35. RIBA Drawings Collection X16/18. See also *Moderne Bauformen* ix 1910.
36. The catalogue of the Paris exhibition held by the National Art Library at the V&A contains pencil notes giving specimen prices of exhibits. For example, pulpit and sounding board in carved oak £100; chafing dish with thead-spinning goddess finial £75; Gloucester chalice £85; MacRitchie mace £200. Many jewels also have scribbled prices beside them: gold necklace with amethysts and enamels showing signs of the zodiac £45; gold necklace with pearl, moonstone, emerald and opal with a pendant depicting enamelled winged figure £95 (compare that of 1905 in Ch. 5 above); gold haircomb decorated with a peacock embellished with moonstone, peridot and three rubies £45; gold and silver haircomb with an opal and a moonstone £12; gold and enamel corsage with eight moonstones £350; gold and enamel pendant and chain with vine leaves and cherubim embellished with a ruby, sapphire and emerald £70; enamelled gold buckle with stag design enriched with rock crystal and chrysophrase £50; gold and enamel brooch entitled 'Cherubim' £80; 'Rose' pattern brooch decorated with enamel and crystal drops, designed by Wilson and made by Harry Murphy £15 (compare Edgar's gift to his mother-in-law in Ch. 5 above); cloak clasp with plique-à-jour enamel and rock crystal £55 (compare Cupid cloak clasp, see Ch. 5 above).
37. *Jnl RSA* 8 May 1914 p. 559.
38. *Studio* vol. 62 1914 p. 238-42.
39. Whall's Gloucester Cathedral cartoons are visible in the illustration in the 1914 Paris Catalogue. His plaster cross with a close resemblance to Wilson's work (see above Ch. IV n. 76) stood on the altar in the exhibition, and is no. 1128c in the Catalogue.
40. *Studio* vol. 62 1914 p. 238-42.
41. Ibid.
42. *Jnl. RSA* 15 January 1915 p. 166.
43. *Jnl. RSA* 7 July 1916 p. 606.
44. H. Wilson. Catalogue of 11th Arts and Crafts Exhibition 1916, Introduction.
45. H. Wilson. Circular to A.C.E.S. members 1916 (Wilson Archive RCA).
46. See n. 44 above.
47. See n. 45 above.
48. *The Nation* vol. 103, 30 November 1916 p. 524-5.
49. ACES Minutes 9 February 1916 (V&A).
50. *Studio* vol. 69 1916 p. 190.
51. H. Wilson. Circular to A.C.E.S. members 1916 (Wilson Archive RCA).
52. Ibid.
53. *Studio* vol. 69 1916 p. 70.
54. *The Nation* vol. 103, 30 November 1916 p. 524-5.
55. *Jnl RSA* 20 October 1916 p. 819.
56. Ill. *Studio* December 1916 p. 123.
57. Ibid.
58. *Morning Post* 4 November 1916.
59. *Burlington Magazine* November 1916 p. 342.
60. *Studio* vol. 69 1916 p. 124.
61. *Jnl RSA* 10 November 1916 p. 853.
62. *Morning Post* 4 November 1916.
63. *Burlington Magazine* November 1916 p. 342.
64. *Burlington Magazine* November 1916 p. 341-2.
65. *Burlington Magazine* December 1916 p. 388-40.
66. *The Nation* vol. 103, 30 November 1916 p. 524-5.
67. More beginnings of the D. I. A. November 1916.
68. Harold Stabler. ACES Minutes 16 June 1916 (V&A).
69. More beginnings of the D. I. A. November 1916.
70. *Jnl RSA* 20 October 1916 p. 819.

CHAPTER 9
ARTS AND CRAFTS IN A MODERN WORLD

1. A. Clutton Brock. A Modern Creed of Work (4th D.I.A. pamphlet). 'The word art does not occur in the title of the Design and Industries Association because art is commonly supposed to be a mystery understood only by artists; and the Association wishes to make no mystery about its aims. The word design has a more precise meaning.... When we say that anything is well-designed we mean that it is well-fitted

to its purpose.'

2. Sedding's lecture appears in the D.I.A. Jnl. VIII 1918, Ruskin's in Jnl. IV 1917.
3. Modern Crafts and Manufactures exhibition catalogue, Introduction. (B.I.I.A.1920).
4. The jewels sent by by Wilson to the 1923 exhibition included the Cupid cloak clasp, the chrysophrase buckle/ pendant, a gold and enamel gem-set necklet with repoussé stag, and portrait medallions struck from dies he had cut personally. W.E. Micklewright, carpenter and cabinet-maker, was Trask's closest colleague.
5. H. Wilson. 'Brightening of Human Life: a Bradford Exhibition'. *Yorkshire Daily Observer* 3 December 1922. See also review of 1923 exhibition, *Studio* vol. 86 1923 p. 263-5.
6. Ibid.
7. Ibid.
8. Ibid.
9. 'Industrial Art for the Slender Purse' exhibition catalogue, Introduction. (B.I.I.A. 1929).
10. *Art and Industry* pamphlet for Ministry of Reconstruction, 1919.
11. Wilson's font cover for St. James's Church was subsequently lost; this cover and its mechanism, the font (by Goodhue), and Cram's reredos were transferred to another Cram, Goodhue & Ferguson building, the 1910 chapel of St. Luke's Home for Convalescents, 149 Roxbury Street. In 1968 St. John and St. James (Episcopal) Church took over St. Luke's Home Chapel and the parishes merged to form the modern church complex of St. John's and St. James's, Roxbury, Mass. Wilson's font cover was illustrated in Montgomery Schuyler's article on Cram in *The Architectural Record* (New York) XXIX No. 1 January 1911 p. 79; and in *The Architectural Review* (Boston), vol. II 1913 pl. 10. See also D. S. Tucci, *Church Building in Boston 1720-1970, with an Introduction to the work of Ralph Adams Cram and the Boston Gothicists* (Concord, MA, Rumford Press 1974) p. 132; and *Boston Bohemia 1881-1900*, vol. 1 of *Ralph Adams Cram: Life & Architecture* (University of Massachussetts Press, Amhurst 1995) p. 301; ill. 76a p. 302.
12. *Boston Evening Transcript* 2 July 1927. An equally positive review, 'Art in Business Enters Through Great Bronze Doors', appeared in *The Boston Herald* (Rotogravure section) 5 February 1928.
13. H. Wilson. Letter to Edgar from Hotel Hudson, 53 Washington Square, New York, 1 July 1927 (Wilson Archive RCA). While Wilson was catching his breath in America, the Weisenhoff settlement, comprising workers' houses and apartments built in the International style by 16 European architects including Gropius, Le Corbusier and Bruno Taut and with Mies van der Rohe as coordinator, opened to the public on 23 July 1927.
14. Although the doors remain *in situ*, the opportunity for examining the story they tell is limited by their having been fixed flat back by the present occupiers, as if flung fully open, with modern glass doors (these dwarfed by Wilson's at twice their height) hung beyond them, opening into the building. The photograph taken for the Gorham Archive (Brown University, Mass.), and those reproduced in the press of the time, record the appearance of the doors on completion in 1927. The Salada contract, between Larkin, designer and foundry was drawn up in 1922. Salada Tea was later purchased by Redco Foods Inc., before being sold to Lipton's (Canada) and becoming part of Unilever.
15. 'New Schools in Art', 1917 (Wilson Archive RCA).
16. Ibid.
17. *Reports on the Present Position and Tendencies of the Industrial Arts as indicated at the International Exhibition of Modern Decorative and Industrial Arts, Paris, 1925.* (Department of Overseas Trade, 1927) Introductory Survey p. 10.
18. *Reports on the Present Position* ... opus cit, p. 12. The Introductory Survey was written by Sir Hubert Llewellyn Smith in his capacity as Chairman of the editorial committee, which included Sir Reginald Blomfield, Eric Maclagan, and Sir Frank Warner.
19. Ibid.
20. Ibid.
21. Ibid p. 19. The contemporary element of the show was highlighted by Warner (p. 16) in relation to the textiles, where 'a true style which will be associated with 1925' could be seen.
22. Ibid p. 37.
23. H. Wilson. *Reports on the Present Position* ... 'Metal Work', opus cit. pp. 117-119.
24. Ibid.
25. Ibid.
26. H. Wilson. Ibid pp. 120-122.
27. H. Wilson. Ibid pp. 120-122.
28. H. Wilson. Ibid p. 125.
29. H. Wilson. Ibid p. 121.
30. *Reports on the Present Position* ... Introductory Survey, opus cit. p. 11.
31. Ibid. p. 28
32. The Leipzig Fair (6 March-31 August 1927) was an international exhibition, meant to show the development of design since the war, and to coincide with the opening of a new gallery in the Grassi museum. The British section, with over eighty artists and firms, appeared under the auspices of the D.I.A., though reviewing the event for *The D.I.A. Quarterly Journal* (New Series) no.1 (September 1927) pp. 6-11, H.H. Peach explained that the British contribution had been unavoidably rushed. Conceding that it was 'not very exciting as against what the modern schools abroad may offer', he insisted it was 'sane, good and could hold its own against anything the others may produce'. The most representative part was the pottery, which included 'simple hand-painted design, fitter shapes, handles that are handles and not art ornaments ...' by Carter, Stabler & Adams; amongst the silver was the Swiney Cup, an 'outstanding' example of 'clean, fresh metalworking'. Peach conceded that 'we have no special school or movement such as the Deutscher Werkstatten', but picked out individual 'pioneers of the modern movement' in the textiles section. Some toys, knitted goods, embroidery, fittings by Hope & Sons and Dryad, two reliefs by Eric Gill and two motor bus insignia by Stabler also caught his attention. However, the Commentary added by M. McLeish complained that the display lacked the 'directness of other countries', was too 'miscellaneous,' and the glass cases 'cut up' the space. Phyllis

Baron, and the 'Modern Textiles' group including Paul Nash and Alec Walker, had struck a 'modern' note, but 'broadly speaking ... we do not understand it'.

33. H. Wilson. Letter to Edgar from Hotel Hudson, 53 Washington Square, New York, 1 July 1927 (Wilson Archive RCA). While Wilson was catching his breath in America, the Weisenhoff settlement, comprising workers' houses and apartments built in the International style by 16 European architects including Gropius, Le Corbusier and Bruno Taut and with Mies van der Rohe as coordinator, opened to the public on 23 July 1927.
34. The gross value of Wilson's estate was £4506-12-4, estate duty of £219-18-6d and legal fees having been paid on that sum. Administration of the will was carried out by Sydney Morse & Co. of 6 Aldersgate Street, London EC1, Margaret's uncle. Dated 3 October 1903, the will had appointed Margaret as Wilson's sole executrix, and had been witnessed at The Thatched House by Olga Johansen, the Wilsons' cook, and Erikka Eriksen, nurse; in the event (Margaret having predeceased him) it was executed by his daughter Pernel on 28 December 1934.
35. Letter to Wilson c/o Leonard Stokes, 2 Great Smith St, Westminster from R.A. Cram, 21 October 1907 of Cram, Goodhue and Ferguson, 15 Beacon St, Boston and 170 Fifth Ave. NY. (Wilson Archive RCA). By the time of the cathedral commission, the firm had become Cram & Ferguson.
36. Letter from R.A. Cram to Bishop William T. Manning, 9 February 1928 (Archive, Cathedral of St. John the Divine, New York). Cram's 'twenty four panels' refers to the doors' regular panels, exclusive of the scenes and figures that would fill their top tier.
37. Ibid.
38. Letter from R.A. Cram to Bursar Canon Robert E. Jones, 28 June 1928 (Archive, Cathedral of St. John the Divine, New York).
39. The 'Portal of Paradise' carvings were finally executed during the Carving Project of 1988-97. They depict figures from the Old and New Testaments, arranged in upper and lower ranks, 8' and 3'6" tall respectively, the upper rank painted with pigments authentically formulated from ingredients described in the Book of Revelation. The workmen were drawn from the city's unemployed, trained by the winner of the 1988 portal statuary competition, the English sculptor Simon Verity, assisted by Jean-Claude Marchionni. The figure on the central pier, St. John the Divine gazing upwards to Christ in Majesty, was carved in the 1970s by John Angel. Flanking the Christ in Majesty roundel are low relief spandrels with figures representing the four evangelists. The low-relief lintel frieze depicts modern Americans of every race carrying palms. For Haley Fiske obituary see *The New York Times* 4 March 1929.
40. Letter to F.H. Ecker, President, Metropolitan Life Insurance Company, 1133 Broadway, New York, from Committee of Cathedral Trustees, 8 June 1929 (Archive, Cathedral of St. John the Divine, New York).
41. Letter from R.A. Cram to Bursar Canon Robert E. Jones, 28 June 1928 (Archive, Cathedral of St. John the Divine, New York).
42. 'I want all the Wilson family to be on top in everything. I haven't got to the top in sculpture yet, but I hope to before I go over to the other side.' Undated letter (c. 1928) from Harry, 1 rue Feudon, Quai President Carnot, Paris, to his brother Edgar. See above Introduction n. 19.
43. The Bishop wrote to thank Larkin for his recommendation on 24 January 1930, addressing his letter to 'The Right Honourable Peter Larkin', who was staying at the Hotel des Indes in The Hague, perhaps on tea business: 'I greatly value your testimony in regard to Mr. Wilson's ability as an artist and sculptor. I feel myself in no doubt as to this and hope that arrangements will speedily be completed for him to make the Bronze Doors for the Cathedral....' Never enthusiastic about their gilding, the Bishop did not choose to use the term 'Golden Doors'; see also his letter to Wilson on the same day, 'hoping work could start as speedily as possible' on the 'Bronze Doors' . (Archive, Cathedral of St. John the Divine, New York).
44. Troup included the work Wilson carried out at 'Batsford Park' in his Obituary on Wilson, *Jnl RIBA* 24 March 1934. The house, designed for A.B. Freeman-Mitford (later the third Lord Redesdale) 1888-1893 by Ernest George and Harold Peto with Guy Dawber as site architect, replaced an earlier Georgian mansion. Built of Boughton stone quarried on the estate, it is in a gabled Cotswold-Elizabethan style, to an H-shaped plan. The entrance hall has Art Nouveau enrichments and timbered ceiling; leading up from it is the carved grand staircase. It is unclear exactly what the alterations, made to the house by Wilson at the beginning of Lord Dulverton's ownership, involved. When the estate was purchased in 1919 by Sir Gilbert Alan Hamilton Wills (1880-1956) of tobacco fame, modifications were made to the house, but the records of these changes were destroyed. During his ownership, it became a noted venue for fashionable house parties, and the gardens (now Batsford Arboretum), were restocked. Sir Gilbert was elevated to 1st baron in 1929 as Lord Dulverton of Batsford. Mentioned in despatches during World War 1 and awarded the OBE in 1919; he was MP for Weston-super-Mare 1918-22, becoming chairman of the Imperial Tobacco Co. in 1927. The Bishop wrote to him at Batsford Park about the New York doors 10 February 1930, 'agreeing fully' with all that he had said about Wilson, 'hoping that the questions that have arisen may be satisfactorily settled' and that Wilson be 'authorized to proceed with this work which he is 'so eminently qualified to carry out'. (Archive, Cathedral of St. John the Divine, New York).
45. R.A. Cram. 'The work of Henry Wilson'. *Christian Art* Vol. 2 Number 6, March 1908.
46. Letter from Wilson, 1 rue Feudon, S. Cloud 20 July 1928 to his brother Edgar, referring to the illustrated article in the *Boston Herald* of 5 February 1928 (Wilson Archive RCA).
47. Letter from Chester N. Godfrey of Cram & Ferguson to Bishop Manning, 31 Jan 1930 (Archive, Cathedral of St. John the Divine, New York).
48. Ibid.
49. Contractual agreement 12 February 1930 (Archive, Cathedral of St. John the Divine, New York).
50. Sinclair had written to Wilson on 24 January 1930, noting

his request that the first payment be made, and that the matter would be sorted out 'without delay'. (Archive Cathedral of St. John the Divine, New York).

51. 'I cannot see why I should be called upon to pay any partial payment for the sculptor's or the bronze work ... in case of death before the completion of the work, who would reimburse me for the money spent?' Letter from Donald Sinclair to Bishop Manning 15 November 1930 (Archive, Cathedral of St. John the Divine New York).
52. Letter from Dean Milo Gates to Donald Sinclair 20 November 1930 (Archive, Cathedral of St. John the Divine, New York).
53. Letter from Bishop Manning to Lord Dulverton 4 March 1931 (Archive, Cathedral of St. John the Divine, New York).
54. Letter from Cram to Dean Gates 27 November 1930 (Archive, Cathedral of St. John the Divine, New York).
55. Letter from Wilson to Bishop Manning 9 February 1931 (Archive, Cathedral of St. John the Divine, New York). See also Ch. 4 n. 10.
56. Letter from Dean Gates to Cram 15 February 1930 (Archive, Cathedral of St. John the Divine New York).
57. Under Ferdinand Barbedienne (1810-1892) the firm became one of the most celebrated and prolific foundries in the world. In 1838, he had joined manufacturer Achille Collas in making bronze reductions of classical figures, and casting models from contemporary sculptors. Later they produced decorative objects (chandeliers, vases, furniture, enamelwork) in a variety of revival styles. Barbedienne took over the business with its 300 employees when Collas died in 1859; at the 1862 International Exhibition in London it won medals in three different classes, and between 1875 and 1886 made the 152' iron armature and copper cladding for F.A. Bartholdi's Statue of Liberty. When Ferdinand's nephew inherited the business, his name was incorporated into its title, becoming Leblanc-Barbedienne. He opened offices in Britain and the US, concentrating after World War 1 on memorials and on the work of sculptors such as Emmanuel Frémiet. Between 1929 and 1952 he cast many busts by Daumier. The firm closed in 1954.
58. Letter from Dean Gates to Cram 15 February 1930 (Archive, Cathedral of St. John the Divine, New York). Godfrey's letter of 25 March 1929 to the Bishop included Wilson's estimate of $84,800 for the doors, assuming Barbedienne would cast them; it also mentioned a commission that was to be awarded to Gorham – the 'bronze shrine for the 'Golden Book' – in which would be recorded the names of all the donors both to the Golden Doors and the building of the cathedral as a whole. The cost of Gorham's proposal, to be carried out 'in accordance with our drawings S-14, revised 17 October 1928, including our commission', amounted to $33,528.00. Godfrey also recorded that 'Other proposals for this shrine have been taken from Yellin of Philadelphia and the Birmingham Guild of England', whose prices 'range from $4,000 to $15,000 higher than the Gorham figure'. (Archive, Cathedral of St. John the Divine, New York). In the event the job went to the Birmingham Guild Ltd., of Grosvenor Street West, Birmingham, England. Standing on the east side of All Souls' Chapel, the shrine is 13'2" tall, its marble base 6'4" by 3'2". Its gold-plated bronze design evokes a Gothic chapel, with its slender buttressed and pinnacled uprights, from which spring cusped arches. The cornice borders a steeply-pitched hipped roof, the lower intervals between the uprights are filled with a quatrefoiled protective grille. In their 'Orders to the Contractor' of 30 August 1929 Cram & Ferguson set out their specifications, countersigned by the Bishop. The Guild (represented by Henry L. Norton) was 'to furnish all materials and labor and make, finish and erect the Shrine of the Golden Book, as in drawing S-14 revised Oct 17, 1928.... The pedestal is to be of Belgian Black Marble with Blue Belge marble panels, selected for its fine veining.... The superstructure is to be of solid bronze ... its modeling ... done with the greatest delicacy ... to produce the finest possible finish. All exposed portions on inside and outside are to be heavily gold-plated.... One section of the the quatrefoil grille is to open as a door ... secured by two cylinder locks. A recess with suitable reflector is to be provided in the ceiling for an electrical outlet. All materials are to be first class and completed as rapidly as is consistent with the best workmanship. The amount to be paid is $24,700.00'.
59. This initial agreement between Barbedienne and Cram of 1 March 1930, would be superseded by the revised, Finch version, signed on 25 February 1931, countersigned by the Bishop on 25 March 1931.
60. Letter from Cram to Bishop Manning 29 November 1930 (Archive, Cathedral of St. John the Divine, New York).
61. Letter to Bishop Manning from Judge Edward Finch 14 March 1931 (Archive, Cathedral of St. John the Divine, New York).
62. Report by Adrien Dumas, representative of the firm of Jacques Gréber, architecte diplomé par le gouvernement, 4 rue Vernier, Paris, 26 December 1932 (Archive, Cathedral of St. John the Divine, New York).
63. Ibid.
64. St. Matthew's church, Westminster (by George Gilbert Scott, 1849-51) stood in a poor parish where so large a processional cross, commissioned for the Anglo-Catholic Congress of 1923, was made possible only after appealing to members of the congregation for their silver christening cups, to be melted down and recycled for the purpose. The symbols of the evangelists appear in repoussé roundels at the tips of the crosspieces, encircling the silver-gilt crucified Christ and the walled structure of the heavenly city which is depicted above him.
65. The text roundel to the left is inscribed 'To the glory of God and in thanksgiving for the life and service of Haley Fiske these doors are dedicated'; that to the right, 'The names of the donors are inscribed in the Golden Book of Remembrance'. Later, on 28 and 29 July 1936, Chester Godfrey wrote to solicitor Sydney Morse asking him to see that the plaster casts were destroyed, as the Cathedral 'did not care to have them shipped to New York'. (Archive, Cathedral of St. John the Divine, New York).
66. Letter from Barbedienne to Dean Gates, 22 October 1931 (Archive, Cathedral of St. John the Divine, New York). Godfrey's having stopped the Cathedral making so rash a promise featured in Cram & Ferguson's justification of

HENRY WILSON 1864-1934 – **CHAPTER NINE**

their 6% commission, this amount having been questioned by the Dean in 1936. As Godfrey pointed out in his letter of 16 April 1936, they had saved the Cathedral some $6000: 'We can assure you that if you had attempted to hold Barbedienne to the original amount of $29,500 you would never have received the doors, for he could not have finished them. Had payments been made by the Cathedral on the gold basis, in accordance with the agreement of the Trustees, the total amount they would have had to pay Barbedienne would have been $46,000, whereas the actual cost to the Cathedral is $40,130.63'. (Archive, Cathedral of St. John the Divine, New York).

67. Letter from R.A. Cram to Bishop Manning 29 November 1930 (Archive, Cathedral of St. John the Divine, New York).
68. A letter from Godfrey to the Dean on 11 Oct 1933 confirmed that the 'full amount' was now payable to the Cathedral by the Haley Fiske Memorial committee, so that in their turn, the Trustees could pay Wilson the rest of his fees. Edward W. Shaldon, Treasurer of the Cathedral Building Fund, compiled an account on 15 June 1934 of payments to Wilson: 27 March 1931 – $15,000 for full-size models of first pair of doors; 13 July 1931 – $7,500 'in connection with the doors'; 1 August 1931 – $15,000 for second pair of full-size models; 10 August 1932 – $5,000 'for models of bronze doors'; total payment to date $42,500. Godfrey wrote to the Dean on 22 June 1935 explaining that 'we have had several requests from Sydney Morse & Co., the attorneys representing the Wilson estate, concerning the balance.... It has been pointed out to them there are certain obligations into which Wilson entered that would reduce the total due him by $3,000. He is owed $8,000, which, after reduction, amounts to $5,000. We suggest $2,500 be paid at present, the certificate made out to Pernel Imogen Yolande Wilson, [and] forwarded to Morse at 6 Aldersgate Street London.' Those 'obligations' related to advances he had received from Cram, whose final record clarified the matter: 'Contract dated Mar 25 1931. Pernel Imogen Yolande Wilson administrix $50,500, less credit $3,000=$47,5000; contract dated 25 March 1931 F. Barbedienne $29,500, amount added $13,630.63 = $43,130.63'. Cram's letter to the Dean on 8 April 1936 confirmed the final payment of $2,500 to the Wilson estate, and $6,635.88 to Barbedienne (Archive, St. John the Divine, New York).
69. Letter from Cram to Wilson, Hotel Splendid, Menton, 10 July 1933 (Archive, Cathedral of St. John the Divine, New York).
70. Letter from Dean Gates to Chester Godfrey, 30 March 1933 (Archive, Cathedral of St. John the Divine, New York).
71. Letter from Godfrey to Barbedienne 31 Mar 1933. The term 'Owners' had been adopted in the preliminary agreement drawn up by Cram & Ferguson in 1928 to mean the Cathedral, 'Donors' to signify the Haley Fiske Memorial Committee, and 'Sculptor', Wilson. (Archive, Cathedral of St. John the Divine, New York).
72. Letter to R.A. Cram from H. Wilson, Splendid Hotel, August 4 1933 (Archive, Cathedral of St. John the Divine, New York).
73. G. Leblanc Barbedienne, quoted in Adrien Dumas's report of 1932. See also n. 41.
74. Ibid.
75. Godfrey wrote to Bishop Manning on 4 December 1935, warning him not to be surprised by the doors' very bright gold appearance, unlike the sample they had approved, which had been a 'dull colour that [would] harmonise with the surroundings'; Barbedienne was leaving the 'final toning down finish to be applied after the doors are erected'. Barbedienne (now at 53 ave. Victor Emmanuel III) had arranged through Cram that Thomas F. McGann, architectural and sculptural bronze and brass monger of 114 Portland Street, Boston, should transport the doors to the Cathedral from their point of arrival in New York, and install them at a cost of $2385. The final gilding, toning and glazing was carried out by E. Newton Marshall Co., contracting painters of 522 Harrison Avenue, Boston, at a cost of $494.75.
76. As early as 15 June 1928, Bursar Canon R.E. Jones had sought to establish the doors' status in relation to import tax. The shipping firm he approached, Perry, Ryer & Co. of 29 Broadway, New York, thought that they could be admitted free of duty as 'original works of art'. However, following a discussion with Mr. Ashworth of the New York Customs Office and Chester Godfrey, Assistant Secretary Lowman of the Treasury Department in Washington thought that the Golden Doors should be classed as utilitarian objects, making them liable to import tax. Dean Gates was quick to dispute this, explaining on 21 June 1930 that they were 'unquestionably works of art erected as a memorial at the State Entrance of the building'. Godfrey proposed classing them as 'sculpture', but this would not have exempted them, as the Tariff Act of 1922 defined that word as barring any article of utility, which 'doors' certainly were. Walter Hope, of the Treasury Department in Washington, had the final say: on 16 May 1930 he authorised Ashworth to grant them free entry 'under bond for permanent exhibition under the 1922 Act as works of art imported for the purpose of erecting a public monument'. (Archive, Cathedral of St. John the Divine, New York).
77. The Golden Doors Souvenir Booklet, c.1936. (Archive, Cathedral of St. John the Divine, New York).
78. H. Newton Marshal Co. started work on the doors in February 1936: cleaning, gilding where necessary, toning and lacquering – though the final coat was delayed by the cold weather. Pernel Wilson recalled the plan to have the doors painted grey for her Biographical Note (see Library, V&A). On 23 May 1939 Bishop Manning wrote to Godfrey about the 'deplorable state' of the surface finish of the doors. A.L. Ferguson (the Cathedral's assistant bursar) consulted the builders William Crawford, 7 East 42nd Street, New York. They in turn approached John Williams Inc., who recommended washing the doors with lukewarm water and soap containing 'little or no lye,' then rinsing with clear water; if this did not produce a better effect, the doors would need 'completely recoating' in gold leaf. When this washing failed, the Bishop announced on 19 October 1939 that, rather than being regilded, the doors would look better with the gold removed completely. Crawford sought estimates for the work. Williams provided one, of $1,350, but could not guarantee to remove every trace of the gold

without dismantling the doors. Another came from the American Bronze Company, at $750. Crawford worried, as he wrote to Ferguson, 1 November 1939, firstly that the bronze surface beneath the gold would be rough and would need rubbing down, and secondly, that different types of bronze, each varying in hue, had been used in the doors (rolled and extruded for the rails and stiles, cast for the panels). The choices that the Cathedral would face when the bronze was revealed were to simply clean and wax the surface, another was to apply mild acid to unify the colour, a third, the most radical, was to use an 'experimental' technique – sandblasting – which would 'run into thousands of dollars' and which would give a satin rather than polished surface. The Bishop concluded on 10 November 1939 that until money for the removal of the gold surface became available, it would be best to 'leave the doors as they are, but to clean the parts which are dark and dirty'. A regime of washing the doors with the proprietry cleaner 'Oakite' was instituted in July 1940, but a year later, Crawford obtained estimates from the American Bronze Company for sandblasting sample areas of the doors – setting up the equipment alone would cost $100, carrying out the process using fine sea sand would be $250, then would come the application of lacquer, at $425. On 19 June 1941 Ferguson authorised A.B.C. to proceed with a sandblasted sample. Soon after, approval was given to proceed with the whole job, which was finished in September 1941. (Archive, Cathedral of St. John the Divine, New York).

79. Letter to Pernel Wilson from R.A. Cram 31 August 1934 (Archive, Cathedral of St. John the Divine, New York).
80. 'Manning blesses Cathedral Doors'. *New York Times* 3 February 1936.
81. C.R. Ashbee 'Masters of the Art Workers' Guild from the beginning till 1934'. Unpublished m/s, c. 1934 (Art Workers' Guild, Queen's Square, London).
82. Preface to the 2nd edition of *Silverwork and Jewellery* (1912). In this passage, Wilson was thanking the craftsmen who had participated in the 1911 Coronation Exhibition at the White City and who had posed for the photographs in the book. These craftsmen, including Indian engravers, stonecutters and polishers, Sinhalese repoussé workers, and Benares brass chasers had given continuous demonstrations of traditional skills for the duration of the exhibiton.

EPILOGUE
"THE ARCH-INDIVIDUALIST"

1. Letter from Emily Stables, The Vicarage, Far Headingley, 3 July 1906. She explains that she ought not think of the cross until she had 'put by enough for the pulpit' (for Ripon Cathedral, see Epilogue below). In fact, 'the cross', made of oak with brass enrichments and enamel shield at its centre (see also Ch. 3 n. 71) was completed by October 1907. A letter of 21 October 1907 from the Rev. E. B. Ward, St. Matthew's Rectory, Ardwick, Manchester congratulated Wilson on its completion: 'The cross is very nice indeed and I really think that the good people of St. Chad's will soon begin to feel that they have got something out of the common beautiful.' He closes his letter hoping that Wilson had 'had a good time in Italy'; the purpose of that visit is unclear, but it highlights Wilson's familiarity with continental Europe. The Rev. Ward's own church, St. Matthew's, Ardwick, also boasted work by Wilson – an altar cross (lost when church dem.), which he had made working with a rough sketch from Ward: 'Can you do anything like it for £20? The height must be 2'9"or thereabouts. The consecration of the church is Oct. 18. Will it be possible for you to get it done by then?' It is visible in a photograph of the time of the church interior (Central Lib., Manchester: I am grateful to Wendy Armstrong for locating this picture). In an earlier letter of 19 September 1907, the vicar had mentioned a processional cross for St. Matthew's. Again he sent Wilson a drawing 'as you have asked', and enquired 'When do you think you can provide it to us?' Wilson's propensity for embellishment emerged in his drawing for this cross, which Ward was reluctant to approve: 'Personally I like the two pendants very much, but my people do rise to them, so if you can leave them out without doing too much violence to your artistic conscience, perhaps you would not mind dropping them.' (Wilson Archive RCA). Wilson would find other opportunities to incorporate 'pendants' into his designs, eg the altar cross ill. in Cram's 1908 article in *Christian Art*.
2. The established and deliberate choice of 'Peter' in their correspondence is confirmed in Wilson's letter to Cram from Menton in 1933 regarding the gilding of the New York doors: too weak to write himself, Pernie typed it, ending with the words 'Signed pp Peter, by Pernel'. The letter to Edgar Wilson signed 'P' is dated 27 Nov. 1928.
3. Letter from J. Miller, 14 Airlie Gardens, Campden Hill, London 2 April 1911 (Private Coll.). Miller's role is not recorded, but his words suggest he played a significant part in the appointments made at the Royal College of Art.
4. H. Wilson and J.P. Cooper. 'The Work of J.D. Sedding' (i) *Architectural Review* III 1897 p. 35.
5. H. Wilson. 'On Education: Definitions'. (Wilson Archive RCA).
6. Letter to Wilson from J. Hoffman, *Verlag fur Kunst und Kunstgewerbe*, Stuttgart 21 November 1907. (Wilson Archive RCA). It is doubtful whether this book on Wilson's jewellery was ever printed, though Hoffman goes on to predict that about 300 copies could easily 'be sold to Libraries, Schools of Art, etc.' for £2-10-0 each.
7. F.W. Troup. Obituary: Henry Wilson. *Jnl RIBA* 24 March 1934.
8. Margaret's grave is recorded in the burial register without a number, but with an asterisk in the margin, between graves no. 244 and 245, indicating its location not in the main part of the churchyard but in the adjoining area that abuts it. The contact address given for the burial is the Westminster Hospital's Radium Annexe at 66 Fitzjohns Avenue, London NW. Her age is recorded as 61, as on her death certificate, where her occupation is given as 'wife of Henry Wilson a sculptor'. The child for whom Wilson had designed a gravestone in St. Mary's churchyard was for Percival Turner. He was the younger brother of architect and churchwarden Captain Austen Charlewood Turner, whose rank reflected his First World War service and after whom 'Captain's Walk'

– the almshouses adjacent to the church – was named. The family lived at 'Millwood', Wrotham Heath. Wilson's cross with its two supporting squirrels, lies between the Garden Meeting Room at the east end of the church and the row of yews beyond. It is inscribed 'In loving memory of Percival Francis Charlewood Turner aged 13 who fell asleep May 15 1904. Blessed are the pure in heart for they shall see God'; on the back appear the lines 'Fair son and is risen so soon, Thy star of eve before the noon. Thy star of eve, ah care not thou, God's morning will be along ere now'. Inside the church is further example of Wilson's work, a simply inscribed memorial to George Billing, of 1907: 'To the glory of God and in affectionate memory of George Billing vicar of this parish 1898-1907. This bas relief is erected by the parishioners of St. Mary Platt by the followers of God as dear children'.

9. The service of dedication was conducted by Bishop William T. Manning and, as reported in the *New York Times* 3 February 1936, the congregation included the architect Chester N. Godfrey, the President of the Metropolitan Life Insurance Company Frederick H. Ecker, and George A. Weigel, manager of the Morrisania office, chairman of the Door Committee, and following the death of Donald Sinclair in 1933, treasurer of the Haley Fiske Memorial Fund. The ceremony signalled a shift in the Fund's relationship with the doors; by the time of their dedication the gilding saga was only just beginning, but on 14 October 1941, Godfrey wrote to the Bishop with two recommendations – that financial reserves for the doors' upkeep be secured, and that the stonework around them be carved. Weigel's comments on the matter, sent to the Bishop on 22 October, gave a businesslike response to the prospect of an ongoing maintenance fund: Donald Sinclair's 'effective handling' of the Fund had 'enhanced it beyond the cost of the doors', and the surplus had been 'turned over to the late Dean Gates.... The letter sent you by the architect is returned herewith'. (Archive, Cathedral of St. John the Divine, New York).
10. C.R. Ashbee. 'Masters of the Art Workers' Guild from the beginning till 1934'. Unpublished m/s p. 315-6, Collections of Art Workers' Guild, Queen Square, London.
11. H. Muthesius. *The English House* (trans. J. Seligman) pp. 45, 14, 196.
12. H. Wilson. 'New Schools in Art' 1917 (Wilson Archive RCA).
13. Letter to Wilson from Robert Catterson-Smith, 16 Frederick Road, Edgbaston 9 January 1916 (Wilson Archive RCA). Catterson-Smith was recounting his heated exchange with an agitated delegate who, misunderstanding Wilson's architectonic philosophy, had accused Wilson of wanting 'to scrap all that existed'. See also Ch. 8 n. 3.
14. F. Russell (ed). *Art Nouveau Architecture*: Ch. 1 'Great Britain, Arts and Crafts and Art Nouveau' by Tim Benton. Other commentators identifying Wilson as an Art Nouveau designer include Andrew Saint, seeing him as 'one of the most idiosyncratic artists of the movement' (*Richard Norman Shaw* p. 320), S.T. Madsen who notes the 'Art Nouveau' metalwork at Holy Trinity, Sloane Street (*The Sources of Art Nouveau* p. 282), and Nicholas Pevsner, who thought the inglenook at Welbeck 'as charming as anything which that movement of English Art Nouveau produced' (*The Buildings of England: Nottinghamshire* p.198). This judicious qualification is also made in *The Architectural Review* CII 1947 p. 144, which states that Wilson belonged to 'that purely English trend of English Art Nouveau' – indeed the qualification lends a useful refinement of the classification whenever Wilson is mentioned in an Art Nouveau context (cf. N. Taylor in 'Byzantium in Brighton' p. 287: 'It may be questioned whether apart from the chalice [his] work at St. Bartholomew's justifies the title Art Nouveau').
15. H. Wilson. Undated letter to Edward Prior (Wilson Archive RCA). Wilson continues 'Horta the Belgian architect ... says that "proportions" and other vignoleries must go the way of all rubbish because a house is constructed to live in.'
16. Letter to Wilson from William Danks, The Residence, Ripon, 14 January 1907 (Wilson Archive RCA).
17. H. Wilson. *Reports on Present Position and Tendencies of the Industrial Arts as indicated at the International Exhibition of Modern Decorative and Industrial Arts*, Paris, 1925: 'Metal Work' p. 117.
18. H. Wilson. 'The Crafts in Education and Reconstruction' in *Handicrafts* (1919), by members of Arts and Crafts Exhibition Society pp. 12-17.
19. Ibid.
20. The French Symbolist painter Maurice Chabas (1862-1947) was influenced by Swedenborgian mysticism. Emanuel Swedenborg (1688-1772), argued for the essentially spiritual structure of the universe, and claimed to have visions and to converse with angels. Wilson was aware of such beliefs through his studies of William Blake, who had been a follower from c. 1750. During the 1890s Chabas depicted dark Brittany landscapes imbued with a sense of the supernatural, which evolved in the 1920s into abstract interpretations of religious feeling.
21. H. Wilson. New Schools in Art, 1917 (Wilson Archive RCA)
22. H. Wilson. 'The Crafts in Education and Reconstruction' in *Handicrafts* (1919), by members of Arts and Crafts Exhibition Society pp. 12-17.
23. H. Wilson. Notebook 5 (Wilson Archive RCA).
24. H. Wilson. Letter to Winifrid Wilson, 13 March 1922 (Coll. I. Howden, BM.).
25. Ibid.
26. 23. H. Wilson. 'The Art of a Nation is the Expression of its Moral Condition' 1914-18 (Wilson Archive RCA).
27. 24. H. Wilson. Notebook 5 (Wilson Archive RCA). See also *Boston Evening Transcript* 2 July 1927.
28. Ibid.
29. H. Wilson quoted in *Boston Evening Transcript* 2 July 1927. See also Troup Obituary, *Jnl RSA* 24 March 1934.
30. H. Wilson. 'The City Beautiful' 1915, see Ch. 7 n. 45.
31. Postcard from G. B. Shaw, Torquay, 1915 (Wilson Archive RCA).
32. Letter from H. Wilson, Platt to G. B. Shaw, October 1915 (Wilson Archive RCA).
33. H. Wilson. Notebook 5 (Wilson Archive RCA). These words bear a striking resemblance to the sentiment famously attributed to Julian of Norwich: 'Not what you are that God judges, but what you long to be....'

ACKNOWLEDGEMENTS FOR ILLUSTRATIONS

In the case of photographic copies of original drawings and photographs, see caption, text or chapter notes for origin.

PLATES:	Geoff Harris	*1, 4 - 25, 27 - 31, 46 - 49, 56, 58*
	John Taylor	*3*
	Kate Cooper	*7 (left)*
	Peter Grosvenor	*7 (right)*
	Keith Gillies	*26, 34 - 42, 51 - 53, 57*
	Arthur M Procter	23
	Rob Orland	*32*
	Cheltenham Art Gallery & Museum	*56*
	David J. Ovens	*59*
	Doug Houghton	*60*
	Jonathan H. Robbins	*62*
	Penny Sparke	*64*
INTRODUCTION	Geoff Harris	*Fig. 1*
CHAPTER ONE	Colin Manton	*Fig. 6*
CHAPTER TWO	Geoff Harris	*Fig. 11, 13 - 18*
CHAPTER THREE	Keith Gillies	*Fig. 19, 21*
	Geoff Harris	*Fig. 22 - 25, 31 - 34*
CHAPTER FOUR	Colin Manton	*Fig. 37*
	Geoff Harris	*Fig. 38 - 48, 50 - 53*
	Keith Gillies	*Fig. 49*
CHAPTER FIVE	Keith Gillies	*Fig. 54, 56 - 58, 60, 63*
	Geoff Harris	*Fig. 61, 62*
	University of Aberdeen	*Fig. 64*
CHAPTER SIX	Geoff Harris	*Fig. 65, 72, 73, 74*
	Keith Gillies	*Fig. 66, 67*
CHAPTER SEVEN	Geoff Harris	*Fig. 82*
CHAPTER EIGHT	Keith Gillies	*Fig. 87*
CHAPTER NINE	Penny Sparke	*Fig. 95, 96*

Index

W

Y

Z

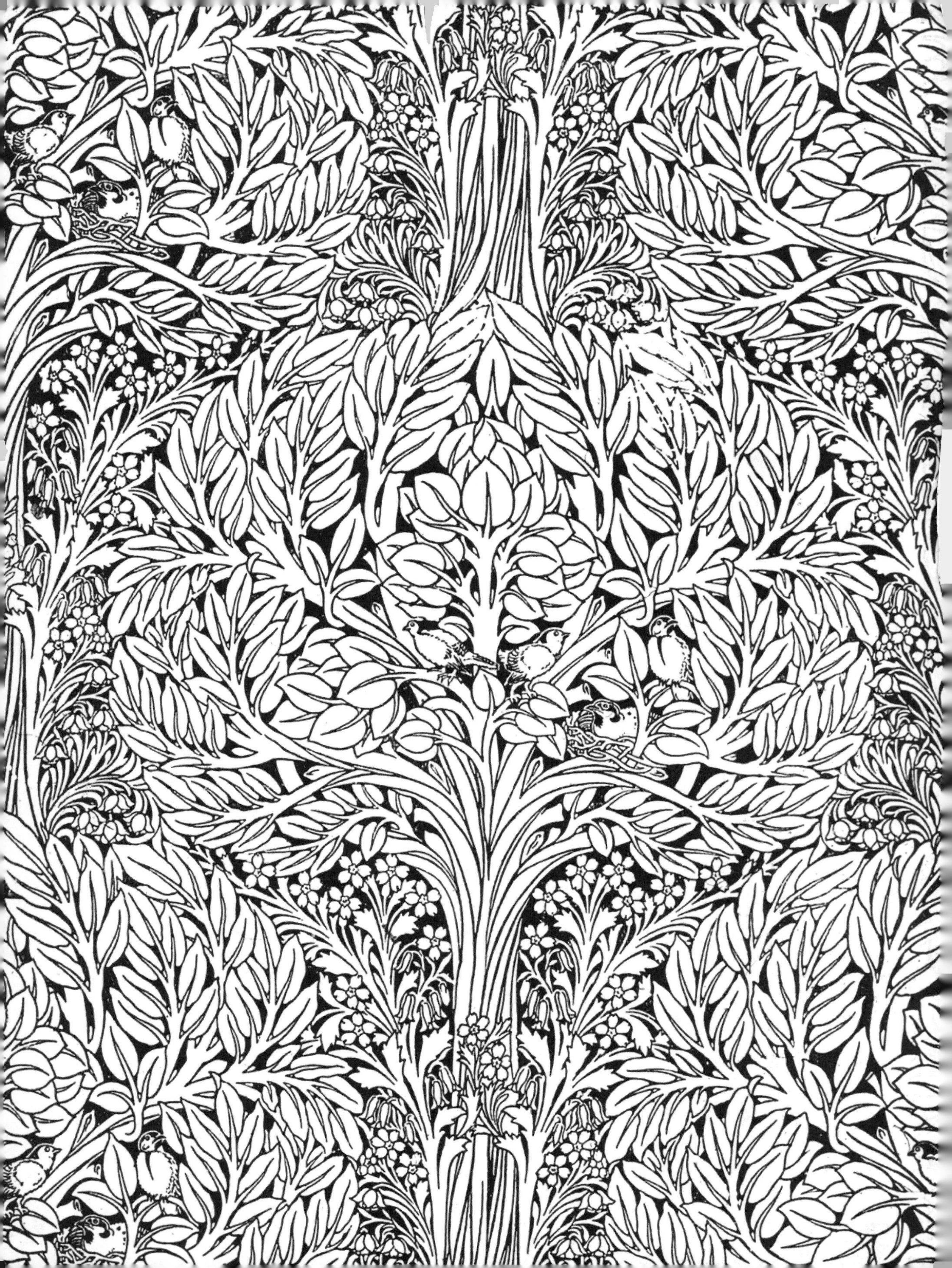